In Search of Adam

In Search of Adam

The story of man's quest for the truth
about his earliest ancestors

BY

HERBERT WENDT

TRANSLATED FROM THE GERMAN BY
JAMES CLEUGH

*Illustrated with photographs
and line cuts*

HOUGHTON MIFFLIN COMPANY BOSTON
The Riverside Press Cambridge
1956

W

PRINTED IN THE U.S.A.

ACKNOWLEDGMENTS

I ought not to allow this book to appear without thanking all those who have come to my aid with valuable suggestions and the provision of material. I am especially indebted to Frau Doktor Dorka of Berlin, Professors Weinert of Kiel, Heberer of Göttingen, Falkenburger of Mainz, Absolon of Brünn, von Koenigswald of Utrecht, and Herr Brandt, Director of the Herne Museum. Professors Weinert, Heberer, and von Koenigswald, as well as Herr Brandt, were so good as to read the proofs of the German edition and in so doing to call my attention to the latest investigations and discoveries that I was thus enabled to take into consideration.

I must also take this opportunity to thank all those who have courteously co-operated in the provision of illustrative material or granted permission for individual pictures to be used. My thanks are due in particular to the Anthropological Institute of the University of Kiel, the Zoological Institute of the University of Göttingen, the Ems Valley Museum at Herne, and the firm of Holbein at Basel, whose exceptionally fine production, *Die Kunst der Eiszeit* by Hans-Georg Bandi and Johannes Maringer greatly inspired me.

The many drawings that had to be made for the book were supplied by Herr Gerhard Bluhm of Stockum near Hamm in Westphalia.

PREFACE

IN A CONFINED SPACE, damp and cold, one hundred and thirty feet below the surface of the earth, two men are crouching. Their torches illuminate an underground passage, half full of water. The silence is deathly. Now and again a drop of moisture falls from the roof into the black lake with a harsh clicking sound. After hesitating for a few minutes the men remove their clothing, put away their torches and matches in a rubber case, plunge into the water, and try to find their way along the passage, into the unknown, by swimming. The roof becomes gradually lower and lower. They have to dive and they begin to get out of breath. At last, in the darkness they bump into a rock. They clamber onto it like seals, noticing that the passage has come to an end. They open their rubber case, light their torches, and find themselves looking into a broad lofty hall thickly festooned with glittering stalactites.

Shortly afterwards their excavation picks are digging into the tough clay of the cave. One of the men utters a soft exclamation as he takes up a hand axe and holds it to the light of his torch. The cracks and bulges of the wall of the cavern are illuminated. Suddenly, scratches made by the claws of cave bears and the imprints of human hands become visible, together with human figures and animals painted in color. In this hall deep in the interior of the mountain primitive man once made his home.

This scene took place in 1923: the names of the two men were Norbert Casteret and Henri Godin. They had found the now world-famous cave of Montespan. Many such caves have since been discovered. Many remains of prehistoric animals and men, together with evidence of early civilizations, have been dug up. Scientific detective work that has been going on for two hundred years has now given some answers to the question of the origin and course of the evolution of humanity.

The adventure of cave exploration is only one of the many aspects of the story told in this book. The quest for Adam was also made by biologists and geneticists, looking for clues to the mysteries of life in their laboratories, by thinkers breaking with old prejudices, by professors who proclaimed revolutionary theories of the origin of species, and by talented amateurs whose chance finds opened up new paths of research for prehistorians. All these achievements and discoveries are described.

The uncovering of prehistory is probably the most dramatic chapter of natural history, full of incident and intrigue, as well as of human tragedy. Each skull and hand axe that lies in a museum today, and each book that deals with the origin of mankind, has had a career of its own. If the evidence of prehistory is examined with the eye of the professional student it acquires an uncanny reality. It emerges from the museums, the cabinets of specimens and the libraries, dissipating the mists of ignorance that obscure the epochs of human and cultural evolution by which the fate of our world has been decided.

In this narrative of scientific fact I have therefore stressed the man himself, the investigator, possessed and inspired by genius, who first makes the facts come to life. For this reason I was obliged to enter upon other scientific fields beyond my actual theme, citing documents, letters, and reports that enabled the setting in which each separate event occurred to be reconstructed. Thus I hope the reader will be able to participate in the adventure of research, in the works of excavation, in the unveiling of relics of the days before history, and in scientific disputes that victimized so many misunderstood discoverers.

H.W.

CONTENTS

PREFACE   vii

PART ONE

ADAM KNOCKS AT THE BACK DOOR

CHAPTER I. EVIDENCE OF THE FLOOD
Under the town gallows at Altdorf   3
Philosophers, fables, and fossils   5
A complaint by the fishes of Lake Constance   11
The persecuted skeleton of an ancient sinner   14
A fossil called Beringer   17
Voltaire objects   19
Did Caesar bring elephants to England?   21

CHAPTER II. THE MAN WHO CLASSIFIED NATURE
Fins become wings   25
The swallow at the bottom of the sea   29
The wedding customs of flowers   31
Discovery of the mammoth   34
How fearful are Thy creatures, O Lord!   40
Man is a superior animal   44
Who can count the species or know their names?   51

CHAPTER III. LINKS BETWEEN MAN AND BEAST
Animals too have a soul   56
The highly objectionable "machine-man"   58
Nature knows no system   63
The unclassifiable bastards   67

Man is a decadent ape   72
Buffon writes the story of the earth   78

CHAPTER IV. SECRETS OF EVOLUTION

Eve — the mother of mankind   85
The quarrel about the germ in the egg   91
A forgotten ancestor   96
Under the sign of Venus   99
Natural scientists revolt   106
Open competition for animate beings   112

PART TWO
ADAM DISOWNED

CHAPTER V. THE ANIMAL IS THE ELDER BROTHER OF MAN

Man, too, has an intermaxillary bone   123
God and nature are one   129
Beast and Man from one archetype   138
Can apes become men?   140

CHAPTER VI. THE HISTORY OF THE EARTH IS WRITTEN IN
    CATASTROPHE

The Devil is a vegetarian   144
Human fossils do not exist   149
Animate beings are the products of their environment   157
The condemnation of Jean Baptiste Lamarck   162
The pope of bones and the red lady   166

CHAPTER VII. ALL LIFE COMES FROM THE CELL

Man as an unknown mammal   172
The enfant terrible of zoology   177
Cell chemistry   184

CHAPTER VIII. HUMAN FOSSILS DO EXIST!

The Flood was an ice age   191
The monkey of Pikermi   197
An argument about Adam's ancestors   200
The paradise of primitive man   207
A poor wretch from Neanderthal   215
The hand axe system of chronology   225

PART THREE
MONKEY BUSINESS OVER ADAM

CHAPTER IX. THE ORIGIN OF SPECIES

In the shadow of Erasmus 235
Jemmy Button gets his rights 239
Birth of a theory 248
A globe-trotter starts an avalanche 254
The affair of Mr. Huxley's grandfather 259
To hell with the gorilla! 266
Eve follows the flag 271

CHAPTER X. NATURE'S STORY OF CREATION

Mechanized man and the riddles of the universe 278
Bombs in the powder barrel 283
The ape man of Java 290
How did life originate on earth? 301

CHAPTER XI. THAT WHICH THY FOREFATHERS HAVE
    BEQUEATHED UNTO THEE

Mice sacrifice their tails 307
The miracle in a monastery garden 309
A mysterious field near Hilversum 314
Nature makes "quantum" leaps 317
Suicide of a natural scientist 320

CHAPTER XII. ARTISTS OF THE ICE AGE

Don Quixote of Altamira 327
The artists of the caves 333
Cave explorers 343
Cain buried his brother Abel 352
The prolific Venus of Willendorf 358
The expressionist painters of Valltorta 364
Herds on African rock faces 373

PART FOUR
ADAM UNMASKED

CHAPTER XIII. THE DAWN OF HUMANITY

A prehistoric Pompeii 383
Two men sold for 160,000 gold marks 387

At the cradle of European man   395
Herr Rösch's sandpit   398
An imitation coconut   405
Comedy of errors   410
Storm over Oldoway   417

CHAPTER XIV. THE PROTOTYPE

The Dayton Monkey Trial   424
Do you speak Chimpanzee?   427
Do animals come from men?   431
Was our original ancestor a lemur?   434
Blood is a very special kind of fluid   436
The baby ape in Man   439
Back to the gibbon   442

CHAPTER XV. PROMETHEUS AND THE GIANTS

Racial politics and the Steinheim skull   448
Homo sapiens rises from the mist   450
The secret of the Chinese chemists' shops   455
The Dragons' Mountain   460
A race of giants   466
Dynamite in Sterkfontein   474
The Transvaal Garden of Eden   481

CHAPTER XVI. THE EARLY CULTURES

Brain, club, and stone   489
The conquest of the fifth continent   497
Comrade cave bear   500
The battle of Krapina   504
My house is my castle   507
The Flood once more   514
The Maya and the mastodon   519
A visit to Adam   527

INDEX   529

LIST OF PLATES

FOLLOWING PAGE 224

1. Scheuchzer's *Homo diluvii testis*. Contemporary broadsheet
2. Skull of a saurian
   Dragon fountain at Klagenfurt by Ulrich Vogelsang, 1590
3. Carolus Linnaeus in Lapland dress (from Knut Hagberg's *Karl Linnäus*, Claasen-Verlag, Hamburg)
4. Anatomical collection from *Thesaurus anatomicus* by Fredericus Ruysch (Amsterdam, 1710)
5. Count Buffon
6. The negroid albino, Genoveva of Dominica. From *Buffon's Natural History of Man*, translated by Freyherr zu Ulmenstein (Berlin, 1805), in the library of J. Pauly
   Paradisal family
7. Female orangutan
8. "Human animals" as depicted in the eighteenth century
9. Duckbill
   Melanesians of the Solomon Islands
10. Cave bear's skull from Wildensee, Austria
    Petrified palaeohippid from Geiseltal
11. Goethe's jawbone collection, Weimar
12. Giordano Bruno, Benedict Spinoza, Immanuel Kant, Arthur Schopenhauer, from engravings
13. The village of Les Eyzies in the Vézère valley, 1867. Drawing by W. Tipping from *Reliquiae Aquitanicae* by Edouard Lartet and Henry Christy (London, 1865–67)
    Houses in Laugerie-Basse
14. Les Eyzies, castle, 1867. Drawing by W. Tipping from *Reliquiae Aquitanicae* by Lartet and Christy

Large rock shelter at Les Eyzies, with statue of Neanderthal man by Paul Darde

15. Neanderthal skull from La Chapelle-aux-Saints
    Native of Melanesia

16. Negrito Semang tribesman from primeval jungles of Siam
    Member of the Moken Vedda race
    Primitive Ice Age skull from the Grimaldi Grotto at Monte Carlo
    Cro-Magnon skulls of old man and young woman at Oberkassel, near Bonn

FOLLOWING PAGE 352

17. Human embryo in fertilized membrane after six weeks' development

18. Human embryo, front view

19. Ernst Haeckel

20. Primitive man without power of speech. Drawing by Gabriel Max

21. *Pithecanthropus erectus*: skull vaulting, thighbone, and reconstruction of skull
    Silver-gray gibbon

22. Mount Smeru in eastern Java

23. Bull bison from Altamira

24. Male and female bison from Tuc d'Audoubert, Ariège
    Wild horse showing wounds from Gautier-Montespan, Haute-Garonne (both illustrations taken from Bandi and Maringer, *Die Kunst der Eiszeit*, Basel: Holbein-Verlag)

25. Entrance to the cave of Lascaux

26. Bull bison from Font-de-Gaume, Dordogne (after Breuil). Sketch on stone for above from La Genière, Ain

27. Climbing South Sea Islanders
    Honey gathers from Cueva de la Araña, Province of Valencia (after Hernandez-Pacheco)

28. The Venus of Willendorf
    Female figure in bas-relief from Laussel, Dordogne (from Bandi and Maringer)

29. Female figure from Lespugue, Haute-Garonne (from Bandi and Maringer)

30. Ivory head of man from Dolní Věstonice, Moravia

31. Ivory carvings of woolly rhinoceros and wild horse from Vogel-
    herd cave, Württemberg
32. Rock engraving of buffalo from Tel Issaghen, North Africa
    Rock painting of family scene from Kargour-Talh, Africa

FOLLOWING PAGE 512

33. Le Moustier from a bridge over the Vézère
    Otto Hauser on the day of the excavation of the "Le Moustier
      boy"
34. Double grave, Grimaldi Grotto, Monte Carlo
35. Intelligence test of orangutan, zoological garden at Hellbrunn
36. Goblin lemur
    Proconsul africanus, reconstruction drawing
37. Professor Weng Chung Pei
    Sinanthropus skull, reconstruction by Franz Weidenreich
38. Geological stratification in Sangiran, Java
    Von Koenigswald and assistants looking for fossils
39. The Child of Taungs (Australopithecus africanus)
40. Plesianthropus transvaalensis, reconstruction drawing
41. Skeleton from the Oldoway Gorge, found by H. Reck
    John Talbot Robinson
42. East African savannah
43. Hand mill, Hesse
    Primitive bone needle from Wildensee, Austria
44. Bone dishes from Thuringia
    Bear's jawbone axe from Thuringia
45. Australian dingo (Canis dingo)
    Mouthless divinity from Australian rock drawing
46. Headless bear from Montespan Cave, Haute-Garonne
    Footprint of primitive man from Aldens
    Bear ritual of the Ainu
47. Painting of hut-type building from La Mouthe, Dordogne (from
      Bandi and Maringer)
    Lake dwellings at Unteruhldingen, Lake Constance, recon-
      struction
48. Man and woman from Hoggar Mountains in the Sahara

Part One

ADAM KNOCKS AT THE BACK DOOR

*It is dangerous to let man see
too clearly how closely he resembles
the beasts unless, at the same time,
we show him how great he is.*
BLAISE PASCAL

EVIDENCE OF THE FLOOD

Under the town gallows at Altdorf

MANY STATUES have been erected to the men who devoted their lives to scientific discovery, but there is no monument to the spirit of research itself. It would have to be represented by some amateur researcher, sunk in a dream of speculation, with a halo of error round his head, and his feet resting on a pedestal of unflagging industry. From Columbus to Schliemann there have been dabblers in science who have explored its territories and spurned the conclusions of the professors for new theories of their own. All too often their ideas only led them astray, and they never reached their goal; but here and there these amateurs of exploration discovered a new world.

Johann Jakob Scheuchzer of Zurich, a doctor of medicine, was one of these amateurs. One summer evening, about the year 1705, he was taking a walk with his friend Langhans over Gallows Hill near the hop-growing town of Altdorf in Franconia, Germany. Altdorf had rather a bad reputation at that time, not because of its hop growing, but because of its university, founded eighty years previously, which had aroused much adverse comment. It was notorious for all kinds of scandal and the citizens and hop dealers of Altdorf were heartily thankful when the university at last closed its doors in 1809.

But the somewhat overripe flavor of this ill-famed institution must have attracted Hansjakob Scheuchzer, as he was called, for he deliberately chose to leave Switzerland to study there. He was undoubtedly an eccentric, for he believed, just as Schliemann a hundred and fifty years later was to believe, in the literal truth of Homer, and in the accuracy and reliability of the Biblical story of creation. He intended to search underground for relics of those long vanished days. His walk to Gallows Hill was not, therefore, simply an evening stroll, as his gossiping neighbors in Altdorf supposed, but a scientific expedition.

The town gibbet, black and ominous, rose into view, with bats skimming over it. Langhans began to feel uncomfortable and suggested that they return home. Scheuchzer, however, refused to do so. He picked up a few stones, examined them, and let them drop again. "I must find proof," he said.

"Proof?" Langhans was standing directly beneath the gibbet. "Of Adam and Eve? Of the Fall? And the Flood? Surely it's all much too long ago? Isn't it enough just to believe in it?"

"No," said Scheuchzer. "Hitherto we simply have not taken the trouble to look for such proofs. But there is evidence that I am right." He counted it up. The great Athanasius Kircher had talked about giants' bones in the earth. Otto von Guericke, the mayor of Magdeburg, had found the skeleton of a unicorn. The fossilized remains of dragons, griffins, and other fabulous beasts were always turning up. They must certainly at one time have fallen victims to the great Flood. "And here, in Franconia," cried Scheuchzer, "relics of it are particularly frequent. Think of all those fossilized fish and huge serpents people have dug up in the neighborhood of Altdorf alone. Don't they point to the Deluge mentioned in Genesis?"

Langhans knew Scheuchzer's collection of fossilized marine animals. He was already quite sick of studying it, and remained unconvinced. It was the opinion of the scientists that such stone images were only freaks of nature, though simple people believed that fabulous monsters existed underground and a few cranks told weird stories about an extinct race of petrified creatures of gigantic size. It might be so or it might not. In any case curios of that description had nothing to do with the Flood.

"Just look at that now!" Scheuchzer suddenly seized his friend's arm and pointed to a fragment of ashen-gray rock below the gallows. Eight black bones could be seen in the stone, gleaming as if they had been polished. "Those are vertebrae, Langhans, real human vertebrae!"

"Phah! They're the bones of a man who was hanged," retorted Langhans, disgusted. "He was a condemned criminal a long time ago." He shivered. "Come on, Hansjakob, let it alone. Let us be off!"

And as Scheuchzer bent down eagerly to pick up the piece of rock, Langhans did a thing no one but an ignoramus, beside himself with fear and superstition, could have done in such a case. He snatched the gruesome thing his friend had found out of his hands and tossed it down the hillside. "Away with the old sinner!" he cried in a tone of relief. The fragment of rock struck hard ground down the hill and smashed.

Then an extraordinary thing happened. Scheuchzer, with a furious glare at Langhans, picked up the skirts of his coat and rushed down the slope after his find. Rapid strides took him to the place where the splinters lay. Langhans heard him raking and scraping, panting with exhaustion. Then he shouted up to his companion by the gibbet in a strangely excited and half-strangled voice, which sounded more like some frenzied fanatic than a learned Zurich doctor.

"Oh, Langhans," he cried, reprimanding his friend, "what an utter fool you are! Do you think you can get rid of facts by hard knocks? If that fellow was an old sinner, Langhans, he dates back to the time when the great Flood came! He saw the Flood, I tell you!"

Langhans hung his head sulkily. How was it possible to identify a witness of the Flood up here on Altdorf Gallows Hill? Hansjakob was a decent fellow and a clever doctor, but his head was in the clouds. Now he was tearing up the hillside again, with two of those black, gleaming vertebrae in his hand. "I managed to save those two at any rate," he said, nudging Langhans in the ribs. "You fool! What we've got here is the proof of my Deluge theory at last!"

Scheuchzer ran the tips of his fingers repeatedly over the shining black surfaces. "Yes, he was an old sinner all right," he agreed, smiling. "He was one of those who, as it says in the Bible, had grown corrupt and full of wickedness, wherefore God destroyed them, together with all else that breathed."

Langhans made no reply. He did not dare touch the vertebrae. Neither he nor his exultant companion was in a position to realize that they had both fallen victims to an absurd error; but an error that would in fact bring on the birthpangs of paleontology, the science of the ancient life of the earth.

Philosophers, fables, and fossils

That firm believer in the Bible, Johann Jakob Scheuchzer, intended the two fossilized vertebrae from Altdorf Gallows Hill to testify against the skeptical rationalism of his time on behalf of the truths related in the First Book of Moses, called Genesis. It was an admirable and pious plan and Scheuchzer, in his simplicity, was convinced that it would win him the esteem of all his contemporaries, both learned and unlearned.

But Scheuchzer's contemporaries, or at least the scientists among them, were completely unimpressed. They turned up their noses at Hansjakob's enthusiasm and thought that he was pulling their leg. When he referred in emphatic terms to the remarkable stone formations discovered in many places, in Franconia, Swabia, and the Alps, in central France and in England — pointing out that they resembled fish, snakes, and crustaceans — the professorial body calmly replied that such things were in no sense traces of organic life in early times, but merely freaks of nature created by a *vis plastica*, a mysterious molding force that imitated the shapes of all sorts of animals and plants by way of a joke, so to speak.

The *vis plastica* theory was at that time exactly seven hundred years old. From A.D. 980 to A.D. 1037 a learned man of Arab descent lived in the Persian city of Hamadan. Doctor of medicine, naturalist, and philosopher, by name Ibn-Sina, he gave an oriental cast to the thought that inspired the immense labors of Aristotle, the "father of the sciences," and reinterpreted it for the appreciation of his contemporaries. Like his predecessor Aristotle, he considered that every form of life had its assured and immutable place and purpose in the world. Each specimen was metaphorically labeled in his collector's cabinet. Ibn-Sina was even more convinced than Aristotle, who had shown such keen and comprehensive insight in this field, that forms were immutable, that nature did not evolve and had no history. He thus reached the conception of a "plastic force" working like a sculptor. This Arab thinker was known to the West as Avicenna. His writings were translated into Latin at a time when Christian Europe was doing hardly any scientific work of its own, and after being adapted to early medieval taste, they were read in all the universities.

The intrusion of Avicenna and other Arabs into the closed world of Western scholarship was an event of great importance for the beginnings of natural history. The Western world had hitherto derived its knowledge of nature from Aristotle alone, taking over his work precisely as it stood and not daring to modify it in the slightest degree. Even in the seventeenth century the old Greek's authority was still so respected that when the Jesuit astronomer Scheiner discovered the spots on the sun in 1611 he was reproved by his spiritual superior on the ground that Aristotle never wrote anything about spots on the sun! This hidebound attitude toward science naturally annoyed the experimentally minded, who numbered quite a few even then. Already the vanguard of science was turning its attention to the East, which lay at its feet awaiting exploration. One after another, discoveries and inventions were being made there. Aristotle was not only being studied in the Orient but also interpreted afresh, commented upon, and brought up to date, and the eager European students of science were fascinated by these activities.

They got hold of the works on natural history written by their Mohammedan archenemies. Their enthusiasm led them into strange bypaths, as the case of Averroës shows. The writings of this Spanish Moor — his real name was Mohammed ibn-Rushd — reached Europe, acording to later critics, merely in the form of the Latin translation of a Hebrew version of a Syrian version of the Greek text of Aristotle. It is not difficult to imagine the result. Nevertheless the influence of Averroës, even in garbled form, became so strong that for some time it actually endangered the supremacy of the scholastic teachers of natural science.

Arab discoveries, inventions, and numerals gradually became known to the Western scientists, and as they did so the rationalist Arab outlook upon nature gained ground. "Wisdom" became "knowledge." Experiment took the place of book learning. Unfortunately, the new principles simply congealed in the subservient medieval mind. They were taken over without any particular investigation, worked into Aristotle's lectures, and embodied as fixed elements in the scientific thought of the age.

In this way Avicenna's *vis plastica* theory outlasted the centuries. The opinion of the wise man of Hamadan that there could be no such things as extinction and renewal of species and forms in a changeless world carried the day against the far more plausible popular idea of the remains of ancient monsters still existing below the earth's surface. The learned stigmatized these explanations of fossil phenomena as fables. Until the middle of the eighteenth century it was held that no runic characters or antediluvian traces were to be found buried in those rocks and that no vanished era had bequeathed its stony records in this manner. The figured rock was no more than a whim of nature, a sort of pattern-in-stone of the living forms of creation. This was the only reason why so many fragments of rock and slate looked like a fish, a crustacean, a leaf, a skull, a tooth, a human bone, or even, as that abusive town councilor and naturalist Konrad von Gesner of Zurich maintained in 1565, the sun, the moon, and the stars.

Long before Scheuchzer's time a few laymen had tried to challenge Avicenna and the official men of science. They were mostly poets, painters, philosophers, or craftsmen — students of nature who had other interests. They were not, strictly speaking, scholars. But they were aware of the views of nature held by classical antiquity — for example, by Empedocles, Xenophanes, Pausanias, and Herodotus.

The ancients had drawn the logical conclusion from the existence of fossilized fish and crustaceans on dry land. They inferred that the continents had formerly been inundated by the sea. They had described the figured rocks as true relics of animals, plants, and monsters and so went on to create their legends of giants, dragons, and basilisks. And the rebellious laymen who subsequently attacked the professors held the perfectly reasonable view that in classical times people had been more sensible than in the age of Avicenna.

In the fourteenth century at Trapani in Sicily, Giovanni Boccaccio, author of the *Decameron*, came across fossilized remains of bones which included a skull of gigantic size with a great hole under the forehead. The Greek philosopher Empedocles had already mentioned such finds, calling them the "bones of Polyphemus." Boccaccio shared his opinion. He gave a detailed account of Polyphemus in the Fourth Book of his *Genealogy of the Gods*.

Three hundred years later the learned Jesuit father, Athanasius Kircher, inventor of the burning-glass and the magic lantern, convinced himself with his own eyes of the existence of the Sicilian bones. Though Kircher was a supporter of the theory of Avicenna, he drew the line in this case. The "Polyphemus," he said, was no freak of nature but a true giant's skull and bones. Boccaccio had made only one mistake, he added. The skeleton of the Cyclops did not measure three hundred but at most thirty feet.

A skeleton of still more uncommon appearance was discovered on January 11, 1613, in a sandpit near the castle of Chaumont in the Dauphiné. The French surgeon Mazurier examined it, declared it to be the skull and bones of Teutobochus, king of the Cimbri, and had it exhibited in a number of French and German cities at so much a head. He made a very good thing out of it, for he was an extremely clever publicist. His account represented the sandpit as a brick grave thirty feet long and Teutobochus as a giant. He even asserted quite seriously that he had read the name of the king of the Cimbri in an inscription on a wall near the place of the find.

For five years the professors discussed Mazurier and his Cimbrian skeleton. Many arguments and counterarguments were published during the dispute over old Teutobochus. At last the wily surgeon was unmasked as a fraud, and the Chaumont bones were transferred as curios to the royal collections in Paris.

A few decades later Otto von Guericke, mayor of Magdeburg and inventor of the airpump, took his researches on fossils more seriously than Mazurier. He conducted exhaustive excavations in the gypsum quarries of the northern foothills of the Harz Mountains. He collected vast quantities of fossils and compared them with descriptions of fabulous creatures in the Bible and ancient sagas. One day at Zeunicken Hill, near Quedlinburg, he unearthed a hoard of enormous bones and teeth. He was perfectly certain that it could only be the skull and bones of the unicorn mentioned in the Book of Job. He arranged the heap of bones in the form of a fantastic skeleton, notified the public, and had his reconstruction of a unicorn printed. Later the philosopher Leibniz gave his approval to the reconstruction

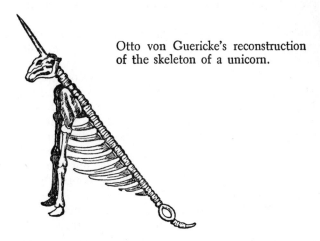

Otto von Guericke's reconstruction of the skeleton of a unicorn.

thus achieved. Leibniz published a copy of it in his *Protogaea*, and the professors were then forced, willy-nilly, to include it in their textbooks.

The giants and unicorns were joined by other monsters that from time to time aroused uneasiness in people's minds about the fanciful conception *vis plastica*.

A spring near Vienna produced a basilisk. A dragon turned up near Klagenfurt. Dragons' teeth were found lying about in caves in the Alps. From the East travelers brought back the talons of the winged griffin. It was not until a later age abandoned all legendary and fantastic stories that it proved possible to take comprehensive stock of such finds. The Polyphemus turned out to be a prehistoric elephant, the Teutobochus a *Dinotherium* of the Tertiary period, and the unicorn a mammoth. The dragons, basilisks, and griffins were found to be in some cases mammoths and in others woolly rhinoceroses, while the "dragons' teeth" were finally identified as having belonged to cave bears of the Ice Age. Meanwhile many years passed, many disputes arose, and many investigators were laughed out of court.

Strangely enough, by far the most intelligent theory of the origin of fossils remained wholly neglected right up to Scheuchzer's time. It was proposed by Leonardo da Vinci, who had often dug up fossilized marine shellfish as a young man while engaged in the construction of canals in northern Italy. He believed that they could only have been carried inland by the sea, and he concluded that the land had probably risen from the ocean, bringing a number of marine

Fossil finds give rise to stories of dragons: a dragon and lion, after a drawing by Leonardo da Vinci.

animals with it in the process; then the slime in which the animals lay embedded hardened and turned into stone, and the organisms themselves decayed, leaving hollows in the fossilized mud that they had occupied. At a much later stage, when fresh layers of mud deposited by the ocean found their way into these hollows of the rock, they flowed into the grooves like liquid metal into a clay mold. This mud, too, finally hardened and became a "fossil," preserving a clear copy of the shape of the creature long since completely dissolved.

In all probability Scheuchzer would not have been able to make much of this astonishingly modern explanation if he had ever come across it. It was too rational for him, unhesitatingly overstepping the boundaries of the Mosaic account of the Creation. Scheuchzer's own favorite was John Woodward. A few years before the discovery of the Altdorf vertebrae this eccentric Puritan had published in England a vast work on the Flood, attributing the cause of the catastrophe to inundation by a subterranean sea. Hardly anyone took Woodward seriously. But Scheuchzer adopted his theory with enthusiasm and set himself to find proof of it.

He took the two Gallows Hill bones back to Zurich with him, where he became chief physician of the town and a canon. He added to his collection, continuing his researches and biding his time. A number of disciples gathered about him, defiantly calling themselves "Diluvians," or "Floodists." They kept a sharp lookout for traces of those old sinners, whose thoughts and desires had once grown so evil that God repented of having created Man on the face of the earth and He drowned them, together with "beast, and the creeping thing, and the fowls of the air."

A complaint by the fishes of Lake Constance

In 1708 Scheuchzer denounced the professors' *vis plastica* doctrine in a pamphlet. He called his preposterous treatise — in Latin — *The Fishes' Complaint and Vindication.* A large pike from Lake Constance opened the prosecution on behalf of his fellow water dwellers and made a fiery speech in Latin attacking the injustice and unreasonable attitude of mankind.

The pike alleged that in the past the innocent fish had appeared before a tribunal set up to judge the sinful conduct of Man. The poor fish had been condemned to atone for human wickedness, and when the Flood subsided they had been left high and dry to die a miserable death. And as if that were not enough, at the present time the hardhearted human race declined to recognize them as companions in misfortune, or even as existing at all. Man had degraded their remains by classifying them as the product of mineral rock and marl.

Scheuchzer let his pike ramble on for a time in this accusing vein, putting into his mouth several nasty little digs at the experts. Then he played his trump card. He described the two vertebrae from Gallows Hill and declared that they proved, for the first time, the discovery of an antediluvian human being, one of those who had been punished by the great catastrophe and who, in accordance with God's will, had been forced to lay down his life in company with the guiltless fish and been embedded at their side in the form of an eternal warning symbol in stone.

It began to look as though the lawyer-pike might win his suit. The pamphlet made quite a stir. The public, always eager for sensation, bought it enthusiastically. Woodward, the original Flood specialist, gave the document his support and the Church itself added its blessing.

The professional scientists, to be sure, cold-shouldered Scheuchzer now as they had done before. His learned fellow countryman, the Swiss Langius, at once published a counterblast. How was it, he wanted to know, that the marked rocks as a rule only represented separate components of an organism instead of the complete animal? His own explanation was as follows. A "seminal gust" came in contact with the soil and started its tricks there by turning the rock into parts of a body, vertebrae, teeth, bone splinters, or shells. Although the gust in question took living nature as its pattern, it copied the wrong object and so brought only fragmentary images into being. The Altdorf vertebrae, he maintained, were simply incomplete creations of this kind.

Scheuchzer could only smile at such a hypothesis. It was Avicenna run mad and turned into a mystic. In addition to which, the idea was an indecent one. The reactionaries now really began to lose ground. The dispute would have looked very promising for the Floodists if a hitherto absolutely unknown man named Johann Jakob Bajer had not suddenly taken a hand in it.

This second Hansjakob was a mineralogist, so he knew something about rocks. He had been collecting in the same regions as Scheuchzer and, like him, had explored the hill country round Altdorf. His investigations were inspired neither by Avicenna nor the Mosaic story of the Creation; instead they were enthusiastically based upon the geological writings of the old French master potter Palissy and those of the Italians Fracastoro and Colonna. These Renaissance thinkers too had once been unimportant laymen. They had held views similar to those of Leonardo da Vinci and had declared, like him, that fossils were the remains of marine animals. Palissy, being a Huguenot, had been sentenced to lifelong imprisonment. Bajer carried on the ideas of these men. He published a book at the same time as the fishes' advocate issued his pamphlet. Bajer's work could not have been called with the best will in the world either original or tendentious. It was a sober geological study of the Alps and contained illustrations of certain vertebrae exactly similar to those from Gallows Hill at Altdorf. Bajer described them, in so many words, as fossilized fish vertebrae.

When he read this, Scheuchzer sprang up from his desk in a rage and at once proceeded to call the unimaginative mineralogist to account. Hansjakob Bajer was not a supporter of Avicenna, to be sure. He believed neither in freaks of nature nor in seminal gusts making love to rocks. On the contrary, he considered it self-evident that living beings might turn to slate, chalk, and marl. He was almost on Scheuchzer's side. But fancy mistaking human bones for fish-bones! Scheuchzer felt obliged to call attention to this absurdity in no uncertain terms.

His attack did not sway Bajer from his opinion. Those doubly perforated bones Scheuchzer had found underneath the gibbet could only be, as any zoologist could tell at a glance, parts of the skeleton of a fish. Antediluvian men indeed! Bajer shrugged his shoulders; that was a theological question which might be important for a canon, but not for a mineralogist. The matter under dispute in this case was not the Flood, but simply a couple of black, doubly perforated vertebrae, pieces of the bony structure of a large fish. They had been fully discussed in his book on rock formation and so far as he was concerned that was the end of it.

The delighted academic spectators of this dispute applauded Bajer. Though they might not be completely in agreement with his opinion that these curious pictures in stone had once belonged to living fishes, they did admit that the Altdorf finds bore a striking resemblance to the vertebrae of fish. Human vertebrae, they strenuously maintained, had quite a different appearance. And they rejoiced at the salutary check administered to that nuisance of a Zurich canon and the relegation of the "Flood man" to the fossil room, where he would be unable to cause any further confusion.

There the Gallows Hill bones remained. Until the end of the eighteenth century they were considered parts of the skeleton of a fish. It was not until the era of the great fossil discoveries that both Scheuchzer and Bajer were found to have been mistaken. The bones were in fact the vertebrae of that star exhibit of the paleontologists, *Ichthyosaurus*.

Scheuchzer did not believe that his defeat at Bajer's hands had settled the question. After that he did keep quiet about the two vertebrae, and he may have secretly lost his implicit faith in them to some extent; but he stuck grimly to his Flood theory and converted more and more young people to its enthusiastic acceptance. One of these days I will definitely find that old sinner of the Bible, he thought. At length, eighteen years later, he was able to play his last great trump card.

The persecuted skeleton of an ancient sinner

The village of Oningen in upper Baden was economically depend-
ent on its limestone quarries, as Altdorf had been on its hops. Both
limestone and hops have only an indirect connection with natural
science. It was pure chance that made Altdorf and Oningen in particular the starting point of the investigation of the dawn of history.
It was merely one of those twists of fate which certain people are so
fond of referring to some kind of general law — twists of fate that,
in the course of history, have led to the discovery of electricity, of
bacilli, of Neanderthal man, and even of America itself. It was
quite by chance that Scheuchzer, in the Oningen limestone quarries,
stumbled across a regular hotchpotch of what were unquestionably
fishbones. It was by chance that a few quarrymen were present who
were sharper witted than their companions. It was by chance that
these particular quarrymen came upon the one slab of calcareous
slate in a condition to set off the avalanche of discovery that was to
follow.

Even in those days stonemasons were glad to unearth fossils. They
could be used as charms against illness, or could be placed in cattle
troughs to cure the staggers. They could be pulverized and their
dust sold to people suffering from stomach trouble, bites, or im-
potence. The men in the pits were therefore always pleased to see
those figured rocks, which brought them a welcome addition to their
wages. Consequently, when they saw Scheuchzer hunting about in
the Oningen chalk pits and heard his request to have all their future
finds, the laborers exchanged knowing winks, assuming that the respectable Zurich canon wanted to go in for the business himself.
Well, let him, if he was willing to pay.

"Here, look at this one," said one of the Oningen stonemasons,
beckoning to his companions, soon after Scheuchzer had left. He
showed them a slab he had extracted from the chalk. "Doesn't look
like a fish to me."

"No!" His fellow worker stared in bewilderment at a queer-looking pattern of bones half buried in the splintered slate. "Got an
eye and a hand, hasn't it?"

The finder nodded.

"Like a child, eh? Think it's worth anything?"

"Might bring ten gulden," said the other sagely. "What do you
say?"

The finder agreed with him. Accordingly, they carried the slab carefully out of the pit, wrapped it in straw, and deposited it at the post station. A few days later the parcel reached Scheuchzer.

The canon immediately summoned his friend David Reding, a sculptor. The former's hands trembled with excitement as he fingered the bones from Oningen. "Look at the one on top, that's the frontal bone," he exclaimed. "Underneath it you can see the eye sockets! And behind it the remains of the cerebellum are still recognizable!"

"Yes," replied Reding thoughtfully. "It certainly looks remarkably human."

"Human? I should think so!" Scheuchzer rapped his knuckle against the slab of slate. "Look at that nasal bone! And here's the pelvic bone! And this one is a fragment of humerus." He stared at Reding with sparkling eyes. "You say it looks human? Well, I tell you that, as sure as I stand here, it's genuine human bone. Human evidence of the Flood!"

Reding became infected by the other's enthusiasm.

"Well, so you've got him at last, that old sinner of yours?"

"I have indeed," Scheuchzer said in a positive tone. "I knew it all along, David. I never doubted I should find him one day. Could you make me a woodcut of him straightway?"

He was already planning a fresh pamphlet. And this time, he swore with the holy fire of a prophet to see to it that no Bajer stood in his way.

Reding started sketching the "old sinner." Meanwhile Scheuchzer began his manifesto, not in the obscure disguise this time of a fish-plaintiff, but as the passionate advocate of God's word. He called his treatise *A Most Rare Memorial of That Accursed Generation of Men of the First World, the Skeleton of a Man Drowned in the Flood.* It was a forthright title which surely no one would dare to criticize.

"In addition to the infallible testimony of the Divine Word," he began, coming at once to the main point of the argument, "we have a number of other proofs of the occurrence of the universal and terrible Deluge. They are plants, fishes, quadrupeds, insects, shellfish, and countless snails. Hitherto very few traces have been found of the human beings who perished on that occasion. Their corpses floated on the surface of the waters and soon decayed. It is not always possible to prove that their bones, which have been found from time to time, are human." It certainly isn't possible to do so, he was thinking, when ignoramuses like Bajer deal with them.

He then flourished his new discovery in the face of science.

The accompanying illustration, a carefully executed woodcut now offered for the consideration of the learned and inquiring world, is an indubitable and indeed unmistakable relic of the Flood. It does not merely present certain features in which a vivid imagination could detect something approximating to the human shape. On the contrary, it corresponds completely with all the parts and proportions of a human skeleton. Even the bones embedded in the stone, and some of the softer components too, are identifiable as genuine and may easily be distinguished from the remainder of the rock. The skeleton is seen from the front, buried in a sepulchre which exceeds in age and authenticity every Roman, Greek, Egyptian, or other oriental monument.

Even in this critical hour Scheuchzer could not resist moralizing. He added a couplet that has outlasted the centuries. It was often quoted at students' gatherings, and has won a place for the father of prehistoric research in the history of unconscious humor.

Afflicted skeleton of old, doomed to damnation,
Soften, thou stone, the hearts of this wicked generation!

Scheuchzer knew well enough whom he meant by the "wicked generation." He only wished he could saddle all the adversaries of his Flood theory with a new Day of Judgment.

It was in the year 1726 that his treatise on the Flood man appeared. The public fought for copies and the professors were obliged to sit up and take notice. The clergy announced that the statements in the Bible were now at last demonstrably true. Simple people were astonished at the time it had taken to discover this fact. And even levelheaded skeptics were left without a word to say in the face of this stone document. The witness to the Flood really existed. He could be seen lying in state in the museum by anyone who cared to go and look at him. The devout stood rooted to the spot, shuddering with awe, as they contemplated their remote ancestor, who, so Scheuchzer calculated, had fallen a victim to Divine justice exactly 4032 years ago. There were only a few who smiled cynically and put rather less faith in the anatomical knowledge of the Zurich canon.

Sixty years later their cynicism turned out to have been perfectly justified. The "afflicted skeleton" was not that of any human being, but had belonged to quite a different sort of creature, of no very special interest. Its precise nature formed the subject of a long discussion. Prehistoric research was still haunted by the "ancient sinner," which occupied the thought of the greatest brains of the ensuing decades. The reader will meet him again in various disguises before finally witnessing his unmasking.

Far more important than the Oningen discovery itself was the tidal wave of controversy and enthusiasm which it aroused in every direction. Scheuchzer's Floodists grew to be a powerful and influential body. They set off zealously in pursuit of fossilized dragons, unicorns, fish, crustaceans, and giant snails, as well as the remains of those who had shared the ancient sinner's fate, stuffing the natural history showcases with their specimens. Some of the less romantic among them were actually gradually groping their way to the truth. They observed that fossils found at various depths of the soil did not resemble one another. They were forced to conclude that Europe had had a different climate at the period of the Flood. They produced excellent sketches of "Ammonites," "Thunderbolts," and other prehistoric marine animals.

Scheuchzer himself made no further important discoveries, with the exception of a few species of plants. He completed his collections and published a large work on *Physica sacra*, or *Holy Nature*. Seven years after the excavation of the Oningen bones he died famous and greatly respected, at the age of sixty-one. He lived long enough to enjoy a further unexpected triumph over the upholders of the *vis plastica* doctrine. He did not, however, owe it to his Flood man, but to a mild practical joke played by some students on their too credulous professor.

A fossil called Beringer

Johannes Bartolomäus Beringer held the chair of natural history at the University of Würzburg and was physician in ordinary to the bishop of that city. He had been infected by the widespread mania for collecting. He spent all his spare time in the Würzburg quarries looking for fossils. He never found anything of importance, and would certainly never have won fame if it had not unfortunately occurred to him to invite his students to take part in his excursions.

The Würzburg undergraduates were by no means delighted at the prospect. They took no interest in fossils and had something better to do with their spare time. But they had to obey. And the odd thing was that no sooner had they begun to help Professor Beringer than his luck changed. He started unearthing fossils such as no man had ever yet seen. There were frogs in the act of breeding, a spider seizing a fly, queer-looking birds, the most peculiar lizards and salamanders, and insects of species hitherto unheard of.

Beringer, in his rapture over these incomparable treasures, lost all sense of proportion and judgment. It was impossible, he considered, that the specimens found in such lifelike attitudes could have been victims of the Flood. Frogs surprised by the Flood would scarcely have gone on copulating, and a spider surprised by the Flood would have stopped interfering with flies altogether. Triumphantly Beringer concluded that old Avicenna had been right, after all. A natural creative force had shaped the stone, imitating processes in life itself. Had done so, did he say? No, Nature was still at it, she first modeled her creatures in stone and then breathed life into them. The things he had found in the Würzburg shell-lime were embryonic, the first stage in creation from dead, rigid matter.

There was no end to Beringer's surprising finds. He dug up a fossilized sun, a crescent moon, and a star with all its rays. At last he actually found a tablet inscribed with Hebraic characters. It seemed, therefore, as though that mysterious creative power had designed everything in the world by producing a preliminary sketch in stone. This was a discovery with incalculable consequences that would turn all natural history upside down. Beringer was overjoyed.

He set to work and described his treasure trove in a stately folio, illustrated by a number of decorative copperplate engravings. Here could be seen those frogs in their amorous frenzy, and the fly-catching spider, as well as those other puzzling creatures, the celestial bodies and the Hebraic characters. And the professor, in an exhaustive presentation of his views, ingeniously supported the *vis plastica* doctrine, rounded off by his own theory of spontaneous generation from stone. He repudiated with zest all hypotheses involving the marine origin of fossils. But it was the Floodists who elicited his wittiest sallies.

His book burst like a bomb into the middle of the debate over Scheuchzer's Flood man. Nobody laughed. The book was read with the same intense interest as the description of the Oningen skeleton. The defenders of the plastic creative force praised Beringer's demonstration to the skies. Even his "spontaneous generation" did not perturb them. The general belief at that time was that frogs, beetles, flies, and maggots might well be generated from mud or rotting flesh. So why could they not equally well originate in Würzburg shell-lime?

But their triumph was short lived. Further excavations in the professor's favorite quarry brought to light, in addition to some other curiosities, a stone with Beringer's name on it. Then at last the Würzburg students unsealed their lips and confessed to the trick they had played. Beforehand they had modeled all the fossils in clay, fired them, and hidden them in the places where their professor was most likely to look.

Peals of mocking, diabolical laughter assailed the ears of the unfortunate Beringer. He at once raised all the money he could to buy up the whole edition of his work and destroy it. Some copies, however, escaped him. Later on, collectors of curiosities paid high prices for them. So after forty years had elapsed and the scandal had long since been forgotten a second edition of the *Book of False Fossils* appeared, and found many buyers. Many of the latter had never heard of the students' trick and once more discussed the possibility of spontaneous generation from stone. It is tempting to dismiss the whole story with a smile. But the history of paleontology includes plenty of similar puzzles, and not only overcredulous laymen, poets, philosophers, and kings have been deceived by them, but eminent scientists, too, have fallen into the trap.

The Beringer case made the *vis plastica* theory look so absurd that the doctrine seemed to have no scientific future. The whole of prehistoric research fell temporarily into disrepute. Something of the ridicule poured upon the unlucky Würzburg professor attached itself to every collector of fossils. Even Scheuchzer's ancient sinner suddenly grew unpopular as a subject of fashionable conversation. No one now knew what was true and what was false in this connection.

However, in the end the Floodists managed to save their faces. The Nuremberg copperplate engraver, botanist, and mineralogist Georg Wolfgang Knorr followed in Scheuchzer's footsteps. He sought eagerly for further traces of the epoch of the Flood. About the middle of the century he published, in association with Johann Ernst Immanuel Walch, who shared his views, four stout folios containing two hundred and seventy-five illustrations, with the pompous title, *A Collection of the Curiosities of Nature and Antiquities of the Soil Bearing Witness to a Universal Deluge*. This work contained all the available knowledge to date regarding the early history of the earth and fossils. The volume put an end to the era of fantasy and charlatanism and ushered in an age of truly scientific research.

Voltaire objects

But in France a cool blast of criticism was already making itself felt. The forerunners of the Revolution were raising their voices, and they were not greatly impressed by the Biblical story of creation. The Flood did not interest them in the slightest. They preferred to talk vaguely of natural law, freedom, equality, and progress. Circles of atheists were formed, and the cleverest men among them ruled the roost. Rousseau, the Noble Savage, dressed as an Armenian, roamed the drawing rooms of Paris, proclaiming that man was a child of nature.

In this sort of intellectual climate a certain man, who understood very well the art of needling an adversary in argument, was able to floor the Flood theorists with a few elegant phrases without difficulty. His name was François Marie Arouet. He was an author, a dramatist, a philosopher, and an opponent of the Jesuits. History, although not natural history, knows him under the name of Voltaire.

Voltaire was very far from being an apostle of nature. He wrote to Rousseau after reading one of his books: "It really makes one want to go on all fours! Come and have a drink of my cow's milk with me. And if you must eat grass, you can do it here!" Rousseau replied: "I don't like you. In fact, I hate you." Therefore it is clear that Voltaire did not pick up his pen with the intention of hurling a Rousseauesque "Back to Nature!" at the students of prehistory who believed in the Bible. On the contrary, he attacked the Floodists because the whole fuss about "nature" was anathema to him.

Thirteen years after the discovery of the "afflicted skeleton" he was writing, in a humorous vein:

> There are some errors which only concern simple people and others which concern philosophers. Perhaps this last category includes the idea of so many investigators of Nature that some revolutionary change once took place. They are determined to find evidence for it scattered over the entire surface of the globe. A stone has been found in the Hessian hills which apparently bore the impression of a turbot and a petrified pike has been discovered in the Alps. The conclusion was drawn that the sea and the rivers flowed, in succession, over the mountains. It would have been more natural to suppose that some traveler had brought the fish with him to eat and thrown them away among the mountains because they had gone bad during the journey, whereupon, in due course, they petrified. But this idea was too simple for the naturalists because, you see, it didn't fit into a system.

A young compatriot of Voltaire's, the talented Jean Etienne Guettard, could have told him that petrifaction of rotten fish would be an impossibility and that the "pikes" and "turbots" referred to looked very different from the kinds one could buy in the Paris fish market. But Guettard, a man of the same stamp as the unlucky potter Palissy, had something else to do. He was having an argument with the Sorbonne, the Paris school of theologians. The latter could not do much against literary freethinkers. But they could do a good deal against heretical natural scientists. According to Guettard's researches, fossils had not been caused by a single deluge but by a large number of marine inundations. Old fossils had been found in deep layers of the earth and later ones in the upper layers. This observation was pioneering work. The censors at the Sorbonne waxed very indignant over it and called upon Guettard to recant in public. In the end he did so. But his theory of a periodical inundation of the continents nevertheless stuck in people's heads, to the annoyance not only of the Sorbonne but also of that archenemy of the Sorbonne, Voltaire.

"In Italy and France," Voltaire reported, "small shellfish have been found which are alleged to be native to Syrian waters. But how is it we don't remember those innumerable swarms of pilgrims and crusaders who took their petty cash to the Holy Land and brought back shellfish in exchange? Ought we to believe, instead, that the sea off Joppa and Sidon came flowing over Milan and Burgundy?" Fashionable society followed Voltaire. In France people began to put their fossils back into their drawers of mineral specimens and turn their attention to more interesting matters.

The Floodists sulked. But they did not mean to let themselves be defeated so easily. They formed, in the midst of all the fuss over the unraveling of prehistory, a brotherhood pledged to mutual support, like the theosophists, spiritualists, vegetarians, and opponents of vaccination of today. They construed every new find to fit their own theory, continued to build up their collections as industriously and imperturbably as bees and took no notice of mockery and intellectuals who professed to know better. Their school outlasted the great age of discovery itself. It was not until the middle of the nineteenth century that the last remnants of the Flood theory were demolished. But the doctrine still lives today in popular tales of prehistory and fantastic newspaper reports.

Did Caesar bring elephants to England?

The first discoverer of human prehistoric remains whose name has come down to us was called Conyers. He was a London apothecary and antique dealer. But his find remained quite unappreciated.

Contemporary observers, who had been deceived by Scheuchzer's ancient sinner and Beringer's false fossils, could not make head or tail of Mr. Conyers' "stone axe." After cracking a few jokes on the subject and making the worthy apothecary's life a burden to him for a time, they finally turned their backs on him and forgot what he had tracked down and identified.

His discovery involved those mysterious bones that so long as one could remember had always been turning up in gravel and stone quarries. They were called "fossil ivory." They had been attributed to unicorns, giants, or dragons and sold for hard cash to the apothecaries, who produced miraculous remedies from them. No one had hitherto thought of comparing them with true ivory — elephants' tusks.

But now Conyers came across a collection of bones of this type in the ancient deposits dredged up from the Thames near London. He made a close examination of them. This took place in the year 1715, some time after the Altdorf finds and before the discovery of the "afflicted skeleton." Conyers, as a keen businessman, would probably have troubled himself very little about the significance for natural science of his find and would have metamorphosed the fossil ivory at top speed into a powerful cure for something or other had the prices for "unicorn" at the time been anything like steady. Just at that moment, however, they were falling in a most distressing manner. Pieces that had been worth their weight in gold at an earlier date now fetched only a few shillings. A member of Conyers' guild complained that unicorns' amulets were set "no longer in gold and silver but hung on iron chains. The efficiency of the unicorn is apparently declining. Its former high repute has gone."

The bones were therefore hardly worth displaying in Conyers' shop. Obviously, he ought to treat them differently and exhibit them as curiosities to antiquarians. He knew that curio collectors were quite willing to pay out a few gold pieces for anything they really wanted. He stared hard at the fossils. Then he suddenly saw that he had picked up not only bones and fossil ivory but also a stone cut in a very peculiar fashion. It looked like an axe. At once he began to think out the terms in which he would commend this rarity to potential buyers. A hunter of the old days had made a stone axe and slain with it the monsters who were responsible for the fossil ivory. What sort of monsters could they have been? Conyers twirled and twisted the bones and teeth this way and that. I'll be dashed, he thought, if these aren't a real elephant's!

A crowd of grinning Cockneys assembled outside Conyers' shop. An elephant in England killed by an ancient Briton with a stone axe — that was rich indeed! Why did the bold elephant hunter not use a decent iron axe? they asked the apothecary. Or what about a spear, like those of the Indians and Moors? A wag suggested that a short time ago an elephant might have escaped from an English menagerie. The rest nodded. Yes, no doubt the elephant had come to grief somewhere, someone had thrown a rock over its carcass, and then that practical joker Conyers had got the idea of trying to talk the collectors into accepting the thing as a curio from the days of our ancestors.

Conyers saw his chance of profit melting away. He argued stoutly that no one denied there had once been unicorns and dragons in England. Why on earth, then, shouldn't his elephant be a genuine one? As for the axe being made of stone, he declared (without suspecting how near his declaration came to the truth) that the ancient Britons had in their time not known the use of metal, and had therefore been obliged to resort to stone weapons.

The crowd only laughed the louder. Some patriotic gentlemen knitted their brows, exclaiming, "Impertinent fellow!" Conyers would have had to throw his axe, and the elephant's bones, too, onto the rubbish heap, if his friend Mr. Bagford had not called to give him some good advice. "Why is it," inquired Bagford, "that you are so determined to make your hunter prehistoric? That's nonsense, you know. No one is going to swallow that. Just think a minute. Who could have brought elephants to England? You don't know? Well, I'll tell you. The Romans did. Just the Romans, no one else. The things you found are souvenirs from the time of the Romans." He added consolingly, "I expect they're valuable souvenirs."

Conyers took that hint. A few days later Londoners started debating whether Caesar had once overrun the Britons with elephants, or whether this inconsiderate method of waging war was not rather to be ascribed to the Emperor Claudius. One thing at any rate they were sure of. One of the plucky defenders of his country seventeen hundred years ago, having no other weapons, had carved out one from a stone and attacked a Roman elephant with it. Interesting, to be sure, but that was about all. Mr. Conyers found a buyer, the Londoners went home in a good humor, and the axe and the bones accumulated dust in a collection of curios.

The ancient Romans, so kindly provided with tanks in the shape of elephants by the imaginative Mr. Bagford, were distinctly better acquainted with early human civilizations than the fellow citizens of Conyers the apothecary. They had been perfectly well aware that men had fought and obtained their food, first with "tooth and claw," then with wooden spears and stone knives, later with swords of bronze, and only at the final stage with iron weapons. But this knowledge had been lost with antiquity itself. It was not until the age of the great voyages of discovery, when Europeans met primitive Stone Age men in other parts of the world, that the lost information came to light again. The greatest zoologist of the Renaissance period, Ulisse Aldrovandi, an exceptionally enlightened man for his time, published a monumental work on the animal and vegetable kingdoms. He was also the first investigator to assemble zoological and botanical specimens in modern style. He was a vigorous upholder of the opinion that all humanity had at one time or another passed through a "stone age" similar to that still prevailing in the primeval forests of Africa and America. Since, however, Aldrovandi had spent a great part of his life in prison on charges of heresy, he was not considered by his contemporaries a wholly reliable guide to prehistory. Other Renaissance scholars who followed in his footsteps were just as little appreciated. It was terrible to think that the ancestors of Western man had been nothing better than barbarous savages armed with knuckle-dusters! It was altogether more consoling to believe that humanity, apart from the dark-skinned heathens, had been furnished with civilization in the shape of tools, iron weapons, and utensils at the moment of creation.

A few years after Mr. Conyers' original disappointment, a German historian named Eckart was at work on the rise and development of the ancient Teutons. His researches did not take him very far back into prehistory, nor did he venture to risk the slightest consideration of those early elephant hunters. But the few Teutonic burial places and barrows subsequent to that time which he did investigate gave him quite a shock. He found no trace of iron in them, but plenty of bronze swords and shields, bronze domestic articles, and bronze ornaments. In still older Teutonic burial places even bronze was absent. The knives, scrapers and spear points were made of antlers, nephrite, and hornstone.

Eckart composed a treatise in which he advanced conclusions which are still valid today. A Stone Age, corresponding with primitive cults, was succeeded by a Bronze Age that introduced civilization, and finally by an Iron Age that has lasted up to the present time.

Hardly any notice was taken of this essay. The innovating student of the ancient Germans, who had been so far ahead of his time, joined Bajer and Conyers in the ranks of the great host of the forgotten.

THE MAN WHO CLASSIFIED NATURE

Fins become wings

THE STUDY of prehistory is a direct descendant of the study of biology. At a time when biology as a science hardly existed, interest in fossils did not count as science either. It was considered a hobby for amateurs, a plaything for visionaries, quacks, and speculators. It was not until a man arrived who classified natural phenomena and assigned them degrees of importance and names that it became possible to do the same for the surviving traces of prehistoric times. The age of fantasy which listened to Hansjakob Scheuchzer gave place to the age of systematization with Carolus Linnaeus as its director.

Of course a prehistoric find is by no means adequately explained by giving it a name and a place in nature's system. If an ancient pitcher is dug up, people are not going to be satisfied with naming it and identifying the material it is made of and the cultural cycle to which it belongs. It will also be compared with other pitchers produced by the community in question before and after the date of the find under investigation. Attempts will be made to throw some light on the cultural history of the community. The pitcher, in short, will be examined with the eye of the historian.

This process seems obvious to us today. But it appeared very late in the sphere of natural history. The continuous historical development that was recognized in human affairs — the rise, prosperity, decline, and disappearance of nations and civilizations — was still not supposed, a hundred years ago, to apply to nature. The very men who brought order into the bewildering exuberance of nature, Aristotle in antiquity and Linnaeus at the threshold of the new scientific age, were those who most strenuously opposed the dynamic method of observation of nature. They preferred a system that gave every phenomenon its own immutable position in the pattern, to groping in the dark and dubious purlieus of history and prehistory. No wonder! Anyone who has had anything to do with government officials knows how much they prefer paragraphs and documents to living matter. And the systematizers are the government officials of natural science.

The Greek natural philosophers, who were not only thinkers but also scientists and men of the world — a happy but unfortunately rare combination — had in most cases believed that nature developed, that species died out and were renewed, and that mankind originally came from the animal kingdom. Aristotle put an end to this approach for more than two thousand years. In his view everything in nature was duly arranged and ticketed in accordance with a permanent design in which any kind of progress or transition from species to species was allowed only to a very restricted extent. His successors behaved still more like officials. They even canceled the slight exceptions he had made. They would have nothing to do with experimental investigation. They did not consider nature to be a maze of puzzles and surprises, but a big picture book with pages that zoologists and botanists could turn over so long as they did not add anything.

Such was the extremely unsatisfactory situation when Linnaeus took a hand in the game. For some time now the first "development theorists" had been proclaiming their opinions. They boldly expressed their doubts of Aristotle's rigid system and could not reconcile themselves to the belief that nature had remained unchanged like a stone statue since the days of its creation.

The first criticism of the doctrine of the immutability of species was worked out, so far as we know, between the years 1603 and 1616, behind the prison walls of the Tower. Sir Walter Raleigh, seaman and explorer, favorite of Queen Elizabeth and founder of Virginia, was confined there, waiting for his death sentence to be confirmed. But he did not idle away his time. He compiled a history of the world in five volumes, containing detailed descriptions of his American experiences and impressions. And since he appreciated nature as much as seamanship or love he set himself to answer the question whether the many newly discovered species of animals in America, as well as the familiar creatures of the Old World, could have been squeezed into Noah's Ark. The problem was a very serious one. Many of the learned men of his day had already begun worrying over this increased number of species and formations. How on earth had old Noah ever managed to find room in the restricted space of his ship for a pair of each of them?

As an admiral, Raleigh felt certain that even Noah could not have built an ark large enough to contain all the kinds of animals in existence. The answer to the riddle must be that only the animals of the

Old World were rescued from the Flood. Later on some of them must have migrated to America, undergone certain transformations because of the climate, and thus originated new species. In this simple statement lurked the germ of the modern environmental theory of mutation.

Fifty years later another Englishman took up Raleigh's idea. He, too, had never been concerned with natural science for its own sake, though he was interested in it. This was Matthew Hale, a learned lawyer and Lord Chief Justice of England. He went a little farther in the matter of Noah's Ark than had Elizabeth's great admiral. In his view God had only created the primitive and rudimentary forms of the animal species, thus assembling a relatively small menagerie that could easily be stored aboard a single ship. From this nucleus of breeding stock the manifold varieties of later times had developed.

Leading theologians indulgently endorsed the opinions of Raleigh and Hale. Consequently, their worries over the tonnage of Noah's Ark came to an end. But before long a third layman entered the field. He was the French Consul Benoît de Maillet, and what he had to say was by no means so congenial. He made no reference to the Deluge and left the Biblical story of creation entirely out of consideration. Instead, he again advanced the old classical theory of the production of land masses from the sea. The seed of the first animals and plants, he said, had arrived from other parts of the universe, raining down into the primeval ocean. Marine creatures were first originated in this way, and they gave rise to all further forms of life. Benoît de Maillet explained the process as follows. A few among the thousands of living forms gradually grew accustomed, as the ocean retreated, to breathing air. They went through an amphibious stage, thus little by little turning into animals with lungs, or true land dwellers.

There can be no doubt [wrote the consul-naturalist at the same period as Scheuchzer was tracking down his Flood man] that fish, in the course of hunting or being hunted, were thrown up on the shore. There they could find food, but were unable to return to the water. Subsequently their fins were enlarged by the action of the air, the radial structures supporting the fins turned to quills, the dried scales became feathers, the skin assumed a coating of down, the belly-fins changed into feet, the entire body was re-shaped, the neck and beak being prolonged, and at last the fish was transformed into a bird. Yet the new configuration corresponded in a general way with the old. The latter will always remain readily recognizable.

Seldom has a man been so laughed to scorn as was this first protagonist of the theory of evolution with his mumbo jumbo about fish turning into birds. With remarkable foresight he took care that his book on the subject should not appear until after his death. Otherwise he would have been boycotted by society. His ideas were too much for even the Age of Enlightenment to swallow.

A recognized expert of those years approached the problem far more cautiously. The natural scientist and philosopher Leibniz noticed in studying fossils that the fossilized species of marine creatures seemed to have quite died out. No one had ever found a living one. This remarkable fact had already attracted the attention of the first Floodists. They wondered at first whether the raging waters of the Flood might have destroyed a number of species. But there was nothing about that in the Bible. They consoled themselves with the belief that specimens of these puzzling creatures would one day be found in some remote corner of the ocean. In other words, as we should say today, they believed in the sea serpent. Leibniz, however, though he had been taken in by Guericke's unicorn, would not accept the sea serpent. He posed the pertinent question: "May we not reasonably conclude that the great changes which have taken place in the past transformed a large number of animal species?" He meant, in fact, that the fossils might be the ancestors of the forms of life prevalent today.

This was not a revolutionary theory like that of Benoît de Maillet. It was no challenge to current opinion, but merely a modest question. Leibniz did not intend to encroach upon the provinces of the zoologist and geologist. But he felt the problem to be so important that he returned to it in another connection. "Perhaps at some period, somewhere in the universe, several sorts of animals, all resembling the cat to some extent, such as the lion, the tiger, and the lynx, were members of a single race and may perhaps today be no more than subdivisions of the single species cat." Two "perhapses" in one sentence! Leibniz knew better than the French consul how far he could go and how much he could expect from his enlightened fellow citizens.

These were the tentative advances over the frontier of knowledge made just before the advent of Linnaeus. Almost immediately afterwards the whole picture changed. People began debating the age of the earth, the kinship between animals and plants, and even the origin of mankind. Scheuchzer's ancient sinner was actually exhumed and examined for signs of life. Subsequent treatment of him would certainly not have pleased the worthy canon of Zurich. A new era began, rich in new observations and conclusions, but also bristling with error and false inference. This was the period of Carolus Linnaeus.

The swallow at the bottom of the sea

On May 13, 1707, at Rashult in the parish of Stenbrohult, a son was born to the curate Nils Ingemarsson Linnaeus, who christened the child Karl Nilsson and called him Kalle for short. Kalle wrote a good deal, later on, about the landscape of southern Sweden, in which he grew up. He described the moors, the oak forests, and the lakes of Smaland, the purple heather, the luxuriant beauty of the flowers, and the variety of bird song. We may therefore assume, to the extent that autobiography can be trusted, that such impressions had a profound effect upon his character at an early age.

Historians declare that he was lazy at school and took more interest in the flowers that grew in his father's prettily designed garden than in science. If that is correct he had already at that time instinctively entered upon the only course appropriate to his future mode of life. If he had shown as much industry and talent as his younger brother Samuel he would undoubtedly have been sent to the theological seminary, to enable him to follow in his father's footsteps later on. As it was, his brother Samuel became a pastor, and Kalle, with his idle ways, after a few false starts could only take up the career that was destined in the end to make him one of the greatest Swedes who ever lived.

Nils Ingemarsson, his father, who had meanwhile exchanged his Rashult curacy for the Stenbrohult living, did not know whether to laugh or to cry as he contemplated the eccentric inclinations of his eldest son. At first he encouraged the boy's love of flowers, for he too loved them. He even assisted in bringing about the final catastrophe. As soon as Kalle had mastered the rudiments of Latin he presented him, in the innocent hope that it would give him a taste for learning, with the *Historia animalium* of Aristotle.

Kalle found Aristotle's book a real revelation — it was the most exciting thing he had ever come across. He suddenly saw nature not as a chaotic mass of wonders and puzzles, but as an orderly hierarchy, disposed and organized by Divine providence. He learned that all species and forms were merely illustrations of eternal and immutable

ideas, that they were as eternal and immutable as the original patterns themselves. Plants and animals could be classified, according
to their structure and mode of life, into divisions and subdivisions.
The world became simple and intelligible. Every phenomenon,
rock, herb, and tree, fish, bird, and quadruped, and Man also, was
firmly rooted in its proper place. All one had to do was to turn the
pages of the book, look up what one wanted, and read about it.
Then one had the key to the magic kingdom. Kalle Linnaeus, the
Stenbrohult parson's son, had the same experience as so many other
young men eager for knowledge were to have after him. He became
positively intoxicated by the open-sesame of the systematizers. There
was no room for anything else in his head, in spite of the disapproval
of the headmaster of the school at Vaxjo which he attended.

Man, too, said Aristotle, was a part of nature which had to be
fitted into the system. Kalle turned the page and read on. "We must
start by describing Man. For of all animals Man is the one we know
best." Of all animals, he thought. That wasn't in the curriculum
at Vaxjo. After due reflection he took a note of that sentence. He
took more notes, and they made him still more uneasy. He read that
storks and swallows were not birds of passage, but went to sleep in
winter. And though he had seen the Smaland storks and swallows
fly south every year, he still believed Aristotle. He went on believing
him even when he had to utter, at school, that verse from Jeremiah:
"Yea, the stork in the heaven knoweth her appointed times; and the
turtle and the crane and the swallow observe the time of their
coming." He shook his head stubbornly. The Bible was wrong.
Aristotle made that clear.

Forty years later when he was a famous man, he still declared,
with the obstinacy of a child, that swallows and storks wintered
at the bottom of the sea. He stuck to this belief and could never,
throughout his life, be convinced of his mistake. He preferred to
credit Aristotle's statement rather than his own experience.

The inevitable occurred. The Vaxjo teachers reported to Parson
Nils Ingemarsson that Kalle was inattentive, and Nils Ingemarsson
took the usual steps of zealous fathers in such cases: he gave his son
a hiding, took him away from the school, and apprenticed him to
a cobbler. Kalle might then have gone on indefinitely stitching away
and patching up soles, instead of meditating on the winter slumbers
of swallows, if it had not been for Rothman, the family doctor,
the first of the long series of helpful foster fathers to whom Linnaeus
owed his success in life. Rothman was an unlucky man. He was a
student of science who had never been able to follow his bent. He
had all the talents that make a great botanist, but he had never

mastered the instrument upon which the son of Nils Ingemarsson was later to play with such virtuosity. He did not understand how to make his way in the world and take advantage of his opportunities. That was why he was still a country doctor at Stenbrohult. He had become infatuated with Kalle. He hoped against hope that this boy, to whom nature was everything, would be able to achieve the ambitions that had been denied him.

Rothman tactfully pleaded with Linnaeus senior. He called attention to Kalle's exceptional zoological and botanical knowledge, and said it was a sin to banish such a gifted boy to a cobbler's stool. At last he succeeded in obtaining permission for his protégé, at the age of twenty-one, to lay aside his awl and thread, and to enroll himself as a medical student at the University of Lund.

The wedding customs of flowers

Kalle Nilsson Linnaeus, equipped with Aristotle and Rothman's essays on plants, started his climb to the top. He thought that he would be able to absorb knowledge with as little trouble as mother's milk. In imagination he already saw himself seated with bent head before collections of botanists' specimens, classifying plants, and ransacking libraries. Whatever Aristotle knew, the professors at Lund would surely know better still.

A great disappointment was in store for him. Lund was not Heidelberg, Leiden, or Paris. It looked more like a rubbish heap than a university town. The streets were full of filth and mud. There were dead dogs and cats lying about all over the place. Every day Linnaeus had to wade through disgusting slime to reach the fountains of wisdom. And the worst of it all was that at Lund those fountains were only miserable trickles. Nothing indicates more clearly the state of natural science at the beginning of the eighteenth century than the poverty of the zoological and botanical collections at this small university. There was no museum, only a "Cabinet of Curios" filled with a hotchpotch of extraordinary, weird-looking objects. The library contained hardly a single work from which Linnaeus would have been able to learn anything. The rector, Anders Rydelius, was a follower of the philosophy of Descartes, according to which animals and plants were soulless machines. He frankly detested — there is no other word for it — every kind of experimental study, called admiration for nature a "betrayal of reason," and refused to allow at his university the representation "of anything so Godless in this world of the spirit."

It was hardly the best spot for a budding botanist and zoologist.

But there was one good thing about it. The place drove Linnaeus to an act of desperation, by which he was diverted from adopting the career of a country doctor and vegetating in a corner like Rothman. One day he discovered that the only useful books on nature which existed in Lund were to be found in the private library of Professor Kilian Stobaeus. Consequently, he broke into this stern person's house at night in order to study them. He was caught in the act, and naturally expected Stobaeus to box his ears with the books, call the beadle, and have him expelled from the university.

But a surprising thing happened. Stobaeus, grumbling and snorting, sat himself down and told his midnight visitor to do the same. Then he began talking, at first in surly fashion, but gradually warming to the theme. He, too, like Rothman, had failed to catch up with his will-o'-the-wisp. In the Lund of Anders Rydelius, so hostile to nature study, he had found no opportunity for the work he wished to do. He had gradually developed from an enthusiastic lover of nature into a frustrated and embittered enemy of the human race, the terror of all high-spirited students. But in the person of the young freshman who had burst in upon him in so unusual a manner he suddenly seemed to recognize his former self and youthful ideals. He forgave the lad for forcing his way into the library, embraced him, gave him all the books he wanted, and thenceforth made him his favorite pupil.

Soon afterwards two more learned graybeards intruded upon Linnaeus' career. They were Olof Rudbeck and Olof Celsius. Linnaeus met them in Rudbeck's botanical garden at Uppsala, the only reputable establishment concerned with natural science that then existed in Sweden. The solicitous Stobaeus, who saw no prospects for his adopted godchild in Lund, had advised him to go there.

The man to whom Sweden owed this center of nature study, Olof Rudbeck the elder, had only taken up botany as a hobby. He had begun his career as a speculative historian and archeologist, mainly devoted to the attempt to prove that Plato had really meant by his Atlantis nothing more nor less than Sweden. Later on, this many-sided genius had entered history as an anatomist, engineer, aesthetician, and musicologist. He died before Linnaeus' time. But his son, Olof Rudbeck the younger, no less versatile a gentleman — at this date seventy years old — had taken over his father's vast field of erudition and was glad of any assistance he could get. He watched for a time the young man recommended by Stobaeus, came to the conclusion that he was meticulous in his work to the point of pedantry, instructed him in the basic theory of plant study, and finally put him in charge of the botanical garden.

Linnaeus was gratified by this appointment. But the small remuneration allowed him by Rudbeck for his work in the garden did not enable him to meet his living expenses, buy books, and pay his college fees. In order to make himself entirely independent of subsidies from home he began to look about for further possibilities of earning money. He discovered that the other scientific luminary at Uppsala, Celsius, the professor of theology, was hard at work on a plan for the publication of a study in several volumes of the plants and animals mentioned in the Bible. He immediately called upon Celsius and said he would be willing to undertake the section of the work concerned with plants. Once more he was in luck. Celsius gave him the job and offered him, by way of remuneration, board and lodging in his own house.

Linnaeus was now really in touch with the source of wisdom. Rudbeck and Celsius realized with amazement that they had accidentally stumbled upon a youthful genius. They took him under their protection, spoonfed him, stuffed him full of facts, and encouraged him, at this early stage, to try his wings.

At the age of twenty-two he was already following a fashion just then coming into vogue among students of natural history. He devised a new method that facilitated the identification and classification of Swedish birds. The graybeards applauded heartily. Linnaeus already visualized himself as something like a new Aristotle. He opened the *Historia animalium* and noted on the fly leaf the amount of author's royalties the old Greek had once received for his works on natural science from Alexander the Great. It was a fabulous sum, which he dreamed about at night. Soon afterwards appeared the book that was to make him famous overnight. It was a treatise on flower fertilization bearing the poetic title *Preludes to a Plant's Wedding*. The result was that at barely three-and-twenty he took over Rudbeck's lectures on botany and could thereafter consider himself one of the master minds of Uppsala.

His essay on the private lives of flowers was really a very unusual one. It even bordered on the scandalous, but it was popular at Uppsala. Linnaeus had made a very close study of the wedding customs of plants and compared them, most daringly for the age in which he wrote, with the sexual habits of animals. It was a striking comparison, but not new. Botanists had long known that male and female plants existed and that those virginally delicate blossoms adorning gardens and parlors were in reality nothing more than sexual organs. But hitherto no one had drawn the logical inferences. No one had yet ventured to give the layman a correct and intelligible idea of the processes operative in the lives of plants. The moralizing attitude toward nature — an attitude that has not yet died out — caused flowers to be contemporaneously regarded as symbols of chastity and animals as those of unchastity. And now Linnaeus, to the disgust of many puritans but to the joy of his generous patrons, was making a clean sweep of this charming delusion.

The reaction to *Preludes to a Plant's Wedding* was a considerable one. But Linnaeus had not yet reached the summit of his fame. He was still only on the lowest rung of the ladder. Many possibilities lay open to him. He might go in for an academic career; he might become an explorer or an author, a system builder or a garden expert. The land stretched fallow in all directions, awaiting the plow. He might become a modern Aristotle or a rebel like Benoît de Maillet. He might demolish the rickety edifice of the wisdom of the schools and set up a new building in its place. Or he might even repair and replaster it.

Linnaeus took the line of least resistance. He settled for restoration, for Aristotle. He was often reproached for this decision by his adversaries, by later biologists, and in particular by the great renovators of the natural sciences in the nineteenth century. But as so often happens, the apparent step back was in reality a step forward. The bold but unproved theories of a Benoît de Maillet could not form the basis of new construction. A surer foundation, a simple system, intelligible to all students of nature, permanently distinguishing the species, genera, divisions, and subdivisions of the animal and vegetable kingdoms, was needed before any attempt could be made to plunge deeper into the secrets of life and growth. Linnaeus had already suspected as much in Uppsala. He had at that time sketched out and scrapped one method of procedure after another, returning again and again to the question of whether Aristotle's long since outdated classification could not be salvaged by some inspired improvement. He could not give up his adored Aristotle, and it was for this very reason that he became famous.

Discovery of the mammoth

A strange procession of men came trickling back to Sweden in those years. Ragged, brutalized, and bearing all the signs of starvation, frostbite, and hardship of every kind, they were the survivors of the three thousand Swedish officers who had been captured by the Russians after their defeat at Poltava and exiled to Siberia and Tartary. They brought back with them from their places of exile a scientific sensation of the first order. It duly reached Uppsala. The ex-prisoners' drawings and maps were copied there, and it was discovered that the world was even more wonderful and mysterious than the treasures and curios in the geographical and natural history cabinets had disclosed.

These three thousand unlucky victims of the war between Charles XII of Sweden and Peter the Great of Russia, or at least as many of them as had not succumbed to the cold of Siberia and the privations of life in the taiga (the eastern alpine region), had used their opportunities to make a profound study of north and east Asia. Their activities left the Russians more or less indifferent. No obstacles were placed in their way, and it was merely a matter of amazement to their captors that the prisoners took the trouble to spread European civilization among the inhabitants of Siberia, setting up schools for the study of languages and mathematics in the deserts, and turning the clay hovels and shacks of the Tartar khans and Tungus (north Asiatic) chiefs into educational centers. The scientific and pedagogic zeal of these compulsory exiles came to the ears of the authorities in St. Petersburg, and some of them were employed as surveyors, cartographers, and collectors of objects of natural history. Accordingly, officers like Philipp Johann Tabbert of Strahlenberg, Gustav Johan Renat, Heinrich Busch, Ambjörn Molin, and Baron Kagg, who actually received the district of Katorga as a gift, traveled, at the orders of the tzar and his subordinate governors, across all northern Asia as far as the Chinese frontiers and those of Manchuria and Kamchatka, coming to know the taiga and tundra regions, their wild animals, and primitive inhabitants, better than any Russian explorer or scientist of the period.

On their return home they produced firstrate maps of the Siberian, Tartar, Kalmuck, and Turkestan countries. They reported that "two or three kinds of Tartar peoples and languages existed," and described beings of so low a cultural level in some respects that the question arose whether they were more than half human. They mentioned roughly hewn stone implements and barbaric customs and cults. The learned world of Sweden absorbed this information with the greatest enthusiasm, realizing that the presence of an enormous body of evidence dating from prehistoric times and freely open to investigation had just been revealed.

Cavalry Captain Baron Kagg's narrative sounded particularly interesting. He had returned to Sweden as early as 1722, bringing with him a most intriguing drawing by his colleague Tabbert von Strahlenberg, still at that time employed as a surveyor in Siberia. The draw-

Herr von Strahlenberg's idea of the appearance of the unicorn.

ing represented an animal something like an ox. But it had claws like a dragon's and two great, much contorted horns growing out of its head. The captain declared that monsters of this sort were still to be found in the Siberian tundra and that he himself, in Strahlenberg's company, had come across their horns buried under the ice. The natives regarded them as a species of gigantic mole, living in burrows deep underground, and called their ivory-like horns *mamontoko-vast*.

What could this beast be? Was it a unicorn? Or the Biblical "behemoth"? People in Stockholm and Uppsala racked their brains. All sorts of theories were advanced, some of which, indeed came near to the truth. There can be no doubt that Linnaeus, too, made a close examination of the *mamontokovast* under the microscope and would have liked to know more about it. To the chagrin of the Swedish naturalists, the supplementary information provided by Strahlenberg some years later did not throw much more light on the subject than the drawing had. No orderly-minded systematizer could possibly fit the creature into his classifications.

Strahlenberg's explanation, supported by the pronouncements of St. Petersburg scientists, Cossack furriers, and Tungus hunters, was that all Russian and Chinese ivory came from *mamontokovast*. Russian businessmen and the native inhabitants, so he had heard, had been for decades in the habit of exploring the country in order to collect or buy up such horns. Isbrand Ides, Peter the Great's ambassador in China, had once talked with one of these ivory buyers while traveling through Siberia, and learned that, although no living *ma-montokovast* had ever been found, here and there a head or a whole carcass of one of these animals did turn up, with fragments of putrid flesh adhering to the blood-stained bones. A practically intact bone, massive, and resembling an elephant's, was to be seen at the St. Petersburg academy. There, too, a report by the German physician and botanist Messerschmidt could be read, according to which the monster "had a hide of long hair like a goat's and might well be the Biblical behemoth." Messerschmidt, a thoroughly reliable man who was one of the many naturalists sent by Tzar Peter to explore Siberia in search of furbearing animals, mineral ores, and other useful products, had discovered in 1724 on a bank of the river Indigirka the complete carcass of a *mamontokovast* in the melting ice. He had made a careful examination of the beast. The obvious inferences to be drawn from all these finds and observations were that in northern Asia a mysterious animal as large as an elephant, with goat hair and horns several yards long, existed and, though no one had ever seen it alive, was the main source of ivory.

If Linnaeus had taken rather more interest in fossils it would certainly have occurred to him that the horns of the *mamontokovast* bore a surprising resemblance to those of Guericke's unicorn. The antediluvian monsters of Zeunickenberg belonged to the same species as the Siberian ivory-bearing animals. They were mammoths. And their "horns" did not ornament their heads, but were carried in their upper jaws as tusks. But neither that titanic genius Kalle Nilsson nor any of the Swedish scientific luminaries ever thought of making such comparisons. They frowned over the bluish-green fragments of ivory from the tundra, brought home by returning travelers as souvenirs, and announced that the Lord God's menagerie was truly vast and manifold. They stumbled over the Tungus word *mamontokovast*, turning it into "mammoth." But they did not venture to include this obscure species in their natural history books. Linnaeus carried his own skepticism even farther. He noted that the alleged ivory looked almost exactly the same as one of the many fossils that had been taken by those daydreaming Floodists as evidence of the Deluge. He told himself, though he kept his own counsel, that Kagg, Strahlenberg, and Messerschmidt might very well have been deceived by queer-looking rocks and freaks of nature. As for the blood-stained carcass found in the ice, that might easily be attributed to mistaken information and native gossip.

But as time went on the Siberian mammoth could no longer be ignored. Hunters in the tundra were perpetually coming across shapeless blocks of ice surrounded by hungry bears, wolves, and foxes. Month after month and often year after year both men and animals made regular pilgrimages to the frozen carcasses and waited for the ice to melt. When at last the thaw came the men took possession of the ivory, the animals devoured the meat, and wind and weather accounted for the bones. Even the Tunguses eventually realized that the mammoth could no longer be regarded as a living animal like the bear and the elk. Perhaps, they thought, it came from the underworld and only bobbed up now and again, in its panoply of ice, to bring ill luck and disaster. Greedily as the men of the tundra sought for tusks, they were awestruck when they came across a whole carcass of the *mamontokovast*. The rumor spread that each finder of a mammoth would perish, together with his entire family.

Seventy years passed before the typical animal of the European and Asiatic Ice Age became recognizable in detail to the keen eyes of a new generation of naturalists. Linnaeus had missed his chance of making this revelation and did not survive to see it. In any case he would not have been able to include it in his system. In 1799 the Tunguse Ossip Schumachov found the carcass of a mammoth in the ice of the Lena estuary, which did not begin to thaw to any extent until 1801. In accordance with the superstition of the time Schu-

The ivory dealer Boltunov's mammoth.

machov fell ill. But when he recovered he began to have doubts about the disastrous effects of finding a mammoth. His conversion was in the end so complete that in 1803 he guided the Russian ivory dealer Boltunov to the carcass, by that time wholly free from ice, and sold him the tusks for fifty rubles. Boltunov was extremely interested. He drew the animal, though without its trunk — which had long since decayed — and sent his drawing to St. Petersburg. From there it made the round of the more important European academies. Blumenbach in Göttingen and Cuvier in Paris, the recognized authorities on zoology and prehistory in their day, immediately diagnosed the phenomenon correctly. It was a prehistoric elephant, which the Siberian ice had preserved.

A modern reconstruction of the mammoth.

Some years later the naturalist Adams visited Ossip Schumachov's mammoth with an expedition. He dug up what the wolves and foxes had not yet devoured and took the remains to St. Petersburg. From this time onward the carcasses of mammoths were discovered in the Siberian ice practically every year. If we take all the finds of

Stone Age drawing of a mammoth.

Siberian ivory into consideration we reach the astonishing conclusion that up to the present time the remains of over 47,000 mammoths have come to light in northern Asia. A third of the ivory in commercial circulation is taken from mammoths. All Chinese ivory carvings are made of mammoth tusks. Mammoths, too, supplied the material for the famous ivory throne of the Khan of the Golden Horde. No other prehistoric animal is so familiar to modern man as this large arctic beast about which the officers of Charles XII sent such mysterious reports, and the fragments of whose tusks Linnaeus supposed to be nothing more than absurd freaks of stone formation. The mammoth played a still greater part in the lives of the men of the Ice Age. The much ridiculed apothecary Conyers had already suspected the truth. The ancient hunters had in fact lain in wait for the monster, snared it in pits, and killed it with their stone weapons. They made drawings of it, too, and adorned themselves with its ivory. But it was not until the two-hundredth anniversary of Linnaeus' birthday that the world obtained a clearer idea of these proceedings.

How fearful are thy creatures, O Lord!

Reports of the journeys of prisoners of war in Siberia had aroused in the avant-garde of young Swedish naturalists a desire for exploration and discovery. Even Linnaeus set out on his travels. Two years after the publication of his book on flowers he put on Lapland dress and went off to investigate the northern Scandinavia. A grant from the Literary and Scientific Society had rendered his excursion possible. He lived for months in the wilderness, studying plants that no one before him had thought worth looking at, enjoying the sun, cursing the rain, and describing the hardships of his journey of exploration — the only one he ever undertook — in a profusion of superlatives that would have done credit to an expedition through the most lethal and fever-stricken of jungles. On his return from these travels in the north, the results of which were actually far from exciting, he was greeted like a reincarnation of Marco Polo. He was obliged to exhibit himself everywhere in Lapland dress and have his portrait taken. He courted publicity like a prima donna, long before his most important work had brought him into the limelight. The few who shook their heads dubiously were not so much concerned over his precocious fame as with his immodest theory of the sexual propagation of plants, which he put into use for the first time in his analysis of Lapland vegetation.

Linnaeus now attempted to apply this method to botany in general.

He proposed to the university that in the future plants should be classified solely in accordance with the structure of their blossoms, for only in this way, he asserted, "can all herbs be identified at a glance." And since he wrongly supposed that he had been the first to suggest such an ingenious idea, he simultaneously struck a shrewd blow at the whole corporation of natural scientists. "All botanists have hitherto been mistaken in this matter and have consequently built new systems on the wrong foundations." At first the good-natured patrons of science at Uppsala were startled. But they eventually came to the conclusion that Linnaeus' new system was not so bad after all. At any rate, it seemed more useful than all its predecessors in the classification of plants. They encouraged the young man to go ahead with his researches. All they really wanted was the publication of a handy guide to plant identification. But they would not have been so complacent if Linnaeus had chosen to reveal to them at that time what he actually had in mind.

The fact was that he not only was looking for a method to enable plants to be more easily identified and classified, he was looking for a system that should be valid for all time and so far as possible in accord with nature's plan of creation. It was a dream of natural scientists that dated back to the dawn of history and one that, in the view of many skeptics, could no more be realized than the manufacture of gold, the squaring of the circle, or perpetual motion. Aristotle had indeed taught that the multiplicity of nature could only be due to its ultimate unity, the significant order and firm design that held it together. But how could such a weak and inadequate creature as man discover the Divine order? How was he going to deduce the essential characteristics of the plan of creation?

Many had already tried to do so. It was for long believed that the Italian Andrea Cesalpino, private physician to Pope Clement VIII, had solved the problem when he classified plants in 1583 in accordance with Aristotle's philosophy. But it was afterwards found that even his system had been purely artificial. Newly discovered plants could not be included in it. The labels on the specimen drawers suddenly became obsolete and the whole question was again shelved.

A hundred years after Cesalpino, the Englishman John Ray tried to see what he could do with plants and animals. He was a strange character. The son of a blacksmith in an Essex village, he had worked himself up to the status of an itinerant preacher and had then explored a number of countries in Europe, becoming in the course of his travels an exceptionally sharp-witted student of natural science. In an inspired moment it occurred to him to get at close quarters with nature through mathematics. He invented the "species" — the small-est inseparable unit in the whole mass of phenomena. In his view the species was the cornerstone of the organic world. Several species that resembled one another made a "family," just as several cornerstones made part of a wall. These families, too, could be arranged in accord-ance with their outward features and brought into relationship with one another. They then composed the "divisions" of the animal and vegetable kingdoms.

With Ray the age of the methodologists began. The "Methodi-cal Synopsis" of the Essex preacher was accepted, as well as his idea of the "holy, inseparable species." Only one element in Ray's teach-ing was disputed. The species in a family were not, as he had declared, related to one another by blood and possibly descended from a single original pair. On the contrary, their resemblance arose from the Creator's plan to group everything in nature by numbers. Every natural scientist now developed his own method of classifying living beings in accordance with certain features which he believed to be decisive. And each method differed from the next. No one had yet discovered the basic outline of creation, the one and only true method.

How far Linnaeus was influenced by Ray cannot be established for certain. He himself says nothing on the subject. But one may, if one chooses, draw a number of parallels between the methods of Essex and Uppsala. Linnaeus, too, made the rigid conception of species the cornerstone of his system. He, too, believed that Nature had designed her creatures on the basis of a numerical series. So many species be-longed to a genus, so many genera to an order, and so many orders to a class. A geometrical figure could include them all. Gaps in the lines would indicate hitherto unknown forms and groups of forms.

The system worked excellently in the case of plants. One look at the blossom would tell the observer at once how to classify it. But in the case of animals difficulties arose. The sexual method was inap-propriate here. And other methods were inapplicable. For the present one would have to stick to Aristotle's own division into four classes of animals with blood and two without blood. Linnaeus remained somewhat dissatisfied with this arangement, since there were many animals that could not be included in any of these classes even by the most generous interpretation. But he did not know enough about zoology to trust himself to tidy up Aristotle's drawers of specimens. Moreover, he was not particularly attracted by ani-mals, and by the cold and slippery amphibians least of all. He once called them "a horrible, naked, gruesome rabble." He was so dis-gusted by them that later, in composing his System of Nature, he headed the Amphibious Section with the motto: "How fearful are thy works, O Lord!" It was really only birds that he liked.

The knotty problems presented by the classification of animals were solved when Linnaeus began to employ an assistant. The new arrival was Peter Artedi. He was a fellow student, shared the views of Linnaeus, and luckily took an interest in the very creatures the latter so abominated — that "horrible, naked gruesome rabble" of fish, lizards, and frogs. Thenceforth they divided the work between them. Linnaeus dealt with botany and Artedi with zoology. The latter soon found a principle for distinguishing between fauna. It was that driving force of life, the heart. Quadrupeds and birds — the two highest classes of animals — had two cardiac ventricles and two auricles, whereas amphibians and fish had only one of each; and those proletarians of the animal kingdom, the insects and worms, did not possess an auricle. Linnaeus approved this method and gave it his blessing. Both men deliberately disregarded the fact that the heart sometimes defied their system and that animals even existed which had no hearts at all.

Linnaeus and Artedi were now as inseparable as Castor and Pollux. For the first and only time in his life the great classifier of nature, formerly so self-reliant, ungrudgingly presented another with a field which he himself could have tilled. He knew what he was doing. Artedi was a man without prejudices, with a cool, logical head, and quite unemotional. He was not particularly ambitious and was indifferent to impracticable speculation. He cared nothing for fame, but everything for the truth. He would have been quite at home in a modern experimental laboratory. He was thus the ideal complement to the highly imaginative and quite uncritical seer from Smaland. Linnaeus learned to value Artedi; he developed a passionate attachment to him and frequently followed his advice blindly.

In the Swedish mining town of Falun, where he occasionally gave lectures on mineralogy, he became engaged on January 2, 1735, to a rich heiress named Sara Lisa Moraeus. Thereupon a new stage in his career began. For Johan Moraeus, an extremely class-conscious gentleman, scrutinized the suitor of his daughter in great detail, made certain inquiries about his professional prospects at Uppsala, his System of Nature, and Rudbeck's botanical garden, and finally frowned disapprovingly when he discovered that the young lecturer had still not taken his doctor's degree. Linnaeus promised to remedy this oversight as soon as possible. "Where?" asked Moraeus. "At Uppsala, by any chance?" And when this prospective son-in-law agreed, he learned at the same time, and to his surprise, that it would not be as easy as all that to obtain the hand of the girl from Falun. The Moraeus family thought nothing of a doctor's degree unless it had been obtained at a foreign university — for example, a Dutch one.

Linnaeus saw no objection, provided his future father-in-law would be good enough to dig into his purse and meet the expenses of study in Holland. The System of Nature could only benefit from the appearance of its author in Holland, the country of master minds and untold wealth. The great Hermann Boerhaave, as famous as a mathematician, physician, and expert in Eastern languages as he was in chemistry and botany, was lecturing there. Doctors and natural scientists made pilgrimages from every country in Europe to sit at Boerhaave's feet, and to gain his favor meant that one was a made man.

Equipped with a substantial subsidy from Falun, Linnaeus set out once more on his travels, taking the plan of his System of Nature with him. Artedi also left Uppsala, though not overburdened with money. He visited England first, in order to extend the range of his knowledge of fish and John Ray's Methodical Synopsis. Castor and Pollux arranged to meet later on in Holland. These journeys of research began in the style of provincial tourists' adventures. But they sealed the fate of each of the two friends. In the one case the road led to fame, in the other to death.

Man is a superior animal

Leiden University was more than an educational institution. It was the contemporary headquarters of the study of medicine and the natural sciences. Minute forms of life were investigated there in drops of water under the microscope, the scalpel was applied to the human anatomy, and the animals and plants brought by trading vessels from foreign lands were collected and exhibited. Anyone who had studied in Leiden possessed a blank check to draw on the future.

To be sure, the great Hermann Boerhaave did not now actually lecture, because of his advanced age. But he had gathered a circle of young and talented scientists about him to whom he continued to impart his views on nature. These views did not always meet with the approval of his fellow citizens, for Boerhaave still privately adhered to the teachings of Spinoza, who held that spirit and matter, soul and body, creator and creation could not be separated. And Spinoza's doctrine was at that time considered equivalent to atheism. Yet Boerhaave was shrewd and tolerant enough not to involve himself in any disputes with those who represented different outlooks upon the world. He was satisfied if his pupils learned a little skepticism in addition to the ABC of natural science, and was content simply to sow his seed. In other respects he only desired to be left alone.

He was gradually exhausting his large fortune in research and the support of deserving talent and philanthropic works. He himself lived as simple a life as Diogenes. The whole world, including his adversaries, honored him for doing so. He was considered a saint of science. It was not until long after his death that he was found to have been helping not only hard-working chemists and doctors, not only highly respected men of learning like the Swiss, Albrecht von Haller, but also impious villains of heretics and materialists, such as the Frenchman Lamettrie. It seemed that Boerhaave was not greatly taken with the practice of hunting down like hares the unorthodox in every country. He much preferred to hear what they had to say and talk it over with them.

Linnaeus called upon this gentleman, Mijnheer Boerhaave, laid his scheme for a System of Nature on the table, and asserted, without batting an eyelid, that he had discovered nothing less than God's own plan of creation. It is easy to imagine what this meeting must have been like. Here was an amiable old gentleman, cool and clearheaded, familiar with all branches of science, being casually informed, out of the blue, by a young man twenty-seven years old, that all naturalists hitherto had been utter idiots and that he alone, Kalle Nilsson from the backwoods of Sweden, had got hold of the philosophers' stone. Boerhaave might have laughed, he might have told his visitor where he was wrong or he might have reluctantly given him a patient hearing. He chose the last alternative, and time proved that he had been right.

"I have been looking at the natural science collections in Holland," began Linnaeus. "They are said to be the most complete in the world." He paused for breath and then stared hard at the professor. "I am disappointed with them, though. For I found no order in their arrangement. I found disorder. I found no lucidity, but wasteful confusion, no plan, only an inextricable heap of stones, plants, animals, monsters, and curios."

Boerhaave said nothing. What could he have replied to such a truism? He thought of the Ruysch and Seba collections. They were treasure chambers of nature, certainly, but they were lumberrooms, too. They contained, side by side, pressed plants, frogs and fish preserved in spirits of wine, dried birds in sealed bottles, the skulls of apes, the skeletons of beasts of prey, calves with two heads, flint knives, minerals, oddly shaped stones, stuffed crocodiles, and heathen idols. What sort of order was one going to put them all in? Was one to follow Aristotle, who had described barely five hundred species of animals and not many more species of plants? Or Aldrovandi? Or Cesalpino, Gesner, or Ray? There was no end to the "methods." Not one of them could stand up to strict examination. All systems, thought Boerhaave in his heretical fashion, were nothing more than asses' bridges. Disorder was an essential element in nature.

"Without order," Linnaeus continued inexorably, "there can be no science. Without system no study of nature can be anything but frivolous."

Boerhaave was just going to object that there were, in fact, plenty of such systems in existence already and he could not see the necessity of adding to them, when Linnaeus started to pull out his manuscript. He pushed it over to the professor, informing him that every previous treatment of the theme would be thrown on the scrapheap as soon as the first accurate and true system had been published, the system that corresponded with the plan of creation — the "systema naturae," in short, of Carolus Linnaeus.

Every plant and animal, Linnaeus proceeded, possessed some definite external feature by which its species, genus, and order could be identified. In plants it was to be found in their blossoms, in insects in their wings, in fish in their scales, in birds in their beaks and talons, in quadrupeds in their teeth. These features revealed the plan of creation to the investigator. He had written it all down on these ten folio pages, which he hoped the professor would be so good as to read for himself.

Ten folio pages! Boerhaave was really getting excited now. He began to study the manuscript more closely. There were three pages of introduction, two pages about animals, three about plants, and two about minerals. That was all. Could those ten pages really comprise the whole hitherto disorderly prodigality of nature?

"That is merely a preliminary sketch," retorted Linnaeus calmly. "It covers only the most important genera or orders. But I consider that I ought to publish it at once, so universities and natural history museums may be enabled to conform with its principles."

Boerhaave thought the matter over. Actually, when you came to look into it, that young man from Uppsala had arrived exactly at the right moment. There were so many systems and methods of classification about that it was impossible to decide between them. Learned men could no longer understand one another. Every institute and museum used a different technique of arrangement and the babel of terms that resulted had made scientific work intolerably difficult. Of course it was nonsense for Linnaeus to assert that he had discovered the plan of creation. But the summary he had drawn up on those ten folio pages did not look at all bad. Classification of plants by the shape of their blossoms, classification of the animal kingdom by cardiac structure and of separate classes of animals by clearly recognizable external features! It was an artificial method, to be sure; but still it was an illuminating one, and it might perhaps be possible to persuade all natural historians to adopt it. Any child could find its way about by playing with such a "systema naturae" and its lucidity would be sure to delight everybody. Moreover, the revelation of nature in numerical series and relations had a certain aesthetic charm about it.

He gave a sudden start. There, on the fourth page of the manuscript, at the head of the animals, stood Man. Was Man an animal? Was Linnaeus, after all, another materialist in disguise like that young Frenchman Lamettrie, who had once proposed in all seriousness, here at Leiden, that an attempt should be made to teach apes to speak and give them a human education?

Linnaeus looked obstinate. "We must begin by describing Man," he quoted from Aristotle. "For of all animals Man is the one we know best." The revered Aristotle could not be regarded as anything but a reliable witness. "That's where the apes come in. For Aristotle said they were animals structurally halfway between mankind and the quadrupeds. Men and apes" — Linnaeus raised his voice a little — "together compose the Order of the Master-animals."

Master-animals! Was that a blasphemy? Was it open contempt for religion that caused Linnaeus actually to refuse a separate classification to mankind, to Man made in God's image, and bring in the apes as his companions and neighbors? Or was it just naïveté? Boerhaave shook his head slowly. Then he smiled. What a frantic uproar of abuse that would start among orthodox scientists! Well, why not risk it? If one only took Man's physical constitution into consideration, and left the soul out of account altogether, one might get away with it. After a certain amount of further discussion, Boerhaave unreservedly gave his support to Linnaeus. A fifth gray-headed patron had now come into Kalle Nilsson's life. Gronovius, a wealthy Leiden resident, paid at Boerhaave's request the cost of the publication of the ten folio pages. They came out in the form of posters, which Linnaeus sent, with a recommendation from Boerhaave, to all universities, museums, and libraries.

The longed-for miracle happened. The posters were read everywhere and attentively studied. This man Linnaeus might be a bit arrogant and slightly odd but, anyhow, there was no denying his unique talent for organization. It was as easy as ABC to classify collections in accordance with his system, to lay out botanical gardens, label menagerie cages, and divide books on plants and birds into their appropriate chapters. Whether the system was a natural or a contrived one was not a matter in which people at first took much interest. The main thing was that the method worked.

Scarcely anyone even worried over the dethronement of mankind. For Linnaeus had rendered this maneuver palatable to the professors by some extremely clever marginal notes. "Man," he had written in his synopsis, "the last and highest-ranking of the servants of nature, to whose profit and convenience almost all her creations contribute, understands how to make Nature herself serve him. He alone is capable of explaining her. But he, too, is subject to her laws."

Linnaeus thus refrained from attacking the idea, characteristic of his age, of Man as the center of the universe. He left mankind's unique spiritual position unassailed, merely asserting that, anatomically speaking, the lords of creation belonged indisputably to the animal kingdom. There was therefore no reason for people to get excited. Such was the physiological situation, as any doctor could confirm, and it just had to be accepted.

Meanwhile, of course, Linnaeus had experienced no difficulty in securing his doctor's degree. He did not at first show any sign of wanting to return to the narrow puritanical world of Sweden, though a bride and her dowry were awaiting him there. Holland was making him far too attractive offers, as a result of the success of his *Systema naturae*, for him to think of any such thing. Artedi, too, had now arrived from England, with somewhat depleted financial resources, and was looking for a salaried post. As he had been of such great assistance in the work that had now been so brilliantly launched, it would be only fair and reasonable for him to share in the profits. The two friends resolved to probe the state of affairs, give serious consideration to the Dutch offers, and also, by working together on the ten folio pages, to compose a stout volume to cover every species of animal and plant, arranged in accordance with the new method now before the public. It went without saying that they could only accept appointments which would give them the opportunity of studying animate life in foreign countries, and thus drawing up a comprehensive balance sheet of the position in natural science.

The enormously rich apothecary Albertus Seba of Amsterdam, who had a large collection of natural history treasures, urgently needed a curator for his museum. Seba had been toiling for years on end at the task of describing all the "curios" he possessed in a series of stately folios. Linnaeus and Artedi were the very men he required for the job. But the even richer banker George Clifford, the British ambassador in Holland, kept up the most magnificent botanical garden in the world at Hartecamp near Haarlem, with several hothouses, a big menagerie, a natural history museum, and a unique collection of dried plants. He had long been most anxious for some capable man to take over the management of this Garden of Eden. There was the keenest competition between these two men, Seba and Clifford, for Linnaeus' services. The latter eventually decided that at Seba's place he would have too much to do with fish, salamanders, and other creatures not to his taste. He unhesitatingly left this field to the exploitation of his brother-in-arms Artedi, and chose Clifford.

Both scientists now began thoroughly to enjoy themselves. They had hitherto not learned much about any animals and plants except those of Scandinavia. But in Seba's museum and Clifford's garden they found vast quantities of exotic creatures from the West and East Indies, Africa, China, and the Arctic, as well as plants from all the four corners of the world. Was it humanly possible to bring them all together in a single volume covering all the animals and plants that existed or ever had existed on the face of the globe? Linnaeus thought it over. He had written in his *Systema naturae:* "The number of species is the same as that which existed at the start of creation." That sentence could not be altered. It was the alpha and omega of any system meant to last. If it were contradicted, if it could be proved that species might vary, the whole framework would fall to the ground. Only if the tissues of the pattern of creation could be regarded as valid for all eternity would it be possible to identify and record them. Yet in Sir George Clifford's parks and hothouses this did not seem to be the case at all.

Linnaeus daily discovered innumerable variant species and "monstrosities" that had evidently not been formed by God when time first began, but had been bred or cultivated by human agency. It was a complicated affair. For species different from those originating in the workshop of creation really ought not to exist. After much deliberation, Linnaeus eventually found a way out of the problem. He wrote: "All species come ultimately from the hand of God. But God indulgently permitted nature, at one time, to modify some of them, and gardeners have taken advantage of the fact." The first doubt had occurred, and the first crack had appeared in the structure. Suppose God, in an indulgent mood, had given many or even all species permission to change whenever they liked? Imagination boggled at the thought! Linnaeus proceeded, by using arguments of Machiavellian subtlety, to try to outwit nature. "The species," he wrote, "that come from God seem to me superior to those contrived by gardeners. The former have existed ever since the beginning of the world. But the latter are growths contrary to nature and can only claim a short life. If they are neglected they disappear and vanish like fugitive shadows. I ignore them!" The observation that underlay this statement was of course correct. Artificially cultivated plants, as Linnaeus knew from his gardening experience, soon lose their characteristic features if they are not duly tended, and apparently regain their former wild state. Could they, for that reason, be ignored in this casual fashion? Could anything be called contrary to nature which existed in nature? It was clear that certain species of plants and animals did change, at least for a time. Ought any systematizer to disregard the fact and pass it over? If not, how could he squeeze these apparent exceptions into his scheme?

Linnaeus discussed the matter with Artedi. No such doubts had occurred to his friend. It seemed that there were no variant species or monstrosities among Seba's fish. Artedi declared, in his usual cool manner, that it was no business of a natural scientist to concern himself with the influence exercised upon species by climate, living conditions, or arbitrary breeding or cultivation. The primary object was the identification in precise terms of the species in question. He was just then writing, at Seba's request, a big book on ichthyology which "in the first place named all the component parts of a fish, secondly recorded the correct genera and the names of the various species of fish, and thirdly mentioned, here and there, such special features of them as were worthy of note." To do any more than this would, he considered, be to indulge in useless speculation.

"But is that really enough?" Linnaeus insisted. "Should not any system of nature also include descriptions of the lives of plants and animals, with all the changes they undergo?"

Artedi shook his head. He answered, "Such long drawn out descriptions of life cycles serve no purpose whatever." He was a methodologist through and through and wished to keep their common task entirely free from all fabulous and anecdotal matter. "We need not trouble," he went on, "about our creatures' actual experiences, how they react to their environment, and the changes that may perhaps occasionally affect them as the result of external pressure. Our only important concern is to be sure of what they are like today and to give them their correct names from such observation alone. If we don't know the names of things, our knowledge of them will in itself be valueless."

Linnaeus was not particularly edified by this program. For it was precisely those long drawn out descriptions, with their colorful comparisons and the practical morals to be inferred from them of which he was so fond. A systematizer, as Artedi had rightly pointed out, could not possibly deal with the thousands upon thousands of episodes occurring in a life. His duty was to provide science with a clear guide to its studies and nothing more. As for the exceptions to his rules, he could only say, "I ignore them!"

The two men began to hunt up suitable names for their species, genera, and orders. Poor Artedi had not much more time to give to his task. One autumn evening in this eventful year 1735, as he was making his way, deep in thought, through the darkness from Seba's house to his own quarters in Amsterdam, he fell into a canal and was drowned. The influence he exercised upon his time only survived in a single sentence from the preface to his work on ichthyology, a quietly challenging statement, expressed in mathematically precise terms, which represented until the end of the eighteenth century the last word of wisdom for the majority of natural scientists: "Long, tedious descriptions of habits and characteristics serve no purpose in natural history, since the true and natural method of distinguishing creatures by their genus and species is of necessity the sole task of urgency confronting natural historians."

This unfortunate formulation of the problem was afterwards attributed to Linnaeus. The attribution was not wholly unjust. For, though he did not invent the principle, he did work in accordance with it. After the loss of his friend, which he felt deeply, he followed his advice blindly. He raised the statement that Artedi had made for purely technical reasons and in rather too uncompromising a fashion to the status of an irrevocable decree.

Who can count the species or know their names?

Linnaeus continued his work in Clifford's garden. Because of Artedi's death he now had to apply himself also to the troublesome business of assigning names and places in his scheme to animals hitherto treated only in a highly superficial manner. After surveying the names that had so far been given, he came to the conclusion that the whole system of names was in a chaotic state. Each authority applied any names he liked to the creatures, so that they all had to drag round with them a string of labels in the ancient Greek, ancient Latin, medieval, and popular languages. "Less than a tenth of the names current for genera is correct and none of those of the species is appropriate," Linnaeus complained. He wondered whether the best plan would not be to make a drastic revision of the entire nomenclature "from my own sources of knowledge."

He soon found a magic formula to bring order out of the chaos. It was the most brilliant idea that ever occurred to him. One word with a Latin root was to designate the genus and another the species. The two linked together would form an unmistakable and internationally recognizable term for the animate being in question. The invention would of course prove useful only if the whole learned world agreed not to employ any other names but those supplied by Linnaeus. Since that world had swallowed the new "systema naturae," there was no reason why it should not also swallow the new "binary nomenclature." Those who had recognized the advantages of the former and supported the system were bound to take over the names assigned into the bargain and vice versa. One proposal, in short, involved the other.

No evidence has come down to us of the extent to which Artedi had co-operated in this venture. Linnaeus, in any case, was not the first to whom this convenient and useful plan had occurred. But the earlier natural historians had never got beyond the first stage of the double appellation. In this case, too, "Nature's Law giver" succeeded in erecting an imposing structure from other people's designs.

It was not until fifteen years later that Linnaeus' nomenclature received official sanction. Another five years passed before he completed, in the tenth edition of his *Systema naturae*, the task he had set himself — to provide all the organisms known to him with a twofold designation. The idea that came to him at the age of twenty-eight among the mazes, hedges, and thickets of Clifford's garden assured him of immortality.

In the Teyler Museum at Haarlem, a bare hour's journey from Clifford's estates, Scheuchzer's "ancient sinner" had long been patiently waiting to be included in the System of Nature. He was slumbering away peacefully among stones, shells, and fishbones. Linnaeus had heard of him. Had he been merely a petrified human being, a *Homo sapiens* showing all the features of an ordinary contemporary person, he would not have needed any special place in the System. There were plenty of dead people about. But — Linnaeus frowned when he saw that slate from Oningen for the first time — the thing did not look like a man. It was easier to believe with Avicenna that it was a freak of nature. It was foolish of the Floodists to try to prove that every oddly shaped stone had been a witness of the Deluge. Antediluvian plants, animals and men had looked exactly the same as those of today, for species were immutable. And if fossils ever had a different aspect, instantly to be detected by the sharp eye of a systematizer, the reason was that they were not the remains of animate beings, but simply stones of a peculiar shape.

He inserted fossilized matter into the section of his system called *Regnum lapideum*, the mineral kingdom, making a special subdivision for it entitled *Fossilia*, on the same level as the two classes of True Stones and Minerals. Here he placed the *Homo diluvii testis* — the man of the Deluge — among Jean Etienne Guettard's stone snails and fish, those greenish-blue teeth found in ancient caves, Otto von Guericke's unicorn bones, and finally the *mamontokovast* from Asiatic Russia, reported by Messrs. Kagg and von Strahlenberg, all elegantly and tidily arranged and firmly set in their respective positions. The fossils occupied only a single page in the *Systema naturae*, which had meanwhile grown to bulky dimensions. A page was quite enough for such perverse fancies of nature.

In so doing Linnaeus struck a heavy blow at prehistoric research. Those who accepted his system were bound simultaneously to accept the degradation of fossils to the level of stones. Paleontology could now be rescued only by the adversaries of the System — men thinking along comprehensive, unmethodical lines, who did not consider species immutable, descriptions of life cycles unprofitable and the assignment of names the only aim and object of natural science. Such men were to be found mainly in France.

Although Linnaeus visited the Paris Jardin du Roi and made friends there with the leading French botanist, Bernard de Jussieu, Paris enraged him. Everything he most detested originated in the French capital — from cynical materialism, the rejection of the idea of species as changeless, and the theory of constant variation in the structure of the earth and its inhabitants to the belief in the origin of life through spontaneous generation. Linnaeus and the leaders of natural science research in Paris represented two mutually antagonistic worlds that could never be reconciled.

Toward the end of the year 1738 Linnaeus returned to his native land, shortly after the death of his benefactor, Boerhaave. He founded there, on the Parisian model, an academy of sciences; he was ennobled, taking the name of the Chevalier Carl von Linné, and soon came to be universally considered the highest botanical authority in the world. It was only in France that people scoffed at that "crazy nomenclator's" mania for classification.

CAROLI LINNÆI

Naturæ Curioforum *Dioſcoridis Secundi*

SYSTEMA
NATURÆ

IN QUO

NATURÆ REGNA TRIA,

SECUNDUM

CLASSES, ORDINES, GENERA, SPECIES,

SYSTEMATICE PROPONUNTUR.

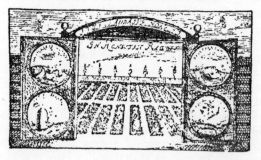

Editio Secunda, Auctior

STOCKHOLMIÆ

Apud GOTTFR. KIESEWETTER.

1740

Title-page of the *Systema naturae* by Carolus Linnaeus.

I. PETRIFICATA.

36. ZOOLITHVS. Petrificatum *Mammalis.*

Hominis. 1. ZOOLITHVS Hominis. *Syft. nat. 201. n. 1. Gefn.*
     peirif. 73.
     Anthropolithus totius corporis. *Carth. min. 81.*
     Anthropolithi praecipuum fpecimen. *l. l. Scheuch.*
     Homo diluuii teftis. Tigur. 1762. quart. c. fig. Act.
     Angl. Act. Vratisl. etc.
     1. Petrificatum Hominis. *Happel Schatkamm. 579. Hen-*
     kel. Saturn. 532.
     Habitat α in Schifto Oenihgenfi. β Aquis Sextiis 1583.
     effoffus.
     Hic *α Partes capitis; offa capitis et vertebrarum; par-*
     tiam an molliorum Cerebri, Mufculorum reliquiae indu-
     ratae?

Cerui. 2. ZOOLITHVS Cerui. *Syft. nat. 201. n. 2. Gefn.*
     petrif. 70.
     Petrificatum Cerni totalis. *Spada p. 45.*
     Cornua Cerui Tarandi. *Act. angl. n. 227. p.* 489.
     Habitabat in-montibus di Valmenara di Grezzana; *in*
     Hiberniae *montibus.*

Eburfos- 3. ZOOLITHVS Trichechi Rosmari.
file.   Zoolithus Phocae dentibus caninis exfertis. *Syft. nat.*
     201. n. 3.
     Sceleton Elephantis. *Tenzel. act. angl. n. 234. p. 757?*
     Offa foffilia. *Spleiffii oedip. ofteologic. Seaphuf. 1701.*
     quart.
     Monumentum diluuii in agro Bononienfi. *Mont.*
     Bonon. 1719. quart. cum icone.
     Mammotowakoft *Ruthenis.*
     Habitat ad Mare album, *frequens effoditur.*

Turcofa. 4. ZOOLITHVS dentis viridi-caerulei. *Syft. nat.* 201.
Turcois.   *n. 4.*
     Turcofa gallica. *Reaum. act. Parif.* 1718. *p. 230.*
     Petrificata animalia dentium quadrupedum; nitorem
     et polituram gemmeam admittentia, colore cyaneo.
     Wall. min. 359.   37. OR.

A page from the *Systema naturae* showing Scheuchzer's
"ancient sinner" included among the "Stones."

III

LINKS BETWEEN MAN AND BEAST

Animals too have a soul

EVER SINCE that remote day when some primitive human being first picked up a beetle and took a closer look at it there have been two categories of natural scientists. One wants to learn the differences between one animate creature and another, the other the resemblances. Some scientists delight in making fresh subdivisions, others are happy if they can succeed in introducing a little fresh air into the tunnels of the systematizers. The first set look for multiplicity in nature, the second for unity.

Linnaeus belonged to the first category, his French adversaries to the second. This was quite natural. Linnaeus had been grounded in Aristotle and the scholastic philosophers, the rebels of Paris took their stand on the French skeptics Montaigne and Gassendi. "Nature is the great teacher of mankind" had been proclaimed as early as 1570 by that jovial man of the world, Michel Eyquem de Montaigne. He had added the amiable advice, "Enjoy your life in accordance with nature's rules," and both counsels were followed in France, to the great satisfaction of the French.

Montaigne, the inventor of the essay, also gave his fellow-countrymen another cause for speculation. He breached the barrier which in the opinion of all philosophers up to his time had been set up between Man and beast. His *essais* contain some remarkably bold statements about animal psychology. "We men," Montaigne had declared, after making a lengthy and profound study of the animal world, "consider ourselves, though for no very good reason, rather from senseless conceit and obstinacy, superior to other forms of life." He did what no one else, right down to the present day, has ever done: he placed Man in the middle of the animal kingdom, but without giving him a leading position in it. Animals, in Montaigne's opinion, were just, intelligent, ready to help one another, morally good, and sociable. These qualities were nothing like so highly developed in mankind.

A few decades after Montaigne's death a vigorous dispute flared up over the question whether men and beasts were to be treated as one category. The animals' advocate was Pierre Gassendi, provost of the Dijon chapter and professor of mathematics at the Collège Royal in Paris. Mankind's defender was René Descartes. The latter was at that time engaged in making a sharp distinction in his philosophical works between natural phenomena and those of the soul. Suddenly Gassendi appeared, with his firm determination to enroll man in the realm of nature, as the "principal and most perfect of animals," to be sure, but all the same as a beast among beasts. Descartes resolutely opposed this view. The soul, he explained in his *Discours de la méthode*, was to be identified, in its essence, with conscious thinking. And as animals could neither speak nor think, they had nothing in common with human beings.

This dispute between Descartes and Gassendi has not, like so many philosophical controversies, become unimportant through the passage of time: it is just as significant today. It will last as long as some men refuse to tolerate any contact between their own aristocratic race and the plebeians of nature, while others demand equality and fraternity in the treatment of all living beings. Descartes's view that animals have neither intelligence nor a soul, that they are "animated machines," that they are like clockwork which runs down when the time comes, was a new offensive weapon in the hands of those who contended that Man was the center of the universe. Gassendi's arguments to the contrary were the battle cry for those who loved and protected animals and defended the theory of mankind's animal origin.

Gassendi was a man of unusual views. He advocated, as one could do only at the risk of one's life in those days, the astronomical system of Copernicus. He admired the Greek natural philosophers, hated Aristotle, and tried to revive the atomic theory of Democritus, which materialists have always regarded as the only source of wisdom. But he was cautious, too. He made concessions, disguised his heretical beliefs, and played his part so well that it resulted in his being allowed every conceivable liberty of behavior. It is significant that Molière, France's most famous writer of comedies, was his disciple. His enemy, Descartes, had an altogether less supple character. He was more than once accused of skepticism and atheism, was often obliged to flee the country and had far more difficulty than Gassendi in "throwing dust in the eyes of the Inquisition," as he himself put it. Consequently Gassendi did not run much risk when he started tearing Descartes's whole philosophy to pieces, making statements in the process which if they had been made by anyone else would have brought the police about his ears.

He attacked the doctrine of the "animal-machines" at close quarters, with biting sarcasm. He seized upon the great philosopher's most vulnerable spot at once. "Naturally, one can't expect animals to talk in human language. They are intelligible to one another in their own tongues." He went on to explain why animals, too, have a soul. Everything that an animal's body experiences, he said, is converted into emotions felt in the soul, just as in the case of mankind. The soul is attached to the body in similar fashion, "as with mysterious and invisible bonds" and is not located only in the human pineal gland, as Descartes declared. To Descartes's key phrase, "I think, therefore I am," Gassendi opposed the natural scientists' principle, founded on experience: "Thought deceives; only the senses can be trusted."

Man had thus been assigned his position in zoology long before Linnaeus gave him the label *Homo sapiens* that confirmed his classification. Descartes's answers amounted to little more than a deplorably inadequate rearguard action. He did what so many Titans driven into a corner have done in such cases: he gave vent to a stream of foul abuse, called Gassendi an insolent rascal who had misconstrued all his utterances, and finally retired, shrugging his shoulders, from further participation in the affair, with the comment that no one could possibly know how animals draw their distinctions and conclusions. He did not advance any plausible grounds for his "animals as machines" theory.

In the dispute that then arose between the supporters of Gassendi and those of Descartes it really would not have been very difficult for the disciples of the animal psychologist and atom physicist to gain the day; but the event proved otherwise. The fact is that men are extremely reluctant to resign their privileges, and those who attempt to rob mankind of its unique position and grant animals a soul as well may advance as many reasonable grounds for so doing as they please, but will always find that it is their adversaries who are believed. Descartes conquered from the grave. And the survivors of the school of Gassendi found it difficult, well into the eighteenth century, to hold their own against an institution which had no particular intellectual justification but was all the more powerful for that very reason. This was the censorship of public opinion.

The highly objectionable "machine-man"

In 1742 a man arrived in Paris who provoked this censorship even more strongly than any Gassendist, heretic, or animal psychologist. He took up Montaigne's and Gassendi's idea that mankind belonged to the animal kingdom, accepted the theory of Descartes that animals were animated machines, and deduced that men, too, were machines. This man was the same Julien Offray de Lamettrie, of St.-Malo, who had studied with Boerhaave in the time of Linnaeus and tried to teach apes how to talk.

Lamettrie became the whipping boy of the materialists. Even today he is considered by many serious-minded people as one of the most infamous, cynical, and immoral troublemakers who ever lived. Learned men, philosophers, and theologians heaped scorn and ridicule on him. Idealists called him the devil incarnate. Even cryptomaterialists, who surreptitiously stole his ideas and exploited them, could cover up their tracks by pointing at Lamettrie and shouting, "Stop, thief!" The school of Hegel, which, as everyone knows, sets great store by the notion that everything in history happens in precise and orderly fashion according to a pre-established sequence, with unconscious humor called Lamettrie an ignoramus who had shamelessly plagiarized Diderot, Holbach, and Buffon. They only forgot that Lamettrie had pronounced his views of nature ten whole years before Buffon's great work on natural history was published and that Diderot and Holbach did not appear on the scene till long after the scandalous philosopher of St.-Malo had ceased to live.

Like many later materialists Lamettrie had originally been a theologian. Subsequently he became convinced "that a good prescription is a better investment than absolution" and transferred his allegiance to medicine. After studying in Leiden he obtained the appointment of surgeon to the Guards in Paris. During a campaign in Germany he caught a high fever, which caused the blood to rush to his brain and decided the course of his subsequent career. During his convalescence he experimented on himself and came to the conclusion that thought was no more than a bodily function. He believed that he had discovered that the soul, too, depended upon the organs and senses. It could not exist, he considered, apart from the body of which it formed one of the functions.

He innocently sat down and wrote a *Natural History of the Soul*. The consequences were appalling. The regimental chaplain sounded the alarm. His superior officers dismissed Lamettrie from the Guards. The *Natural History of the Soul* was publicly burned and Lamettrie had to flee in haste, from probable incarceration in the Bastille, to Leiden. His adversaries rashly expected that his downfall would teach him a lesson and keep him decently quiet in his Dutch exile. But they were mistaken. In 1748 a second book by Lamettrie appeared, with the title *Man As a Machine*. It was a far more objectionable publication than the first.

"The human body," he had written, "is a machine which winds up its own works. It is a living instance of perpetual motion. The soul, however, is merely an unintelligible expression to which one cannot attach any meaning. Bodies have everything they need to enable them to move, feel, think, and have regrets, in short, to find their way about in the physical domain and the moral one that depends on it.

Man As a Machine was, in contrast to the *Natural History of the Soul*, a polemical work. With that uninterrupted flow of eloquence peculiar to all prophets of materialism, Lamettrie sought to convince his contemporaries, not by proofs of the truth of his views, but by brilliance of style, by piquancy of approach and by impressive rhetoric. It was noticed that he had read Montaigne and Voltaire with zealous appreciation. He took all the philosophers who had preceded him severely to task and tore their ideas to shreds without mercy. The last lines of his book were briskly provocative. They ran: "Such is my system, or rather, if I am not very much mistaken, such is the truth. It is short and simple. Contradict it if you can!"

No one contradicted it. He was simply turned out even by the easygoing Dutch. He finally found refuge at the court of a king who was fond of collecting intellectual rebels about him and letting them give vent to their ideas in any form they liked. "The appeal of one who is both a philosopher and unhappy," wrote Frederick the Great to the persecuted Lamettrie, "is enough to make me offer him protection in Prussia." Apparently he considered the denial of the soul's existence as a form of philosophy. In Potsdam, Lamettrie joined the circle of emigrants around Voltaire and Maupertuis. He worked in the Academy, became Reader to the King and entered enthusiastically into all the intrigues and conspiracies of that brilliant and frivolous society.

He had a sense of humor, as the titles of his numerous pamphlets and lampoons reveal. He described the medical fraternity as "charlatans unmasked," called Linnaeus a "human plant," and his former teacher Boerhaave the "Medical Machiavelli." But he did more than let off intellectual squibs. He also experimented on many occasions with men and animals with a view to lending further support to his materialist theories. His aim was to conduct his research and write down its results "as though you were alone in the universe and had nothing to fear from the jealousies and prejudice of men." Stimulated by the *Systema naturae* of Linnaeus, he hit upon a daring notion. Did classes, orders, genera, and species of the animal and vegetable kingdoms in fact exist independently of one another, as the "human plant" of Uppsala taught, or did they not rather arise one from another? Linnaeus had emphasized the differences between individual categories. He, Lamettrie, now meant to reveal the connections between them, concentrating chiefly on the link between man and beast.

"It is a mistake," he observed, "to suppose that human beings may be distinguished from animals through the operation of a natural law which enables the former to tell the difference between good and evil. For such a law operates in the case of animals also. We know, for example, that we experience remorse when we do wrong. And we conclude, from certain signs which we perceive in ourselves in such cases, that other men have the same experience. Well, identical signs may also be perceived in animals." Dogs acknowledge their guilt by groveling. They feel sorrow, depression, and gratitude. They understand the moral instructions they are given, and behave accordingly, just like men. "All this proves that men and animals are composed of the same elements."

"What were men like," Lamettrie asked his critics, "before the invention of language? They were beasts among beasts, at the mercy of their instincts." Men first became human beings when certain highly developed representatives of the genus invented words. The inventors then imparted their new accomplishment to the rest, "just as when we train animals." It was training, therefore, and education, that turned a mere beast into the lord of creation. Education, according to Lamettrie, would enable us to raise apes to the level of mankind. Education changes species and is responsible for continuous development in nature. These ideas indicate for the first time a belief, still somewhat nebulous and hazy, in a pedagogic strain in Nature, forcing her creations, like a schoolmaster with his cane, to make progress and get on in the world. It was an alluring notion, and despite all the attacks to which it has since been exposed it still retains its hold on humanity.

People were determined to put the worst interpretation upon everything that Lamettrie said and wrote, but what infuriated them most was his statement that there were no absolute moral standards. The well-being of all forms of life, including human life, depended on pleasurable feeling, which was relative, differing from individual to individual. "The sense of well-being is the great faculty through which nature has conferred upon all men the same right and claim to contentment and rendered existence agreeable to them all in the same way." Lamettrie made it very clear indeed what he meant by pleasure. He did not confine it to food, drink, and women, though he had nothing against such amusements in themselves, but laid stress upon the pleasure taken in the exercise of intelligence and taste. This emphasis did nothing to help his case. "Now we can see," raged his opponents, "that he is in fact nothing more than an impudent voluptuary, trying to find justification for his own profligacy in materialism." Even Frederick the Great became rather cool toward his protégé.

Not much is known about Lamettrie's profligacy apart from these unproved assertions. He certainly sang the praises of sensuality in some of his books. But Ovid, Goethe, and Balzac, among others, did the same thing without being called impudent voluptuaries. Lamettrie neither consigned his children to an orphanage as did Rousseau, nor plighted his troth to two women at once like Swift. He was neither charged with bribery and corruption like Bacon nor with forgery of documents like Voltaire. His only crime was his honesty. What others thought in secret and practised more or less openly he publicly announced as his philosophy of life. He scandalized his contemporaries in the same way as Sigmund Freud shocked the twentieth century when he analyzed unconscious impulses.

It was the manner of his death that really did the most harm to his reputation and his work, although the story seems to have been greatly exaggerated. The official version is that on November 11, 1751, when he was barely forty-two years old, he attended a festive gathering at the French ambassador's house in Potsdam, where, "in a vainglorious exhibition of his capacity for enjoyment," he swallowed a truffle and liver pie, whereupon he "immediately expired in a violent and pitiful fit of delirium." His enemies considered it a just punishment from heaven, and the rumor spread like wildfire that the villain had at last gobbled himself to death. Decent people nodded with pious fervor, telling each other that it was an unmistakable sign of the evil of his materialistic doctrine.

But a document exists that gives a completely different account of Lamettrie's death. It is a confidential letter, dated November 21, 1751, from Frederick the Great to his sister, the margravine of Bayreuth. He informed her that Lamettrie had been quarreling with German doctors about the expediency of blood-letting. In order to prove that he had been right he had given instructions that he himself should be bled while suffering from slight stomach trouble. This was what had killed him. "He was a cheerful, kindhearted fellow," wrote the king at the end of his letter, "a good doctor but a shocking bad writer. He was likable enough if you didn't read his books." Lamettrie's work was like a bomb with a time fuse. It did not really begin to have any effect until after his death, but a whole generation of thinkers and scholars were more or less influenced by it, including Voltaire in his old age, Diderot's revolutionary group, d'Alembert, Holbach, and Count Buffon's school of natural science. Forty years later Lamettrie's ideas were inscribed upon the standards of Danton and Robespierre, and a hundred years after that they turned up again in Karl Marx.

Nature knows no system

Lamettrie's case had attracted the attention of the French censors. They now began to examine, with particular care, the latest publications of the natural historians. In Linnaeus, Jussieu, and the other methodologists they found hardly anything to take exception to. But they were exceedingly suspicious of a certain man who was said to believe secretly in the common origins of horse and donkey, dog and wolf, lion and cat. In the end this otherwise highly respectable gentleman might come to believe in the common origin of ape and man, and that was a good enough reason to watch him closely.

A hundred or so censors seized eagerly upon the first of his writings to appear. They read till their heads ached, but only the seven most energetic found anything there to criticize. He was certainly clever enough, this marquis turned natural scientist! His writings were neither one thing nor the other, neither orthodox nor heretical. All sorts of conclusions, or no conclusion at all, might be drawn from his *Histoire naturelle*.

Georges Louis Leclerc was the name of the sly fox that thus slipped through the meshes of the censorship. He came of an old noble family of Montbard in Burgundy. In 1739 he had been appointed one of the commissioners of the Jardin du Roi in Paris and shortly afterwards had been raised to the rank of count, under the name of Buffon, by Louis XV. He was the same age as Linnaeus and as famous, at an early age, as he, but that was the only thing the two men had in common.

Count Buffon was known in society as a man of the world and a pleasant gossip. He was on intimate terms with princes, at home in drawing rooms, and, according to the philosopher David Hume, looked more like a marshal of France than a writer on natural science.

But this behavior was mere camouflage. He had assumed the mask of a *grand seigneur* in order to be left in peace. His real character only came to light when he was sitting at work in his plainly furnished study at the top of a tower. Accordingly, only his very closest friends ever discovered what he secretly thought and believed. Outwardly he seemed very different from the intellectual forerunners of the Revolution. Nevertheless, he supplied them privately with his essays on nature. When Linnaeus classified man as part of the animal kingdom, it was Buffon who first went into operation against this "humiliating truth." He admitted that he thought mankind was related to the apes, but took the line that matter ought not to be made the subject of discussion. This was not mere duplicity on his part. Buffon in his work was always haunted by the phantom of Riballier, the royal censor, whose power he had reason to fear.

The greatest brains in France revered him. "He has the body of an athlete and the soul of a wise man," said the usually cynical Voltaire, who had by no means a high opinion of natural scientists in general. But was Buffon, then, nothing more than a natural scientist? He could talk in the most fascinating way of his work, of the spontaneous generation of new life perpetually taking place in decay and putrefaction, of the mighty force impelling plants, animals, and human beings, all alike, to love one another, and of the multiplicity of creation which no professor had ever yet been able to confine within a system. Those "tedious descriptions of life cycles" which Artedi and Linnaeus had wished to banish from natural history altogether were considered by Buffon to be its main concern. "Information, facts, and discoveries," he wrote on the flyleaf of his works, "can never hold the attention for long. They are external to mankind. Well-written books are the only ones which will be read by posterity. Style is the essence of man." Buffon was undoubtedly a poet — a poet of nature. When Rousseau, the philosopher of nature, came to see him one day, he was so moved that he kissed the threshold of Buffon's study.

Buffon made nature fashionable in France. Duchesses, court ladies, and maids of honor visited him at the Jardin du Roi and looked through his microscope. They admired the exciting, colorful pictures of animals and plants he had prepared for his forthcoming *Histoire naturelle, générale et particulière.* They wore pressed plants in their corsages to please him. At the hairdresser's they exchanged whispered confidences about the piquant behavior, hitherto unfortunately so completely ignored, of animals and plants. The microscope showed them tissues, blood corpuscles, eggs, and germs of life. Buffon had even told them about a discovery of the book-keeper and optician Leeuwenhoek, over in Holland — he had made it, to be sure, some seventy-five years ago, but it was still a novelty to the Parisian public — that male semen, when examined under the microscope, was found to be composed of tiny animalculae, which swam about briskly in a drop of water. Was this another proof of the barrier between man and beast, or was not nature, in fact, one great organism spontaneously built up from the most minute particles, producing both mankind and all its other forms of life from such materials?

Buffon also talked to ladies in drawing rooms about the Swedish doctor of genius, Carl von Linné, who had trumpeted forth his doctrine from Uppsala across the whole world. "That fellow Linnaeus," said Buffon, "does of course take the greatest pains to convince humanity how useful and profitable an interest in nature can be. Nevertheless, he has no idea of what nature really is. Judge for yourselves, ladies!" He read out a passage from Linnaeus' writings. "People who are unacquainted with natural science can never manage their domestic affairs properly. It is the most considerable of sciences, for it has the greatest number of practical applications. That is why I wish it to be regarded as the most important branch of philosophy and to be taught and practised at the university."

"Well, isn't that correct, then?" the ladies asked. "Don't you agree? You write about nature, too, and consider the subject of your research more important than any other branch of science."

Count Buffon's aristocratic face lit up in a mocking smile. "But I don't see any purpose in nature," he said, "except that, possibly, of pleasing mankind." He added with suppressed indignation that he could not understand, with the best will in the world, what right the "nomenclators" of Linnaeus' type had to call themselves investigators of nature. After all, the investigation of nature — he put forward this objection in all modesty — was primarily the investigation of life, directed to discovering the unity of nature's grand synthesis. It was not a frivolous game to be played with numbers and names. "I have studied nature pretty thoroughly, *mesdames*. But I have never found a sign of any such thing as a system. Those classes and orders and genera exist only in the imagination of our respected friend Linnaeus. In nature — " he smiled again — "in nature there simply aren't any."

The ladies nodded in delight. Yet occasionally one of them would venture upon a contradiction. For if, as was now the fashion, one knew one's way about the Cabinet du Roi and turned over the pages of the stout folios that were delivered there month after month, coming from all the academies of the world, one did get a little puzzled. Wasn't Buffon rather overdoing his hostility to his Swedish archenemy? Every natural historian with a good opinion of himself brought out a new system. In Danzig, for example, there was Jacob Theodor Klein, in Jever, Heinrich Gerhard Möhring, and they all used Linnaeus' nomenclature. Klein and Möhring were admittedly foreigners, but even in France, for some years, people had been starting to arrange natural phenomena in neat, tidy, and aesthetically pleasing groups and subgroups. There was Pierre Barrère, for instance, the brothers Jussieu, Mathurin-Jacques Brisson, and above all the count's great rival, the collector and museum curator René-Antoine Ferchault de Réaumur. Were these champions of science wasting their time? Might it not be that Linnaeus' system was merely not the right one? Might not the methods of others be better?

Buffon snapped his fingers. "Think of every naturalist having his own system! One with this and one with that — " He bowed deeply, and laughed. "*Voilà!* Shuffle the cards!" Then he grew serious. The mask dropped, revealing a glimpse of the real Buffon, the materialists' friend who knew his Lamettrie. "In nature," he declared, glancing through the window at the rustling trees of the Jardin, "only individualists have any real existence. Species are merely intellectual conventions. They are just — paper!"

It was annoying and yet exciting at the same time. Only a worldling, an atheist of the stamp of Voltaire, Condillac, Helvetius, or Diderot, could have uttered the phrase. Was Buffon really, after all, as people whispered, in touch with certain revolutionary circles? There could be no doubt that species were ultimately to be referred to God's own plan of creation. He had formed them in clear distinction from one another and made them immutable. All natural historians said so, one learned it at the Sorbonne, and it corresponded, too, with the structure of human society, in which the various classes stood in a fixed order, one above the other. When even an aristocrat like Buffon, a court scholar in charge of the royal collections, attacked this hierarchy, it was no wonder the times they lived in were unsettled.

"You think species are constants and last for ever?" Buffon shook his head slowly. "That is just what they are not," he explained. "Nor does the story of creation mention such a thing. Dr. Riballier of the Sorbonne himself would have to agree with me there. No, *mesdames*. The so-called species are perpetually changing under the influence of climate and nutrition. They degenerate and produce illegitimate offspring. How long do you suppose the world has been in existence? You don't know. Neither do I. But we do know that it has already lasted a very long time. How things must have varied, improved, changed, and degenerated during so extended a period! What a vast number of combinations have been possible! Yet, what does Linnaeus still stick to? Petals, talons, teeth, and scales! He makes accidental features which may have quite a different aspect at some future epoch of the world's history into distinguishing characteristics." The ladies shivered slightly at this prospect. If that were so, what would the fate of mankind be — was it also destined to change? Buffon nodded. "Man is already changing, from day to day and from hour to hour." His face cleared, and once more he was smiling. "I myself, *mesdames*, am growing old and crotchety, while you grow lovelier every day. Surely that proves that nature changes?" He made another slight bow, then added in a lower tone, "Nothing stands still. Everything moves. Even the seed of man does so, otherwise it would never reach its goal. May I show it to you under the microscope?"

"Oh, how shocking!" cried the ladies, frowning severely. "Please don't even suggest such a thing!" But they were smiling behind their fans.

The unclassifiable bastards

Ferchault de Réaumur, Buffon's rival for the laurels of French natural science, was already an old gentleman of seventy. He was one of the last representatives of the versatile scholars of the Age of Enlightenment. In contrast with those of later generations, their inquiries were extended to every branch of natural science. Ferchault had in the course of his long life discovered a new method of steel production, invented a new kind of porcelain and a thermometer, studied marine animals and insects, and founded a great museum of natural history. He taught his pupils hitherto unheard-of methods of preparing natural phenomena for exhibition, pursued researches on instinct, and admired — altogether in the spirit of Montaigne and Gassendi — the intelligence shown by animals in obtaining their food, rearing their young, and constructing their dwellings.

Taking him all in all, he was a man of great learning and industry, such as natural science needs for repairing its structure. Nevertheless, he was no Buffon. He possessed neither the latter's geniality nor his supple and less than scrupulous mentality. He was consequently overshadowed all his life by the other's genius. He never visited Paris if he could help it, but lived in the country, in Bas Poitu, where exotic animals and plants were sent to him from all the four corners of the world by its most daring explorers. He arranged them on Linnaeus' principles and thus gradually achieved a reputation as the leading French systematizer.

Yet it was from Réaumur, his spiritual brother, that Linnaeus was to receive the heaviest blow of his career, which came near to annihilating the whole System of Nature. It was launched from the blue. Réaumur did not realize what he was doing, and Linnaeus never foresaw it — for that very reason it hit him all the harder.

The two men understood each other very well; they corresponded and exchanged experiences. It is true that Réaumur did not entirely accept Linnaeus' classification, because he thought there were too few genera in it. He got his assistant Brisson to work out some new systems of classifying birds and quadrupeds. Nevertheless, in principle he pursued the same objective as Linnaeus. However, one day this alert scientist, who was always dabbling in experiments, took a step that would have been more in character with his frivolous opponent Buffon. He tried to find out whether species would mix, by instituting experiments in crossbreeding.

If one believed in the immutability of species, this alone was enough to make one's hair stand on end. If a breeder could produce hybrids, they could also be produced in a state of nature, which reduced everything to vagueness and uncertainty. The "sanctity of species" would be nothing but a vain delusion, and the "systema naturae" a fiction that might at best only serve as a guide to people who pressed flowers and impaled beetles and butterflies and who would be glad to do it in some kind of orderly fashion. That was exactly what Linnaeus thought when he first heard of Réaumur's crossbreeding experiments. The idea made him tremble in every limb. He was still hoping against hope that nothing would come of it when he was attacked from another quarter.

This time the fly in the ointment was named Sjöberg, or Zioberg, a student from the tiny village of Roslagen. He had found, on an islet near Uppsala, a certain plant that he could not, try as he would, fit into the master's System. Linnaeus gave the plant a casual glance and was about to exclaim, with his usual virtuoso's confidence, "*Linaria*. Toadflax!" when he noticed that the flower of the supposed flax had not one spur, as is usual with the *Linaria*, but five. He jumped up from his chair in a rage, believing that Sjöberg had stuck four additional spurs on the flower in order to lead him, of all people, astray.

But the student swore that he was innocent. When Linnaeus examined the herb more closely he perceived that it was a natural one. But it still did not fit into his System! He stared at the five-spurred flower as a farmer would stare at a cow that suddenly laid eggs instead of giving milk. "It's a malformation," he told the student curtly. When the latter looked surprised, he thundered: "Yes! A botanical monstrosity, like a calf with a wolf's head! I shall call it *Peloria*, a monstrosity!"

A crossbred type? suggested the student. Might it not be that the pollen of some plant with five spurs had fertilized a *Linaria* and the monstrosity had been produced from this improper connection? Linnaeus scouted the suggestion, and brooded over the phenomenon. If the five-spurred *Linaria* were only an exception, a pathological case of degeneracy, he could with a good conscience ignore it. But if it propagated itself, producing further "malformations" with five spurs, what then?

In spite of the System, it did so. Linnaeus found himself breeding, with sullen anger, five-spurred flaxes from his *Peloria*. He was tormented by unwelcome doubts that brought him reluctantly to a new decision. "This *Peloria*," he wrote, "not only differs from its maternal genus, but is also distinct from the whole class. It sets an example wholly without parallel in botany." He set his teeth and wrote on: "It may therefore happen that new species of plants may arise, that genera with diverse types of organs of fertilization may have identical origins and characters, even that variant organs of fertilization may exist in one and the same family. Consequently" — he groaned, it was like committing suicide — "the fundamental structure of the theory of fertilization is hereby demolished and with it the entire science of botany itself, involving the dissolution of the classes of nature."

Finished! The *Systema naturae* could be scrapped. His whole life's work had been destroyed by that satanic plant. But he could not shrink from the facts. He would have to make the new discovery public. He announced with the calm courage of a combined hero and martyr, the "dissolution of the classes of nature" by the *Peloria* and awaited his sentence of condemnation.

To his astonishment nothing of the kind happened. The world was quite happy with his System of Nature and felt quite at home in it. People did not want any revisions. They were determined not to have the former chaos back, with its rambling notions. Here and there a scholar read Linnaeus' self-accusation, took it upon himself to reply, and protested strongly against these "ingenious rather than accurate views." The rest did not take the slightest notice. Linnaeus resignedly thrust that sinister *Peloria* into a drawer.

The devil, however, is not so easily silenced. Linnaeus discovered that some of old Réaumur's attempts at crossbreeding had succeeded. He remembered again, then, what Sjöberg had said when he brought the plant. Might not the *Peloria* be just a by-blow, the illegitimate fruit of a marriage between two different genera? Might there not be several other such "by-blows" in nature? Indeed, that must be the case. Species were not immutable. Only genera, the higher categories, did not change and new species might regularly arise from crossing them.

This was, almost word for word, the doctrine of his opponent, Buffon. The species of any group, Buffon maintained, resemble one another only because they are mutually related, having a common ancestor. And the mixture of these various kinds of descendants continually produced new forms. Linnaeus might now easily have extended his hand to the French count as a gesture of reconciliation. Instead, he sulked. No reconciliation was possible with Paris, the home of the sworn enemies of methodology, those who were demolishing, piece by piece, the structure so laboriously built up by natural science ever since the days of Aristotle. In Paris lived — Linnaeus sketched a bitter caricature of the worldly count — "those monkeys that clamber about on my shoulders, gnashing their teeth at me, in horrible laughter." To him, Paris was definitely not worth much.

He jotted down a new theory of evolution, admitting mutability in nature, but designed to rescue the System all the same. Everything that did not fit into his classification was accounted for under it as a bastard type. The public liked that much better than the "dissolution of the classes of nature." Botanists and zoologists, with cries of approval, instantly dashed to their collections and sought eagerly for bastard types. Linnaeus could now sleep peacefully at night.

The innocent little *Peloria* that had caused all the trouble was, as we now know, not illegitimate at all. It was not even a new species. It was a common toadflax that had undergone a mutation, a sudden alteration of its hereditary features. The formation of peloria occurs in many ringent and labiate types of flowers, in certain species of violets, and in orchids, usually increasing the number of calcaria, coronal sections, and stamina. Consequently, any artificial system based on features of this kind is obviously destined one day for the scrapheap.

Linnaeus remained keenly on the watch for any hereditary alterations. He had an inkling that there was something wrong about the theory of these apparent "bastard types" and that the formation of peloria ought really to have been explained in quite a different fashion. "It will be a great century that solves the problem of this phenomenon," he once told his pupils. But meanwhile the concept of illegitimacy had met with approval. Linnaeus went on working at it, and never returned to the subject of genetics.

It was a rumor, due to a grotesque misunderstanding, which brought back his fearful doubts. He heard that Réaumur had managed to cross, not only different genera, but also different classes of animals. This meant that the higher categories, too, were no longer immutable, so that cracks were appearing all over the System. He noted, with desperate anxiety: "Réaumur had a hen fertilized by a rabbit. The resultant eggs produced chicks precisely similar to the normal bird of their kind, except that they were covered with sparse fur." There is no doubt that Réaumur neither carried out nor could have carried out such an experiment. Linnaeus believed that he had, or at any rate that such a thing was possible. He got into a state of great excitement over it.

His first thought was to wonder whether men, too, could be coupled with animals. What conclusions could one draw from such a possibility? The first would be that mankind would no longer be able to lord it, in solitary grandeur, over the rest of creation. But that was far from being the end of it. "Appalling consequences would follow. One would be forced to conclude, in the case of men, that Negroes originated in an altogether extraordinary manner."

One could play with the idea. But it would be dangerous in the extreme to think it out logically. Suppose not merely a few of the present-day forms of life were crossbred but all of them. Perhaps God had only created certain basic types, from which a wild promiscuity had produced the entire range of organisms. Did animals with undivided hoofs couple with those with divided hoofs? Did quadrupeds couple with birds and apes — with men?

At one bound Linnaeus had abandoned the rigid certainties of his System for the treacherous swamp of evolutionary theory. He announced his new ideas for the first time in a work called *Plant Metamorphosis*, a book whose very title was calculated to disturb the scientific world. Some decades later a very different sort of author, the creator of *Faust* and *Wilhelm Meister*, wrote a *Plant Metamorphosis* that dealt not cautiously but in clear, positive language with the evolution of nature "through thousands upon thousands of forms."

Linnaeus had not yet reached that stage. He only advanced very circumspectly into this deceptive field, making tentative suggestions. He began with a statement that could be read as compatible with his

System and the theory of "illegitimacy." "The many species which belong to the same genus appear to have been originally a single species and to have come into existence at a later date by the combinations referred to. According to this view, a genus would simply be a collection of such forms which had a common mother but different fathers." He proceeded to risk a further advance. "Species of animals and plants, as well as genera, take time to develop. Only the natural orders are due to the Creator. If these latter forms had not been available, the former would never have been able to arise." Finally he showed some hesitation about accepting the orders themselves as fixed. He now made a complete break with his previous confession of faith. "Life originated at a single initial point from which creation began and gradually spread." This was pure evolutionary theory, fifty years before Lamarck and a hundred years before Darwin.

At the same time Buffon was writing: "Everything seems to have been shaped in accordance with an original and general structural scheme which can be traced very far back. It may be assumed that all animals arise from a single form of life which in the course of time produced the rest by processes of perfection and degeneration."

Buffon's hypothesis of evolution was eagerly discussed. It was hailed in some quarters and damned in others. But many people supported it. Linnaeus, on the other hand, listened in vain for a response to his appeal. He was not mocked, nor applauded. The experts simply ignored his revolutionary statements. They loved and admired the Linnaeus of 1735, the systematizer. They could make neither head nor tail of the skeptic of 1759. The authority of the Classifier of Nature had become so great that no one, not even himself, could challenge it.

He took up his pen and struck out, in the new edition of his *Systema naturae*, the sentence upon which the system had really, in the last analysis, been based — the statement about the immutability of species. Even this attracted no attention. The unsuspecting cause of the whole dispute, Réaumur, could no longer be consulted about the logical consequences of his experiments in "bastardization." He had meanwhile quietly passed away, without feeling any doubts about his position as an uncompromising systematizer.

Man is a decadent ape

A dense crowd of inquisitive sightseers jammed the Zoological Gardens of the Prince of Orange at Het Loo, not far from the

Residence at The Hague. A most extraordinary creature was on view there, half man, half beast, with a flame-colored hide. It could "walk upright on its hindlegs and also run on all fours." The monster was called an orangutan, a wild man of the woods or a night-man. Mijnheer Vosmaer, director of the Zoological Gardens, explained to the excitedly attentive spectators that it came from the island of Borneo.

"We have known for a hundred years," said Vosmaer, continuing his lecture, as he gave the dazed and unhappy-looking orangutan an apple, "that these wild men of the woods existed in the Indian Archipelago. Our fellow countryman Dr. Bontius made their acquaintance in person. He considered them to be savages who had taken refuge in the woods so as not to have to work. But this specimen — the first that could be captured and brought to Europe — shows us clearly that it is more like an ape than a man. As a matter of fact, it is a young female, very tame and good tempered. You can put your hand into its mouth and it won't bite!"

"Is it true," inquired an eager member of the audience, "that the wild men of the woods could speak if they wanted to?"

"I have heard that they can," replied Vosmaer. "But the young female we have here has hitherto shown no sign of intending to do so. On the other hand, she understands the arts of undoing shoelaces, unlocking doors, and using toothpicks as well as any human being. She also feeds in human fashion and very much appreciates a good bottle of Malaga." He raised his voice. "After she had been caught and was being examined by her captors, she had a feeling of shame. She moaned, covered her nakedness with her hands, and shed tears, which proved that she was still a virgin."

The visitors were quite touched. They pushed sweets, strawberries, cooked meat, and other kitchen odds and ends through the bars of the cage to the female orang, and nodded wisely when the "wild man" sniffed cautiously at their gifts and then popped them into the large receptacle of its mouth. Only one man regarded the modest young lady from Borneo with some skepticism. "Mijnheer Vosmaer," he murmured to the menagerie's curator after a time, "that ape is suffering from consumption. When it dies, let me have the carcass. I'd like to dissect it."

"By all means, Mijnheer Camper, provided His Highness the Prince has no objection," Vosmaer promised. "I hope, though, that she'll be with us a little longer."

But the virgin of the woods did not live up to Vosmaer's hopes. She succumbed to phthisis shortly afterwards. Peter Camper obtained the carcass, cut it up, and found to his astonishment that the internal organs resembled in all respects those of a human being. The discovery would certainly have enraptured a man like Buffon. It would have bewildered a Linnaeus. But Camper's mind was of a different cast from either of theirs. He merely shook his head, wrote down an account of what he had found, and reflected privately that, owing to Vosmaer's mania for importing queer creatures, he would no doubt be having further opportunities of dissecting orangutans. He was sure that in so doing he would one day light upon some fundamental difference that had hitherto escaped him between that big ape from Borneo and his majesty, Man.

Peter Camper of Leiden had at one time, like Linnaeus and Lamettrie, belonged to the school of that wise ignoramus Boerhaave. He later dabbled in medicine, painting, architecture, and sculpture and was a man who loved beauty, "a Rembrandt of anatomy," more of an artist than a scientist. He cared little for systems or theories of any kind. Instead, he gave his Dutch colleagues in painting and drawing anatomical and osteological advice, while he sought for formulas and principles that might account for the beauties of nature and the human countenance.

He had not been able to recognize any such principles in Vosmaer's female orang. But he thought he might succeed in finding them in the bones of an antediluvian human being. He traveled to Haarlem to inspect Scheuchzer's ancient sinner and studied him for a long time. "If you'll excuse my saying so," he said at last, smiling half in mockery and half in disappointment, "these bones are nothing more than the remains of a lizard!"

After saying this he returned home and resumed his researches into apes' organs and human facial structure. The "wild man of the woods" from the Het Loo menagerie — short as its life in civilized conditions had been — gained a permanent place in the records of natural history, for its advent started a new chapter in anthropology. Honest citizens gaped at it and behaved precisely as we should if we were suddenly confronted by a Neanderthal or Peking man in the flesh. The most daring hypotheses began to be advanced from many quarters concerning the origin of the human race, and everywhere potential associations of mankind with the animal kingdom were sought. The hairy female from Borneo was considered an incarnate insult by conservative natural scientists, while to the rebels she represented an obvious connecting link between Man and the ape.

How was it Man first appeared upon the earth? Linnaeus had labeled him *Homo sapiens* in the *Systema naturae*, and named his genus and species in the same way as those of all forms of life. But he had simultaneously taken a step that now suddenly seemed interesting and significant, and made a separate order to include mankind and those animals which, according to Aristotle, "occupy, in view of their build, a central position between mankind and the quadrupeds." This order Linnaeus called the Primates. Not only was man a master-beast; the apes were, too. And, if Linnaeus could be trusted, so were the prosimians (semi-apes) and the bats. Up to a short time ago that would have been the worst one could expect. But now this same Linnaeus was declaring that the various genera and species included in one order "took time to develop" — were blood relations, so to speak. Did all primates, then, originally spring from a single root? Did they start "from a single small initial point that gradually spread"?

The worthy systematizers, as we have already seen, had taken no notice of these statements. However, supporters of the idea of evolution and the many amateurs of research in that century of the worship of nature were seriously disturbed. The question had already been raised at that time as to whether mankind had descended from the ape. It had been hotly discussed, not indeed in serious scientific circles, but certainly by laymen and outsiders. Amazing stories of hairy men, with tails, went the rounds. The owners of traveling fairs profited from the circumstance, and exhibited abortions of this sort in the towns they visited. Sensational journalists rushed into print with hairraising "guaranteed true" accounts of the rape of Malay girls by gigantic apes. Travelers proclaimed in all seriousness that the "wild men of the woods" were the offspring of unions between apes and Indian women.

Very little was yet known about the anthropoid apes. Such knowledge as was available became the subject of popularization and misunderstanding. Nearly all the investigators and authors who concerned themselves with the "wild men" of Indonesia and Africa believed them to be primitive human beings. Scarcely one thought they were brutes. The natural historian of ancient Rome, Pliny the Younger, had long ago called the great apes of the Black Continent "men with animals' faces." Saint Anthony had mentioned a hobgoblin, half man, half beast, "sent by his tribe to ask the saint whether he would consent to invoke the Universal God on behalf of such creatures." The most interesting report in antiquity was made by the Carthaginian Hanno, who sailed to West Africa about 500 B.C. and had discovered an island in a bay there, probably in the region of the Cameroons, "populated by many wild beasts." He describes them precisely. "Most of them were females with clumsy, shaggy bodies whom our interpreter called gorillas. We chased them. When we tried to capture them, three of the females resisted our people by biting and scratching to such an extent that we had to kill them. We skinned them and brought their hides back to Carthage."

Similar "shaggy, wild beasts" were encountered about 1590 by the English pirate Andreas Battel, while a prisoner for several years of the Portuguese in West Africa. "All their measurements correspond with those of men. But their shapes resemble those of giants rather than men. For they are very tall, with human features, deep-set eyes and shaggy eye-brows. The face and ears are hairless, as are also the hands. The body, however, is covered with hair. There is hardly any difference between these monsters and men."

It was perfectly clear to the scientists around 1760 what sort of creatures Battel had meant. They had been arriving occasionally for the last hundred years in European menageries under such names as insiego, enjocko, chimpanzee, or mandrill. Count Buffon kept one of these chimpanzees in the Jardin du Roi in Paris. The little "mandrill" obeyed every word he said like a well-behaved child. It offered him its arms, went walking with him, sat down to table, poured out its own wine, toasted him, and after the meal wiped its mouth with a napkin. Could one still describe a being that behaved like this as an animal? Buffon watched his well-mannered young charge very closely and reflected deeply about it.

Linnaeus never made the acquaintance of the orangutan of Het Loo. He did know a few chimpanzees and he fancied he had also heard of some other members of this half-bestial, half-human family. There was the mandrill, for instance, of which old Gesner had said, in his plain, downright fashion: "if you threaten him with your finger he turns his back on you." There were also the "guinea Pygmies," the little bushmen from darkest Africa, who were said to live in trees and caves like apes. Linnaeus included them all under the heading "Tailless Apes," lumping together the human pygmies, the true anthropoid apes, and presumably by some error — the mandrill, which has no resemblance to a human being at all. He pigeonholed them next to *Homo sapiens*. And a popular *General History of Nature*, composed by the respected doctor of medicine Friedrich Heinrich Wilhelm Martinus of Berlin, followed up the idea and informed a wide circle of readers that there were two kinds of "wild men," first of all the "bushmen, earthmen, mandrills, man-shaped apes, copse-dwellers, wild men, night-men, orangutan, fauns and wild men of the woods or pongo," and secondly the "little bushmen, satyrs, barris, little forest or wild men, jocko or guinea Pygmies."

Did that agree with the notion of the creation of mankind in God's image? It was no great consolation to the disgusted public to learn that the chimpanzee and orangutan were covered in hair and were unable to speak. They might lose their hair and, it was then believed, be taught to speak. People did not breathe freely again until Peter Camper once more came into the limelight with the bold assertion that he had now discovered the decisive difference between man and beast, as well as that between man and anthropoid ape. It consisted of a bone that Camper emphatically affirmed was possessed by all mammals except man. Camper's bone, which put a stop to the general confusion, was called the *Os intermaxillare*, the intermaxillary bone. It consisted, in fact, of two pieces of bone between the two halves of the upper jaw, and in animals carries the incisors.

Camper had studied the human skeleton more closely than any other anatomist in Europe, and his conclusions could be trusted. The special position occupied by mankind in zoology was thus retrieved. Unfortunately, however, Camper had only dissected orangutans, not chimpanzees. In the case of the latter he would have sought the intermaxillary with as little success as in the case of man. But orangutans possessed the bone. "Man alone," proclaimed Camper, "carries his incisors in a continuous upper jaw, without any intermediary bone."

As a matter of fact, this was an old story. The reason for this peculiarity had already baffled the anatomist Jacobus Sylvius at the beginning of the sixteenth century. He eventually reached the conclusion that men, too, must at one time have possessed an intermaxillary but "had lost it owing to their excesses." Camper refrained from any such excess in his thinking. In his view the absence of the intermaxillary in human beings was a clear proof of the eternal separation intended by nature to subsist between man and beast. All scientists agreed with him in this respect. They elevated the humble little bone to the status of a top-ranking exhibit.

A Frenchman, Félix Vicq d'Azyr, was the only one to protest. He was of opinion that Man, too, showed traces of an intermaxillary. He went even farther than this. "Anyone who examines a quadruped after acquiring precise knowledge of the human skeleton finds them to be so closely related that he may proceed from investigation of the one to the other without difficulty." But his voice died away unheard. The question of the intermaxillary was not reopened until an amateur natural scientist dealt with and finally solved the problem. His name was Goethe.

Count Buffon expressed no opinion in the matter. He looked after his well-mannered chimpanzees, glanced through the systems, which continued, in accordance with the arrangement sanctioned by the great Linnaeus, to place this little monkey in the same group as mankind, and laughed heartily. He told his most intimate friends that this classification was neither new nor surprising nor, indeed, precisely accurate. "The truth, gentlemen, is by no means so bizarre as to oblige one to describe it in Latin formulae. If I may be allowed to be perfectly frank, I will say that I don't find the slightest difficulty over Man. The fact is, he is no more than a *decadent ape*."

Buffon writes the story of the earth

The meetingplaces of the Encyclopedists were the drawing rooms of distinguished men and brilliant women. It was there that literature and science were discussed in a light and agreeable fashion; there that the leading spirits came to love and hate one another; there that reckless individualists, apprehensively watched by Dr. Riballier and his censors, fanned the flames of the intellectual revolution. The Encyclopedia had originally been an idea of the Paris bookseller Le Breton. He wanted to collect all contemporary knowledge in a single work of many volumes and obtain contributions to its various parts from the greatest scholars, philosophers, and creative writers of France. Since, however, these great men were usually engaged in flirting with the conception of a "reversal of ordinary modes of thought," the Encyclopedia became something of a nuisance to the authorities, while its circle of contributors, to quote their spokesman, Cabanis, formed "a holy alliance against fanaticism and tyranny."

Denis Diderot, their leader, indicated their aims in phrases that rang in the ears of the censorship like a defiant challenge. "Whenever a national prejudice has sufficient currency to justify it, its particular bearing, including the whole array of pretexts advanced in its support, should be explained with all due respect. Once this has been done, the rubbishy edifice should be overturned, the futile dustheap scattered to the winds, and the evidence produced which contains the solid principles upon which the contrary truths are based. This method of refuting error very soon convinces reasonable minds and infallibly affects all others, secretly and silently, without disagreeable consequences."

Unfortunately the first consequence of this method was the banning of the Encyclopedia, because "its artistic and scientific merits in no way compensate for its attacks on religion and morals." The booksellers who retailed the work were imprisoned in the Bastille. It was not until Madame Pompadour discovered that the Encyclopedia also contained interesting articles on the art of applying face powder and cosmetics that the censors were obliged, by royal command, to withdraw their ban and look on sourly while one volume after another appeared and "refuted errors."

As well as Diderot, the members of the "holy alliance" included the sober mathematician d'Alembert, the arrogant Helvetius, a former tax farmer, the melancholy and shy Friedrich Melchior Grimm of Regensburg, and the atheist Baron von Holbach. They all inclined to the materialist point of view, without representing it so uncompromisingly as Lamettrie had in his day.

They met at the house of Julie de Lespinasse, the "pockmarked Muse of the Encyclopedia." Other meetings took place at the house of Madame Geoffrin or under the patronage of Madame Necker, wife of the banker and finance minister who later invented paper money and whose dismissal was one of the causes of the popular riots in Paris which ignited the French Revolution. At Madame Necker's the combatants against fanaticism and tyranny came into contact with the man whom the banker's wife looked on as her best friend, Count Buffon.

Buffon, who had long advised the king of France on matters of science, could not officially have anything to do with the rebellious Encyclopedists. In the hallowed precincts of the Cabinet du Roi he inveighed lustily against all of them, d'Alembert in particular. Diderot and his henchmen returned his abuse with interest, calling him the "king of the Gasbags." In Madame Necker's salon, however, he arranged to collaborate with them in their "offensive" work. The zoological articles in the Encyclopedia are written by him. The Encyclopedists found to their alarm that Buffon's articles were almost more "offensive" than Diderot's at times passionate, at times marmoreally chilling sarcasms.

Confidentially, I will tell you what I think [wrote Madame d'Epinay, the excitable mistress of Melchior Grimm, to her constant correspondent, Abbé Galiani]. I am afraid Buffon's writings contain more fiction than fact. In his essay on Man he makes him the chief and most perfect of all animals. But in his essay on quadrupeds it is clear that he took the greatest delight in placing them, if not above mankind, at any rate only just below. You may remember that he ascribed human domination of the world to mere chance. Birds, he says, have the advantage over human beings of being able to fly, of having keener vision and superior faculties of reproduction and perception in certain directions, while quadrupeds enjoy the advantages of being able to run faster, of a superior sense of smell, bodily strength and perception in certain directions. So Man has nothing left but his feelings and his taste. It seems to me that if the best of all rhinoceroses had taken the trouble he could have formed a more correct judgment of his race than Buffon has of his. He ought to have been content to define the limits of every form of life and not have allowed one to trespass upon the other's ground. Nevertheless, his genius is a very fine one and his style has nobility, simplicity and charm.

Madame d'Epinay's letter reveals what the Encyclopedists thought of their new, clandestine member. Revolutionary as they might be themselves, they found Buffon's rough sketch for a theory of evolution somewhat intimidating. The count wrote like a poet. He intoxicated people like a mob-orator. He disported himself on the quivering tightrope of natural science like a champion acrobat. No one was quite sure if it was safe to believe in his hypotheses of evolution, or whether he was really only pulling his readers' — and Nature's — leg.

Even more astounding and daring than Buffon's speculations about humanity and the animal kingdom were the contents of his subsequent work on geology, *Theory of the Earth*. He made a clean sweep of all previous ideas on the subject, including the fancies of the Floodists, Linnaeus' explanation of fossils, and the traditions of the Mosaic story of creation. Physicists and astronomers had long been teaching, though they did not always evade punishment for so doing, that the cosmos had developed in quite a different fashion from that asserted in religious dogma. The time had come to apply their observations to the history of Mother Earth as well.

"Ages ago," Buffon wrote, "the Earth was a dislodged fragment of the sun, which gradually congealed in the chill of outer space. It was not until this splinter of the sun had cooled to a certain extent that life began upon it. For life is not the salamander of the legends, which live on fire. It exists at an intermediate stage between the heat of the sun and the cold of ice. Its pre-eminence on our planet will not last long."

How long had that pre-eminence existed? The theologians suggested a few thousand years. That was too short, Buffon thought.
The multiplicity of forms in nature could never have developed in
so brief a period. He performed an experiment that has become a
classic and which, despite its mistakes, cleared the way for future
research in prehistory.

He heated two metal spheres and then allowed them to cool. In
so doing he took note of two moments: that at which he could touch
the spheres again without burning himself, and that at which the
temperature of the spheres coincided with the average temperature
prevailing in Paris. He converted the figures thus obtained to apply
to a sphere of the size of the earth. The first moment represented
that at which life began, and the second the contemporary period.
The intervening time indicated the duration of life from its beginning to the day of the experiment.

It would take 168,123 years, Buffon calculated, for a white-hot
sphere of the size of the earth to turn to ice. The earth was 74,832
years old, and life could have existed upon it, theoretically, for the
last 40,062 years. It had another 93,291 years before it froze over.
These figures, of course, differed completely from those extracted
of old from the Book of Genesis, which had hitherto been used. But
what possible justification could there be for a scientist to transfer
observations taken of metal spheres to the globe, without further
calculation? Buffon saw no reason why he should not. The laws
of nature were bound to apply to all bodies, great or small. "Similar
temperatures," he stated, "everywhere create similar conditions,
everywhere breeding and supporting the same forms of life."

In his calculations he had forsaken the earth for a rapid journey
through space. If the same process of evolution were going on all
over the cosmos, if all the planets had once been sun-splinters and
had changed, on cooling, into stars similar to the Earth, then they,
too, "during the interval between glow and frost, would be covered,
like the Globe, with plants and populated by creatures with senses,
which would necessarily be very similar to the animals on earth."

Today we are not much better off than Buffon, so far as our knowledge of the forms of life on other planets is concerned. We talk
about Martians, saurians on Venus, and the sinister inhabitants of
the satellites of Jupiter. We wonder how we should deal with them:
whether they could be converted to our morality and customs,
whether they have immortal souls, and all the rest of it. We fear
that one of these days they may brutally invade and occupy our
native star. In short, despite Schiaparelli's canals on Mars, despite

all sorts of hypotheses concerning the composition of the atmosphere of Venus, despite spectral analysis and the observatory on Mount Palomar, we simply have not the slightest idea what form of life may exist, create, feel, think, or quarrel beyond our own earth's atmosphere. But we have gradually familiarized ourselves with the notion that seaweed, bacteria, monsters, or even supermen may exist out there.

In Buffon's time such thoughts were at once new, absurd, and terrifying. Could one still call that natural science? The Parisians shrugged their shoulders as they read. Most of them considered Buffon's book a wonderfully exciting and highly imaginative piece of fiction about the earth. Dr. Riballier, however, regarded it as heretical. He was determined to show this darling of society that even Count Buffon could not overstep certain limits. He suddenly began to make the count's life extremely unpleasant for him. Buffon had to bottle up his witty retorts and sparkling jests and listen, without contradicting, to what Monsieur Séguier, the advocate general, had to say about scientists who "give their support to materialism, subvert religion, spread licentiousness, and promote moral depravity."

The Encyclopedists, at whom these charges were primarily aimed, observed bluntly that before there could be any prospect of freedom for scientific inquiry "the last king would have to be strangled with the guts of the last priest." Voltaire expressed himself similarly in one of his letters. "Everything I see around me is sowing the seeds of a revolution, which will infallibly take place." But the court scholar, Buffon, kept quiet. He was not going to surrender, but on the other hand he was not going to involve himself in unnecessary dealings with the authorities, and he probably did not believe in strangling, anyway. In his view the Encyclopedists were intellectual chatterboxes and salon revolutionaries. Science could not be renovated, he remarked, either by grandiose declarations or by staging a bloody revolution. Nothing could help but scientific proof itself; facts and realities were needed.

In order to solve the problem of the early history of the earth, he turned again to the explanation of fossils given by Jean Etienne Guettard and concentrated upon the petrified objects in the lumber-rooms of the curio collectors. If the earth changed, and in the course of its cooling process convulsively ejected fiery masses from its crust, quenching the flames in the waters of the oceans, the forms of life would also necessarily change, perish, and revive in a series of Earth revolutions. There had not been one, but many creations; not one Flood, but many catastrophic floods and fires; not one set of flora and fauna since the beginning of the world, but many such sets, each of which, except that of the present day, had fallen a victim to the conflict between intense heat and water, lava and the sea. "The fossils," Buffon concluded, "are the remains of extinct forms of life."

Buffon had thus at last pointed the right direction for paleontological research and opened the road to prehistory, and to past geological epochs. The situation which Empedocles and Leonardo da Vinci, Palissy and Guettard had vaguely suspected could now be proved by the school of Buffon. The earth had once been inhabited by creatures different from those of the present day. They died out and now survive only in the fables and fancies of the Deluge. Some of their remains turned to stone, others to coal. Some left their traces in the soil like the tracks of an animal. Others were preserved, either wholly or in part, by being enclosed in lava, chalk, clay or ice.

There was only one weak point in this otherwise perfectly correct deduction — its theory of Earth revolution. Buffon saw the history of the earth in terms of a series of violent events. Completely destructive catastrophes continually interrupted the flow of life. And thereafter, when the earth lay desolate and empty as on the first day of its existence, new species and shapes arose, by spontaneous generation, from organic "molecules." This theory was not yet, of course, that of "catastrophes" in the sense of Cuvier and Agassiz, but it did amount to a preliminary sketch for it. Buffon continued to believe it perfectly possible that bridges had existed between the separate eras of the earth's history. His disciples, however, broke down these bridges and replied to the question whether present-day forms of life had developed from the fossil types with an unhesitating negative. Already in its early stages paleontology lay under the shadow of a fateful error, which even today has not been quite obliterated.

On this occasion the Sorbonne had no grounds for attacking the director of the Jardin du Roi. Closer study of the fossils proved him, in every case, to have been right. A German, Samuel Christian Hollmann, established the fact that "dragons' bones" found in the Harz Mountains were actually the remains of prehistoric rhinoceroses; and his fellow countryman Johann Friedrich Blumenbach revealed the "unicorns" and "behemoths" to have been primitive elephants which, as he was able to prove a few decades later, were to be identified with the wondrous Siberian beast reported by Messrs. Kagg and von Strahlenberg, Ossip Schumachov's mammoth. The "bones of Polyphemus," too, were those of antique elephants, the "meteors" were giant cuttlefish and Scheuchzer's vertebrae from the Gallows Hill at Altdorf had belonged to a creature that was half fish and half dragon, a saurian. As for the much persecuted "ancient sinner," opinions were divided about him. He might have been a lizard, as Camper maintained, or even a fossilized whale, as Blumenbach believed — but in any case, not a man.

All sorts of puzzles remained to be solved, but scientists were not shy of tackling them. Research, excavation, and picture-making continued. People formed collections, classified survivals of the past in the system of the living, and described them, as Buffon described the creatures of the wilderness and of the menageries in the thirty-six volumes of his *Histoire naturelle*.

The subject was also discussed in the salons. If the earth could make revolutions and do away with saurians and mammoths, it was about time that Man, too, achieved something equally effective and startling. "All the same, Count," said Madame d'Epinay, "I'm not so much in love with your theory as all that. It makes the earth seen so insecure and untrustworthy!"

Buffon smiled. "So are we human beings, are we not?" he asked. "Where will you find security, *madame?* Where will you find permanence? In politics, I suppose? Or — in marriage, perhaps?"

"No, not in politics or in marriage," Madame d'Epinay admitted. "Your doctrine of catastrophes meets their cases all right." She was thinking of her rebel friends, who wanted to get rid of the king, and of her husband, who was so fond of the *petites maisons*. "But it really must be different in nature. There must be fixed, immutable principles in nature, not this mad chaos of burning and inundation, annihilation and new creation — "

"*Madame*," said Buffon, "nature is just the same as life. So long as conditions remain stable in the heart and those of nature in equilibrium we can have faith. But if trouble starts, if the mammoth grows too strong or the sharer of one's heart overtyrannical, nature will change her fauna as a disappointed woman changes her lover."

SECRETS OF EVOLUTION

Eve — the mother of mankind

It is not only in politics that slogans are so useful. Not only statesmen, members of parliament, and journalists, but also scientists find them useful to convince their supporters and convert their adversaries. Two slogans ruled biology right down to the beginning of modern times. They were considered valid scientific principles that no one would oppose unless he were absolutely determined to make a laughingstock of himself. The first maintained that "Nature does not proceed by leaps and bounds," and the second that "All life originates in the egg."

These propositions sounded convincing. They seemed obvious. "Nature does not proceed by leaps and bounds" meant that a fish could not suddenly become a salamander, nor an ape a man. "All life originates in the egg" meant that every form of life was created by and born of another, spontaneous generation from dead matter being nonexistent. We know today that neither of these statements is true. Nature is quite good at leaps and bounds. New stocks may arise as the result of abrupt alterations of hereditary character. And many forms of life do not originate in a maternal womb at all. The viruses, for example, are albumen crystals. But it was a very long time before these facts were understood.

It is usually a hopeless task to try to discover who first invented a catchword. The wonderworking phrases suddenly come into current usage from nowhere. We use them, and soon stop speculating about them. This was not the case, however, with those two biological propositions. The name of the guilty party was Leibniz. It is true that before Leibniz' time the Jesuit Eusebius Nieremberg and the English systematizer John Ray both denied nature's ability to make leaps and bounds, while long before then antique scholars had made use of the doctrine about the egg. But it was the philosophy of Leibniz that first fixed these two concepts in men's minds, where they were to remain until the twentieth century.

It was from Leibniz that Buffon got his notion that all forms of life had grown out of tiny organic molecules. These molecules corresponded in some respects with the Leibnizian monads — those "true atoms of nature" which compose the world. Buffon was content to consider every form of life as a compound of indestructible particles of body and soul. Leibniz regarded the universe as a progressive series in which "each member has to follow its predecessor without a break. Both organisms and events proceed by infinitely small gradations, thus forming a continuous set of stages the individual steps of which differ only quantitatively, not qualitatively, from one another. For if the differences were not infinitely small, gaps would occur and certain possible forms of life would be absent from the scheme of creation. Such a contingency would involve an inconceivable contradiction in the perfection of the Creator."

The perfection, therefore, of what Leibniz called the "best of all possible worlds" allowed nature no leaps and bounds. And since, according to his doctrine of monads, everything "in the whole wide world happens mathematically to the exclusion of all error," we may of course admit the possibility "that animal species are subject to mutation," while at the same time denying all arbitrary mutation, not already provided for in the original scheme of creation. "The entire future of the world," Leibniz declared, "is contained in its present, completely planned in every detail." Consequently, no novelty can be imposed from any outside source, the future reposes in the present like an embryo, all species are guided by their eternal archetypes and every form of life originates in the egg of another.

As philosophy these ideas are perhaps tenable. In Leibniz' time, too, they represented a positive advance on the uncompromising dualism of Descartes. The doctrine of monads built a bridge between spirit and matter, rendering nature a single great unity, though one composed of many particles. Matter and force, body and soul, beast and man were no longer irreconcilable in this philosophy. On the contrary, they formed an inseparable, harmonious whole.

Disaster ensues only if speculatively minded natural scientists swallow these propositions whole and try to make practical use of them in their fields of research. For the character of philosophical systems, however brilliant they may be, is such that they tend to break down when faced by the facts of nature. There was a certain fascination, for all methodical minds, about Leibniz' logically graduated world. It could be graphically illustrated and creatures could be grouped in it, by similarity, in networks and circles of relationship. The gaps and fissures between the separate groups, upon which Linnaeus laid such stress, would no doubt in time be closed by fresh discoveries. If infallible nature never proceeded by leaps and bounds, surely the "System of Nature" ought not to contain anything, either, that progressed in this way.

These speculative graphs were accompanied by the theory of "preformation," the predetermination of every form of life in the original design. The souls of mankind had, according to Leibniz, "always existed, as organized bodies, in their forebears, right back to Adam and consequently since the beginning of the world." This meant that every egg, even before fertilization, contained a tiny "homunculus." The creative part played by the father would accordingly be limited to stimulating this slumbering mite to growth and development. No fresh evolution took place, but only the "extraction" of something that was already there. Any reference to the transformation of primitive organisms into higher ones, as of marine animals into land animals, was called by Leibniz "insolent presumption." His disciples in natural science considered the conception that the ovum underwent any alteration from the time of procreation to that of birth as equally insolent. The separate form of life resembled a microcosm. It developed on the pattern of an "archetype," as the whole of nature did on its monadic, archetypal models.

Leibniz' philosophy coincided with the views of natural scientists in the seventeenth century. The anatomist Fabricius ad Aquapendente had himself considered that all the parts of a body were already formed at the time it came into existence. The papal private physician Marcello Malpighi confirmed this belief by his thoroughgoing investigation of respiration, blood circulation, and procedure in the hen's egg. The discoverers of the micro-organisms, Leeuwenhoek, Swammerdam, and Spallanzani, who had an excellent understanding of embryos, ovum, and sperm, Infusoria, the larvae of insects, and other evolutionary phenomena, also proclaimed without hesitation that each form of life sprang into existence fully fashioned in the ovum and emerged like a butterfly from its chrysalis.

A sensational proof of the doctrine of preformation was furnished when the Geneva schoolmaster Abraham Trembley discovered the fresh-water polyp in 1740. No matter how Trembley dissected the creature, the parts invariably grew together again to form perfect specimens. So it seemed to be true that all forms of life were already complete in the ovum from the start, and when attempts were made to destroy this original form nature renewed it by the mysterious power of regeneration. Many natural scientists now started eagerly cutting up all sorts of animals — earthworms, chrysalids, crayfish, and salamanders. In some cases all the parts, and in others at least one part, grew afresh, in precisely the same form as before. Réaumur was one of these worm dissectors. He did not himself believe quite so blindly in the preformation theory, and observed that regeneration might perhaps depend on the methods and efficiency with which the experiment was carried out. But a still greater authority in the fields of procreation and growth theory, the Italian Lazzaro Spallanzani, attracted more attention than Réaumur when he declared emphatically that truncated worms and legless lizards had really not been provided for in the plan of creation and consequently the amputated creature, if it survived, must itself replace the components of which it had been deprived.

Spallanzani not only divided worms into their component parts; he also carried out the first artificial fertilization of frogs' ovules. This was genuine pioneer work. He was able to prove by his experiment a fact that had long been known but would otherwise never have come to be employed in affiliation cases. The maternal ovum can develop only when stimulated to such development by the paternal seed. The latter, however, in Spallanzani's view, was no more than a stimulant to *extrication*.

People who regarded nature as a complete, unbroken series of gradations and each form of life that it contained as the realization of an archetype existent from all eternity would have to accept the ultimate logical consequences of their belief. Two Swiss scholars, who were simultaneously zoologists, anatomists, philosophers, and moralists, did so. They wished, like Linnaeus, but not in the Aristotelian sense — on the contrary, in the Leibnizian — to define the magic network of nature and establish it as a revelation of the Divine order in the world.

One of them was called Jacques de Bonnet. Though he came from Rousseau's Geneva like Trembley, who dissected the polyp, in other respects he did not resemble Rousseau in the least. He, too, did what all self-respecting natural scientists and believers in preformation did in those days: he turned one worm into twenty-six, waited until the separate parts had joined up again, divided them afresh, and went on in that fashion as long as the patient worms could stand it. Nor were polyps, tree lice, caterpillars, or butterflies safe in his hands. And while he thus tested the tenacity with which they clung to life, he meditated on the nature of life after death. That was not so much of a digression as it sounds. He observed that tree lice increased in numbers even when no fertilization took place, consequently that their ova did not require Signore Spallanzani's stimulant. That was already, he reflected, really something like immortality. At any rate, it seemed to him that it could only prove that the forms of life that crept out of the virginal ova of the tree lice must have existed in embryonic shape ever since the beginning of the world. "These ova," he remarked, "slumber in the womb and only develop into active creatures when circumstances permit."

The other Swiss, Albrecht von Haller of Berne, went farther than Bonnet. He was interested not only in worms and the virgin births of tree lice, but also in human immortality. "Six thousand years ago God created the earth," he maintained, in opposition to Buffon's calculations. "At the same time he created the ova of all future plants, animals, and men and placed them in the bodies of their first parents." Bonnet had declared that neither spontaneous generation nor transformation existed in nature, but that one generation was set inside the other like a tiny image. The butterfly was contained in the chrysalis, the chrysalis in the caterpillar, the caterpillar in the ovum, the ovum in the butterfly and so on. Haller completed the picture by the statement, often quoted and ridiculed since, but perfectly logical to a supporter of the preformation theory: "The ovum of two hundred billion human beings was once placed by the Creator in the womb of our first mother Eve, in so light and diaphanous a form as to escape notice."

The incasement hypothesis of Bonnet and Haller had an unexpected sequel. The metaphysicians, who had always rather looked down on the speculations of zoologists and botanists, were overcome with enthusiasm. If preformation could be proved a correct theory, Buffon's utopias would collapse; materialism, too, would be given a setback, and natural science could once more fall into the outstretched arms of a reconciled orthodoxy. Every ovum, according to Haller's teaching, already contained, in the germ, the complete organism of the future creature, and consequently its ovary. And in this ovule reposed the next generation — in miniature form, of course, but already complete in every detail. In its ovule squatted, in their turn, the grandchildren. The static, unchangeable world of the scholastic philosophers reappeared in a new guise. There was no further need to make wild conjectures about the mutation of species and the origin of mankind from the animal kingdom. Evolution simply meant a jump out of the box and nothing more.

Before long the distortion of Leibniz' doctrine of monads by the natural scientists led to a positive masquerade. Certain investigators took it upon themselves to defend the honor of the male sex. They did not accept Spallanzani's idea that the only task of the male in procreation was to stimulate the growth of homunculi already in being. Nor could they accept the notion that the receptacle for the entire human race, if Haller were to be believed, had been a female — Eve. If it had to be someone, it must have been Adam who had carried the germs of two hundred billion people inside him.

An otherwise perfectly reasonable man, G. F. Meier of Halle, a professor of philosophy and admirer of Klopstock (who, in his *Essay Toward a Theory of the Soul in Animals*, had actually argued, like Lamettrie, that every animal had a soul capable of development and a gradual rise to equal status with the human), now became infected by all the fuss about Adam and Eve. He felt impelled to act as counsel for our first parent. "Adam bore all mankind in his loins, including, for example, the spermatozoon that became Abraham. And in this spermatozoon were already contained, as spermatozoa, all subsequent Jews. When Abraham afterwards engendered Isaac, the latter emerged from the body of his father and at the time brought with him, contained in his own person, his entire posterity."

Eve's defenders replied scornfully that if that were so then the spermatozoa must also have a kind of soul. And what about the souls of those that were expended without doing any good? The soul-components concerned might perhaps become merged in the soul of the child actually generated, or they might even go straight to Paradise. People did not seem inclined to commit themselves either way. There were no limits to the various fantastic theories that were held.

Albrecht von Haller, who supported the Eve hypothesis, was unquestionably a profound scholar and one of the most important anatomists and physiologists of his century. He had learned precise methods of investigation under Boerhaave. Doctors could rely, until the time of Johannes Müller and Virchow, upon his analyses of respiration, the circulation of the blood, and muscle and nerve action. His hobby was *vis vitalis* — vital energy. He established the fact that even the muscles of animals of which the spinal cord had been cut could still be stimulated. Consequently, the impulsive force of life did not reside exclusively in the brain: animating impulses flowed through the entire body. In contrast to those who shared the opinions of his former fellow student Lamettrie, he drew a sharp distinction between organic and inorganic nature. In the former, vital energy held sway, but not in the latter. He thus founded the still influential vitalist school.

But he did not confine himself to medicine. He wrote a didactic poem entitled "The Origin of Evil," which set a fashion for a regular spate of extremely labored productions in verse on philosophical subjects. He wrote novels of social criticism. He had himself appointed to manage salt mines, orphanages, and maternity homes. He settled the frontier disputes of two of the Swiss cantons. He put the ecclesiastical affairs of the Pays de Vaud in order, and when barely fourteen he perpetrated an epic poem of four thousand lines on the origin of the Swiss confederacies. In short, he tried his hand at everything, with more or less success.

Bonnet went rather the same way. As soon as he had had enough of his worms, tree lice, and caterpillars, he began to study philosophy, with a view to adducing proofs of the existence of God. He also took an interest in the theory of the transmigration of souls and actually attempted, though in vain, to convert the Jewish thinker Moses Mendelssohn to Christianity. Both Haller and Bonnet were men of that autocratic, proselytizing type that turns up so very often among natural scientists and has apparently taken over the historical task of continually clipping the wings of rebels who overdo their revolutionary fervor. The abstract systematizers of the stamp of Linnaeus and the utopian evolutionists who followed Buffon and considered nature quite capable of making leaps and bounds were accordingly now joined by a third group. Their disorderly systems could not at first imperil Linnaeus' lucid classifications of nature, but their views on procreation and development finally gained acceptance, their catchwords became the current coin of science, and anyone who doubted them did so at the risk of his career. The classical example of this situation is that of Kaspar Friedrich Wolff.

The quarrel about the germ in the egg

In September 1759, while Linnaeus was brooding over apes and Buffon over fossils, the professors of the University of Halle summoned to their presence a young student, a candidate for a doctor's degree. They pointed with indignation to the thesis he had had the impertinence to submit. This wretched affair was entitled "Theoria generationis" — Theory of Generation. The author, Kaspar Friedrich Wolff, son of a Berlin tailor, had been shameless enough to declare in this work that the whole preformation theory of Messrs. Haller and Bonnet was utterly mistaken. He had even attempted to prove it.

In the addled egg, the thesis stated, there is no trace at first of any body in process of formation. All we have is a small round disc of a white color, floating on the yolk. And this disc (Wolff was insistent that he had examined the process in detail) broke down after a short time into four layers. The first subsequently grew into the nervous system, the second into the flesh, the third into the heart and blood vessels, and the fourth into the digestive apparatus. "We are not therefore here concerned with the development of organs already formed," concluded this remarkable work by a twenty-six-year-old student, "but with a series of new formations. One part arises after another. All at first appear in quite a simple structure, altogether different from what is formed later. The complete body is only gradually developed through a succession of remarkable transformations."

The worthy Halle professors shook their heads. Wolff had probably been asleep at lectures; otherwise he would have known perfectly well what Spallanzani and other authorities had taught concerning germ formation in the egg. Meier, the lecturer in philosophy, was particularly annoyed. For Meier had told his listeners, including the rebellious Kaspar of Berlin, over and over again, that the body, fully formed in all its parts, was contained within the spermatozoon and penetrated with it into the egg. What Wolff had taken to be a small round disc was already, in fact, the complete body. There was no need for it to break down into layers, nor were any "remarkable transformations" of any kind necessary. It simply grew up, and that was that.

Wolff modestly suggested that his respected professors might like, nevertheless, to have a look through the microscope and so convince themselves of what went on in the egg. But his suggestion did not meet with any favorable response. What was the good of using a microscope when you had the textbooks of Spallanzani, Haller, and Bonnet handy, where everything that was worth knowing about development had been recorded? It was too much to ask them to test the theory of a perverse young crank. They put their heads together and deliberated what they should do with Wolff. He was not, of course, untalented. He had concentrated hard on his slide and used his eyes. Naturally he would have to be reprimanded, and after that perhaps he would leave the authorities' venerable teachings in peace. Once he had sown his wild oats he might make quite a useful embryologist or obstetrician.

After a certain amount of fuss they finally allowed him to take his degree. It would have been better for them if they had not done so. For Wolff was by no means cowed by their attitude. He had his "Theory of Generation" published at once. At the same time he announced its practical application. It was not only in the egg that a little bubble gradually gave rise, through a series of new formations, to a highly organized type of living being. A similar process took place throughout nature. First came the simple phenomenon. This underwent transformations, and in the course of time the compound phenomenon arose. The manifold creatures of the present day took shape.

Sixty years later a vine-dresser's son from Baden, Lorenz Oken, taught something of the same kind at Jena, not very far from Halle. A hundred years later, in the same town of Jena, the son of a Potsdam lawyer, Ernst Haeckel, ensured the triumph of the theory. Both Oken and Haeckel were persecuted, as if for spiritual forgery and assassination, though in their day Haller's preformation theory had long been discredited. We can therefore well imagine the fate of their unfortunate predecessor when preformation was in its heyday. Albrecht von Haller, an attentive reader of all the latest publications on natural science, immediately joined issue with Wolff. "There is no such thing as growth!" he thundered. "No part of an animal's body is constructed prior to another. All are created at the same time!" Haller left no doubt that he was condemning Wolff's work.

Wolff could not find a post in any university. No one wanted to have anything to do with him, and he had no choice but to enlist in the army of Frederick the Great. He took part in the Seven Years' War, worked for a time as a surgeon in Silesian military hospitals, and subsequently made an attempt to give private lectures on physiology in the tolerant atmosphere of Berlin, where even a Lamettrie had been accepted. He hoped that the generous Prussian academic caste would not refuse such a favor to one of Frederick's soldiers.

But even there Haller's powerful influence cast its threatening shadow. The Berlin professors firmly declined to permit a fellow subject who was surreptitiously trying to reinfect science, by the circuitous route of ovum and germ research, with the stupid and damnable idea of gradual development, to take over any of the hallowed Chairs of a decent university.

Wolff, in desperation, retorted: "What have you people made of nature? She is a living force! She has produced an infinite number of variations by her own power alone! But in your opinion her structure never alters, except in the sense that she is gradually being used up!"

For the time being he was allowed to give a few lectures of a more or less official character, under the intently watchful eyes of the professors. What they were obliged to hear confirmed all their suspicions That radical tailor's son not only referred to the four layers he pretended to have observed in the hen's egg, but even went so far as to demolish the lofty and solid boundary wall that had been erected between animate and inanimate nature. "We first come into existence as an inorganic secretion, then we are rendered organic by being provided with an organization in the form of minute bubbles and ducts." Haller's vital energy, which of course constituted the real difference between organic and inorganic, was not mentioned by Wolff.

Horrible, thought the professors. Man, at the moment of his generation, to be nothing more than an inorganic secretion, a tiny drop of liquid! In the spirit of the words later addressed by Josef Hyrtl, rector of the University of Vienna, to the nineteenth-century Darwinists, they felt that he was turning "the proud lord of creation into an anatomical exhibit, a pinch of manure for the soil!"

Neither in Wolff's case nor in Darwin's was the reproach justified. On the contrary, Wolff took the greatest possible trouble to discover what kind of power it was that turned the inorganic into the organic. He was by no means utterly averse to assuming the existence of something not yet, for the time being, to be explained, which caused the germs of life to arise, in water or in air, and to develop into complete bodies. It would have been perfectly possible to reconcile his theory of generation with Haller's vitalism, if both sides had been ready to meet each other. Wolff himself was prepared to discuss the matter.

He made a personal appeal to Haller and proposed that all the subjects of dispute between them should be publicly debated. That seemed to him the only right and proper course. But Haller was not at all keen on public debates. Hitherto he had always been clever enough to avoid them. When Lamettrie tactfully dedicated to him his *Man As a Machine*, in order to force him to define his attitude, he had only growled out a few curses of the more respectable sort. But he would not take on the sharp-tongued Frenchman. And when Linnaeus wholeheartedly was unable to approve of his extremely involved *Natural System*, Haller made no direct approach to the father of all systematizers but published a pamphlet against him under the name of his fifteen-year-old son, Gottlieb Emanuel. It culminated with the reproach: "This fellow Linnaeus has not yet even learned Latin properly!" Linnaeus replied, for his part, to the young Gottlieb, who had thus been thrust into the foreground, with a certain humor absent from his other writings: "I have been knocking about for so many years with Finns, Lapps, and Norwegians that I have become quite a barbarian."

Haller could not make any further use of Gottlieb in the Wolff case after the boy had attained his majority. The father had to take up the cudgels himself. What was it that this incorrigible troublemaker now wanted to argue about? Was it the origin of life from nonexistence, spontaneous generation, mutation, and similar improprieties? No dispute was possible about such rubbish. It was only fit for burning. Haller retorted icily to Wolff's challenge: "The question whether organic bodies proceed from an invisible to a visible state or whether they are formed from empty air does not in my view provide any basis for discussion. I am not prepared to support either hypothesis." He added an ironical postscript: "And that's what you really think, too, my distinguished friend!" He ended his refusal to be drawn by making a statement of principle which later authorities often quoted when they wished to adorn themselves with the halo of pure science. "Our inquiries are solely directed to the elucidation of the truth. Why, therefore, should I engage in controversy with you?"

He meant that a polemical discussion with Wolff was quite unnecessary, since the problem would solve itself, as the rebel from Berlin would soon find. The professors, enchanted by Haller's dexterity in getting rid of persistent bores, hastened to emulate his tactics. They declined to allow Wolff to give any more lectures and harried him to such an extent that in the end he left Berlin. In 1766 he emigrated to Russia, where he worked in the St. Petersburg academy and was soon forgotten by his adversaries. They took no notice of what he taught in Russia. No breath of it penetrated scientific circles.

It is perfectly possible, and even probable, that Wolff worked out a theory of evolution in exile which may have resembled Lamarck's or Darwin's. There seems no reason why he should have abandoned his belief after leaving Prussia. He had not the slightest grounds for doing so. Libraries and records are silent on the point. We have only a single, and not very reliable, indication that Wolff's teaching may have had some further effect. In 1829, almost thirty-five years after Wolff's death in St. Petersburg, the Königsberg professor Karl Ernst von Baer joined the Russian Academy of Science as a zoologist and anatomist. When he later attended the German Congress of Natural Scientists he brought with him some new data, which are still valid today, on the subject of germ development in the ovum.

They correspond with the conclusions reached by the unlucky, ridiculed Kaspar Friedrich Wolff, driven into exile by recognized experts.

A forgotten ancestor

In Franconia, where Scheuchzer had once found the first "witness of the Flood" under the gallows at Altdorf, another amateur was now at work. He made a discovery that might have put an end to the futile arguments over Adam and Eve, the age of the earth, and the origin of mankind at one blow, if science had been only slightly more alert and less prejudiced. What he discovered was nothing more nor less than the first specimen of Early Man.

No scientific epic has ever been written about the finder and his treasure. He is occasionally given two or three lines, but they are always followed by a big note of interrogation. The dust of time lies thick upon his notes. His specimen itself has been forgotten. It is no longer even possible to say for certain from which cave it was brought out into the light of day. Probably it was somewhere near Gailenreuth.

Even after Scheuchzer's time people went on digging industriously, inspired by the books of the Floodists and Buffon's paleontological writings, in the caves of Franconian Switzerland. Ammonites, belemnites, petrified fish, and the imprints of plants were unearthed. But the chief finds were of fossil ivory. This *ebur fossile* did not at first attract any attention from scholars, for Professor Beringer's mistake remained in their heads for long afterwards. It was the businessmen who took an interest in it. The situation resembled that in the England of Conyers' time. In spite of Linnaeus and Buffon, popular belief in the Flood, in giants and monsters, in the curative and magical effects of the strange objects found under the earth's crust remained undisturbed. The masses did not wish to be deprived of their faith either by the interpreters of stones who followed Linnaeus or by the collectors of documents who followed Buffon. This superstition, like every other, could be used as a source of profit. Now as before, quacks flourished, and the advertisers of patent medicines persuaded humble men and women that the best remedy for sickness of every kind, the most effective means of postponing old age and increasing sexual potency, resided in a powder prepared from the mysterious *ebur fossile* — that primitive osseous rock, hazy with the aura of legend.

The cave investigators of those years did good business. They pulverized the substances that should properly have graced the natural history museums and collections of fossils. They gradually grew so expert in tracking down fossils that they were usually a jump or two ahead of serious collectors. Anyone in search of fossil ivory for a museum would have to keep a very sharp lookout if he wanted to preserve his finds from passing rapidly into the hands of obscure assistants to his colleagues of the apothecaries' guild for further exploitation.

As all this dealing in magic and fraud was unworthy of a God-fearing Christian, one day in 1774 a priest named J. F. Esper went off to the cave region to exercise a moral supervision, in person, over the transactions. As a good Floodist he had no doubt that all zoolites were to be referred to the Deluge. He considered their pulverization by greedy quacks extremely regrettable and found it most painful to stand by and watch the proofs of Genesis, one after another, being transformed into unprofitable aphrodisiacs, and thus becoming lost to science. Consequently, he determined to dig for them himself and rescue what could still be preserved.

In a cave beneath a massive ledge of rock he came across a layer

The cave bear as drawn by an Ice Age artist.

of clay that contained the bones of a gigantic animal. Esper generally knew what things were made of, and he was an alert observer into the bargain. He was aware that such bones had previously been found quite often, especially in Styria, Switzerland, and Transylvania. They were popularly supposed to be the remains of dragons. However, since Buffon scholars had believed otherwise. They were perfectly right, as Esper saw at first glance. For these, as he correctly supposed, were the bones of a large antediluvian bear. The monster appears in natural history as a "cave bear."

Esper went on digging. He found more bones, of other animals, and collected them carefully. Suddenly, to his amazement he found something lying in the clay near the remains of the bear which had never belonged to an animal. It was beyond question a human lower jaw. His hands trembled as he raked and shoveled the earth away. What was this other thing? It could only be a human shoulder blade! Human bones were lying side by side with the traces of antediluvian forms of life in the depths of the earth!

Esper thought of Scheuchzer. He could not help smiling. The professorial body would certainly not be able to describe this "old sinner" as a fish or a lizard. He might have been a bear hunter surprised in his cave by the Deluge or a corpse of the primitive age, buried with his quarry. There was no need to bother about it any more: the solution of the problem was the scholars' business. The modest priest did not sound the big drum, like Scheuchzer. He packed up the bones, took them home without saying a word to anyone, and then proceeded in the manner of a conscientious modern archeologist or paleontologist. He examined cave after cave. He described and drew what he saw, and at last he had the luck to dig up a well-preserved human skull.

It was not until then, after he had done all he could to guard against the possibility of any error, that he sat down and wrote for the learned world a *Detailed Account of Newly Discovered Zoolites*, to which he added a large number of accurate drawings, and in which he inferred the consequences of his discovery in as lucid and logical a fashion as any man of science. "If human bones are found buried in this cave-mud beside the remains of antediluvian animals, human beings must have lived at the same time as the animals."

It was Esper's misfortune that he supported the theory of the Floodists. Half a century before, the whole world would have been set by the ears if it had heard something about human beings existing in the days of the Flood. But since then, after the painful revelations concerning the "Scheuchzer skeleton," Buffon's convincing theory of geology, and the correct interpretation of previous finds of "unicorns" and "dragons," no one any longer believed in antediluvian human beings. The idea of mankind being contemporary with the mammoth and the cave bear was considered utterly ridiculous. Scholars shook their heads when they read the *Detailed Account* of the cave-investigating priest. All the same, they did not feel quite easy in their minds about it. Were they now in for a fresh hullabaloo about old Father Adam? Scheuchzer's "persecuted skeleton" was sleeping the sleep of the just, though plagued by a certain amount of mockery, in the form of fish or lizard or heaven only knew what,

in Mijnheer Teyler's Haarlem collection. It would be most irritating
if a new monster were now to take his place and start further trouble.
Esper excitedly awaited the reaction to his pamphlet. When the
experts' opinions began to come in he was thunderstruck. He read
that a layman without geological knowledge cannot expect everything he says to be believed. The find had probably been made in
a grave of a later period containing the bones of bears as well as
those of human beings. It was even possible that Esper had worked
in careless fashion and, owing to his amateurish digging, had allowed a human skeleton from some old cemetery to find its way
into a bear's cave. In any case, the matter was of no importance.

Esper had not, unfortunately, inherited any of the talent for
controversy displayed by his predecessor Scheuchzer. He denied the
charges timidly, and because he made so little fuss, no one took him
seriously. The "newly discovered zoolites" disappeared after his
death. The quacks were soon busy again in the bone-producing
caves of Franconian Switzerland. More cunning than the amateur
prehistorian, they pulverized the bones of the "witnesses to the
Flood" and turned them into money.

Twenty years after Esper's ignominious failure something similar
occurred at Hoxne in Suffolk, England. A man named John Frere
discovered four yards under the earth's crust, in a layer of gravel,
certain elephants' bones accompanied by wedge-shaped and other
stone tools. The story of the find sounds like a replica of the Conyers affair. Frere, too, concluded from the mingling of the remains
of mammoths with wedge-shaped tools that early types of Man
must have been contemporary with extinct monsters in England.
As he refused to be put off as easily as Conyers and Esper, he actually
managed to get his observations published in a technical journal
of archeology. But the publication did not do him much good,
and only exposed him to the scorn of the authorities. By that time
geologists and paleontologists had long since developed a "theory
of geological catastrophe" from Buffon's "theory of the earth."
They maintained that present-day forms of life had nothing to do
with those of earlier epochs. It followed that there could be no such
thing as fossil human beings. And when the facts seemingly contradicted them, people reacted like the philosopher Hegel a few decades
later. To the objection that his philosophy did not agree with the
facts he is said to have replied, "So much the worse for the facts!"

Under the sign of Venus

Four years after Esper's discovery Linnaeus died. While he still lay on his deathbed his wife, Sara Lisa, the former buxom beauty of Falun, began to quarrel with the master's son and heir over the inheritance. Linnaeus' books, manuscripts, and collections of plants were valuable, as both knew only too well. Every museum longed to possess them. Sara Lisa wanted to sell off the lot as quickly as possible at top prices. Linnaeus junior objected that the collections ought to form part of the sacred national property of the Swedish people. What he really wanted to do was to employ them for his own purposes.

The squabble went on for months. At last the English botanist Sir Joseph Banks, president of the Royal Society, intervened. He tried to tempt Linnaeus junior with a large sum of money. "An offensive offer!" exclaimed the hopeful heir with indignation. "No one is going to squeeze even one single plant out of me!" Shortly afterwards, however, he accepted the offensive offer. Unknown to Sara Lisa, he had the property left him by the great father of natural science secretly packed up in several cases and shipped to England. Linnaeus' treasures, to the last labeled item, found their way into the British Museum and Sir Joseph's private collection.

This same Sir Joseph Banks, who transferred Linnaeus' former possessions to the British nation, was one of those chiefly concerned in certain activities which opened a new era of discovery in natural science. The star that inspired him and all his associates was Venus. Operation Venus had begun long before Linnaeus' death. It lasted, on a generous estimate, from the strictly scientific point of view, well into the twentieth century, until every corner of the earth had been investigated by first-rate zoologists, botanists, and geologists.

The planet Venus, our neighbor, which Buffon had thought to be populated by beings of delicate perceptions, was due, according to the calculations of astronomers, to pass across the sun on June 3, 1769. And as it had been known for nearly a hundred years that observations of this event from various points on the earth's surface would enable the solar parallax to be ascertained with a high degree of probability, the governments and academies of France, England, and Russia sent out important expeditions to every quarter of the globe. There had been nothing really novel about expeditions since the days of Columbus. The only novelty in the case of the expeditions to study Venus was their expressly scientific character. They did not set sail — or at any rate that was not their only object — in order to occupy certain peaceful strips of coast, adorn certain harmless natives with European civilization, and turn certain hitherto idyllic spots into strategic points for military purposes. The intention was rather to make scientific studies, calculate the paths of stars, collect animals, plants, and minerals, and take notes of the habits and customs of those "natural human beings" whom Rousseau had made so popular.

Natural scientists then found themselves for the first time attending a kind of international congress, to ensure that this unique opportunity would be thoroughly exploited. Linnaeus and Buffon had turned their fans, who had previously been little more than a mutually abusive set of enthusiastic amateurs, into a promising body of professional instructors. The intention now was to close the many gaps in the museums and systems of classification and to hunt down new species and forms of life in wild nature and out-of-the-way corners of the world. The days when explorers had taken only surgeons and cartographers with them were definitely over. The academically trained expert openly staked his claims to a share in the conquest of the earth.

Sir Joseph Banks got into touch with the English naval lieutenant and geographer James Cook, went aboard the latter's ship, the *Endeavour,* and put himself at the head of the scientific staff of the first of Cook's expeditions. In his botanical capacity he took with him, as might have been expected in England, where Linnaeus was so much admired, a disciple of his, the Swede Daniel Solander. Buffon staffed the French expedition, which was headed by the lawyer Louis-Antoine de Bougainville, with his own followers. The scientists on Bougainville's sister ship, *L'Etoile,* were led by his pupil Philibert Commerson. The Russian empress, Catherine, engaged for the Asiatic exploration she had planned Peter Simon Pallas of Berlin, a follower of Linnaeus, together with a group of German, Swedish, and Russian zoologists and botanists. In this way the preparations to observe the transit of Venus were transformed into a common enterprise in which natural scientists from all the leading powers participated.

It proved a great success. Cook and Banks discovered that the hitherto hardly known coasts of Australia and New Zealand were a new quarter of the globe, full of the most extraordinary forms of life. Primitive mammals were to be found there, the females of which gave birth to their young in the embryonic state and reared them in a pouch. Banks even came across a creature that was amphibious like a lizard, had a beak like a bird's, and a hide like a mammal's. It did not fit into any system, and looked as though it had been created to make fun of Linnaeus. A hundred years later the still more embarrassing discovery was made that this zoological puzzle laid eggs and yet suckled its young. Banks named it *Ornithorhynchus Anitinus.* Our textbooks record it as the duckbill.

Even the human inhabitants of Australia seemed rather difficult to classify. They looked like apes and also lived like apes, in shockingly primitive conditions. They possessed only a single talent, which Banks, baronet as he was, could never master. They could kill the fastest kangaroo with a piece of curved wood which they called a boomerang. If they missed the animal, the boomerang would come obediently whizzing back through the air into the hunter's hand.

Were they complete human beings, semihuman, or a more efficient kind of ape? They roamed about the country in hordes, like wild beasts. Marriage did not exist among them, only promiscuous intercourse whose rules were rather hard to understand. They had no sense of shame whatever. To the explorer their religion seemed limited to a fear of evil spirits, their art to the scratching of images of men and beasts on vertical rock surfaces. Yet they could pick up the trails of game and follow them like well-trained hunting dogs. It was true that they performed certain ceremonies, danced and built primitive huts, like cages, of branches and bark. They also understood the use of fire. Nevertheless, on the whole their habits seemed more like those of brutes than men.

The other expeditions also returned with exciting news. Bougainville and Commerson, like Cook, had thoroughly explored the South Seas. Being French and subject to Rousseau's influence, they believed that they had discovered the earthly paradise. The Polynesians of the eastern islands were light brown in color and enjoyed a distinctly higher cultural level than the Australian boomerang throwers. They closely resembled Europeans. The women and girls in particular made an extremely agreeable and alluring impression. The dark-skinned Melanesians of the Western islands were rather different. They made meals of one another and behaved, in general, in a very crude fashion. But both the brown and black inhabitants of these islands of the blest seemed to confirm in striking fashion the opinion of Rousseau that mankind is happiest in a state of nature.

Commerson also explored the Sunda archipelago and the large island of Madagascar. In the latter place he found animals nearly as strange as those of Australia. It was the country of the lemurs — apelike creatures with foxes' faces. No doubt they were "master-animals" according to Linnaeus' system. Yet they were of a more elemental type than most other mammals. Their shrill, mocking laughter in the Madagascar nights sounded like scorn of all industrious methodology. Commerson, as a disciple of Buffon, considered that perfectly right and proper. He was unable, however, to communicate his observations of the wondrous islands of Lemuria to the

Grand Master of the Jardin du Roi. For Commerson died of tropical fever on the island of Mauritius in 1773.

It was Pallas who stayed longest abroad. Until 1795 he traveled with a number of expeditions all over northern Asia, following in the footsteps of the Swedish prisoners of war who had discovered the mammoth. He visited the wild tribes of Siberia and noticed that they used stone tools similar to those found in the old burial places. His colleagues got as far as Mongolia, Persia, Daghestan, and Alaska. The result of Pallas' twenty-eight years of exploration was a natural history of animals in several volumes, based on an adroit synthesis of the principles of Linnaeus and Buffon.

These first explorations were only a beginning. Cook set sail a second time. On this occasion he was not accompanied by that fussy nobleman Banks, who had found the cabins abroad too small for him. Two German natural scientists went with him, the former pastor, Johann Reinhold Forster, a somewhat pedantic man, and the latter's highly gifted son Georg, a boy of seventeen. They were joined by the Swedish naturalist Anders Sparrman, a follower of Linnaeus, as were also the two Forsters. The elder Forster initiated theories of extensive maritime migrations by the Polynesians in historical times, while the younger fancied he recognized an ideal type of early communism in their social behavior. Sparrman, after a voyage of two years, disembarked in South Africa, where he studied two more primitive peoples, the Hottentots and the Bushmen. The outcome of this second of Cook's expeditions in the spheres of botany, zoology, and anthropology exceeded anything yet achieved.

Cook's third voyage, which ended with the tragic death of the great circumnavigator of the world, was shared by the naturalist William Anderson, who collected vast quantities of specimens for the museum owned by the wealthy and eccentric Ashton Lever. Anderson, too, died before he could return home. But his treasures reached England in good shape.

Nor did the French remain idle after Bougainville's return. Pierre Poivre, a disciple of Réaumur, and the former's nephew Pierre Sonnerat, explored Indochina and Madagascar. They sent Buffon the skins of innumerable animals hitherto unknown. Sonnerat did not always tell the truth in this connection. In his mania for systematization, he fraudulently added many other species to those newly discovered, although they did not exist in the regions he visited. He thus created a considerable amount of confusion in zoological textbooks.

Finally, the adventurer François Levaillant, the idol of all youth who long for distant lands, roamed for years about Africa. He brought home more than two thousand birds and wrote, quite in Buffon's style, a poetically phrased, disorderly and unmethodical but magnificent work on the animal world of the Black Continent. Levaillant opposed Linnaeus' decree as to the unprofitableness of diffuse descriptions of life cycles with the attitude of an impartial observer of nature throughout the world.

At the risk of incurring excommunication by scientific bodies I must continue to repeat that bulky volumes are of no importance in comparison with the great book of nature and that an error does not cease to be an error on being hallowed by the assertions of a hundred facile pens. All our usual classifications will be inadequate so long as we lack complete knowledge of all species of animals and above all of the habits of each individual species. Precise observation of every department of animal behavior, though it is beyond question the most effective means of ascertaining the proper situation to be occupied by every species in the order of nature, has been entirely neglected by those responsible for systems of nomenclature.

Naturalists have been pursuing the secrets of the earth ever since. They still continue to do so. From the observations of Venus in 1769 to modern deep-sea diving, there has been an unbroken series of scientific expeditions. Even in Cook's day it was tending to reconciliation between the two mutually opposed methods. The animal and vegetable kingdoms were far more multifarious than Linnaeus had ever suspected. Humanity, from the beastlike Australians, Melanesians, and Bushmen to the white lords of creation, was equally multifarious. Buffon's supporters recognized that some sort of system was necessary to find one's way about the multitude of species, and the followers of Linnaeus dimly suspected, in the words of Pallas, "that nature does not submit to artificial scholastic systems and diagnoses of her species. She will tolerate observation, but not confinement."

After Linnaeus' death a new generation of naturalists, with new principles, came on the scene. The theorists retired before the practical investigators. Haller had been carried to his grave two years before the death of Linnaeus. The former's anatomical and physiological discoveries remained valid, but his doctrine of preformation, which had made such a tremendous stir in its time, was quietly and good-humoredly shelved. People smiled, too, over those methodically minded persons who, as Pallas put it, "relied on the permanence of infallible indications of genus, consisting of a few propositions only."

The great scientific expeditions themselves had proved that everything in nature was in a perpetual state of flux and that nothing lasted forever. The ghosts of Linnaeus and Buffon were made to compromise. The earth was not six thousand but several hundred thousand or even million years old. The animal and plant species of the present day were far from having existed ever since the beginning of things. Systems could not be erected in the same way as arithmetical series or geometrical figures, but had to present natural relationships, which it was impossible to determine mathematically. Finally, Man had not received civilization as a gift in his cradle. Once upon a time, like the Australians, he had followed trails in the wilderness, as other beasts did. It was only after a hard struggle that he had emerged from primitive conditions.

In the year of Linnaeus' death the first of the new generation occupied a chair in a German university. He was Johann Friedrich Blumenbach of Göttingen, destined at a later date to unmask the mammoth. He announced his program to the students at Göttingen in the following words: "It will be our task to discover a method in conformity with nature. For this purpose we must examine, not individual features in abstraction, but all the external characteristics and habits of animals as a whole."

He brought zoology into direct association with comparative anatomy — a branch of science, in other words, that had hitherto been mainly concerned with human beings. It was only in this way, he explained, that clear views and well-grounded ideas could be obtained of the nature of animals and the relationships subsisting among them. He studied the reports of explorers concerning primitive peoples, considering human beings as natural phenomena like animals and plants, in order to reach a similar understanding of them. He identified the paradoxical duckbill as a very primitive toothless mammal, in opposition to the English scholars who had described the creature as an indefinable mixture of mammal, bird, and amphibian.

Blumenbach also struck a new note in another direction. He called for an end to be made once and for all of the senseless dismemberment of the animal kingdom which had been prevalent in the era of Bonnet and Spallanzani. Hitherto only a few people had objected to animals being skinned alive or having their eyes or intestines extracted to satisfy mankind's mania for experiment. Blumenbach was the first scientist to protest against all unnecessary vivisection and thus draw practical conclusions from the recognition that animals, too, are sensitive beings.

In this way biology took its first step into the new age. Meanwhile, men were growing up in France and England who would soon enable it to make further progress by revealing prehistory and formulating the laws of evolution. Before this stage was reached, yet another dispute, in reality already out of date, flared up in Paris between the followers of Linnaeus and those of Buffon.

Natural scientists revolt

Buffon in his old age could boast, "I have lived all my life between four walls," but the disciples he was then gathering about him had long been finding the four walls of his study too cramped a domain. Most of them personally took part in voyages of exploration or at the very least remained in permanent sympathy with the zoologists and botanists who sailed round the world or hacked their way through its jungles.

They worked away at steadily expanding the *Histoire naturelle*, which Buffon alone would never have been able to do. They inserted in it the new arrivals from Madagascar and Abyssinia, Cambodia and Cayenne. The stylistic mannerisms, in many places, caused very serious blemishes in the work. It was already quite evident which of them were likely to step into Buffon's shoes. There was, for instance, Philibert Gueneau de Montbeillard, with his somewhat speculative turn of mind; there were the two Daubentons, Jean-Marie and Edmée-Louis. The abbé and ornithologist Gabriel-Leopold Bexon had also well-founded expectations of succeeding to the throne of scholarship in the Jardin du Roi. Sonnini de Manoncourt, too, the extremely youthful explorer of South America, who was enthusiastically devoting himself to the final sections of the master's *Natural History*, dreamed constantly of a rosy future.

Little remained of the work of Réaumur, Buffon's dead rival. His assistant, Brisson, had turned to medicine, and his collections were now housed in the Cabinet du Roi, under Buffon's protection. The young guard of scientists consisting of the Daubentons, Bexon, and Montbeillard, amused themselves by arranging the collections in as unmethodical a manner as possible, in order to annoy the systematizers. If any follower of Buffon had then prophesied that it would not be long before systematizers of the stamp of Linnaeus, Réaumur, and Brisson would be disporting themselves in these hallowed halls and chambers from which nearly all Buffon's young men had vanished, he would certainly have been certified as a lunatic.

Two men may have had a better inkling than anyone else of what was coming. They were Buffon himself and his favorite pupil and secretary, the Marquis de Condorcet. These two took the Encyclopedists seriously. In fact, Condorcet was one of their most zealous supporters. They also knew that the booksellers and traveling stationers were carrying the radical ideas born in the salon to every peasant and artisan in the country. If a political revolution ever occurred it would not stop short of the noblemen and scholars in the Jardin du Roi. The scientific opposition to Buffon gradually spread into radical circles. A secret Linnaeus Society was founded in Paris. Its members read to one another "Latin descriptions of nature, based on philosophical and critical principles." Systematizers in both politics and natural science were coming together.

Strangely enough, the future revolutionaries inclined toward the conservative Linnaeus rather than the progressive Buffon, even though he was still their occasional collaborator. For example, Diderot's friend, the leader of the Encyclopedists, Baron von Holbach, called a work in which the Revolution was foretold as an inevitable process of nature, *Nature's System*. This literary bombshell had, to be sure, apart from its title, nothing to do with Linnaeus' *Systema naturae*. However, one may safely assume that Holbach meant something by giving his book this name, and intended it to convey his respect for the Classifier of Nature. The events that took place in the Jardin during the Revolution reinforce this assumption.

Holbach's "System" was the concentrated essence of materialism. It went even farther in its radical phraseology than Lamettrie's books, and the Baron was shrewd enough to issue it under a pseudonym and to keep quiet in the midst of the uproar that arose when it appeared. The pseudonym, strictly speaking, was perfectly justified, for the publication, which was setting the whole educated world by the ears, was by no means concocted by Holbach alone. Some of it was taken word for word, with the author's benevolent acquiescence, from Diderot's private memoranda.

In addition to a number of philosophical, political, and sociological questions, *Nature's System* also dealt with Nature herself, as she was regarded by revolutionary thinkers and scientists. The only thing that really existed, according to the book, was matter. The movements and changes that affected it — how Linnaeus would have torn his hair! — had neither purpose nor moral significance. The actions of all creatures were dictated solely by the principle of self-interest. Its practical application to the case of mankind was automatic.

Buffon would have been able to accept many of Holbach's propositions without hesitation and might even have described them as borrowed from his own teachings. He would have agreed, for instance, to the following passage. "Nature is the great Whole and man is only a part of nature. His only misfortunes arise from the fact that he does not understand nature. Nothing exists or can exist outside the circle that contains all Being." Buffon would also certainly not have objected to the statement that men are wont to set up divinities "in consequence of their lack of understanding of Nature," and that such divinities are "not only superfluous but actually harmful to the contentment of the nations." And he would have been entirely at one with Holbach in arguing that "the world shows us nothing but matter and movement. It is an unending chain of cause and effect. Matter and movement are eternal. The idea of creation from nothing is meaningless."

Accordingly, there would have been no real need for any breach between the nature-studying count and the nature-worshipping baron. Yet a breach did occur. Anyone who cared to look could see Buffon's statue at the entrance to the Cabinet du Roi. It had been put up during the subject's lifetime as though to a king, a work of the great sculptor d'Angivilliers. Anyone could read the dedication, in Latin: "The majesty of nature is rivaled by the mind of man." Statues of the hated Louis stood not very far away, looking regrettably like that, cast in bronze, of Buffon, the *roi de la nature* — and there were those who muttered under their breath that all kings should be treated alike.

Holbach's book appeared at a time when Louis XV, the master of Buffon's garden and collections, was dissolving parliament and imprisoning its members, when his *lettres de cachet* were spreading anxiety and terror among his people, when Madame du Barry ruled, and Rousseau had only just returned from exile. The landslide was beginning, and even Louis XVI, who was happiest when quietly doing locksmiths' work and had left his people to their own devices, would no longer be able to stave it off. The glimmers of the first Revolution, in which natural scientists had a substantial share, could already be discerned.

During this disturbed period Count Buffon was looking for a traveling companion and tutor for his young son. He found one at last in the person of an obscure abbé from Picardy. His choice was to have important consequences. The stranger from Picardy was the only member of Buffon's school who later managed to survive the Revolution. Twenty years after the storming of the Bastille he flung the incendiary torch of the scientific revolution into the

Jardin and the former royal museums. In true Picardy style, his name was a long and sonorous one, Jean Baptiste Pierre Antoine de Monet de Lamarck.

Lamarck was miserably poor. Ever since childhood he had suffered from the economic distress that afflicted so many of the sons of officers with large families, the fathers having hardly a penny to spare for the expenses of education in spite of their rank. It was pure hunger that obliged him to put aside the cloth and take part in the Seven Years' War as a private soldier, though on the opposite side, naturally to Kaspar Friedrich Wolff. Being an indifferent soldier, he had no luck in the army, and so went to Paris, worked as a bank clerk, and also studied medicine some, as a hobby. Consequently he had no very special qualifications for the post of private tutor at Count Buffon's. Nevertheless, the director of the Jardin felt sorry for him and confided his son to his care.

From that moment the young man from Picardy devoted himself not only to the education of his aristocratic pupil, Leclerc de Buffon junior, but also to natural science. He eagerly absorbed the teachings of Buffon, the Daubentons, Jussieu, Brisson, and other scholars working in the city that had recently grown so restless. They found him eager to learn. The first independent study upon which the novice embarked was, of all things, a new system of plant classification. Buffon growled when he heard about it and observed that every amateur sooner or later became infected by the disease of systematization, a sort of childish ailment, a symptom of scientific arrested development. Lamarck growled back at him, taking no notice of his comments.

A year before the outbreak of the Revolution the novel entitled *Paul et Virginie*, by Bernardin de Saint-Pierre, was read in Madame Necker's salon. This tear-jerking best-seller of the age of Rousseau described the happiness of two children of nature on an island paradise and their wretchedness in civilized conditions. When the reader came to the passage in which Virginie, corrupted by the conventions of civilized life, is drowned in the roadstead under the very eyes of her despairing lover Paul, because she suddenly finds that she is ashamed to take off her clothes, Buffon stood up. He declared, to the indignation of the Parisian highbrows, that the book was a tasteless concoction. Madame Necker gave him a long look, and reflected that all the same, quite a number of people were soon going to be in danger of drowning, if they did not take off their clothes in time and show everyone what they were really like.

Buffon did not live to see what was coming. He died soon after this scene. When the storm broke only two of his supporters were to be found on the side of the rebels. They were Lamarck's young pupil, Leclerc de Buffon, and the Marquis de Condorcet. The rest fled, begged the National Convention to give them certificates of immunity or were taken to prison.

In the Jardin du Roi, under Jussieu's famous cedar, the revolutionary Linnaeus Society of Paris set up a bust of the great systematizer, with the inscription: "To Carl Linnaeus, from the Naturalists." The methodologists invaded Buffon's realm to a flourish of trumpets. For a short time they got on well enough with the remnants of Buffon's school. It even seemed as though Buffon's protégé Condorcet was going to be one of the leading men in the new state. It was he who made the opening speech for the prosecution at the trial of Louis XVI. He, the naturalist, got himself elected president of the Legislative Assembly. At the king's trial he voted for the severest form of imprisonment.

But when the decapitation machine invented by Dr. Guillotin and first tried out on a sheep began to come into operation, the lives of the scientists belonging to the dominant school were also endangered. France's greatest chemist, Lavoisier, the discoverer of oxygen, lost his head. Condorcet, suspected of sympathy with the Girondists, poisoned himself in prison. Jean-Marie Daubenton hovered for months between life and death. He was only able to save himself in the end by suggesting improved methods of wool production to the Convention.

It was the younger Buffon who met the most tragic fate. In his fury against the Duke of Orleans, who had seduced his wife, he became one of the fiercest of the Jacobins. This proceeding did not prevent his being blackmailed by a scoundrel who called upon him one day, wearing the Jacobin cap, and told him confidentially that a former count and son of the foremost scholar at court must always remember that he might be arrested at any time. There was only one chance of escaping such a contingency, he went on, and that would be for Citizen Leclerc to put his hand deep in his pocket and pay the honest bearer of this information a good round sum of money. Citizen Leclerc de Buffon did not share his visitor's views. He had the blackmailer arrested.

A few hours later he was himself imprisoned on the charge of having played a reprehensible trick on a patriot. He applied to the public prosecutor, Fouquier-Tinville, to whom he wrote, in some excitement: "I call down blessings upon the Revolution! I have always been a true patriot and most zealously supported the Convention. What reason could I have for not doing so? The statues of the tyrants lie in the dust. But that of my father still stands in the Jardin and is daily admired by the People. I am sure that the Tribunal will be just." The letter did him no good. In the general purge that followed Robespierre's rise to power he was sentenced to death, on June 10, 1794, as "a nobleman and supporter of the former regime." On the scaffold he uttered a last despairing cry, "Citizens, I am the son of Buffon!"

A short time before, the obscure abbé from Picardy, Jean Baptiste Lamarck, had been appointed professor of Zoology at the Jardin, for when the mob stormed the Tuileries in 1792 and forced the king to abdicate, it was Lamarck alone who had faced, with imploring gestures, the excited crowds intent on trampling down the royal gardens. He had then managed to get the Convention to agree to the Republic of France taking over Buffon's and Jussieu's venerable and useful institution under the new name of the Jardin des Plantes. It was now staffed almost exclusively by formalist members of the Linnaeus Society, headed by Count de Lacépède, whom the Revolution had spared and who later became president of the Legislative Assembly, where he was luckier than Condorcet. Lamarck had impressed these people by his courage. He insinuated himself among them and acquired the reputation of a reliable and nonpolitical believer in systems, as in fact he was. The hour of his fame was still to come.

Another new personality appeared at the very time the head of Louis XVI fell beneath the guillotine, when the Jacobins had seized all the power in the state and the Christian calendar had been replaced by a Revolutionary one. The newcomer was scarcely twenty-one years old. He had abandoned theological studies for medicine and zoology at the Collège de Navarre. His name was Etienne Geoffroy Saint-Hilaire. It was assumed on all sides that he would be a thoroughly suitable recruit to the revival of interest in Linnaeus in Paris, for he came from the ranks of the supporters of Réaumur and Brisson, who had formed the keenest opposition to Buffon's theories of evolution. Just as Lamarck had been attracted to botany by Buffon, so Saint-Hilaire had been attracted to zoology by Brisson. It was for this reason that this callow young man became the occupant of the second chair of zoology rendered vacant by the man-eating Revolution.

Yet one of Geoffroy Saint-Hilaire's first remarks to his colleagues was, "I have the very gravest doubts of the permanence of species." This statement was made at a time when the glorification in France of the doctrine of Linnaeus, which had been forbidden under Buffon's regime, meant practically the same thing as the glorification of Robespierre's "Supreme Being." However loyal a servant of the Revolution Geoffroy Saint-Hilaire might be, he nevertheless realized that hatred of the former court scholars was leading to the petrifaction of science. People had been fighting on the wrong fronts. The true scientific revolutionaries were not the pedants who were working along traditional lines, the men who had been accidentally carried into the Jardin on the stormy flood that had assaulted the Tuileries, but the others — the men who had been driven out by it and in some cases were caught in the trap of the guillotine.

The natural scientists' revolution had been a setback for natural science itself. It had not created rebels among scholars, but petty doctrinaires of the type produced a hundred and thirty years later by the no less scientifically minded revolution in Russia. Progress, however loudly it may have been proclaimed by the Jacobin successors of Baron von Holbach, was in reality to be found among the supporters of the two quiet outsiders, Lamarck and Geoffroy Saint-Hilaire. But the latter's influence first became noticeable, as we shall see, when a somewhat less than petty doctrinaire took over the protection of scientific research. His name was Napoleon Bonaparte.

Open competition for animate beings

During the years in which the ideas of Rousseau, Voltaire, Lamettrie, Diderot, and Holbach were being realized in France a tall, heavily built man who suffered from an impediment in his speech was writing, in the little English town of Breadwall near Derby, a long and didactic poem called *Zoonomia, or the Laws of Life*. One is tempted to compare it with Albrecht von Haller's moralizing epic in verse. But though, like Haller, the author was a practising doctor of medicine, a philosopher, a naturalist, and a poet, he had nothing in common with the theorist of "preformation." He did not adhere to any school or method of research, but went his own way in a rather eccentric and peculiar fashion. He was called Erasmus Darwin.

A cooler atmosphere than the Continent's prevailed in the British Isles. Their spokesmen were not hotheaded zealots and world reformers, but sober collectors and curators. The treasures that Banks, Solander, Anderson, Sparrman, and the two Forsters had brought home were piling up in the museums. Year after year they were increased by the produce of further expeditions, and still awaited classification and arrangement. In the universities and in private libraries the systems and theories from across the Channel were being carefully examined, their minutest details weighed, and the greatest pains taken to make the best of them. For the moment the English were of the opinion that the best was still the well-tried method of Linnaeus, supplemented, to be sure, by the rather more elastic views of nature current among the practical explorers of the globe.

Sir Joseph Banks, president of the Royal Society and superintendent of the royal gardens and flocks of sheep, occupied a somewhat similar position in England to that of Count Buffon in prerevolutionary France. The only difference was that, as the heir of Linnaeus, he did not play the part of a poet in scholar's robes, but that of a strict systematizer. He collected everything he could lay hands on and avidly searched for anything that attracted him. He had designs, in particular, upon the Forsters' treasures. That unlucky fellow, Johann Reinhold Forster, had run into debt on his return and been temporarily imprisoned at the suit of his creditors. His fortunes did not mend until at last the Duke of Brunswick and other German princes obtained his release and repatriation. All the specimens he had discovered while accompanying Cook around the world, which had been duly mounted and brought home with him, had to be left behind in England. Banks bought them up as a job lot, so to speak, and added them to his collection.

The second largest private collection in England, that in the renowned Leverian Museum, shared with those of Banks and the British Museum the reputation of being the nucleus of the new, world-wide activities of research in natural science. The Leverian's history had been a most remarkable one. The rich amateur naturalist, Ashton Lever, devoted the wealth he had inherited to erecting a large building in Leicester Square in London to house his specimens. The principal attraction of the exhibition was the Sandwich Room, containing the items contributed as a result of Cook's third voyage. Banks wanted to get possession of these valuable objects, but Lever outbid him. It was not long, however, before Lever's passion for collecting had made a very deep hole in his pocket. In order to recoup his losses he organized a lottery. He offered thirty-six thousand tickets at a guinea each. There was only one prize: the ownership of the Leverian Museum. Lever had bad luck. On the day of the draw a dentist named James Parkinson actually received the winning number. The unfortunate owner had to throw all his blanks into the fire and hand his museum over to the dentist.

Shortly afterwards he drank himself to death, out of sheer vexation, at the Bull's Head tavern in Manchester.

Parkinson called in George Shaw, a Linnaeus enthusiast and the leading zoologist at the British Museum. With the latter's assistance he turned the collection of curiosities he had acquired for a guinea into a spectacle of the first order of scientific interest. It is true that he finally went bankrupt and had to sell everything by auction, down to the last of the stuffed birds. But the transaction was all to the profit of natural science. The British Museum and other large public collections, which would hardly have outstripped the Paris Jardin in such a short time if it had not been for the zeal and financial sacrifices of private collectors, took these stored wonders of the world into their keeping. As a result, London became far superior to all the research centers of the Continent — so far, at any rate, as the abundance of its exhibition pieces was concerned.

The man from Breadwall, author of the *Zoonomia*, of course knew the now resplendent London museums quite well. They were the very thing he wanted for his studies. In them he could meditate upon the amazing adaptation of many plants and animals to their environment. He could speculate, as he examined poisonous insects, armored reptiles, and the color camouflage of birds, on the means employed by living creatures to protect themselves from their enemies. In the halls and domed chambers, from the walls of which Australian lyrebirds, Antarctic penguins, and sapajous — little South American monkeys with prehensile tails — stared at him, he could set himself many a problem, the solution of which he felt to be more important than the labeling of cases of stuffed animals and plant specimens with Linnaean titles.

He wondered how parents transmitted their characteristic features to their children, how social instincts developed in separate genera, and what the very word "instinct" — that puzzling expression — really meant. There was something in Erasmus Darwin of the spirit of the French globe-trotter Levaillant, who had said that the books of scholars were of no consequence in comparison to the great book of nature. Darwin could not travel abroad, since he had to keep his medical practice going, so he became an armchair traveler, seeing at least as much in that way as the explorers did on their expeditions. He read their reports with critical attention. He studied the communal life of great herds of animals in the tropics, the mystery of insect-eating plants, symbiosis, mimicry, and a thousand different kinds of phenomena which the professors of the age of scientific formalism hardly troubled themselves about. In the museums he compared the species of the Old and New Worlds, those of the tropics and the Arctic. He tried to puzzle out the reasons for their striking mutual differences. He absorbed everything he came across like a highly sensitized photographic plate and retained it in his memory. Then he returned to Breadwall, to his desk and absorption in certain heavy and venerable tomes.

His favorite books — another curious trait in this curious man — were unexpectedly not treatises on natural history, but the works of the two philosophers, Adam Smith and David Hume. He did of course read technical literature in addition, for he read absolutely everything that had the slightest bearing upon the field of his interests. It was they who inspired his studies in natural science, but these philosophers had hardly written a single line about nature, hardly a word that might have served as a signpost to any ordinary investigator. Smith was an economist with a nationalist outlook. Hume described himself as an "anatomist of the human soul." Smith laid down economic principles and Hume criteria of knowledge. Neither Linnaeus nor Buffon would have found them of any practical use. Darwin, however, shaped from them the foundations of his new didactic edifice of natural science.

Adam Smith's book was called *An Inquiry into the Nature and Causes of the Wealth of Nations*. It was the Bible, in questions of national economics, of the Whigs, the British liberals. The motive power of human development, it maintained, was free competition among various forces. Erasmus Darwin picked up his pencil and underlined that sentence. If Smith were right — and he certainly was right — it meant that in nature, too, the competitors for the prize of life were engaged in a mutual struggle that developed their capacities to higher and higher levels. For human beings, it could not be doubted, were not subject to any special laws of their own. Man had adapted himself to his environment. He had grown certain organs and developed social instincts. The reason was not that he could not help doing so under the compulsion of some mysterious life-force. The causes were purely economic. The same thing happened in the case of all animals and plants. The "free competition of forces" eliminated purposeless action and promoted purposive action. Just as in the economic affairs of a country, if they were not subjected to interference, prices, wages, and profits found their own level automatically, so in nature everything was automatically regulated if no irrational factor intervened.

Erasmus Darwin thus transferred the liberalism of Adam Smith and the English Whigs to the processes of nature, and in David Hume he found further material to complete his picture. Hume had taught that there was really no such thing as metaphysics, but only sense impressions and practical experience. Even the philosopher, reflecting upon the things of this world and seeking to transcend the limits of the perceptions of his senses, was merely, according to Hume, associating one experience with another. Like the student of the exact sciences, he expected similar causes to produce similar effects. And experience proved that all things — personalities, civilizations, and political constitutions — evolved. Hume concluded that the world, too, must have gradually evolved from small beginnings. The theory that it had been created as a complete structure contradicted all the data of perception available to a human being.

"This idea," Erasmus Darwin noted in his diary, "agrees with all the observations that we are regularly able to make. Throughout creation we see no persistence of any one phenomenon but a constant tendency of each to improve. We watch the multiplication of the stable and inhabited parts of the earth and in our own persons the steady increase in our knowledge and prosperity." In this passage a genuine forerunner of the age of natural science expresses the unbounded optimism that was to be so characteristic of the nineteenth century. Evolution meant for Erasmus Darwin, as it meant for his physically and spiritually related successor Charles Darwin, in every case higher evolution. Retrograde steps in nature or in human history were inconceivable to them.

Erasmus Darwin's theory, almost forgotten today, works so amazingly well that one wonders why it had to wait for more than another generation before it entered upon its victorious career in modified and improved form under the name of his grandson Charles Darwin. The resistance that Charles had to overcome hardly existed for Erasmus. The great adversaries of the theory of evolution, Cuvier and Agassiz, had not yet come on the scene. In France, Buffon had been teaching a similar doctrine. In Germany Goethe, Herder, and Kant had been considering the same questions, and in England, though Linnaeus was popular, people were nevertheless tolerant enough to discuss new opinions seriously. But at first no one dreamed of discussing Erasmus Darwin's ideas. The reason may well have been that in his principal works he did not write in the style of a scientist, but in rhyming verse, which was rarely taken seriously, and as a rule did not reach the occupants of professorial chairs. When Erasmus Darwin wanted to say that animate beings reached higher stages of development in their struggle with the external world, it sounded like this:

> *Where milder skies protect the nascent brood*
> *And earth's warm bosom yields salubrious food;*

Each new descendant with superior powers
Of sense and motion speeds the transient hours;
Braves every season, tenants every clime,
*And Nature rises on the wings of Time.**

Behind the brooding author of Breadwall's many ponderous stanzas — so tedious to read — lay the belief that every created being had the chance of improving its lot by taking pains. In the "free play of forces" each put the other to the test. Each species did what it could to perfect itself and outstrip competition. Thus nature reached higher and higher stages of evolution, each of its elements grew more and more perfect, and yet the balance of the whole remained poised because of the operation of economic laws.

Erasmus Darwin treated very thoroughly a number of questions at that time which were far from being regarded as of any practical importance. It was only a hundred years later that they came to occupy a central position in scientific thought. The ideas of heredity, protective adaptation, and sexual selection were first brought into notice by him in connection with the theory of evolution. "Every animate being," he declared, incidentally contradicting orthodox modern Darwinism, "possesses the power of transforming itself in accordance with the requirements of its environment. Animals assume the colour of their surroundings the better to escape observation. Plants protect themselves with thorns, nettles and bitter juices against the attacks of their enemies. In the course of many generations all those qualities which assist creatures to survive have grown steadily more effective. In addition, the struggle for the female of the species promoted the development of weapons. For only the strongest animal has any prospect of winning a female and propagating his kind." This passage already anticipates, in principle, his grandson Charles's "selection in relation to sex." The poet of the *Zoonomia* is also really entitled to precedence over Lamarck, for he maintained that, since every being was a new type of formation, bearing the signs of conflict with its environment, it would be capable of transmitting all its qualities, including those newly acquired, to its offspring. "In this way a few imperfect original types have produced the multiplicity of the existing types of animals and plants."

Nor did Erasmus evade the question of all questions: the origin of mankind. He attacked it quite in the spirit of Lamettrie and Holbach. "What, then, is all our seeing and hearing, smelling and touching, which enable us to perceive phenomena and accumulate

* "The Temple of Nature," Canto II, 11, lines 31–36.

experience? To what is our digestion to be referred, to what our breathing and our reproduction, that which gives us life and that which maintains it? They are to be referred to innumerable tiny, living clusters of nerves, distributed throughout our whole body and reacting to every stimulus."

Man was a piece of nature. He had gradually developed from the many other forms of life, but remained a competitor in the struggle for survival. Like his fellow creatures, he saw and heard, smelled and touched, breathed, digested, and reproduced himself. Erasmus Darwin did not hesitate to infringe the ancient taboo. That was, after all, what Hume and Smith had taught. He was merely applying it to natural phenomena, including human existence. He said emphatically: "We are not degraded by recognizing this fact, but only the more in duty bound to strive for perfection and accomplish great things — in short, to be *men!*"

He worked for a number of years, between 1781 and 1798, at his rhyming epic. In addition, he wrote didactic poems entitled "The Botanical Garden" and "The Temple of Nature," inspired by the same idea. The English, who rejected with horror the science of the Parisian sans-culottes, read his verses and saw nothing in them; they placed the *Zoonomia* on the shelf that held their volumes of Shakespeare, Swift, Hume, and Smith. They did not realize that their versifying and philosophizing countryman from Derbyshire was thinking along far more revolutionary lines than the whole Jardin des Plantes with its militant Jacobin band of natural scientists put together. Erasmus Darwin was considered an unpractical dreamer, as in the same way Swift had been considered an amusing teller of nursery tales.

The dust of bookshelves was also gathering upon the works of another Englishman that were no less revolutionary, though no one paid any particular attention to them. This man, the philologist Lord Monboddo — who remembers his name today? — might have served as the complement which the works of Erasmus Darwin still needed. His ideas, if one applies them to the theory of evolution originating at Breadwall, result in a theory of the descent of man in Charles Darwin's sense. He had made extensive studies of primitive peoples and apes, instituted comparisons between them, and found a feature common to both: the mimetic instinct — in other words, a typical characteristic of children. Just as every child "apes" grownups in order to learn from them, so do, in an astonishingly similar manner, the inhabitants of bush and jungle when they come into contact with white men.

This conception seemed merely comic to most people. They saw nothing more exciting than that in it. Monboddo, however, treated "aping" as a serious phenomenon. He maintained that such apelike behavior, which enabled children and tribes living close to nature to learn languages and good manners with ease, had been one of the chief causes of the rise and development of civilization. He considered that early man once must have imitated the sounds of nature, thus exercising his vocal muscles, and that later on men came to understand one another in this way, by memorizing and refining upon the sounds they had learned.

"The tongue," the ancient Roman Lucretius had written long ago, "existed long before speech arose." It followed, for Monboddo, that imitation existed long before civilization. And it was only logical to add to this conclusion that early man, speechless and imitative, like an ape, could not have been anything more than a kind of ape walking on its hind legs. Monboddo did not give any expression to his ideas in this connection. He was a philologist and linguist. Biological problems did not come within his province. Natural historians, in their turn, took no interest in stammering babies and jabbering bushmen. So this hypothesis, too, sank into the sea of forgetfulness, without causing a ripple.

Erasmus Darwin preserved for years the well-founded hope that his intellectual achievement would be a permanent one. He expected that his three sons — Charles, Erasmus, and Robert Waring — would carry on the work as he had begun it and continue to rack their brains over the question how the "free play of forces" had in reality brought about evolution in nature. But at this stage misfortune after misfortune came to afflict the house at Breadwall. Charles, the most talented of the heirs apparent, died of blood poisoning. Erasmus junior went out of his mind and committed suicide. The only son left was Robert Waring Darwin, a doctor of medicine who was no intellectual genius and still less a rebel in natural science, but a man of thorough practical mentality, a devoted specialist in midwifery and optics.

Robert Waring Darwin received his father's bequest as if it had been a valuable family heirloom. He guarded it carefully, but did nothing with it. Still less did he venture to refashion it. Fifty years were to pass before the grandson of old Erasmus began to pay attention to it and eventually, in the quiet, meditative style of his grandfather, turned it into a masterpiece of almost Copernican eminence. This grandson, Charles Robert Darwin of Down House, who now rests close to Isaac Newton in Westminster Abbey, had not yet been born.

Part Two

ADAM DISOWNED

There can be no greater impediment to progress in the sciences than the wish to detect its outcome at too early a stage.
GEORG CHRISTOPH LICHTENBERG

V

THE ANIMAL IS THE ELDER BROTHER
OF MAN

Man, too, has an intermaxillary bone

"HE's MESSING ABOUT with those horrible bones again," said the
worthy citizens of Weimar, wrinkling their noses as they pointed to
the windows of a house that remained alight far into the night.
They shrugged their shoulders. A minister to the court of His Highness the Duke Karl August of Sachsen-Weimar-Eisenach, they observed, had no need to encroach upon the province of the natural
scientists. And if nature really were such a hobby of his, why not
chose, instead of ancient skulls, teeth and bones, pretty flowers, or
sparkling precious stones, as was usual in high society?

The man they were talking about was a lawyer by profession. He
bore the title of Acting Privy Councilor, and as well as being President of the Chamber, managed all the building, mining, and forestry
activities of the little Thuringian state. In addition to his many
other duties, he had taken over, out of sheer interest in the work,
the supervision of the scientific institutions in Weimar and Jena.
He was therefore perfectly entitled to concern himself with scientific
questions. But was the work that he did scientific at all? He compared human and animals' skeletons, made drawings of them, and
tried to find out in what respects they were similar. It was a frivolous
undertaking, his fellow citizens thought — the whim of a poet.

Johann Wolfgang von Goethe had begun his studies of bones in
1784. He was then thirty-five years old. He had been impelled to
the task by Peter Camper's much praised statement that man differed anatomically from the beasts by having no intermaxillary bone.
Goethe did not believe in the existence of such a distinction. "Nature," he proclaimed, "can only succeed in her creative intentions
by proceeding from one thing to another." She would not, for example, be able to create a horse if all the animals previously existing
had not formed a kind of ladder, by mounting which she could
arrive at the particular structure of the horse. Thus the individual
always exists in relation to the whole, and the whole in relation to

the individual, for the simple reason that the individual itself is also the whole. Of couse this interpretation of Leibniz's idea of nature's stepladder of phenomena differed completely from the theories of Leibniz' disciples, Haller and Bonnet. For Goethe Nature was not static, but dynamic. Her forms did not repose side by side, motionless, like beetles in the showcase of a museum. They continually blended into one another. Species had not remained unaltered since the beginning of things, but had gradually evolved.

> *Nature hath neither core nor shell,*
> *All things at once in her we tell,*

was Goethe's rhyming answer to Albrecht von Haller's prose theory of preformation. And if Nature forms one great unity, in which one thing has evolved from another in a continuous series, Man, too, must have originated in her womb. Man, like most other mammals, possessed incisors. In animals the incisors had their roots in the intermaxillary. It would be perverse to assume that Man had the same dental formation as the animals but quite a different jaw formation. No. In Man the intermaxillary had merely become atrophied. One had only to make a thorough search for its traces and then the question would be cleared up. Goethe was firmly convinced that at some time or other he would come across that little bone.

He set about his investigations with the fanatical patience of an archeologist assembling and comparing shards and stone implements so as to reconstruct from them a whole cultural epoch. He examined in detail the skulls of all sorts of mammals, had drawings of them prepared, corresponded with zoologists and anatomists, ransacked the entire osteological collection of the Weimar museum, and attained a standard of technical knowledge in this field which was at least equal to that of his learned contemporaries. Yet hardly anyone came to his assistance or shared his views. The professors were utterly indifferent to his researches. Only two friends — Herder, who was five years older than Goethe himself, and that rather wild participant in the literary "storm and stress" movement, Johann Heinrich Merck — awaited the result of the bone inspection with intense sympathy and excitement. Each in his own way agreed with Goethe's view of nature, and found nothing shocking in the idea that man and beast might in principle possess the same skull structure.

Merck, who had at first been the most convinced supporter of Goethe's intermaxillary thesis, did not enter literary history on account of his poems, but owing to the fact that he furnished Goethe with a model for Mephistopheles. It was no wonder that he did so. For Merck was himself a stormy petrel, "a spirit of eternal contradiction." This eccentric character could never feel at home in Weimar. After a brief sojourn at the court of Duke Karl August, he was politely given his discharge and returned to his native city of Darmstadt. But he continued to keep up a lively correspondence with Goethe, and, as he became infected with Buffon's theories, began enthusiastically collecting fossils, and actually discovered some new prehistoric species of animals. Goethe received a good deal of scientific stimulation from the man who was his model for the devil!

He got his philosophical stimulation from the ecclesiastical superintendent-general and court preacher Herder. The latter, too, was a restless and wayward character, utterly unsuited to occupy the position of a very senior cultural official in the dukedom of Weimar. In the same year when Goethe started his quest for the human intermaxillary, Herder completed the first part of his chief work, *Contributions to a Philosophy of the History of Mankind.* It contained certain propositions about humanity which must have made his orthodox colleagues see red. In creation, he explained, "a series of ascending forms and forces" prevailed, while the sun ensured "the continuance of our earth and of all organisms born" and the animal was "man's elder brother." These observations unquestionably suggested the outline of a theory of evolution. Nor could Herder's qualifying clauses alter the fact. "As soon as the gates of creation had been closed, the organisms previously selected for existence served as definite avenues and entrances through which in the future, within the limits of nature, the lesser forces were to make their way and continue the work of construction. But they created no more new forms."

Goethe was more impressed by the implications than by the qualifications of his friend Herder's work. In his view the gates of creation had by no means yet been closed. Other readers in Weimar, too, could not help feeling that Herder was implying that men were descended from animals. Frau von Stein, for example, shortly after the appearance of Herder's book, wrote in a letter to Knebel, controller of the duke's household: "Herder's latest work makes it look as though we were originally plants and animals. As to what nature is going to do with us in the future, that we can't possibly tell. Goethe is now giving his whole mind to the subject and anything upon which his imagination has been working always turns out to be extremely interesting."

It did indeed turn out to be interesting. For soon after Herder's appearance on the scene, Goethe followed him with an essay, *On the Intermaxillary in Man and the Animals*. He had been able to prove the existence of Camper's bone in Man also. Admittedly, the actual evidence was barely visible. It could be detected only as a uniting seam. But it did exist. "I was busily engaged upon the search for a type of bone common to all," he wrote, "and I therefore had to assume that all the separate features of any creature, both in their details and as a whole, ought to be discoverable in all animals, as comparative anatomy itself is based upon this preliminary condition. Accordingly, I looked for traces of the intermaxillary alleged to be characteristic of the difference between apes and human beings, being attributed to the former and denied to the latter. I found them without difficulty."

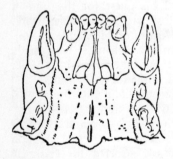

Drawing by Goethe of the upper jaw of a lion. The intermaxillary, holding the incisors, is clearly recognizable. In the case of Man it has become so closely associated with the two jawbones that the conjunction can hardly be discerned. It is only at the embryonic stage of development that the intermaxillary appears as an unmistakably separate bone.

He triumphantly informed Herder of his discovery. "You ought also to be very pleased about it because it is as though the cornerstone of human structure were not lacking after all, but is actually there. Most definitely! I have also been thinking the matter over in connection with your own general theory and realize how well it fits in with your ideas." Herder's opinion that animals were the elder brothers of men was in fact given first-rate confirmation by the discovery of the intermaxillary. Goethe's instinct led him on to a daringly imaginative conclusion: there perhaps actually was some original type from which all vertebrates, including mankind, had proceeded — some primal animal? And was there some primal plant?

Herder reflected. He asked for more details. And Goethe explained what he had conjectured. The multiplicity of nature, its abundance of diverse forms, had not been there from the beginning. They had gradually evolved from simple primitive forms, the structure of which could still be traced in every animate being. "Once the conception of this archetype has been grasped — it sounded as though Buffon had been resurrected in a German poet — "it will then be easy to see the impossibility of regarding any genus as sacrosanct. The individual can never represent a pattern of the whole, consequently we must not look in the individual for the pattern of all things. Classes, genera, species and their separate members resemble cases in law. They are contained in the law but they neither contain it nor promulgate it." This was a restatement of the methodology of Linnaeus. It has never been so ingeniously and thoughtfully expressed from that day to this. "But the means by which we can discover such an archetype are provided by the very idea of the type itself. Experience is bound to teach us what components are common to all animals and how such components differ in the different animals. Abstraction will then come to our aid to enable us to set the matter in order and construct a general picture of the position."

In this passage Goethe had formulated a notion which, to use the expression of the youthful Linnaeus, "no natural scientist had yet understood" By the combined efforts of his intelligence, his imagination, and his talent for observation, the author of *Werther* had reached the only possible explanation of the abundance of forms in nature, and had at the same time shown the scientists, too, the road they would have to travel for the future in order to classify related phenomena and reconstruct the archetype. But it was not until seventy-five years later, in the time of Charles Darwin, that this revelation was recognized and properly appreciated. In the Weimar of 1784 the time was not yet ripe for the enthusiasm for Goethe later expressed by such men as Ernst Haeckel and Rudolf Virchow. Even Herder shrugged his shoulders. He did indeed call Goethe's bone theory "very simple and excellent." But he did not agree with Goethe's ideas on evolution. He doubted whether nature ever "creates and organizes new species" and refused to associate himself with so bold an interpretation of his own extremely confused ideas on evolution. Man might well stand in a fraternal relation with the beasts. But the skeptical superintendent-general could not bring himself to admit that man might once have been, in actual fact, a real archetypal beast.

Goethe experienced a similar disappointment with Merck, his second associate. Merck had taken it upon himself, as an expert connoisseur of bones, to inform Camper of the discovery of the human intermaxillary. He sent Camper Goethe's essay. But he seems to have been intimidated by his own rashness in doing so, for he added: "You will be astonished at the industry of an amateur who, in spite of his duties as a Minister of Finance and the obligations of close friendship with a Prince, still finds the leisure to perform work which is not, perhaps, unworthy of your attention." The phrase scarcely sounds like that of an enthusiastic devotee, and certainly not a fanatical one. When Camper took not the slightest notice of this communication, Merck lost still more of his confidence. He made a second approach to the great Dutch anatomist, in which one cannot deny that he played Goethe false to a certain extent. "Though you may find his system ludicrous," he wrote deprecatingly to Camper, "you must confess that it is quite consistent. If he had not pressed me to send it to you, I should never have dared to do so. Nevertheless, this piece of research by a man of the world, who spends his time immersed in business and, what is even worse, has a great reputation as poet, seems to me remarkable."

Goethe's interests were by no means in good hands, even though he himself did not suspect the baseness of his friend Merck. He awaited Camper's opinion with much anxiety. In his view the man who dissected human beings and orangutans in Amsterdam and Leiden still remained an authority "equipped with powers of observation and logical thinking all his own," and he believed that a scholar of such eminence would be just the man to admit a mistake and be grateful for its correction. He was therefore greatly disappointed when Camper, after putting his patience to a prolonged test, bluntly rejected his "conjecture regarding the intermaxillary bone." Goethe wrote, with much bitterness:

I communicated my short essay to Camper, taking so much trouble over its format and style that the man I was addressing received it with a certain amount of surprise. He praised my work and pains and expressed himself in friendly fashion, but continued to maintain that man does not possess the Os inter-maxillare. Well, it certainly proves a strange lack of knowledge of the world, and a degree of childish egotism, for a pupil of lay status to venture to contradict past masters of the trade and it is even sillier to dream of convincing them. Repeated attempts of this kind have taught me a further lesson, namely that phrases uttered over and over again harden in the end to obstinate conviction which makes the speaker utterly deaf to persuasion.

The second great authority in the field of osteology — that disciple of Buffon, student of the mammoth, and adversary of vivisection, Blumenbach — showed himself equally indifferent to the "Goethe-bone." This was particularly surprising, for Blumenbach did not generally behave dogmatically. Goethe knew him to be a tolerant and open-minded man, sympathetic to all innovation. Yet even the most tolerant of professors still considered Goethe to be a mere layman, an amateur of natural science whose tastes deserved hearty applause but did not justify entering upon a serious dispute with him. "A negative attitude of this kind," Goethe complained, "is worse than contradiction, for it implies a rejection of that interest in a subject which enables any scientific project to reach due fulfillment." It was not until many years later that Blumenbach saw his mistake and lent his aid to the excision of Camper's alleged distinguishing feature from books on natural history. Goethe had meanwhile drunk the cup of scholarly disdain to the dregs.

God and nature are one

On Christmas Day 1784, when Frau von Stein celebrated her forty-second birthday, Herder sent her a book that was destined to become the guide not indeed of himself or of the recipient on this occasion, but certainly of Goethe and a new German school of natural science. It was the *Ethics* of the Jewish glass cutter, schoolteacher, and philosopher Benedict Spinoza. Herder accompanied his gift with the recommendation — an amazing one for a theologian — "May you ever consider Spinoza to be the model of a saintly Christian."

Three persons who were allied and yet already secretly at odds with one another were now reading the audacious doctrines of a rebellious outlaw from Holland, who had died over a hundred years before of hunger and pulmonary consumption. Each interpreted the propositions in question in his own way. Spinoza was being rediscovered, and with him that philosophy of nature which, with the materialism of the followers of Lamettrie and the liberalism of Adam Smith, formed the third intellectual influence. This philosophy was to contribute decisively to a revision of the natural sciences and the absorption of humanity into the kingdom of nature.

In Goethe's time revival of interest in Spinoza was in the air, just as beyond the Rhine the teachings of the Encyclopedists and beyond the Channel those of the Liberals had been commonly accepted. It

was a natural reaction against the theory that had now been taught
for two thousand years and had hardened into dogma, tending to
separate body from soul and matter from spirit. As scientific knowledge increased, people began to have doubts about the special position occupied by spirit and the human soul. It was recognized that
earthly phenomena could be far more easily explained by the assumption of a nature comprising all things and unifying within
itself both creator and creature, while matter and spirit were merely
attributes therein of a single primal substance. On this assumption,
too, there would be no need to invoke a mystic act of creation in
considering the question of the origin of mankind, since man was
a part of Universal Nature, born of it and forever inseparable from
it in the same way as plants, animals, and minerals were. This
theory had been taught long ago by the Greek natural philosophers.
Giordano Bruno, Galileo, and Spinoza had proclaimed it. It is
tantalizing to reflect how near these thinkers came to discovering
the secrets of life and the origins of humanity. Fascinating ideas
were to be found in their writings, but it was left to other minds
intoxicated with nature to carry them to their logical conclusions.

The first philosophy of the West — that of the pre-Socratics
— was a pure natural philosophy, the first attempt made to grasp
the character of the primal substance ultimately responsible for the
production of phenomena. The creators of this school of philosophy
were colonists. They were Greek settlers in Asia Minor and Sicily,
men already disposed to receive and ready to absorb new impressions. There can be no doubt that they not only constructed systems
of thought but also thoroughly investigated nature and life. Thales,
in the flourishing Ionian colonial city of Miletus, taught that all life
had originally arisen from moisture. His pupil Anaximander went
still farther in his declaration that man, too, had at first resembled
the fish and had gradually, under the influence of the sun, been
transformed into a terrestrial creature. Finally, the third Milesian,
Anaximenes, considered that the cosmos as a whole possessed a
soul. In the Sicilian colonies the Pythagoreans discovered mathematics. They described the Earth as one star among many, revolv-
ing through the universe at distances calculable from a fixed point.
They also emphasized the relationship between Man and beast.
Xenophanes, in Colophon, proved from fossilized crustaceans and
fish that the structure of the earth and its fauna are subject to
periodic modification. And in Ephesus the greatest of the pre-Socratics, Heraclitus, summarized all these doctrines and set out in obscure, highly metaphorical language his theory of perpetual change,

of the life-provoking and life-consuming conflict of opposites in nature and human life.

"Everything flows" was Heraclitus' key phrase. It was also the motto of the other natural philosophers of ancient Hellas. In their view there was no "Being," only a continual "Becoming." "We can never step twice," said Heraclitus, "into the same stream, for new waters never cease to flow into it." It was not an easy idea to agree with and has at no time made any special appeal to the instinctive human longing for certainty and permanence. Nor was it long before the first voices became audible, proclaiming that human thought could only be based upon the existent, that perpetual change was inconceivable, and that if sensuous perception found nothing but growth and movement in the world, then appearances must be deceptive. "That which is moved," Zeno of Elea objected to Heraclitus, "moves neither in the space it occupies nor in the space it does not occupy." Consequently, it does not exist. Natural philosophy was attacked by the dialectical method, the art of tricking one's adversary by a disguised false inference, of which people are still so fond today. Thus it was triumphantly proved by logic that a flying arrow did not move, but was at rest and that the swift-footed Achilles would never overtake the slow tortoise. Of course these fallacies, thought out by subtle Greeks, who had suddenly become obsessed with the delights of reflection, were great fun. Even today schoolboys still enjoy them. But they gradually dug the grave of natural philosophy. The clever wordplay of the Eleatics had already started the period of the decline of the Hellenic spirit.

During this period of decline, when philosophy was degenerating into sophistry and retreating farther and farther from concern with nature, once more three great scientific thinkers appeared, who made attempts to rescue thought from perpetual change. They were the popular orator, engineer, and apostle of nature Empedocles, from Akragas in Sicily, the statesman and cosmographer Anaxagoras, who emigrated to the still conservative Athens as the first representative of the enlightened school of Ionia and Asia Minor, and the Athenian Democritus, with his atomic theory. Just over four generations separated these men from Thales, the father of philosophy, and in those generations from 600 B.C. to 450 B.C., the Hellenes had made more contributions to the knowledge of nature than all the rest of mankind during the next two millenniums. As biologists they advocated theories of evolution that have a surprisingly modern ring; as physicists they had already approximately sketched the main outlines of the theory of gravitation and the law of the conservation of

energy; as mathematicians they laid down the first elementary foundations of geometry; and as astronomers they produced descriptions
of the universe which remind us of those of Copernicus, Kepler, and
Galileo. They were acquainted with all the kingdoms of nature.
They related them to one another and sought in the abundance of
phenomena for the primal cause that unified their multiplicity.
Man, too, they were convinced, obeyed the laws of nature, as one
creature among many.

Yet only a few decades later their wisdom ceased to be valid.
The Sophists taught that Man was "the measure of all things."
Plato affirmed that the world of appearances was an illusion and
the body "a prison of the soul." Aristotle turned the eternally flowing nature of Heraclitus into a well-arranged museum and declared
that the "essence and cause of every phenomenon are identical with
the purpose residing in it." Man, it was now alleged, was the navel
of the universe, the crown of creation. Other forms of life had
been expressly produced for his benefit. Every natural object had
its fixed place and a task assigned to it from the very beginning, in
this" best of all possible worlds." There was no longer any need
to rack one's brains over biological, physiological, physical, and
evolutionary problems. The only subject in which a thinker could
now be interested would be the moral nature of man.

The invention of ethics was the decisive turning point in the
history of the West. Henceforth natural science was separated from
mental science and eked out a stunted existence, like a plant growing in the shade, beside its younger, triumphant sister. Even the
last three great natural philosophers, Empedocles, Anaxagoras, and
Democritus, were also writers on ethics, prophets, and moralists.
Their efforts to unify topics that had a powerful tendency to diverge
were wrecked on a fatal institution, that of the cultural dictatorship of the police state.

Empedocles, who had laid the foundations of the doctrine of cosmic construction from elements and sketched a theory of the origin
of species that came near to being an early anticipation of Darwin's,
died a political exile in the Peloponnese. Anaxagoras, the first thinker
to assume the formation of the universe from the eddyings of primal
mist, was arrested for heresy and escaped a death sentence only
through the intervention of the statesman Pericles. The sixty books
of Democritus, which expounded the cosmos as seen by exact natural
science, reasoning directly from physiology to the theory of atoms,
proved the Athenian father of materialism to be the spiritual ancestor of all the great physicists from Galileo and Newton, through

Dalton and Faraday, to Bohr and Einstein. But his works were sacrificed on the bonfires of the censorship. Plato himself is said to have instigated this first case of the burning of books to occur in the history of civilization. And since this method of gagging undesirable thinkers worked so well, it was also applied later on. Giordano Bruno paid for his teachings of natural philosophy, which recalled those of the pre-Socratics, with his life. Galileo, a reincarnation of Democritus, was forced to recant his beliefs under torture. The Renaissance scholar Petrus Ramus, who had dared to criticize Aristotle's teleology, was murdered. Ever since Plato had degraded the investigation of nature to the status of a mere preliminary "to the return to serious concern with the world of ideas," anything that went beyond the bare assembly and description of natural objects was regarded as objectionable. Every attempt to dislodge Man from his pedestal and reinstall him in the kingdom of nature encountered vigorous protest from philosophical, scientific, and theological authority. For two millenniums, natural philosophy was equated with spiritual high treason.

It is one of the bitterest ironies in world history that a natural scientist, of all people, should have been mainly responsible for this development. It was that baldheaded, paunchy, shortsighted Aristotle of Stagira who achieved immortality as the omniscient "professor." His ability was undoubted and he was an industrious zoologist, botanist, and physiologist. He jotted down the first System of Nature, was the first scholar to take up embryology, and even believed in a gradual evolution of animate beings, in spontaneous generation of the lower organisms from decomposing matter, and in some relationship — in a distant one, at any rate — between Man and the apes. But the very fact that he knew so much and bequeathed all his knowledge to posterity in such good order sealed the fate of science. The ensuing generations considered that he had known positively everything, that there was now nothing left to discover, and that the problems of natural history had thus been once and for all defined and settled by him. The most fascinating contribution of the professor from Stagira was his opinion, which has remained current down to our own day, that Nature had created all animate beings in accordance with a single conception, an ideal aim she had in view. To put it crudely, the fly had been made for the tomtit, the tomtit for the sparrow hawk; the grass for the goat, and the goat for the wolf. Everything in nature existed in order to be useful to something else, and the final object of all of them taken together was to serve mankind.

This was the exact opposite of what natural philosophy had taught. "Phenomena," Democritus had written, "have no reason or object for their existence. They simply exist. The question why the atoms exist is as foolish as the question why the lion is carnivorous." Aristotle retorted: "Nature never does anything without a reason." And to the assertion of Anaxagoras that Man was the cleverest of all animate beings because he possessed hands, Aristotle replied: "Quite the opposite. Man acquired hands because he is the cleverest of all animate beings." This statement indicated in the clearest possible manner the difference between the pre-Socratic investigators of nature and the natural historians of the Aristotelian era.

The Romans took over Aristotle, the neo-Platonists, the Arabs, and the scholastic philosophers. Those pallid successors of Democritus, the Greek Epicurus and the Roman Lucretius, on the other hand, could make no headway. Aristotle survived the Renaissance and the Enlightenment. He eventually found expression in Linnaeus. For centuries all contradiction of his teaching ranked as heresy, all rejection of the idea of purpose in nature as sacrilege, and all attempts to dethrone humanity as crime of the first magnitude. Scientists considered that their principal task for the future would be to make a series of fresh translations and interpretations of Aristotle. There was no further question, for the time being, of inductive research, unbiased observation, or analysis of natural phenomena.

The first objections to the teachings of the professor from Stagira of which any notice was taken at all were heard at the time of the Reformation. Luther, in his downright fashion, simply called Aristotle an ass. Contradiction grew louder when Copernicus banished the earth and mankind from a central position in the universe in 1543. But another hundred years passed before anyone came on the scene who proved capable of bringing about a revival of natural philosophy in the spirit of the ancient Hellenes. He did not find it easy to do so. In the very year in which a solemn sentence of excommunication was pronounced in Amsterdam against the twenty-three-year-old rabbinical student Benedict Spinoza for "abominable false doctrines," the famous phrase of Blaise Pascal, a disciple of Descartes, was uttered. "Everything natural is godless. Natural philosophy, in my opinion, is not worth an hour's study." And Pascal spoke for his age.

Those "abominable false doctrines" on whose account Spinoza had been banished from the Jewish community had not been, as a matter of fact, natural philosophy at all. They were the completely dualist and anthropocentric theses of Descartes. The studious young man had made their acquaintance at the house of the Dutch physician and free thinker Franz van den Enden. It was only gradually, at first, that Spinoza turned from a Cartesian to a stern critic of the great philosopher of the theory of knowledge. It almost looks as though he had betaken himself to the promulgator of the doctrine of the soullessness of nature only in order to erect his own system in accordance with the form and content of the other's. His enthusiasm for Descartes had not been aroused by the strict separation of spirit from matter or the theory of animals as machines, nor by the bold assertion that only thought could be taken for granted, whereas the existence of the corporeal world could not be so taken. It was only the mathematical, the geometrical method that Descartes had been the first to introduce into philosophy which attracted him. One could dip into the thought of Descartes as though into a mathematics textbook. It was a period when mathematics, physics, and astronomy were celebrating their greatest triumphs; when the discoveries of Copernicus, Galileo, and Kepler were gradually becoming recognized, and when the culmination of the age was reached in the cosmos of Isaac Newton, constructed from mathematical physics and the chemical data of Robert Boyle. At such a time it was tempting to arrange and decipher all the phenomena of nature and the spirit as cause and effect by means of the magical expedient of mathematics.

But the very way in which Spinoza went to work contradicted the teachings of his master Descartes. He did not analyze, he did not argue from effects to causes, but, like his revered model Democritus, did just the opposite. He took phenomena as a whole and proceeded from the first cause to its consequences, working by synthesis. Spirit and matter were not, in his philosophy, two separate substances, but simply two attributes of the one eternal substance, God. His God did not work upon phenomena but within them, being identical with what people called *nature*. It was an unprecedented idea, simultaneously alarming and soothing. There was neither good nor evil, neither angel nor devil in Spinoza's world of universal unity. His ethical system discarded the doctrinaire straitjacket of the schools. Everything that happened was natural and part of God's being. In this world animals did not take their places as "animated machines" but as "individuals with souls," like men.

Spinoza declared war more remorselessly than had any critic of

Aristotle hitherto, more remorselessly than Giordano Bruno, Francis Bacon, and Gassendi, upon all teleological purpose and concern with Man in nature. He knew only too well that this was the Achilles heel of the prevailing views of life. Man, he taught, possesses no special, eternal rights, but is subject, like plants and animals, to the mechanism of cosmogony. He called the indefatigable quest of the Aristotelians for purpose "an inversion of cause and effect derived from human habits of thought." It was this phrase in particular that delighted his later supporters in the ranks of natural science. They felt that Spinoza had handed them just the right spiritual weapons to overcome the cold, rigid thought of Aristotle. It was the worshippers of Spinoza who, in the nineteenth century, were fond of uttering the witticism that if everything in nature had some use or purpose, the existence of Siamese twins could only be explained by supposing that God had thus afforded cannibals the chance to eat one of their dearly beloved brethren if they felt like it.

Spinoza's contemporaries reacted to this greatest of all revolutions in the history of philosophy in the traditional way. His family disowned him. He had to resign himself to the loss of his inheritance. In order to earn a livelihood he learned the trade of glass cutting. He lived the life of an outlawed pariah in Holland, that much admired country of natural scientists, where at that time the first microscopic researches were being conducted, blood corpuscles and spermatozoa had been discovered, and embryology and histology founded as new branches of science. The same people who had established the fact that under the dissecting knife the differences between man and beast disappeared were alarmed when a thinker drew the philosophical inferences from their discovery. Hardly any philosopher has been so relentlessly abused and attacked as Spinoza. On one occasion an attempt was even made by fanatical zealots to murder the "atheist." Leibniz himself, who resembled him in many respects mentally and had once actually gone to see him in Amsterdam, could make nothing of him. A world without good and evil, without moral laws inscribed on tablets of bronze or fixed notions of order, a world purposeless and profitless, in which creator and created were one and human beings were fundamentally of no more importance than a micro-organism, was simply inconceivable even to the most tolerant.

Only Rembrandt the painter and Jan de Witt the republican had anything in common with Spinoza. The lonely, brooding man often felt stimulated by Rembrandt's pictures, was intimate with Jan de

Witt, and shared the latter's democratic outlook in politics. He lived to see Jan de Witt and his brother done to death and literally torn in pieces by the rabble in the year 1672, after the defeat of the Dutch Republic in its war against England and France. It was at that time that he wrote his confession of political faith. "The purpose of the State is in truth to achieve liberty." It was a pregnant phrase. But it has remained inoperative down to our own day. Five years later Spinoza died at The Hague, unappreciated, misunderstood, and a social outcast.

Even then, after his premature death, he was treated "like a dead dog," as Lessing put it. The followers of Spinoza, until well into the nineteenth century, encountered the greatest difficulties imaginable in their dealings with political, scientific, and theological authorities. As late as 1850 a public appreciation of the work of Spinoza by the young German lecturer in philosophy Kuno Fischer cost the latter his appointment. Yet seventy years previously practically the whole of Goethe's circle had believed in Spinoza, and fifty years previously the poet Novalis had exclaimed in ecstasy: "The philosophy of Spinoza is saturated with a sense of the Divine order. It is an epitome of religious feeling." In fact, the point at issue was not the religious feeling of the rebellious glass cutter, which could not be doubted; the real controversy concerned that question of all questions, the place of mankind in the world.

It was therefore altogether an exceptional book that Goethe, Herder, and Frau von Stein read around Christmastime, 1784, and it was more than courageous of Goethe to attribute his view of life to Spinoza's teaching: "I feel that I am very near to Spinoza," he wrote to Knebel with considerable emotion, "though his mind is much deeper and purer than my own." Of the three Weimar residents concerned, it was only he who had correctly understood the views of the lonely man from Holland, for he was immediately inspired to make a practical test of them.

And the final inference from the idea of God as Nature was the conception of "metamorphosis," the evolution of all animate beings, including Man, from a primal form. Many thinkers and scientists had already been busy with this hypothesis. But they had all drawn back from it in alarm in the end, the last being Kant, who had called it "a rash adventure of reason." Goethe, however, in referring to Kant's expression, announced with emphasis: "Nothing can now stop me from embarking upon the adventure of reason with all the courage at my command."

When in 1788, immediately after his return from Italy, he began writing his *Essay Toward an Explanation of Plant Metamorphosis*, he was feeling very lonely. He had at last definitely broken with the hypochondriac Herder, who was forever going abroad. His relations with Charlotte von Stein were steadily changing for the worse. Schiller had not yet entered his life. His discovery of the intermaxillary bone had already set many people against him and brought him few friends. What a terrific opposition he was to arouse when he came out into the open with a theory of evolution based on Spinoza!

"With this work," he wrote in the introduction to perhaps the most interesting of all early theories of evolution, "I am entering upon a new career which I shall only be able to pursue with a great deal of difficulty." When Schiller paid his first visit to Weimar, Goethe soon found how difficult the task was going to be. "A worship of nature amounting to affectation," was how Schiller, scornfully, characterized the Goethean investigations, "an artificial simplification of logic, a piece of extravagance." His opinion was shared by the whole of Weimar society, including Herder, who had grown cold and snappish, and the disappointed Frau von Stein.

Beast and Man from one archetype

In Bertuch's summer residence at Weimar, Goethe was now pursuing his quest for the primal plant and the primal animal, for that "internal and primitive common feature which lies at the root of all organic forms." He got out the notes of his travels, in which he had described how plants lived and developed under altered conditions in the Alps and in Italy. He visited botanical gardens and conservatories. He grew flowers. He studied date palms and prickly pears. He also continued those investigations, considered so highly disreputable by the citizens of Weimar, of the bones of animals and men, trying to prove that the vertebrae of various animals had a common origin.

Soon an all-important question obtruded itself. He perceived that all animate beings were endowed with an amazing flexibility and tractability which enabled them to adapt themselves to the manifold conditions of their environment. Plants and animals suited their attributes to their surroundings and transformed themselves accordingly. Yet such transformations did not proceed in any arbitrary or ill-considered manner, but in accordance with quite definite rules of hereditary transmission. Goethe found that there were two kinds of formative impulses in nature: a "primitive formative direction propagated by hereditary transmission" and responsible for the development of the aptitudes observed, and a "continuous process of transformation," an adaptation to external conditions of existence, which produced new aptitudes and forms. Both impulses worked in opposition to each other. The compulsory specialization to which every creature is committed by its inheritance from its forebears is repeatedly cancelled out by its need for elastic conformity with the data of its own existence. Conversely, the environment cannot produce new forms without restriction but is obliged in such activities to take into consideration the "obstinate generic and specific perseverance" of animate beings. This mutual relation between the two formative impulses was called by Goethe "the highest conception to which nature has risen." It was, in his view, the driving force of evolution.

Goethe was here already broaching the most vital problems of modern biology. He was the first to see in the evolution of animate beings not an obscure process of growth, but manifest obedience to law, a subtle interaction between heredity and environment. The mechanism of this interaction was not to be laid bare for another hundred years.

How did Man come into the picture? Spinoza had never given direct expression to his views of the origin of mankind. Linnaeus had shirked committing himself. Buffon had camouflaged his ideas in witty aphorisms. Wolff had been forced into exile for his more timid opinions. But Goethe spoke out frankly. He also smiled complacently to think how appalled the faces of his Weimarians were soon going to be. "We should then have reached the stage of being able to declare without fear that all complete organisms, among which we may include fish, amphibians, birds, mammals and at the head of the latter mankind, have all been formed in accordance with a single primal image, the component parts of which alone undergo more or less important changes in one direction or another and which is still day by day developing and transforming itself by propagation." His contemporaries were not merely alarmed; they were stupefied. Goethe suffered far more from this lack of comprehension than he would have from contradiction and hostility. Even the new member of the Weimar circle, Schiller, who had studied physiology while he was still at school, and whom, therefore, Goethe must have assumed to possess an adequate interest in natural science, had no inkling of the importance of these theories. He merely uttered a mild reproof: "The many pursuits in connection with natural science to which Goethe is addicted as hobbies distract him far too much. I almost despair of his ever finishing his *Faust*."

Goethe made desperate efforts to explain his ideas to Schiller. The two men had made each other's personal acquaintance for the first time in 1794 at a session of the Natural Science Society in Jena. After the conference they strolled off together, chatting away, through the ancient streets to Schiller's cottage. On the way Goethe elaborated his theory of the development of animate beings from a single primal type. Schiller listened, shaking his head dubiously, and put certain questions. Goethe spoke with more and more emphasis. At last they came to a halt outside Schiller's door. It was a moment of destiny. Schiller asked Goethe to come in. They entered the dark little hall and went up the winding staircase. Schiller laid his hand on his chest, for his lung was paining him, and Goethe helped him up the last few stairs. Then they sat down and Goethe continued to elucidate the *Plant Metamorphosis*, exerting himself to gain the other's intellectual support.

Schiller was most sympathetic. But his sympathy did not extend to that strange evolutionary hypothesis. He was attracted only by the eccentric personality of this exceptional man, who had the nerve to retail such stuff in plain and unflinching terms. After a long pause for reflection he shook his head, staring at Goethe uncomprehendingly, almost dully. Did the author of *Werther* and *Götz von Berlichingen* really believe in an earthly origin of species, in the descent of man from brutes, or was his meaning only symbolic? It was to be hoped the latter was the case. "That is not knowledge derived from experience," he said firmly, in a quiet and positive tone. "It's a mere idea."

Goethe assumed a sulky expression. Schiller smiled amiably. At the bottom of his heart he considered everything Goethe had said to be simply nonsense, a poetic inspiration disguised in the language of natural science. The great opportunity had been missed. Goethe and Schiller shook hands and parted. They became friends, but in their attitudes to nature they remained worlds apart.

Can apes become men?

In Königsberg, about this time, the man from whom Schiller had obtained his philosophical panoply was tackling a knotty problem. Immanuel Kant had long been concerned, though in different fashion, with questions similar to those being studied by Goethe. This seems surprising in the case of one who was a critic of the theory of knowledge and convinced that fixed and eternal ideas and maxims were valid in the life of nature as in the life of Man. But Kant was by no means as indifferent to natural philosophy as may appear from his *Critique of Pure Reason.* On the contrary, he had begun his career as a natural philosopher, and he ended it as the apostle of a crude theory of evolution, of which natural historians, to be sure, have taken very little notice.

"Give me matter," ran his theory of the origin of the world, "and I will construct a world from it." Anaxagoras and Democritus, too, had said something of the same sort. According to this doctrine spherical bodies, planetary rings, suns, planets, and moons had arisen from primal matter existing in the form of mist. And since processes throughout nature must logically correspond with those operative in the construction of the universe, the origin of life on the earth had occurred in a similar way. "The whole of nature's technique seems to be derived" from crude matter. Mosses and lichens were first produced, from which the vegetable kingdom developed, together with small animate beings of the polyp type, which gave rise to one genus of animals after another "until mankind was reached."

It was not pure thought that led Kant to this conclusion. He had also studied comparative anatomy and, like Goethe, found structural similarities in the most diverse kinds of animals. As the result of these investigations he declared in his *Critique of the Power of Judgment:* "The analogy of forms reinforces the presumption of their actual kinship through production by a common primal matrix." The entire animate world was for him "one great family." Accordingly Kant too, though he qualified this vision of evolution by calling it a "rash adventure of reason," may be considered a genuine product of the dawning era of natural philosophy.

In old age he returned once more to these thoughts on evolution. He wrote a work dealing with mankind, entitled *Anthropology.* It gave expression to ideas that previously only Lamettrie had dared to discuss.

The shape of animate beings, he maintained, was not a gift of nature, or immutable. It was liable to change under the influence of the conditions of existence. Every creature learns and practises, creates new organs and skills in order to deal effectively with its situation. It bears within itself the potentiality of rising in the scale of evolution, even of developing human characteristics. "It is possible for a chimpanzee or an orangutan, by perfecting its organs, to change at some future date into a human being. Radical alterations in natural conditions may force the ape to walk upright, accustom its hands to the use of tools, and learn to talk." And if such a possibility existed, it might well lead to the conjecture that modern human beings had at one time in the past been apelike mammals. Adam had worn the hide of an arboreal beast of the primeval forest.

The author of the much reviled and vigorously disputed proposition, "Man is descended from the ape," was therefore not Darwin, who expressed himself with decidedly greater caution, but the idealist philosopher Immanuel Kant. And the second great thinker, who repeated the proposition sixty years later, was also an idealist philosopher, Arthur Schopenhauer. The latter was to write in his *Parerga and Paralipomena*, years before the publication of Darwin's theory of the descent of man: "We must imagine the first human beings as having been born in Asia of orangutans and in Africa of chimpanzees, and not born as apes either but as full-fledged human beings." Thus his view of the world also necessarily implied the mutability of species.

Schopenhauer concerned himself even more than Kant with the question how such mutations could have taken place in nature. In this connection he came into violent conflict with the venerable statement that "Nature makes no leaps." But nature does make leaps, his intelligence told him, otherwise the mutation of one species into another remains inexplicable. The new form must already have developed in the womb. The first amphibians were hatched from the eggs of fish. A female ape gave birth to the first human being. Schopenhauer did not mean, of course, that a form of animal existent today had produced one entirely different. He was thinking of tiny steps leading from fish to amphibian, reptile to mammal, ape to Man. "That is the only reasonably conceivable mode of the origin of species that can legitimately be supposed."

We know today that Schopenhauer was right. Biologists now call his "leaps" "mutations." The natural scientists of his own time could make nothing of such hypotheses. The idea that an ape might have given birth to the first human being seemed so crazy that even the most advanced theorists of evolution thought it unworthy of notice. Schopenhauer died shortly after Darwin's doctrine had been announced. He never heard anything about it.

Kant's *Anthropology* met the same fate. It gave rise to a minor scandal and called down a reproof upon its author. But that was absolutely all. People were particularly irritated to find that the old gentleman from Königsberg derived not only the body but also the mind of humanity from the animal kingdom. It would be possible, he had observed, for the compulsion of the struggle for existence to have originated an organ in the apes for the use of intelligence and for this organ to have gradually evolved "by means of social cultivation." According to Kant the much lauded brain of humanity would thus be nothing more than an animal's organ transformed by natural influences. And this was the opinion, positively, of an intellectual, a man who knew how to use his intelligence better than any other thinker in Germany before his day. It did not seem to accord with the Kantian critique of human intellectual capacity. Even Schiller, that enthusiastic Kantian, never made the slightest reference to the *Anthropology*.

VI

THE HISTORY OF THE EARTH
IS WRITTEN IN CATASTROPHE

The Devil is a vegetarian

THE YEAR 1794, in which Schiller shook his head over Goethe's *Plant Metamorphosis* in the marketplace at Jena, and in which Kant studied the possibility of apes turning into men, was also one of historic importance for the Jardin des Plantes in Paris. It was at this time that a young man — who like Lamarck and Geoffroy Saint-Hilaire had failed to come to terms with theology — applied for an appointment on the scientific staff. His name was Georges Cuvier.

Cuvier immediately made an excellent impression on the professors of the Jardin, less on account of his views than on account of his appearance. His frail little body was crowned by a gigantic head, with a mop of wavy reddish hair. Lightning flashed from his blue eyes. All his gestures were as vehement and impetuous as those of a fanatical mob-orator. So exceptional were his looks that Schiller, who had been a fellow pupil with him at Duke Karl's military school in Stuttgart, would have had no difficulty in recognizing him. Though Cuvier was still a child at the time, he had learned much from Schiller during excited discussions in the dormitory, and may even have received from him his first encouragement to take up science. He had been present when Schiller gave a clandestine reading of *The Robbers* to his schoolmates and when he provoked the Duke in person with his medical treatise *The Philosophy of Physiology*. Cuvier had listened with interest when his school friend from Marbach, who was many years older than himself, spoke of his *Study of the Connection Between Man's Animal and Intellectual Natures*. He regarded Schiller rather as a future physiologist than as a coming playwright, and could not quite understand why his admired model went a different way and chose as his guiding stars, instead of Linnaeus or Buffon, the philosopher Kant and the Muses. The two young men separated when Schiller left Duke Karl's school. They never saw each other again.

Cuvier's Burgundian native town, Montbéliard, had belonged to

Württemberg as Mömpelgard until the French Revolution. Cuvier did not become a French citizen until after the victory of the revolutionary forces. Material poverty obliged him to end his theological studies. He returned to his native country, took up botany, acted for a time as private tutor in the family of a Norman count, then hung about the military hospital at Fécamp, as something of a pauper, giving lectures on botany to the young doctors. At nights he studied the works of Linnaeus, Buffon and Réaumur, as well as the theories of the Encyclopedists and natural philosophers, cramming his enormous head with all the learning of the century.

Just as Buffon had formerly patronized the hungry Lamarck, so now Lamarck patronized the poverty-stricken Cuvier. He took him into the Jardin, talked a good deal to him, and soon found that the young fellow from Montbéliard possessed the sharp eye of genius in zoological and anatomical contexts. The newcomer made a good impression on the Jardin scholars, for he supported Linnaeus rather than Buffon and in all discussions upheld the dogma of the immutability of species with positively fiery zeal, taking quite a different line from that of the eternal skeptic Geoffroy Saint-Hilaire.

Cuvier was soon able to submit a new and surprising theory to the Paris professors, who were already well used to surprises. The theory had occurred to him while observing, collecting, and sketching fish, mollusks, crustaceans, starfish, and polyps on the seacoast of Normandy. He perceived — it sounds obvious today, but it was still a novelty at that time — that all the parts and organs of any animate being stood in a mutual relationship to one another. He was thus led to formulate a law, his famous "Law of Correlation." The law stated that if an animal develops one of its organs in an unmistakable manner, a particular development of its other organs can be counted on. Animals with horns and hoofs, for example, invariably possess teeth adapted to vegetarianism. Animals with claws and anklebones are necessarily equipped with carnivorous teeth. Reptiles with a closed system of teeth are vegetarian, while those with interlocking systems feed on other animals. According to Cuvier, this correlation applied even in the smallest details. It must even be theoretically possible, he said, to reconstruct the entire body of an animal of which only a single organ is known.

This brilliant flash of inspiration at once ensured Cuvier the profound respect of the Jardin. It led to unexpected results in zoology. Comparative anatomy, which had hitherto been quite an unimportant branch of zoology, now took the lead, becoming its chief department. Cuvier was thereupon encouraged to come out with a second theory, which in his view followed from the first. This was the theory of the four types of animal structure. Linnaeus had taught that creation had been completed in accordance with a single plan. Buffon had assumed the existence of connections between the separate classes of animals. Cuvier did not believe in either of these ideas. There had been not one plan of creation but four. The first provided for vertebrates, the second for insects, spiders, and crustaceans, the third for mollusks, and the fourth for worms, starfish, polyps, sponges, and Infusoria. And these four sets of animals were entirely separate. No connections existed between them.

He discussed the matter with Lamarck. This time, however, the expected approval was not forthcoming. The little man from Picardy had accepted his correlation law amiably enough. But he bluntly rejected his four plans of creation. "Why limit yourself to four?" he asked, with subtle irony. "You might just as well assume dozens of plans and acts of creation. The result would be inextricable confusion. To be quite frank, I should prefer the evolution theory."

"Species are immutable!" cried Cuvier, defensively. "There is no such thing as evolution; there can't be! How could the accidental play of evolution produce that significant mutual relationship between the parts of a body?" He added with harsh emphasis, "All the phenomena of nature are arranged in accordance with the laws of logic. Anyone with eyes in his head can see the four plans of creation identified by me staring him in the face."

Lamarck gave a slight start at the words, "Anyone with eyes in his head." Did Cuvier know that he, Lamarck, had been obliged for years to struggle against eye trouble? Was he sneering at him? I don't see those plans of creation, he thought. On the contrary, I see communication and connections between form and form. The lower gradually builds itself up into the higher — but that's philosophy, he thought suddenly, zoological philosophy, not exact natural science.

Cuvier had more luck with his four plans of creation among the other professors, especially those who were unswerving supporters of Linnaeus. His theory gradually gained ground. By the time the National Convention was dissolved and the Directory had replaced the rule of the Jacobins in France, Cuvier already occupied the post of assistant to Mertrud, the professor of comparative anatomy in charge of the Jardin. He could concentrate on making a clean sweep of the differences of opinion and the extremely various hypotheses, theories, views of life, and private beliefs of the intellectual world of Paris. There was the most urgent need for scientific reform. It was high time for natural science to take its stand on solid ground again after all the dreams and speculations of the pre-revolutionary period. Such solid ground would be provided by the Law of Correlation, the first to render possible a correct classification and arrangement of the animal kingdom, and the Theory of Plans of Creation, which sent all bewildering evolutionary notions packing.

Cuvier's first opponent was a man three years younger than himself but far more experienced in the habits and customs of the Jardin — Geoffroy Saint-Hilaire. So far the latter, despite all the sneers of the orthodox disciples of Linnaeus, had been able to express his doubts about the immutability of species with impunity. But now that upstart of an anatomy assistant was confronting him with excited asseverations of his correlation law. "It proves beyond doubt," Cuvier exclaimed, "the existence of eternal and immutable plans of creation! It is irresponsible, to go on talking about evolution now! Evolution means attributing the genius of a purposeful and farseeing Constructor to the whim of undisciplined nature. And that is manifest perversity!"

"How are you going to explain the extinction of animate beings, then, if new growths don't exist?" asked Geoffroy Saint-Hilaire, just as vehemently.

"By catastrophe," Cuvier replied. "By a series of geological revolutions. Apparently you don't know your Buffon, my dear colleague. In my view there can only be one answer to that problem."

Geoffroy Saint-Hilaire knew his Buffon very well. It was only Cuvier's overingenious interpretation of *The Theory of the Earth* that was a novelty to him. "In your view, then, there were several acts of creation, and every one of them ended in a catastrophe?" He smiled. "That may be. The evidence of prehistory seems to confirm it. But Buffon never said that after each catastrophe the earth must have been devastated and empty and then started off again as on the first day of creation. That notion is scientific mysticism."

"You believe in the Flood, don't you?" demanded Cuvier. "And the Flood, according to our traditions, destroyed all life on the Earth. Well, any geologist can prove to you not only that there was one Flood, but that there were many, exactly as many as the known periods of the earth's history. I am perfectly aware that Buffon made the further assumption that a great many species survived into the subsequent geological period after these catastrophes. But this assumption has now become untenable. Have you ever heard of William Smith's investigations?"

William Smith? Geoffroy Saint-Hilaire nodded. He had heard

talk of him in the Jardin. Smith was a twenty-six-year-old English geometrician, a queer fellow who got on the nerves of miners and quarrymen by crawling about in shafts and conduits and collecting fossils in order to prove that every layer of the earth had its characteristic type of petrifaction. Smith had drawn up a table of thirty-two principal layers found in England and given them such names as Carboniferous, Devonian, and Cretaceous. Very interesting for geologists. But what had that to do with zoology?

"Each of William Smith's layers," said Cuvier stubbornly, "corresponds to a geological period. Fossils are found in each of them which do not occur in the others. The layers do not overlap. One can even, as Smith has pointed out, use these fossils as guides to identify the separate geological periods."

"Obviously," Geoffroy Saint-Hilaire agreed. "And geology will be benefited by the fact. I still don't understand why that should be an argument against the evolution of species."

Cuvier ran his hand excitedly through his hair. "You really don't understand? Each epoch has its own animals and plants. They arise with it and perish with it. Catastrophes obliterate. Nature creates anew, in accordance with those four plans that are clearly recognizable in all periods."

"Well, how did it happen, then," Geoffroy demanded imperturbably, "that the inferior types of plants and animals appeared on the earth first and the most highly organized, including Man, came last?" There were not four plans of creation, he went on, but only a single general plan, in accordance with which animate beings had gradually evolved from lower to higher forms throughout successive floods and geological periods.

"And what proves the existence of such a general plan?" Cuvier asked sharply with an angry frown.

"I do the same as you do," Geoffroy Saint-Hilaire explained. "I compare. But while you deduce differences from your comparison I deduce similarities. If I may cite a few examples, gills, for instance, resemble lungs and may be their forerunners. A bird's wing resembles the leg of a reptile and may have evolved from it."

Cuvier laughed aloud at this dreamer who was looking for similarities where none existed. His fancies were like those of the natural philosophers, the Germans and that fellow Goethe, with whom Cuvier's old school friend Schiller was now staying. "We need not discuss this matter any further," he said. "I am a natural scientist, not a natural philosopher. And my intention is to remain a natural scientist."

"I suppose you don't yet know," Saint-Hilaire retorted, "that your friend and spokesman Lamarck thinks exactly the same as I do?"

"Lamarck?" cried Cuvier. He trembled. "That's impossible!"

"Lamarck and I," said Geoffroy Saint-Hilaire, "are each writing a philosophy of zoology!" he added enthusiastically.

"Am I in the Jardin or a lunatic aslyum?" Cuvier growled. He turned on his heel abruptly and left the room.

Later on, when Cuvier had reached the height of his fame, an incident occurred that caused even amateur naturalists to extol his correlation law. Some students plotted to play a trick on him. One of them dressed up as the Devil, stuck horns on his head, put on shoes shaped like a cloven hoof, and broke into Cuvier's house by night in this garb, while his companions crowded round the window and stared in.

Cuvier was lying fast asleep when suddenly a great voice roared in his ear: "Wake up, thou man of catastrophes! I am the Devil!" Cuvier at once opened his eyes, lit a candle, and observed the monster with interest. "I am the Devil!" cried the disguised intruder once more. "I have come to devour you!"

"Devour me?" Cuvier shook his head. "I doubt whether you can. You've got horns and hoofs. According to the Law of Correlation you only eat plants." He turned on his other side and went to sleep again. And the students outside the window, instead of laughing, gave him an enthusiastic ovation.

Human fossils do not exist

Most fossils have not been discovered by purposeful excavation, but by accident. A fragment of bone turns up somewhere after a landslide, during the building of a railway or canal, or in mining or quarrying. It arouses the curiosity of some interested laborer or passer-by. Many are again lost without attracting any attention. Only a few come into expert hands and provide a starting point for more intensive researches.

This happened in the case of the find of bones that led Cuvier to undertake his great excavations. For decades white scribbling chalk had been extracted from the subterranean labyrinth under Peter's Hill near Maastricht. These passages were supposed to date back to Roman times. Many fossils must often have been found there and been thrown away again. But it was not until 1780, when a scientist happened to be poking about in the chalk galleries, that it was realized what treasures lay hidden in Peter's Hill. The scientist who made the discovery was the German military surgeon Hoffmann, who was working at the time in the Teyler Museum at Haarlem. He had seen Scheuchzer's "old sinner," which was reposing there, and had also studied other fossils. But the huge skull that he suddenly saw sticking out of the wall of one of the chalk galleries, during his visit to Peter's Hill nevertheless startled him. No such monsters as this had ever so far been dug up. The ancient legends of dragons seemed to be coming true. Hoffmann immediately recognized it as the skull of a reptile. But what a reptile it was! It must have been as big as a whale. Its footsteps, if it had feet and not fins, could have crushed trees to pieces and demolished houses.

Hoffmann made up his mind to transfer the monster to the Teyler Museum at all costs. He found that the owner of the quarry was a certain Canon Godin, a priest with a keen business sense who was in the habit of investing his money in all kinds of industrial undertakings. It was clear that all he cared about was the extraction of scribbling chalk. Old bones did not interest him. Accordingly, Hoffmann did not hesitate to have the skull cut out at his own expense. He carried it off to Haarlem and there showed it to his colleague Peter Camper. The latter, too, was astounded at the sight of the giant reptile. So were all the scholars who were told of the discovery of the mosasaur, the lizard of the Maas. The designation "saurian" was at once adopted. Stories about saurians began to go the rounds in the same way as the old traditional tales of dragons had once been current. People shuddered at the idea that such creatures had formerly lived in the world.

The delight of the scientists did not last long. Canon Godin, the owner of the chalk quarry, learned of the sensational discovery made by a trespasser upon his property and flew into a passion. He sued Dr. Hoffmann for return of the skull. As the canon had the law on his side the doctor was obliged to hand back the valuable curio. Thenceforward Godin kept the saurian locked up and would not allow any scientist access to it. Hoffmann died shortly afterwards — rumor said that he died of grief over the loss of this epoch-making monster.

News of the Peter's Hill excavation had reached the Jardin. It proved impossible, because of the canon's peculiar behavior, to find out what had become of the saurian. Another fifteen years passed before Cuvier could obtain possession of the papers in the case. The troops of the French Republic were then approaching Maastricht. It would be a first-rate opportunity, Cuvier thought, to seize the saurian and again make it accessible to science. He sent a message to the people's commissary, Freicine, who commanded the French troops in Holland, requesting him, whatever happened, to do no damage to Godin's house but to confiscate the skull and bring it to Paris.

Freicine complied with his request. Godin by that time had got wind of the affair and had hidden the saurian in another part of the city. The revolutionary troops searched his house from cellar to attic, found nothing, and swore heartily. Some of them in their loyal enthusiasm, suggested tickling the canon a bit with the bayonet. He might then be more inclined, perhaps, to part with his beloved dragon's bones. But Freicine knew a trick worth two of that. He sent his soldiers into the city, told them to search every nook and cranny of it, and offered a reward of six hundred bottles of wine to anyone who discovered the saurian. The soldiers combed Maastricht, forcing their way into the houses and disporting themselves there in the usual fashion of soldiers. Early next morning twelve grenadiers, in a triumphant procession, brought in the skull. They got their six hundred bottles of wine and drank the health of the old saurian to the accompaniment of songs and laughter.

The Republic of France had to meet the cost of the wine, but it did so with pleasure. For as a result of Freicine's inspiration the Jardin des Plantes had once more, at one stroke, become the center of prehistoric study. And Cuvier now resolved to dig for fossils himself in the valley of the Seine and at Montmartre. He regarded the discovery of the Peter's Hill saurian as an unexpected triumph for himself. If such monsters had existed at earlier epochs of the earth's history, it would be foolish to talk any more of the evolution of species. What could a giant saurian have evolved from? An ordinary lizard? And what present-day animals could have been derived from the brute? Obviously none. Saurians, as Cuvier now gradually came to recognize, were typical beasts of the geologic Middle Ages — that secondary epoch now called, following William Smith's example, Triassic, Jurassic, and Cretaceous. Before and after this era there were no such animals, so they were products of their age, beginning and ending with it.

Equally typical of their periods were the fossils of geological antiquity, the primary epoch, such as ammonites and belemnites, giant crustaceans, sea lilies, and armor-plated fishes. They died out when their hour struck. Finally, in both periods of the modern geological age, Tertiary and Quaternary, the story was similar. They were separated by the last of the floods, the Biblical one. Its fury left no Tertiary animal alive. Cuvier reviewed the animate beings of the Tertiary period in his mind's eye, reconstructing them. There were fearful creatures among them, shaped as if concocted from elephants, tapirs, and sea cows, such as *Dinotherium*, which the charlatan Maurier had once advertised as the skeleton of a Cimbrian. Another monster of the Tertiary age, which could not possibly have been an ancestor of any modern form of life, was *Megatherium*, the giant sloth from Argentina, as big as an elephant. Its skeleton had been discovered by chance in a precipitous bank on the river Luján near Buenos Aires. The viceroy of Argentina, the Marquis of Loreto, had sent the skeleton to Madrid, where the Spanish scientist José Garriga had examined it and told wonderful stories about it. Cuvier possessed drawings of it which had been secretly purloined from Madrid, without permission, by a French colonial official. Soon the *Megatherium* became as popular as Hoffmann's Maas saurian. Painters depicted it as a colossal brute walking on its hind legs and trampling down forests. Sensational writers described in dramatic language how it fell a victim to the great catastrophe. A few decades later Viktor von Scheffel composed a students' song about it.

> *It stared in sloth upon the world*
> *And yawned in dreamful ease*
> *And dug its talons sharp into*
> *The Embahuba trees.*
> *With gentle nod and pleasant smile*
> *Its owlish features peep,*
> *For after a successful meal*
> *Its next job is to sleep.*

Geoffroy Saint-Hilaire himself did not go so far as to suppose that this ancient voluptuary of the Tertiary period might have blood relations among present-day fauna.

Cuvier was now the undisputed expert on extinct animals, not only in France, but throughout the world. He started an anatomical collection that soon exceeded in importance all the museums and naturalists' showrooms both in France and elsewhere. His excavations in the Seine valley unearthed vast quantities of fossils, revealing, in particular, the entire range of Tertiary fauna. He classified and named all the prehistoric animals, had plaster casts made of them, and identified with precision, by the aid of his correlation law, the most minute fragments of bone.

The philosophizing zoologists of the Jardin, Lamarck and Saint-Hilaire, were now completely overshadowed by Cuvier. He was appointed in rapid succession member of the National Institute, professor at the College of France, director of the Natural History Museum, formerly managed by Buffon, and inspector-general of public education. At his instigation both professional and amateur investigators in France, England, Germany, and Holland, and even in Egypt and Russia, started excavations in search of the remains

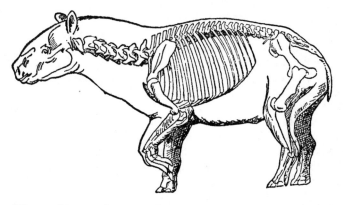

The prehistoric beasts, whose skeletons Cuvier excavated from the gypseous soil of Montmartre, included the *Palaeotherium magnum*, a primitive hoofed animal.

of antediluvian forms of life. He corresponded with Blumenbach about the mammoth and the *Megatherium*. He dug up *Palaeotherium* — a primitive hoofed animal — from the depths of Montmartre and an extraordinary marine lizard, *Ichthyosaurus*, from the basin at Le Havre.

The credit for the actual discovery of the subsequently far-famed *Ichthyosaurus* is still the subject of dispute. This creature, too, was celebrated in verse by Scheffel as follows:

> There's a rustle among the horsetails,*
> An ominous gleam in the sea,
> An ichthyosaurus comes swimming
> And a tear in his eye hath he.

* Equisetales, the most abundant order of Sphenopsida during the Paleozoic Era. They resembled the modern horsetail (*Equisetum*) but were tall trees, not plants.

The tears of Scheffel's saurian had something to do with Cuvier's theory of catastrophes, for there is an equivocal reference to these monsters at the end of the song:

They got too deep in the chalk pit
And that was the end of them

Many bones and skeletons found at earlier periods in the German and French Jura country and believed to be the remains of fish or dragons belong to the ichthyosaurian tribe, as did Scheuchzer's Altdorf vertebrae. It had long been known that the creature was half fish and half lizard, but it was Cuvier who definitely classified this puzzling beast, after his Le Havre find, among the relatives of Hoffmann's Maas saurian. And it was owing to the fact that a twelve-year-old English girl was fond of playing with marine animals that Cuvier was able to introduce a further series of different members of the great saurian family to his contemporaries.

The girl's name was Mary Anning. She was the daughter of a man who earned his living in the coastal resorts of southern England by selling attractive seashells and odd-looking marine creatures. Mary helped her father in the business. But she was also interested in the appearance and shape of the objects that Richard Anning sold to the tourists. She made a collection of her own. It thus happened that she found, among other things, the bones of an *Ichthyosaurus*, which the tide had uncovered on the beach. Cuvier heard indirectly of this discovery and encouraged the child to continue her researches industriously and send him everything she could find. Mary complied. She discovered the *Plesiosaurus*, the big marine saurian with a snake's neck that still haunts the imaginations of superstitious seafarers as the "sea serpent." She discovered the winged saurian, the pterodactyl, which made the air dangerous with its batlike activities in the geologic Middle Ages, and some further types of giant lizards. After her father's death she continued to earn her living by selling shells. A tongue-twisting line of verse in English mentions her trade and has made her popular among children as elsewhere: "Mary Anning, she sells seashells." But she also went on supplying, as long as she lived, scientific institutions and especially her great patron Cuvier, with saurians from the Jurassic deposits of southern England — the first female fossil merchant in history.

Cuvier identified all these fossils unerringly. He really was able to reconstruct the complete specimen from a single bone, a fragment of the jaw. Anyone could see that his correlation law was correct in every detail, so his theory of catastrophes must be correct too. At his lectures he made sketches that could hardly be understood and had a poetic, dreamlike quality. He unveiled the earth's portrait gallery of ancestors, showed his listeners the mammoth drama of geological events, the periodical upheavals, scenes of the destruction and of the engendering of life, and gave the fossils a striking name, calling them "the medals coined by creation." He spoke of geological

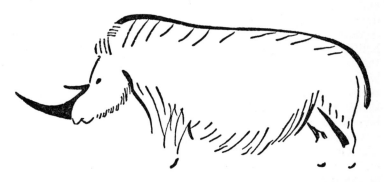

The woolly rhinoceros, a typical European animal of the time of the Deluge, was not destroyed by the Flood, as Cuvier believed. It survived to the end of the Late Ice Age. Early Stone Age man has left us in his magnificent drawings an idea of what it looked like. The woolly rhinoceros is related to the modern white rhinoceros of South Africa.

antiquity, of Silurian, Devonian, Carboniferous, and Permian formations. He described the rustling forests of "horsetails," the Echinodermata, the giant crustaceans, and armored fish. Then he went on to the secondary epoch, with Triassic, Jurassic, and Cretaceous formations and saurians resembling the hallucinations of a fevered brain. He talked about the weird mammals of the Tertiary period, the paleo-, dino- and megatheria. Finally he gave a graphic account of the last flood, the Deluge, which eliminated the mammoth, the woolly rhinoceros, the cave bear, and the *Megaceros* (Irish elk). And just as between the Tertiary period and the present day, so also between the other periods came the gloom of an age of ruin.

The theory of catastrophes came to be almost universally accepted in all countries. The data of William Smith and the new English school of geologists appeared to give first-rate confirmation of it.

Subterranean traces of inundation, volcanic eruption, earthquakes, and glaciation were found everywhere. And as at that time separate geological periods were reckoned, not as they are today in units of a million, but in units of a thousand years, the notion of a series of devastations must have positively forced itself upon naturalists. Even human history, if it were telescoped into a period of a few decades, would look to us like a sequence of catastrophes. It was not until geology in the nineteenth century was able to prove the Ice and Diluvial ages did not come with a rush but only spread quite gradually in the course of tens of thousands of years over certain parts of the Earth, and our planet was not a hundred thousand but a few billion years old, that Cuvier's theory ceased to hold its own. Around 1800 it had only three adversaries worthy of the name: Geoffroy Saint-Hilaire, Lamarck, and Goethe. The last named considered it no more than so much "empty gabble." His whole being revolted against Cuvier's attempt to force the earth into this "infernal torture-chamber." No one listened to him. The gabblers had it all their own way.

Cuvier's museum also contained documents relating to the case of *Homo sapiens*. Human beings and apes, according to the theory of catastrophes, were children of the last, the present, geological period. Antediluvian men and Tertiary apes could not have existed. Scheuchzer's old sinner was finally unmasked by Cuvier, amid the cheers and laughter of his supporters, and as a giant lizard of the Tertiary period. It had to be acknowledged that he was right, and Camper and Blumenbach shamefacedly confessed their mistake. Once again the "Pope of Bones" had proved to be infallible. As for the other traces of prehistoric man that had been found, Cuvier considered that they had all been wrongly identified. Frere's "primitive tools" could easily be splinters of flint that had accidentally found their way into the remains of a mammoth. Esper's "bones of primitive man" might be contemporary human bones that had subsided into lower geological layers. The teeth found in Tertiary deposits, which had been thought to be apes', looked more like the teeth of hoofed animals.

"The human fossil does not exist!" This declaration seemed to Cuvier to settle the question of Adam. *Homo sapiens*, in his present form, had been created at the beginning of the last geological period. All the scientists who talked about primitive human beings or even the descent of man from the beasts were on the wrong track.

Cuvier's statement was eagerly received. It had a reassuring sound. In all quarters — in Blumenbach's circle at Göttingen, in that of

Smith and his disciples in England, in zoological and anthropological institutions, and from chairs of mineralogy and "geognosy" — it was now proclaimed an indisputable dogma, that the Floodists, theorists of evolution, and natural philosophers had been chasing a will-o'-the-wisp, that creatures remained as immutable, until their extinction, as the masterpieces of mankind, and that the human fossil did not exist.

Animate beings are the products of their environment

Napoleon was one of the few dictators who gave an impetus to science. He had no prejudices, imposed no conditions upon scientists, and put no obstacles in their way. In strong contrast to Cromwell the Puritan, Robespierre the system builder, Hitler the mystic, and Stalin the materialist, the great Corsican had no intention of forcing the scholars within his sphere of influence into the straitjacket of any particular view of life, but rather of promoting their free development to the best of his ability. Under him Paris became once more the stronghold of natural science.

The greatest spirits of the age came into contact with each other there. Laplace, the idol of young students, took up Kant's theory of the origin of the universe and proved to a breathlessly attentive audience that everything in the cosmos had grown up out of eddies of primeval matter in accordance with the laws of mechanics. Gay-Lussac, ruler of the Sorbonne, confronted the heirs of the Revolution with a picture of the world in which only physical laws and chemical reactions existed, to the exclusion of any mysterious "vital principle," spirit, or transcendental power. Life, so the new men in Paris taught, is a chemico-physical process, nothing more. Both its cornerstones, the *elements* of Empedocles, and its smallest components, the *atoms* of Democritus, were known. A mysterious current, too, had been accidentally discovered by the Italian, Luigi Galvani, which made the muscles and nerves of dead animals twitch. It was called electricity. Napoleon sponsored the researches of Count Alessandro Volta, Galvani's successor, into the problem of electricity, and the latter constructed the first generator of electric current. A new era of natural science had dawned which could only be compared with that of the great Hellenic age between Thales and Democritus.

The intellectual giants of Paris did not confine themselves to scientific experiment. They were also appointed to important public offices. Laplace was made Napoleon's chancellor, Volta an Italian senator, and Cuvier adviser to the Imperial University and head of the committee of scholars charged with the erection of academies on the French pattern in the occupied countries. And Geoffroy Saint-Hilaire, the dictator's special favorite, put on officer's uniform and accompanied the Bonapartist armies, intent on scientific conquests of his own. No totalitarian system of the past or present has ever understood so well as that of the French soldier-emperor how to win the confidence of men of outstanding intelligence and give them political and cultural employment. The policy succeeded and Western science is still living on its results.

The tendency had begun while Napoleon was still a mere general. His Egyptian adventure was a unique scientific expedition on a grand scale. Important archeologists, historians, philologists, and zoologists took part in it. They stood in awe before the pyramids of this ancient civilization, examined the mysterious tombs of the kings, tried to puzzle out the meaning of the sphinxes and statues, and made efforts to decipher the strange language of the hieroglyphs. "A thousand years are looking down upon you!" Napoleon had cried to his soldiers and the learned men in his suite as they stood among the wonders of Egypt. It was not only a thousand years that were in question. Millions of years confronted Geoffroy Saint-Hilaire in his search for fossils in the deserts and in the mud of the Nile. In these months he became the great authority on prehistoric Egypt. He excavated settlements in the Valley of the Nile dating from aeons before the priests of Isis and the Pharaohs. He founded the first European scientific center on African soil, the Cairo Institute of Natural Science.

His discoveries led him to formulate theories entirely different from those of his opponent Cuvier. The extinct prehistoric fauna of Egypt included several species of large and small elephants, various kinds of rhinoceroses, sea cows, and big beasts of prey. They were creatures, accordingly, by no means widely divergent from the existent African fauna. It was quite easy to suppose the former to have been ancestors of the latter. Such transitional forms were undoubtedly to be found in all geological formations. They had merely hitherto been overlooked by geologists concerned only with the search for "guiding fossils" that would enable them to identify the separate strata. Fluctuating forms, or those that recurred in a number of different layers, could not, of course, be used as aids to the construction of a systematic history of the earth. Some transitional forms were still in existence and did not fit into Cuvier's scheme. There was the duckbill, for example, intermediate between reptile and mammal. Were not such fossils and existing transitional types the best proof that the earth had not in fact passed through a series of convulsions, but had undergone a steady, gradual alteration since the very beginning?

Geoffroy Saint-Hilaire had not yet quite satisfied himself as to the way in which such changes came about — how, for instance, a fish became a salamander, a salamander a reptile, a reptile a duckbill, and a duckbill a warm-blooded mammal, born alive. He plunged into philosophical speculations, describing nature in a manner that was bound to antagonize and even disgust the learned world of the Napoleonic era, which had grown accustomed to proceed on a basis of rules, formulas, and facts. But his students continued to applaud him — they were, however, applauding the officer of Napoleon, the hero of the Egyptian campaign rather than the theorist of evolution. He did not understand nearly so well as Cuvier how to charm an audience, describe events on a grand scale, and astonish his hearers with zoological demonstrations and conjuring tricks. If he had ever seen a devil in his bedroom he would have been most unlikely to have examined the creature for horns and hoofs. At best he would have relegated it to the sphere of that "science of organic deformity" which he founded in these years.

Accordingly, someone else took over the task. This was Cuvier's patron, Jean Baptiste Lamarck, professor of the natural history of the lower animals. The dreams, conjectures, and inspirations of Saint-Hilaire were transformed by Lamarck into a solid edifice of doctrine. The little abbé from Picardy had secretly been in doubt for years about the immutability of species. He had industriously studied systematic botany and zoology. He had compared all the extinct and existent forms and often thought, while doing so, of a statement by his master, Buffon. "The idea of species is an artificial one. In reality there are only individuals." Yes, he thought, Buffon had been right. There were no species, genera, orders, and classes in nature. All her forms had originated in variations, minute departures from the radical type.

> The almost universal assumption [he wrote in his *Zoological Philosophy*] that organisms form species permanently distinguished from one another by invariable features, arose at a time when observations were as yet incomplete and the natural sciences had hardly yet come into existence. The farther our knowledge advances the greater grows our embarrassment when we attempt to define what we mean by species. The more products of nature we assemble the more obvious it becomes that almost all gaps

between species tend to fill up and obliterate our dividing lines. We are obliged therefore, to take refuge in an arbitrary definition which forces us at times to have resort to the most insignificant divergences of the variety under consideration in order to establish the character of its species and at times to explain a type which others consider to be a particular species as in our view simply a variation of the species in question.

In other words, what had hitherto been accepted as the very foundation of zoology and botany was in reality nothing but an extremely questionable expedient.

But if the truth lay elsewhere, if species did change, how did such changes come about? Lamarck meditated on the same question as had troubled Geoffroy Saint-Hilaire. How did a fish become an amphibian, a reptile a bird, a mammal a man? The conclusion he reached was actually astonishingly simple.

When he read geological history he was less impressed by the influence of catastrophes than by the fact that the conditions of existence had been undergoing constant alteration from primitive times until the present day. And being the typical product of the French Revolution that he was, Lamarck took the line that new conditions of existence create new requirements. Such new requirements demanded in their turn new skills, new habits, and new organs. Fins become legs, legs become wings, when environment exercises its irresistible compulsion. Animate beings are simply the result of their surroundings.

Such was the origin of the "environment" theory, the foundation in natural science for the socialism of the nineteenth and communism of the twentieth century. The theory was already mature in Lamarck's work, and the Lamarckians, who came later, could hardly add anything to it. It stated that in the seas and swamps of prehistoric times no need yet existed for a bony skeleton, legs or wings, hoofs or claws. When dry land came into being animals had to develop special limbs and organs to enable them to survive. Those that lived on foliage had to stretch their necks to reach the leaves on the trees. If they did so for several generations they took the same sort of exercise as an athlete does, thus stimulating the growth of new organs. Prolonged employment of the new organs strengthened and perfected them. But if their use was neglected, existent organs became atrophied.

This explanation of the abundance of species and of growth and decay in the world was extremely enlightening, though only if one assumed that the newly inherited capacities were handed on to posterity. A single generation could not suffice to turn a leg into a wing, the short neck of the prehistoric giraffe into the long one of the present animal, and the five-toed foot of the prehistoric mammal into the hoof of the horse. Countless generations would have to pass before a slight variation could produce, through progressively improved adaptation to the needs of environment, a new species, genus, and order. "Everything obtained or lost by an animate being owing to the influence of persistent living conditions of a certain type," ran the basic statement of Lamarck's environment theory, "is rendered a permanent condition by heredity and transferred to the next generation." It was a fateful announcement. If it were true, if acquired characteristics were transmissible, all systems, all the zoological and botanical writings of the past, became so much lumber and all the great scientists from Aristotle to Cuvier had been barking up the wrong tree. Lamarck himself did not draw any such inferences. He could not have dreamed that a hundred and fifty years later intellectual opinion would be divided on this very question.

Cuvier knew very well why he himself, from the start, had resolutely opposed "zoological philosophy." He was the only one who grasped its true significance. He saw clearly that his whole work would be at stake if Lamarck's theory were to be accepted. He was enraged most of all by what he called Lamarck's unjustified and offensive statement that living species of animals and plants had developed out of fossil forms. "In reality," the Zoological Philosophy had asserted, "what we describe as the system of animals and plants is a genealogical tree, a line of ancestors. Species have no hard and fast limits, they blend into one another, proceeding from simple Infusoria right up to humanity. The fossil forms of organic life are the genuine and actual predecessors of our present forms." That was an open dig at the theory of catastrophes. He, Cuvier, who daily demonstrated to packed audiences that the creatures which lived at earlier periods on the earth had perished utterly, could no longer afford to disregard this insult.

Lamarck did not hold back even when he was confronted with the mind of Man. Human intelligence, he said, was not an exceptional phenomenon. There must have been a time when animals, in obedience to the compulsion of their environment, had accustomed themselves to walk upright, had changed their forepaws to hands, and raised their eyes to heaven. "This new attitude led to the higher development of the senses, to the growth of the brain and to the faculty of speech. The creatures, walking on their hind legs, organized themselves in communities, communicated intelligibly with one another, enacted laws and climbed to the top of the ladder of reason." From which animals, then, did Lamarck mean that men were derived? He answered, without hesitation: "From the higher apes." It followed that Lamarck believed in the existence of human fossils.

Cuvier muttered angrily: "It has been an excellent practice in universities only to teach what you can prove. Unproved hypotheses have no business in a university chair." He considered it both his right and his duty, however much he might himself owe to this philosophizing fraud, to unmask him publicly.

Laplace, Gay-Lussac, Saint-Hilaire, and the other leading lights of the learned world in the Paris of Napoleon now found themselves watching from the stalls a drama that was like a continuation, on more violent and tragic lines, of the old disputes between Linnaeus and Buffon, Haller and Wolff, Camper and Goethe. But this time the struggle was fought out to the end. It was a case of conquer or die. On the high plateau of Parisian science there could be no evasions, no compromises, no truces, and no flight. Persistence or development — that was the question in the last resort: being or becoming, multiplicity or unity. It was a very ancient problem. And the disputants in this decisive trial of strength had sharpened their weapons well.

The condemnation of Jean Baptiste Lamarck

Lamarck's eye trouble had got worse. He was nearly blind. He had to be led into his lecture room by one of his daughters. As a rule his favorite daughter, Cornélie, took care of him; but the students had encountered others of his children, for their professor had married four times and brought more posterity into the world than he could support on his salary. It was maliciously suggested that he had done so in order to prove his environment theory and transmit as many of his characteristic features as possible to future generations.

The hall was never very full for his lectures. Nor did the students show any particular enthusiasm. There was no trace of the rapturous excitement produced by the demonstrations of the doctrine of catastrophes. Lamarck was rather surprised at the lack of interest. Was the world blind, then? Did he alone see the truth? Geoffroy Saint-Hilaire had uttered a few disparaging phrases about the *Zoological Philosophy*. Cuvier ignored it. Its opponents made the wholly frivolous objection that its guiding spirit was not that of any kind of order, but sheer hazard, not that of immutable law, but only that of supposititious caprice. An ornithologist had gone back to Aristotle for a refutation of the environment theory. "Just as the body of an animal is divided into a number of organs and a political or military society into different sets of functions, so it is with animals themselves in Nature. And as notes in music are grouped into concerted form, so the same sort of stratification is expressed in Nature by her concrete phenomena." That was no argument, of course. Bureaucracies, army ranks, and music had, in Lamarck's view, little to do with events in the course of nature. If that were all the counterevidence available, people ought at least to allow public discussion of the new doctrine in the academies, instead of passing it over in indifferent silence.

On the day on which his fate was to be decided he was lecturing on the cave salamander. He was fond of referring to this classical example. The creature lived in the caves of the Illyrian alps and had, according to the environment theory, lost its sight because it had no need of vision in the darkness of the caves. But if it were kept for any length of time in an illuminated aquarium its sight returned. As Lamarck was explaining how his salamander grew genuine little eyes under the influence of light a stir of excitement passed through the hall. But this reaction was not caused by the miracle of the salamanders. It was because someone had suddenly entered the lecture room and sat down on one of the rear benches. The students turned round. Some of them clapped. Cornélie Lamarck looked up. She turned as white as a sheet. For the newcomer was Cuvier himself.

Cuvier listened for some time to the story of the salamanders. Then he stood up. He called out in a rude and tactless way that was unlike him, "If that is so, Monsieur Lamarck, one can only conclude that you, too, have made no use of your eyesight, and have consequently lost it!" Not a sound came from the hall. Lamarck had nothing to say, for he possessed very little presence of mind. He fiddled nervously with his collar. "If you used your eyes a little more," Cuvier went on ironically, "you would get a better idea of nature, instead of indulging in obscure fancies. Then perhaps you might get your sight back, eh?"

Several of the students laughed. Cornélie laid her head on the desk and began to cry quietly. "I beg of you, Cuvier," said Lamarck in a faint voice, "let us not make this a personal matter!"

Cuvier snapped back, "You didn't make any personal attacks on me in your philosophy of zoology, did you?"

"Not that I am aware of," Lamarck mumbled. A further wave of excitement ran through the hall. Some of the hostile students cracked jokes. They suggested that Lamarck ought to be asked how it was that he had not bequeathed his blindness to his numerous offspring. Seizing her father's arm, Cornélie tried to pull him out of the hall, away from this agonizing scene. He resisted her, and glared in the direction of Cuvier. Then he said in a defiant tone that sounded above the uproar, "I stand by everything I have written and taught. And I must now ask you, Cuvier, to leave the room!"

"Are you afraid?" Cuvier inquired. "If you are not, kindly answer one question, will you? Do you still maintain your assertion that fossilized forms of life are the predecessors of present-day species?"

"Certainly," replied Lamarck.

"You dare to tell me that to my face?" Cuvier banged the desk with his fist. "You know perfectly well that I have proved the contrary!"

"I don't believe in your doctrine of catastrophes," retorted Lamarck imperturbably. But no sound of agreement reached him. "Your demonstrations, Cuvier," he went on, "do not constitute proof, so far as I am concerned."

"That is an insult!" Cuvier thundered back. "I formally challenge you to produce your counterevidence or publicly retract your theory!"

Lamarck shook his head. "My theory cannot be proved any more than yours can," he said. "Not yet. Posterity will decide between us."

"Then you are no scientist, but a dreamer!" Cuvier glanced round the room. Most of the listeners were gazing at him excitedly. "I can prove anything I teach," he said. "I propose that the audience adjourn to my own lecture room. Find out for yourselves, gentlemen, which theory is correct, mine or that of this pitiful creature!"

The students followed Cuvier out of the room. However painful the incident might have been, even those of them who supported Lamarck did not want to miss the promised entertainment. Only Lamarck and Cornélie remained behind.

Cuvier's lecture hall was furnished with blackboards upon which sketches of antediluvian monsters had been drawn. Cuvier discussed them. He chose one, *Palaeotherium magnum*, which looked like a mixture of rhinoceros, tapir, and horse. He asked his listeners whether they thought it conceivable that any living creature could be derived from such a monster. No one did think so. "The type," said Cuvier, "is immutable. *Palaeotherium* never was and never became anything but a *Palaeotherium*. For nature is not subject to caprice, but to order, not to the play of chance, but to correlation."

He pointed to a stone slab lying on the table before him. "I should like now to try to reconstruct for you, from a single bone, an animal that I have never yet seen," he told the students, who were breathless with excitement. "If I succeed, you will be so good as to accept it as a proof that I understand fossils better than Monsieur Lamarck!" Only a tiny fragment of bone protruded from the slab. Everything else lay hidden in the stone. "I have never come across such a fossil before," he went on. "But I believe that from the small bone visible I can deduce the invisible form inside the stone. And I don't only believe it, gentlemen, I am sure of it; for I know that nature works in accordance with fixed, unalterable plans. This animal is an opossum dating from the early Tertiary period."

The students were torn between faith and skepticism. No one could yet identify the typical pouch bones and the typical opossum teeth. Perhaps Lamarck was right, after all, and some quite different animal might come out of the stone, stamped in some special way with the character of its environment. Cuvier chiseled away chip after chip from the slab. Nerve-racking minutes and quarters of an hour passed. Everyone was staring, spellbound, at the stone. At last, just as one of the students uttered a low cry of astonishment, with a jovial laugh Cuvier held up the pouch bones to the light. The fossil was in fact an early Tertiary opossum, as he had foretold.

The victorious expert was carried triumphantly through the Jardin. No one any longer doubted the truth of his teaching. Lamarck's utopian visions faded before the realities which Cuvier conjured out of stone and identified with calm certainty. It did not occur to anyone that this sort of reconstruction, though it might well prove the law of correlation, did not prove the theory of catastrophes. The fascination exercised by the magical art of this zoologist was so great that even Saint-Hilaire, who had always opposed Cuvier, set aside his scruples and worked in close collaboration with him for some time. In any case, Geoffroy Saint-Hilaire had never really felt confident about the environment theory in the emphatic form given it by Lamarck.

The latter's lecture hall thenceforward remained empty. In deep distress the little man from Picardy waited day after day in vain for his pupils to return. He was shunned like a leper. Soon after the collision with Cuvier he had to resign his professorship on account of total blindness. He lived almost another twenty years, in miserable circumstances, giving occasional private lessons in natural science for low fees and preparing frivolous students who had been idling through their school year for their final examinations. It is amazing that he nevertheless retained enough energy to dictate from memory to his loyal daughter Cornélie and her sister the eleven volumes of his natural history of invertebrates. Even completion of this work did not suffice to rescue him from poverty. It was ignored until the age of Darwin. Finally, about 1890, the zoologist Alfred Giard gave Lamarckism currency in France.

Toward the end of his life Lamarck had one more piece of good fortune. The first French socialists appeared and proclaimed that nature and mankind could be altered by a change in the constitution of society. Lamarck's idea that animate beings are created by their environment suited their political program. They visited him in his tenement and did their best to obtain some support from him in natural science for their social theories, but Lamarck had grown too old and weak to throw himself once more into the struggle. He courteously declined the invitation of the eager party theorists of the school of Count Saint-Simon and François Marie Charles Fourier to impart enlightenment.

When he died at the age of eighty-five, he was penniless and forgotten. The only person who troubled to preserve his memory was Cornélie Lamarck, as she eked out a beggarly existence in the Paris of the victorious Georges Cuvier.

The pope of bones and the red lady

It is always extremely disagreeable for a scientist if, while looking for evidence to support his theories, he discovers a fact that has the precisely opposite effect. He does not always allow it to influence him. He often closes his eyes to it. Sometimes he even denies the existence of what he has himself detected. Such behavior is not exactly in accordance with the sacred principles of science. But it is natural to mankind. The inner struggles involved are known to him alone. The highly respectable Baron Ernst Friedrich von Schlotheim, who refused in these circumstances to acknowledge the teeth of his ancestor, therefore may be allowed a smile of forgiveness by posterity.

Schlotheim was one of the first German paleontologists to follow the example of William Smith and Cuvier in considering fossils from chronological points of view. He had specialized, in particular, in plants of the Carboniferous period and fossil mollusks. He was not nearly so well acquainted with vertebrate animals, to say nothing of human beings. As a loyal supporter of the theory of catastrophes he always calculated in the case of every fossilized plant that came into his possession just which geological revolution had annihilated it. He was able to prove that the fossilized ferns of the Carboniferous period, despite their likeness to still-existent species, had completely died out. It was this achievement that attracted the attention of Cuvier's school to his work. He did the same thing in the case of prehistoric shellfish and snails. And no doubts would ever have occurred to him, throughout his long, industrious, and successful life, as to the truth of the teaching of the master, Cuvier, had he not conceived the unlucky idea of excavating the gypsum quarries of Thuringia for mammals, too, of the Diluvial, the last catastrophic period.

At first he did not find anything really new. His bones of mammoth, cave bear, and rhinoceros did not greatly excite the scientific world. All museums of any standing now possessed such fossils. But when in 1820 he suddenly came out with the statement that he had unearthed human teeth among some mammoth remains at Köstritz, it caused quite a stir among the academies and natural history museums. Was there such a thing as a fossilized human being, then, after all? Had Cuvier and all the other catastrophe theorists been criminally mistaken? Schlotheim produced the fateful teeth and announced, though somewhat reluctantly, that this find meant that human beings must have been contemporaries of the mammoth. Yet the mammoth, according to Cuvier, had belonged to quite a different period of creation. And between the latter and the final creative period there had occurred, as was then believed, a mighty inundation of the entire earth. In Cuvier's day the Ice Age had not yet been heard of.

Cuvier was informed of Schlotheim's discovery. He remained calm. He could not dispute the fact that the teeth were really human. But that meant nothing. Probably the grave digger had buried that ancient native of Köstritz rather deep in a Diluvial layer. Schlotheim thought it over and agreed to this explanation. Reassured, he continued to search the Thuringian gypsum quarries for evidence of the last geological revolution.

Fate would not let him rest. Two years later, in Bilzingsleven, he encountered Adam for the second time. Once more human remains lay side by side with the bones of extinct animals. And a year after that workmen dug out of the loess — a kind of loam — at Lahr in Baden the teeth and fragmentary bones of a third primitive human being. That was distinctly awkward. Schlotheim either had to drop altogether the theory of catastrophes, on which his life's work had been built up — and that was not easy for an old gentleman of sixty to do — or else he had to say what was hardly credible: that all three of his discoveries represented relics of interments dating from a later period. After an internal struggle, which did not enable him to draw any logical conclusion, he announced with some trepidation that it might not perhaps, after all, be quite out of the question that mankind had at one time been contemporary with diluvian animals. The statement sounded ominous to Cuvier and his adherents. For Schlotheim was not a mere nobody. His paleontological works ranked as exemplary in their lucidity and precision.

The authorities put the worthy Schlotheim through a stiff examination. They were very insistent. And in the end he allowed himself to be persuaded that they knew better. He threw the teeth and bones away, admitted that fossilized human beings did not exist, and returned to his ferns and mollusks.

Cuvier had the same experiences in his old age as Linnaeus. He began to have doubts. It was not absolutely necessary, he now declared, to assume a completely new creation after each geological revolution. Some catastrophes had perhaps devastated only part of the earth's surface, so that certain kinds of animals might have survived at isolated points and later on re-entered the ravaged areas. He thus prudently once more established precarious communication, as by bridges of rope, across the ground that had been cut from under his feet.

A number of disputes, darkened by the shadow of Lamarck, arose between him and Geoffroy Saint-Hilaire. The latter raised the question whether it might not be possible for the survivors of the catastrophes to develop into new species as a result of the changed circumstances. Cuvier denied the possibility. Species were immutable. But Saint-Hilaire would not give in. If development did not occur, if flood and volcanic eruption reaped a periodical harvest and left only a few animals and plants to survive until modern times, a quite fantastic profusion of forms of life must have prevailed at the earlier stages of the earth's history. Yet all the evidence of geology and research into primitive conditions contradicted such a view.

Cuvier had nothing to set against this argument. He replied, more generously than he had in the days of Lamarck, that the science concerned with prehistoric forms of life was still only in its infancy, and that it was far too early to come to any definite decision about so abstruse a problem. Its solution could safely be left to the coming generation of natural scientists. This was not the sort of language used by the quarrelsome "pope of bones" in the old days. Cuvier had won every distinction a man could. He had outlasted the fall of Napoleon with less difficulty than his colleagues, and now held several public offices under the new regime, including that of Councilor of State. The whole world honored him as the father of zoology. He now no longer felt it difficult to make concessions, and made them accordingly. Nevertheless, with senile obstinacy, he continued to adhere to the two weakest points of his doctrine: the dogma of the immutability of species and the principle that fossilized human beings did not exist.

In this connection the Schlotheim case had already caused him a certain amount of anxiety. Nor was this the end of it. In England the "Red Lady," a headless skeleton (now known to be that of a young man) dyed crimson by being embedded in red soil, had been discovered and was making a great stir. "She" had been found in 1823 in the so-called "Goat's Hole" at Paviland in Wales. There could be no doubt whatever that the skeleton had been reposing at a level far below the strata of modern times. This time it would be making too much of a good thing to talk of grave subsidence. The discovery at Paviland aroused such interest that certain unprejudiced amateurs once more, as in Scheuchzer's day, started off in pursuit of the "Man of the Deluge."

One of them was the English clergyman McEnery. He eagerly searched the caves of the southern coast of England. And two years after the discovery of the Red Lady he came across, in Kent's Cavern in Devonshire, a regular workshop of stone weapons and tools. All around them lay the bones of mammoths, primitive rhinoceroses, cave bears, primitive wild horses, and other extinct animals. It looked exactly as though prehistoric human beings had encamped there and piled up their kitchen waste round the fire. English geologists made pilgrimages to Kent's Cavern. They were able to confirm the truth of McEnery's discovery in detail. Man had known the mammoth. He had consequently lived before the last geological revolution. It was time for Cuvier and those who shared his views — Brongniart and the brothers d'Orbigny in France, Blumenbach in Germany, and Buckland in England — to confess the error of their ways.

They did nothing of the kind. For lack of proof, they allowed Adam to escape them again. Such conduct might be appropriate in a court of law. In science it proved disastrous. Cuvier pronounced the same sentence on the Red Lady and McEnery's stone tools as he had pronounced on the worthy Schlotheim's ancient Thuringians. All these discoveries were without significance, he said, because their age could not be determined with absolute accuracy. It was the most famous, the most momentous error of judgment in the whole history of paleontological research.

His negative attitude toward the problem of early man was reinforced by his contempt for apes. If fossil man existed and human beings had at one time developed out of the animal kingdom, their ancestors must, as Lamarck's *Zoological Philosophy* had already asserted, logically have been the higher apes. This idea disgusted Cuvier. He had a positive horror of apes. He did keep a young orangutan for six months and let it play with a couple of cats, noting that "it sat with its legs crossed under it in the oriental style." He also kept other apes in the Jardin. But he did not use them for psychological experiments as Count Buffon had. He considered them vile caricatures of creation. He described his mandrill — a venturesome, robust species of ape, of striking appearance — as follows: "Its cries, its expression and its lower tones bear witness to its utterly brutish effrontery. One has the impression that nature intended it as a picture of vice in all its hideousness." A similiar abhorrence of our bestial cousins was shown subsequently by the majority of Darwin's critics. As late as 1900 Haeckel's generous publisher categorically refused to print an illustration showing, as proof of the theory of evolution, a human female surrounded by apes. This "ape complex" is very ancient. It was painful for mankind, from time immemorial, to recognize itself in the shape of an unpleasant-looking animal, that resembled a human being as if reflected by a distorting mirror. Cuvier's phrase, "Man cannot be derived from the ape," should really have run: "Man ought not to be derived from the ape!"

The year 1830 was approaching. The opposition between Cuvier and Saint-Hilaire grew stronger, as in the days when they had first met. Goethe followed the progress of their disputes from Weimar and took a lively part in them. His interests, too, were at stake in the Paris conflict. A session of the French Academy on February 22, 1830, at which Geoffroy Saint-Hilaire handled the old lion pretty roughly, was described by Goethe as "an important event, which is bound to have consequences of the highest significance." He rounded off his scientific works with a study of this wrangle, observing that he "entertained views similar" to those of Geoffroy Saint-Hilaire and was "working along the same lines." He ended with the hope that "generic principles would be more widely adopted in future."

It was a vain hope. The sessions of 1830 were to be the last of their kind in Paris for a long time to come. They closed a brilliant era. Only a faint echo of its achievements remained. Cuvier was made a peer of France. He was about to be appointed Minister of the Interior when on May 13, 1832, he died, leaving his loyal disciples Brongniart and Alcide d'Orbigny to carry on his work. They reinforced the theory of catastrophes, piled up paleontological evidence in favor of it, and drew up, in far more dogmatic form than their dogmatic master, a "system of twenty-seven successive acts of creation," according to which no form of life survived from one geological catastrophe into the ensuing period, not even Man himself. This system — a typical product of the Restoration — suited that age. It met with great success, not only in France but also in the rest of the continent, and lasted well into the second half of the century. Geoffroy Saint-Hilaire and his most eminent pupil, Prince Charles Lucien Bonaparte, exerted themselves in vain to demolish it.

Cuvier's influence remained so strong that even the most indisputable of all the discoveries of primitive human remains hitherto made hardly aroused any interest in the learned world. This took place in 1833, a year after the master's death. The Belgian doctor of medicine Schmerling, who had gained particular credit for his researches in the field of the history of domesticated animals, was ransacking certain caves near Lüttich, looking for the bones of prehistoric watchdogs. At that time dogs were already thought to have had an origin in those early times, but this was not admitted in the case of mankind. Explorer's luck led Schmerling to the Engis cave. There he stumbled upon such vast quantities of animals' bones belonging to d'Orbigny's "penultimate period of creation" that no doubt could be entertained as to the age of the subsoil in question.

Schmerling sorted the bones. He recognized those of cave bears, mammoths, and rhinoceroses. Suddenly, to his surprise there appeared an unmistakable human skull. He continued his search, and eventually collected the remains of three human skeletons, including two skulls, and a large number of bone and flint implements. Primitive hunters, therefore, their weapons, their tools, and the game they had killed were all lying together in that cave. A clearer proof of the existence of Diluvial man could not be imagined. Schmerling, enraptured, buried his find and wrote a work in two volumes on the subject. But he had the same experience as Father Esper. He received a large number of letters and was praised for his industrious scientific investigations. But no one could bring himself to the point of wholehearted agreement with his conclusions.

Fortunately, the Engis skeletons and the Red Lady of Paviland were preserved. We know today that they belonged, except for one Neanderthal type, to members of the Cro-Magnon stock, which lived toward the end of the last Ice Age and already possessed an advanced culture at that time. We shall never know what Father Esper and the Baron von Schlotheim found, whether those remains were of Cro-Magnon men also, or of primitive, brutish Neanderthal human beings.

VII

ALL LIFE COMES FROM THE CELL

Man as an unknown mammal

THE LITTLE university town of Göttingen on the Leine River contributed much to early anthropology, the science of mankind. During the years in which people were beginning to decipher the early history of animals in Paris, in Göttingen others were studying the natural history of the most interesting of all animals, Man.

Intellectually, the French and the Hanoverian capital cities of natural science were closely allied in Cuvier's day. Albrecht von Haller, who had once taught at Göttingen, had packed the whole of humanity into the womb of our ancestral mother Eve. The mathematician Kästner and the satirist Lichtenberg had subjected professors and the common people alike to the lash of their wit. And it was there that Joachim Campe, in his *Robinson,* had drawn an idealized picture of human existence in early times, while the travelers Georg Forster and Alexander von Humboldt were associated with the university. In short, the town had long been an intellectual arena, not unlike Paris. But in one respect the study of natural science on the Leine differed from that on the Seine: the duels were not fought with unbuttoned foils, but with wooden swords.

Lichtenberg's mocking laughter was directed against everything that happened in Göttingen. His miniature essay on natural science had left an indelible impression on all those who discussed scientific problems in the town.

If we regard Nature as our schoolmistress and ourselves, poor human creatures, as her pupils, we shall be apt to take a very odd view of the human race. We all go to her lecture and possess the rudimentary knowledge necessary to enable us to understand it and yet we regularly take more notice of the chatter of our companions than of what the lecturer says. Or if one of our neighbors does start writing something down, we look over his shoulder, crib what he himself probably didn't quite understand, and add our own spelling mistakes and misunderstandings to it.

The Cuvier of Göttingen, Johann Friedrich Blumenbach — that disciple of Buffon, antivivisectionist and discoverer of the mammoth and the duckbill — took Lichtenberg's words to heart. He did not merely imitate the Parisian expert in zoology. Though Blumenbach denied the mutability of species and the existence of fossilized human beings, he nevertheless tried to form opinions of

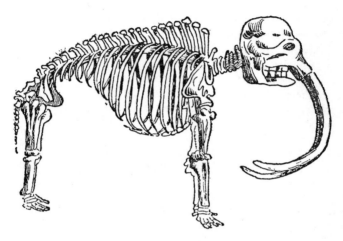

The papers left by Blumenbach, discoverer of the mammoth, after his death included a sketch of the skeleton of a mastodon, which had been found in Ohio. He called it the "Ohio mammoth." It was only established at a later date that the mammoth and mastodon belong to different genera and that their tusks turned upward. Animals related to this American mastodon were still alive in America 1600 years ago.

his own about phenomena. The first time he showed he was doing so was when he made a formal recantation and acknowledged to Goethe his mistake in the matter of the intermaxillary bone. The second time was when Pallas, the Siberian explorer and a disciple of Linnaeus, submitted a "genealogical tree of animals" to him. Pallas, a secret adherent of the evolutionists, had hit on the notion of representing the mutual relationships of animals, not by the old system of juxtaposition, but in the form of a family tree. Others took up the idea, and it might have ended in another Lamarck episode in Germany. But Blumenbach did not take the offensive. He merely remarked quietly that we had better wait "until still further observation presents us one of these days with a key to the secrets of nature."

Blumenbach ranked as the highest authority on all questions of natural science in his native land, the *magister Germaniae*. Many of his ideas recall those of Goethe, with whom he came to be on friendly terms in his later years. He talked, for instance, of a "creative force" which caused all animate beings to assume harmonious forms and actually produced crystals from apparently dead rock. He took the line that it was this creative force, not the compulsion of environment, which had brought species into being. But in prehistoric studies he was on Cuvier's side. He postulated four separate epochs of geological history, calling them, rather vaguely, the "mythological, heroic, historical, and present" ages. He was deeply interested in the question of the aspect of the chaotic interval between each of the separate ages. Enormous boulders, which seemed to have been flung by a gigantic hand, were to be found on level ground, providing evidence of destructive geological revolutions. Blumenbach considered it impossible for even a single creature to have survived such catastrophes, to pass from the mythological to the heroic age and from the historical to the present epoch.

He was not nearly so attracted by "dark surmises" about fossilized human beings as by mankind in the flesh. Little enough was known about this subject. Man was really the least understood of all animals. Before a start could be made with his introduction into the system and the investigation of his past, one would have to ascertain the truth about his organs and capacities, races and varieties. This was what Blumenbach did. He set to work and wrote the first natural history of humanity.

It was he who was originally responsible for the conception, which was accepted until well into the twentieth century, that the human being differed basically from all other mammals by walking upright, possessing skilled hands, a jutting chin, and a well-developed brain. Men are two-handed creatures, apes four-handed. The intermaxillary bone was thus replaced by a new, far more conspicuous distinguishing characteristic. It was applicable to the entire race, whether white and yellow-skinned representatives of civilization, black and brown barbarians, or primitive dwellers in the Australian bush. Blumenbach had no doubt whatever that all these varieties of mankind were derived from a common stock.

Whatever his feelings about a genealogical tree for animals, he certainly believed in setting one up for human beings. He examined skulls from all parts of the earth, reflected on the ways in which humanity had split up into races under the influence of climate and landscape, and imagined the first type of man as a brown-skinned, adaptable creature, something like the Australian aboriginal, inhabiting flat, tropical country. This early specimen had developed into a "Caucasian" in the civilized land of Europe and Western Asia, into a "mongol" in the Far East, into an "Ethiopian" in Africa's primeval jungles, into a "Red Indian" in the New World, and into a "Malay" on the islands of the Indian and Pacific Oceans.

Blumenbach's anthropological writings were the first works of any scientific value to deal with the racial characteristics of mankind. They accepted the assumption of development from an original type. But the obvious next step of studying its bones had not yet occurred to anyone in the circle around him.

Human anatomy and physiology were now much better understood. But here, too, many gaps remained to be closed. For his part alone, the Göttingen master published seven volumes containing illustrations of human skulls. He scrutinized every part of the human body. He also wrote on what he called the "procreative process" of man and analyzed *Homo sapiens* so thoroughly that generations of anthropologists were able to profit from his work. And, strangely enough, no one got into a passion over it. The prejudices of earlier ages against consideration of the bodily processes and growth of mankind had been swept away at last.

As Blumenbach wandered about the Zoological Institute or paced the halls of the natural history collection, he often caught sight of the newly fledged private tutor in natural history, Lorenz Ockenfuss.

Ockenfuss was a strange man who in Göttingen was generally thought to be mad. He certainly looked mad enough: his tanned face was crowned with a bush of black curly hair, and he spoke very fast in a hoarse voice with an unmistakable Swabian accent. In discussions he was hot-tempered and quick to provoke a quarrel. Young and inexperienced as he was, Ockenfuss perpetually irritated his worthy older colleagues: for although much of what he said sounded quite remarkable, much, too, sounded like the ravings of a drunken poet. Among other things, he said that all animals were cases of arrested development. They were, so to speak, immature men.

Ockenfuss was a typical example of the self-educated man. His father owned a small vineyard in the village of Bohlsbach near Offenburg and was notorious for his quarrelsomeness. He had brought up his son in the usual peasant style. Lorenz had anything but pleasant memories of his youth. He never forgot, as long as he lived, the ache of overworked muscles, the reek of manure and vines, the squabbles in the tavern, and the scuffling in the village streets. Instead of tending the cows and keeping his ill-tempered father company in the latter's daily wrangles with his neighbors, he became, in spite of this background, fired by ambition for higher things, and began to read German and Greek philosophers, zoological, botanical, and medical works, Linnaeus' *Systema naturae,* and Goethe's *Plant Metamorphosis.* After a few clashes with his father, he finally obtained permission to study medicine. But he did not adopt, as his father had hoped, the steady career of a country doctor. He wrote, reflected, and indulged in speculative ideas. He studied embryos, frogs' spawn, and the seeds of plants. While still a student he published a book on procreation which was practically identical with the forgotten *Theoria generationis* of the Berlin tailor's son, Kaspar Friedrich Wolff. Every animate being, it stated, was a product of ovum and sperm, beginning as a tiny bubble. In its development from conception to maturity it had to pass through all the lower organic stages, becoming a worm, a fish, and an amphibian in turn, till it could grow into a fowl, a horse, or a human being.

Now, after admission to the faculty at Göttingen, he had written a second book, called A *Summary of the System of Biology,* which was even more unusual. It contained propositions that elicited, at the very least, murmurs of disapproval from the venerable Göttingen professors. All life had originated as a primeval slimy substance in the sea. A network of mutual relationships connected the species, genera, and classes of the animal kingdom. And Man, the "measure and register of creation," was the divinely ordained goal of a complex evolutionary process. Some of the book seemed to have been borrowed from the ancient Hellenes and some taken over from Leibniz.

"Undigested natural philosophy" was the verdict of the professors of Göttingen, half mockingly, half indulgently. If Ockenfuss had arrived in the city on the Leine a little earlier, they argued, he would certainly have joined the Grove Society, a noisy *Sturm und Drang* club which drank the healths of Klopstock and Goethe in Rhine wine and banished Voltaire and Wieland to outer darkness. But since then the bards of the Grove Society had grown old and staid, and perhaps Ockenfuss, too, would soon follow their example and become more reasonable, if he were given a bit of encouragement.

"Well, what have you got there under the microscope?" asked Blumenbach, laying his hand on the shoulder of his unruly protégé.

"Tadpoles," said Ockenfuss. "All the stages of development from the fertilized ovum to the full-grown larva." He stared hard at his professor. "We men, too, once looked exactly the same. In early geological times we were little bubbles. Then we formed groups of bubbles, acquired a skin and an intestine, turned into a kind of worm. Then we grew gills, changing into fish and batrachia."

"And then into reptiles, quadrupeds, and human beings," replied Blumenbach, thinking it was really about time the boy had his hair cut. "How many glasses of wine did you have today, Ockenfuss?"

But Ockenfuss refused to be sidetracked. "A mysterious law of nature," he said defiantly, "obliges all animate beings to develop steadily to higher levels, till they reach the top."

"And the name on the top is Lorenz Ockenfuss, eh?" Blumenbach, still smiling, shook his head. "If you really believe that sort of thing, my young friend, I should like to ask you just one question. Why is it that, apart from us men, other creatures exist which are organized on a totally different system?"

"Because all other animals have tripped over the manifold obstacles of life." Ockenfuss struck the table with his fist. "Every animate being except Man is a case of repressed growth!"

"In that case frogs, lizards, dogs, and apes must have got out of breath a bit prematurely, eh?" said Blumenbach jokingly. "No, Ockenfuss, that's a delusion. Nature is not so frivolous as to leave the development of her budding formations to caprice and chance. If she did, it would be the end of all order in the physical world." He, too, was becoming a little excited now. "And that would be intolerable!" he exclaimed. "If there were no order in nature, there would be none in the moral world, in religion and ethics, in anything which humanity had brought into being!"

"Do you call that an argument?" Ockenfuss demanded in his turn.

"There are certain people about today," said the other, half seriously, half ironically, "who deduce a particular view of life from the possibility that new species may arise. Perhaps they would even like to replace our good old, still serviceable religion with natural philosophy. I hope," he concluded, "that you are not one of them. Be content with things as you find them at present. Study them as well as you can. The most insignificant result of observation, if there is no mistake about it, is more valuable than the boldest hypothesis."

He left the room. If I were Cuvier, he thought, I should have had to expel him. But I'm not Cuvier. Ockenfuss interests me: I should like to know what's going to become of him.

The enfant terrible of zoology

Ockenfuss was fond of making excursions into the Harz Mountains with his students. He took the view, at that time highly unusual, that nature could be better studied in the open than in lecture rooms. And we may take it for granted that he did not roam the fields and woods with a butterfly net and specimen box like a professor in the comics. His excursions were probably more like a philosopher's stroll. With a countryman's craft he analyzed vegetation, animals, and minerals. Then, with a poet's imagination he reassembled them into a microcosm of their own. No doubt it was more exciting and amusing for the Göttingen students of medicine and natural history to tramp through the Ilsetal and climb the Brocken with this eccentric professor than to brood in stuffy classrooms over an old bone, a foetus preserved in spirits, or a pressed plant.

During one such excursion, near the Ilse Rock, Ockenfuss suddenly came to a halt, staring as though spellbound at a whitish object lying among the trees. The students looked at one another in astonishment. Some were sure that their tutor had relapsed into one of his periodical fits of lunacy. For the thing lying in the moss and undergrowth was simply the bleached skull of a hind. Why on earth did the sight of it disturb Ockenfuss so deeply?

"Now I have it!" he cried at last, still gazing fixedly at the hind's skull. "Pure chance! If that skull had been lying in a slightly different position, I might never have realized it!" He seized one of the students by the arm and shook him. "Do you see it? Take a good look at it! Do you see it too?"

The student saw nothing. The others gathered round, giggling while Ockenfuss shouted, "Do you know what that skull is made of? Don't you see it even now? It's made of vertebrae — transformed vertebrae!"

Vertebrae? The students shrugged their shoulders. The thing was unmistakably a skull, not vertebrae at all. Was their teacher trying to play a joke on them? Even they knew enough about anatomy to distinguish a skull from vertebrae.

"You've got to use your imagination as you look at it," Ockenfuss adjured them. "Then you can clearly see what I mean. Skulls are simply transformed vertebrae!" He collected his pupils about him and started giving them one of those notorious lectures that exasperated the whole of Göttingen "Animals with skulls, gentlemen, such as fish, amphibians, birds, quadrupeds, and human beings, formerly developed from animals that had none, merely by recasting their frontal vertebra. The skull — that privilege of the aristocrats among animals, containing the sense organs and the brain, the skull, which turns the worm into the fish — is no longer a secret! On the back of certain wormlike animals a sort of gristly lump formed, rendering the body more stable. The gristle hardened into bone and became vertebrae. The first of the latter grew into a capsule in which the nerve fibers collected. The skull, with its brain, came into being!" He concluded triumphantly: "From worm to Man — a direct route! This discovery, gentlemen, is a striking proof of my theory of perpetual metamorphosis."

As soon as he got back to the university he sat down to study Blumenbach's collection of skulls and the vertebrae in the natural history museum. He made comparisons, took notes, and drew diagrams. He believed that he had now solved one of the greatest problems of evolution — if there were such a thing as evolution at all. His fingers ached as he wrote out a draft of his *Vertebral Theory of the Skull* for the professors. And at last he actually received a perfectly friendly and affirmative reply. But it did not come from a professor. It came from Goethe, and enclosed a most flattering invitation to move to Jena and take up an appointment as assistant professor of medicine and zoology there.

A remarkable combination of circumstances had induced Goethe to summon Ockenfuss to his side. Exactly the same idea that had struck the imaginative Ockenfuss at the Ilse Rock had occurred to the poet of Weimar years before. During his second visit to Italy he had found the smashed skull of a ram in the sand of the old Jewish cemetery at Venice. He picked it up and "at once perceived that the cranial and facial bones must be derived from vertebrae." But he felt that this discovery did not yet justify publication. He continued his bone studies for some decades afterwards. In the drawer of his desk lay an unfinished manuscript entitled "Framework of the Skull Constructed from Six Vertebrae," as well as several drafts of an introduction to comparative anatomy. He talked his vertebral theory over with friends "who cautiously assented and followed up the notion in their various fashions." In this way he learned that someone else — Professor Meckel, from Halle — had also discovered the secret of the origin of the skull. He built up his evidence carefully, piece by piece, with a view to bringing out, one day, a finished work, proof against any cut or thrust of criticism, on the whole complex problem.

In Ockenfuss he believed he had found someone who shared his views. It was true that there was a good deal about this eccentric character that he found difficult to accept. For example, he was not at all happy about the idea that Man was the "measure and register of creation." He expressed it in another way: "Man only knows himself in so far as he knows the world; he is only aware of the world within himself and alone in the world he *is* aware of himself." But Goethe looked indulgently at this notorious hothead.

Ockenfuss accepted his offer. He dropped his surname, which meant "bullock's hoof," and which he considered inappropriate to high society, and in the future called himself simply Lorenz Oken, expressly indicating his readiness to suit his manners to those of the illustrious Jena and Weimar circles. He was not unwilling to bid farewell to the solemnities of work in the home of the *magister Germaniae*. In the group of poets and scholars gathered about the Grand Duke of Sachsen-Weimar-Eisenach he hoped to rise to fame and contribute to the final victory of the theory of evolution that was denied by Cuvier and doubted by Blumenbach.

On arrival at Jena he found the atmosphere positively intoxicating. Ecstatic young men, romantic poets disguised as scholars, were preaching natural philosophy as if it were a new view of life. Their leader was named Schelling. Though he no longer lived in the grand-ducal university town, since its literary disputes had caused him to dislike the place, he still exercised great influence there, and everyone was still obsessed by his teaching. It had hardly anything in common by this time with the clear pictures of the world offered by Spinoza, Goethe, and the pre-Socratics. It consisted of a hymn to nature that amounted to frenzy. It acted on Oken like an opiate. He threw himself into Schelling's company, declaring that this was what he had been seeking for so long but had never found in the dry air of Göttingen.

Schelling and his disciples were primarily responsible for the fact that the theory of evolution, which had already gained a good deal of ground by about 1815, was now being more and more depreciated by serious naturalists. For Schelling's school had annexed this conception for its own use, associating it with Plato's doctrine of Ideas, Aristotle's teleology, and the mysticism of the Romantic movement. They turned it into a religion of nature, which at first sight seemed very impressive but when more closely examined was found to be extremely unstable and vague. Goethe's and Blumenbach's "creative force" was transformed by Schelling into a "mighty spirit, embedded, with all its senses petrified, in nature, stirring and stretching in uneasy slumber and striving with vast efforts, in both dead and living things, to attain consciousness." This mighty spirit of Schelling's forces nature to engage in a perpetual process of becoming, with the definite intention of manifesting eternal ideas. There are many obstacles in its way: every natural phenomenon has first to pass through a certain series of possible forms before the idea that lies within it can be realized. In this way, according to Schelling, the abundance of forms in the fossilized and living animal and vegetable kingdoms came into existence.

This theory coincided to an amazing degree with Oken's own reflections. He soon found himself at the head of the new direction of thought. It was possible, if one followed Schelling, to believe in evolution without abandoning the systems. For the genera, orders, and classes were "ideas." The world of nature was derived from the world of spirit, and not the other way round. The realm of phenomena had been set up on an eternal basis which could easily be understood by the exercise of a little imagination. "The true task of the natural scientist," said Oken, soon after his arrival in Jena, speaking like a reincarnation of Linnaeus, "is to expound nature's gradual advance. All forms represent successive stages in the evolution of a single impulse to growth. They can all be apprehended logically. There are as many classes among vertebrate animals as there are organic systems in mankind. Each class has the same number of orders. There are analogies everywhere." In other words, though nature is not, as Linnaeus, Haller, and Bonnet had stated, a rigid piece of architecture constructed according to mathematical rules, it has nevertheless evolved in accordance with the laws of mathematics.

The young natural scientists of the Romantic epoch now became hysterically active. They drafted "systems of nature according to geometrical principles, gradations of natural phenomena, logical bases for types" and similar fabrications, which really differed in no way from those of the old worm-dissector Bonnet. It was therefore no wonder that the majority of scholars turned their backs on them and preferred to take sides with Cuvier and Blumenbach. It made them shudder to hear talk of mutability, natural gradations, spontaneous generation, and the descent of Man. They abandoned both the theory of evolution and the mysticism of Schelling's followers and refused to have anything more to do with them. A Berlin professor of zoology said with great emphasis to his students: "This mysticism, which so many people are taking up nowadays, and which deliberately seeks to convert the ignorant, is having a considerable success. But I can assure you, not faith but doubts will lead you to the truth." Goethe, of course, was of the same opinion, though he may never have definitely said so.

Armed with Schelling's doctrines, Oken set about shaking the world to its foundations. He was the first to proclaim the vertebral theory of the skull against Goethe's advice, making rather a great deal of noise about it. He declared it alone to be a clear proof of sound government by the world-spirit. Schelling's disciples greeted the announcement with a storm of applause. It was echoed from all directions — from Munich, Erlangen, Würzburg, Bremen, and Leipzig. But the levelheaded scientists frowned, maintaining that this was not an arguable theory, but merely mysticism disguised as zoology. Their criticism affected not only Oken but also Goethe. For, after all, it had been Goethe who had first described the framework of the skull as transformed vertebrae. The attacks aimed at Oken's rash assertions rebounded on the prudent Goethe, darkening his reputation.

Goethe was genuinely alarmed. His agitation was increased by the fact that Oken, in that aggressive spirit which he had inherited from his father, stated in public that the right honorable gentleman had stolen his theory. The affair began to assume the dimensions of a scandal. Goethe, deeply shocked, disassociated himself from Oken's vertebral theory by announcing that it had been "sprung upon the public precipitately and prematurely, so that it cannot fail to arouse much antagonism." He added a gloomy prophecy. "The extent of the damage done to the theory by the crude way in which it has been presented will possibly be made clear by history in days to come. The trouble thus started, by which a perverse twist has been given to excellent work, will undoubtedly become more and more evident as time goes on."

This prophecy was fulfilled even more drastically than Goethe had foreseen. Oken did not shake the world to its foundations. On the contrary, he contributed to the achievement by Cuvier and the executors of his legacy of a victory that had lasting effects even in Germany. For fifteen whole years the bogy of the *enfant terrible* of zoology disturbed Weimar and Jena society. Innumerable young scientists positively worshipped him, ecstatically proclaiming that it was he who first dared to leap across millenniums and draw the veil from the first act of creation.

One of these enthusiasts was the chemist Justus Liebig. Ten years later he confessed, "I, too, lived through that period, so rich in words and ideas, but so poor in real knowledge. I wasted years of my life over it. I can't describe my horror and disgust on coming to my senses after that nightmare!" The great influence Oken exercised upon his contemporaries can only be explained by the fact that he, like Cuvier, possessed a unique genius for discovering and interpreting zoological and anatomical details, and he understood even better than Cuvier how to popularize his field of research. He translated the obscure jargon of the scholars into plain German, rammed home such ideas as "mammals," "reptiles," "batrachians," and "insects," and cleared away the abstruse tangle of verbiage that had overgrown the system of nature. He wrote in a lively and vivid style. One did not need to have studied the subject in order to understand him. Anyone, for instance, could grasp Oken's simple statement that "mates and associates must be reckoned as one species." It was he who inaugurated the era of "knowledge for the common man."

As a natural philosopher the son of the Bohlsbach peasant was a fraud; his critical colleagues were perfectly justified in maintaining this. His theory of evolution, compared to the theories of Goethe, Lamarck, and Saint-Hilaire, was fanciful and artificial; but in research he was far ahead of his time and possessed an intuitive grasp of the truth. The "little bubbles" from which he believed all animal and vegetable bodies to have been constructed were later identified as "cells." His opinion that every animate being recapitulated the family history of its species in its individual evolution represents a first draft of the "fundamental law of biogenetics" today associated with the name of Haeckel. He recognized essential processes in pro-creation and fertilization, bridged the gulf between inanimate and animate nature, and vigorously defended, though admittedly not with the lucidity and exactitude of Jean Baptiste Lamarck, the thesis of Man's animal origin. Oken possessed two souls: that of a romantic poet and that of a modern biologist.

The last act of the tragedy was played out in 1819, when the notorious *Isis* case, now a part of literary history, became the talk of Weimar and Jena. *Isis*, a magazine of natural history edited by Oken, suddenly published among its scientific essays not only the usual complaints, grievances, and accusations aimed at professors in the opposite camp, but also articles ferociously attacking the character of the Grand Duke and administrative conditions in Sachsen-Weimar-Eisenach. Oken's unfortunate aggressive streak had led him to stray on to the slippery ice of politics. The articles made an extraordinarily painful impression, especially since Oken had not been entirely unjustified in his attack. The conditions both of science and of public life in Sachsen-Weimar-Eisenach left a very great deal to be desired.

The government was on the point of instituting proceedings against Oken for high treason. The trial would in all probability have taken place if Goethe, as the Minister concerned, had not intervened. He knew Oken only too well and realized that an intelligent and ready speaker of his type would have no difficulty in check-

mating the Grand Duke's stolid lawyers and court officials. To muzzle him prematurely would be to endanger the principle of freedom
of speech. Yet if one did not do so Oken might well prove the
victor in the affair, to the disgrace of the prince and the whole realm.

Goethe proposed a solution of the problem which has proved an
extremely useful expedient right down to the present time. He suggested leaving Lorenz Oken, in person, out of the question altogether
and transferring responsibility to the publisher of the *Isis*, who could
himself be arrested, and thus precluded from issuing further copies
of the paper. In this way, he pointed out to the government, they
would deprive the "insolent young fellow" of his weapon without
letting matters come to an open scandal. The Weimar lawyers took
his advice. And Oken found himself suddenly without an outlet
in which to vent his spleen and ill-humor. In his resentment, and
faced, moreover, with the dilemma of either giving up his political
ambitions or his professorship, he chose the latter, and turned his
back on the University of Jena. It was just what the Weimar government had wanted.

Oken lived on for some years as a private scholar in Jena. He became the center of a large group of adherents who formed the germ
of the congresses of natural scientists that afterwards achieved such
fame. Later he obtained an unsalaried lectureship at the University
of Munich. As he annoyed people there, too, he accepted an invitation from the University of Zurich, thus becoming the second of
the German biologists to emigrate, after Kaspar Friedrich Wolff. He
remained the leading spirit of the natural science congresses and
played the part of a pike in a carp pond at their meetings. He stirred
up trouble, enthusiasm, and strife wherever he went. The inexorable
sentence of condemnation pronounced by the old school of scientists
followed him implacably.

Cell chemistry

As soon as a science leaves its happy and romantic youth behind, it
engenders a particular breed of mankind — the specialists. Some of
them spend their whole lives in exclusive concern with the parasites
of whales. Others are interested in absolutely nothing but fossilized
sea urchins. Others, again, are wholeheartedly devoted to the canine
tapeworm. They perform useful services of a restricted kind, and
science could not do without them. Yet by their nature they get out
of touch with other specialists and, owing to their preoccupation
with whale parasites, fossilized sea urchins, and canine tapeworms,
lose sight of nature as a whole.

The nineteenth century, with its accumulation of discoveries and inventions, very nearly became an age of specialists. Scientists with a truly comprehensive training, experts in all the realms of nature, grew rarer and rarer. Cuvier and Saint-Hilaire in France, Erasmus Darwin in England, Goethe, Blumenbach, and Alexander von Humboldt in Germany were replaced by indefatigable technicians, each of whom extended in his own field the work initiated by the previous generation, though he already regarded the adjacent field as a book with seven seals.

In Germany it was the much abused Lorenz Oken, of all people, who at an early period recognized the danger inherent in this development and set himself to counteract it. He kept his colleagues from the other faculties in close touch with one another and took care that they met periodically to exchange news. And those very colleagues of his — the sober physicists, the practical chemists, the masters of scalpel and microscope — formed a sound counterbalance to the intellectual speculations of the school of Schelling. The pendulum swung the other way. At Oken's natural science congresses the realists obtained a more and more attentive hearing.

The physicists explained that all processes in nature obeyed the laws of mechanics. Justus Liebig, chemist, showed how science could help to improve men's lives. His friend and collaborator, Friedrich Wöhler, proved the possibility of the production of organic substances by artificial means in the laboratory. The gulf between inanimate and animate nature was bridged in several directions. The natural scientist was obliged to take leave of many a cherished illusion. In the domain that the physicists and chemists of the new era had founded and fortified there was no more room for Schelling's dreaming world-spirit. It was ruled by mechanical forces, electromagnetic vibrations, atoms and molecules, acids and alkalis. Nature had grown sober and prosaic. Many regretted the fact. Others found it peculiarly fascinating.

The biologists were at first somewhat reluctant to draw conclusions from the new knowledge. The idea that life might be nothing more than a chemical process struck them as altogether too alarming. They felt that if the wonders of the structure of animals and plants and the remarkable capacities of the human mind were to be explained, one really would have to assume, in addition, a mysterious and consciously creative "life-force." Such, at any rate, was the opinion of the great physiologist and supporter of Cuvier, Johannes Müller. Most of his colleagues accepted the doctrines of his "vitalism."

Johannes Müller became professor of anatomy and physiology

at Berlin in 1833 and taught there for twenty-five years, until his death in 1858. This quarter century, the "era of Müller," was an important period in the development of natural science, though he himself did not make any outstandingly novel contributions to it. "These were the years," wrote a contemporary, "of the rise of embryology, of the discovery of cells in the organisms of plants and animals, of the more precise definition, based upon this last discovery, of histological characteristics, and of the first systematic utilization of the data of detailed anatomical and chemical research." They were the years in which the physicist Helmholtz, the biologists Schleiden and Schwann, and the physician Rudolf Virchow were active; in which the unlucky doctor of medicine Robert Mayer established the "principle of the conservation of energy" and was robbed by technical specialists of his birthright in this connection; and in which a Potsdam lawyer's son, Ernst Haeckel, who at that time still believed in the literal truth of the Bible and opposed the materialists, was beginning to make his first advances to Mother Nature, without dreaming of the consequences that would ensue.

All these scientific stars revolved like planets round their sun, Johannes Müller, who remained to the day of his death tenaciously and imperturbably loyal to Cuvier's views. They were all passionately devoted to him, though they did not by any means entirely agree with his vitalism and conservative concept of nature. It was only in secret that a few rebels grew restless.

Müller kept a strict eye on them. For instance, there was Jakob Schleiden of Hamburg, a former lawyer, who had one day abandoned his clients and gone over to the study of natural science, which he liked better. At the time he was doing botanical work at Müller's institute, and was in the habit of asserting in confidence to his intimates that at some early geological period "forces which may indeed still be in existence today but under such conditions and in such combinations as do not seem possible any longer on this earth" had generated the first germs of organic beings from highly soluble and chemically unstable organic substances in the sea. Then there was the young anatomist Theodor Schwann, assistant at the same institute. He was a keen student of the *Amphioxus* — a small, headless, wormlike fish known as a "lancelet" — and took the view that the existence of this creature proved species to have developed by slow degrees from very simple forms. Neither Schleiden nor Schwann could be suspected of the slightest flirtation with the natural philosophy of Schelling, which Schleiden called "that insufferable, obscurely delving rigmarole, with not an atom of meaning in it." They had already taken a long step forward out of the fanciful world of Lorenz Oken into the realities of the world of modern scientific research. They announced in clear and unmistakable terms that science could be made to "appear attractive and captivating in itself without resorting to the adornments of those conscious or unconscious lies with which poets would like to replace thought, cranks knowledge and dreamers the truth." The sentiment was one with which Johannes Müller heartily agreed. It seemed all the more reprehensible to him that such exact scientists, of all people, should be addicted to damnable hypotheses about spontaneous generation and the origins of phenomena. They did not even refrain from laying hands on man. He had, according to Schleiden, "entered the society of the inhabitants of earth, in some inexplicable way, as the result of a long series of evolutions."

It happened that it was just these two black sheep in Müller's flock who made the greatest biological discovery of their age. One day in 1838 Schleiden was examining sections of a plant through the microscope. He saw something that many had seen before without taking any further notice of it. The plant consisted of a mosaic of tiny particles pitted like a honeycomb. Wondering exactly what was wrong with the particles, he made a more precise examination. Each cavity or "cell," he found, had a stable envelope enclosing a nucleus. It could split up, as Infusoria do. It was, accordingly, a small organism contained in the large one of the plant.

Schwann at the same time was studying animal tissue under the microscope. He made the same observation. Animals too consisted of cells of this kind, and their bodies grew in consequence of the splitting up of the cells. It was true that animals' cells were not enclosed in a stable envelope like those of plants. In other respects the members of both kingdoms of nature possessed the same structure. The cell was the cornerstone of every organism, and all life originated in it.

Little as Johannes Müller cared for the theories of evolution held by the two experts with the microscope, he at once recognized the importance of their chance discovery. He had the matter further investigated. One of his pupils, Max Schultze, was able to prove twenty-three years later that the cells of both animals and plants in fact arose from the same substance. The physical basis of life, the secrets of which Müller had supposed to be impenetrable, turned out to be albumen and protoplasm circling indefatigably, like the eternal flux of Heraclitus, in the cells.

The discovery of the cell was a scientific sensation of the first order.

There was no further need for human intelligence to resort to theory in order to explain the metamorphosis of animal and plant structure, for the whole of animate nature had been built up on foundations of the same sort of material. Embryologists perceived that the ovum was a single cell, which divided upon fertilization and grew up in this way. Zoologists and botanists discovered primitive forms of life consisting merely of agglomerations of cells. Physicians dropped the old medical notion that diseases were to be accounted for by vitiation of the bloodstream and founded "cellular pathology," the theory of the diseased cell.

A new sun rose beside Johannes Müller's into the heavens of science. It was that of Rudolf Virchow, a Pomeranian farmer's son, physician, biologist, and student of prehistoric ages, who described the cell as the simplest expression of life, the initial and central point of all animate phenomena. While still a youthful assistant at the Berlin charity hospital, he had defined living bodies as communities of cells in which individual groups produced everything we call life, from physical movement to the activities of the mind and the soul. And each cell, as laboratory experiments proved, was a complex association of chemical elements that broke down into their component parts at death.

Johannes Müller accepted the facts disclosed by his industrious workers on the cell. But he was reluctant to give up his belief in a supernatural life-force. This was the straw at which a whole generation of transition between Cuvier and Darwin clutched. The new generation thought differently. Müller's own assistant, the former clockmaker Emil Du Bois-Reymond from French Switzerland — a stately gentleman of somewhat ceremonious manners who produced the effect, according to Wilhelm Bölsch, "of a statue of Humboldt holding the textbook of the world-wide laws of natural science on his knees" — had long since broken with vitalism. He considered that only physical forces existed, even in animate nature. In his view natural science was merely the recognition of activities of such forces. Nor did he alone hold such opinions. Müller was deeply shocked to find in the last years of his life that though the brilliant group of young scientists he had gathered about him had certainly taken his advice never to abandon the field of exact science, they did not now consider the theory of life-force to be exact science.

The era of Müller was succeeded by the era of Virchow. It was true that even Virchow described himself as a vitalist, no doubt out of respect for his master. But fundamentally he represented the same train of thought as the most extreme materialists among the biologists. He supported experimental science as the only justifiable kind, opposed all anthropomorphism and all attempts to smuggle metaphysics into natural science, emphasized the inseparable connection between spirit and matter, and ended his "medical confession of faith" with the words: "I am convinced that I shall never find myself in a position to deny the principle of the unity of human life with all its consequences."

Such was the situation by the middle of the century, when the great decisions were taken. The ground had been well prepared. Microscope and dissecting knife had revealed the most secret processes at work in the bodies of plants, animals, and human beings. Levelheaded and practical-minded investigators had come to the fore and everything was ready for the rise of a new Lamarck. People were no longer looking to Paris, where hardly any new discoveries had been made since Cuvier's time, but to the rising young metropolis of Berlin, where Virchow taught, boldly proclaiming that the animate and inanimate were inseparable, that the cell was capable of producing the most highly developed of forms, and that every living being must at some time or other pass through the unicellular stage.

During this period scientific materialism flourished as it never had before. The works of Ludwig Feuerbach, Ludwig Büchner, and Karl Vogt excited extraordinary interest in the minds of the people, who were rendered still more restless by the revolution of 1848. Feuerbach declared any speculation going beyond the boundaries of the real world to be a retrograde step. Büchner, with his formula that nothing existed but forces and matter, made nature wholly abstract. Vogt, who seemed to be a reincarnation of the *enfant terrible* Lorenz Oken, described the vitalists, with unqualified contempt, as "a set of foolish children" and shocked honest citizens with his announcement that "the mind bears the same relation to the brain and the nerves as urine does to the kidneys." The great men of Berlin, Virchow and Du Bois-Reymond, saw no objection to this scientific radicalism. On the contrary, in 1848 Virchow joined the men of the Left at the barricades and supported their political and social demands. Du Bois-Reymond waxed positively enthusiastic over Vogt's witty epigrams, considering that it was "difficult to condemn the implied representation of psychological activity as the product of material conditions in the brain, seeing that the soul gradually came into existence as the result of material combinations and has, like other hereditary talents, increased and perfected itself through countless generations."

And if such a man as Karl Vogt were "difficult to condemn" one might have supposed that it would have been easy for any thoughtful theorist of the origin of species and a few conscientious students of early man to have stormed the scientific citadel of Berlin. But oddly enough nothing of the kind happened. When at last the question of the descent of man could be introduced into the discussion, the same Du Bois-Reymond who had previously emphasized the relationship between human and animal psychology refused to have anything to do with it and coined the phrase "We know nothing and we never shall know anything!" And the same Virchow who considered a human being to be a community of cells like an animal or a plant, turned his coat and joined in the hue and cry against Darwinism, relegating the existence of early man to the realm of a fable with a bluntness worthy of Cuvier.

Yet both Virchow and Du Bois-Reymond remained perfectly well disposed to the theory of evolution. The reasons for their bias against Darwin, Huxley, and Haeckel, and the Neanderthal and Taubach finds troubled many contemporary historians. Some believed it proved their excessive caution. Some suspected that they were still influenced by Johannes Müller from beyond the grave. Others, again, maliciously insinuated that it was the very nature of a dictatorship, whether political or scientific, only to recognize its own decrees. Whatever the reason, in the case of Adam, Virchow was not consistent with his "medical confession of faith." He followed in Cuvier's footsteps. For nearly fifty years the moment any trace of early man was discovered or some theory of the origin of species put forward, he thundered out a decisive prohibition against its discussion.

The great turning point was reached elsewhere, in a country given to even more sober and practical thinking than Prussia — England. And it was no natural philosopher like Oken, no materialist like Vogt, no student of the cell like Virchow, and no physiologist like Du Bois-Reymond who first successfully stood up for Adam. It was a man whose chief business was rocks, ores, and volcanoes, the geologist Charles Lyell.

VIII

HUMAN FOSSILS DO EXIST!

The Flood was an ice age

IT IS ONE of the most astonishing facts about natural history that the
name and work of Darwin have been subjected to a crossfire of discussion right down to the present day, whereas for a hundred years
now the name and work of Lyell have not given rise to any serious
dispute. Both men in principle came to the same conclusions, and
Darwin's theory of 1859 necessarily derived from Lyell's of 1830.
This extraordinary circumstance can only be explained when we
remember that Darwin's special field of biology only too obviously
touched upon mankind and Lyell's field of geology could do no harm
to anyone. Animals are closer to us than rocks: the way in which
the earth grew to maturity does not seem of overwhelming importance to the general public, but when the same laws that hold good
on our planet are applied to organic nature and to the lords of
creation many people are horrified.

Geology had only just emerged from an embittered dispute when
Lyell came on the scene. The old opposition between Thales, who
had once described water as the prime cause of all things, and
Heraclitus, who said it was fire, had cropped up again. Two schools
were at feud and each had inscribed the name of a Roman god upon
its banner. The Saxon mineralogist Abraham Gottlob Werner
taught — under the sign of Neptune, the water god — that the origin
of all geological formations was to be sought in the ocean, which
had gradually constructed layer after layer of rock on a foundation
of crust, as when boilers become furred. This view was sharply
contested — under the sign of the fire god, Vulcan — by the Scottish geologist James Hutton. He ascribed to volcanoes, not to water,
the main contribution to the origin of the earth's crust. Every natural
scientist at the beginning of the nineteenth century joined the
"Neptunists" or the "Vulcanists." People discussed the question
of the formation of the earth as eagerly as they now discuss the
theory of relativity and the splitting of the atom.

Hutton and the god Vulcan finally defeated Werner and the god Neptune, and Cuvier and the supporters of the theory of catastrophes played a conspicuous part in bringing about the victory. Volcanic rumblings, the abrupt alteration in the appearance of an earth that had perhaps existed from all eternity, suited their doctrine better than the slow, furtive action of water. Geologists now represented the history of the earth as a tremendous drama, the protagonists of which were violent eruptions, torrents of lava, earthquakes, and outbreaks of fire. Interested laymen searched for these strange "erratic" boulders that lay about like giants' playthings in level country, and stood amazed, regarding them as traces of bygone geological convulsions on an enormous scale.

But those same "erratics," which the Floodists believed to have been washed up by the Deluge and the Vulcanists considered to have been hurled to the surface of the earth from its interior, soon gave evidence against both the god of water and the god of fire. They originated, as geologists had long known, in the Diluvial epoch, that puzzling span between the Tertiary period and modern times — as to the character of which experts could never quite agree. Was it identical with the Flood in the Bible? Had a vast, catastrophic inundation taken place at the time? Or had the god Vulcan set the earth blazing and rocking in those days? Agreement could only be reached as to one aspect of the matter. The Diluvial age must have invaded the earth with inconceivable rapidity. That was the very point at which a capital error had been made in calculation.

Goethe and the geologist Karl Ernst Adolf von Hoff of Gotha were the first to notice it, eight years before Lyell came on the scene. Von Hoff, a disciple of Lichtenberg and Blumenbach, discovered that the earth's history had been reckoned in periods that were far too short. Events that if telescoped into a few decades and centuries resembled catastrophes became gradual modifications if they were considered in terms of a few hundreds of thousands of years. The Diluvial age need not have been a deluge or a geological convulsion. It might just as well have taken aeons over its gradual conquest of various regions. If that were so, its erratic boulders could be quite naturally interpreted as normal formations and deposits. Goethe shared von Hoff's view, and he made further discoveries. Neither water nor volcanic activity could have strewn those erratic boulders of the Diluvial age over the land. There was only one substance in nature that could carry great fragments of rock on its back like ships. That was ice. When he heard one day that huge icefloes laden with granite had floated through the Skagerrak he was, in his own words, "thrown into raptures." The vision of an "ice age" rose before him for the first time. Glaciers or oceanic currents full of drift-ice had once covered the plains where erratic boulders now lay. They deposited rubble and rock there. And that ice age had not suddenly descended upon level country like an avalanche. An inconceivable length of time had been required before it could leave its indelible runic inscriptions upon the surface of the earth.

Charles Lyell knew nothing of either Goethe's or von Hoff's ideas while he was investigating the formation of the earth at King's College, London, in 1830. He was a barrister by profession but by the time he was twenty-two had already become a member of the British Geological Society, having a natural taste for the subject. At that time geology in England was dominated by Hutton's vulcanism and prehistory by Cuvier's theory of catastrophes. The recognized authority in both fields of knowledge was William Buckland, a rigid adherent of the French school. Like most scientists of his day he regarded the Diluvial age as a period of vast inundations brought about by geological convulsion. He believed neither in gradual geological change nor in the metamorphosis of forms of life, and still less in any great antiquity of the human race. When, after Cuvier's death, the finds of Frere and McEnery and the Red Lady of Paviland began to be discussed again and the question was once more raised whether man had been contemporary with the mammoth, Buckland represented the hostile camp. He did refer to these finds in his book *Reliquiae diluvianae,* but strongly advised the geologists and prehistorians of England against demolishing the edifice of the prevailing theory in favor of a few stones and bones of doubtful origin.

Accordingly, it was a daring step for the young former barrister Lyell to declare war against the great Buckland. He knew perfectly well what the result would be, for it not only raised the issue of whether the earth had assumed its present aspect in consequence of catastrophes or gradual alterations, but also the extremely knotty problem of prehistoric man, which had already obliged many a rebel to give up the struggle. Lyell was made of sterner stuff than the vacillating Baron von Schlotheim. He studied geological history profoundly for ten years. He found that such geological processes as could be observed in modern times would be quite enough to account for the structure of the whole of the solid part of the earth's crust if they had only occurred often enough and over sufficiently long periods. His conclusions, which were the same as von Hoff's unnoticed theories, were announced in three volumes published between 1830 and 1833 under the title, *Principles of Geology*. This publication marked an epoch. It began modern geology, the exact scientific investigation of prehistory, and ultimately the unmasking of Adam.

According to Lyell the history of the earth had not included any of Werner's floods or Hutton's rivers of fire. What scientists had thought to be catastrophes were deceptive and deluding pictures. Nature had worked upon the earth's crust over enormously long periods by the agencies of water and ice, volcanoes and geological convulsions, just as she does today, and in this way slowly changed its appearance, without making any destructive onslaughts. But since men had only been able to observe the effects and not the processes of such changes they had erroneously inferred that geological revolutions must have taken place.

The *Principles of Geology* upset all the notions of time hitherto conceived by geologists, reckoned the duration of the various epochs in millions of years and dated the production of the different types of minerals, plants, animals, and humanity itself so far back that the units of time assumed in Buffon's story of the earth shrank, by comparison, to seconds. Nor did Lyell hesitate to apply his geological principles without qualification to organic nature. If insignificant causes had produced, over a long period, such great changes in the surface of the earth as to seem like geological revolutions to present-day observers, similarly insignificant causes over a similarly long period would be able to produce alterations in animate beings which today might well be regarded as new creations, new species, genera, and orders. Geological evolution logically implied the evolution of the inhabitants of the earth.

The English public gave this revolutionary work a most friendly reception. Lyell had been prudent enough to eliminate any possibility of misunderstanding and error from the start by employing a whole staff of like-minded scientists to assist him in his profound geological investigations. He could support every assertion made in the *Principles* by a wealth of evidence. His old adversary Buckland, who stubbornly opposed him by arguing alternately for the Biblical story of creation and Hutton's vulcanism, was defeated again and again. He fell into the worst trap of all when he tried to refute Lyell's conjecture that the Diluvial age had been a glacial period and restore the Flood to the enjoyment of its former authority.

Lyell's work had not been out very long before this very question of the Ice Age was decided once for all. A Huguenot born in Saxony, living in the Pays de Vaud, and belonging to a respected family of geologists of the name of Charpentier, had been inspired by a conversation with a Swiss chamois hunter to publish a sensational paper affirming that the much discussed erratic boulders and the entire subalpine landscape had been formed solely by gigantic glaciers of a former era. Louis Agassiz, the young professor of natural history at Neuchâtel, got into touch with Charpentier. He took a learned staff, including that radical Karl Vogt who repudiated the existence of the soul, on an expedition to the Alps, confirmed Charpentier's conjectures, and expanded them into a "glacial theory." Central Europe, it was proved as a result of these investigations, had been subjected to glaciation on one or even several occasions during the Diluvial age. It was ice that had carried the erratic boulders and deposits of rubble to the plains. The Diluvial animals, the mammoth, the rhinoceros, and the cave bear, had been children of the ice — polar creatures.

Lyell's work was thus strikingly substantiated in one essential point. The Deluge, whose traces had been so desperately sought by all Floodists from Scheuchzer to Buckland, now finally had to resign its place in prehistoric times both early and late. Lyell's opinions on other questions of geology, too, gradually made their way in England. His country's mentality and history were a great help to him in this connection. In the rest of Europe history had consisted from time immemorial of an incessant series of quarrels, riots, wars, and revolutions. It was easy to assume a similar series of events in nature. But in England greater moderation had been shown in the conduct of affairs. British habits of life and thought therefore rendered men far more prone to believe in a gradual process of growth. Just as Cuvier had been a product of the bloody French Revolution, so Lyell was a product of the bloodless Liberal movement in England. He received the respectful, if not boisterous, applause of his fellow countrymen, was soon appointed a professor, and at barely forty years of age became England's leading geologist.

It was not until he set himself to do away with the "successive acts of creation" postulated by the school of Cuvier, to identify fossils correctly, and to look for traces of Ice Age man that the conflict flared up afresh. Though geologists had accepted almost unanimously his principles relating to a slow and steady alteration of the earth's surface, the paleontologists and prehistorians remained as refractory as ever and would not hear of plants, animals, and men being subjected to the same laws as minerals. It had hitherto been most convenient to be able to refer every fossil to a definite geological layer and, following William Smith, actually to distinguish between the various geological formations by indicating their "fossil guides." But if the various layers and acts of creation could no longer be regarded as separate — if for example, as Lyell maintained, apes and primitive men had existed in the Diluvial age or even earlier, though according to Cuvier these creatures were the "fossil guides" of the present age — the most reliable means of identifying eras would break down and the whole system would have to be abandoned.

The result was that the paleontologists suddenly closed their ranks against the man who was renovating geology, not because they doubted his geological discernment, but because they wanted to preserve fossils and the problem of mankind from his interference. William Buckland, by this time Dean of Westminster and more and more inclined to turn his geology into theology, found allies in Alcide d'Orbigny, Cuvier's loyal executor, and Richard Owen, the leading collector of and expert on prehistoric animal remains in England. They were joined by the most strenuous defender of the doctrine of creation, Louis Agassiz, of all people, the very man who had pioneered the Ice Age theory. He believed that the Ice Age had been a sudden geological revolution of diluvial type. It was not until it ended, he maintained, that apes and human beings had appeared on the scene. Once again the mortally wounded theory of catastrophes rose to aim a blow at the renegade geologists. Geological formations and their fossils, Agassiz proclaimed, indicated that there had been a number of separate acts of creation. They were, so to speak, an illustrated report on God's activities since the production of the world. Agassiz subsequently became the most serious antagonist of Charles Lyell and the latter's later adherent, Charles Darwin.

Lyell's demonstration of the existence of prehistoric apes and human beings is a masterpiece of natural science detective work. His researches lasted thirty years and were crowned with success. Though he himself did not discover any prehistoric men, he had a hand in all the important finds of his time. It was thanks to him and his collaborators that the cases of Conyers, Esper, Frere, Schlotheim, McEnery, and Schmerling did not recur and that Darwin, in his reflections upon the descent of man, was able to use an abundance of material — beginning with the Tertiary anthropoid apes, passing on to primitive Neanderthal man, and ending with the Cro-Magnon type of the Late Ice Age.

In this connection it is interesting to think that Lyell regarded these elaborately planned researches simply as a hobby for his spare time. Tertiary apes and Diluvial human beings attracted him less than the geological transition from the Tertiary to the Diluvial age and from the Diluvial to the present. He only needed Adam's bones as additional props for his principles of geology.

The monkey of Pikermi

If a fossilized ape is discovered nowadays hardly anyone but a few professional experts gets excited. In 1838 it was different: if the ape came from an early geological period it would demolish the whole theory of catastrophes.

The hero of the following incident did not know this, and in any case he was not in the least addicted to speculations on prehistoric and zoological problems. His name has not come down to us. All we know is that he was a Bavarian soldier from Landshut who accompanied the Wittelsbach Prince Otto to Athens after the latter's coronation as King of Greece. The lad from Landshut did his duty there as a loyal subject, went on patrol, mounted guard, taught the Greek girls Bavarian customs, and enjoyed all the weird and wonderful adventures that fall to the lot of soldiers on foreign service. During lectures in the courtyard of the castle at Athens he and his comrades listened to learned noncommissioned officers and budding elementary schoolteachers spouting Homer and Hesiod. On those occasions they heard of Zeus and Apollo, that she-devil Helen, Agamemnon, Odysseus, and all sorts of bloody combats and heroic deeds. For King Otto was a connoisseur of Greek history and wanted his men to find out everything about the country they were in.

The foot soldiers from Munich, Rosenheim, Straubing, and the Bavarian Alps couldn't make head or tail of it. Most of them were less interested in ancient Hellas than in the modern resinous wine and the local women. But a few of them took the songs of Homer and Hesiod for gospel and set out, the spiritual forerunners of Schliemann, in search of relics of the times of fair Aphrodite and fairer Helen. Our friend from Landshut was one of them.

In 1838 he happened to be on patrol with a single companion near the little village of Pikermi in Attica. The pair of them suddenly stumbled across a few moldering bones in the dry bed of a brook. Calcareous spar crystals glittered in the medullary cavities. They looked like diamonds. The man from Landshut felt quite interested. The place might once have been a cemetery, where the heroes of ancient Hellas lay buried, or it might even have been a battlefield, full of treasures and precious stones, one of those waste pieces of ground so circumstantially described by Homer, on which the heroes fought. He urged his companion to fix his bayonet and start digging.

The result was amazing. All at once, the man from Landshut found himself staring at a whole lot of skulls and skeletons that a few thrusts of the bayonet had unearthed and sent rolling about all over the place. He picked up one of the skulls and examined it. It was certainly a bit on the small side. But perhaps the hot Greek sun had shrunk it. He opened his pack to stow away the thing.

"I shouldn't do that!" his comrade warned him. He added that a cemetery was a cemetery, whether Achilles or only old Alois Moosbacher happened to be buried in it. Better leave that sort of stuff alone!

The Landshut man could already see himself regaling his people at home with tales of the Hellenic warriors, and was looking forward to shoving the proof of his stories under the noses of his brother Wastl and his neighbor Hiasl. He resolutely packed the grinning death's head among his rations, took one more look at the pile of bones, picked up what he thought were diamonds, and gave the command: "Come on, off we go!"

The world would probably never have heard anything about the treasures of Pikermi if the finder had not shortly afterwards been granted his well-deserved leave. Six months later he might have forgotten all about the skull and the sparkling, hollow, cylindrical bones. As it was, he proudly carried his souvenirs of the "heroes' cemetery" in his knapsack on his arrival in Munich after a long journey, and fetched them out every time he got a chance to boast of his find. And as he wanted to celebrate his return to Bavaria in style, he didn't take the next stagecoach to Landshut, but stayed on for a while in the nearest tavern. He sat there, tanned as brown as a berry, the center of an inquisitive group, and told tales of his experiences abroad. He talked about King Otto in Athens, the hot sun and the dark women, Achilles and Agamemnon, and drank one pot of beer after another. At last, when some of his boon companions started staring at him incredulously, he slammed the Pikermi skull angrily down on the table. "There you are, there's Achilles!" he shouted. "I got him out of a churchyard, the old devil!"

A few minutes later a policeman in a spiked helmet tapped him on the shoulder. The man from Landshut turned round in astonishment. Then he gazed guiltily and gloomily at the skull, with its toothy grin, lying in a pool of beer. "Come along with me!" thundered the guardian of the law. He added, by way of explanation, in a most indignant tone: "That's a disgraceful thing you've done, my lad! It's a desecration of the dead!"

In great dejection the adventurous student of Hellas followed the representative of public authority to the police station. The inspector listened to the charge with the serious attention it deserved, picked up the exhibit in the case with the tips of his fingers, stuck a numbered ticket on it, and then made a set speech. Did the delinquent realize what it meant to rob a churchyard? Had the delinquent forgotten all moral restraint and decency while resident among the heathen in that distant land? Was the delinquent ready to confess and repent of his offense?

"Well, I was drunk," declared the defendant plaintively. He added that he had not been telling the truth at the tavern but just bragging a bit too much. The skull, he said, wasn't that of Achilles, but —

"But what?" demanded the inspector sternly. He had meanwhile discovered the "diamonds" in the knapsack and found the case still more puzzling.

The man from Landshut took a deep breath. He stammered for a moment, then stood rigidly at attention and exclaimed with the courage of despair, "Well, I mean, it was a dog's skull!"

"What about these then?" The inspector pointed to the calcareous spar crystals.

"They're dog's bones," murmured the man from Landshut defiantly.

Dog's bones? The inspector looked dubiously at his subordinate. He didn't know much about bones. The case would have to be investigated at a higher level by experts. He let the man from Landshut go to sleep and passed on the hero's skull and the "diamonds" to his superiors. They informed him, next day, that the confiscated bones were neither those of human beings nor those of dogs. Still less were they diamonds. The skull was doubtless that of an animal and would be subjected to a further special examination. Consequently Schliemann's forerunner might be allowed to go on his way to Landshut unmolested, but minus his Pikermi baggage. The objects in question passed through a number of different hands, for the file about "grave desecration in Attica" would of course have to be brought to a proper conclusion with a clear and satisfactory statement. Thus the articles discovered eventually found their way into the hands of Professor Wagner of Munich. It turned out that the man from Landshut had unearthed a fossilized ape, not very different from the modern *Semnopithecus*, the long-tailed species of monkey.

Many years later the French paleontologist Albert Gaudry traveled to the locality of the find and actually came upon a cemetery there, though it did not contain human bones, but those of innumerable species of animals dating from the early Tertiary period. The remains of many more monkeys were among them. Today the Pikermi skull is called *Mesopithecus pentelicus*. It belongs to one of the most important groups of extinct monkeys, that from which all antique genera of apes probably arose.

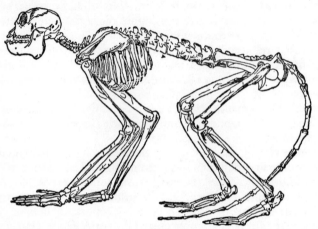

The Pikermi monkey. Albert Gaudry's drawing of the skeleton of the *Mesopithecus pentelicus*.

The facts had proved the followers of Cuvier to have been wrong. So early a period as the Tertiary, the epoch of the *Dinotherium* and the giant sloth, had known monkeys of extremely modern aspect. In France people were prudent enough not to draw any hasty conclusions from the discovery. But in England the search for the Ice Age was immediately undertaken all the more intensively. And the first traces identified by Lyell and his pupils led to the very country that had for so long refused to listen to anything about Adam — France.

An argument about Adam's ancestors

The two Frenchmen who started the ball rolling were amateur investigators like Canon Scheuchzer and Father Esper. The learned world had scoffed at them before the English geologists began to communicate with them. One, an unassuming lawyer named Edouard Lartet, assisted the farmers of the little village of Gers in various legal transactions. The other, a less unassuming man of letters named Jacques Boucher de Crèvecoeur de Perthes, acted as surveyor of customs in the town of Abbéville. It was the longing for knowledge that induced the lawyer Lartet to study prehistory. It was ambition that led the man of letters Boucher de Perthes to do the same thing. Lartet worked at his discoveries with pedantic thoroughness; Boucher de Perthes made sensational revelations. And as at all times sensations have been more effective than disinterested industry the decisive step was taken, not in Gers but in Abbéville.

Lartet first resolved to devote himself to prehistoric investigation when a farmer brought him a gigantic molar he had plowed up. The lawyer immediately looked up his Cuvier and identified it as the masticator of an aboriginal elephant. The animal was called a mastodon by scientists. How long could the tooth actually have been lying in French soil? Could mankind have been already in existence at that time? Lartet decided to pursue the matter and undertake excavations on his own account. It made an agreeable change in his extremely monotonous life, which had hitherto mainly brought him into contact with human baseness and sordid greed.

As early as 1830, while Cuvier was still alive, he began digging in the environs of Gers. He found nothing important, but he did not give up. He heard about the learned disputes on the question whether mankind had been a contemporary of the great extinct elephants or not. He discovered that people in England were beginning to have doubts about Cuvier's denial of the existence of fossilized human beings, and as time went on he extended his excavation work to other regions of France. His most brilliant inspiration was to investigate the natural caves of the rocky districts in the south of the country. He believed that the earliest types of primitive humanity might well have made their dwellings in such places. His theory was destined to be confirmed later on, in a way that he would never have believed possible.

Before these discoveries began, Lartet had made quite a different find, dating from a much earlier period. It was regarded right down to the present time as one of the most important props of the theory of evolution. In 1837, a year before the Pikermi affair, he dug up at Saint-Gaudens, on the north gradient of the Pyrenees, the bone of the upper arm and several fragments of the skull of a creature resembling a human being. It had been slightly smaller than a chimpanzee, apparently combined the characteristics of ape and man and had undoubtedly lived in the Middle Tertiary period, which was the main thing from Lartet's point of view, so that contrary to the prevailing opinion, as early as this epoch there existed in Europe, beings that in part resembled the gibbon, in part the chimpanzee, and in part Man.

This was news that ought to have made the academicians of Paris sit up. But these gentlemen, led by Alcide d'Orbigny, merely shrugged their shoulders. They did in the end admit that they had been wrong about the antiquity of apes. But they refused to recognize that the *Dryopithecus*, as the creature from Saint-Gaudens was called later, had anything to do with mankind. After a certain amount of coming and going a formula was eventually agreed upon. The *Dryopithecus* had been a large-sized relative of the South Asiatic gibbon. It was most remarkable that gibbons should have lived in the European Tertiary period. Still, the sky was not going to fall for that reason.

It was not until the time of Darwin and his forerunners Huxley and Haeckel that the *Dryopithecus* was again taken up and more closely examined. Many other bones of similar type were discovered in Europe, Asia, and Africa. It was established that Lartet had actually unearthed the first representative of an antique group of anthropoid apes, now regarded as the radical form of all the higher apes and very nearly related to the brutish ancestors of mankind. The structure of the *Dryopithecus*, that cave-dwelling contemporary of the monstrous mastodon and *Dinotherium*, which was more primitive than the chimpanzee and gorilla, already comprised certain basic features that were to lead to the later *Homo sapiens*.

Meanwhile the second amateur of the spade had come to the front in the shape of the fashionable author and surveyor of customs Boucher de Perthes. He had astonished his French fellow citizens with the statement that he could prove the existence of Tertiary man. Lartet was induced by him and by his own find at Saint-Gaudens to follow a false trail. Henceforth he searched Tertiary layers indefatigably for the remains of primitive human beings, for he had concluded, like many later investigators of prehistory, that at a time when apes had lived men too must already have existed. It was not yet realized at that date that the epoch of geological history between Tertiary and modern times, in other words the Diluvial age, with its glacial periods, had lasted over half a million years. The Ice Age was believed to be a phenomenon of relatively short duration. It was consequently thought that primitive human beings, if they existed at all, were only to be found in the Tertiary period. And as Lartet, despite all his efforts, could discover no human traces in the Tertiary layers in France, he eventually gave up the struggle. But he stuck to his opinion that mankind had formerly shared accommodation with the cave ape of Saint-Gaudens.

For the first time, the question assumed a different aspect when Lyell arrived in France with a group of colleagues and seized upon the material supplied by Boucher de Perthes. The latter had hitherto cut more of a figure in sensational newspapers than among scientists. The Abbéville surveyor of customs was generally regarded as a sentimental composer of books with a peculiar tendency to expatiate not only upon love, women, morals, and the fascination of foreign countries but also upon minerals, and he was considered a bit of a crank. No one thought it worth while to deprive him of his theory about Tertiary human beings.

As a young man Boucher de Perthes had belonged to the circle of political-minded authors at the court of Napoleon. He had written numerous comedies and tragedies for the Parisian stage and had also traveled over half of Europe on various missions. The Restoration put an end to these activities; but he retained his literary ambitions. His work in the dull little port of Abbéville did not satisfy him. He began by taking up political economy, then championed the emancipation of women and drew tears from the readers of his epistolary romance *Emma*. Next he broke a lance on behalf of the theory of evolution, and, inspired by the spirit of Geoffroy Saint-Hilaire, he wrote a work on natural philosophy in five volumes which dealt with the origin and development of animate beings. Nevertheless, these excursions into economics, sociology, and science did not achieve the success he desired. The reading public thought that everything he produced must be fiction, and fiction was of no interest to politicians and scholars.

Then he heard that workmen in the quarries of Moulin-Quignon in the Somme valley had made all sorts of prehistoric finds, the kind of stones and bones of animals that the brothers d'Orbigny were collecting in Paris. He immediately set out for the spot, which was situated not very far from Abbéville. The environment was one Boucher de Perthes must surely have contemplated with silent veneration. For here Lamarck had been born. We may assume that the surveyor, as a student of nature, knew the *Zoological Philosophy* of the unlucky man from Picardy and that it had greatly stimulated him. But he was not content with inspecting the landscape and turning his thoughts to natural philosophy. He also wielded the spade. He dug it into the chalky soil of Moulin-Quignon and burrowed deep into several layers of sand and clay that covered one another like the skins of an onion.

He may be forgiven for not proceeding on wholly scientific lines. He knew very little about geological conditions in the chalk hills of Picardy. They were explained by Lyell when he visited the neighborhood. Ever since early times the sea and the river had been sinking channels there and depositing sand and clay. The topmost layer dated from the modern period. It consisted of fine sand in which innumerable shellfish had been buried. Below that lay the characteristic coarse sand of the Diluvial period, the Ice Age. It contained the bones of mammoths, woolly rhinoceroses, the ancient bison, the ancient wild horse, the elk, the cave lion, and other Diluvial animals. Deeper still one came upon the argillaceous earth of the Tertiary period. The whole series had the effect of an impressive display. The trained investigator only needed to make a proper division between the layers to ascertain what creatures had lived in the Tertiary, Diluvial, and post-Diluvial, or Alluvial, ages, the latter having lasted down to the present time. But the author of *Emma* was not this kind of trained investigator.

He unearthed, as Conyers, Frere, and Schlotheim had done before him, the bones of animals belonging to the Ice Age. And among them he found, like his predecessors, a number of curiously hewn flints shaped like almonds, with one thick end suitable for being held and the other pointed, with sharp edges. Some looked like daggers, others like spear points, scrapers, and awls. They were not the first Paleolithic hand axes (one of the most ancient types of tool made by man) ever to be found. Such flints had often been picked up from the ground and thrown carelessly away again, being considered merely freaks of nature. The thought at once flashed through the mind of Boucher de Perthes that they must be primitive men's tools. And as he had not made a very careful division between the layers and thus mixed Diluvial sand with Tertiary clay, he attributed far greater antiquity to the flints than they really possessed. On his return he reported to the Paris Academy of Sciences that he had discovered the culture of mankind in the Tertiary period.

The professors were rather disagreeable about it. Such paleoliths, they politely informed the enthusiastic layman from Abbéville, were produced by the silicium secretions of lower marine animals and in course of time became hardened and fossilized. It was not the hand of man but natural processes of decay and demolition that had given them their present form. Boucher de Perthes refused to be put off by this professorial explanation. He had at last obtained the great opportunity of his life. The discoveries at Moulin-Quignon were more precious to him than any successful comedy or novel. He intended to fight for them to the last. And as he knew only too well that facts alone do not convince people if they are not accompanied by the right sort of propaganda, he began to publicize his discoveries for all he was worth.

The works on *Celtic Antiquities* which he now produced in quick succession appealed in a unique way to French patriotism. The Gallic race, he declared in these books, was of high antiquity. Picardy had been the cradle of human civilization. As early as the Tertiary period "Adam's ancestors" had been hunting monsters of the elephant type on the soil of France. This sort of thing was found to please readers. This aggressive searcher for Adam achieved a result which only that apostle of the Flood, Scheuchzer, had obtained before him. The masses of the people became inquisitive and scented a sensation.

The academicians in Paris, forced by public opinion to take action, determined, for better or worse, to send a committee to the Somme valley to examine the finds. But to the boundless disappointment of Boucher de Perthes the gentlemen concerned soon established the fact that the worthy customs officer, that poetical surveyor, had treated the separate geological layers in very arbitrary fashion. There could be no question at all of flints from the Tertiary period. The writings of Boucher de Perthes on *Antediluvian Man and His Works* bristled with the errors of an amateur. The author of *Emma* did not seem to understand anything whatever about prehistory. He had exaggerated and produced an unidentified stone as evidence of the oldest of all human cultures.

Though the professors had been prejudiced when they began their investigation and had not by any means subjected their finds to a proper examination, the blow had fallen so suddenly that Boucher de Perthes was thrown into a state of complete despair. His sensation-mongering readers felt they had been taken in by a dishonest piece of journalism, and they revenged themselves by laughing at him. Even those who had hitherto backed and admired him thought that he had tried to bamboozle the hallowed representatives of science, and that his prehistoric studies were really only disguised romances. People enjoyed the notion that Adam's ancestors had once lived in Picardy, but in the same way as they enjoyed Jules Verne's novels about the future.

Boucher de Perthes made every effort to clear up the misunderstanding. He had been fifty when he first took a glance into prehistory in the valley of the Somme. At the age of seventy he was still fighting in vain for recognition of prehistoric man. The public

had long since grown bored with the topic: the vision of a journey
to the moon replaced the vision of an antique mammoth hunt, and
the learned world considered the persistence of this argumentative
man of letters scandalous. Boucher de Perthes had actually founded
a Société d'Emulation in Abbéville, to break with scientific prejudice,
and made himself president of it. In the eyes of the scientists he
was not merely a harmless lunatic like most of the sons of the muses
in the Latin Quarter but, owing to his perpetual complaints and
accusations, a public danger.

Such was the situation as Lyell found it; but he was not in the
least perturbed by the opinion of the French experts. Boucher de
Perthes might be this, that, or the other. The only important point
was, what had he found? The great geologist, accompanied by his
friend and pupil Hugh Falconer, traveled at once to the valley of
the Somme. He had a talk with the elderly surveyor and carefully
examined all the chief localities in which stone tools had been found.
He himself dug up no less than seventy paleoliths. They were unmistakable lanceheads, knives, hand axes, and other small implements of different kinds. However inaccurately Boucher de Perthes
might have worked, his interpretation of the objects was correct in
principle. In one respect, neverthless, he was wrong. All the flints
belonged to the Diluvial, not the Tertiary, epoch. They were productions of the Ice Age man.

The workmanship of these hand axes and stone tools was so neat
and accomplished that Lyell and Falconer could not imagine how
they could ever have been misinterpreted. Primitive man had not
improvised. He had not hastily chipped a few flints to serve as make-
shifts. The whole arsenal of weapons and tools showed that they
were the result of hereditary skill practised over a long period. They
represented a stage of genuine human culture, existing at a time
when the saber-toothed tiger, the cave bear and the cave lion, the
woolly rhinoceros and the elk had lived. The teachings of Cuvier,
d'Orbigny, and Agassiz received an unprecedented shock.

A year later a group of English scientists carried out a second series
of excavations near Abbéville and authoritatively revised the statements of Boucher de Perthes. Such were the admittedly tentative
beginnings of the victorious career of a completely new science, the
prehistory of mankind. Cuvier's line of demarcation was erased.
The existence of prehistoric man was a fact. All that now remained
to be done was to try to establish the antiquity of the human race,
the appearance and mode of life of Adam, and the course of development of his culture. The tenants of the citadels of the theory of

catastrophes at first, to be sure, shut their eyes to all this. Paris did not capitulate until Edouard Lartet, the modest lawyer from Gers, resumed his excavations with English support, and this time at the proper place.

Boucher de Perthes enjoyed a triumph at last. He was not, however, quite satisfied with the support given him by his colleague Lyell. The Tertiary man had bewitched him; since his whole work had been founded on this idea he refused to give it up. Five years after Lyell's visit to Moulin-Quignon, Boucher de Perthes found a fossilized human jawbone and once more proclaimed that he had discovered the real Adam. As a result, he dated the antiquity of Man so far back that even his British supporters grew slightly impatient. They pointed out that although the jawbone was of course of epoch-making importance he ought not to spoil the effect of his discovery by drawing unjustifiable conclusions from it, for it could hardly be doubted that the bone dated from the Ice Age, not from the Tertiary period. The old gentleman at Abbéville declined to be convinced. Tenacious, like Cuvier, he stuck to his main point that antediluvian man exists, right up to his death in 1868.

The paradise of primitive man

Christian Jürgensen Thomsen, son of a Copenhagen merchant, had had an extremely respectable career mapped out for him. He was to take over his father's business and concern himself with bookkeeping, the balancing of accounts, and similarly useful but scientifically unproductive matters. For a man interested in art, who had begun collecting coins, medals, and all sorts of antiquities at an early age, the prospect was not very satisfactory. Nevertheless, such activities did bring in money. He was able to increase his collections and soon made a name for himself as the highest authority on the history of art and prehistory in all Denmark.

Accordingly, whenever his countrymen turned up an ancient burial ground with the plow or unearthed a sword covered with the green patina of antiquity they went to his house and asked him whether the find was important. He had all the objects discovered in Danish soil brought to him and set up an "Ancient Nordic Museum" in Copenhagen, the first of its kind. Here he exhibited the products of early European cultures. Thomsen confirmed what Eckart, the misunderstood student of the ancient Germans, had revealed a hundred years before: human civilization had gradually developed to its present high level from extremely remote beginnings.

Scandinavian and German collectors of antiquities followed in Thomsen's footsteps. Half-obliterated sepulchral barrows began to be investigated. Skeletons, ornaments, and weapons dating from the times of the ancient Germans and earlier were unearthed. Finally three great epochs of human history were established, the Stone Age, the Bronze Age, and the Iron Age.

Since Thomsen's time the Iron Age had been held to be the epoch of human civilization that has lasted down to the present day. It was preceded by the Bronze Age, in which men had used for the manufacture of their implements at first copper and subsequently an alloy of copper and tin. This was the period in which states and civilizations arose, reaching their culminating points in the realm of the Pharaohs and Homeric Greece. Farther back still, as abundant discoveries proved, lay an era in which metals were unknown, that of the Stone Age. Men were already engaged in agriculture and pastoral pursuits in this period, as well as in the production of decorative pottery. But their weapons and tools suddenly assumed an entirely different aspect. They were made of hornblende, nephrite, flint, obsidian (vitreous lava), and other stones. Mineral axes and chisels, saws and borers, arrowheads and lanceheads, knives, scrapers, and burins of this kind, often fastened to a wooden haft with a clamp of stag's horn, were repeatedly found in the oldest burial places. Even traces of workshops, in which the Stone Age men had worked up their materials and chipped, split, and ground them into their proper form, were discovered.

Such data, supplied by Thomsen and his successors, had by Lyell's time long been the common property of scientists. Nor did they annoy the learned in the opposite camp. For the Stone Age, apparently the earliest stage of the development of civilization, lay at most, according to Thomsen's investigations, 6000 years back. Sepulchral barrows, the tombs of warriors, buried settlements, and destroyed cities might prove that civilization had slowly progressed from the use of the stone knife to the invention of the railway by Stephenson. But no such developments could have gone as far back as the twilight of earlier geological eras.

However, Lyell and Falconer then appeared on the scene and declared that before the time of nephrite borers and obsidian knife-blades humanity had lived on a still more primitive cultural level. Simple, roughly flaked scrapers and hand axes, made of flint, had then been the only weapons and implements. Thomsen's Stone Age should more properly be called the "Late Stone Age," because it belonged to the present geological epoch. But the "Old Stone

Age," the genuine primitive culture discovered at Moulin-Quignon, was Diluvial.

The English scientists systematically explored their own country in order to prove their point. As early as 1850 the geologist Godwin Austen visited Kent's Cavern and inspected the place where Parson McEnery had found his hand axes. Other geologists followed him. It was proved that the parson had been right. Eight years later Hugh Falconer, backed by the Royal Society, undertook excavations in the so-called Windmill Cave near Brixham in Devonshire. Another year passed. Then the geologist Prestwich opened up the John Frere file again and explored the neighborhood of Hoxne in the county of Suffolk. The picture turned out to be the same everywhere. Broken stone tools lay scattered among the bones of mammoths and other animals of the Ice Age. It thus became clear to the learned world in England that human beings and mammoths had lived at the same time.

There was nothing their adversaries could say. The chief of them, old Buckland, withdrew from the struggle. He went out of his mind and died in 1856 at Clapham near London. Agassiz accepted an invitation to the United States, founded a great zoological museum at Harvard University with the support of rich businessmen, gained a considerable reputation for his services, especially in the domain of ichthyology, and took no further share in the conflict until Darwin's theory began its triumphant tour round the world. The professors of France finally confessed themselves convinced by the documents which Ice Age man himself had submitted as proofs of his existence.

Edouard Lartet, stimulated by the finds of a truffle hunter in the Dordogne, had resumed his investigations in the grottoes and caves of southern France. But with less obstinacy than Boucher de Perthes he now limited his researches to the Diluvial age, abandoning the Tertiary. He was given generous support from England. Henry Christy, an industrialist extraordinarily interested in prehistoric matters and a keen partisan of Lyell's, financed Lartet's excavations and thus relieved him of the need to earn a living. Christy's faith was rewarded. In September 1860 Lartet and his friend Alfred Fontan came across a layer at Massat in the department of Ariège which to all appearance consisted of the kitchen waste and cultural relics of the Ice Age. In addition to the bones of animals and flints, litter left by mankind — such as antlers, the fragments of tools and so on — lay about in such profusion that Lartet immediately cried, "There must have been a human settlement here!" He looked more closely at the heaps of rubbish. And there he found part of the antlers of a stag. The unmistakable head of a cave bear had been crudely scratched on the horn.

His heart beat excitedly as he examined this primitive work of art. He remembered an incident of some twenty years before. A professional colleague of his, the lawyer Brouillet, had found a remarkable bone in a grotto near the town of Savigne. Two does were engraved on it. Brouillet had been of the opinion that the engraving had been made by a primitive man, but the learned world had described it as a crude sketch done by children in play. Brouillet was now justified. For no human being of the present day, apart from a few scientists, knew what the long extinct cave bear had been like. Only a man of the Ice Age could have scratched such a picture. In 1861 Lartet published his views in an article accompanied by an account of Brouillet's long forgotten discovery.

Then even his most stubborn adversaries climbed down. They revised their earlier views about the beginnings of human civilization and pushed the line of demarcation a bit farther back. And when, shortly afterwards, Lartet and Christy, who had hurried out from England to join him, were able to announce the discovery of vast quantities of Ice Age artifacts in the Vézère valley, in the department of Dordogne, widespread interest was aroused. The Vézère valley came in the course of time to mean the same for prehistory as the Valley of the Kings meant for Egyptology. One surprise followed another in this "paradise of primitive man." The first collection of prehistoric engravings, coming from a grotto near the village of Bruniquel, was taken to London and lodged in the British Museum, where it aroused great admiration and soon made the Vézère valley popular. Other finds remained in France, and were destined to occupy a place of honor at the Paris International Exhibition.

The opening of the Vézère valley inaugurated the period of excavation on a scientific basis. It was not only geologists and prehistorians who participated in it. Connoisseurs of art, anthropologists, and zoologists, including the Belgian natural scientist Henri Milne-Edwards, who lived in Paris and had published the posthumous works of Lamarck in eleven volumes, accompanied the expeditions. France was quickly catching up on England's flying start. The former Gers lawyer was joined by Gabriel de Mortillet, the second pioneer of the science of primitive man, who tried to arrange the early human cultures in a systematic order and to date them as precisely as possible. A new era had dawned.

In 1864 Lartet and Christy crowned their work in the paradise of primitive man by finding a mammoth's tusk. It lay beneath an overhanging cliff near La Madeleine and bore the picture of a mammoth incised with a sharp flint tool. The layer was a virgin one. No one had been near it since the Ice Age. No more convincing piece of evidence could be imagined. It was, so to speak, a written document, positive proof that primitive man had lived early enough to have known the mammoth. This engraving was the showpiece at the International Exhibition of 1867. A dense mass of spectators gathered in front of it. The drawings of the cave bear and the deer, as well as the hand axes and lanceheads from the Vézère valley, soon became the subject of daily conversation in Paris. The general opinion was that the people of the Ice Age, capable of artistic production of this quality, could really hardly have been primitive barbarians.

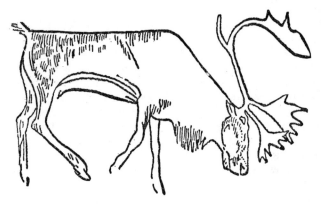

The first information about the art of the Old Stone Age was provided by drawings of animals scratched on fragments of antlers.

A year after the Exhibition in Paris the world learned what the creators of the art of the Dordogne had actually looked like. Henry Christy, the great patron of the investigation of remote antiquity, did not live to see this historic event. He had died in 1865. After his death Lartet was left without financial resources. He was beginning to fear that he would only be able to carry on his work in the future to a very limited extent, when he heard that a new cave had been discovered in the course of railway construction near the village of Les Eyzies in the Vézère valley. His son Louis visited the spot, inspected this "Cro-Magnon" cave, which was completely filled with rubbish, and had it cleared. Under the rubbish lay not only carefully chipped flints, carved reindeer antlers, the perforated teeth of animals, ivory pendants, and the shells of marine snails pierced with holes, but also the skeletons of a whole family of Ice Age human beings! The Cro-Magnon cave was a natural museum of prehistory, a primitive dwelling that displayed the domestic life of late Diluvial men, from weapons, tools, ornaments, and the game hunted, to the inmates of the dwelling themselves.

At the back of the cave lay the "old man of Cro-Magnon," a strikingly convex male skull with a high forehead, a prominent nose, a pronounced chin, and a broad face. These were not the features of a semibrute, a savage cave man, but unquestionably those of a splendid specimen of genuine humanity. The skull differed mainly from those of modern Europeans in the powerful formation of the zygomatic arch, which gave the head an almost angular look. Three skeletons of younger men were found close by, as well as a female one, remarkable for two reasons. This Stone Age woman, as Louis Lartet, Mortillet, and other workers who investigated the find saw with the greatest astonishment, had undergone a cruel fate. Her skull showed a deep wound due to some cutting instrument, and close to the skeleton lay the remains of a child not yet completely out of the womb. What could have happened to her at that time, perhaps 30,000 years ago? Had some enemy, possibly a cannibal, attacked her during her pregnancy and tried to kill her? And was she then watched over and tended by the old tribal chief and his sons or followers in the Cro-Magnon cave? It was evident from the state of the wound in the skull that she was already recovering from it. But before the birth of her child death had suddenly overtaken her and her male companions in some other obscure manner. Had these Cro-Magnon people fallen victims to a battle, a pack of beasts of prey, or a geological catastrophe?

Lartet drew up an enthusiastic account of the lives and activities of these Ice Age people, as he firmly believed them to be.

The traces of repeated human occupations of the Cro-Magnon grotto [he wrote in his report on the find] are attributable to the same type of hunters. They may at first only have used the grotto as a shelter for gatherings to share the quarry hunted down in the neighborhood. Later on they occupied it as a permanent abode. And finally, as their kitchen waste piled up, continually raising the level of the floor and considerably diminishing the height of the cave till it was only just over three feet and made the place unsuitable to live in, they gradually abandoned it, only occasionally returning to bury their dead there. After they ceased to do so the cave became inaccessible or at most visited, perhaps, by foxes. The gradual process of decay covered this remarkable sepulcher with a layer of great depth, testifying, by this fact alone, to its high antiquity.

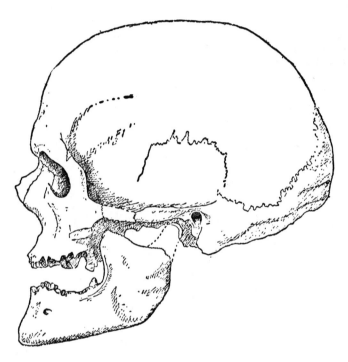

The old man of Cro-Magnon. Louis Lartet's great find: a representative of the Old Stone Age culture. The skeleton of the young woman and that of the embryo are no longer available, with the exception of the woman's skull, which is now in the Musée de l'Homme in Paris.

Gabriel de Mortillet, the system builder of prehistory, poured cold water on this enthusiasm and pronounced a dispassionate verdict that very much disappointed the young Lartet. In his view prehistoric but post-Ice Age men had rediscovered the old cave and used a recess in it to bury their dead. The old man of Cro-Magnon, his three companions, and the unfortunate woman were therefore not Diluvial human beings. The investigators of primitive man began to divide into two camps: with Lartet, on the one side, warmly extolling the Cro-Magnon people as the creators of the Ice Age culture of the Vézère valley; or with Mortillet, the skeptic on the other, believing them to be of a far later date.

It was again the valley of Vézère itself which decided the issue. Enthusiasm defeated skepticism. In Laugerie-Basse, at a spot where great landslides of rock had jammed vast quantities of stone tools and the bones of animals into a tight mass, a skeleton lay hidden which also belonged to a member of the Cro-Magnon race. A similar

This was the Old Stone Age man's idea of himself. A portrait of man with pointed beard, from a wall engraving in Les Combarelles, Dordogne.

find was made at Brantôme. Some half-dozen other accumulations of the remains of Cro-Magnon people then came to light in quick succession. The museums and private collections were sifted. Schmerling's man from the cave of Engis and the Red Lady from the Goat's Hole at Paviland were also proved to be racial and temporal associates of the old chieftain and his kinfolk. Who could then still believe in the misleading tricks supposed to have been played by crazy antiquarians?

A robust, heavily built, big-boned type of man — with a skull formation which according to some anthropologists, "might equally well have been that of a philosopher or an ancient Athenian" — lived among the large animals of the Late Ice Age, slaughtered and skinned them, cracked their bones and roasted their flesh. He was particularly fond of frequenting places where animals, pursued by beasts of prey, ran down steep gradients and perished on rocks, for he lived on their carcasses. In the so-called "slaughter yard" near the small village of Solutré, under a steep crag over a thousand feet high, more than fifty thousand bones of wild horses were discovered, mingled with tools and weapons. Two human skeletons lay close by. The men of the Ice Age must have held regular battles there. Yet these same men, who hunted wild beasts to survive in a pitiless environment, adorned their women within their caves with festoons of ivory and shells. They were able craftsmen and engravers. They had their own conceptions of death, and buried tools and food with their corpses. The *Homo sapiens diluvialis*, as Cro-Magnon man came to be called, did not differ essentially from the proud *Homo sapiens* of European civilization, but only in the degree of his culture.

Ethnological investigations were able to establish beyond the possibility of contradiction that the people of the Vézère valley were genuine ancestors of modern man. According to French scientists traces of their type had survived through the Late Stone Age down to the present day in the Dordogne. In central Sweden, Westphalia, and Hesse also, but especially among the Basques of the Pyrenees, the Berbers of North Africa, and the aboriginals of the Canary Islands, persons of decidedly Cro-Magnon aspect could still be found. They and other races closely akin to them had once inhabited the whole of northern Asia. They were the first to migrate to America across the Bering Strait. It proved that while Man was still a mammoth-hunter, he had conquered the world with his hand axe and flint knife.

What had the situation been like before then? That was now the great question. Once more excitement ran high, and the professors of the old school were to find the Fuhlrott case far more disturbing than those of Boucher de Perthes and Lartet.

A poor wretch from Neanderthal

Joachim Neumann, the author of the hymn "Praise to the Lord, the

Almighty, the King of creation," organist at Düsseldorf, and vicar of St. Martin's, could certainly never have dreamed that the name under which he wrote would one day serve to designate a brutish type of primitive man. In accordance with the practice of his learned age he had given his simple surname Neumann a sonorous ring by translating it into Greek as Neander. And later on his native town called a highly picturesque little vale between Düsseldorf and the village of Mettmann by the name of Neanderthal in his honor. This valley of Neumann's slumbered peacefully for nearly two hundred years, only disturbed by the occasional sounds of quarrying. It first became popular in 1856, when a secondary schoolteacher from Elberfeld heard that a strange discovery of bones had been made there.

There had originally been a large number of limestone caves in the Neanderthal. But they had gradually been demolished by the quarrying. We may assume that in this process many precious bones, misunderstood and disregarded, had been burned in the lime kilns. Only two caverns were now left, called the Feldhof grottoes. They were situated in the face of the cliff, some sixty feet above ground level. But they too were now attacked with blasting powder and pickaxes. Occasionally the workmen glanced into the grottoes. The entrances to them were so narrow that it was only just possible to see inside, and not practicable to go in. Later, this circumstance turned out to be important.

In the summer of 1856 the quarrymen blew up part of the cliff face. The entrances to the caves widened. Thereupon, as usual, the men entered the caves in order to remove the coating of loam from the interior and get to work on the rock face. The pickaxes came into action and lumps of earth came tumbling down the slope. The men swore a little, for the loam was tough and nearly six feet thick. Suddenly one of them pointed to some fossilized bones, remarking that they must have belonged to a human being buried there a long time ago. His mates nodded. Their feeling of reverence had only been faintly stirred, for without further ado they shoveled the bones out of the grotto and sent them showering down into the valley.

They fell at the feet of the owner of the quarry, who was going his rounds. He glanced upward. One of the workmen shouted down by way of explanation, "We're just clearing out an old skeleton's bones!" "Nonsense!" retorted his chief. He picked up one of the thick unwieldy fragments of bone. "These belonged to a bear. Collect them, will you? The schools may be able to do something with them."

Johann Karl Fuhlrott, teacher of natural science at the Elberfeld high school, was childishly delighted when he was told he could go and fetch a few cave bear bones from Neanderthal. He knew his natural history, being one of those pedagogues so numerous in Germany who wander industriously about their restricted native environment, examining every form of life and every stone they come across, and thus performing valuable small scale services to science. In his youth he had written a book about the various systems of plants proposed by the French botanists. He was well acquainted with zoology, too, and the geology of the hill country between Wupper, Düsselbach, and the Rhine was his special hobby. But genuine cave bear relics had never yet come his way. If what he heard were true his school collection would be enriched by a real treasure.

His delight turned to boundless astonishment when he saw the bones from one of the Feldhof grottoes. They were not the remains of cave bears: they were undoubtedly the bones of a manlike being of extraordinarily coarse and brutish build. He noticed that the vault of the skull lay low, was long, and much retracted. The brow ridges were massive above the eyeholes, like those of the giant gorilla first discovered a few years before by the English missionary Savage. The upper parts of the thighbones were so thick and heavy that it was no wonder they had been mistaken for the bones of a bear. They showed a curvature of a peculiar kind that at once caused Fuhlrott to suspect the creature must have walked, or rather crept, along in a bowed posture, with the upper part of its body thrust forward. This attitude in moving was at that time also ascribed, in consequence of the earliest descriptions given, to the gorilla. The formation of the pelvis, so far as could be seen from the fragments available, reinforced this conjecture. Instead of modestly remaining in the background and consulting the authorities before committing himself, the schoolmaster from Elberfeld immediately diagnosed the find correctly. The thing must have been a beast-man, an intermediate form between gorilla and *Homo sapiens*.

Eagerly he searched further among the rubbish. He collected the left elbow and the right radius belonging to the lower arms, as well as parts of the shoulder blade and a few ribs. Everything else, including the jawbone and teeth, had disappeared. Nevertheless, these bones of different types from all parts of the body were enough to give an excellent idea of the aspect of this primitive being. No one, in Fuhlrott's opinion, could now doubt that this was actually the first of all the inhabitants of the earth to deserve the name of human being. He was far older than those found at Engis and Paviland, which were still at the time the subject of dispute. The coating of loam covering the Devonian chalk that formed the floor of the cave probably originated in the Middle Diluvial age. Owing to the narrow entrance to the grotto, there could be no question of explaining the remains as those of a later burial.

Fuhlrott, however, went to work with the most extreme care and attention. He knew for certain that the public revelation of the discovery would raise a storm of indignation. He began by taking steps for the preservation of the bones, which age had rendered soft and brittle. Then he procured all the technical literature in existence on human prehistory. There was not much of it. At this period even Boucher de Perthes had not yet quite made his name. Finally Fuhlrott invited some anthropologists to pass judgment on the find. They were just as astonished as he had been, congratulated him, and shared his opinion. The most eminent of them, the Bonn professor Hermann Schaafhausen, had the "Neanderthal man" transferred to the provincial museum at Bonn and took measures to ensure that the specimen would be discussed at the next congress of natural scientists, due to take place at Kassel in 1857.

In this way Schaafhausen, assisted by the finder Fuhlrott, began a campaign, the fluctuations of which for thirty years aroused the most lively interest among the public. The writings concerned with the Neanderthal man, or *Homo primigenius,* as science subsequently named him, together with the controversial essays against him, are alone enough to fill a small library. Schaafhausen's main reason for taking a favorable view of the fossilized bones from Parson Neumann's valley derived from his long standing approval of the theory of evolution. He, too, had been a pupil of the great Johannes Müller. But, like Schleiden and Schwann, he had soon parted company with the ideas of his master and worked out a theory of the descent of man — which, to be sure, hardly attracted any attention — in a book entitled *The Stability and Transformation of Species.* He considered Fuhlrott's discovery to be an unmistakable proof of the origin of Man from the beasts. He wrote a study of the bones in question and invited the schoolmaster Fuhlrott to Kassel to give a lecture to the masterminds of science on the subject.

That was the greatest and at the same time the saddest day in the life of the modest high school teacher. The men who listened to him at Kassel, first with interest, then with boredom, and finally with impatience, had hitherto been the objects of his boundless veneration. They included Rudolf Virchow, at that time thirty-six years old, the zealous champion of the freedom of science, admired by all prehistorians, archeologists, and anthropologists, who had personally excavated ancient burial grounds in his native Pomerania and always lent an attentive ear to the problems of the dawn of history. They included Rudolf Wagner, the disciple of Cuvier, who occupied Blumenbach's chair at Göttingen and who plunged into an embittered dispute — his views in this case being wholeheartedly shared by Fuhlrott — with the materialist Vogt (Wagner arguing for a complete separation of the fields of science and religion). They included great men like Schaafhausen's colleague at Bonn, Mayer; like the Frenchman Pruner-Bey and the Englishman Blake. They must surely see how important this Neanderthal business was! Fuhlrott excitedly pointed out the extraordinary formation of the bones, the strange shape of the skull, and the curved structure of the thigh.

The answer he received was merely a shake of the head. He was told that he was obviously not yet in a position to prove that the bones really dated from the Ice Age. Neither the bones of Diluvial animals nor tools of the Old Stone Age had been found in the cave. The place, as Fuhlrott himself had implied, was practically inaccessible. Probably rain water had carried the bones into it at some time or other. "Do you remember the Cossacks who were on the Rhine. in 1814?" Professor Mayer demanded of the disconcerted Fuhlrott. "They looked barbarous enough, those fellows! I'm convinced that we have here the bones of a fallen Cossack whose corpse putrefied in Neanderthal, the remains reaching the interior of the grotto by the agency of animals or water." Blake thought differently. "No. The vault of the skull is so deformed that the man must have been diseased. He had water on the brain, was feeble-minded, and no doubt lived in the woods like a beast." The rest nodded their agreement.

A number of other similar views were expressed, some of the remarkable skulls in Blumenbach's collection being adduced in support of them. Rudolf Wagner called the Neanderthal man an "old Dutchman." The French authority Pruner-Bey was more inclined to regard him as a "member of the Celtic race." Other anthropologists considered he had been a hermit. Only Schaafhausen stood up for Fuhlrott and firmly declared that no human being in historical times, whether Celt, Dutchman, or Cossack, anchorite or insane could have possessed bones so clearly resembling an animal's. He glanced at Virchow. The undisputed ruler of their circle had not yet committed himself.

When at last he rose a deep silence fell. Fuhlrott's heart was thumping. The decisive moment was at hand. It depended on Virchow's opinion whether the assembly would allow itself to be persuaded or not. No one yet knew the views of this man, who was considered the soundest authority on humanity, on the question of early man.

"For some time the opinion has been current," Virchow began in his quiet, cool, and slightly ironical way, "that the beginnings of human civilization must have involved men of inferior physical build as well as others. But that is a mistaken idea. Dwellings erected on piles have been discovered in the Swiss lakes. Those who set them up have been extinct for tens of thousands of years. Their magnificent skulls would take a high place among those of civilized people. Finds have been made in a number of different places which would appear to indicate that long before the period of the lake dwellings man had lived contemporaneously with the mammoth and kept himself alive in the fashion of the beasts. But no one remembered to mention in this connection that Siberian hunters today are in the habit of extracting the carcasses of mammoths from melting ice and devouring their flesh. Our ancestors must have done exactly the same. It cannot be safely assumed that mankind lived as early as the mammoth. There is no justification for the statement that the human race in prehistoric times was more primitive than it is at present. On the contrary, the men of the Stone Age, who maintained the struggle for survival under the most difficult conditions and at the same time adopted more and more of the rudiments of civilization — thus furnishing us with the best of all examples of cultural progress — must have possessed natural talents of an unusually high order for intellectual progress. They were of the same flesh and blood as ourselves."

Applause broke out. Schaafhausen frowned. The speech had sounded plausible enough, but it did not refute the fact that the Neanderthal skull showed characteristics that were decidedly more reminiscent of apes than of all the living and past races of mankind which had hitherto been known. Schaafhausen replied that Virchow himself had substantially agreed in his teaching that every individual consisted of an organized assembly of countless animal cells, the theories of a blood relationship between man and beast. It was hard to see why he should have refrained from drawing the ultimate conclusion and set aside a most valuable piece of evidence with a few empty words.

Virchow explained why he had done so. The Neanderthal skeleton, he said, had not belonged to a normal individual, but to an

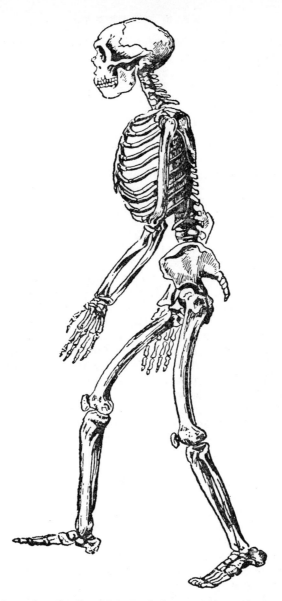

Virchow thought that Neanderthal man was a rachitic idiot afflicted with arthritis, but that he was a genuine primitive human being. He walked in a markedly stooped position, was of small size, and had very long arms.

unfortunate man whose anatomy had been changed by disease. He went on to give details of what he had to say on the subject as a doctor of medicine. The gathering of natural scientists heard from his lips the whole story of the life of this miserable wretch from the Feldhof grotto. The Neanderthal man had been born with a peculiarly long skull and a deeply hollowed frontal cavity, like those of the men of ancient Friesland. In his youth he had been afflicted with rickets, which had curved his legs and deformed his pelvis. Despite this cruel illness he had grown into a physically strong man, apparently fond of fighting. For his skull had received several heavy blows. The ridges over the eyes and the flat forehead proved it. He survived all these combats, and as an old man had the further misfortune to be attacked by painful arthritis. It completed the distortion of the bones. Anatomy of this sort, Virchow concluded, could naturally not provide a basis for any kind of general statement.

The gentlemen at Kassel found Virchow's hypercritical views amusing. They waved Schaafhausen aside and dismissed Fuhlrott and his documents. The matter seemed settled. The allies, the Bonn professor and the Elberfeld teacher, were not convinced, and tried to interest the public in their opinions. Schaafhausen brought out an essay on the Neanderthal skull. Fuhlrott joined in with a paper entitled *Human Remains from a Grotto in the Düssel Valley*. Further publications followed, and a new and vigorous controversy arose. Interested laymen wished to know the age of the skeleton. And numbers of people wondered whether the Neanderthal man could think, light a fire, and manufacture tools. Bitter attacks upon Fuhlrott became common among scholars, and when at last Darwin's theory struck like a flash of lightning into the conflict the argument about the Neanderthal man reached grotesquely spectacular heights.

In Germany Virchow's authority lasted until the end of the century. It was reinforced when a skull discovered near Cannstatt turned out to be relatively modern, although the supporters of the Neanderthal man had cited it as contributory evidence of the truth of their beliefs. Curiously enough, the French prehistorians had previously accepted the erroneously identified Cannstatt skull as the genuine Neanderthal specimen and for a long time gave *Homo primigenius* the name of "the Cannstatt race." Whenever anyone who took Darwin's side pointed to the apelike being described by Fuhlrott and Schaafhausen, he was loudly informed that Virchow had long ago put this evidence out of court. And Virchow himself seized every opportunity to maintain against the Darwinists that his successful denunciation of this irrelevant exhibit in the case necessarily involved the cancellation of the entire conception of "Man's descent from the monkey" from the program of science.

Once more it was Charles Lyell who started the reaction. In England people had already made up their minds about the Neanderthal man a few years after his discovery. As soon as Lyell heard about the affair, he went over to Germany, called on Fuhlrott, examined the place of the find in his company, and wanted to hear everything worth knowing about this remarkable creature. This was at least some small consolation to the much harried schoolmaster. He also heard that Lyell's assistant, King, had coined the term "Neanderthal man." Neither Fuhlrott himself nor Schaafhausen had ever ventured to render the valley of the organist Neumann immortal in this way. To his satisfaction, he learned from Lyell that his first impression had been correct. This was in fact a new species of human being, altogether distinct from *Homo sapiens*. But he was not granted the pleasure of celebrating the triumph of this opinion in his native land. He had long lain in his grave when Virchow lost the last round.

How did the story end? The English scientist Busk remembered, during the discussion over the Neanderthal man, that he possessed an entirely fossilized skull. It had come to light as early as 1848 during the construction of fortifications at Gibraltar, but at that time no one knew exactly what to do with it and so it had remained a mystery. Now, however, the skull from Gibraltar suddenly became interesting. In 1864 Busk took it to the anthropologists' congress at Norwich and presented it to the Hunterian Museum of London. The belief gained ground that this too was a case of Neanderthal man.

Two years later the Belgian geologist Dupont discovered the fragment of an underjaw of very primitive appearance in the cave of La Naulette near Dinant, among mammoth, rhinoceros, and reindeer bones. An anthropologist named E. T. Hamy immediately made the bold assertion that this underjaw belonged to the same species as the skeleton from Neanderthal and the skull from Gibraltar. If he were right, the Neanderthal man had jaws that protruded like those of a monkey but possessed human teeth. Some slighter finds in Bohemia supported this hypothesis. The point could not yet be fully established, though the English had long ceased to doubt the existence of a primitive species of beastlike human beings. Then suddenly, in the years 1880 and 1886, two more discoveries were made which put the last stone of the edifice into place.

In the cave of Schipka, near the Moravian village of Stramberk, a Czech named Maschka came in 1880 upon a massive underjaw which irrefutable investigations proved to have belonged to a teething child, in spite of its size. No illness or bone deformation could have caused the jaw of an infant to have assumed so gigantic a size. Virchow said that this bone, like the one of La Naulette, was pathological; but the majority of anthropologists now inclined to the view of Schaafhausen and his party. In 1886 the confirmation came at exactly the right moment. In the cave of Spy d'Orneau, not far from the town of Namur, the Belgian geologists Fraipont and Lohest were confronted with an impressive panorama of the Neanderthal age. Five layers of soil were here superimposed on one another. The lower four contained the bones of mammoths and woolly rhinoceroses, as well as crude stone tools, knives, and lanceheads. They were therefore undoubtedly of Ice Age origin. And in the fourth layer from the top, in other words the second oldest, two skeletons were found, in the huddled attitudes of sleepers. They were Neanderthal men.

The skulls showed a somewhat higher vaulting than that from the Feldhof grotto but the same massive ridges were above the eyes. The one lower jaw that remained corresponded in size and in its coarse structure with those from La Naulette and Schipka and lacked, as they did, a normally developed chin. The bones of the limbs were thick and curved. There could be absolutely no question in this case of modification by disease. No savage, not even the Australian aboriginal, no Late Stone Age or Cro-Magnon type had so primitive a physique.

The Spy find was the first of its kind to be recorded in full scientific detail. The geologists checked the subsoil. It belonged to the Last Intermediate Ice Age and was twice as old as the layer in which the Cro-Magnon human remains had been found. The prehistorians examined the stone tools. They were attributable to a far more remote stage of culture than the implements discovered by Lartet. Then, even in Germany, the anthropologists could no longer keep silent.

The Strasbourg anatomist Gustav Schwalbe compared the skeletal remains from Spy with those from Neanderthal and established such extensive similarities that even the greatest skeptics and critics had to confess they had been mistaken. Only the veteran Virchow protested once again, but no one echoed his objections.

The men with the spades had done their work. The cultural historians now took up the tale.

1. Scheuchzer's "miserable sinner." This broadsheet depicting the alleged evidence of the Flood started the search for Adam.

2.   Remains of prehistoric animals such as the saurian's skull shown above were reconstructed in fabulous forms. Below is the famous Dragon Fountain at Klagenfurt, carved in 1590 by the sculptor Ulrich Vogelsang after the skull of a woolly rhinoceros found as early as 1335.

3. Carolus Linnaeus, with a good sense of publicity, was fond of having himself delineated in Lapland dress.

4. An engraving on copper from the *Thesaurus anatomicus* of the anatomist and natural scientist Fredericus Ruysch, published at Amsterdam in 1710. The composition consists entirely of human organs and is intended to symbolize the elements of which the body is built up.

5. The "grand seigneur" of natural history: Georges Louis Leclerc, Count Buffon.

6. Two illustrations from the chapter on mankind in Buffon's *Natural History*.
Left: the negroid albino Genoveva from Dominica, whom Buffon himself examined and described.
Below: a paradisal family group.

7. The "wild man of the woods" in the zoo at Het Loo near The Hague was a female orangutan, the largest anthropoid ape then known.

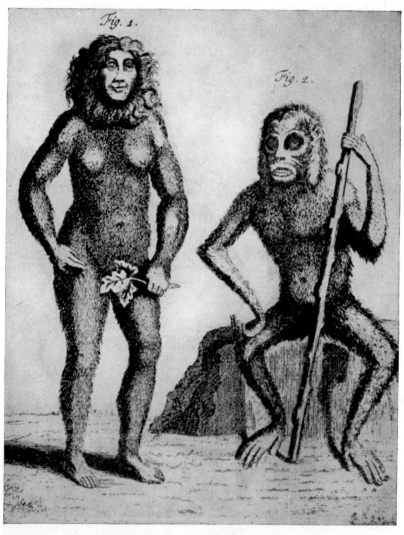

8. An eighteenth-century idea of "human animals," inspired by anthropoid apes, which were at that time still unfamiliar and the subject of many legends.

9. The explorers of the world in Cook's time discovered "living fossils," prehistoric animals and ancient human beings that had survived the ages in Australasia. *Above:* the egg-laying duckbill of Australia. *Below:* marriage ceremony of a Melanesian family of very primitive type from the Solomon Islands.

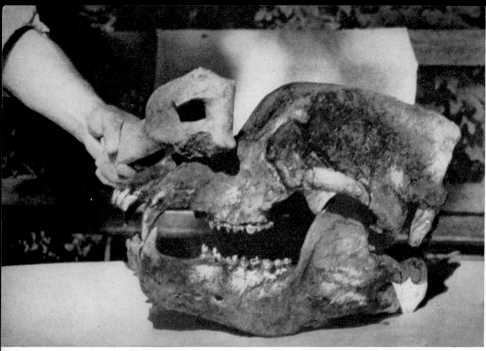

10. Skull of a cave bear brained by a heavy blow. Even such manifest traces of human activity as this did not lead, before 1850, to the recognition that prehistoric men and prehistoric animals had been contemporary. *Below:* petrifaction of an ancient horse the size of a dog.

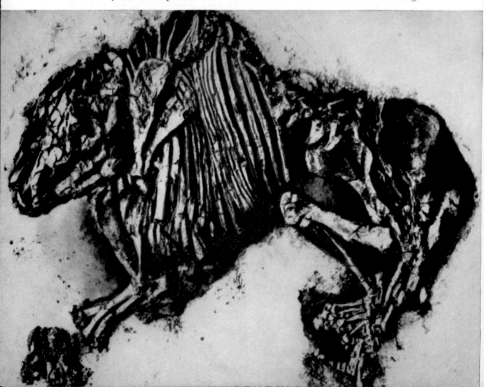

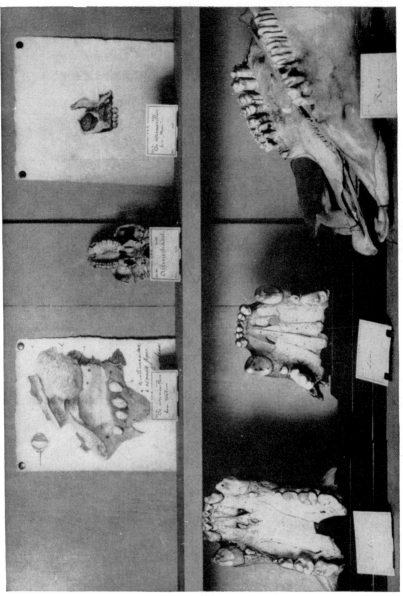

11. Goethe's material for his studies of the human inter-maxillary.

Giordano Bruno   Benedict Spinoza

12.   It was not natural scientists but philosophers who prepared the way for the idea of evolution. Giordano Bruno and Spinoza proclaimed the unity of nature. Kant and Schopenhauer considered the descent of man from the apes possible.

Immanuel Kant   Arthur Schopenhauer

13. *Above:* a drawing, made in 1867, of the village of Les Eyzies, the focal point of excavations in the Vézère valley in Lartet's time. *Right:* under massive, beetling cliffs, which once sheltered primitive human beings, stand the old houses of Laugerie-Basse.

14. The ancient castle of Les Eyzies, shown here in a drawing of 1867, was also situated under overhanging rocks. To the left of the ruins, which today accommodate the museum, the sculptor Paul Darde set up a monument to Neanderthal man (*below*).

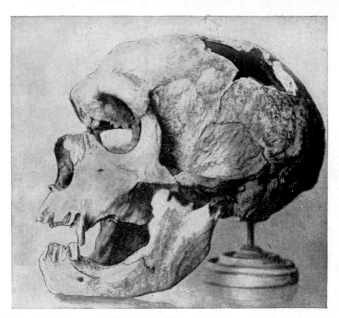

15. Since Fuhlrott's find, many skulls of Neanderthal man have been dug up. The best preserved and also the most typical was discovered by Marcellin Boule near La Chapelle-aux-Saints. *Below:* Neanderthal man perhaps resembled this primitive native of Melanesia.

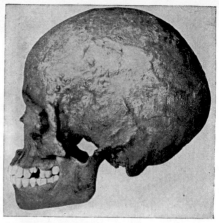

Skull of a primitive man of the Ice Age from the Grimaldi Grotto, Monte Carlo.

16. We may perhaps conceive Grimaldi man to have been like this Negrito-type Semang tribesman from Siam (*above*) and Cro-Magnon man to have resembled this member of the Moken Vedda race from the Mergui Archipelago (*below*).

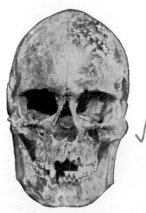

Cro-Magnon skulls from Oberkassel near Bonn. *Above:* a young woman. *Below:* an old man buried with her.

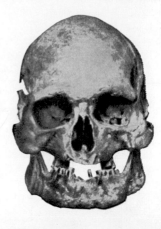

The hand axe system of chronology

Ever since the days of Linnaeus nothing has been able to stop scholars from classifying all their finds in a closed system. The habit is of course a useful one, for systems can be excellent guides through the worlds of nature and humanity. It becomes disastrous, however, when the system builders stick rigidly to the letter of their schemes and are thus led to forget the living phenomena with which they are dealing.

Prehistorians are very proud of the complex system they have laboriously worked out in order to determine the various cultural stages of the Ice Age and fit them into a chronological sequence. The idea behind their methods is derived from the times of Cuvier and William Smith. It supposes that the various cultural periods can be distinguished, like the geological, by "fossil guides," exclusively indicative of their own age and no other. The fossil guide of prehistory became the hand axe.

As early as 1852 Lartet had divided the Old Stone Age into three sections: the Cave Bear Age, the Mammoth and Woolly Rhinoceros Age, and the Reindeer Age. He had observed that the weapons and tools found could easily be distinguished from one another. In some cases they were crudely formed lumps of flint, in others implements of the knife type, while elsewhere scrapers, notched and pointed stones, and weapons with laurel-shaped blades came to light. Some flints were rough-hewn. But others, again, were finely carved and given finishing touches. In older layers stone implements only were found, while in later ones, needles, harpoons, and ornaments made of bone, horn, and ivory turned up. It obviously followed that human civilization had begun as soon as the first man picked up a hard stone and used it to hammer a flint into the shape he wanted, and that only after long periods had elapsed were the inventions of the stone knife, the awl, the lancehead, and the engraving tool added to the rest; until finally, at a more refined stage of civilization, raw material of a more tractable kind replaced the stubborn stone.

This basic idea was taken up by Lartet's colleague Gabriel de Mortillet. An expert, like many Frenchmen, at rigorous system-building, he used it as the foundation of a schematic method carried to extremes, which has turned the history of early cultures into a kind of secret science. Most unfortunately, he also gave his cultural stages names extremely difficult to understand and not easy to bear in mind. In this connection he followed a long established custom

Years Ago	Age of the Earth	Duration of Epoch	Soil Climate	Animals
10,000 —	Holocene	Recent Past	Later Alluvial Soils	Modern Fauna
15,000 or 20,000		Postglacial	Steppe Climate	Steppe and Tundra Animals
100,000 —		Fourth or Würm Ice Age (97,000 years)	Formation of later loess. Cold occasionally temperate	Reindeer Elk Bison Musk Ox Wild Horse Mammoth Woolly Rhinoceros Cave Bear
		Riss-Würm Warm Age (65,000 years)	Large-scale erosion and removal of soil; multiplication of caves. Warm	Cave Lion Cave Hyena Elephant Rhinoceros
200,000 —		Third or Riss Ice Age (53,000 years)	Lower layers of caves formed; earlier loess. Cold	Mammoth Woolly Rhinoceros Cave Bear
300,000 —	Pleistocene or Diluvial	Mindel-Riss Warm Age (193,000 years)	Large-scale erosion and removal of soil; terrace formation. Mild to warm	Antique Elephant Merck Rhinoceros Primitive Hippopotamus Saber-toothed Tiger
400,000 —				
		Second or Mindel Ice Age (47,000 years)	Cold	Mammoth Woolly Rhinoceros
500,000 —		Günz-Mindel Warm Age (65,000 years)	Alluvial soil on plateaux. Warm	Southern Elephant Etruscan Rhinoceros Wild Horse Deninger Bear
600,000 —		First or Günz Ice Age (49,000 years)	Cold	?
	Pliocene	Last Tertiary Period	Tropical Heat	Mastodon Dinotherium Okapi Monkey

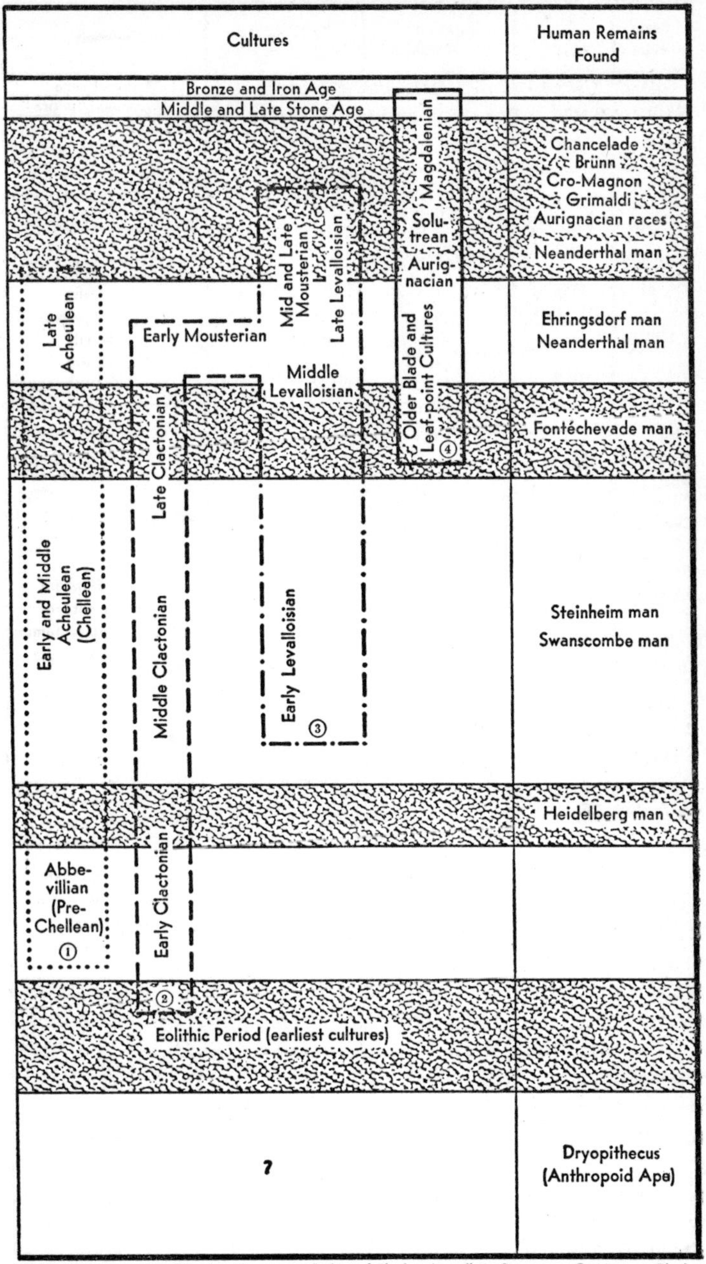

Cultures				Human Remains Found

Bronze and Iron Age

Middle and Late Stone Age

Chancelade
& Brünn
Cro-Magnon
Grimaldi
Aurignacian races

Neanderthal man

Magdalenian

Solu-trean

Aurig-nacian

Mid and Late Mousterian

Late Levalloisian

Older Blade and Leaf-point Cultures ④

Late Acheulean

Early Mousterian

Middle Levalloisian

Ehringsdorf man
Neanderthal man

Late Clactonian

Fontéchevade man

Early and Middle Acheulean (Chellean)

Middle Clactonian

Early Levalloisian ③

Steinheim man
Swanscombe man

Heidelberg man

Abbe-villian (Pre-Chellean) ①

Early Clactonian

Early Clactonian ②

Eolithic Period (earliest cultures)

？

Dryopithecus (Anthropoid Ape)

① Hand Axes ② Clacton Group ③ Broad Blades, Levallois Group ④ Narrow Blades

European chronology on the Hand-axe System.

of geologists, who were in the habit of calling each period after the place where its characteristic relics had been found: thus the names of small villages in France, near to which hand axes had been discovered entered scientific terminology.

Mortillet believed that men had always and exclusively produced, at any particular period, instruments of quite definite kind. He considered that different instruments had then come into fashion which could be used as fossil guides for the ensuing epochs. Such cultural changes, he supposed, had not only taken place over a certain small area but simultaneously throughout the whole world inhabited by mankind. Layers that only contained rough-hewn lumps of flint belonged to the Middle Diluvial age and thus at the same time to the earliest stage of culture. If the hand axes were smaller and more regularly formed the layer was then to be attributed to the last third of the Ice Age. And if notched and pointed tools, gravers, awls, and bone implements were found, it meant that one was dealing with the latest cold period, with which the glacial epoch gradually came to an end.

This system of Mortillet's was subsequently supplemented and improved in various ways, especially by the eminent investigator of the cave paintings of the Ice Age, Henri Breuil, of whom we shall have much to say later on. But the basic idea remained. The prehistorians strenuously opposed, as many still do today, recognition of the simple fact that higher and lower cultural levels in the history of humanity as a whole have always existed not only in succession but also in combination. There were tribes that had long been capable of sharpening and retouching stone at a time when others, perhaps actually inhabiting a neighborhood valley, still had to put up with the blunt axe. Just as in many areas animal forms were preserved which had been extinct for aeons in other places, so also culturally backward races of mankind continued to exist in favorable environments, though these people were really no longer suited to the age they lived in. The evolution of mankind proceeded in the same way as that of other animate beings, not in orderly succession, but in the form of keen competition, in the course of which the champions often finished off their weaker rivals. While the Egyptians were building their pyramids, people in central Europe were living in much the same way as the old man of Cro-Magnon. While James Watt was inventing the steam engine in England, people in Australia had scarcely passed the cultural stage of Neanderthal man. The recognition of this fact really means that we ought to abandon Gabriel de Mortillet's scheme. Yet since it continues to be used, at any rate as an auxiliary and determinant method, it is inadvisable to suppress it in the picture of early cultures.

The oldest implement employed by humanity according to Mortillet was an almond-shaped *coup de poing*, produced by chipping and pointed at one end, in other words a simple "hand axe." In modern opinion it is accepted as a standard form of Paleolithic tool. Such stones were first found near Paris, close to the little village of Chelles, together with the bones and the remains of the teeth of Ice Age rhinoceroses and elephants. The cultural stage at which it was supposed to have been exclusively used was accordingly called the Chellean. And when it became clear that the so-called Ice Age had in reality consisted of four glacial periods and three intermediate glacial ages the Chellean era was given a more or less central position, being placed at the beginning of the second intermediate glacial epoch.

The climate of this later period was mild. The animals that lived in it were mostly antique elephants, primitive hippopotamuses, and a type of rhinoceros named after Goethe's friend Merck. No human remains dating from Chellean age were known.

A still earlier stage, with more primitive "fossil guides," was proposed at the beginning of the present century by Henri Breuil and his German colleague Hugo Obermaier. They had discovered that in addition to the primitive hand axe many small instruments had existed in the Chellean age, while at an apparently lower level, especially near Abbéville and Amiens, only the crudest lumps of flint, sharpened at one end, were to be found. This latter culture was called Pre-Chellean, or Abbevillian, and attributed to the first intermediate glacial age, that of the southern elephant and the Etruscan rhinoceros.

The Chellean age was followed in Mortillet's scheme by a period during which men produced, in addition to hand axes, knifelike tools with straight cutting edges. These ancient toolmakers had learned to chip fragments of stone from a good-sized block in so dexterous a manner that they could be used to cut up meat and slash human flesh. The village of Saint-Acheul, in the Somme valley of Boucher de Perthes, gave its name to the period of the first knives, the Acheulean. It was the time when the Second Intermediate Ice Age was ending. The climate was growing colder and the first mammoths were joining the antique elephants. No relics of mankind were discovered.

The classic valley of the Vézère, Lartet and Christy's sphere of operations, was immortalized in Mortillet's fourth epoch. Lartet had discovered there, in the Le Moustier grotto, certain small, triangular stone tools that might have been used as daggers or scrapers. They did not seem to have been roughly chipped, but methodically produced in workmanlike fashion by a quantity of light touches. Similar pointed implements had subsequently turned up in La Naulette, Schipka, Spy, and other places where the remains of Neanderthal man had been found. It followed, accordingly, that Neanderthal man had been the creator of this Stone Age craft and the representative of the "Mousterian" culture. He lived, in the opinion of the system builders, toward the end of the third and Last Intermediate Ice Age and had to hold his own against the mammoth, the woolly rhinoceros, and the cave bear.

When Mousterian man died out in the last glacial period, *Homo sapiens* came on the scene. The mammoth and the woolly rhinoceros were becoming rarer. They were being replaced by the elk and the reindeer, the bison, and the wild horse. The culture flourished. Man invented applied art. Mortillet's system, as improved by Breuil and Obermaier, distinguishes three stages of this period. There was the Aurignacian, called after the town of Aurignac in southern France and characterized by small, flat, oval instruments, beak-shaped, curved awls, long scoops, and the first bone, horn, and ivory implements. Then came the Solutrean. The name derived from the village of Solutré between Lyons and Chalon-sur-Saône, where the bones of fifty thousand wild horses had been discovered in the "slaughter yard." In the Solutrean period the hard stone was not merely chipped but also shaped, by lighter touches and compression, into lanceheads having the form of a laurel leaf. Finally, there was the Magdalenian, called after La Madeleine, a promontory in the Vézère valley. This was the period of the advanced culture of Cro-Magnon man.

In the Magdalenian era the Diluvial age was already ending. Mammoth and woolly rhinoceros, elk and cave bear were dying out. The transitional "Mas d'Azil" stage, the typical instruments of which were harpoons made of elk's antlers, lasted into the Middle Stone Age, which became in its turn, some millenniums later, the Late Stone Age. From then onward man took up agriculture, cattle breeding, and pottery, traded, founded the first political communities, built ships, and sailed them to distant shores.

Such is the history of Adam as we find it in Gabriel de Mortillet's Hand Axe System. It sounds splendid and is in many respects correct, but, as in the case of all systems, a number of adjustments had to be made in this one too. For a long time it seemed beyond question that extensive chronological gaps lay between the various periods. When attempts were made to fit Stone Age implements from other European countries and other continents into the French system, one difficulty after another was encountered. Periods that corresponded in geological age with the Chellean or Acheulean in France proved elsewhere to be entirely lacking in hand axes. It followed that the Old Stone Age cultures had prevailed for long periods simultaneously, in combination with one another, exercised mutual influence, and in certain localities even intermingled. It became obvious that the Middle Stone Age had already begun in Egypt while northern Europe still remained in the Magdalenian era. Neanderthal man, with his Mousterian culture, was proved to have by no means died out at the time the Cro-Magnon race came into the picture. The striking identification of cultural stages with definite divisions of geological history had been reduced to an absurdity by the very industry of the investigators themselves.

All that remained was the realization that the stone tools of the European Ice Age had been bequeathed to us by at least two different kinds of human beings. There was the primitive type that could at best produce knives, scrapers, and daggers, in addition to the earliest hand axe; and there was the advanced specimen that made steady progress and even showed proof of artistic capacity. The anthropologists came to exactly the same conclusion. The former species of man was their Neanderthal type and the latter belonged to the Cro-Magnon and related races.

A fresh problem was raised. Was the Neanderthal type the first man? What was his origin? What did his ancestors look like? The evolutionists believed they had found the answer long ago. They immediately presented the students of primitive man with intellectual weapons. At the very time when Lyell, Boucher de Perthes, Lartet, and Fuhlrott were beginning their researches on Adam's trail, the Darwinian era dawned.

Part Three

MONKEY BUSINESS OVER ADAM

*The moment we want to stop
believing in anything we have
hitherto believed in we not only
find that there are many objections
to it, but also that these objections
have been staring us in the face all
the time.*
GEORGE BERNARD SHAW

THE ORIGIN OF SPECIES

In the shadow of Erasmus

CHARLES DARWIN remained throughout his life a true Whig, a genuine British Liberal. And when one is a Whig one is a man of principle. In the first half of the nineteenth century this meant that one hated the Tories and the slave trade, respected the political economist Adam Smith and the progressive Lords Helbourne and Palmerston, welcomed the English Reform Acts, favored religious toleration and emancipation, and was most profoundly convinced that "welfare, happiness and civilisation follow wherever the English flag is hoisted."

One of the many revolutions without tears which characterize English history coincided with Darwin's youth. The fluid merchant class was replacing the rigid structure of the aristocracy. Open competition was reorganizing the social strata. King Cotton had begun his rule. English merchant vessels plowed the seas. Englishmen set foot on every continent. It was a time of hope, except for the recently constituted industrial proletariat, with its steadily growing numbers and loud demands for enough to eat. But the Whigs saw no danger from that quarter either. They read the *Essay on Population*, in which the English country clergyman Thomas Robert Malthus urged the control of overpopulation through sexual restraint and advocated families of two children only. They considered that if the poor were to exercise a little more self-restraint poverty would soon be eradicated. They themselves, of course, were not concrned in the matter. They could afford more than two children.

Meanwhile the Darwins had moved from Breadwall to Shrewsbury on the Severn. Here the medical practitioner and obstetrician Robert Waring Darwin continued to cherish the memory of old Erasmus and his theory of evolution. Weighty tomes, copper engravings, and collections of dried plants and minerals filled the doctor's house. He told his patients stories about his eminent father, read out stanzas from his didactic poems in the evenings, and saw to it that young Charles, with every breath he drew, inhaled something of the spirit of the *Zoonomia*. This bottle-nosed boy, timid to the verge of clumsiness, was the last scion of the Darwins, and the fact was continually hammered into him. All the resources of pedagogy were vigorously employed to teach him that it was his duty to carry on the family traditions, rival his grandfather, and continue his work. The idea alarmed him. The figure of the deified Erasmus grew to the proportions of a gigantic phantom in his mind. If he were to adopt the profession of his grandfather and father he would have to become a doctor. But the sight of a single drop of blood was enough to turn Charles's stomach.

By a twist of fate the critical moments of his life coincided with the critical moments in the conflict over the doctrine of evolution. He had been born in 1809, the year in which Lamarck rebelled against Cuvier. In 1830, while Cuvier and Geoffroy Saint-Hilaire were contending in the Paris Academy and Lyell was revolutionizing geological science, Charles Darwin became a professional student of nature. In 1844, when Geoffroy Saint-Hilaire was carried to his grave in France and the young Virchow first encountered the wonders of the cell in Germany, Darwin formulated his theory for the first time. And in 1859, after Lyell and Boucher de Perthes had proved the existence of primitive men, he published his much admired and much disputed masterpiece on the origin of species, the work which in Haeckel's phrase made him the "Copernicus of biology."

In Shrewsbury it did not look at first as though he would achieve any such success. Dr. Darwin was extremely dissatisfied with his offspring. The schoolmasters described Charles as a mediocre pupil, or even as a slow-witted youngster. The only things he took any interest in were insects, shells, plants, and minerals. Even in these studies he showed himself so sensitive to pain that his father completely lost his temper. When he started a collection of beetles and butterflies he only looked for dead ones. When he was asked why on earth he did not use a net to capture his treasures, like all other young students of nature, he replied sadly that he could not bring himself to take the life of any animate creature merely for the sake of adding to his own possessions. Could such a supersensitive character, tormented by such inhibitions, ever develop into a good doctor and scientist?

Charles did his best. With persistence he endured medical lectures and practical work at the University of Edinburgh for two years. Then he could stand it no longer, and Robert Waring Darwin reluctantly decided to betray the memory of Erasmus. He determined that if Charles refused to study the human body he should at least try to study the human soul. He sent him, accordingly, to Christ's College, Cambridge. Perhaps it would be possible to make a tolerable parson or missionary out of him.

Charles cared as little for theology as he had for medicine. His hesitant stammer hampered his preaching. His shyness impeded his ministrations to the soul. And when he played with the idea of transmitting the doctrines of Christianity and the Whigs to barbarous head-hunters and cannibals, the appalling thought occurred to him that he would then inevitably come into contact with slave dealers, hard-boiled ruffians, thoroughly unsympathetic to Christianity and the Whigs, who were putting a stop to head-hunting and cannibalism by the far more drastic methods of whips and chains, hunger and misery, consumption, and syphilis. Consequently, the only result of his studies at Christ's College was the conviction, dictated by compassion, that every decent Whig ought to regard the fight for the abolition of slavery as his most urgent task. And a man on the other side of the ocean, who happened to have been born on the very same day as himself, a certain Abraham Lincoln, actually put this idea of Charles Darwin, B.A., and those who shared his views, into practice at a somewhat later date.

For Charles Darwin it was only a short step from the slave problem to natural science. He began to study the habits and customs of alien peoples. He read the reports of the scientific explorers James Cook and Alexander von Humboldt, as well as the crowning achievement of the literature of travel — the German poet Adelbert von Chamisso's descriptions of the South Seas. Seas and islands, rivers and mountain ranges, exotic plants, animals, and human beings fascinated him. And now for the first time something of his grandfather Erasmus appeared in him. He wondered how it was that in different parts of the earth, under the same climatic conditions, creatures existed that did indeed resemble one another but yet were not precisely similar. Why did the fauna of South America differ so fundamentally from those of Africa? What was the reason for the animals of Australia having quite a different aspect from those of the neighboring islands of southern Asia? Did the principle of the free competition of forces, as laid down in the *Zoonomia*, in fact also apply to nature, and was responsibility for the dissimilarity in question to be attributed to such rivalry? It was an interesting problem that science would one day have to consider.

Darwin took his speculations to the botanist Professor J. S. Henslow of Cambridge University. Henslow took a fancy to the serious meditative young man and carried him off whenever he could on his excursions into the Cambridge marshes. He introduced him to botany and zoology, and finally spoke to him frankly about his future. He said that to feel pity and respect for living beings was by no means the sign of a weak character, but gave a budding scientist a better start than the usual chilly routine of slaughter and dissection. He himself, said Henslow, thought very highly of any biologist who took greater pleasure in living than in dead creatures. He suggested that Darwin should give up theology and take refuge under his own wing.

The offer was very tempting, but Darwin did not wish to offend his father by yet another change of profession. He divided his time between lectures at Christ's College and visits to Henslow in his spare moments. It was inevitable that in this process zoology should gradually obtain the upper hand over the liturgy. Henslow's intuition had been correct. Darwin was a born natural scientist. The twenty-one-year-old student could occupy himself for months on end with a single small animal. He possessed the patience and perseverance of an elderly levelheaded man of science. While other undergraduates were loafing about or visiting taverns, he was huddled over his books or gazing into the microscope. While others had long been fast asleep in bed, he was still sitting there, his brain on fire, thinking about moss animals, Cirripedia, and earthworms.

When at last he actually discovered a new English species of insect, Henslow earnestly besought him to devote himself to natural science for good, cleverly appealing to his weak point, his interest in foreign countries. The professor had just received a letter from the Home Office, signed by Viscount Melbourne himself, asking him to recommend a suitable young scientist for participation in an expedition to South America. This was just what Darwin needed. By taking part in such a journey he would have the best chance of developing his latent capacities.

Darwin accepted at once. He thanked Henslow quietly, almost coolly. Henslow felt secretly pleased at this behavior. For the young man's detached attitude proved that he was no visionary enthusiast, but a true Englishman who knew what he wanted to do. It was not the prospect of adventure that attracted Darwin to foreign climes, but, on the contrary, the perfectly calm realization that it was time he freed himself from the pressure of family tradition by a decisive act. When a young man is constantly hearing that he is good for nothing compared to his grandfather he is bound to feel sooner or later, with all due respect, that his grandfather and all his

works can go to the devil and that he does not want to have anything more to do with them. Perhaps, thought Henslow, Charles
will be inclined later on, for this very reason, to think more highly
of old Erasmus.

Charles Darwin started, accordingly, on a journey round the world
which was to be of equal importance in the history of biology to
that of Christopher Columbus in the history of humanity. Darwin
took leave of his family, kissed his cousin and childhood playmate
Emma Wedgwood goodbye, packed up his personal belongings, and
put in his sea chest, on top of everything else, a book that would
be his permanent stand-by for the future — the first volume of the
Principles of Geology, by Charles Lyell.

It was through Lyell's spectacles that he thereafter examined coasts
and mountain ranges, islands, rivers, and geological deposits. In his
mind's eye he could see the continents slowly rise and fall, the waters
slowly eroding the rocks, as the world worked on incessantly, wrinkling its brow and smoothing it out again in an endless, uninterrupted
process of growth. It made a deep impression on Darwin. He became an unquestioning disciple of the man who had resuscitated
geology. And when, four years and nine months later, he returned
to England, the two scientists met. It thus happened that Charles
Lyell, who had assisted at the birth of the study of primitive man,
also rendered decisive services as the midwife to Darwinism.

Jemmy Button gets his rights

The ostensible reason for Captain Robert Fitzroy's voyage to South
America was such an unusual one that it alone was bound to appeal
to the young Darwin. His Majesty King William's ship *Beagle,*
which had hitherto rendered excellent service in surveying operations
and hydrography, had received orders to restore three slaves from
the remote island of Tierra del Fuego to a life of freedom. This
special act of generosity was intended to show the world that Liberal
England would in the future no longer be willing to participate in
the capture and sale of slaves. The fact that H.M.S. *Beagle* happened also to go on to the Falkland Islands, where Fitzroy hoisted
the Union Jack, though England had no particular business in that
part of the world, was only a trifling blemish on this admirable
enterprise.

The events that led up to the *Beagle's* proceedings were no less
unusual. About the year 1830 the two political parties of England,

the conservative Tories and the liberal Whigs, had fallen out badly over the question of slavery. For some considerable time the Slavery Abolition Acts had prohibited the British from engaging in the lucrative "black ivory" trade. But now the Liberal government of Lord Grey, the Prime Minister, and Lord Palmerston, the Foreign Minister, was also demanding the liberation of all colored slaves in the English Crown Colonies. The Tories were against this proposal. But the Whigs succeeded in putting it through and passed a law accordingly.

At this very moment H.M.S. *Beagle* returned from a voyage to Tierra del Fuego, and cast anchor in the Port of London. She had aboard not only Captain Robert Fitzroy and his white crew but also four brown-skinned natives from the island. Fitzroy, an out-and-out Tory, grandson of the Duke of Grafton and, despite his mere five-and-twenty years, already a recognized meteorologist and cartographer, had not the faintest suspicion of Palmerston's new law. He announced without a blush in the Naval Officers' Club that he had brought the four savages with him as slaves, to teach them morals, decency, and the Christian religion. And his sailors supplemented this hair-raising fact, in the taverns round about the West India Docks, by the further appalling statement that one could buy Tierra del Fuego children from their parents for no more than a single mother-of-pearl button.

Hitherto, so far as Captain Fitzroy could remember, no living being had troubled himself in the slightest if an honest seaman had landed in Old England with a few "niggers, or Injuns." At first he couldn't quite understand the point of the scandal that broke out. It was not until he was called to the Home Office and its chief, Viscount Melbourne, dumfounded him with the thunderous accusation of being a brutal slave hunter that he realized he had become involved in a question of high politics.

"Is it a fact," inquired his lordship, "that these Tierra del Fuego people were brought to England against their will?"

"Certainly, my lord," Fitzroy admitted. "I arrested one of them as a public nuisance, because the members of his tribe had been so unchristian as to steal one of my boats. He was baptized aboard by the highly respectable name of York Minster."

"And why did you not afterwards release him, Captain?"

"Because, begging your lordship's pardon, I wished to make him a useful member of society."

Viscount Melbourne raised one eyebrow and asked crossly for details of the other Tierra del Fuego natives. He learned that the second victim, an adolescent girl, had been given the new baptismal name of Fuegia Basket. Fitzroy, according to his own account, had purchased this charming little savage in order to clothe her decently. The third native was a half-grown boy. His name was Jemmy Button.

"Button?" repeated the viscount, filled with uneasy suspicions. "Button? How on earth did you hit on such a name, Captain?"

"Because he cost me a mother-of-pearl button," explained Fitzroy in some embarrassment. "His parents, my lord, were quite satisfied with the bargain."

"A mother-of-pearl button!" groaned his lordship. "It's true, then!"

"Well, yes," Fitzroy replied, somewhat conscience-stricken. "I intended to educate him at my own expense. I beg your forgiveness, my lord. But I don't understand this new law."

Viscount Melbourne was not very interested in the powers of understanding of a man who could offer such an insult to the dignity of humanity. He gave Captain Fitzroy brief and concise instructions, in the name of His Majesty's government, to fit out the *Beagle* for a further voyage and take the four Tierra del Fuego natives forthwith back where he had fetched them from.

"Four?" Fitzroy interrupted. "My lord, there are only three of them. The fourth has just died here in London, unfortunately."

"That only makes matters worse," retorted his lordship with emphasis. There was a short pause. Then he eyed Fitzroy sternly. "You understand, Captain? These three unfortunate people are to be resettled in exactly the same place as they formerly lived in. You will be responsible to me, Captain, for carrying out my instructions to the letter."

"Jemmy won't be very pleased," Fitzroy remarked. "He's taken quite a fancy to me already."

But Jemmy's opinion was not asked. Fitzroy's case was made a precedent. It soon became well known. Before long there was not a Whig in England who was not consumed with the deepest sympathy for Jemmy Button, York Minster, and Fuegia Basket. The preparations for their return to freedom were followed with great emotion and satisfaction.

Fitzroy had to put a good face on the matter. He took aboard a missionary named Matthews, who had been ordered by the Home Office to take up residence at Woolya Bay, Tierra del Fuego, in order to guide Jemmy's cannibal tribe gently and tactfully into the bosom of civilization. The captain had been rather surprised at first that he had not been more severely taken to task and called upon to answer for his infringement of the law. But he soon found out the reason. His Majesty's government still needed him, not only to take charge of the passage to Tierra del Fuego, but also in his capacity as an expert on South American islands and waters. As the *Beagle* was making a voyage to Tierra del Fuego, she might just as well explore some of the localities that interested England. There were the Falkland Islands, for example. They were the subject of dispute between Argentina, Spain, France, American seal hunters, and the Hamburg merchant Louis Vernet. They were quite near Jemmy's native land.

Fitzroy immediately understood this second object of the voyage. So his instructions were to sail to Tierra del Fuego, settle Matthews, the missionary, and the brown pair of lovers, York and Fuegia, somewhere in the wilderness, exchange Jemmy back again for the mother-of-pearl button, then do away with the impossible situation in the Falklands, and finally decide the question of their legal possession. He changed his mind about Viscount Melbourne, who now seemed to him an astute politician who had designed an agreeable mission for him.

But he was not quite so pleased with the third object of the voyage. He had been ordered to take a natural scientist aboard, some learned landlubber or other, who was to collect insects, plants, and minerals in Tierra del Fuego, on the Patagonian and Chilean coasts, the Falklands, and other islands of equal interest to England. Of course he understood why. If a scientist were aboard, no one would suspect the voyage of any political intention. H.M.S. *Beagle* would be serving the cause of humanity by her voyage and at the same time enriching science. So far, so good. But the fellow sent aboard his ship by Professor Henslow, that twenty-two-year-old bachelor of theology and amateur zoologist, Darwin, was by no means to his taste. He looked just the sort to be frightfully seasick and probably come to a miserable end in the bleak climate of the Strait of Magellan. All the same young Mr. Darwin did have the decency to confess that hardly any natural scientist could ever have started on a voyage so imperfectly equipped as himself, and this admission did win Fitzroy around a little. He sent for the ship's surgeon, Mr. Bynoe, told him to keep an eye on the young fellow, and hoped against hope that all would be well.

On December 27, 1831, the *Beagle* set sail on a southwesterly course into the Atlantic. Thereafter, for a whole year, Darwin had the opportunity to study Jemmy Button, York Minster, and Fuegia

Basket and give himself up to serious thoughts about the evolution of human civilization. It is clear from his diary that the three Tierra del Fuego natives, ostensible reasons for a political mission, gave him the first foundations of his subsequent theory of the descent of man. Little Jemmy Button, whose fate had been accidentally illuminated by the searchlight of public interest, thus took his place in the history of natural science.

The three natives soon perceived that they were the center of interest and took prompt advantage of it. They were in high spirits — at any rate at the outset of the voyage — over the prospect of returning to their homes, told astonishing stories about their compatriots, and assumed the airs and graces of prima donnas under the affectionate care of Matthews, the missionary. Fitzroy was obliged from time to time to reprimand them rather sharply. Every such occasion gave him an excuse to grumble over the ill-starred law of the right honorable Lords Grey and Palmerston and to express himself in favor of the retention of the institution of slavery.

Darwin became excited. After all, Fuegia, York, and Jemmy were not simply wild animals, but decently clothed, duly baptized, enlightened human beings, eager to learn, and with as much right to a free life as any white man. The seamy sides of their characters were harmless in comparison with those of the rough sailors from East London and Devonport. Fitzroy only laughed at these observations. He told his sentimental fellow voyager that there was a natural law by which the stronger made his way and used his power. Without slavery, he proceeded, expounding the wisdom of a lifetime, the colonies could make no progress, human society could not be controlled, nor could any culture exist throughout the world.

These were the principles of a scion of the aristocracy. They must have sounded positively obscene to the Whigs. Darwin, nothing if not an objective-minded scientist, had the feeling that there might be something in them. He thought the matter over. A law of Nature? Was Nature really so cruel as to allow the stronger to make a meal of the weaker? Yes, she was. Every glance at a meadow or a pond proved it. What was the object of such behavior? There must, after all, be some kind of sense in the brutal struggle for existence. Mysterious as it might be, it was perhaps extremely important for science. He remembered once more the free competition of forces, advocated by the Whigs and transferred by his grandfather Erasmus to nature. Basically, that was the same idea, the only difference being that competition in that case did not result in the ethical chaos of the jungle but in the rationally grounded selection of superior types for survival. Darwin gasped a little. He felt a sudden sense of relief.

The ticklish problem of the Tierra del Fuego natives still remained obstinate, despite his recognition of this principle. It was clear that the colored races had been defeated by the white in the struggle for survival. But this fact, in the opinion of Darwin as a Christian and a Whig, laid special obligations upon the victor. Man, as distinct from all other creatures, was a moral being. He had been charged in the cradle with the duty of loving his neighbors, even those weaker than himself. This high estimate of mankind that Charles Darwin of Christ's College had conceived was destined to receive a rude shock on the island of Tierra del Fuego.

A year had passed since the start of the expedition by the time the *Beagle* reached Tierra del Fuego and cast anchor in Woolya Bay. The three brown protagonists then had to be returned to the bosoms of their families. They had suddenly grown very silent. They were staring with something like dread at the wild, deeply indented coast. And as soon as they met the first members of their tribe they showed every sign of alarm. Apparently they had quite forgotten, during their contact with civilization, what it was like at home. The wild natives, on the other hand, received the returning travelers without surprise, without, in fact, any sign of emotion. They looked at them, so at least the men of the *Beagle* could not help thinking, in practically the same way as one might inspect a prime joint of meat.

Darwin, too, was much alarmed. He had imagined the natives of Tierra del Fuego to be not very different from Jemmy and Fuegia, a bit more naked and unrefined perhaps, but any rate recognizably human. The mob he saw rushing out of the woods of Tierra del Fuego consisted of utterly bestial creatures, devoid of all appearance of modesty and morality. It was a horde of savages that tried to steal everything but the fixtures. They might be described as a superior troop of monkeys, the individual members of which, whether male or female, behaved in utterly brutal and indecent fashion. How had civilization been able to bring about such a change in three human beings taken from this rabble of cave dwellers? A sudden thought, sinister and deeply disturbing, shot through Darwin's mind. Had all human beings originally been animals like these natives and only developed true humanity and civilization after a long process of growth?

Darwin fell into reverie while the captain, the missionary, and the crew did all they could to smooth over the return of their protégés. Little Jemmy had taken refuge at Darwin's side. He was trembling from head to foot and staring at his compatriots in wide-eyed terror. He had remembered that it was the custom in Tierra del Fuego to beat sick and weakly members of the tribe to death and devour them. And he had already become so English that the very thought made him feel faint with horror. Darwin, doing his best to console the boy, wondered anxiously what was going to become of Jemmy and the other two natives in this barbarous place. Would they be able to teach the savages what they had learned and start humanizing them? Hardly, he thought, for English habits and customs — as he very soon found — did not suit the primitive conditions of Tierra del Fuego.

A second idea occurred to him, as overpowering as the first. Might it not be that the natives of this island at the end of the world had become bestial, cruel, and greedy on account of the very harshness of nature in these parts and the remorseless struggle for existence? He noted in his diary that since Nature made habit all powerful and its effects hereditary, she had suited the native of Tierra del Fuego to the climate and the produce of that miserable country. How did she do this? By annihilating what was inappropriate and only allowing what held good to survive. It must be the same with animals and plants. They were passed through the sieve of the struggle for existence; this accordingly decided which were to remain and which were to leave the stage.

Then he remembered his Lyell. Environments, it was stated in the *Principles of Geology*, changed in the course of millions of years. The conditions of existence, the rules of the game of the survival of the fittest changed with them. What had formerly been appropriate and passed the severe test of selection would be appropriate no longer and be doomed to disappear. Darwin had a vision of a savage landscape inhabited by prehistoric animals and primitive human beings. He watched them, in his mind's eye, gradually changing because of the cumulative effect of a number of different, extremely small variations: the primitive forms died out one after the other and only those best suited to the new conditions maintained themselves, continuing to propagate, and thus after enormous lapses of time developing into the species of the present day. In the case of Jemmy, Fuegia, and York this process of change had been compressed, under the English sky, to a period of a few months. Would there now be a retrogression? Or did Nature in Tierra del Fuego annihilate, by some deed of violence, what had become foreign to her?

This last question was soon answered. York Minster, being robust, was the first to return to the old way of life. The islanders made the acquaintance of his fists and began to respect him. Since he had learned from the whites all sorts of technical accomplishments into the bargain, he came in a short time to occupy a most important position in the tribe. He paid fewer and fewer visits to the settlement that the missionary Matthews had built for himself and the better behaved of the natives. Fuegia, too, now formally united to him in marriage, began to lead the old savage life again. Both of them, to Matthews' disgust were very soon going about completely naked, taking part in heathen ceremonies, and acting as though they had quite forgotten England and the *Beagle*.

One day when Jemmy in his smart European clothes was taking a walk at a little distance from the settlement, his former comrade York Minster attacked him, stripped him to his very shirt, and robbed him of all his possessions. Jemmy fled in despair to the missionary's hut, called his compatriots a set of wicked and ignorant rascals, and begged with tears to be allowed to return aboard the *Beagle*. Matthews did his best to comfort the boy. Shortly afterwards he in his turn had such unpleasant experiences with the natives that he came to the conclusion that no sort of missionary work in such a place was likely to succeed, and went off to see Fitzroy.

The captain listened to him with a malicious smile. He made no comment, merely inquiring when Matthews had finished what the reverend gentleman proposed to do about it. The latter was at his wits' end. "Those brigands tried to strip me naked and pull all my hair out," he complained, in great distress. "I think it's a hopeless case. We shall have to abandon the settlement."

"Without the application of a cat-o'-nine-tails," Fitzroy observed imperturbably, "it is impossible to teach such people how to behave. The authorities ought to have realized that in London before we left. It's a thousand pities," he added, "about those three pets of ours."

"It is, indeed," Matthews agreed. He went on diffidently, "So you don't think, Captain, we can take poor Jemmy aboard again?"

"No," replied Fitzroy. "We should be disobeying the government's orders."

Matthews bowed his head, examining the misty landscape of Tierra del Fuego with a melancholy air. He proceeded to have his possessions brought aboard the *Beagle* and took leave of Jemmy Button. However much the boy might plead, he would have to stay with his wicked kindred. Politics took priority over the longing of a little brown native for civilization.

A few months later, after Fitzroy had completed his survey of the most southerly point of South America, the *Beagle* returned to Woolya Bay. Darwin met Jemmy again. The experience crushed him. He saw an emaciated, wretched savage with long, disheveled hair, naked except for a rag of cloth about his loins. There never was such a complete and deplorable change in anyone. Jemmy's opinions had changed, too. He no longer wished to return to England. The reason he gave was a cogent one. Beside him squatted a naked young girl, toward whom Matthews cast a highly censorious eye. The boy, in such English as he still remembered, introduced her as "Jemmy Button's wife." He accepted valuable parting presents. The other natives looked on avidly, ready to seize their share of the booty as soon as the ship departed.

Neither Darwin nor anyone else ever heard what happened to him and the ferocious York. Fuegia Basket met a tragic fate ten years later. In 1842 a sealing vessel anchored off the coast of Tierra del Fuego. The crew were greatly astonished when a strange sort of female native came aboard who could speak a little broken English and showed a childish pleasure at meeting white men again. The seal hunters naturally had not the remotest idea of the identity of their delighted visitor or the story of Fuegia Basket. All they understood was that she was a woman; they treated her accordingly. Fuegia was not strong enough to endure the demands of these robust seamen. She died a few days later. No doubt she had imagined that her return to civilization would work out rather differently.

The humanitarian part of the enterprise, accordingly, failed utterly, though we may add that the Falklands operation on the contrary succeeded. Fitzroy and his learned passenger took different views of the fiasco. The captain considered that his distaste for sentimental nonsense of this kind had been brilliantly justified. Darwin, on the other hand, drew the conclusions of a natural scientist from the affair. He now realized how greatly the characters and peculiarities of animate beings could alter under the influence of environment and the high degree of risk of permanent displacement run by all plants, animals, and human beings in consequence of the struggle for survival. The Tierra del Fuego natives who had been softened by their lives in England could not easily adapt themselves to an existence among savage hordes. They either had to return to primitive ways or perish. Was that really a law of nature? And what followed from it?

While the *Beagle* cruised off the American coast tentative conjectures and flashes of inspiration gradually shaped themselves into a theory in Darwin's mind.

Birth of a theory

H.M.S. *Beagle* sailed along the coast of Patagonia. During his rides over the pampas, Darwin saw the bleached bones of innumerable cattle and horses that had fallen victims to a great drought. He discovered other heaps of bones close by, under the soil. They had belonged to prehistoric animals, Megatheria, mylodonts, and toxodonts. According to Cuvier these animals had been destroyed in a catastrophe. But how was it that similar, if smaller forms — such as sloths, armadillos, and anteaters — still existed in South America today? Why should horses have died out in America, whereas in the Old World the equine species managed to survive down to the present day? Were the fossils deposited in the pampas to be attributed after all to periods of drought and similar perfectly natural events that had nothing to do with geological catastrophes? And were there perhaps actual connecting links between extinct and modern forms of life? Had the stronger, more ingenious and more adaptable types resisted the cruel law of natural selection?

Always the same question! It buzzed in Darwin's ear like a persistent fly every time he went ashore. Guanacos, long-necked wild llamas, which could defy the severest drought, wandered over the pampas. And in the soil trampled by their hoofs lay the bones of the *Macrauchenia*, a long-necked, llama-like animal supposed to have utterly vanished millions of years ago. Utterly? If so, why did the *Macrauchenia* resemble the guanaco in the same way as a remote grown-up ancestor might resemble his small descendant? It was a queer sort of principle according to which forms disappeared and similar forms appeared for the first time in the same part of the world!

This surprising relationship between dead and living animals on the same continent will, thought Darwin, shed more light in the future upon the appearance of organic creatures upon the earth and their subsequent disappearance than any other class of facts. He added, quite in the spirit of Lyell, that if some catastrophe had destroyed the animals of America, the entire framework of the globe would have felt the shock. Moreover, examination of the geology of Patagonia supported the view that the land formations had been brought about by slow and gradual changes. A much more probable hypothesis than annihilation by catastrophe would be that unfavorable living conditions render a species rarer and finally extinguish it altogether. And once we admit that species become rarer before they die out and yet continue to believe in a catastrophe, it is as though we were to admit that sickness is the forerunner of death and yet believe that a sick man dies as the result of violence.

H.M.S. *Beagle* sailed on. Fitzroy hoisted the English flag on the Falklands and charted the Chilean coast. Darwin climbed in the Andes. The new theory took on more and more definite shape. At last, in 1835, it was reinforced in startling fashion on the Galápagos Islands west of Ecuador. Darwin visited one island of the group after another. He found that the animal and plant world of the Galápagos Islands roughly corresponded to that of the American continent. But the similarity was not complete. Each island possessed its peculiar species, varying slightly from those of the other islands and rather more from those of the continent. No one had noticed such a thing before. It surprised Darwin and set him thinking.

There was every indication that the islands were satellites of South America. According to the prevailing theory their fauna and flora must have originated in the same act of creation as those of South America and must correspond to them. However, in fact special forms peculiar to the islands had developed from the preceding species on the continent and each island showed a different one. Each living thing on the islands, whether finch, iguana, rat, beetle, snail, or flowering plant, suggested a unique and specialized form of descendant of immigrants from Ecuador, Peru, or Chile. Was that still to be attributed to mere accident, or to the arithmetical series of some occult plan of creation?

During the thirty-six days Darwin spent on the Galápagos Islands his new theory reached imposing heights. Continental forms of life seemed to have migrated to the islands by air or water. They had made themselves at home in their new environment like truant children. Those that survived the struggle for existence became new varieties and new species.

On October 2, 1836, the *Beagle* returned to England. During the voyage, Charles Darwin had grown from a dreaming boy into a coolly reflective adult, content to let the knowledge he had gained mature quietly in his mind. He was able to submit much information to his country as the results of his voyage. They comprised a comprehensive collection of South American fossils, a novel explanation of the origin of coral reefs in the Indian Ocean and interesting zoological, botanical, and geological data. These achievements soon brought him recognition from English scientists. For the time being he kept the "secret of all secrets" — that of the first appearance of our race on this earth — to himself.

He parted from the bluntly outspoken Tory Robert Fitzroy on

the best of terms. The captain of the *Beagle* continued in his pre-destined career. He became in turn a member of Parliament, gover-nor of New Zealand, and eventually an admiral. It was not until twenty-three years later that Fitzroy again heard of his traveling companion, the natural scientist. He was even less pleased by what he heard than he had been by Darwin's views on the slavery question. He told himself that it was just what might have been expected from such a softhearted, persistently seasick fellow.

Meanwhile another man had come into Darwin's life. It was Charles Lyell. They corresponded and exchanged notes of their ex-periences. It was thanks to Lyell's patronage that the English natural scientists soon adopted Darwin as a full-fledged member of their circle: some species of animals and certain places were named after him. And when he took his M.A. degree Robert Waring Darwin could now be unreservedly proud of his son.

There was no reason why Darwin should not have revealed his ideas to the public at this juncture by applying Lyell's theory of gradual geological alteration to organisms as well. But he was an irresolute character, the Hamlet of natural science. He hated un-proved hypotheses from the bottom of his soul, was repelled by the fancies of the natural philosophers, and wished to be quite sure of himself before he assumed the right to bring down Cuvier from his pedestal. Moreover, he was seriously ill at this time. The hard-ships of the voyage had painfully affected his digestion. He was continually plagued by violent headaches. Attacks of giddiness, articular spasms, and retching made his life a misery. Robert Waring observed these symptoms with great anxiety. Would Charles, in such circumstances, ever be able to embark on a scientific career, marry, and perpetuate the race of Darwins?

Charles answered this question in his usual quiet, unruffled fash-ion. A substantial legacy enabled him to purchase a country seat, Down House, at Downe in the county of Kent, which carried with it the post of a county magistrate. His future was thus assured. He could work at Downe as a private scholar and allow the vague specu-lations that had occurred to him under foreign skies to mature slowly. The continuance of the family of Darwin was ensured by his giving his cousin Emma Wedgwood so long an account of the breeding habits of South American animals that she eventually realized he was proposing to her. He married Emma, submitted himself to her care, and thenceforth lived within a strict program. After three years in London they moved to Downe.

Darwin's first works were modest scale-models of his later *mag-*

num opus. He set himself marginal aims only and used them to prove separate points of the theory that still lay asleep in the drawer of his desk. Each of his subjects, whether he wrote of earthworms, coral reefs, cirripeds, creeping plants, or the fertilization of orchids, was treated so precisely and exhaustively that the scientists of England could make practically no further contribution to it. The professors were delighted and showed it. They placed Darwin's books on the same shelf as Lyell's *Principles of Geology.* It never occurred to them that their acceptance of the ideas therein contained amounted to repudiation of the static methods of natural science hitherto accepted.

Meanwhile Darwin had at last found the key to the secret of all secrets. Ever since 1838 he had been carrying a book about with him which constantly repeated that spell-binding expression he had been so much concerned with on his voyage round the world. "Struggle for life" was the phrase in question. And the book was the standard work consulted by all politicians dealing with problems of population, the *Essay on Population* by Malthus. The fascination of this essay for Darwin consisted not in the gloomy vision of a future starving and overpopulated earth, nor in its somewhat unrealistic advice to control the instincts and procreate reasonably, but in the reverend gentleman's recognition that all creatures had a tendency to multiply without restraint. In nature, Malthus stated, the struggle for life checked this impulse to multiply, but in human society Man himself must apply the drag. Darwin was interested in the first part of this proposition. He did not consider the second particularly important.

He glanced through the pages of statistics published by natural scientists and assembled certain familiar but astonishing data. They proved that the total descendants of a single pair of animals, if they had remained alive and fertile, would have covered the entire earth in a relatively short time. Each female sturgeon produced five or six million eggs every year, each mawworm forty million, and each tapeworm no less than sixty million. The number of children and grandchildren that a single tree louse might theoretically have in three hundred days could only be expressed by thirty-two figures. Every organism, Darwin concluded, procreates under natural conditions a number of descendants far greater than the earth could ever support. The enormous majority of such descendants are destroyed in the struggle for life before they can themselves propagate. A single small fish the size of one's finger exterminates in the course of its life about a million water fleas, each of which in its turn has annihilated an astronomical number of micro-organisms. Seven thousand such fish are eaten by one pike in the course of a year. Consequently, if you catch a ten-year-old pike you are confronted by a creature that has consumed directly and indirectly seventy billion other multiple-cell animals and an incalculable quantity of unicellular organisms.

This was in fact a truism. It had long been known that the struggle for life performs a regulative function in nature, governing the quantitative increase of animate beings. In Darwin's opinion this was not the only function it performed. So prodigal an expenditure of life must have a deeper meaning. What was defeated in the struggle for existence? That which was diseased, weak, and ineffective. And what conquered? That which was strongest, most resistant, and most adaptable. If, among all the millions of animals and plants that were born, only one survived, it was not mere chance that had enabled that single individual to last. The creature had passed through the finest filter imaginable and been sifted over and over again by its environment, its climate, its enemies, and by the struggle for food and reproductive partners. It could be regarded as a choice specimen, a high-level product of its species. Darwin accordingly deduced that the Malthusian struggle for life also acted as an inducement to breeding for quality in a species. Just as man artificially bred new stocks, so nature bred new species and genera by "natural selection." Lyell maintained that geological formations and environments were always changing. The choice animals and choice plants that had formerly survived natural selection would have to succumb to the struggle for existence under fresh conditions. Its place would then be taken by a different, more suitable type from among the countless germs of life procreated, and this type would proceed to hold its own and propagate its qualities. This was the very same flash of inspiration that had come to Darwin off the misty coast of Tierra del Fuego, but this time the lonely scholar at Down House knew what he had to do to prove his theory.

It could only be true if Linnaeus' cut and dried notion of species were found to be wrong, if the descendants of a single couple of parents were not of exactly similar type but inclined to variation without limit. And such capacity for variation could be precisely determined by the breeding of animals and plants, keeping all their descendants alive and watching to see how far they inclined to vary and whether they transmitted their peculiarities to their posterity. Accordingly, Darwin began to breed animals and plants.

Before long Down was swarming with pigeons, dogs, rabbits, and chickens. The quiet country seat turned into an animal farm. Darwin analyzed the breeds of domestic animals and traced them back to their primeval forms. He made use of ancient breeding methods to prove that it was a simple matter to produce from the posterity of a pair of original ancestors, in a relatively short time, new stocks more divergent from one another than the so called "good" species of the system builders. The capacity for variation was far greater than he had supposed in the cases of domestic animals, cultivated and wild plants, flowers and fruit trees. Such capacity could be used by man for the methodical breeding of certain types. And if Man could do it then obviously nature could.

Darwin experimented for almost twenty years in this way, with the patience and endurance of Jacob, without revealing any of his conclusions to a single human being except Emma. As soon as he had done with domestic animals he turned to wild species. For at that time it was believed only domestic animals and cultivated plants possessed this amazing flexibility, since they existed in order to serve mankind. In the case of wild varieties, however, no such potentiality was thought to be available. Darwin was able to refute this naïvely utilitarian argument. Creatures in the wild state varied in just the same way as those bred by man. But in this case extreme variants were as a rule obliterated again, since there was no need for them. Domestic animals had formerly developed out of the wild state, not because it was their destiny to do so but because gardeners and cattle breeders had eliminated free competition between the forms of life and replaced it by purposeful and deliberate management. Such was the solution of the puzzle.

Now and again Darwin thought of those three natives of Tierra del Fuego. If the principle of natural selection for breeding could be applied to all forms of life, it could be applied to mankind also. This action had already been taken, thirty years before, by a certain Dr. Wells, who had remained almost entirely obscure. He had stated that the races of mankind were products of the climate and living conditions prevailing in the areas they occupied. In his view climatic disease eliminated all the individuals that could not adapt themselves to the region and left alive only those resistant enough to withstand the peculiarities of their environment. Dr. Wells's theory sounded harmless enough, but the consequences it involved were clear to Darwin. Man had been implicated in the great process of selection and had not only branched out into certain definite races, tested and shaped in the struggle for existence, but had also at some time or another escaped, as a species of a peculiar kind, from the sphere of other animate beings and emerged victorious from competition with other mammals of similar type, at the same time developing his mind to a high level by taking advantage of favorable conditions. Man, therefore, had originally — there were no two ways about it — been an intelligent variant from the stock of anthropoid apes and favorable economic conditions had given him the opportunity of becoming lord of the earth.

Darwin maintained his ultra-prudent attitude and kept this opinion to himself. A single letter, dated 1844 and addressed to Lyell's friend Joseph Hooker, director of the botanical gardens at Kew, proves that he had soon come to break completely with the current scientific dogmas. "It is getting light at last," he said, "and I am almost convinced . . . that species are not (it is like confessing a murder) immutable."

A *globe-trotter starts an avalanche*

In the spring of 1857 Darwin's hands trembled a little as he read a letter from Alfred Russel Wallace. Then he pulled himself together. Of course this was bound to happen. Someone else had anticipated him.

The letter came from Celebes. It contained the main ideas of what Darwin regarded as his own theory. He had been trying to prove them experimentally for almost twenty years. The following year a more explicit letter from Wallace reached Down House on June 18, at the very time when Darwin had practically determined to publish his studies, under pressure from those who shared his views. There was no point in doing so now, for Wallace had meanwhile made exactly the same discoveries and was asking him to arrange publication. In fairness, Darwin ought not to suppress Mr. Wallace's letter with the essay enclosed.

He told Emma about it. She turned pale. He consoled her, smiling. "This is not a personal matter, Emma. It is the discovery that is important. Wallace was the first to have the courage to speak out in this affair. So it is only right and proper that the theory should bear his name." And he informed Lyell further of what had occurred.

A series of events then began which were typically English. A group of leading scientists learned of the unusual circumstance in which a certain investigator, out of exaggerated modesty, desired to allow someone else to take precedence of him. They imposed a gentleman's agreement on the two parties. As a first step, Lyell informed the Linnean Society, to which the best minds in England belonged, of the breeding data ascertained at Down and of Mr. Wallace's flash of inspiration. He wrote that it was considered desirable that these ideas, founded upon a very broad basis of reasoning from facts and tested over years of reflection, should now be accepted as forming a point of departure for future investigators. The Linnean Society also considered it desirable. They resolved to publish Mr. Wallace's discoveries on condition that "Mr. Darwin does not refrain, as he intends, from publication of his own work covering the same ground, in favour of Mr. Wallace." In other words, both or neither were to take the credit. It was a truly sportsmanlike decision.

Alfred Russel Wallace, whom fate had thus singled out to be Darwin's companion, was neither a famous scholar like Lyell nor a quiet student like the lonely owner of Down. He was an adventurer and globe-trotter who had experienced a certain amount of bad luck. He had been obliged to earn his living by toiling as an obscure surveyor, engineer, and schoolmaster before being attracted by foreign travel. He became a hunter of animals and explored the banks of the Amazon for years in the company of a wandering industrialist named Henry Walter Bates. But he had only been able to supply the London dealer who had financed the expedition with a few insects and birds, for almost the whole of his collection had been destroyed by fire aboard ship on his return voyage. He did not allow himself to be discouraged by this misfortune and obtained funds from certain collectors and heads of museums to enable him to equip a second expedition, this time to southeastern Asia. During this journey he became, thanks to his tenacity and thoroughness, an explorer, in the true sense of the word, of the Sunda Islands. He clarified the geographical distribution of animals and plants in this frontier area between India and Australia, collected over six thousand insects, studied the magnificently colored bird of paradise of New Guinea, and watched the great orangutan's mode of life and behavior in the family group. These last observations were to acquire much importance later on. He also concerned himself with the human inhabitants of districts in Australia and Malaya. He took skull measurements of primitive natives, compiled dictionaries of their languages, and presented anthropologists with a great quantity of valuable and highly informative data relating to hitherto practically unknown primeval peoples. All in all he was an ideal complement to Darwin.

It sounds almost incredible, like the plot of a novel, that he, too, should have hit upon the idea of evolution from reading the works of Lyell and Malthus. Lyell proved to him that the earth had evolved. Wallace, as an expert on animals, drew the conclusion that they, too, had evolved. Malthus emphasized the fact that hunger, disease and conflict had limited the diffusion of animate beings. Wallace considered this an answer to the problem of how evolution had proceeded. At the same time as Darwin he gained the same knowledge from the same sources.

In the fever-stricken jungles of Malaya he saw how species varied and how each variety sought to win a place for itself in life by strenuous effort. Nature went unfeelingly to work with her children, continually put them to the test, and eliminated all that were not pliable enough to adapt themselves to new circumstances. He encountered animals that showed so little fear of him that he could have shot down the whole lot of them. Some of them very soon learned that Man was dangerous and took their measures accordingly. Others never learned the fact and were consequently doomed to perish. He saw some insects that were bound to attract the attention of their enemies immediately and others that by resembling leaves, bark, or poisonous insects escaped the danger. Such mimicry could not be due to chance or any deliberate and purposeful adaptation since the beginning of things. It was the final result, Wallace recognized, of a prolonged process of selection, in the course of which the ineffectively disguised variants fell victims to the struggle and the rest had steadily perfected the effectiveness of their own disguise.

He had heard of Darwin's breeding experiments. And his object in first writing to him from Celebes in October 1856 had only been to inquire whether his observations could be of any use at Down and in London. Without suspecting what an avalanche he had let loose he continued his explorations. It was not until almost a year later that he received an answer to his first letter on the Moluccan island of Ternate. Darwin invited him therein to develop his theory at length in an article for the Linnean Society. Wallace was so amazed at this request that at first he could not realize what it meant. When he did, he almost wept for joy. Shaken by malaria, he sat down in his tent, to the accompaniment of the singing of tropical birds, drafted an essay with the title "On the Tendency of Varieties to Depart Indefinitely from the Original Type," and sent it off to Darwin with the request that he would pass it on to Lyell. It was the happiest hour of his life.

Darwin read the essay, found it excellent, collected some of his own manuscript notes made between 1839 and 1858, added them to Wallace's work, and sent the lot to Lyell. And Lyell, greatly struck by this "ingenious theory designed to explain the appearance and propagation of varieties and species on our planet" immediately drew the attention of Joseph Dalton Hooker, the greatest botanist in England, to the matter. For if Hooker took an interest in anything no one in England could afford to ignore it. Hooker belonged to an old English family of natural scientists, was a man of undisputed authority, and had, moreover, corresponded with Darwin for many years. He had participated in important expeditions to the Antarctic, the Himalayas, and India, discovered thousands of new species of plants, and made the botanical gardens at Kew the best in the world. He also held views similar to those of Darwin. It was he who subsequently induced the adventurer Henry Wickham to purloin seeds of the rubber plant from Brazil on the quiet, thus laying the foundations of British predominance in the rubber industry.

The Darwin-Wallace variations theory instantly aroused Hooker's enthusiasm. He declared himself ready to do all he could to promote it. On July 1, 1858, the two papers were read before the Linnean Society and published subsequently in the Society's *Journal*. England's leading natural science society, the Linnean — which, as the name implies, was the guardian of the legacy of Linnaeus and should really have stood by the principle of the immutability of species — deliberated on the affair and complained that "Mr. Darwin has not yet published his opinions, although we have repeatedly urged him to do so." They considered it was high time this step should be taken. And since Darwin was more accessible at Down than Wallace in his jungles, the trustees of Linnaeus' bequest brought urgent pressure to bear upon him to write a book forthwith on the origin of species.

Nothing like this had ever happened before. All the earlier evolutionists, those, that is, who received the slightest encouragement, had been obliged to fight desperately against the opposition of the scientific authorities. Now the authorities themselves were actually pressing a hesitant scholar, for all they were worth, to raze the fortress of recognized doctrine to the ground. The peculiar situation of science in England was responsible for this state of affairs. The ground had long been prepared, in the land of David Hume and Adam Smith, for such a man as Darwin. Not only Lyell and Hooker but also the shrewd anatomist, physiologist, and marine biologist Thomas Henry Huxley and the much discussed philosopher Herbert Spencer had each made similar discoveries in their own fields of research. Highly respected men, such as Dean Herbert of Manchester, Patrick Matthew, the expert on trees, the publisher Robert Chalmers, the astronomer Sir John Herschel, and the father of General Baden-Powell, founder of the Boy Scout movement, did not hesitate to write on evolution in the periodicals. The time was more than ripe for the theory itself. The only element of it that had not been supplied by Darwin's predecessors was the magic phrase "struggle for life."

Darwin retired to the Isle of Wight. In fourteen months he had written a book to which he gave the title *On the Origin of Species by Means of Natural Selection, or the Preservation of Favoured Races in the Struggle for Life.* It was the first work of an evolutionist that had been based upon fact and not on speculation. Neither Oken's creative world-spirit nor Lamarck's shaping environment was to be found in it. But above all the idea of purpose, that eternal apple of discord among scientists and philosophers, was not mentioned. According to Darwin neither hidden meaning nor premeditated plan was required for the development of even the highest degree of fitness of animate beings for their purpose. It was sufficient to assume that species were capable of infinite alteration and that nature always selected the best out of this abundance of forms by allowing the struggle for life to take its course. This conception must have sounded most attractive to the English, who believed that the same principle operated in the case of human society.

They also found Darwin's renunciation of Lamarck attractive, for the little man from Picardy had been the child of a frankly didactic age. He was thus led to suppose that environment educated its creatures in the same way, by the force of example and training. Darwin, however, was the child of a practical age which had ceased to believe that training could make a tree frog green, a giraffe longnecked, and a fool intelligent. According to current opinion, anything advantageous had lasting qualities and could be further developed, while the unprofitable would be bound to give up the struggle and perish. Darwin, as a practical man, felt himself rather repelled than attracted by the dogmatic and speculative character of Lamarck's theory. He expressly stated that Lamarck had not influenced the development of his own thought in the very slightest degree.

What he felt on completing his manuscript may be deduced from a letter to Huxley. He said that he was undergoing hydropathic treatment and would be all right again as soon as he had finished his "accursed" book. It would have been easy enough for anybody else. But it had half killed him, and he was very far from expecting that he would be able to convert Huxley to many of his heresies. He expressed himself in equally reserved and almost anxious fashion when dedicating his work to the leading scientists of Europe before

it reached the book trade. He stressed his desire that it should only
be regarded as a kind of preliminary study. He wrote to a friend
that he felt almost like a monomaniac. He told Lyell that he had no
intention whatsoever of calling in question the descent of man and
the Biblical story of creation. He expressly affirmed that he was
only stating facts and drawing such conclusions from them as he
considered fair. He carried his caution to the uttermost limit.

The *Origin of Species* came out in November 1859. The first
edition was sold out on the very day of publication.

The affair of Mr. Huxley's grandfather

The causes that send a book on a career of conquest round the world
have often been subjected to penetrating analysis. These studies
seem to prove that two preliminary conditions are indispensable.
The subject must be topical and it must be shocking. Both con-
siderations applied to Darwin's work. This purely technical volume,
which was not even easy to read, passed from hand to hand and set
going a regular series of intellectual reactions.

Philosophers and natural scientists, clergymen and laymen fell
upon it with cries of delight or indignation and at once took up their
positions. Everywhere people began to prick up their ears and take
an interest in a matter so controversial and for that very reason
worthy of special attention. The luck that Lamarck, Geoffroy Saint-
Hilaire and Oken had never been blessed with came to Darwin
wholly against his will. The world resounded to the battle cries of
the contestants, but to Darwin's intense dismay they disputed less
about the origin of species than about the origin of mankind. Both
friends and enemies were convinced that this was the true issue at
stake.

Yet Darwin, in his prudent fashion, had only touched upon the
problem of the descent of man in a single sentence. "Light will
also be thrown upon the origin of mankind and its history." Lamarck
and Oken, Kant and Schopenhauer, and even Linnaeus and Buffon
had been far more outspoken in this connection. But Darwin's very
caution was deplored as much in the ranks of his friends as in those
of his adversaries. The former had expected him to make a bold
profession of faith in descent from the apes. The latter wanted an
uncompromising statement that man did not come from the apes
but from God. Darwin was not the sort of person to adopt either
alternative.

He remained silent throughout the controversy, not out of cowardice, but because he was almost physically revolted by it. He shunned the natural science clubs, in which, as he put it, the members growled at one another in a far from gentlemanly manner. Others took the initiative, chiefly his correspondent Huxley. Contrary to Darwin's expectations, Huxley declared himself of his own accord in favor of all the "heresies" of the theory of natural selection. "How extraordinarily stupid of me not to have thought of it myself!" he wrote to Darwin. He set about making amends for this stupidity as quickly as possible. He became the loudest of the disputants, the blockade-runner on behalf of Darwinism, and immediately raised the painful question of the apes.

His most prominent adversary among scientists was the Cuvier of England, Richard Owen, the director of the natural history section of the British Museum, the same Owen who had already crossed swords with Lyell. According to tradition, Owen appeared as the resolute champion of Cuvier's point of view against Darwin. But there are passages in Owen's correspondence — Darwin himself referred to them in a *Historical Sketch of the Progress of Opinion Regarding the Origin of Species* — which imply that Owen had already drafted a theory of natural selection before Darwin did so and that it was only later, when he saw with profound vexation that another had been more successful than himself, that he went over to the opposite camp. There is much to support this supposition, for Huxley had no great difficulty in checkmating the leader of the English paleontologists.

Owen's arguments against a descent of man from apelike mammals included, in addition to Blumenbach's statement that man is a two-handed but the ape a four-handed creature, yet another special trump card, the structure of the brain. A human brain could never have developed from that of an ape, he asserted, for certain parts that exist in the former are completely lacking in the latter. Huxley made a close examination of the relevant facts. He studied exhaustively all the species of ape acessible. So far as the criterion of four-handedness was concerned, he was able to prove that the resemblance of the ape's foot to a hand was "only skin deep" and that the feet of both apes and human beings were exactly similar in bone structure. And as for the structure of the brain, the similarity between that of the despised race of apes and that of the lord of the earth was even more disconcerting. In fact the human brain, with the special capacities of which we are so proud, was in Huxley's view a genuine ape's brain.

Most of his contemporaries were disgusted when Huxley announced that the surface of an ape's brain represented a sort of sketch for that of a man. In the case of the anthropoid apes more and more details were inserted, until finally the brain of the chimpanzee and orangutan could only be structurally distinguished from that of a human being by a few subordinate characteristics. People were still more disgusted by the conclusions drawn by Huxley from this observation. As if Nature had wished to prove by a striking example the impossibility of erecting a barrier between ape and Man founded upon the structure of the brain, she had graded the brains of monkeys in an almost continuously ascending series, from primitive forms only slightly superior to that of the brain of a rodent to developed structures only slightly inferior to the brains of men. It was especially remarkable in this connection that the only gaps in this series did not occur between anthropoid apes and man but between the half-ape and the genuine ape. Huxley, in his dogmatic fashion, at once lays down a guiding principle that the difference between the lowest and the highest types of ape is far greater than that between the highest type of ape and the lowest type of Man. He proceeded coolly and imperturbably, as if it were the most obvious thing in the world, to insert *Homo sapiens* into the despicable family of anthropoid apes. Whereupon the gentlemen in the other camp of course made the most strenuous efforts to remove the human species from the appalling situation to which it had been thus degraded. But Adam stood his ground firmly shoulder to shoulder with the chimpanzees, gorillas, and orangutans. He still stands there today.

A large number of English scientists felt obliged to agree with Huxley about the "ape question." The churches and the leaders of society, profoundly shocked, now took the field. The trumpets sounded for a general assault. Darwin's theory, which he himself had never regarded as a dogma but merely as a working hypothesis, was accordingly made a religious issue. Bishops, puritanical clergymen, Tories proud of their aristocratic descent, and conservative professors rose up and called upon science to account for its actions. Thereupon Huxley, decidedly more of a fighter than Darwin, Lyell, and Hooker, conceived it his duty to be the Saint George of the theory of evolution. He unsheathed his sword to clear these obstacles from the path of free inquiry.

Battle was joined in the University Museum at Oxford before an audience of the most respected scholars in England. Darwin, however, was not there. But his most fanatical opponent, Samuel Wilberforce, Bishop of Oxford, a most eminent natural scientist, who could meet Huxley the ape-theorist on his own ground as a technician, duly took his seat.

The bishop did what was expected of him. When Huxley started to develop his ideas before the professors, some of whom agreed while others disagreed with him, Wilberforce brusquely interrupted. All this talk about variability and natural selection, the hands and feet of apes, cerebral formation, and that sort of thing, he said, seemed to him unimportant. In his opinion the point at issue was quite different. He put to Huxley the simplest and plainest question that anyone could think of in this connection. "I should like to ask you whether you really believe that your ancestor was an ape. If so, I should be interested to know something else. Did that ape come into the family on your grandfather's or your grandmother's side?"

By asking such a plainly biased question, the bishop had knocked the sword out of his own hand. Even so, some of his quarrelsome allies resorted to the same methods later on. But cudgel play of that kind was resented by English scholars. Huxley retorted that he would not be ashamed to have a monkey for his ancestor, but he would be "ashamed to be connected with a man who used great gifts to obscure the truth."

It is clear that in those days one did not mince one's words at Oxford. One of the ladies present was so shocked that she fainted. Robert Fitzroy, the former captain of the *Beagle*, brandished a Bible in a threatening manner in Huxley's direction. There were a few other excited interruptions as Huxley proceeded to prove that his zealous adversaries had not in fact the faintest glimmer of under- standing of Darwin's theory. This demonstration won him the game. The gentlemen on Wilberforce's side did not see the weak points in the theory of natural selection, particularly the difficulty about hered- itary transmission, and wasted their time in vain efforts to preserve mankind from the general bankruptcy of previous beliefs. Their criticisms finally culminated in a charge of heresy. That, however, cut no ice in the practical England of those days. The dispute over Mr. Huxley's series of apes ended with a landslide in favor of Darwin.

At that very time Huxley had just received a grievous personal blow, which would have prevented many others in his position from engaging in further propaganda for the brutish origin of mankind. The most precious thing in the world to him, his little son, had died. A friend of his, who was a clergyman and also a well-known author, Charles Kingsley, tried to make him reflect and revise his opinions by attacking him on this tender ground. The loss of a beloved being, he wrote, can only be borne if, instead of degrading mankind to the status of an ape, one believes in man's immortal soul and a reunion in the beyond.

In his reply, which is certainly one of the most interesting letters in English literature, Huxley declined this consolation. He made a profession of faith in the "scientific view of life" which deeply impressed his contemporaries. At that time, such a view was quite a novelty, but soon afterwards it combined with Darwinism to represent the typical intellectual attitude of large sections of the public in the latter half of the nineteenth century.

I do not deny the immortality of the soul [Huxley told Kingsley], nor do I affirm it. I see no reason why I should believe in it. On the other hand I should not know how to refute it. What I have to do is to induce my intense desire to take due account of the facts, not to try to force the facts into agreement with my wishes. Accept a fact as a little child does. Be prepared to give up every preconceived idea. Follow Nature humbly wherever, into whatever abysses she may lead you, or you will learn nothing. It was not until I resolved to do all this that I began to experience any peace of mind. I know very well that ninety-nine out of a hundred people call me an atheist. Our laws would not allow my evidence to be of any value against the most miserable thief who may steal my coat. But I can only say with Luther, God help me, I can do nothing else!

Such was the man whom Bishop Wilberforce wanted to have tried for heresy. People in England might think as they pleased about the "ape question." Huxley and the Darwinists had won a moral victory, which was a serious consideration in a country of "fair play." Even the more liberal type of churchman now inclined to take the view that it would be foolish to reject the new doctrine out of hand. At worst it was no more incompatible with the Biblical story of creation than Cuvier's theory of catastrophes. If it were ignored there would be a risk of the materialists, atheists, and other radical elements seizing upon it and using it as an advertisement for their own wares. It was better therefore to decide to treat it with benevolent indulgence.

The swing of the pendulum to Darwin's side was complete when the case of Spencer arose. The philosopher Herbert Spencer, who like Darwin was an out-and-out Whig, had embarked upon the brilliant scheme of applying the theory of evolution to all the departments of science and human life and writing a series of works intended to trace the "development of matter and spirit from the nebula to mankind and from the savage to Shakespeare." But he was a poor man and had also been obliged to resign his post as editor of *The Economist* in order to find time for the realization of this super-Darwinian ambition. While writing the first part of his *Principles* he had to live from hand to mouth.

At this point Lyell, Hooker, Huxley, and many other eminent men in England intervened. They helped him to make progress, stood security for him, got up subscriptions to guarantee purchase of the work, and succeeded in having Spencer's *First Principles* issued shortly after the publication of Darwin's theory. The results were appalling. The storm that had arisen against Darwin and Huxley assumed the dimensions of a hurricane. Spencer, the Wilberforce faction raved, had had the nerve to give a biological explanation even of politics, the nature of society, morals, and aesthetics. He had deprived the cosmos of all spiritual content and was a shameless materialist and atheist. The attacks were so furious that many of Spencer's patrons and subscribers, who had already been disturbed by the scandals arising from the ape question, suddenly became terrified and discontinued their support. Lyell's group met with refusal after refusal. Spencer's financial resources and also his courage, soon ran out. He was obliged to announce with the deepest distress that he had surrendered to the harsh realities of the situation and could make no further progress with the planned volumes on biology, psychology, sociology, and ethics.

At this juncture he received a letter from his fiercest opponent, the positivist philosopher John Stuart Mill. These two men had a cat-and-dog relation to each other. Mill had been a prodigy in his childhood, mastering Greek at the age of three, the whole of elementary mathematics at ten, and all the systems of philosophy at fourteen. He was a socialist, belonged to the radical wing of the House of Commons, and enjoyed such prestige in that assembly that the great statesman Gladstone felt it to be a "moral and intellectual degradation of Parliament" if he were ever absent from one of its sessions. Spencer, on the other hand, did not think much of socialism and believed that a socialist age would be the greatest disaster that mankind had ever experienced and would inevitably end in a military despotism of the sternest type. Mill was pious. He belonged to the puritanical Manichean sect. Spencer, however, was an agnostic, taking the view that one could know nothing about God and must therefore exclude Him from philosophical consideration. In Mill's opinion the process of nature consisted of a conflict between two opposed principles. Spencer thought there was only one principle — that of evolution. Mill rejected Darwin; Spencer supported him. Accordingly, when Mill sent a letter to his antithesis,

Spencer, one might assume that it was very unlikely to contain anything agreeable.

Actually it stated that he, John Stuart Mill, while of course setting no value whatever upon Spencer's philosophy of evolution, nevertheless deeply regretted the decision to abandon the work as planned. As he was in comfortable circumstances himself he would be prepared to see to the financing of the project for the future, not in order to do Mr. Spencer a personal favor but to promote an object of general importance. Mill reinforced his generous proposal with a promise to obtain subscriptions from American millionaires with whom he was on friendly terms. He put a sum of seven thousand dollars at his adversary's disposal there and then.

Spencer at first politely and resolutely refused the offer, but Mill would not be put off. He took action himself on behalf of Spencer's project, talked the matter over with him personally, and finally convinced him that he had no object in view but that of introducing to the public a great and noteworthy piece of work though one which he himself repudiated. Spencer was thus enabled to complete, over a period of almost forty years, his "synthetic philosophy," one of the most sagacious philosophical productions of the nineteenth century and one that ensured the penetration of Darwin's ideas into metaphysical thought itself.

This event caused a great stir. If such a man as Mill could show himself so impartial then surely even the most implacable critics of "monkey descent" could refrain from their coarse abuse of Huxley and his disciples. The theory of natural selection was accepted. It was taught in the universities. And monkeys, which had suddenly become so interesting, were made the subject of more intensive study.

A chance discovery put the finishing touch to Darwin's victory. Three years after the publication of the *Origin of Species* he had summarized his researches on orchids in a book containing the suggestion that a creature probably existed on the island of Madagascar which possessed a device for fertilizing the large species of orchids to be found there. No such animal was known at the time the book appeared, so Darwin's statement was considered a vague hypothesis. Very soon afterwards the news reached England that a gigantic butterfly with a proboscis fitting precisely the calyx of the orchids in question had actually been discovered in the woods of Madagascar.

This disclosure made a great sensation. It did not, in fact, reinforce the proof of the theory of natural selection, for a creative spirit might just as well have caused the butterfly and the orchid to fit each other as exactly as a jar and its lid, and the proboscis might just as well have come to suit the calyx of the flower as a result of Lamarckian adaptation. Nevertheless, most people were immediately convinced that the man from Down who had caused so much argument must be infallible. And perhaps even Vice-Admiral Robert Fitzroy of Grafton, who had previously considered all Darwinism to be nothing but the typical product of a seasick Whig, growled out a word or two of appreciation of his former traveling companion's butterfly.

To hell with the gorilla!

The first colonists of North America had been English puritans — crude, practical people who stuck to the Bible and had a hearty contempt for every sort of intellectual activity. Their descendants in Darwin's time, no less crude, practical, and Biblically minded, did of course by then regard science and other unremunerative studies with more favor, but they were nevertheless somewhat taken aback when they heard of a certain Mr. Darwin who considered that man had not been created from a lump of clay but from a lump of protoplasm. Several of the states immediately passed a law forbidding such nonsense to be taught in elementary schools from that time on.

On the whole, natural science, if it did not lead to any effective practical application, had at first no particularly high reputation as current coin in the land of unlimited possibilities. Fanatical sectarian preachers and agitators conducted a deliberate crusade against those suspicious characters who squatted over slimy indefinable substances in their mysterious laboratories and discussed "mutability of species" in the Boston *Journal of Natural History*. Public opinion decided that it was all humbug and firmly opposed the wonders of biological research with the miracle of the late lamented Jonah and the whale.

The affair first began to become more interesting when discoveries were made in the United States which seemed to go considerably beyond those of the infamous Mr. Darwin and his supporters. Gold miners in Pennsylvania and Missouri had for a long time been digging up massive bones and trading them for a drink of spirits or a good breakfast to farmers with whimsical tastes, who fixed them up in their houses as clothespegs and doorknobs. A certain Mr. Parker Foulke noticed these unusual articles of furniture in Pennsylvania farmhouses. He bought up all the bones he could find from the backwoods humorists and placed his collection at the disposal of the Academy of Natural Sciences in Philadelphia.

The anatomist Joseph Leidy of that institution identified the clothespegs and doorknobs as the remains of saurians larger than any hitherto known. The monsters were given the name of dinosaurs. George Peabody, a millionaire, heard about the affair and did what several American millionaires, including Carnegie, have since done. He opened his wallet and set aside a great part of his fortune for the benefit of "bone grubbers." It was in this way that the great era of prehistoric research began in America. The fossil hunters sent out by the philanthropic Mr. Peabody were so successful that even in the most remote settlements of Kentucky and Tennessee people pricked up their ears and began to have some respect for the "dubious" science.

The men who handled the spades came for the most part from highly exalted circles. Peabody's own nephew, Othniel Charles Marsh, and Edward Drinker Cope, a scion of one of the most important Quaker families of Pennsylvania, as well as a number of qualified geologists and engineers, were among them. They ventured into districts inhabited by rebellious Indians and at the risk of their lives dug up saurians, Tertiary mammals, and gigantic birds. They showed such diplomatic ability that even ferocious Sioux chiefs left them in peace. Their exploits pleased their compatriots. A further development was that Marsh and Cope, the two leaders, soon quarreled and started an embittered competition for depriving each other of the likeliest areas and the best fossils. This guerrilla warfare between paleontologists in distant Wyoming, Nebraska, and Dakota amused the public. It was at least as exciting as a football game between Harvard and Yale. We do not know, of course, whether bets were placed on Marsh and Cope in sports circles; but it is quite probable.

No one like Cuvier or Owen had ever succeeded in bringing to light such vast quantities of prehistoric animals as the expeditions of Marsh and Cope now brought back with them. The primeval world of America was suddenly revealed to the astonished gaze of Americans in stage after stage. Gigantic saurians, rhinoceros-like titanotheres, mastodons resembling elephants, and graceful miniature horses filled the museums. People looked at the pictures in which the ancient monsters were magnificently reconstructed, looking like the visions of a Brueghel from hell. People read what the immense crop of writings on popular science had to say about them. They fell into the traps of charlatans like the so-called "Doctor" Albert Koch, who exhibited, at a fair organized on a great scale, some whale skeletons from Alabama as "sea serpents." This same Koch had previously turned up in Prussia, where he had managed with similar talk about sea serpents to get an annual salary of a thousand thalers from King Friedrich Wilhelm IV, who was suffering from softening of the brain. In short, all of a sudden people went crazy about "science facts" and "science fiction."

The only trouble about all this was that the same splendid fellows who had dug up these magnificent bones in the wilderness were simultaneously supplying firstclass evidence in favor of the accursed Darwinian theory of evolution. For example, that champion of prehistoric research, Othniel Charles Marsh, was able to present an almost unbroken line of the ancestors of the horse, from the five-toed *Phenacodus,* no bigger than a hare, to the four-toed *Orchippus,* the three-toed *Miohippus,* and finally the whole-hoofed *Pliohippus.* The advance guard of American paleontologists studied in Europe, met Darwinians, admired the "monkey-theorist" Huxley and considered it a matter of course that the newly discovered fossil material should be classified from the standpoint of the theory of evolution. The Quaker's son Cope even proposed a law, which was instantly accepted by the Darwinians, to the effect that gigantic and highly specialized types of animals cannot adapt themselves to changes in their environment and therefore die out, while smaller, less specialized forms withstand even periods of unfavorable living conditions and thus hand on the torch of life. In Mr. Cope's view, accordingly, *Homo sapiens* showed rather a low degree of specialization, since he had held his own so well and for so long.

The masses in the United States suddenly discovered that Darwinism had been smuggled through gaps in the puritan system of customs control without its having been ever really noticed. The much admired scientists, in some states at any rate, were actually continually breaking the law. This was undoubtedly a painful dilemma. Its existence can only be explained by the fact that while natural science was making rapid progress in the United States, the most remarkable anti-Darwinian theory ever conceived had attracted widespread attention and belief at the very same time.

The originator of this theory was the man who had discovered the Ice Age, Louis Agassiz. He taught zoology and geology at Harvard University, where a swarm of valiant anti-Darwinians gathered about him. Like an Old Testament prophet he hurled anathemas against the cynical English who wanted to make Man a grandson of the gorilla. Wealthy industrialists and merchants were proud to be his patrons. On his behalf they financed journeys to the tropics, and maritime and deep-sea expeditions. They founded for his son Alexander a now world-famous marine laboratory at Newport, Rhode Island. It goes without saying that they were not paying out good money to encourage folly. Nor were the Agassizes, father and son, fools. They were outstanding scientists in their own special fields, above all oceanographers, from whom the line of descent leads directly to modern deep-sea investigators like William Beebe and Otis Barton. But they were not content with this eminence. The father, Louis, intended to do no more and no less than make mincemeat of the whole fabric of Darwinism.

His doctrine was based — how could it be otherwise? — on the venerable if at the same time somewhat decrepit and brittle work of Cuvier. He introduced into it, as the rationalist Cuvier had not, a personal God, who had completely destroyed his earlier work by a series of geological revolutions in order to replace it on each occasion with an entirely new supply of inhabitants of the earth. In the opinion of Agassiz the fact that first the lower, then the higher creatures had come on the scene pointed to purposeful intention, not evolution. "At each fresh creation God started with the forms of the age that had passed away, in order to improve his creatures progressively until they reached the final goal, man made in God's image."

Agassiz regarded the Darwinian view of life as a jungle, destructive of everything that industrious scientists had built up over the centuries, of the clear system they had erected, with its tidy separation of the various groups of animals and plants, its neat marking off of geological epochs and their fossils. Darwin's disciples, for instance, maintained as a fact that both primeval amphibians and reptiles, unspecialized mammals, and finally apes and human beings all had twenty fingers and toes, and considered that this proved all the higher vertebrates to have come originally from the amphibian stock. Agassiz strenuously opposed this argument. To him the number of fingers and toes possessed by the batrachian was a divine prophecy. God had foreseen Man from the beginning and anticipated his attributes at earlier geological periods. The puritanical Harvard professor saw the same kind of prophetic intimation in the surprising similarity between the forms of primeval animals and the embryos of higher types. Primeval fish that looked like the larvae of the land salamander, primeval water salamanders that resembled newts and sharks, with gill slits that could also be identified in the human foetus, were, so to speak, historical statements about the future. The bewildering likeness between ape and human being could be explained in the same way. The gorilla had imaginatively forecast *Homo sapiens* just as John the Baptist had proclaimed the Son of God.

Hardly anyone thought of this "highly anthropomorphic representation of the Creator" — so a contemporary ironically phrased it — "made by a zoologist in his own image" as a blasphemy. The theory of Louis Agassiz, on the contrary, traveled from America round the world, conquered German and French universities, and

The fossilized footprints of primeval batrachians prove that even these oldest of land vertebrates had five toes on each hind foot like a human being. The first batrachian also possessed five fingers on each forefoot. In the course of time the fifth finger disappeared.

was energetically defended by such eminent scholars as the Göttingen zoologist Keferstein. Decades later, when the Darwinians asked what valid objection could possibly be brought against the theory of evolution, the old school promptly answered in the one word, "Agassiz!"

Agassiz must be granted one virtue. His consistency was positively frightening. In his day the search for the "missing links" in the Darwinian chain of proof was just beginning. Zoologists and paleontologists were busily looking for types of animals that connected the various groups with one another, transitional forms between worm and fish, fish and water salamander, reptile and bird, or mammal, ape, and Man. A few of such links had long been known, such as the wormlike surgeonfish, the lungfish that resembles a water salamander, the primitive lizard fish, the egg-laying duckbill, and the lizard-like antique bird known as the *Archaeopteryx*. But according to Agassiz even these prime exhibits of the doctrine of evolution did not represent true transitional stages. He considered them "mixed forms" in which the Creator had for once in a way run two designs together and produced, so to speak, zoological centaurs.

Young and vigorous America digested her Agassiz, as she had digested her immigrants of miscellaneous races, her industrialization, her Negroes, Indians, religious sects, and speculators. The principle of free competition in nature had an even greater effect, in the end, on the land of self-made men than natural science in the guise of evangelism. Those restless years gave birth to men like Henry Fairfield Osborn, undoubtedly the greatest paleontologist of modern times, and Thomas Hunt Morgan, the founder of modern genetics. Both men were consistent Darwinians.

It did of course still frequently happen later on that lecturers who wished to speak on the theory of evolution in some little town in the South or Middle West would suddenly be confronted by a mob of excited people waving garish placards and shouting down in unison every word he said. It still frequently happened that when science ventured too far into the backwoods the cry rang out: "To hell with your gorilla!" And many a rash citizen of the United States who had forgotten that in Tennessee and Kentucky people still gave clay the preference over protoplasm had to be careful he did not get lynched. But these were isolated occurrences. American textbooks accepted the theory of evolution. American children sang

> *When you were just a little newt*
> *And I was a great big fish.*

America, in spite of all her evangelists, crusaders, and iconoclasts, became Darwinian and remains Darwinian to this day.

Eve follows the flag

Adrian Yeflichev, an obscure serf living in the Russian administrative district of Kostroma, would never have dreamed he would one day arouse public interest by his physical shortcomings and make quite a little pile of rubles. It was all due to Darwin's theory. "Little Father" Yeflichev, to his great distress, looked like a monkey. His whole body was thickly covered with hair and he had a face like a French poodle. In other respects, too, he could hardly be called a beauty. He had only been able to grow a few teeth and found it difficult to crack sunflower seeds, a circumstance which often caused him to curse his fate, especially as his little son Fedor showed the same dreadful peculiarities.

One day a foreign gentleman came to see him, dressed him up in new clothes, gave him some money, and told him he intended to take him and his son Fedor on a tour of Europe to show them to learned professors. Little Father Yeflichev felt bashful at first, but when he heard that his monkey-like growth of hair might make him a rich man he agreed to go. Soon afterwards he found himself the greatest attraction at English, French, and German fairs. The public gaped at him, tugged at his hair to see if it was genuine, and the professors kept on bandying about words like "atavism" and "reversion to the brute stage." Little Father Yeflichev gradually got used to it.

Adrian's fame kept Captain Hougston awake nights. He knew a whole family of monkey-haired people in Burma. Their name was Shwe Maong and they lived at the Court of Ava, the ancient capital. Their abnormalities had been transmitted through three generations. Finally a hairy beauty with bristles all over her face, Julia Pastrana, was imported from Mexico. She danced before smart society in Europe, thus proving the brutish origin of mankind to the sound of piano strumming. Natives with tails from India and Greece, a Filipino with a monkey's jaw and monkey's teeth, a Baden recruit from the assize town of Triberg who had six nipples and other monstrosities completed the picture of people who even in modern times had preserved the characteristics of brutes. The anatomists proved them to have been arrested at certain points in the embryonic stages during which the developing human being is distinguished by a covering of hair, a tail, and similar attributes. "Human beings with tails," Goethe had already stated in 1787, commenting upon news that had reached him, "do not surprise me. To judge from the description the phenomenon is quite a natural one." And the evolutionists, who considered that every embryo passed through all the ancestral stages of its species, at once seized upon this phrase and raised these poor misshapen creatures, who still showed signs of their shaggy or tailed forebears, to the status of documentary evidence of the highest importance.

The indefatigable Huxley thought out the structure of the missing link, the still undiscovered intermediate stage between the ape and Neanderthal man. According to him it must have been a most repulsive creature, half an Adrian Yeflichev and half a chimpanzee. The first Eve might well have been even uglier than Julia Pastrana. She would have had a hard job to seduce anybody but her forest monster of an Adam.

A flattish type of skull with very prominent eyebrow ridges and a set of teeth to match [was the description given in a contemporary book on popular science], long and powerful arms hanging to the knee, legs without calves, a rolling, stooping gait would undoubtedly be some of the most conspicuous characteristics of our primal ancestor, still thickly covered with hair and incapable of human speech. The long, powerful arms were still useful to him for climbing trees which, though they might no longer be his actual dwelling, were at any rate one of his favorite places for eating and his usual refuge from stronger beasts of prey which had less practice in climbing.

Alfred Russel Wallace had published on his return from the jungles of Indonesia some astonishing reports of the lives of monkeys in the wild state. They showed that the tiny "goblin" lemur, something like a tree frog, which closed Huxley's gap between the half-ape and the genuine monkey, already possessed certain human peculiarities. And the big orangutan, which means "wild man of the woods" in the native language, was considered by Wallace to be a sort of early missing link, or half-man, even when all the fables told of it in Linnaeus' time were discounted.

A baby orangutan caught by Wallace and intensively studied by this first of a long line of psychologists of the anthropoid apes, behaved "exactly like a human child in similar circumstances." It played with sticks and rags, rocked itself in its cradle, started crying when it did not like the taste of anything "just as a child does in a temper." It differed far more from a macaque (short-tailed monkey) of the same age which Wallace was bringing up at the same time, than from an unweaned Malay infant. The ways in which it teethed, learned to walk, and showed its need for affection were so startlingly like those that Mrs. Smith and Mrs. Brown noticed in their own babies that the Smiths and Browns who read Wallace's report could not get over their amazement. How could one any longer oppose the idea of beast and Man? Man was not a descendant of the animal, he was simply the highest developed of all animals. Anthropoid apes were only slightly inferior to him, and the connecting link had once been formed by the "ape man" — now the main object of search and thenceforth, as both caricature and idol, to haunt the minds of enlightened citizens of the nineteenth century like the sea serpent.

In those days, when people looked at an anthropoid ape in one of the newly founded zoological gardens they positively blushed, out of shame that it should be kept behind bars and also out of embarrassment, for it suddenly seemed so unpleasantly human. Perhaps Darwin, Wallace, and Huxley had been right after all.

At last things went so far that Darwin himself could no longer remain silent. He had still been able to write of the descent of man in 1857: "I intend to skip the whole chapter, as it is too hemmed in by prejudice, though I must admit that it is the most important and interesting problem for students of Nature." But since then he had, in his usual conscientious and pedantic fashion, been busying himself with Huxley's investigations of the brain, Wallace's stories about the orangutan, and the atavistic peculiarities of Maphron Shwe Maong, Julia Pastrana, and Little Father Yeflichev. He had another flash of inspiration. In 1867 he wrote to his loyal henchman Wallace: "I have practically decided to publish a short essay on the descent of man. And I am still firmly of the opinion that sexual selection has been the essential effective force in connection with the origin of the human race."

Sexual selection was a new catchword. While the shock troops of Darwinism were proclaiming with much zeal and ingenuity the descent of man from the apes, their leader was already wondering how it happened, and investigating an idea of his grandfather's. Erasmus had found that in many species of animals the female pursued the most handsomely decorated male "just as the ladies of the feudal age followed the banner of the conqueror." Decorative forms and colors that were much too conspicuous for the purpose of the struggle for existence, and had therefore been considered useless, were now found to have a special meaning. They reached their full splendor at the mating season, when they attracted the females already susceptible to the approach of the male. It followed that the most highly decorative males had the best chances of propagating their species, handing down their beauty and breeding up to a higher level.

Darwin surmised that something similar must have happened in the case of human beings. The old cave dweller, that apelike ancestral type, had collected his harem more or less by violence. But among his descendants were a few who were clever enough to arm themselves with stones and give their rivals a bang on the head. The primeval females were only too pleased by this enterprising behavior, and they ran after the heroes with the stone weapons and presented them with numerous children. Thenceforth, the daughters of Eve regularly preferred the less shaggy, more intelligent, and more inventive variations of the male portion of the human race to the rough-haired, brutal creatures. And the consequence was that the traces of intellect and human feeling, still slight when the process began, increased from generation to generation. These ideas, clothed in scientific language, were formulated by Darwin in his work *The Descent of Man, and Selection in Relation to Sex* which came out in 1871.

To his great distress the book gave rise to a fresh scandal. The world had learned that it must accept Lyell, Wallace, Spencer, and even Huxley. That Darwin himself should now advocate the same views, though after all it was quite logical that he should do so, once more started a commotion. Darwin's book explained bluntly just how human evolution had progressed. Man had begun as a worm, then breathed through gills like a shark, crawled through swamps like a water salamander, carried a bag under the belly like a kangaroo, and finally whimpered all night long like a half-ape. Worse and worse! The indecent baboons were our distant cousins, the repulsive gorillas and orangutans already showed traces of human thought and feeling, primitive man had at one time possessed a hide, practised polygamy, and gradually worked his way up through sexual maneuvers of one kind or another till he reached the level of a William Shakespeare or an Isaac Newton.

The works of Huxley and Wallace had not brought home these facts quite so clearly to the masses. Hitherto people had tolerated the idea, even been ready to admit it to the academies and schools. But this was a bit too much. Even Darwin's old patron Lyell and his otherwise docile disciple Wallace did not quite agree with the theory of sexual selection. "That I have not been fortunate enough to convince you," wrote Darwin in great anguish of mind to Wallace, "is the heaviest blow I have had to bear." These deviations from the general Darwinian line were not really significant: a certain amount of argument took place as to whether it was the struggle for food areas or the appearance of more ingenious Casanovas that had formerly bred mankind from Tertiary apes. Then the waters of debate grew calm once more.

Huxley's statement, made as early as 1863, still remained valid.

The question of all questions for humanity, the problem which lies behind all others and is more interesting than any of them is that of the determination of man's place in Nature and his relation to the cosmos. Whence our race came, what sort of limits are set to our power over Nature and to Nature's power over us, to what goal we are striving, are the problems which present themselves afresh, with undiminished interest, to every human being born on earth.

In this sense research went on while disgust, prudery, and prejudice were gradually conciliated. Huxley set aside Blumenbach's old scheme for explaining the human race and replaced it with a new one based on the theory of evolution, by which Neanderthal man had evolved from a hypothetical ape man. Neanderthal man had then produced primitive races that still survived, such as Australian aboriginals, Veddas, Papuans, Pygmies, and Bushmen. Three human groups — the white, the yellow, and the black races — arose from these primitive types. They had intermingled at the boundaries of their areas of distribution, initiated cultures, and thus produced the modern variety of tribes and peoples.

A London banker called John Lubbock supplemented Huxley's genealogical tree of races with a cultural tree. He had found out that the long-armed gibbons of Indonesia could sing scales perfectly. A chimpanzee in the London Zoo could count better than many a human being. According to the reports of explorers and travelers, anthropoid apes in the wild state used tools, adorned themselves, and performed rites and ceremonies reminiscent of primitive cults. As a result, Lubbock became convinced that human culture was rooted in that of the apes.

When Lyell, who had meanwhile been made a baronet, died in 1875, he was laid to his eternal rest in the most venerable of England's burial places, Westminster Abbey. And when Darwin followed him seven years later he too was buried there. His state funeral was attended by the greatest minds in England, by theologians, by members of the nobility, by statesmen and the ambassadors of America, France, Germany, and Italy. Joseph Hooker, Thomas Huxley, Alfred Russel Wallace, and John Lubbock were the pallbearers. They listened to the bells of Westminster tolling over the mourning city of London and felt proud of the tolerance of their native land. One incident relieved their gloom.

"Do you really believe that Darwin was right?" Huxley was asked by a worried-looking peer after the ceremony.

"Of course he was right," replied Huxley.

His lordship surveyed the Abbey with a pained expression. He observed in a low tone, "Couldn't he have kept it to himself?" He twirled his top hat for a moment, cleared his throat, and walked away.

After Darwin's death one of his paladins deserted him. Wallace took up spiritualism and came to believe more in table turning and prophetic mediums than in the intelligence of orangutans and nature's skill in breeding. The rest persevered and passed on their triumphs to posterity. Today, Julian Huxley — a descendant of Darwin's supporter — is a leading authority on genetics and a stern critic of the Soviet biologist Lysenko into the bargain. The physicist Charles Galton Darwin, grandson of the recluse of Down, has also written an interesting book on the future development of humanity, and supports with Malthusian logic, but without Malthusian prudery, the proposition that in the absence of reasonable birth control, the spiritual and biological substance of mankind is doomed to gradual extinction.

And in the study of a monarch who despite all the revolutions and disillusionments of our century still believes himself to be a direct descendant of the gods, the Emperor of Japan, there hangs as its only ornament the portrait of Charles Darwin.

X

NATURE'S STORY OF CREATION

Mechanized man and the riddles of the universe

THE MOST ARROGANT and pugnacious of the evolutionists, Ernst Haeckel, professor of zoology at Jena, became a legend during his own lifetime and is still one to this day. This tempestuous bearded fighter for Darwin's theory has often been described quite simply — even by those who fully recognized his great scientific gifts — as a materialist, and a boastful, arrant specimen of the breed into the bargain. He has been held mainly responsible for all sorts of notorious brawls and wrangles which for decades transformed the hallowed professorial chairs of science into a parliamentary arena of violent uproar. He has been reproached with introducing vulgar slang and outrageous coarseness into the language of scholars, thus anticipating the profane spirit of the twentieth century.

Contemporary documents give rather a different impression of the Haeckel case. The "ape-professor of Jena" certainly did not mince his words in controversy and his methods were not quite suited to the drawing room. Nevertheless, it is disappointing to have to say that the most robust terms of abuse did not proceed from him but from his adversaries. And Haeckel's view of nature certainly did rest upon hypotheses of a physical character. However, that was not the reason for its materialism. It was in fact, as speeches, letters and autobiographical documents very clearly testify, Protestantism permeated and powerfully inflated by pantheistic ideas. Genuine materialists — like Bebel for example — turned up their noses at it.

The epoch into which Haeckel was born awakened a slumbering fiend, technology. And this fiend in its turn awakened a slumbering horde, the proletariat. Steam and electricity, whirling wheels and thudding hammers won dominion over the cities. Masses of employees accumulated in the industrial towns that shot up so fast. Fettered to their machines, they turned into machine parts of flesh and blood. At the very time when the last civilized states were setting about the elimination of the relics of ancient slavery, they felt themselves becoming enslaved once more and in a far more treacherous fashion. Believing that it must be possible to guarantee all men alike a share in technical inventions, happiness, and prosperity, they did not confine themselves to thinking but acted on their beliefs.

A new era was dawning, which could not help being an era of social struggle and reform. Humanity, intending to create a paradise on earth by the use of reason and the ingenious exploitation of nature, had to roll up its shirtsleeves to solve the economic riddles of the universe.

It was precisely at this time that the man who intended to solve these riddles scientifically raised his voice. Ernst Haeckel was separated by a deep gulf from the political materialists, as his quarrel with August Bebel shows. "I am, of course, no friend to Herr Bebel, who has repeatedly attacked and even slandered me," Haeckel once declared, opposing Bebel's party program with the words: "The conditions of existence are dissimilar in the cases of all individuals from birth, as are also their inherited attributes and aptitudes. How then could their careers and the consequences ensuing from them be the same everywhere?" Bebel, for his part, was no friend to Herr Haeckel. He repudiated these statements as "superficial" and gave it as his opinion that the struggle for life in human society had simply led, as he put it, to the "dominion of the most cunning and the most corrupt." Two worlds were here coming into collision.

Despite these tensions between science and practical life, Bebel's supporters, the masses of the people — eager for education, seeking new paths and new knowledge — seized with enthusiasm upon Haeckel's "riddles of the universe." Of course this did not make Haeckel, as the *Fuldaer Zeitung* wrote at the time, "the spiritual stepfather of socialism, nihilism and communism." But he did introduce socialists, nihilists, and communists, as well as large numbers of the middle classes, to natural science. In this way Darwinism and the theories of generation, evolution, and the ape man acquired a political significance and played a brief but extremely dramatic part in the arena of politics.

On February 16, 1834, at the time when Darwin was noting in his diary the amazing resemblance between extinct and living animals in Patagonia, Haeckel was born in the conservative Protestant town of Potsdam and into a conservative Protestant family of officials. The environment in which he grew up was thoroughly pious and loyal to the throne. Haeckel never abandoned those sentiments. If we are to give faith as broad an interpretation as Lessing and

Goethe gave it, we must call Haeckel, in contrast to many of his later adversaries, a man of faith. Natural science was always for him a matter of one's view of life and one's creed. In this connection he remained a true descendant of the families of Haeckel and Sethe, which had struggled for the recognition of eternal truths from time immemorial, even though he abjured the faith of his forefathers.

He was led to zoology by the writings of Oken and Humboldt, to literature by the works of Goethe and to the doctrine of evolution by the book on plants written by Schleiden, the discoverer of the cell, and Darwin's *Journal of Researches . . . during the Voyage of the H.M.S. Beagle Round the World*. Much of his youthful history is surprisingly reminiscent of Darwin's. He, too, could not kill animals, stand the sight of blood or dissect corpses. His university lecturer, Virchow, cured him of these disabilities completely. From Virchow he learned the wonders of the cell, and from Johannes Müller, with whom he went on several voyages, the wonders of the sea. He relates in his autobiography that when quite a little boy he had already thought of the possibility of Man's descent from apes as the result of a visit to Brockmann's monkey theater in Berlin. In short, he absorbed all the new discoveries of his time, revered the great Johannes Müller, considered the summary materialism of Karl Vogt to be "crazy radicalism," and showed every sign of turning into a respected and highly esteemed university professor.

Then in 1860 a quiet, modest paleontologist from Heidelberg, Heinrich Georg Bronn, who sympathized with the ideas of evolution, read Darwin's *Origin of Species* in the English edition and resolved to translate it into German. To be sure, Bronn thought one ought not to emphasize the daring of this work. He therefore simply cut out the single sentence that dealt with the origin of mankind. Haeckel procured the translation, was surprised to find that it did not mention Man, and, in contrast to Bronn, took the line that this omission ought certainly to be rectified in order to round off the new theory. This decision affected the whole course of his future life.

Until then Haeckel had paid little attention to mankind. The principal objects of his research had been Radiolaria, unicellular marine organisms of wonderful structure, which he had studied in Italy. His monograph on Radiolaria, in the opinion of a renowned expert of cells "one of the greatest embellishments of zoological literature," gained him his appointment to the University of Jena. And there, to the disgust of his older and more experienced colleagues, he at once began to speak enthusiastically of Darwin and the problem of the descent of man. "I have read this remarkable book over and over again and each time I looked through it afresh I found new and surprising examples of insight and far-ranging vision. Evolution is the keyword which will either answer all the riddles with which we are surrounded or put us on the way to their

At a very early stage of development the human embryo produces gill slits resembling those of the shark. It bears an astonishing likeness at this time to other mammals' embryos of the same age. Haeckel concluded from this that every form of life reproduces as a germ the course of development followed by its species. Top row, dog and rabbit; bottom row, bat and human embryo. Each set at third and fourth weeks of development. Drawing after Haeckel.

solution. This brilliant victory of the discerning intelligence over blind prejudice will contribute more than anything else not only to the spiritual liberation but also to the moral improvement of mankind."

His colleagues smiled at his enthusiasm and observed calmly that in a few years' time no one in Germany would even bother to talk about this English crank. They were mistaken. In a few years' time all Germany was talking of him and especially about a man named

Haeckel, who was now starting to close the big gaps in the edifice of Darwinism.

As a marine biologist Haeckel knew something about lower organisms. He could therefore do what Darwin had neglected to do: draft a theory of generation according to which primitive unicellular creatures of aboriginal type, known as Monera, had at one time been formed in the ocean from albumen compounds. As a disciple of Virchow, Haeckel knew a lot about embryology. He therefore ventured to transfer development processes in the germ to the family history of life. Just as the ovum divides, growing into the shape of a mulberry, and then turns in upon itself to produce the earliest form of the intestine, and finally develops organs, so also had the unicellular forms divided, amalgamated into conglomerations of cells, become creatures with intestines, and finally taken their separate ways as echinodermata, mollusks, articulate animals, and vertebrates. And just as the human embryo possesses at different times gills, a tail, and a hide, so also had the ancestors of mankind at one time possessed gills, at another tails and hides.

It sounded plausible. Haeckel presented the public with this picture of evolution at the same time that Huxley was doing so in England. He hoped the learned world would agree with him and recognize that he had, as he put it, made a contribution by his theory to the spiritual liberation and moral improvement of mankind. He was not, to be sure, the first champion of such a logical theory of the descent of man. Long before this time the "radicalist" Karl Vogt had roamed through the countries in which he was still allowed to show himself, beating the big drum for his theory of generation and descent from the apes, winning the nickname of "monkey keeper," a pun on the word Vogt, which means "keeper" in German. That didn't matter to Haeckel. On September 19, 1863, when he rose to speak at the congress of natural scientists in Stettin, he did not talk of harmless Radiolaria, as had been expected, but of Darwin and the origin of mankind.

A storm of indignation broke out at once when he stated, with disarming ingenuousness, "So far as we men ourselves are concerned, we should logically seek our ancestors first among apelike mammals, beyond them among kangaroo-like marsupials, still farther back among lizard-like reptiles, fish at a low level of organization and finally among unicellular aboriginal forms generated from dead matter." The worthy professors gazed at each other blankly, imagining they had not heard him aright. In the ensuing debate some of the gentlemen called Darwinism a meaningless fraud. Others put

it on the same level as table turning. The majority expressed profound regret that such unscientific subjects for discussion could be
raised at all during a congress of natural scientists.

Haeckel was amazed. He was even more astonished when he
heard himself called an atheist and blasphemer. Till then he had
considered himself a good evangelical Christian and had been unconscious of any opposition between his scientific and religious faith.
He now learned that he was being put on the same level as the
radical monkey keeper. He could not quite understand it, and returned to Jena more determined than ever to straighten out the
tangle.

In the most exalted circles in Germany just then, opinions about
Darwinism differed altogether from those expressed at the Stettin
congress of scholars. When he visited Berlin, Lyell found that the
Crown Princess of Prussia was an enthusiastic Darwinian. Haeckel
found the same reaction in Alfred Krupp and his own Grand Duke
Karl Alexander of Weimar.

Shortly after the congress fiasco he told the Grand Duke that he
now meant, in defiance of all the reproaches leveled at him, to
write a book on the doctrine of evolution. The Grand Duke smiled,
laid his hand on Haeckel's shoulder, and observed, "One may think
that sort of thing, my dear professor. But one doesn't have it
printed."

Bombs in the powder barrel

What led Haeckel to abjure the faith of his youth and hammer out
a new view of life from Goethe's pantheism, Luther's rebellious
challenge, and Helmholtz' physics? As often in the history of mankind, a personal tragedy was the cause of this great change. His
cousin Anna, the playmate of his youth, died suddenly. For Haeckel
her death meant a prolonged physical and mental collapse, the
crash of his world. He wrote bitterly to his father, who had only
prevented him with difficulty from committing suicide, that he considered it tasteless to offer religious consolation in such a situation
and that he could no longer feel any confidence in that sort of
thing.

"The abrupt change in my circumstances brought about on the
unlucky day when I completed my thirtieth year," he wrote in a
personal note made at this time, "destroyed at one blow all the relics
of my earlier view of life. Individual human existence now seems
to me so horribly wretched, paltry and worthless that I cannot see

it as destined for anything but annihilation." Haeckel became a monist. The standpoint had hitherto been a most honorable one. It counted among its adherents Giordano Bruno, Galileo, Spinoza, Goethe, and a whole series of other great minds. It maintained that God and nature were one and that no barrier could be erected between matter and spirit, body and soul. It was accordingly a philosophical doctrine that ranked as one of the greatest spiritual achievements of the Western world, and no doubt a substantial number of natural scientists sympathized with it in Haeckel's day. Haeckel made it a substitute for religion. And that was the real source of all his later trouble.

He fought for it quite as sincerely, passionately, and ardently as his adversaries fought for their own view of life. He often made a false step, and his arguments became irrelevant, harsh and contentious. So did those of his adversaries. Because faith is usually bolder than reason he ventured into fields he knew little of. His adversaries did the very same thing. The consequence was that for fifty years in Germany and far beyond Germany's frontiers a strange, often touching, and frequently painful drama was played out in public. A pitiless struggle between a man who sought the divine in nature and other men who sought the divine beyond nature was fought to a finish. In its course both sides tried to turn the facts of natural science into metaphysical articles of faith, and vice versa.

The fight began with the publication of Haeckel's *General Morphology of Organisms,* a thick volume on natural science that contained not only his theory of evolution but also his philosophy of nature. Each chapter was headed by a quotation from Goethe. Some passages were most interesting, though hardly appropriate to a textbook on zoology. The present-day atomic theory, for example, was foreshadowed. At the same time certain ill-natured pinpricks were administered, such as the comparison of the rule of priests and despots with parasitism in nature. On the "question of all questions," the origin of mankind, he wrote, among other things: "It is an interesting and instructive fact that the discovery of the natural evolution of the human race from genuine apes arouses especially intense indignation among those people who have obviously, so far as their intellectual equipment is concerned, hitherto traveled the least distance, themselves, from the apes." In other passages, too, Haeckel distributed charges of this kind with a fairly lavish hand.

As soon as the book was published he sent a copy to Darwin, whom he had in the meantime met. Darwin greatly admired the scientific part of the work, but not the numerous pinpricks.

I have long noticed [he wrote, in a gentle reproof, to his fiery adherent] that excessive severity inclines readers to take the part of the persons attacked. Since you, my dear Professor Haeckel, will assuredly play a great part in science, pray allow me, as your senior in years, to beg you most earnestly to reflect on what I have ventured to say. I know that it is easy to preach and I am not afraid to say that I myself, if I possessed the ability to write with the proper pungency, would enjoy turning these poor devils inside out. But I am convinced that it does no good but merely causes unpleasantness. It always seems to me rather dubious policy to speak too positively on any complex subject. I hope you will pardon my frankness.

Darwin's warning came too late. Haeckel's work did not only cause unpleasantness, but it also caused an open controversy. Even his best friend, the Jena professor Gegenbaur, was shocked. He observed that to serve up a dinner like that "with a hundred courses" to one's esteemed colleagues did not help to achieve the object in view but merely produced indigestion. But Haeckel had the mentality of an ancient prophet. He simply had to pass on the revelations he had received, and he went on serving up dinners with a hundred courses to his contemporaries.

As the professors disapproved of his doctrine, he resolved to take it to the people and thus achieve his purpose. From the winter of 1867 on he held regular free lectures attended by a large audience on what he called "Natural History of Creation," in other words the theory of evolution, generation, the descent of man, and pantheistic philosophy. And it was clear — to the annoyance of many professional people, who could not see the point of this campaign of enlightenment — that uninstructed laymen at once went over to Darwinism without the slightest hesitation. Never had scientific gatherings at Jena been so crowded, never had a professor of zoology enjoyed such popularity among middle-class citizens, workmen, married women, and schoolchildren as that controversial and much persecuted figure, Ernst Haeckel.

The first twenty-four public lectures soon appeared in book form with the title *Natural History of Creation*. Further volumes of the kind were added, one of the last, in 1899, *The Riddles of the Universe*, going into an edition of 400,000 copies, and being translated into all civilized languages, to the joy of its publisher, who had been at first rather doubtful of its success. Simple fishermen in the Orkney Islands, Scottish highlanders, Australian shepherds, and even semi-savage Maoris in New Zealand read this highly controversial and brilliantly written, if by no means flawless, work. Men like the leader of the anthroposophists, Rudolf Steiner, went so far as to regard it as their Bible. Others, like the professor of philosophy Friedrich Paulsen, were thoroughly disgusted by it. And by the turn of the century a whole "Riddles of the Universe" literature had come into existence, with all the arguments for and against.

Haeckel's influence on the masses at that time was described by the literary critic Georg Brandes, one of the few neutrals in this scholars' war: "Haeckel's books acted like a bomb thrown into a powder barrel. In fiery language, in poetic style and with astonishing erudition he gave a creative turn to Darwin's theory and stated its logical consequences with a frankness bordering upon that of the martyrs of old." On the other hand Haeckel's friend and closely associated colleague, Gegenbaur, who was a convinced Darwinian, thought that "it was best to write such books in Latin, so that only a small circle can read them." And Darwin, doubtful of Haeckel's success and full of uneasy forebodings, warned him that "sometimes your boldness makes me shudder."

A hot-tempered man always offers his adversaries plenty of openings. There was much which could reasonably be said against Haeckel's writings. But for a long time the professors of the old school, allied with conservative politicians, orthodox theologians, and idealist philosophers, did not use their foils to such effect. Instead of seizing upon Haeckel's excursions into purely intellectual fields, where he often skated over thin ice, they undertook the hopeless task of trying to defeat him on the ground of natural science. Darwin would have said that they were not very gentlemanly. The paleontologist Rütimeyer reproached Haeckel with deliberately falsifying his drawings of embryos. The ethnologist Bastian called the theory of human descent a "betrayal of the sacred name of science" and a "mockery of human dignity." Professor Michelis at Bonn described the hypothesis of the ape man as an "attempt to destroy morality." Finally the great Du Bois-Reymond stigmatized Haeckel's pedigrees of animals as being "worth as much as the pedigrees of Homeric heroes," though these, as we know today, are by no means as worthless as he thought. Such arguments had very little connection with biology and it was easy for Haeckel to refute them.

The charge of materialism, one of the worst that could be made at that time, was also repudiated without difficulty by the defiant champion in characteristically acrimonious style. Fundamentally the natural scientist says no more than that everything in the world

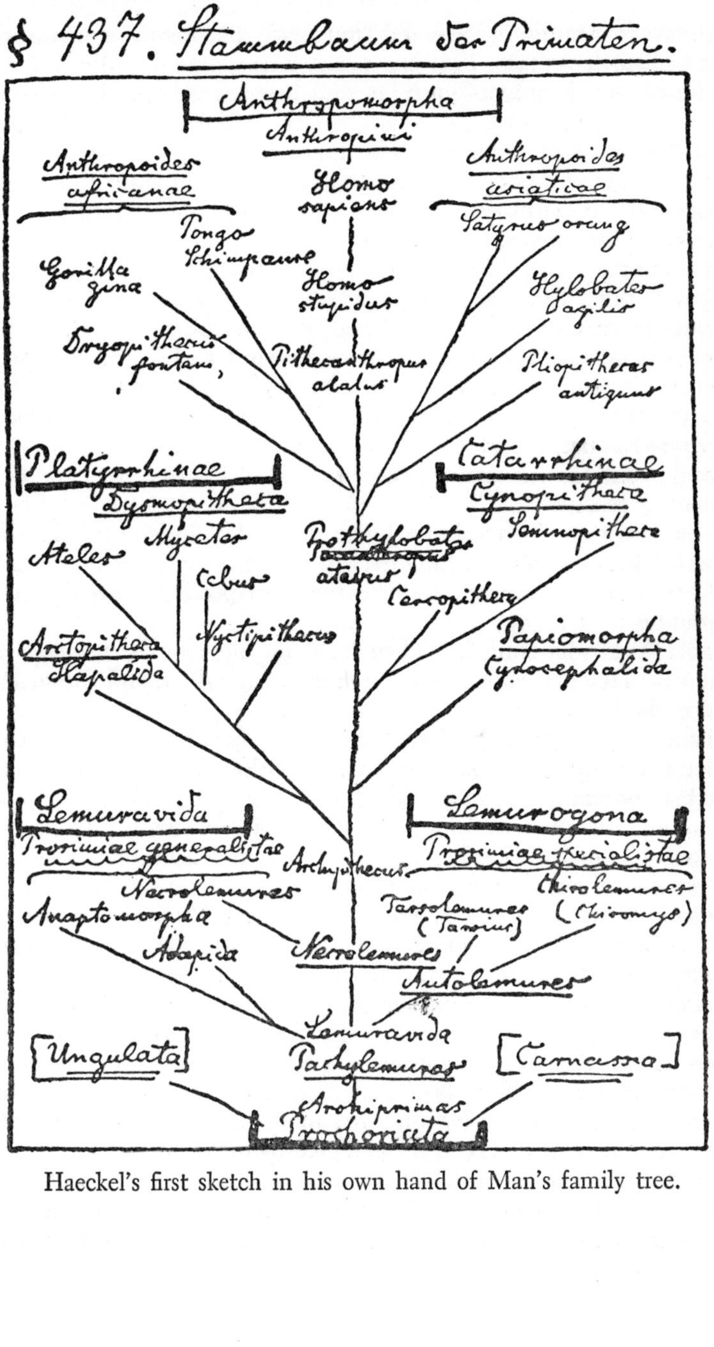

Haeckel's first sketch in his own hand of Man's family tree.

happens by natural agency and that every effect has its cause and every cause its effect. This has nothing in common with true materialism, which pursues no other aim in practical life than that of the most refined enjoyment of the senses. It entertains the unhappy delusion that this proceeding can give mankind true contentment, but has no inkling of the profound truth that the real value of life is based not upon material enjoyment but upon moral action. "You will search for materialism among natural scientists in vain, for it must be sought in palaces." Naturally the inhabitants of the palaces did not much care for this deduction. The affair reached such a critical stage that Haeckel's adversaries determined to call in the state authorities to remove him from his post and forbid all discussion of the theory. One day the Weimar churchwarden Schwarz, at a private audience of the Grand Duke Karl Alexander of Sachsen-Weimar-Eisenach, said the *Natural History of Creation* was corrupting youth and demanded the dismissal of Haeckel from the University of Jena.

"Do you think," the Grand Duke asked the churchwarden, "that Haeckel believes in everything he writes and considers it the truth?"

"Yes, I'm sure he does," replied the unsuspecting Schwarz. "Unfortunately!"

Karl Alexander smiled. "Then he is no more in the wrong than you are!" He escorted his visitor politely to the door, and the matter ended there.

Haeckel's only antagonist of any note was his former teacher Rudolf Virchow. And as Virchow had nothing against evolutionary ideas in principle but merely considered "any suggestion of cosmic planning," whether of Linnaean or Darwinian stamp, "premature clowning" — since, in other words, he was interested in facts — the discussions about Father Adam became for a time somewhat more objective. Anthropology and prehistory were Virchow's own very special fields. He knew more about the races of mankind than any other scientist in Germany. He had done actual spadework for Schliemann in the excavation of ancient Troy and ranked as an outstanding expert in all questions relating to *Homo sapiens*. He only had one fault: he was a confirmed skeptic. His skepticism penetrated in every direction where he failed to find cast-iron proof — in the spheres of bacteriology, Neanderthal man, Ice Age civilization, and even more in that of Haeckel's pedigree of mankind.

He had nothing whatever in common with Haeckel's conservative and orthodox adversaries. He was a man of independent mind, so full of pride in natural science that he paid scarcely any attention to gentlemen like Paulsen, Michelis, and Schwarz the churchwarden. When Haeckel reproached him with co-operating with these people he was most indignant: he differed from them at least as much as the rebel from Jena.

Then in September 1877, at the Munich congress of natural scientists, the question of teaching Darwin's theory in the schools came up. Haeckel had meanwhile undertaken several journeys to the East, had been welcomed by the viceroy of Egypt like a prince and by England's intellectual aristocracy as "an authority of the highest standing." After all the recognition and honors conferred upon him abroad he was determined to ensure the final victory of his ideas in his own country as well. Consequently, his report to the congress, which elsewhere kept strictly to the matter in hand, culminated in a demand for the immediate communication of the outlines of Darwinism to the schoolmasters.

Virchow spoke against him and issued a warning against teaching in the schools "theories whose certainty one could not yet swear to." He referred to descent from the apes as "possible but not proved." He took the opportunity of pronouncing an extremely laudatory obituary of Lorenz Oken and added some very shrewd comments on the situation of the natural sciences. But his next words revealed that he was a politician as well as a scientist. This was the man who had taken part in the founding of the party of liberal progress, at that time involved in strenuous conflict with the Social Democrats. "Imagine the attitude of the socialists to the descent theory today!" he cried to the assembly, who listened to him in shocked fascination. "Some of you may think it absurd: but I tell you that it is an extremely serious matter and I take leave to hope that this theory is not going to cause among us all the frightful consequences that similar theories have actually brought about in France. We must be quite sure we have taken this into account!"

Neither Haeckel nor the Social Democrats, his most implacable enemies, could follow Virchow's bold association of ideas. The anti-Darwinians, however, in whose eyes Virchow had hitherto ranked as nothing but a cynical materialist, understood it all the better for that reason and burst into loud applause. It happened that shortly afterwards two muddleheaded anarchists — a tinker's apprentice from Leipzig, Max Hödel, and a man named Karl Nobiling — made an attempt to assassinate the German Kaiser and wounded him with small shot.

At once Haeckel was again attacked. The conservative Berlin *Kreuzzeitung*, referring to Virchow's speech, accused Haeckel and Darwinism, of being morally guilty of the outrage. Others joined the attack and said that it was now obvious how much harm these theories did in the minds of tinkers' apprentices and individuals of that sort. When Haeckel replied that the theory of the descent of man had nothing to do with Hödel's and Nobiling's ambush, since it showed in the clearest possible way that such bloodthirsty plans were impracticable, he was only greeted with scornful laughter. Incidentally, it turned out afterwards that Hödel and Nobiling had never heard of Darwin, Haeckel, or the theory of evolution.

Haeckel had hitherto refrained from answering Virchow's false political inference. It went against the grain for him to attack a man he respected and one united to him by bonds of friendship. Now he could no longer keep silence, and imitated Mark Antony's tactics toward Brutus. In a bitterly hostile pamphlet entitled *Free Science and Free Teaching* he first recounted all the services rendered by Virchow to science, then expressed his deep regret that so distinguished a man had since grown too old and senile to understand the simplest biological argument, and finally advised him, as a friend, to hold his tongue in the future. He wrote, "It is true that Virchow prints the following sentence from his Munich speech in italics: '*All I am proud of is the knowledge of my own ignorance.*' But it is precisely such pride that I fear I must emphatically deny him. Virchow does not know how ignorant he is. Otherwise he never would have uttered such destructive criticism."

And the students of Jena, enthusiastic disciples of their stormy professor of zoology, composed a new couplet to an old tune, alluding to Virchow, Du Bois-Reymond, and the other Berlin celebrities.

> *If you know the truth and speak it out,*
> *You'll land in jail without a doubt.*

The ape man of Java

The history of research on primitive man is full of incredible occurrences, miraculous accidents, and lucky finds that sound like fiction. Fossilized human beings are rare. Generally they are discovered by chance, not deliberate excavation, by the farmer who comes on buried treasure as he plows his field.

But this did not happen in the case of the discovery of the long sought "ape man," the subject of so many legends and jokes. The search was methodical, like a bad detective story — on a basis of false clues, under the wrong conditions, and apparently in the wrong places. Yet after a relatively short time the long sought object was unearthed. The details of the discovery are more incredible than any chance find.

Archeologists have an easier task than paleontologists. They know more or less where the ancient culture they wish to uncover is to be looked for. Unless they already have some clues to work on, the paleontologists have nothing like this to help them and as a rule research on primitive man has to grope in the dark. In Haeckel's time no one had the slightest idea where the ape man, whose anatomy had been built up by guesswork and immortalized in a number of pretty pictures, might really once have lived. There were plenty of suppositions, but Virchow only smiled mockingly at them. Firmly convinced of the uselessness of all such speculation, he advised the Darwinians to chatter less about the alleged intermediate form and take to their shovels and present their evidence. He was not in fact by any means so skeptical as he pretended. It is interesting to find that he once observed that the "missing link" would turn up, if it ever did, most probably somewhere in the archipelago beyond India. Some years later his adversaries had the chance to remind him of what he had once said.

There was a stir in the learned world when in 1871 quarrymen had found a human skull near Taubach on the Ilm. According to the geological evidence, its owner must have lived before the Neanderthal specimen. Virchow looked over the skull, saw that it seemed of a more refined type than that of Fuhlrott's rachitic cave dweller, and classified it as of the Late Stone Age. The find was forgotten. No one now knows what became of it. At all events it did not look like the skull of an ape man, as Virchow was actually able to prove.

Twenty-one years later some molars came to light near Taubach. The anthropologists could not agree as to whether they were of human or simian origin. In the end they sent the molars to New York, where master paleontologists of course were bound to know everything. The Americans replied laconically that the molars were chimpanzee teeth. The next step obviously should have been for science to make a few further investigations into the secrets of Taubach and the charming valley of the Ilm. For the fact that chimpanzee teeth had been found close to a human skull of by no means primitive type was rather remarkable. But no one took any particular notice of the coincidence. Not until 1914 did further excavation prove that although the Taubach finds had nothing to do with ape men, they had nothing to do with chimpanzees or Late Stone Age man either. They were to be referred to as the Ehringsdorf race, a very ancient type of Neanderthal man which, oddly enough, with its arched skull and lofty forehead, looked more human than the true Neanderthal specimens from Düsselthal and Spy.

Haeckel had been looking for a long time in a different direction. During his researches on the history of evolution he had been struck by the startling resemblance between human and gibbon embryos. While other Darwinians favored the gorilla, the chimpanzee, and the orangutan in turn, the current opinion in Jena was that the ancestors of humanity resembled the gibbon. We know today that this view was mistaken. The long-armed gibbons, so musically gifted according to John Lubbock, are not even so much as anthropoid apes. They branched off at an early date from the common stock and went their own peculiar way.

Haeckel's conclusion that the ape man had probably been at home in the regions still occupied by gibbons in modern times — the Indonesian islands, for instance — was equally questionable. Primitive gibbons, such as *Propliopithecus*, were also found later on in quite different parts of the earth. And the Dutch anatomist Eugène Dubois was in reality pursuing a will-o'-the-wisp when he resolved to visit the gibbons' native land and try to find the ape man there. He really only had one clue. In the Siwalik Hills of India a fossilized anthropoid ape had been discovered by Richard Lydekker, who was certain it was a primitive orangutan. But the characteristic fauna of the Siwalik Hills were also to be found in Java. And Java, as distinct from India, had been spared the Ice Age. According to Dubois, mankind might very well have developed in Java from a primitive gibbon or a Siwalik ape.

Dubois was an adventurous young fellow who had, moreover, no intention of spending his whole life in anatomical institutes. He meant to see the world. The best and cheapest way of carrying out this plan, if you were a medical doctor of Dutch nationality, was to join the colonial army as a surgeon. The islands on which Dubois intended to find the missing link were part of Holland's overseas possessions. Men of his type were in demand there.

The connection between ape and Man, which hitherto only existed on paper, had already been given a scientific name by Haeckel. He called it *Pithecanthropus alalus*, ape man without speech. It was nothing but a working hypothesis, over which Virchow waxed very facetious. The naming of a creature that had not even been found yet appeared outrageously impudent to a man who cared only for facts, but Haeckel and his party took the term *Pithecanthropus* in dead earnest and employed it whenever possible as if they had been dealing with a fact long since proved. And Dubois secretly cherished

the word. Wearing the uniform of a junior surgeon in the Nether-
lands East Indies troops, he went aboard ship in 1889 and sailed away
to Sumatra.

Whereupon he became involved in a fascinating detective story.
He made a few excavations in Sumatra. Apart from a few thousand
teeth of orangutans he found nothing, as may easily be imagined
from the brief and cursory nature of his researches. Then he suddenly began to pull every kind of string to get himself posted to
central Java, for a unique skull had been sent him from that quarter.
On arrival in the highlands of central Java and after a few false starts,
he soon came upon a second human skull of the same sort near
the village of Wadjak. It had a broad flat nasal bone, a prominent
oral section, and a strikingly thick lower jaw. One of the skulls had a
brain cavity about 200 cc. more capacious than that of a modern
man, while the other also afforded evidence of a most imposing
brain. Assuredly the skulls were not those of ape men. At worst
their owners might be compared, if one ignored the size of their
heads, with Australian aboriginals. They came, moreover, from
a geological level identical with that of the later European Ice
Age.

Although scientific circles would undoubtedly have been very interested to hear that Java had at one time been inhabited by primitive Australians, Dubois did not reveal a word about his discovery.
He packed up the skulls in a box, took this home with him to
Holland at a later date, and did not disclose the contents until
1921. Perhaps he had been disappointed with the skulls; or perhaps
he was secretive by nature. Altogether he was a difficult man to understand.

He made his way from Wadjak to Trinil. He had heard that the
more distant surroundings of the latter village were a perfect mine
of fossilized bones belonging to mammals of the Tertiary period.
And *Pithecanthropus*, according to Haeckel, had lived then. The
most extraordinary coincidence of the whole story now took place.
In November 1890, during one of the very first of his tentative excavations, he dug up at Kedung-Brubus, some twenty-five miles southeast of Trinil, a small, undoubtedly human fragment of a lower jaw
containing the stump of a tooth. It is said that he had originally
intended, in spite of his find at Wadjak — or perhaps even because
of it — to return to Sumatra and pursue his researches there. But
he now finally decided to remain in Trinil. He felt like a man who
had found a needle in a haystack at his first attempt.

Nothing much could be done with the fragment of lower jaw. It
was too tiny. He put it, also in a box, together with all sorts of bones

belonging to animals and no one heard anything about it for some time. Dubois believed the layer in which he had found it to be a Tertiary one. Inwardly he exulted. With the detective instinct of a trained paleontologist he made a systematic examination of the banks of the Solo River, near Trinil, for Tertiary relics, picking up every tiny bone of an animal he could find. The boxes that were destined to remain unopened for thirty years — many of them longer still — were soon full.

Trinil is still called by the Dutch today the "hell of Java," not only because of the heat but also because of the sinister traces of periodic volcanic activity. There was one volcano in particular, the Gunung Gelunggung, which had been spewing lava, mud, and ashes over the country ever since primitive times and burying plants, animals, and probably also human beings under red-hot masses. Here, if anywhere, was the very place for Dubois.

An army surgeon who spent his free time tirelessly tramping through the jungle and digging up the banks of rivers, rather than in playing cards and filling himself up with rice wine, must have struck the Royal Dutch troopers as extremely eccentric. Dubois was not to be easily diverted from his purpose. With the gibbons chanting overhead and the vision of *Pithecanthropus* before him, he worked on. He filled more and more boxes. Finally, in September 1891, he discovered in a cavity of the riverbank a most remarkably shaped molar of the right upper jaw. It might be a chimpanzee's tooth. But it might also be the tooth of a human being.

He proceeded to do something that no investigator of prehistory had hitherto dared to do as the result of finding a single tooth. He paraded all the native helpers he could find and had the riverbank removed, layer by layer, at the spot in question, with every possible precaution. The work took several months and the expense bore no relation to such a dubious relic as a queerly shaped molar. Everything Dubois had done, from his crossing to Java to the choice of a region to excavate and the enormous works undertaken at the bank of the Solo River, turned out afterwards to have been uncannily prophetic and correct. He had acted as though in a trance.

A month after the discovery of the tooth his Malays came across something that looked like a bowl, about three yards from the place of the original find. It was as hard as stone, shallow and measured 183 mm. (about seven inches) in length. Dubois immediately recognized it as the top of the skull of an apelike creature with prominent ridges of bone over the eyeholes and at the nape of the neck. Was it a *Sivapithecus*, like Richard Lydekker's? Or was it a prehistoric chimpanzee? Dubois was at first inclined to think it was the latter. After a time certain facts came to light which compelled him to revise this opinion.

The excavations went on. No one in Europe, neither Haeckel nor any other interested party, heard anything about the finding of the skull vaulting. Months passed. All they produced was a molar of the left upper jaw. Dubois persevered. It was as though he guessed that his trouble would be worth while. And then the great moment came, the crowning achievement of a year's work. In August 1892, just as the Malay workmen removed a layer some twelve yards thick from the riverbank, a fossilized upper thighbone protruded from the mass of tufa and soil. It was a bone of extremely strange appearance, undoubtedly related to the skull vaulting. But in that case the supposed primitive anthropoid ape must have walked on two legs like a man. Dubois still hesitated to take the last bold step of his reasoning. He described the creature as *Anthropopithecus erectus*, an anthropoid ape resembling a chimpanzee and walking upright.

Then, however, he proceeded to examine the skullcap more closely. It was relatively easy to find out whether it came from an anthropoid ape or a human being. One only needed to measure the volume of the skull, which would be about 500 cc. in the case of anthropoid apes but in the case of modern Europeans would amount to an average of 1450 cc. One would then know whether the find was to be classified as simian, human, or intermediate. Dubois made careful measurements. He ascertained the volume to have been at least 800 cc., and at most 1000 cc., occupying a precisely central position between that of anthropoid apes and human beings.

Dubois was now quite satisfied. A *Pithecanthropus* at last! What had seemed utterly incredible had been proved true. The objects found, skull vaulting, teeth, and upper thighbone, ought to be enough to convince the professors and the public at large of the existence of the ape man. The skull showed what sort of mentality the creature had possessed. The teeth proved what it lived on and the thighbone how it moved. Dubois wrote down what he had established and had to admit that a good deal of it did not agree with Haeckel's picture of *Pithecanthropus alalus*. The skull vaulting, to be sure, was more animal-like, but far less massive than that of Neanderthal man. And the upper thighbone did not show the characteristic Neanderthal curvature but closely resembled that of a modern man. The Javanese Adam possessed, in addition to primitive features, others that placed him as superior to the much later Neanderthal specimen. Above all — and this was a point that no Dar-

winian had taken into consideration — he did not seem to have
walked in the fashion of the anthropoid apes. He did not bend forward like Neanderthal man. He was a *Pithecanthropus erectus,*
an ape man that walked upright.

It was not until 1894 that Dubois, writing from the Javanese
capital of Batavia, informed the learned world of his discovery and
sent Haeckel an article in German entitled *Pithecanthropus erectus,
a Human Transitional Form from Java,* in which he had set down
everything worth knowing about the ape man. Haeckel was overjoyed. "The situation in the great fight for the truth has now drastically changed," he proclaimed triumphantly to Virchow. "The discovery by Eugène Dubois of *Pithecanthropus erectus* has made ma-
terially accessible to us the petrified bones of the ape man I had
hypothetically constructed. This discovery has an even greater significance for anthropology than the much praised discovery of Rönt-
gen rays has for physics." Virchow, however, retorted coolly that it
would be necessary actually to inspect the bones before pronouncing
judgment. The majority of anthropologists agreed with him.

In 1896 professors from all over the world traveled to the ancient
and venerable university city of Leiden, where Boerhaave, Lamettrie, Linnaeus, Haller, and Camper had left their traces, and proceeded to puzzle over Eugène Dubois's transitional form during the
International Zoological Congress. They made themselves acquainted
with the steps taken by the finder. They heard that the ape man had
been discovered in a Pliocene, that is to say late Tertiary, layer; that
his skull had some resemblance to that of a gibbon; and that it was
possible to establish a genealogical law according to which the weight
of the brain in relation to the size of the body doubled from one
evolutionary group to the other. Then the box, one of Dubois's
many boxes, was opened and the skull vaulting, the thighbone, and
the two molars were revealed.

At once a lively discussion broke out. A quarter of the authorities
present considered the *Pithecanthropus* a genuine though primitive
human being. Another quarter described it as a very large gibbon.
A third quarter was undecided or agreed with Dubois, and a fourth
did not believe that skull and thighbone had belonged to the same
being. All the subjects of dispute that had any relation to Darwinism were once more brought up. A few geologists and paleontologists
were decidedly dubious — and rightly, as we know today — about
the Tertiary origin of the bone. Others denied altogether that the
thighbone at least dated from primitive times. And finally, as once
before in the Fuhlrott case, Virchow rose to enumerate all the objections to our Javanese ancestor.

He pointed to a morbid growth of the upper thighbone which his trained pathologist's eye had detected. "I know those growths," he said, with his ironic smile. "I have treated many patients who had them. Without careful attention those patients would have died. But the creature to which the bone we are discussing belonged did not die. The growth healed, as we can see. Consequently the creature was no primitive human being but a modern one."

Some of those present contradicted him. The paleontologist Nehring pointed to the apelike skull, the low forehead, thick eyebrow ridges, and slight volume of the specimen as evidence against Virchow's interpretation. "The skull," Virchow replied, "shows deep stricture between the lower vaulting and the upper edge of the eyeholes. Such stricture is never found in human beings, only in apes. Consequently the skull is that of an ape. It has nothing whatever to do with the thighbone."

"There can be no doubt," the paleontologist Dames exclaimed, "that skull and thighbone come from the same individual. They were found close together in the same layer, are the same color, and in the same state of petrifaction!"

"I have seen human skulls," Nehring added, "which have the same deep stricture at the temporal section of the frontal bone as the one we have here."

Then the leading American prehistorian, Othniel Charles Marsh, discoverer of dinosaurs, titanotheres, primitive horses, and fossil apes, stood up. He muttered under his breath that Virchow was a damned old skeptic. He said he had seen healed growths of bone like the one Virchow had pointed out on the ape man's bone, belonging to apes in the wilderness. And those apes had certainly not received medical treatment.

Virchow defended himself. He stuck to his opinion and suggested sarcastically that the ape man had been "dreamed up." After this, twelve of the professors present gave their views as to how Dubois's find was to be authoritatively described. Three considered that the bones were those of a human being, three were more inclined to suppose they were an ape's. But six agreed with Dubois. And the chronicler of the Leiden congress, William Dames, who later on published an account of the discussion in the *Deutsche Rundschau*, summed up its results as follows: "Great differences of opinion as a rule involve uncertainty and vacillation. But in this case they may actually be taken as strong arguments for the transitional character of the *Pithecanthropus*." During the ensuing years a number of well-known anthropologists, in particular Klaatsch and Schwalbe, came to share this view of the matter.

Haeckel, who had celebrated the discovery of the ape man as his greatest triumph, did not take part in the Leiden congress. He thus missed a unique opportunity. The spiritual father of the *Pithecanthropus*, he never actually set eyes on the only evidence for it. Dubois did eventually speak on the subject of his ape man at several congresses in France, England, and Germany. But as strenuous attacks were also made on him at these meetings he became deeply embittered and from that time forward kept the bones shown at Leiden, as well as all the other material he brought home from Java, under lock and key.

In compliance with Dubois's directions, his collaborators continued the excavations at Trinil until 1900 and sent more boxes of fossils to him at Leiden. He placed them in his private collection and did not show them to anyone. The professors were most indignant about it. They sent out a second expedition in charge of the widow of the deceased zoologist Selenka, who had already dug up a number of interesting animal fossils in Java near the Solo River.

They were sure that more ape men must still be lying buried there. But Frau Selenka did not find anything of importance. It was only natural, therefore, that the skeptics gained the day. Dubois did not care. He had gone straight to his *Pithecanthropus* like a man with a divining rod. Now that he had found what he wanted he kept it locked up in his safe like a diamond.

Years passed. Haeckel's genealogical tree of gibbons was by then generally rejected. People were more and more inclined to believe as time went on that the chimpanzee was a cousin of mankind. Yet *Pithecanthropus* continued to remain the most mysterious and unexplained of all prehistoric human relics. It was cited respectfully by evolutionists and disrespectfully dismissed by their adversaries. The great German anthropologist Hermann Klaatsch, who had done so much for prehistory, went to Java in 1905 to inspect the place at which *Pithecanthropus* had been found. He did not discover anything. All he did was to catch malaria, which later caused his death. When he came to Leiden and asked to see the Trinil bones Dubois refused to show them. Other investigators had the same experience.

It was not until 1921 that Dubois took the Wadjak skulls out of their box and published a description of them. They furnished valuable support for the assumption that the Australian aboriginals descended direct from *Pithecanthropus*. It proved possible later, as we shall see, to compose an almost unbroken evolutionary series leading from the primeval, very apelike *Pithecanthropus robustus* to the somewhat more human *Pithecanthropus erectus* of Dubois,

Ngandong man — the "Javanese Neanderthal specimen" — the Cro-Magnon type found at Wadjak, and the Australian bush dweller.

The spell was broken during the next two years by the anthropologists Aleš Hrdlička and Hans Weinert. The former was the first investigator for thirty years to be allowed to inspect *Pithecanthropus*. The latter wrote the first detailed account of it, corroborated by Dubois. Scientists were eventually satisfied that that skull vaulting, upper thighbone, and teeth all really belonged to a single creature, which was by general consent given the emergency name of *ape man*, for lack of a better one. It was, however, agreed at the same time that the Javanese ancestral progenitor had lived not in the Tertiary but at the beginning of the Diluvial age, or, to give this its modern name, the Pleistocene.

This is not the only surprising feature of the story. In 1927 Weinert, too, managed to get an interview with Dubois. He induced him to open his many boxes at last and give their contents a thorough scrutiny. The result was sensational. No less than four upper thighbones of "ape men" had been lying unobserved for thirty years, among the ancient bones of mammals. A further search in 1935 revealed a fifth. This overwhelming abundance of evidence would have enabled Dubois to gain a brilliant victory while Virchow was still alive. Weinert made Dubois tell him the story of the find, published it, and came to the conclusion that the Trinil human beings had once been torn to pieces by crocodiles in a crater full of water.

Dubois, who was living the life of a recluse, took practically no notice of his belated triumph. It is even said that for some inexplicable reason he had lost all interest in his ape man. At the very time when new discoveries were filling in the picture it was reported from Leiden that the queer old gentleman was now more inclined to believe the *Pithecanthropus* had been a large extinct species of gibbon. He remained of this opinion until his death in 1940.

No one troubled about these later doubts of his. There were the best of reasons for not doing so, for between 1937 and 1939 the young paleontologist G. H. R. von Koenigswald, who had been following in Dubois's footsteps in Indonesia since 1930, succeeded in putting a stop to all argument. Von Koenigswald, a highly talented prehistorian, born in Berlin in 1902, the son of a Danish student of the American Indians who was then a Brazilian citizen, grew up among stone axes, skulls, and masks. Ever since his boyhood he had wanted to go to the tropics, form collections, and dig. In 1930 he was offered a post as paleontologist to the geological survey service in Java and was thus at last enabled to realize his boyish dream.

He began by settling the question of the age of the various fossil layers in Java. His investigations showed that the Trinil stratum belonged to the Middle Pleistocene epoch. The much disputed ape man had therefore lived about 300,000 years ago and not, as Dubois had thought, about 1,000,000. On the other hand his hopes of discovering further remains of *Pithecanthropus* and thus completing the work of the obstinate recluse of Leiden were not for the present fulfilled. It was a fact that in 1931 one of the geologists belonging to the survey service, C. ter Haar, had found an ancient depository of bones in a former terraced river embankment near Ngandong, just over six miles from Trinil. But the Ngandong, or Solo, men — of whom eleven fragmentary skulls came to light there by 1933 — were unmistakably of old Javanese type, Neanderthal-like descendants of the ape man and much later in date. And it happened that at the very time when von Koenigswald was about to make a closer investigation of another highly promising locality, in the hills near Sangiran in central Java where the periodical rains washed up quantities of teeth and bones, the colonial government had not further funds available for such undertakings.

Von Koenigswald, fascinated by this region that was full of fossils, easy to survey, and quite ideal for a paleontologist, applied to John C. Merriam, president of the Carnegie Institution in Washington. "I have found a new source," he wrote. "If another *Pithecanthropus* is ever discovered, it will be here!" Merriam invited the explorer to come to America. Von Koenigswald, furnished with the necessary dollars, returned to Java through China. He was then able to organize excavation works on a grand scale. He engaged further assistants to collect material, distributed advances of pay, and made a systematic examination of the hills around Sangiran. Only a few months later, at the end of the dry season of 1937, when the rains were beginning to wash more fossils out of the old layers, his assistants brought him a fairly large piece of a human skull.

Von Koenigswald wrote later:

The night train took me to central Java. And next morning I stood at the spot where the skull had been found. It was a bare slope of the bank of the Tjemoro stream. First of all I announced the rewards I was prepared to give, my native helpers were to receive one cent for each tooth and ten cents for every piece of skull they found. I then had every yard of the hill thoroughly searched until late in the afternoon. The result was worth the trouble. We not only found the jawbones and teeth of the small deer and antelopes also characteristic of the *Pithecanthropus* layer at Trinil; we actually found forty fragments of a small human skull with thick walling. The day ended in ceremonial style, with the payment of wages, Javanese *gamelan* music and village dancing-girls.

Many of the skull fragments showed recent breakages. The cunning natives had secretly split them up so as to obtain more than the ten cents promised for each piece. Von Koenigswald was not greatly perturbed over this trick. The splinters could easily be reassembled to form a skull which was undoubtedly that of a *Pithecanthropus erectus*. As time went on von Koenigswald brought to light, in addition to other most interesting relics of primitive humanity — referred to in a later chapter — another fragment of the skull of a *Pithecanthropus erectus*. This did away with all the uncertainty and contention about the existence and aspect of the "ape man of Java." The skull of Sangiran and that of Trinil, in the words of the anthropologist Weidenreich, "were as like as two eggs." It only differed in being much more nearly complete. The structure of the temporal sections and the position of the gap at the back of the head showed unmistakably that the owner had been no ape but a human being, an "early" specimen, to be sure, with a brain volume of 775 cc. The dispute over the nature of the puzzling creature of Trinil, which had used up just as much paper and printer's ink as the argument over the Neanderthal man, was now settled forever.

It was only Dubois who continued to doubt. He even accused von Koenigswald of having tampered with the skull to some extent, but he had no success with his suspicions. In the spring of 1939 investigations carried out by the most modern methods proved that von Koenigswald's reconstruction had been correct. The coronal sutures, no longer visible on the surface of the skull, showed up clearly in the Roentgen photograph. Since then *Pithecanthropus* — primitive Java man, as he is called today — has held a secure position in science.

How did life originate on earth?

Paris, the ancient and venerable mother of the biological sciences, for long emphatically declined to recognize Darwinism. A new intellectual giant dominated public opinion there and fought as stubbornly as Cuvier had against spontaneous generation, the theory of evolution, and other "illusions and errors." This was the founder of bacteriology, Louis Pasteur.

On April 1, 1864, Pasteur conducted an experiment before a large audience at the Sorbonne, where the opponents of free investigation had once gathered in Voltaire's time. It subsequently became world-famous. Many eminent people watched him, including renowned scientists like Cuvier's successor Brongniart and the Lamarckian Milne-Edwards. Authors like George Sand and the elder Alexandre Dumas also came, as well as Pasteur's keenest antagonist, Pouchet, who believed that lower organisms could be artificially produced in a chemical retort. A mood of excitement prevailed, as on the day Lamarck's fate had been decided.

"Today," Pasteur began, "great questions lie before us, questions that never cease to agitate our minds. They are the unity or multiplicity of the races of mankind, the origin of humanity a few thousand years or a few thousand centuries ago, the stability of species or the slow, progressive metamorphosis of one into others, the indestructibility of matter and whether it alone exists, the question whether a God is still needed. Such are but a few of the matters that are being discussed at the present time."

Pasteur, who had long made up his mind that species were stable, picked out one of these questions in order to use it to answer the rest. He meant to prove that organic life cannot evolve from raw material. At that time, while evolutionary theory was still in its early stages, many scientists, including Pouchet, believed that Buffon had been right after all in assuming that micro-organisms regularly originated in putrid matter. Pasteur now incontrovertibly established the fact that this was not the case. Vessels filled with hay and refuse, which he had sterilized years before by heating, did not contain a single germ. Hence Pasteur drew the conclusion that life only arises from life, there being no such thing as spontaneous generation. He added triumphantly: "Today there is no longer any reason for assuming that living beings can come into existence in the absence of germs or parents which resemble them. The theory that asserts such a thing will never recover from the mortal blow dealt it by this experiment."

The defenders of spontaneous generation, with Pouchet at their head, had promised that if Pasteur's test succeeded they would honestly admit defeat. They did not keep their promise. The discussions that arose over the pasteurized vessels were so heated that Joly, a member of the Academy, described them as conflicts in the arena. Louis Pasteur's party deduced from the fact that no fresh bacteria or protozoa had formed in the Sorbonne laboratory the somewhat daring conclusion that this must have been the rule in nature ever since primitive times. Pouchet's party, on the other hand, exhausted themselves, wrathfully but in vain, in the attempt to create unicellular beings in miniature out of all sorts of chemicals. Finally they thrust the whole problem back into the mists of primitive ages, as Haeckel had long since done in Germany.

The author Edmond About, a man of keen intelligence who was a lay intruder into the conflict, listened dubiously to the arguments by which the overzealous adherents of Pasteur now proposed to settle the question of the descent of man into the bargain. It was impossible, they said at Sorbonne, for Man to have been originated by any force residing in matter, for Pasteur's work had shown that the first appearance of any complete organism capable of life could only be accounted for by an act of creation. This argument made About smile. He suggested that at the very beginning of geological history conditions might well have prevailed which were quite different from those in Pasteur's retort and might have enabled nature "to allow the spontaneous generation of tiny creatures no bigger than the hundredth part of a pin's head" out of dead matter. And from such creatures the entire organic world, including mankind, must have arisen. About argued against the gentlemen at the Sorbonne like a true Lamarckian. "Man," he said, "was formerly nothing more than an ambitious noncommissioned officer in the great army of apes."

Since the day of Pasteur's experiment the question of the way in which life arose has lain at the heart of biological study. It turned out during the next few decades that the experiments at the Sorbonne did not by any means discredit the theory of spontaneous generation, for the bacteria, mycoderms, and unicellular organisms of animal type that declined to rise before the Parisian audience, like so many phoenixes, from the pasteurized ashes, were anything but primitive aboriginal forms of life. On the contrary, they were highly differentiated creatures. The first organisms, Haeckel and Huxley in particular affirmed, could not possibly have existed in the form of cells. They must have been formless lumps of albumen, lacking any sort of structure, in the sea. One such undifferentiated mass of mud had been discovered at the bottom of the ocean by a deep-sea expedition. Huxley named this allegedly primitive creature *Bathybius Haeckeli* in Haeckel's honor and believed he had discovered in it the ancestral form of all life. But it soon turned out that the far-famed *Bathybius* was nothing but jelly-like gypsum. Haeckel then grouped together a whole series of Monera, very primitive unicellular organisms which apparently possessed no cell-nucleus, and assumed them to be the ancestral parents of all animals and plants. Critical tests proved, however, that even these Monera were in fact furnished with cell nuclei and had thus already progressed quite a long way up the ladder of life. The theory of spontaneous generation seemed to be incapable of proof, a matter of faith like the story of the Creation.

At this point the physicists took a hand. They had long recognized that the old dream of the automatic generation of energy was an illusion, whence they concluded that the automatic generation of life was equally impossible. But in that case where did life come from? It must have reached the earth from somewhere. The Englishman William Thomson and the German Hermann von Helmholtz thought they knew the answer. Tiny germs of life, coming from other stars, had undertaken a long journey through icy outer space. At a favorable moment they had settled on the cooling planet of the Earth and in the course of aeons had developed into every shape and form of flora and fauna. Life, therefore, was eternal. At the time this supposition became current, between 1870 and 1880, Schiaparelli discovered the "canals" on Mars. Everyone suddenly began to believe it probable that other stars, too, were inhabited. From this belief it was only a step to the theories of Wilhelm Preyer and Svante Arrhenius.

About 1880 Preyer, a German doctor of medicine born in England, an adherent of the theory of evolution, and an outstanding physiologist, looked at the facts from a different angle. He maintained that organic substance had come into existence first, developing in the gigantic organism of glowing, molten stars. The inorganic elements had gradually become disengaged from this substance. Life, according to Preyer, was merely the perpetual motion in the universe. As the stars cooled, everything that no longer participated in this motion and grew rigid, became dead matter. This theory of cosmogony, reminiscent of Greek natural philosophy, was welcomed with enthusiasm. But levelheaded scientists called his hypothesis a frivolous play on words. In their opinion by extending the idea of life to apply to everything that moved Preyer was simply transferring the problem to another plane without solving it.

A more sober-sounding theory was that of panspermia, based on the researches of Helmholtz. It was proposed about 1900 by the Swedish Nobel Prize winner Svante Arrhenius. He supposed the entire universe to be full of life germs, set in motion through the ether by the rays of the sun and fixed stars and scattered upon all planets in course of formation. "From all eternity," he wrote in his much discussed book *Worlds in the Making*, "life may have been borne from planet to planet within the same solar system. But just as out of a billion particles of pollen blown from a big tree by the wind only one, on an average, leads to the growth of a new tree, so too only one of the trillions of germs, probably, happens to fall on a planet hitherto untouched by life and begins to promote multifarious forms of life upon it. On this theory organic beings throughout the universe are all related."

No convincing refutation of the theory of Svante Arrhenius has yet been made. It was given a supplementary amendment thirty-four years later by the French physicist, of Russian descent, Georges Lakhovsky. In his view cosmic rays may have aroused the inert life upon planets in course of formation and stimulated it to further development. The school of Haeckel considered that all these speculations obscured the real problem by romantically taking flight to unknown regions. Haeckel's disciples held fast to a saying of Aristotle, a philosopher in other respects by no means very highly prized by the evolutionists. He had written, "Nature carries out the transition of lifeless into living phenomena quite gradually, so that it is impossible to draw a definite line of demarcation." The school stuck to its pet theory of spontaneous generation.

This doctrine has remained the most logical answer to the question of the origin of life, and at the same time the one most favored by biologists. Ernst Haeckel, its great champion, died in 1919, after a long life full of conflict and unrest, but peacefully convinced that his theory had come to stay and that one day, in laboratory conditions similar to those in which the earth had been formed, lumps of albumen in which life had been artificially induced would be brought into existence. But in spite of every effort scientists have not yet succeeded in this task.

Nevertheless, modern biology has discovered forms of life which the electronic microscope has revealed to be lumps of albumen lacking all shape and structure, just as Haeckel formerly conjectured. These viruses and bacteriophages each consist of no more than a single giant molecule or molecule group of albumen. But they are already capable of growth and multiplication as if they were genuine animals or plants. As they only exist as parasites on alien cells they can hardly have been the aboriginal ancestors of all animals and plants. And yet it is easy enough to imagine that at one time the spark of life was struck in albumen compounds of this kind, that they thus became "living molecules" and gradually, as the result of cosmic radiation, bred to a high level by natural selection, developed progressively, and spread all over the world.

The tale of creation thus narrated by modern natural scientists, however much intellectual wrangling may have arisen over it, has a general similarity in sense to that related by Genesis, the Upanishads of the ancient Indians, and the other great religious compositions of mankind dealing with the origin of phenomena. Today the story is no longer a matter of dispute but, to adopt Plato's phrase, a "probable myth."

XI

THAT WHICH THY FOREFATHERS
HAVE BEQUEATHED UNTO THEE

Mice sacrifice their tails

THE FAMILY of John Lambert aroused a great deal of astonishment
in their day. Ever since 1710 each male member of it had been
covered all over the body with a thick black outer skin and small
horny prickles. This covering was shed every autumn and then
renewed again. For this reason the Lamberts were given the rather
ugly name of human porcupines and the unfortunate John was hardly
ever free from incessant examinations. Some professors even elevated
him to the rank of a representative of a special race of mankind.

John's ancestral progenitor must have inherited this disagreeable
feature because of some kind of accident. It had now become hereditary in the family. The evolutionists suddenly rescued Lamarck
from the neglect into which he had fallen, studied his works, and
read that all animate beings were products of their environment and
capable of transmitting acquired characteristics. In John Lambert,
nature had for once been caught red-handed. It seemed plausible
enough. External influences initiated bodily or mental changes in
certain individuals. These changes were handed down to posterity
and became permanent. Thus new species had been formed and a
creature like a troll, half man, half beast, had developed into the
modern human being.

Darwin's view that environment only influences creatures through
the struggle for existence was thrust into the background. Neo-
Lamarckism flourished and the environment theory was reborn.
Even Haeckel, in other respects a convinced Darwinian, saw the
problem of transmission through the eyes of Lamarck. A great many
paleontologists joined forces with him. Writers on popular science,
headed by Wilhelm Bölsche, signified their agreement. Nor had
the materialists, with the single remarkable exception of the political
theorist of the Socialist Party, Friedrich Engels, anything against the
idea.

As early as 1787 Lichtenberg had referred to the transmission of acquired characteristics. "It has long been observed that Nature has in the end acquiesced in many artificial mutilations whereby man believes he can improve upon her work and allowed herself to be imitated in her own factory." Accordingly, those who desired to track down the secrets of transmission deliberately resolved to cut off their tails and thus prove the validity of the ideas of Lamarck.

The former private physician of the Archduke Stephan of the castle of Schaumburg on the Lahn, August Weismann, who had since been appointed professor of zoology at the University of Freiburg, went to work on a family of mice. He mutilated a number of generations of them this way and, altogether, he reared and amputated 1592 mice, of twenty-two generations. Not a single tailless youngster was born. Other scientists repeated the experiment with the same result. And when Haeckel remarked that the tendency to form a tail must be so strong that it continues to be transmitted after decades of mutilation, Weismann undertook further experiments in order to induce physical changes in the objects of his research. In no case, however, did he discover in their posterity the least traces of such external intervention.

This was a great surprise to most scientists, but Weismann had already thought of an explanation. It was not in the least necessary, he asserted, for the correct completion of Darwin's theory, to assume transmission of acquired characteristics. Two groups of cells were to be distinguished in the organism, the actual cells of the body, which were subject to the influence of environment, and the germ plasm, the transmitting substance, which remained wholly unaffected by external events. All mutations, according to Weismann, took place solely in the germ plasm. It was the scene of a competitive struggle between the individual particles, in which environment and bodily processes exercised no influence, but in which each cell and each transmission germ strove for mastery over the rest. One germ enabled one set of characteristics to triumph and another a different set. A great quantity of varieties thus arose, which were then passed through the sieve of natural selection.

August Weismann's germ theory led to the birth of genetics, the science of heredity. It met with strenuous resistance. The theorists of the influence of environment considered the assumption of a transmitting substance or even of definite laws of heredity to be utter nonsense. They maintained that the whole theory of evolution would collapse if the creative influence of environment were denied. Teleologists like the botanist Karl Wilhelm Nägeli proposed a counter-theory according to which environment demanded certain types which nature then proceeded to breed deliberately, without resort to the struggle for existence. Weismann refused to be put off by these opponents. He had identified the great gap in the Darwinian edifice, that of the problem of heredity, and he meant to close it.

He never suspected that it had been closed long ago and that the laws of heredity which could have proved his germ theory were slumbering unknown and unobserved by anyone in a Moravian monastery.

The miracle in a monastery garden

Although Johann Mendel, a Moravian farmer's son, knew a lot about horticulture and beekeeping, he lacked the ability to pass on his knowledge. When he was left without means on his father's death, ill and half starved, he took refuge in the state school at Znaim as an assistant instructor in natural science. But he made a complete failure of it there. He was absent-minded, his nerves went on strike, and the school authorities sent him to Vienna, so that he could at least sit for his teacher's examination, regain his health, and acquire new knowledge.

Mendel was ignominiously rejected in his examination. To the astonishment of his tutors, it was in natural science — for which he maintained he had special qualifications — that he proved to be utterly without talent. His biology was marked "unsatisfactory." In zoology he could not answer the simplest questions, and he had not the faintest idea of classification. The gentlemen in Vienna voted him a hopeless clodhopper and advised him in a well-meaning manner to keep away from nature for the future.

Mendel tramped home in despair to his native village of Heinzendorf, where he intended to try to get taken in somewhere as a boarder. He broke his journey at Brünn, as a good Christian paid a visit to the Augustinian monastery there, and told the abbot, Cyrillus Napp, about his ruined life. The abbot saw at once that the young man was utterly broken, both physically and spiritually. He advised him to submit himself to the strict and self-denying ordinances of the Augustinian rule. So having failed as a teacher of natural science, Johann Mendel became an Augustinian monk, under the name of Gregor, in the Altbrünn monastery.

Cyrillus Napp was an intelligent man who understood human nature. He allowed Mendel to go on working at natural science in the monastery, put him in charge of the garden, and procured him microscopes, collections of plants, and specimen boxes. And in

Brother Gregor, as he grew flowers and vegetables, grafted fruit trees and collected herbs, there gradually awoke the passion of his peasant forebears for breeding. Eagerly he began to cross various kinds of beans and other cultivated plants and watch the results.

The hybrids produced by crossing varieties with white and red flowers came up pink. Mendel had expected that. He now wanted to know what would happen if he arranged a marriage between two of these pink hybrids. Would the grandchildren also be pink or would the colors of the original parents come through again? He made the test, counted carefully, and worked out the result. Half the grandchildren were pink, a quarter were red, and a quarter white. Further experiments proved that the posterity of the red ones remained red and that of the white white, while the pink ones again split up as before.

He repeated the experiment thousands of times with patient care, and always got the same result. It then became clear to him that he had actually discovered a law of heredity by which in the second generation a quarter of the descendants resembled the grandfather, a second quarter the grandmother, and half consisted of hybrids, the posterity of which varied in exactly the same ratio of 1:2:1.

Mendel, delighted with his discovery, proceeded to devote himself to peas, in order to find out whether the law would also hold good with them. He crossed the smooth and rough-surfaced varieties. Yet, to his boundless amazement, the entire posterity of the first generation were smooth. He was beginning to think that his hope of a law of heredity had been wrong when, on pairing the smooth crossbreeds, rough-surfaced peas suddenly turned up again in the next generation. They were in a minority compared with the smooth grandchildren, for a quarter showed this feature, which had remained passive for a generation.

Further experimental breeding from this second generation of peas showed Mendel that his law of heredity was correct. The posterity of the rough-surfaced types were all rough; that of a third of the smooth ones remained smooth; but of the rest of the smooth ones, half the grandchildren were mixed, three quarters being smooth and a quarter rough. Smoothness, accordingly, was a "dominant" characteristic, which caused the rough type to retreat and rendered it "recessive," without, however, getting rid of it.

Mendel's view that the laws of heredity could be determined merely by counting all the crossbred posterity was one of the most brilliant inspirations that ever occurred to a natural scientist. He went on experimenting for many years, crossing yellow-seeding peas with green-seeding ones and round ones with longish ones. He kept a record of the behavior of each plant and drew up tables in which he entered the figures he obtained and their ratios. The abbot looked on benevolently. Mendel's rows of figures seemed to indicate a stable, immutable world order, and that was just what he liked.

One day, as he worked in the monastery garden with his scissors and bag of gauze, Brother Gregor was severely conscience-stricken. It occurred to him that he was really engaged in very frivolous actions. He was crossing brothers and sisters, interfering with the handiwork of the Almighty, presuming to unravel the mysterious web of creation. He hurried off to his abbot and made a clean breast of the conflicts that were affecting his mind. If Abbot Cyrillus had been a less wise and sympathetic man the world would probably never have heard anything about a scientist named Gregor Mendel. But in a discussion that was to have decisive results for the future Cyrillus Napp explained to the monk and student of nature that since God had chosen Brother Gregor to reveal a law to mankind Brother Gregor must obey and announce that law to the public. Mendel saw the point and repressed the prickings of his conscience. The abbot even happened to know an address to which Mendel could apply. The botanist Nägeli, who had been much concerned with questions of heredity, lived in Munich. Brother Gregor need only just send him his notes and wait patiently to see what the professional verdict would be.

Mendel formulated three laws of heredity. The first ran: "If two breeds of one species are crossed, all the individuals of the first ensuing generation are similar." The second was: "If the hybrids of the first generation are crossed, the distinguishing characteristics of the original parents will reappear in the second generation in a certain numerical proportion." The third law added: "All characteristics are transmitted independently of one another. If they are combined in one generation, they may appear in isolation in the next." Finally, Mendel mentioned the numerical proportion he had discovered, described what he meant by dominant and recessive features, wrote out his tables, packed up all the papers, and sent off the lot to Nägeli with beating heart.

He could not have picked a worse address. Nägeli believed in a deliberately planned transmission of acquired characteristics. He could not make head or tail of the rules, figures, and tables of Brother Gregor. He wondered idly why the inmate of a monastery should have amused himself by crossing plants, glanced casually through all the papers, mumbled "Premature conclusions!" and then sent the material back to Mendel, complimenting him briefly on the trouble he had taken. He did not notice that laws had been formulated in the notes.

Mendel was much disheartened. But Abbot Cyrillus was filled with righteous wrath, and all the more determined to see that something came of the matter. He applied to the national science society in Brünn, composed of worthy but not especially distinguished state-school teachers, university lecturers, and amateur students of nature. He aroused their curiosity about his pea-crossing Augustinian monk. And the gentlemen, who were reluctant to refuse the abbot anything, heard the whole story out and decided that one might just as well call upon Brother Gregor to give a lecture and invite a few scientists to listen to it. They did not expect to hear anything very startling.

On February 8, 1865, twenty-two years before Weismann proposed his germ theory and sought in vain to determine the laws of heredity, Mendel mounted the rostrum and did his best to render his "experiments with plant hybrids" intelligible to Brünn society. He was a bad speaker, had to struggle with his various disabilities, and made a rather unfortunate impression as he chalked up red, white, and pink points on the blackboard and talked about smooth- and rough-surfaced, yellow-seeding, and green-seeding peas.

The gentlemen listened in silence. They had been well brought up and were willing to let him have his say. More and more colors appeared on the blackboard. The peas' pedigree grew longer and longer. After a while some of the audience began to nod. Others got rather impatient and glanced covertly at the clock. Just why was this Brother Gregor delivering himself at such length? Everyone knew there was such a thing as heredity, and that you could grow flowers in new colors. Brother Gregor's law was mere chance, simply a game with numbers.

At last Brother Gregor ceased speaking. The gentlemen clapped politely and had already started to get up and leave the hall in order to drink a glass of beer when Mendel, with the sweat running from his brow, asked in a tone of astonishment whether it was possible that no one wished to say anything about the discovery of the laws of heredity.

One of the professors replied in a very friendly fashion. He thanked the reverend gentleman cordially in the name of the assembly for his interesting account of such a praiseworthy hobby as pea growing, but he did not mention what he thought of Mendel's alleged laws of heredity, as he did not want to vex the good brother. Mendel answered that perhaps he had not expressed himself correctly. He attempted to make a fresh start, but the gentlemen had already left the hall.

Disappointed and greatly put out, Mendel went back to his cell. His respect for science was so great and his self-confidence so slight that he undertook no further investigations. He gave up his studies in natural science and may have consoled himself with the thought that the same thing had happened in the case of his discovery as happened in the case of a recessive feature in peas. It remained inoperative because its time had not come. It would celebrate its resurrection in a later generation. He waited patiently, for nearly two decades. He knew that all over the world people were trying to track down the laws of heredity which he had discovered long ago. He retained the quiet hope that one of these days, in Munich or Brünn, he would be remembered.

After the death of his fatherly friend Cyrillus Napp, Mendel became abbot of the Altbrünn monastery. He then had to engage in an embittered struggle with the Austrian treasury and had no further thoughts to spare for smooth- and rough-surfaced peas. In 1884, on a cold Epiphany Day, he died. Only the local religious periodicals took any notice of the event. They referred to Mendel as a pious son of the Church who had enlarged the estate of the monastery. They did not mention his scientific studies.

It was not until sixteen years later that Gregor Mendel's dormant laws were revived. Three scientists, Erich von Tschermak-Seysenegg of Vienna, Karl Correns of Berlin, and the Dutchman Hugo de Vries arrived independently at the same conclusions as the forgotten Augustinian monk. They found that the characteristics of parents were passed on to their posterity in a certain numerical proportion. They applied this discovery to mankind and eventually heard about the notes in the Altbrünn monastery. The learned world, on being informed of the circumstances, did what is usually done in these cases to vindicate the honor of an unrecognized discoverer: they gave the laws of heredity Mendel's name.

It was in connection with human beings that genetics now rapidly developed into a science of the highest significance. It was proved that hereditary diseases regularly recurred in certain families in mathematically exact succession, according to Mendel's laws. It was ascertained that many hereditary diseases may become recessive in the course of generations but dominant after the union of two carriers of the disease. The chromosomes — nucleoid threads constituted by the molecules of serum albumin and dividing in complicated fashion after fertilization and then again amalgamating — were discovered, as were also the genes, carriers of hereditary characteristics which are strung along the chromosomes like pearls on a necklace. The transmissible material, which is passed on to children and children's children in the ingenious manner noted by Mendel, turned out to be an endowment with potentialities for both good and evil, a creator of both body and spirit — in short, the most important substance on earth.

How was this rigid mechanism of hereditary transmission to be associated with the rise of new forms and types, with Darwin's theory? It was the Dutchman Hugo de Vries, one of the three rediscoverers of Mendel, who came upon the answer by chance, as he was looking at a tract of waste land. He realized, even before Mendel had been rehabilitated, the way in which new species were being born under his very eyes, popping up like jack-in-the-boxes.

A mysterious field near Hilversum

About the year 1880 a doctor of laws named Six acquired certain property near Hilversum to which he gave the name "Hunter's Pleasure." In addition to gardens and fields it comprised a neglected potato patch, of which Six found himself unable to make much use, since it had been rendered inaccessible on three sides by canals. Accordingly, he let it remain fallow and the patch consequently fell into the state of all cultivated land when tilling is abandoned — it became a weed-grown wilderness.

The flowers in Dr. Six's ornamental beds included an evening primrose named after Lamarck. This *Oenothera Lamarckiana* is today a scientific showpiece like Scheuchzer's "Flood man," the Neanderthal specimen, the primeval bird *Archaeopteryx*, the ape man of Java, Cuvier's mosasaur, and Mendel's peas. In Dr. Six's potato patch, which had been lying fallow like the field in the parable, it was responsible for nothing less than an act that created a new world of ideas.

The story of this plant begins with the discovery of America. When on October 12, 1492, Columbus first trod the shore of the New World his foot was touching the land of the evening primrose. These flowers, which today flourish like weeds in European meadows and woodlands, were at that time only to be found on the American continent, in nearly a hundred species. Later explorers admired the *Oenothera*. They took it home with them, planted it in their gardens, and hardly noticed that their foreign guest was stealing away from their flowerbeds and taking possession of waste land and forest glades of its own accord, like a tenacious colonist.

Toward the end of the eighteenth century Lamarck had found in the collections at the Jardin des Plantes a few dried specimens of an evening primrose hitherto unknown. He was the first to describe it and it was named after him. Oddly enough, it was this species, of all others, which was destined to bear witness against Lamarck and his theory of the hereditary transmission of acquired characteristics.

Dr. Six's Lamarckian primroses soon found his flowerbed too small for them, a habit natural to their species. Since the potato patch lay quite close by, they proceeded with the boldness of typical pioneers to settle upon it. They scattered their seeds over the fallow land. Their children and children's children dislodged other weeds. And long after Dr. Six's bed of evening primroses had ceased to exist, a blazing sea of bright yellow *Oenothera* blossoms was covering well over an acre of ground.

Then it happened: a certain man looked at that shining field, not only with a view to picking the flowers, but also to detecting the secrets of nature. In 1886 Hugo de Vries, professor of botany at Amsterdam, was thirty-eight years old. He was no longer, like Huxley's generation, following Mr. Darwin's theories word for word. His motto was, "In order to possess what you have inherited from your Darwin you must first acquire it!" He believed that so long as no one had ever yet seen how a new species arose Darwin's theory could only be considered probable, not proved. Consequently, he had been nosing about for years, like a detective, looking for an example of metamorphosis in an animal or plant.

As his eyes ran over the yellow sea of blossom on the waste land they were automatically in search of types transcending the normal features of the species. He perceived, as he had expected, that the Lamarckian primroses varied to an incredible extent in this instance. But such trifling variations were not of any great assistance to him in tracking down the secrets of the rise of species. Aeons might pass before new species arose from them. He experienced the same sort of feeling as an astronomer undergoes when he sees a comet disappear and knows that it will not be visible again for a thousand years. Suddenly de Vries uttered a loud cry of astonishment. In the midst of the Lamarckian primroses were to be seen two completely new species, differently leafed and with flowers of a different shape. They were so closely wedged in among the host of usual varieties that they were bound to be direct descendants of the latter. It seemed as though one species did not develop gradually out of another but at a single stride.

De Vries proceeded to plant a number of cuttings of the Hilversum evening primroses in the botanical gardens at Amsterdam. And the prodigy occurred. The mysterious plants from Dr. Six's field produced within thirteen years seven entirely new species, including some giant forms, some dwarfs, and one wonderfully beautiful specimen. They were not related types or varieties but genuine species, which transmitted their characteristics unmodified. De Vries had discovered nothing more nor less than the origin of species.

He took out a warrant, so to speak, for the arrest of the posterity of the new types. He engaged other scientists to examine the miraculous field of Hilversum and repeat the experiment. He then published a magnificent work, adorned with many fine colored plates, entitled *The Mutation Theory*. In this book he argued that mutations, abrupt alterations of hereditary dispositions, were the chief cause, if not the only one, of the formation of species.

"A species," he wrote in this publication, "has in certain circumstances the power to develop by propagation, in sudden fits and starts, a new species akin to itself but fundamentally divergent. There is no question in this connection of the usual variations or small individual discrepancies. A genuine evolutionary advance takes place, in which the derivative plants or animals are profoundly reorganized, reshuffled and recast throughout their nature and appear in altered form. This act of fresh creation is the meaning of mutation."

This passage confirmed what Schopenhauer and subsequently the philosopher and former Prussian guards officer Eduard von Hartmann had already discovered by logical reflection: nature does proceed by leaps and bounds. A new species arises directly, all present and correct, in the womb of the parent species. Plants and animals, as de Vries and other geneticists showed, do not experience regular mutation, but embark upon periods of change directly, after long intervals of passivity. The new formations then follow tumultuously upon one another and often throw up huge numbers of each individual type.

Such periods of mutation were thought by de Vries to have been brought about by particular events, by a change of environment, for instance, which affects the species in question, or by extraordinarily favorable conditions of propagation. Hence the conjecture arose that mutations might be nothing more, fundamentally, than sudden, abrupt adjustments to circumstances. The Lamarckians, so far as they believed at all in the validity of laws of transmission, immediately seized upon this point and asserted that the evolutionary stride meets adjustment halfway, setting in the moment any change takes place in the environment.

De Vries was utterly opposed to this view. His evening primroses underwent mutation quite casually. The new species included both appropriate and inappropriate types. Nature made countless experiments which she afterwards tested by the struggle for existence in order to award the prize of predominance to the best. The struggle for life did not therefore, as Mr. Darwin had taught, breed species from very slight variations. It only rejected from the advancing host of new mutations those which were obviously unsuitable. All other forms remained permanent, propagated themselves and supplied scientific systems with their material. And environment did not, as the great Lamarck had maintained, bring about purposeful alterations in order to meet a new need for adaptation halfway. At most it stimulated a wild chaos of mutations. The miracle of the origin of species, so biologists concluded from the theory of mutations, is to be explained neither by environmental influence nor by gradual natural selection. It takes place in the form of a spontaneous act of creation within the organism, in germ plasm.

The lucky find in Dr. Six's field was the prelude to twentieth-century biological research. The theory resulting from it, one of the most revolutionary pioneering acts in the history of science, at last revealed a motive for the transformation of animate beings and one which, as the future showed, was to stand the test of practical experiment. But how were mutations brought about? The question was bound to be one of enormous importance to mankind. Would breeders be enabled to form new species by artificial means in the laboratory? Was man now reaching out, like Goethe's sorcerer's apprentice, for the greatest secret of all, in order to play the creator himself? It was an exciting prospect.

In 1910 the American geneticist and zoologist Thomas Hunt Morgan began to experiment at Columbia University with a tiny insect, the fruit fly — *Drosophila melanogaster* — which propagates with extraordinary speed. A few years later he received the Nobel Prize for certain discoveries that can only be compared, in the importance of their consequences, with that of nuclear fission.

Nature makes "quantum" leaps

Science always begins to prosper when the various fields of research co-operate with one another. The great age of biological discovery, distinguished by the names of Buffon, Cuvier, and Darwin, was at the same time an age of discovery in physics and chemistry. Scientific revolutionaries like Lavoisier, Gay-Lussac, Dalton, Faraday, and Helmholtz flourished in it. And the era that saw the rise of genetics coincided with the development of the theory of relativity and the quantum.

Those were the years in which Albert Einstein founded modern physics, the Curies, husband and wife, investigated the secrets of radioactivity, Ernest Rutherford and Nils Bohr composed their diagrams of atoms, and Max Planck proved that in nature energy cannot be assimilated and given out in small doses of unspecified quantities but only in fixed amounts or *quanta*. The geneticists learned from the atom and quantum physicists and formed the opinion that laws valid for inanimate nature must also hold good for animate nature.

This assumption was confirmed in most startling fashion. Mutations, it was found, were in principle nothing but biological "quantum" strides. Just as physical energy propagates itself by fits and starts, so too, have organisms developed. Procedure within the chromosome began to be compared to procedure within the atom. While the atom physicists were attempting to divert electrons from their course in order to change the structure of the atom, the geneticists were attempting to expel genes from the chromosome in order to change hereditary predispositions. Both these attempts succeeded. Man today can not only split the atom. He can bring influence to bear, by means of the subtle manipulation of short-wave radiation and chemical infection upon the germ plasm of animals and plants subjected to his experiments, and thus produce creatures never seen in the world before. Science is becoming as weird as the box of tricks kept by Albertus Magnus.

Thomas Hunt Morgan had chosen the little *Drosophila* fly because within a short period he could study through it the development process of a long series of generations. These flies need only ten days to become sexually mature. Four weeks later their grandchildren are already in existence. In four years they have produced as many generations as mankind has from the end of the Ice Age down to this present moment. Morgan and his colleagues bred them for forty years and recorded over two hundred million descendants, representing ten thousand generations. The first thing they found was that spontaneous mutations occurred incomparably more often than had hitherto been supposed. The flies changed in all sorts of ways. Some acquired enormous eyes, others became eyeless, bandy-legged, or incapable of flight. A single mutation would sometimes be observed in as many as a hundred flies without the possibility, at first, of determining the cause. Most of these mutations did not stand the test of the struggle for existence. Only a few seemed to be holding their ground.

Tables of mortality were drawn up for the new types of flies that had arisen. Modern microscopes revealed the sites of the germs of heredity in the chromosomes and it gradually became clear that the genes composed a regular administrative body, with a kind of chief-of-state at their head. If the administrative functions were disturbed or pernicious genes appeared, like bomb-throwing anarchists, deformities resulted. But if the government was only reconstructed, without adversely affecting equilibrium in the chromosome, a new and separate species developed.

After innumerable experiments Morgan at last discovered a possible explanation of the occurrence of mutations. He called it "crossing over." Responsibility for this remarkable phenomenon was shared by the two partners that united to create a new being. If their germs did not suit each other the chromosomes, in the process of division, became intertwined, displaced, and lacerated. Certain genes accordingly disappeared or exchanged posts in the government. The offspring, therefore, for better or worse at once became an entirely distinct specimen.

A strange cause of the alteration of species and forms was next discovered by the American geneticist Joseph Muller. He exposed his fruit flies to the influence of Roentgen rays, gamma rays, and ultraviolet rays. And, as though touched by a magic wand, they immediately underwent a hundred times more mutations than usual. The genes proved exceptionally sensitive to such radiation. Their structure changed. Spectral types of flies subsequently came creeping from the eggs. And since in nature every form of life is constantly affected by all kinds of radiation, Muller deduced that physical forces were perpetually at work, penetrating the interiors of organisms and transforming their shapes.

In the "mixing bowl" of modern biology these deductions were given practical tests. Chemistry, too, now took a hand. If plants were treated with mustard gas or meadow-saffron poison, the number of their chromosomes increased and the size of their products grew disproportionately large. The Swedish investigator Haggquist finally began to administer miraculous drugs even to domestic animals. He applied narcotics to their ovarian cells, caused changes in their germ plasm, and bred huge sows — which had such extensive litters that the number of their teats was not sufficient to feed all their offspring — as well as gigantic rabbits, big enough when cooked to make a substantial meal for a very large family.

All these half-fascinating, half-frightening events that took place in the laboratories had also been taking place in the state of nature, in the seas and rivers, in the plains, the woods and the air, for two billion years, ever since the earth had turned from a desolate waste of rock and water to an inhabitable star. Era after era Nature had been working upon her creatures by radiation, by chemicals, and by innumerable other methods. She had made thousands of rough sketches with no definite object before embodying a single one of them in material form. Highly organized marine creatures had emerged by filtration from unicellular types. Vertebrates that conquered dry land had, in the same way, emerged from wormlike creatures with backbones, and gradually, from marsupials, insectivores, prosimians, and monkeys, the first human beings had developed.

The geneticists who followed in the footsteps of Weismann, Mendel, de Vries, and Morgan emphasized that mutations were the offspring of chance and not products of their environment. Nature did not strive to create particularly successful and perfect specimens. She acted like a gambler who stakes all he can afford on a card without knowing which card will win. This prodigality on Nature's part was by no means unanimously appreciated throughout the world. Many people — those who stubbornly continued to believe in the creative power of environment, transmission of acquired characteristics, and consciously planned progress — considered the whole science of heredity, from Mendel's laws down to Morgan's fly-breeding, unprofitable trifling. They declared that the mysterious germ plasm ought not to be separated from the other cells of the body. They maintained that anything which happened to the body must also happen to the generative cells. They stuck firmly to Lamarck.

The dispute between Morgan's geneticists and the neo-Lamarckians nowadays tends to be decided in the political rather than in the scientific field. The Western world follows Morgan and the Eastern his opponents. This dispute has already claimed more victims than the whole series of scientific quarrels since the beginning of modern times. Its first victim was a highly controversial figure, the Austrian biologist Paul Kammerer.

Suicide of a natural scientist

One wet September morning in 1926 two workmen were crossing

the rocky Theresien hills near the Austrian village of Puchberg. They heard two dogs howling, followed the sound, and saw a human figure in a state of collapse on a bench. The body was that of a man about forty-five, well dressed, with intelligent features. He had killed himself with a revolver shot through the head. While the workmen were examining the body they had great difficulty in keeping the furious dogs at bay. At last they succeeded in taking a bundle of papers from the hand of the dead man. They read the superscription: "To the esteemed finder of my body." They read a letter. It was signed with the name Paul Kammerer. Then they ran toward the village at full speed to obtain help.

A few days later, after Paul Kammerer had been buried in the cemetery at Puchberg, all the Austrian newspapers published the details of the affair that had driven this most highly gifted of the pupils of the Viennese geneticist Erich von Tschermak-Seysenegg to his death. Kammerer, the left-wing periodicals announced, had been scandalously treated by the University of Vienna. He had been refused a professorship because he was a supporter of the environment theory and was not of purely Aryan descent. Official opinion retorted that Kammerer's appointment had been discontinued "for other reasons." Every informed person was aware what was meant by these other reasons. Those without inside knowledge were able to find out later by reading the papers. Paul Kammerer had been accused of the disgraceful forgery of evidence to prove a case of hereditary transmission of acquired characteristics.

The property left by Kammerer included papers which showed that he had been asked to succeed the elderly Russian biologist Michurin at the Soviet Academy of Sciences in Moscow. He had declined the invitation a day before his death in apologetic terms, adding the pathetic words: "In view of the existing situation I can no longer regard myself as a suitable candidate for the post, though I had nothing to do with the forgeries in question. But I also find that it will be impossible for me to endure this ruin of my life's work. I hope I shall have enough courage and strength to put an end, tomorrow, to a life which has proved such a failure."

Paul Kammerer's lifework, interrupted in so sudden and mysterious a manner, was directed to supplementing the lifework of Ivan Vladimirovich Michurin. Michurin son of a Russian smallholder, had been having exceptional success in the growing of fruit, vegetables, and corn ever since 1880. He had shown himself, like the Californian fruitgrower Luther Burbank, to be capable of perfect miracles of gardening. Being a purely practical expert, he knew little or nothing of genetics. And when he succeeded in producing

types of fruit that did amazingly well in the special climatic conditions of central Russia he doubted the validity of Mendel's laws
and considered — it was a typical grower's belief — that hereditary
dispositions were unstable and could be reorganized.

He was already old when the October Revolution occurred. His
views were eminently appropriate to the program of the Communist
Party. The early social revolutionaries had long ago announced
that man is a product of his environment and may be altered if his
circumstances are altered. It must be the same with animals and
plants. Hereditary dispositions, the biologists of Soviet Russia said
later, were simply concentrated precipitate of environmental influences and could be artificially diverted into any desired channels.
While in America the theory of the free competition of mutations
was coming to be the prevailing doctrine, the old theory of the
hereditary transmission of acquired characteristics was starting on
a fresh career in the Soviet Union. Michurin, in the last years of
his life, though he had made hardly any further contributions of
any real novelty to science, enjoyed as much popularity as a great
statesman or soldier.

Meanwhile he had grown so old that the Russian scientific institutes began to look around for suitable successors. Their eyes turned
to Vienna. A whole staff of scholars were working there in the
laboratories of the former Vivarium in the Prater. Official science
turned up its nose at them. They were undertaking daring experiments with a view to the extraction of nature's last secrets. Eugen
Steinach, a zoologist and doctor of medicine from Prague, had
broken the taboo on investigations into sex and was testing the
hormones concerned. He based his investigations on discoveries by
the Frenchman Brown-Séquard and the Russian Voronov, who were
trying to rejuvenate people by injecting them with extracts from the
testicles of animals and grafting the glands of monkeys. Steinach
was making every effort — creating an unfortunate impression on
the public at large — to renew eroticism in the aging body by chemical means and stimulate the internal secretions of the germ glands
to functional activity. Viktor Hammerschlag and Hans Przibam,
students of hereditary transmission, were breeding rats, mice, and
the praying mantis and ascertaining with precision the seats of their
instincts. And above all Paul Kammerer, the rebel from Graz, was
attempting to demonstrate the possibility of a reorganization of
nature by reference to processes in lizards, fire salamanders, and
midwife toads.

Kammerer was born on August 17, 1880. He belonged to the

same generation of young scientists as the great American geneticists Morgan and Muller, but he did not follow the same road. He did not believe that evolutionary jumps were due to chance. In principle he agreed with Michurin and the neo-Lamarckians. Like Oken and Vogt in their day he was a constant stumbling block to the adherents of the prevailing dogma. His temperamental outbursts, his violent attacks upon Morgan genetics, and his persistent globe-trotting as "trade representative of the environmental theory," advertising hereditary transmission of acquired characteristics, had made him many enemies.

On the other hand he was a great favorite with his colleagues in the Vivarium, mainly on account of his almost Franciscan love of humanity and animals. He was a champion of the rights of the poor and a zealous partisan of the Austrian socialists. He declined to make experiments that might involve the infliction of pain upon any living creature and built his lizards, salamanders, and toads reserves of novel design, where they could feel as much at home as in their natural surroundings. Like Oken he probably would have entered scientific history as a tirelessly speculative, recklessly pioneering, and somewhat extravagant type of biologist, if fate — sudden and sinister as a hawk from the clouds — had not dropped down to seize him in its talons.

The experiments he was preparing in order to prove that animals transmitted to their posterity newly acquired characteristics appropriate to a certain purpose looked very successful. Lizards exposed to great heat assumed a dark color. Dark colored offspring emerged from their eggs even at normal temperatures. Salamanders changed their markings to correspond with those of the sort of ground upon which Kammerer kept them. Their offspring also showed the newly acquired pattern. Applied to humanity this procedure meant that "nothing is hereditary in any absolute sense. Individuals are repeatedly obliged to adjust themselves to their environment, deal with it and conform with it. Living matter is capable of preserving such impressions. This is in fact what is called heredity." According to Kammerer, therefore, our germ plasm is exposed like a strip of film to the rays of our environment. It digests, of set purpose, everything that happens to the body and passes it on to the next generation. In this way, under the compulsion of environment, in the dim dawn of prehistoric ages *Homo sapiens* evolved from the proto-men of the primeval jungle.

Kammerer's showpiece was the midwife toad. The male of this species of frog possesses, as distinct from most other toads and frogs, no rutting callosities upon the forelegs. Nor does it need them, as it couples on dry land and therefore does not have to immobilize the female by clinging to it. Kammerer wondered what would happen if a male of this species were obliged to mate in the water? Would it then develop a rutting callosity? And would such a callosity be transmitted to the next two generations?

For some years Kammerer made his toads mate in the water. At last, in 1919 he announced to the world that he had caused rutting callosities to form upon the animals under experiment, and that they were promptly transmitted to the baby toads. This information caused great excitement among biologists. It was a major scientific discovery, a far more convincing piece of evidence than any experiment with salamanders and lizards, if Kammerer's statement were in fact true. Geneticists examined the photographs of the metamorphosed midwife toads which Kammerer had sent to the scientific institutes. Then they gave way to doubts. They described the alleged rutting callosities as either insignificant traces of pigmentation, accidental thickenings of the skin, or shadows on the photographic plate. For seven years disputes raged over the miracle of the toads. Not until 1926 did a committee of scholars, led by the English biologist Noble, decide to visit Vienna and inspect Kammerer's specimens.

At this period Michurin's disciples in the Soviet Union already had their eyes on the rebel at the Viennese Vivarium, who declared that he had proved the existence of something that had hitherto been, for Russia's supporters of the environmental theory, merely a scientific and political wish-dream. When Noble, with his staff of scholars, arrived in Vienna, Kammerer had already received an invitation from Moscow. In his indignation at having been denied a professorship in his native land so long, he had almost determined to accept it. But first he wished to convince the gentlemen from England, feeling it due to himself and his work.

To Kammerer's disappointment, the inspection was carried out without any such sensational results as he had expected. Noble walked in, glanced at the specimen toads, whispered a few words to his companions, jotted down some notes, took his leave in a very cool fashion, and departed as he had come. A few weeks later *Nature*, the leading English natural science periodical, published an article over Noble's signature which professors all over the world rushed to read. It left its readers breathless. The article was Kammerer's death sentence.

The alleged rutting callosities, Noble wrote, were in reality black spots that had been artificially applied with India ink to the toads' legs. The committee, which had started on its journey with the object of testing in all sincerity and without prejudice the evidence adduced for hereditary transmission of acquired characteristics, had discovered, instead, the clumsiest and most scandalous forgery in the whole history of biology. The learned world was overwhelmed with horror and disgust. If this were the case, Kammerer was done for, the environmental theory would henceforth bear an ugly stain upon its character, and the science that had admitted such a man to its ranks could only hide its head in utter shame.

Noble's judgment had been only too correct. When Kammerer and his colleagues, in the greatest alarm, opened the cases in which the specimens had been placed, they saw at a glance that the callosities had been forged. Kammerer begged the rest in a low voice to believe that he had not been guilty of the act and had not looked at the specimens for months. His colleagues believed him. They thought the matter over again and again, but could find no explanation for such an unheard-of occurrence. Apart from Kammerer only two other persons had possessed a key to the cases. They were his friend Przibam and one of his scientific adversaries, Dr. Megusar. Suspicion fell upon the latter. But he was no longer there to be cross-examined. He had died only a short time before.

Kammerer made no attempt to clear himself in public. He abandoned his work, went to Puchberg, walked off into the Theresian Hills, and put a bullet through his head. Whether he or someone else had been responsible for the forgery was never discovered.

The environmental theory fell into utter disrepute in consequence of this affair. It was only in Russia that it continued to be upheld, though by methods not particularly calculated to revive the confidence of the rest of the world. Nor, doubtless, were they such as Kammerer himself would have approved. Michurin's successor, the agriculturalist and planter Trofim Denisovich Lysenko, made no efforts at first to discuss the question with the supporters of Mendel and Morgan in his own country. He had them arrested and sent to compulsory labor camps or made them confess in public that their scientific data had been erroneous. It was a method that could not be expected to appeal to the scientists of the Western hemisphere. Genetics, which had begun in so innocent a fashion with experiments on peas in a monastery garden, thus became involved in the machinery of power politics.

Lysenko has carried out numerous experiments that seem to tell against the views of Mendel and Morgan. He grafted cuttings of a different species into fruit trees and asserted that the graftings were capable of altering the hereditary characteristics of the trees so grafted. He heated the seeds of plants in stoves and chilled them in refrigerators, saying that he could thus obtain new varieties suitable for tropical or arctic regions. A practical man to the backbone, he declared: "If one is absolutely determined to achieve a certain result, one really will achieve it."

Beyond the frontiers of Russia this statement carries rather less conviction. Considerable reserve is shown in the reception of Lysenko's public announcements, especially as thorough investigation has hitherto failed to substantiate a single one of his results beyond doubt. "The contamination of his fields of experiment is deplorable." Thus the English natural scientist Ashby, who visited the places where Lysenko worked, sums up his impressions. "He quite definitely neglects to take the most elementary precautions." And the English biologist and president of UNESCO, Julian Huxley, a by no means dogmatic adherent of Morgan's theory, observed after a conversation with Lysenko: "It was as though one were discussing the differential calculus with a man who could not do simple multiplication." It will be noticed that in biology once more the buttons are off the foils, as they were in the days of Cuvier and Haeckel.

Whether Man was a lucky throw in nature's game of dice or a product of his environment — whether he outlasted his brutish competitors like a champion runner or suited his configuration to the conditions in which he lived like Proteus with his changing forms — is the ancient question that is again being debated today between West and East. It is a fateful question, and a complete answer to it has not yet been given.

ARTISTS OF THE ICE AGE

Don Quixote of Altamira

THE HUNTSMEN of the Spanish nobleman Don Marcelino de Sautuola had often been out after foxes in the neighborhood of the castle of Santillana del Mar without meeting with any particularly remarkable adventures. On a certain day in 1869 one of the hounds suddenly vanished among the hillocks of a meadow as though it had been swallowed up by the earth. The huntsmen whistled, made a search, and eventually came upon a crack in the middle of the field with a cold draft of air streaming out of it. They could hear the dog whimpering somewhere underground. They continued their investigations and found that the gap in the ground led to a large spacious cave. They improvised torches, got the dog out and reported the matter to their master.

This chance discovery of the cave of Altamira at the foot of the Cantabrian hills brought about a complete revolution in prehistoric research. All the ideas that scholars had hitherto entertained of the people of the Late Ice Age were turned upside down by it. It now appeared that the ancient mammoth-hunters already included artists of stature equal to that of the greatest painters of all time. The proudest member of Western civilization need no longer be ashamed of his ancestors. Considerable time passed before scientists condescended to recognize this amazing fact. For decades it looked as though the man who had revealed the miracle of Altamira to the world was a Don Quixote tilting at windmills.

Don Marcelino de Sautuola made a superficial examination of the cave, found nothing special in it, and had the place closed when the village boys from Puente San Michel started playing about in it. For nine whole years he hardly gave a thought to the subterranean dungeon on his property. It was not until he visited the Paris International Exhibition of 1878 and admired in the display cabinets and glass cases the tools and engravings from the Ice Age which Lartet, Mortillet, and the other cave explorers had found in the valley of the Vézère that it occurred to him to look for similar implements in the Altamira cavern.

He at once communicated with Lartet's successor, a former magistrate named Piette. The latter was amiable, obliging, and very knowledgeable. He gave the Spanish lord of the manor exhaustive information about the cultural stages of the Ice Age and its hand axes, stone knives, and engravings of mammoths. Don Marcelino also learned what precautions had to be taken in unearthing such objects and the things to be noted down. Then he tore his eyes away from the cabinets and glass cases, returned home, and armed himself with a spade to go digging in his cavern.

He had no luck at first. However industriously he excavated he always came back to his castle of Santillana with empty hands. But he would not give up his idea. He was obsessed by it as Scheuchzer, Lartet, and Boucher de Perthes had been obsessed with theirs. And one day in November 1879 his efforts were rewarded. He pulled a hand axe and some stone arrowheads out of the clay in the cave. This find proved that Altamira had at one time been inhabited by human beings of the kind described by Piette. More and more implements were discovered during the following weeks. And Don Marcelino, anxious to have his finds checked by a recognized authority, traveled to Madrid and paid a visit there to Spain's greatest prehistorian, Vilanova, who heartily congratulated him.

He continued his excavations with fresh enthusiasm, and since his five-year-old daughter Maria said she also wanted to look at the cave, he took her with him. While her father dug, the child played and crawled about in the cave, and ventured into certain recesses where Don Marcelino could not stand upright. There in the flickering candlelight she suddenly perceived, all around the walls, a number of red bulls that seemed to be moving about, charging, running away, or resting. She called out in astonishment and showed her father the pictures. At first Don Marcelino could not see anything, but as he brought his candle closer to a bulge in the rock he suddenly caught sight of the great eye of a dying bison, starting out as if in mortal terror.

His excitement was so intense that at first he stood motionless, staring at it. Then, with Maria as his guide, he searched area after area of the walls. He discovered bisons in all sorts of postures, huge bulls, cows, and little calves, which some prehistoric painter had rendered in so lively and colorful a fashion that no modern artist could have bettered it. The candle shook in his hand. Maria shrieked with delight whenever she found a new animal. Don

Marcelino gently touched the colored surface. It felt greasy. The color stuck to his finger. He glanced up at the roof of the cave. There, in addition to the red bisons, he saw wild boars in flight and a whole herd of horses. Each animal had been painted with such skill over a rounded or prolonged bulge in the rock that the spectator felt as though the body were standing out in three dimensions before his eyes.

At Don Marcelino's request, Professor Vilanova immediately hurried out from Madrid. He congratulated the small discoverer, Maria, and then examined the cave paintings. He shook his head over them. It is impossible, he thought, at first glance. No primitive Ice Age man could possibly have produced such works of art. He put Don Marcelino through a formal cross-examination, as in a court of law. He asked who could have obtained access to the cave. Eventually he was obliged to admit that neither hunters nor village children would have been able to paint bisons of the Ice Age. Digging among the rubbish on the floor of the cave he came upon more hand axes and the bones of cave bears, and at this he was convinced and agreed with Don Marcelino.

The two men then made a thorough examination of every picture. They found that the yellow pigments had been manufactured from ocher in the natural state and the red from iron oxide. The ancient artists had probably dampened red chalk and ocher in water and used fresh bison's blood as a medium. They seemed to have ground the mixture into the porous rock with such skill by their fingertips and the ball of the thumb that the tones, when required, blended into one another with the greatest subtlety. Although the paintings must have been extremely ancient, belonging, at the earliest, to the Magdalenian epoch, they looked quite fresh and recent, as if produced only a few weeks before. This aspect was due, as Vilanova saw, not only to the seclusion of the cave but also to a light, perpetually damp coating of chalk that covered the walls as though with a layer of varnish.

"These paintings are not only in the highest degree amazing because they were made by men of the Ice Age," Vilanova declared in a voice of great emotion, unable to take his eyes off the dying bison, "but also because they may be ranked with the greatest masterpieces of all time. This fact alone must convince the world of their authenticity. I know of no living painter who could achieve such work. I will stake my reputation as a scholar on their genuineness, if anyone dares to doubt it." Don Marcelino interpreted this last sentence as a binding promise.

He gave a lecture, with the assistance of Vilanova, on the paintings at Altamira in the Spanish provincial capital of Santander. The newspapers reported the discovery in large type, photographed little Maria, and made her famous throughout the country. Thousands of people swarmed to Altamira. The isolated meadow became a place of pilgrimage. The King of Spain himself, Alfonso XII, squeezed into the cave, shuddered at the eye of the dying bison, and treated Maria de Sautuola like a national heroine.

A few months later, at the congress of prehistorians in Lisbon, Don Marcelino was roughly deposed from his pedestal of triumph. All the leading personalities of prehistoric research had gathered in Lisbon to pass judgment on the pictures that Vilanova had copied, and were later on to visit the site. Rudolf Virchow came from Berlin; his French opposite number, Emile Cartailhac, from Toulouse; John Lubbock, the anthropologist and gibbon expert, from England; the prehistorian Undset, father of the novelist Sigrid Undset, from Norway; and Montelius, the interpreter of ancient Scandinavia, from Sweden. They did not shudder. They shrugged their shoulders skeptically. Not one of them dreamed of conceding the Altamira paintings an antiquity of more than twenty years at the most.

France's prince of prehistorians, Cartailhac, who knew the engravings in the Dordogne better than almost anybody, firmly declared it to be impossible for Ice Age men, with their primitive equipment, to have produced pictures at least equal, in their up-to-date technique, to the works of the French impressionists. Virchow, cool and lucid as ever, pronounced the whole thing to be a deliberate swindle. The Scandinavian experts inquired caustically of Vilanova what sort of an idea he had of the progress of mankind if he believed that wild prehistoric cave dwellers had already been capable of turning out such artistic masterpieces. Even the Darwinian Lubbock doubted the authenticity of the paintings. He could not rid himself of the notion that primitive human beings had lived a semi-brutish existence. Vilanova became more and more dejected. At the bottom of his heart he had already surrendered. At last he suggested, without any real conviction, that the gentlemen might like, after all, to suspend final judgment till they had seen the cave with their own eyes.

At this moment a Spanish colleague of Vilanova rose and with the pride of a talented detective announced he had ascertained that Don Marcelino had been entertaining for years a certain highly gifted and rather eccentric painter in his castle at Santillana. Anything further he had to say was drowned in an indescribable tumult of cries of "Forger! Swindler! Impostor!" Cartailhac stood up indignantly and left the room. Virchow nodded, mockingly. He had suspected something like that. Undset glared reproachfully at Vilanova, while Vilanova said nothing. He abandoned the owner of the castle at Santillana to his fate and the excursion to Altamira did not take place. None of the professors now had the slightest desire to have anything further to do with the matter. Don Marcelino, without taking leave of anyone, left Lisbon in a hurry and withdrew to his castle, in utter despair.

The newspapers, which had previously published such enthusiastic reports about Altamira, were now filled with spiteful attacks upon the cave-digging nobleman. They accused him of having heavily bribed the mysterious painter to compose the pictures of bisons and of having played a dastardly trick on the scientific world. And when the painter, at the request of his host, gave written testimony that he had never been into the cave, no one believed him.

However, in spite of all his disappointment, Don Marcelino was firmly determined to carry on the fight for the Ice Age pictures to the end. He found an ally in his friend the painter, who had been so unfortunately drawn into the affair through no fault of his own. Don Marcelino showed him the cave paintings and asked him to make exact copies of them for a book he intended to write about Altamira. The painter had never suspected the existence of such things and had hitherto known very little about prehistory. He gazed with astonishment at the red bisons and the multitude of other animals. Then he said that even a layman must surely recognize at the first glance that this was a wholly alien world, which no modern artist could possibly have represented. He at once placed himself at the disposal of the owner of the castle of Santillana.

The book appeared. The pictures must have struck any unprejudiced observer as positive revelations, for they were quite unlike any known portrayal of animals. Since they were still tainted by the suspicion of forgery the public remained quite unimpressed. Don Marcelino took the pictures with him to the congress of French prehistorians at Algiers. He was refused admission by Cartailhac. Then he sent his book to Berlin, where students of remote antiquity from all countries were again to meet in 1883. Virchow did not send him an invitation, nor did he even place the subject of Altamira on the agenda. Don Marcelino had a similar experience in Paris. A wall of mistrust barred him from any scientific gathering. He grew more and more embittered and wore himself out in the vain effort to find a single scholar to take his part.

The last years of his life were spent being derided as a fool and reviled as an impostor, and by the time he died, people had long ceased to discuss Altamira. Access to the cave was closed by a gate, while Maria de Sautuola waited silently in the hope that one day a professor might call, confess his mistake, and present his apologies. At last, in 1903, twenty-three years after the congress at Lisbon, one of them did come. It was Don Marcelino's most important adversary, Emile Cartailhac of Toulouse.

Similar evidence of Ice Age art had meanwhile been discovered in France. As early as 1889 bone-engravings came to light in a cave near Teyjat in the Dordogne. The engraved lines had been filled in with color. This find should have proved to prehistorians that Ice Age men had made use of color. It turned out shortly afterwards that the caves of La Mouthe, Pair-non-Pair, and Marsoulas also possessed colored wall paintings. Nevertheless, after the Altamira fiasco, no one could quite find the courage to assert that these pictures were genuine.

Then one day a young priest and natural scientist, the Abbé Henri Breuil, called on Cartailhac. He asked whether he might take part in the research work going on in the French caves. Cartailhac appreciated the priest's enthusiasm for prehistory, made him his pupil and assistant and took him to Les Eyzies, in the Vézère valley, where two recently discovered caves, those of Font-de-Gaume and Les Combarelles, were just then about to be cleared and examined.

Both caves were chock full of soil deposits and rubbish, and Breuil saw at once that it was out of the question for anyone to have forced his way into these places and worked there as an artist in recent times. Breuil had the rubbish removed, discovered a number of finely wrought stone tools, and then, surrounded by flaring torches, stood speechless before a marvel which no imagination had yet conceived. It was the same in both caves. Great numbers of animals were painted on the walls in vigorous style and accurate perspective, brilliantly colored in yellow, red, brown, and black. A herd of reindeer surged in one direction, in another the ponderous form of a mammoth rose up like a tower. A bear tramped heavily across the face of the rock, a wolf lurked in a corner. There even were human beings, lightly and delicately sketched, in rapid strokes, on the wall. At Font-de-Gaume Breuil was particularly struck by the picture of a huge aging bull bison, given such individuality and breath-taking naturalism that it must have been the work of some unique genius, a prehistoric Rembrandt.

Cartailhac turned pale as Breuil accompanied him round the two caves. Then he whispered, in such excitement as he had never known before, that preparations must instantly be made for a journey to Altamira. A few days later the two French scientists stood face to face with Maria de Sautuola. They asked her to unlock the gate leading to the cave which had been so long the subject of controversy. Maria fetched the key in silence and preceded them along the path she had trodden so often over a quarter of a century, at first in delight and later in despair.

Cartailhac caught at Breuil's shoulder and drops of sweat stood on his forehead as he examined the Altamira pictures. "There is only one thing I can do now," he said to the daughter of Don Marcelino, as she stood silently beside him. "I shall immediately confess to the public, my dear Countess, the unpardonable neglect of which I have been guilty. I shall explain that it was not your father, but I, who was the fool."

Maria gazed at him, with a small smile. "You can do a lot more than that, Professor," she replied in a tone which was only faintly tinged with reproach. "The schoolmaster at Torrelavega is already waiting for you. He knows of an entire series of Spanish caves containing drawings like those we have here in Altamira. You ought to have a talk with him!"

"But for heaven's sake!" cried Cartailhac. "Why on earth did he never say a word about them?"

"Well, you people didn't want to hear anything about cave drawings, you know," retorted Maria with a slight air of challenge. Then she conducted the visitors to the grave of Don Marcelino.

The artists of the caves

Del Rio, the schoolmaster at Torrelavega, was a temperamental southerner. He opened his arms wide when he saw the two French scientists, embraced them both, and explained in torrential fashion that he had been stimulated by the Altamira affair to visit, in company with Father Sierra of Limpias, all the accessible caves in his district. He had discovered fabulously beautiful pictures of horses, bulls, and other kinds of animals. The local people, he said, had long known about such wall paintings in the depths of the earth and believed that it had been the ancient Goths, the Arabs, or even the spirits of pagans who had immortalized themselves in those places. But he himself, as an educated man, naturally believed no such nonsense and was of the firm opinion that the caves had been used as art schools by the painters of antiquity.

"They were not art schools, I think," rejoined Breuil, "but more probably temples. The men of the Ice Age are likely to have cele-brated their ritual cults there. They practised hunting and fertility ceremonies and immobilized on the walls, in color, the dangerous and evasive beasts they hunted, so as to cast a spell upon them."

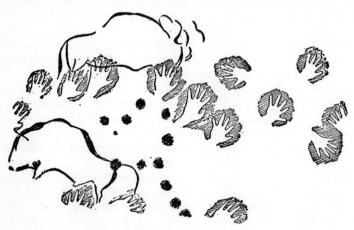

In the caves imprints of human hands were found, their out-lines obviously having been formed by staining the rock with color. Drawings of bison close by.

Del Rio nodded. "That is what Father Sierra thinks, too. But if so, gentlemen, why is it that many of the pictures in the different caves resemble one another? If I am not very much mistaken, the pupils of some old master must have gone from place to place to receive commissions and execute them in accordance with his designs. I shouldn't be surprised," he added, "if art were already an object of commerce in those days."

They crawled through a low opening into a small underground chamber forming the entrance to the cave of El Castillo. Rubbish was lying about all over the place. Cartailhac and Breuil found tools dating from all the stages of prehistoric culture. They realized that ever since early times the most diverse races of primitive man must have lived there. They noticed traces of scratches on the walls, made by cave bears. Elsewhere on the walls these scratches had been copied by primitive human beings, who had drawn lines, circles, and the outlines of figures with their fingernails. They had also dipped their hands in color and clapped them against some con-spicuous part of the wall until they finally discovered light, shade, and perspective; and in the process of a long and painful struggle with materials and forms — which probably lasted for many milleniums — made the first naturalistic picture of a bison. And when primitive man had reached this stage he went on to catch the movement of animals as they rushed along, leaped, or took flight. He reduced a herd of animals to a cloudlike fluctuating mass of strokes symbolic of a charge at full gallop, thus turning from naturalism to impressionism. Later on he became an expressionist. He simplified the forms of life represented, dissecting them into triangles and quadrangles, rhombs and sectors.

"It is as though one paced from gallery to gallery of the Louvre," said Breuil, "reviewing the entire development of painting."

Suddenly remembering the Lisbon congress, Cartailhac felt the greatest regret that Virchow was no longer among the living. Faced with this unique evidence, even that hardened skeptic would have had to give in. "These unexpected paintings of the Quaternary age," so he summarized his impression, "are in every respect magnificent and surpass all ethnographic parallels. However distant these primitive people may have been from us in time, we feel near to them and closely related in the same cult of art and beauty. We need not blush to call them our ancestors."

Cartailhac was expressing what every subsequent observer of the pictures has felt. The Ice Age world, hitherto so alien, had actually been brought close to present-day mankind in this strange manner. The cave men thus showed their distant posterity how they had lived, hunted, and loved, how they had attacked the mighty mammoth, the powerful bison, the dangerous cave lion, and the swift wild horse. The cave paintings disclosed even more than this. The abstract and symbolic drawings of the latest epochs had probably developed into the first picture writing. Man — who had until then only been accustomed to communicate by sounds and gestures — learned, while still a nomadic hunter, the use and the magic of language that could be written down.

The schoolmaster del Rio had yet another surprise in store for Breuil and Cartailhac. He showed them a flat piece of rock on which some hinds had been engraved.

"I know that picture," said Breuil thoughtfully. "I must have seen it before somewhere."

"Yes," nodded del Rio. "In Altamira. In one of the galleries there is a colored wall painting in which exactly similar hinds are represented, though on a slightly larger scale."

It turned out that he was right. The rock engraving was a pre-

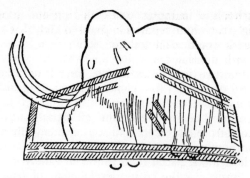

The Ice Age man could not get near monsters with his hand
weapons. This cave drawing shows how he outwitted them
by constructing traps.

liminary study which an Ice Age artist had used as a basis for the wall
painting. But how had the sketch come to be preserved in quite a
different cave? Had there actually been at that date specialists in art
among the cave dwellers? Did they acquire or collect such studies
or even dispose of them as samples to interested persons living at a
distance? This was a question often debated in the years to come.
As time went on, many more such sketches on fragments of rock were
discovered. The study for the picture of the enormous bull bison
of Font-de-Gaume, engraved on a slab of slate and agreeing in every
detail with the colored drawing on the wall, was found in a cave

A magic drawing for casting a spell over the animal,
or perhaps an instructional model for hunters.

nearly two hundred miles away from Font-de-Gaume. It must have
passed from hand to hand across half of France as an inspiration to

the Ice Age schools of painting, unless the ancient master himself was a traveling artist whose reputation stood so high that his kinsmen in distant places would send for him to decorate their walls and supply them with hunting magic.

Why did primitive man draw at all? Breuil and the other explorers of caves, who were now beginning to search eagerly for more Ice Age paintings, published ingenious and often mutually contradictory theories on the subject. They all probably had a certain amount of truth in them. It was not only out of delight in decoration and beauty, not only for ritual and religious reasons, and not only simply to achieve success in hunting by the use of symbolic images. The simple child of nature of the early Aurignacian period began to create plastic art from a profound human instinct that included all these motives. He perfected his talents over a period of fifty thousand years, during the Solutrean and Magdalenian epochs. What had begun for pleasure turned to a dedicated and serious activity. Finally fashion and commerce took a hand, putting art on an organized basis, just as in later times.

No drawings of Neanderthal man and still more primitive human groups are known. But this does not prove that there was no place for art in their harsh and exhausting lives. Man must first have expressed himself artistically in music and the dance. Before a young child takes up a pencil to draw he imitates noises and gestures, and even anthropoid apes are in the habit of singing, drumming on dry branches and the hollow trunks of trees, and also performing rhythmic dances. Footprints in the clay of caves show that early man, too, danced in moods of exaltation, just as primitive tribes still do today if the glittering gifts of European civilization have not yet been showered upon them. And from the delight in movement and the pleasure taken in play there developed ritual and ceremony in the course of time as man awoke to consciousness and sought to unravel the mysteries of his environment.

Women and animals dominate the thoughts and feelings of all hunting peoples. The group desires to propagate itself and ideally to have many healthy and strong offspring. It also wishes to kill plenty of game and escape the attacks of beasts of prey. Accordingly, the Ice Age artists were especially fond of representing hunting and love scenes. They portrayed the girl of their choice, often indeed — as in a recess of Les Combarelles cave — in an affectionate embrace. They painted mammoths, bison, and cave bears, marking the position of the heart, and used these images as targets for spear-throwing and lance-thrusting.

But primitive man did not think of animals only as sources of food. These powerful and violent companions shared his existence, and were only to be attacked with extreme cunning and skill. The men of the Ice Age had keen eyes and excellent memories. They used all their senses to understand what they saw in nature, retaining it, so to speak, photographically and stamping it for ever on their

A man wearing a bison skin. From the cave of Les Trois-Frères.

brains. After their first discoveries of color and perspective, they succeeded in creating large naturalistic portrayals of animals in peculiarly vivid style and, moreover, in representing the movement of a herd of animals in time and space with the effect, almost, of a modern motion picture.

This stage of evolution was already dominated by the wizard, the magician who understood both human beings and animals and the art of drawing them. He painted his wall pictures to serve as decorations and targets and also for ritual purposes. It was formerly the custom among all hunting peoples, such as American Indians,

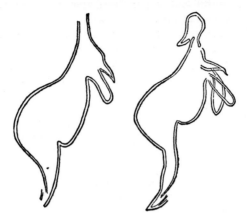

The art of the Stone Age began when the scratches made by cave bears were copied by human beings in clay with their fingers. At first the lines were purposeless and chaotic. Later they developed into primitive representations like the above figures of women.

The men of the Ice Age transfixed the hearts of mammoths with spears of yew. This rock engraving showed them where to aim.

Negroes, and Siberian natives, to dance round a slaughtered animal, transfix it with spears or arrows, and celebrate their triumph. These peoples also danced round and exorcised images of the game they hunted in order to obtain power over the originals and master them in the wilds on the following day. Not only was this the case. Images of young girls were magical inducements to sexual intercourse and those of pregnant women to births, while images of animals carrying their young ensured the fertility of game. In the lives of the men of the Ice Age there also came a day when these magical ideas were represented ceremonially. The great artists of the Magdalenian epoch were at the same time great medicine men, or at least they worked hand in glove with them. The caves adorned with pictures, often difficult of access, became places devoted to ritual and religious ceremonies, where young men, groups of hunters, or fathers of families anxious to be blessed with more children assembled and performed their dances of exorcism under the wizard's direction in front of the magic-inducing wall paintings.

Prehistorians first realized the great part played by ritual and magic, especially in the Magdalenian age, when the caves of Tuc d'Audoubert and Les Trois-Frères in the French department of Ariège were explored. Excavations had been going on in the district ever since 1876, but it was not until 1912 and 1914 that Count Bégouen, the owner of the estate, discovered near his castle of Pujot a regular maze of subterranean galleries, vaults, and dancing halls. With his three sons — after whom the cave was named Les Trois-Frères — he squeezed through small openings and narrow passages. He had to cross rivers as black and sinister as the Styx and lakes full of ghostly murmurs in the bowels of the earth and make his way through caverns with white glimmering stalactites hanging from their roofs like icicles before he succeeded in reaching the actual sanctuaries. Many of the passages were so narrow that the somewhat stout count stuck fast in them and his sons had to push and pull him through by main force. The men of the Ice Age could never have inhabited these inaccessible stalactitic catacombs permanently. Each visit to the actual picture galleries must have meant a grueling physical experience for them too, a kind of test of their courage and fitness. Here in the obscure depths of the earth, lighted by stone oil lamps and surrounded by black waters the great magicians had once celebrated their fertility rites.

The pictures in the first halls of Tuc d'Audoubert represented bison, wild horses, and reindeer, with arrows, and also boomerangs, whizzing round them. Magdalenian man, therefore, was already acquainted with the strange casting implement used by Australian aboriginals. Still more sensational was the sight that Count Bégouen and his sons beheld in the last of the halls, which they were only able to reach with the greatest difficulty. Two sculptured reliefs of bison stood out from the wall, representing a bull mounting a cow. All round the group the footprints of dancers could be traced. In a feverish dance, probably clothed as bison, they had put away child-ish things and learned the secrets of coupling and impregnation.

The great wizard in the cave of Les Trois-Frères.

In the Trois-Frères cave, more than twenty yards underground, the Bégouens, after crawling for hours through passages of extreme dif-ficulty, encountered the great magician in person. All the pictures in this cave had been engraved by the same hand, indicating that hunting magic had been practised there. There were mammoths, woolly rhinoceroses, and bison, with arrows directed against them, a cave bear with its body showing the wounds made by arrows and blood flowing from its jaws, and a man wrapped in a beast's hide who was bewitching two reindeer by playing a flute. But one picture differed entirely from the others. A little over four yards above the level of the floor, beside a vertical protuberance of the rock, there appeared — like the letters of fire on Belshazzar's wall — the artist's self-portrait, that of the magician himself, half engraved and half painted. It is the most powerful, sinister, and diabolical of all Ice Age pictures. A bearded man is performing his dance of exorcism. He is painted all over his body and wears a reindeer mask with widely projecting antlers, the paws of a bear, and a horse's tail. His round, owlish eyes stare the visitor in the face, positively hypnotizing him.

The cave of Lascaux, first discovered by accident in 1940 by four French boys, contains, in addition to delicately sketched paintings of game, whose playful grace is reminiscent of drawings in India ink from eastern Asia, the picture of a man killed by a bison. A bird perches on a pole close by. It may be the man's soul, which has left the body and is getting ready for its flight to heaven, or it may be the dead man's totem bird. We do not know. There are still many puzzles to be solved in the caves of France and Spain.

The connection between art and ritual in the early and middle Magdalenian periods gradually loosened as people began to copy the magical pictures to decorate their dwellings and the articles they used. It seems certain that skilled artists earned their livings by their talents. They traveled from settlement to settlement supplying decorations for centers of ritual and other gatherings. They accumulated all sorts of small-scale works of art, which may be assumed to have lost their magical meaning — such as ivory and bone carvings, stone and antler engravings, and weapons with handles representing various animals — and traded in them. Schools of applied art came into existence. A linear style of drawing developed. Ornaments in the form of stylized bodies of animals and geometrical figures took the place of the realistic and impressionistic representations of nature. The former could only be used with difficulty for magical purposes. They were characteristic of the progress of civilization. They met the cultural requirements of large sections of the population. And when the Ice Age came to an end and the caves were abandoned, when humanity began its great migrations and proceeded to create social communities, tribes, and states, the threads leading to the mysterious world deep below the earth's surface were also broken off. It was only in the subconscious mind that vague recollections of the ancient holy places still stirred, in the form of belief in ghosts and fear of demons.

These ideas of the lives, thoughts, feelings, and spiritual growth of late Ice Age man gradually took shape as more and more caves containing pictures were explored. The discovery of Les Combarelles and Font-de-Gaume broke the spell. Scientists began to acknowledge the artistic gifts of our remote ancestors. Henri Breuil took up the search for Adam, and by his energy rapidly surpassed his master, Cartailhac. He investigated each newly discovered cave with tireless industry and published a series of magnificent works that illuminated the course of the growth of the early cultures.

In 1914 Albert I, Prince of Monaco and one of the great patrons of the study of early man, founded an institute for human paleontology in Paris. Breuil became director and the German prehistorian Hugo Obermaier took a professorial appointment in it. As time went on they worked in close collaboration, collected an exemplary team of scholars and together wrested one secret after another from the subterranean mazes, stalactite grottoes, halls, and chambers in the rock. Count Bégouen, the discoverer of Tuc d'Audoubert and Trois-Frères, succeeded Cartailhac at the Prehistoric Institute of Toulouse. And the former schoolmaster of Torrelavega, now mayor of his native village, the *alcalde* del Rio, took charge of the works of art in the Spanish province of Santander. Later on he was joined by Breuil's friend and colleague Obermaier. The latter settled in Madrid and became a well-known personality throughout Spain as Don Hugo, the cave investigator.

Cave explorers

The discovery of Old Stone Age art was the real turning point between nineteenth- and twentieth-century prehistoric study. It shocked people out of their previous conceptions and obliged them to re-form their ideas on a new and broader basis. They ceased to be concerned exclusively with the bodily evolution of the human race and began to consider its mental growth as well. It was recognized that the primitive phenomenon of early art could not be satisfactorily explained by either the methods of the natural scientists or those of the art historian. In the caves of the Ice Age, as Breuil put it, for the first time man had dreamed, however instinctively and vaguely, of great art and the potentialities of human existence. The cult of beauty that he practised there had clarified his mind, perfected his faculty of reflection, refined his speech, and enabled him to conjecture a world beyond what he could see and touch.

Breuil and Obermaier had been trained from their youth up as

Catholic priests and belonged to the Jesuit order. Their activities started a development that led many other theologians to take up prehistoric study. A chaplain, Ferdinand Birkner, occupied the chair of prehistory at the university of Munich. Father Teilhard de Chardin dug up remains of early man in England and China. The Jesuit Felix Rüschkamp supported human descent from apes in an article that attracted much attention in 1939 in a periodical called *Contemporary Voices*. Other priests of both creeds investigated the traces of early human culture in their restricted native environment, following the example of the Abbé Breuil in deciphering and copying the utterly hopeless tangle of lines and figures, animals, weird faces, and symbols in the caves of the Ice Age, as they made every effort to penetrate through the mists of milleniums to the dawn of civilization.

Theologians were of course by their very nature particularly attracted to the task of groping in the primeval darkness of early ages when the human spirit awoke and man arrived at some idea of the cosmos. Until Breuil's time the churches had maintained an attitude of skeptical expectation to the science of primitive man. The situation at this date resembled that of four hundred years before, when the discoveries of Copernicus caused the collapse of an entire cosmology. It is understandable that the dismissal of traditional ideas should be difficult for those who believe in a fixed order of phenomena. But though the Copernican revolution had to wait a very long time for acceptance, since the new cosmic system was not universally recognized until more than two hundred years later, the second great revolution of thought, in the biological history of evolution, won a relatively swift victory. The keenness of those scientifically inclined theologians who became prehistorians played a special part in it.

As early as the times of Edouard Lartet a priest had set himself the task of tracing Adam back to the dawn of the world's history. The French Abbé Bourgeois was one of the most surprising and interesting champions of prehistoric study. In 1863 he found near the village of Thenay in the department of Loire-et-Cher, in layers apparently dating from the Tertiary period, a number of flints he considered to be in the nature of tools. At two congresses of anthropologists at Paris in 1867 and at Brussels in 1872, this find was the subject of lively discussion. The experts made angry accusations against Bourgeois and called his scientific accuracy into question. The eccentric priest, who contended that the age of civilized humanity should be relegated to unimaginably remote epochs, suffered the same fate as Boucher de Perthes and Don Marcelino de Sautuola. His only defenders were Gabriel de Mortillet, the classifier of Stone Age cultures, and his disciples.

The position of the Abbé Bourgeois was particularly difficult because he found himself, as a priest, confronted with a discovery which to all outward appearance utterly contradicted his religious faith. His adversaries made the most of this new weapon and tried to involve him in conscientious scruples. In his reply, which also served as a statement of his scientific belief, Bourgeois announced in clear and unmistakable terms that he saw no reason for opposition between religious and scientific truth.

> To those who ask me how I intend to reconcile this discovery with the Biblical story I can only answer that I take my stand on the basis of facts without entering upon any attempt to explain them. I am content to say that I have found flints that show obvious signs of treatment by man and that I found them in a soil which people call Tertiary. I assert nothing more. If science compels us to set the origins of humanity further back there is nothing to be afraid of in that, and I would like to remind you at this point of that oft-quoted statement by the Abbé Le Hir: "There is no such thing as Biblical chronology. It is the business of science to establish the date upon which man first appeared on the earth."

Bourgeois died in 1878, but he triumphed from the grave. It is true that at the turn of the century the eoliths of Thenay proved to be anything but tools of Tertiary man. Nevertheless, the view taken of the problem of primitive man by their discoverer came in the course of time to be shared by the majority of theologians. "The Church," wrote the Freiburg theologian Heinrich Schneider in 1946 in his pamphlet entitled *The Church, the Bible and the Theory of Evolution*, "need not be supposed to await the answer to the important questions of the theory of evolution from Divine revelation, nor, consequently, from the Bible. She awaits it from scientific investigation." In this statement Schneider relied on a declaration of Pope Pius XII in 1941 dealing with the origin of mankind: "We can only leave to the future the answer to the question whether science may one day be able to record its definite and final findings concerning this highly important subject." The heated controversies between theology and biology were followed by a sober stocktaking of the discoveries. It was above all in that El Dorado of paleolithic investigation, France, that priests especially, and schoolmasters, set out on Adam's trail and submitted one premature document after another to science. The theory of evolution, a few decades previously still the object of passionate polemics, was thus supported in a fashion that scholars in the lifetime of Darwin, Huxley, and Fuhlrott would never have believed possible.

The men of science having once broken the spell, the men of action, the bold adventurers, followed in their footsteps. The caves of the world — the clefts and grottoes of mountains, the icy vaults and stalactite caverns underground — suddenly became interesting. Secrets were now scented in all directions. It was hoped to find traces of prehistoric times all over the place. And just as the peaks of the earth challenge both the explorer and the sportsman to overcome them, so the riddles underground summoned those in search of danger, as well as prehistorians, to take a hand.

The Frenchman Norbert Casteret was explorer and adventurer, prehistorian and sportsman rolled into one. He had set himself the task of reconnoitering the great caves of the Pyrenees, some of which were still quite unknown. Subterranean rivers and lakes, waterfalls, walls of stalactites, and dizzy gulfs often closed access to their innermost chambers and halls. Casteret and his companions had to unite the abilities of underwater swimmers, navigators, and mountaineers in order to overcome the manifold obstacles within the hills. New types of implements, lighting sets, and boats were manufactured and new techniques of swimming and climbing were developed. At the same time as the assault upon the giants of the world of mountains and the descent into the depths of the oceans began, with modern equipment constructed for this object alone, the advance started — in surprisingly similar fashion and with similar success — into the most remote and secret treasure chambers of the earth.

Casteret's whole family took part in various less dangerous expeditions. Participating were his mother, trained as a mountaineer, his athletic wife and her friends, the cave explorer's two small children, and, in the capacity of interpreter and copier of the drawings and cultural relics to be discovered, his brother Dr. Martial Casteret. The Casterets' mother helped them to find the long sought source of the Garonne in the Monts Maudits on the Spanish side of the Pyrenees. Madame Norbert Casteret bathed in the icy waters of a cave lake in Monte Perdido, 9000 feet above sea level. She crawled through narrow passages, had herself lowered by rope into deep gorges, and struck up a friendship with the real owners of those inky depths — the bats. In the "Hall of the Roaring Lion" the children admired the chamber of state in the cave of Labastide, the various monsters that their early ancestors had placed with so masterly and magical a touch upon the walls. Casteret's helpers and rivals were his brother Martial, the explorer of cave rivers Henri Godin, the industrialist Marcel Loubens, André Mairey, doctor of medicine, Robert Levi, Dupeyron, the Abbé Moura, and other enthusiastic explorers. Each of them grew accustomed to taking his life in his hands and some of them paid the penalty of their daring. One of the most recent victims was Loubens, despite his familiarity with all subterranean hazards. In August 1952 he climbed too far down into a chasm of the Pierre Saint-Martin cave, was suddenly attacked by nervousness, and hurriedly attempted to regain the daylight. The plate securing the cable-clamp worked loose, thus opening the rope loop around Loubens, and he was dashed to pieces against the rocky bottom of the abyss. A year later Casteret, Levi, and Dr. Mairey, while exploring the same cave well over two thousand feet below the surface, were buried by a landslide and only rescued after prolonged efforts.

How had people ever been able to live in caverns so difficult of access? In 1922, after the discovery of the Montespan cave, Casteret wrote: "The study of geology teaches us that the climate at the end of the Ice Age was particularly cold and dry, something like it is now in Lapland. The subterranean rivers and pools dried up for long periods. Consequently the caves afforded a refuge to primitive man." Montespan was the best example of this aspect of the caves. When Casteret and Godin began to reconnoiter it, water was gurgling everywhere in the subterranean catacombs, often rising as high as the roof vaulting. Repeated advances under water through the maze of passages were necessary in order to reach the actual workshops and picture galleries of the Ice Age men. Fabulous scenes then rewarded the explorers for their toil and perseverance. The floor of the dry chambers beyond the rivers and lakes consisted, wrote Casteret, "of a series of highly picturesque 'stair-carpets,' the waved and rippled fringes of which covered a natural staircase. Their hollowed out steps were full of clear water. Elsewhere, a flowerlike expanse of golden-yellow growths and protuberances recalled the coral reefs of submarine landscapes." An abundance of forms and colors had been conjured into existence by stalactites, and close behind them, after the passage had taken a sharp turn, were revealed halls containing reliefs of horses and cave bears, plastic representations of bears, sketches of animals, bone modeling tools, and the imprints of the hands and feet of the Ice Age men.

In 1932 Casteret explored, by climbing, swimming, and wading through thick and deep mud, the sacred grotto of Labastide in the Baronnies hill country, the "land of the forty caves." He had to struggle with nitrogen gas, piles of rubbish in his path, and treacherous bogs before reaching his new marvels, the Hall of the Roaring Lion and the Horse Cavern. He describes his experiences as follows:

How is one to communicate one's impression and thoughts on confronting, alone and underground, one of those manifestations of the art of primitive man, in comparison with which the antiquities of Egypt are positively recent? When it has fallen to one's lot to be the first to find, after tens of thousands of years, the picture of the terrible cave lion that once made the forests and plains of our native land so dangerous? The rich exhibition of prehistoric art to be found here is undoubtedly the most fascinating, most exciting and most ancient of its kind.

The roaring cave lion. This engraving was found by Casteret in Labastide. There are only a few representations of this mighty beast of prey, which was at that time just dying out. It is not yet known whether the animal was a lion or a tiger.

The roaring lion depicted on the back wall of the Labastide cave — which included among many other sketches of animals, a naked male dancer and a strange, weirdly human wizard's mask — was in fact a masterpiece. The over life-sized head of a beast of prey, strikingly realistic in expression, showed long, threatening canine teeth in its open jaws. The narrowed eyes were full of menace and every detail of the drawing indicated terrifying savagery. But was it really a lion? In other cave drawings representing the same animal the paleontologist Othenio Abel had discovered stripes like those of a tiger. He concluded that this most formidable enemy of Cro-Magnon man ought really to bear the name of cave tiger. This opinion is supported by the fact that even today the tiger is found in countries subject to glaciation, like Siberia. However the fact that the lions discovered by Casteret have tufted tails, such as the tiger does not possess, is evidence to the contrary.

Casteret was gradually able to introduce the world to the entire fauna of the Ice Age. He found traces of their activity in deep remotely situated caves and reconstructed their lives of between 20,000 and 50,000 years ago.

There is nothing stranger and more impressive than such indications of the stubborn attempts of the cave bears to climb upward. There are very many marks of their claws visible in the clay of the cave floor. One can imagine the animals falling back into the water, standing up again, growling, and making a fresh attempt at climbing. The clay of a steep bank and the muddy bottom of the lake below has preserved quite clear traces of one of the most remarkable scenes in the life of the cave bear, enabling us to realize it vividly. The bears made use of the natural features of the ground to indulge in games of sliding, which ended in muddy water. Many of the marks made are so clear that they even give the imprint of the hair of the hide in the soft clay. In one corner of the Pène-Blanque cave a bear employed the long and tedious period of hibernation by dancing for hours in the same place, as is proved by the repeated crossing of the impressions of his four feet in different directions.

On the other hand Casteret had one good reason for finding the cave hyenas less attractive. "Paleontologists curse the cave hyena. For it alone is responsible for the fact that the skeletons of prehistoric men and animals are so seldom found." The hyenas were extremely voracious scavengers and they attacked the kitchen waste of the Ice Age people, the bones of their slaughtered game, and their old burying places. They did not even spare the dead of their own species. For this reason all the finds they did spare come from especially deep layers or places so remotely situated as to be quite inaccessible.

Only a fraction of the secret underground chambers has hitherto been explored, and many puzzles and marvels still await discovery. But the history of cave exploration is not made up of adventures and the work of scholars only; it has had its farcical incidents. Just as Harlequin once used to leap from the wings of a theater and interrupt the action of the play with his fooling, so farce is always breaking into the realm of science to elicit wild applause from the audience. One such incident occurred in July 1952 in the Pech-Merle cave in Cabrerets, where times had changed since the days of the young Breuil. Pech-Merle was no longer a shadowy grotto only accessible to explorers and adventurers. It had become a highly popular and comfortably furnished showplace for tourists. The mayor of the village of Cabrerets, by name Bessac and by trade a blacksmith, had rented the cave and its Ice Age picture galleries

A wild horse from the Late Ice Age. A magnificent naturalistic cave drawing at Labastide.

in order to exploit them commercially. Electric light was installed in the passages and chambers. A bar had been erected in a recess, where the tourists could refresh themselves after their subterranean excursions with cognac and aperitifs. A record player sent dance music and the rhythms of jazz hurtling up the walls that were illuminated with arc lamps and adorned with mammoths. Madame Bessac sat with the collection box at the entrance to the cave and sold tickets. The enterprising blacksmith's children raced about the cave offering the interested visitors from all the regions of the earth gaudy postcards illustrating the cave paintings. It was no wonder that many people who came frowned upon these activities and thought them dubious.

One of these skeptics was the French writer André Breton, author of the famous "surrealist manifesto." Breton strolled through the Pech-Merle cave on July 24, 1952. He listened to the dance music and inspected the bar, then he looked at a splendid drawing of a mammoth on the wall. Apparently he thought that this juxtaposition of phenomena was altogether too strange, for he immediately marched resolutely up to the mammoth, rubbed his thumb over its trunk, saw that the color stuck to his thumb and then turned, with a laugh, to Monsieur Bessac. "Forgery, *monsieur*," he said with a grin, indicating the trunk of the mammoth. Three square centimeters of it had disappeared, having been transferred to his thumb. Bessac, red with rage, struck the poet a heavy blow on the fingers, ran him out of his luxury cave, and took out a summons against him for damages of a million francs.

A year later Breton and Bessac appeared before the magistrate in the small town of Cahors. The case of the mammoth of Cahors, which was to decide whether one square centimeter of mammoth trunk was really worth 333,333.33 francs, attracted like flies journalists, authors, prehistorians, and inquisitive laymen from all over France. Breton had powerful figures in French literature behind him: François Mauriac, Jules Romains, André Malraux, and Albert Camus raised their voices, protesting energetically against the "shameful persecution" of their hypercritical colleague. They had, however, to submit to being told by a representative of the museum of fine arts that even a poet must not rub out with impunity what a Cro-Magnon artist had once created and that the effaceability of a Stone Age drawing does not by any means necessarily prove it to have been forged. The Ministry had associated itself with the charge brought. It was however more indulgent than Monsieur Bessac. It only demanded a token fine of one franc. Proceedings at the trial resembled scenes in a witty boulevard comedy. Epigrams and insults were hurled from prosecution to defense and back again. On one occasion Bessac rose and declared resentfully that Breton had behaved in his respectable cave "like a bull in a china shop." If anyone had behaved like a bull there, countered the defense, it had been Monsieur Bessac, who had hit a poet on the fingers. The defense added that the prosecutor was making "a mammoth out of a midge." The court eventually scaled down the value of the effaced portion of trunk considerably. André Breton had to pay over twenty thousand francs to Madame Bessac. The blacksmith and bar owner of Pech-Merle was quite satisfied with this sum, for the numbers of visitors to his Ice Age establishment had meanwhile been multiplying.

Fortunately not all the caves with pictures had been turned into electrically lighted bars. The prehistorians in Henri Breuil's circle soon began to take measures to prevent that sort of thing. They noticed that the respiration of thousands of visitors was very injurious to the preservation of the pictures and vigorously advocated that these ancient works of art should be sealed off, so far as possible, from the outside air. This step alone, Breuil declared, would enable them to survive for a further period of milleniums. Many caves — that of Tuc d'Audoubert, for instance — may only be visited today by experts and other interested persons with special permission.

At the same time that the antique picture galleries were being opened up, explorers were also forging ahead with spades and picks to the graves of their creators and letting in daylight in that quarter. And it was found that the Ice Age man already possessed some idea of a life after death as well as of art and magic.

Cain buried his brother Abel

When the son of the Vézère valley explorer, Lartet, discovered his Ice Age family in the cave of Cro-Magnon he was immediately convinced that these splendidly built people with their high foreheads and angular skulls could not have been rude denizens of the woods, but intelligent and busy architects of civilization. Fifty years later, after study of the cave drawings, there could be no further doubt about the penetrating intellectual capabilities of Cro-Magnon man. When they contemplated the average specimen of contemporary man, quite a number of connoisseurs of the subject felt a certain regret that the intellectual progress of humanity since the days of the Cro-Magnon tragedy, at any rate in the artistic sphere, should have been so disproportionately slight. The extravagant optimism of the nineteenth century, which thought that all the riddles of the universe could be solved and promised to create a paradise on earth, faltered to some extent on being confronted by these early cultures.

Meanwhile graves and skeletons of the Cro-Magnon race began to be found all over Europe. In each case the remains of the bones were not washed up in a cave by chance. They had been buried with

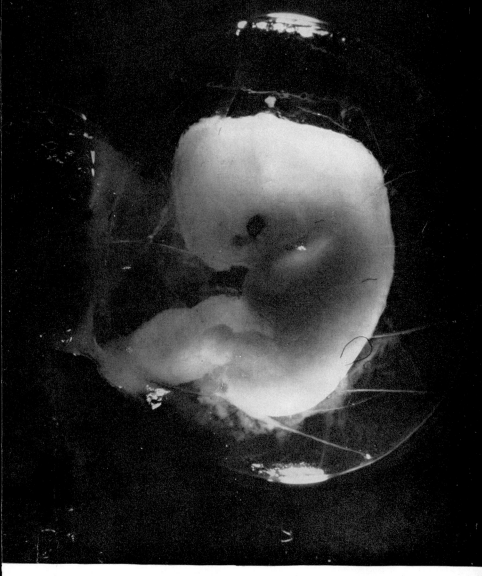

17. Human embryo, six weeks old, in the fertilized membrane.
Original size less than an inch.

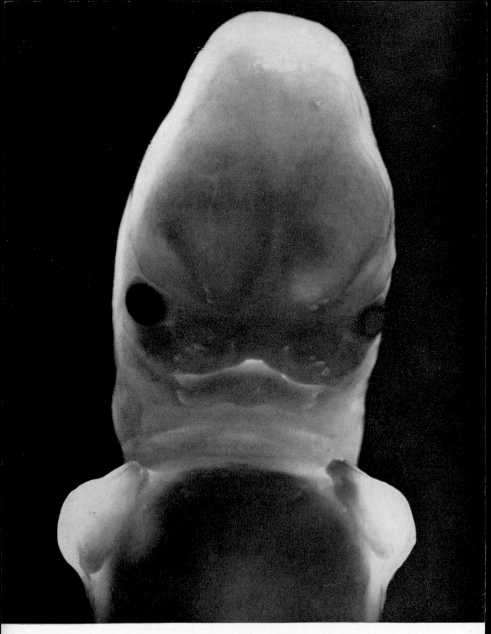

18. The primal form. Enlarged photograph of human embryo seen from the front. The shape still looks reptilian, but the bipartite brain can already be clearly recognized.

19. The "ape-professor" from Jena, Ernst Haeckel with his collection of skeletons. He compared that of a half-grown child (*extreme right*) with that of a gibbon (*second from right*) and was led by certain similarities to regard the gibbon as the nearest simian relative of Man. The deduction was false, but it resulted in a decisive discovery.

20. The "primitive man without speech" as conceived by Haeckel attracted the attention of artists as well as the general public. The painter Gabriel Max imagined him as above.

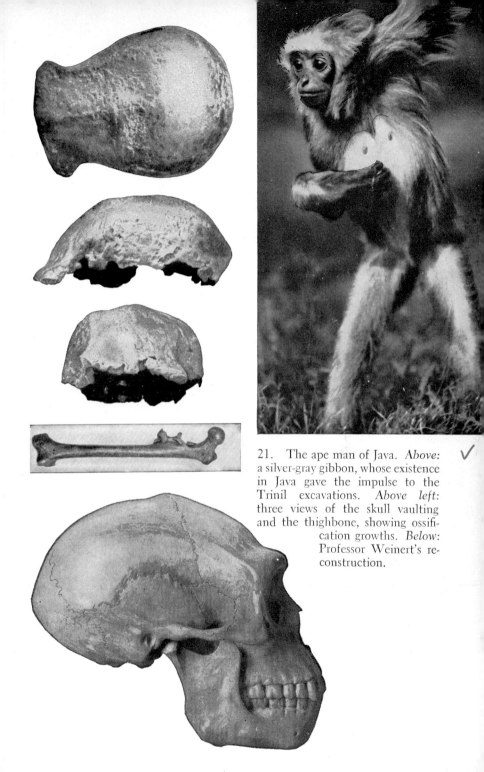

21. The ape man of Java. *Above:* a silver-gray gibbon, whose existence in Java gave the impulse to the Trinil excavations. *Above left:* three views of the skull vaulting and the thighbone, showing ossification growths. *Below:* Professor Weinert's reconstruction.

22. The primeval landscape. The *Pithecanthropus* lived in the volcanic highlands of Java, where ever since the earliest times many living creatures have been buried under lava, mud, and ashes.

23. The Altamira prodigy. This 6-feet-wide wall painting in red and black of a bull bison at Altamira is the work of an Ice Age artist of genius.

24. The sculptors reached the same artistic level as the painters. Probably the finest example of Late Ice Age modeling is that of the two bison from the rearmost chamber of the cave of Tuc d'Audoubert. The animal on the right is about two feet wide. *Below:* relief of a wild horse at Montespan, showing a number of arrow wounds.

25. Entrance to the cave of Lascaux.

26.   *Below:* The great bull bison of Font-de-Gaume (about 3 feet wide).
Above: the small sketch on stone (2¾ inches wide) from which the
traveling Ice Age artist worked. It was found 187 miles away from
Font-de-Gaume.

27. By the same methods as South Sea Islanders still use today Stone Age men climbed trees and smoked out bees' nests to get at the honey.

28. Woman as a fertility symbol. *Above:* The Venus of Willendorf (original 4 inches high). *Right:* basrelief from Laussel, Dordogne (original 18 inches high).

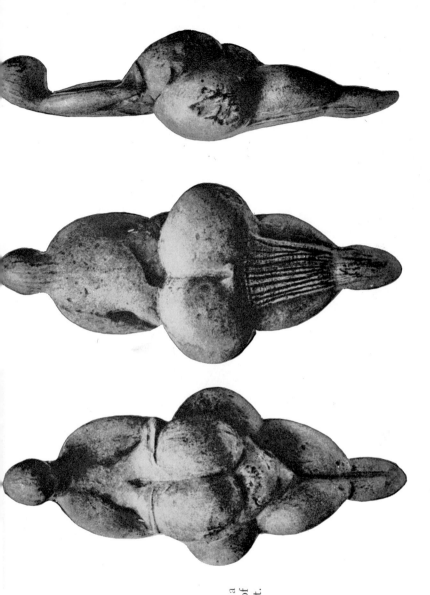

29. Ivory statuette of a woman. An example of almost abstract art.

30. This small ivory carving is the best and most lifelike portrait of Stone Age Man (original height about 1½ inches).

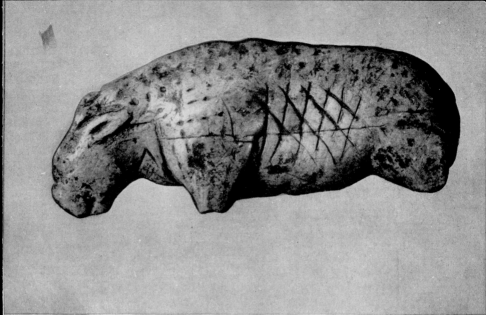

31. Small carvings of woolly rhinoceros or cave lioness and wild horse from the cave of Vogelherd in Württemberg.

32. It was a far cry from these artistic records in Africa to their late echo in the Bushman drawings of the eighteenth and nineteenth centuries. *Above:* a rock engraving from the Late Ice Age, discovered by Leo Frobenius at In Habeter, a dry riverbed. *Below:* a family group in a rock drawing from Kargour-Talh in the Sahara Desert.

care and piety, indicating that the people of the Late Ice Age had had the same attitude to death as present-day man. Some graves were discovered in abandoned domestic interiors, others in pits elsewhere, while still others consisted of artificially constructed heaps of rock. Some of the dead men's possessions had been buried with them. Garlands of the shells of marine creatures and snails, or of the teeth of deer, cave bears and cave lions, decorated the brows and necks, the chests and loins, the arms and legs of the skeletons. Bone awls, flint knives, and attractive carvings lay within reach of the hands of the corpses. Traces appeared in the soil of the remains of animals intended to serve the soul as food during its long journey into eternity.

These ancient hunters of mammoth and bison, only slightly different from the modern Westerner in their artistic, cultural, and religious aspects, also practised — as the opening of their graves proved — a most surprising custom. They were out and out cannibals. Many of the corpses buried with such loving care had previously had their skulls cracked open by a fellow tribesman and their brains eaten. It is possible that the man so killed had been a great hunter, artist, magician, or warrior whose qualities his heirs wished to obtain by this somewhat drastic method. But probably the eating of human flesh was one of the common habits and customs of the Late Ice Age, as it had been in still earlier times. Not only were dead enemies devoured, but kinsfolk too were handed over to the medicine men to be sacrificed with solemn ritual to divinities, eaten, and then honorably interred. The head-hunters and cannibals in the primeval jungles of Africa, Malaya, and South America were therefore not particularly perverse representatives of the species *Homo sapiens*. They had merely preserved their loyalty to an antique cult right down to modern times.

This custom was not supported by the men of the Ice Age, or indeed by modern cannibals, on purely culinary grounds, but was connected with belief in the immortal soul. Today the uncivilized communities of Australian aboriginals still believe that the souls of the dead are dangerous haunters of the dark, capable of doing all sorts of damage if proper measures are not taken in time to restrain them. The aboriginals consider that the best method of controlling them and bringing them up in the way they should go is to devour the bodies of the dead and thus swallow their souls.

The great anthropologist Hermann Klaatsch, who had been concerned to draw comparisons between the customs and cults of Australian aboriginals and the people of the Ice Age — and made some

astonishing discoveries in the process — wrote in this connection in
The Growth of Mankind and the Beginnings of Civilization:

> "Devouring love" has a background of actuality. In the desire
> not to lose beloved persons the attempt is made to cast a spell
> upon their souls and immobilize them within oneself by eating
> the body. The mother herself eats the flesh of her dead child
> and carries her darling's bones, stripped clean and painted red,
> about with her. Here the wish to retrieve and retain what has
> been lost is the decisive factor. When a dead enemy is devoured
> the idea of the transfer of power plays the chief part. If it is not
> practicable to eat the whole body, the brain at any rate or the fat
> in the neighborhood of the kidneys is consumed, as this substance,
> oddly enough, is considered to be the seat of special capabilities.
> This idea of being able to assimilate physically the qualities of
> another person has been retained by mankind partly in the form
> of superstition and partly as an accompaniment to religious con-
> ceptions.

Obviously, if one wished to assimilate the characteristics of someone else, there was no need to wait till he died naturally. If a special
cultural motive for doing so existed, one could just as well put him
to death by force. Such was the origin of the custom of human sacrifice, and it was already familiar in the Ice Age.

Nevertheless, this sort of spellbinding was not considered by primitive man to be entirely reliable. It was believed that the dead man,
in spite of having been eaten and especially if he had been a great
warrior or wizard, might return and make mischief as a spirit. According to Klaatsch, the fear of an undesirable resurrection of this
kind was responsible for the special rite of burial in a crouching
position. In the great majority of graves from Aurignacian, Solutrean,
Magdalenian, and later Stone Age times the skeletons lay in a peculiar crooked posture, like a child curled up asleep. The more romantically inclined scholars, when they investigated these graves,
jumped to the conclusion that primitive man had been influenced
by the wish to give his dead back to Mother Earth in the same
embryonic attitude in which they had come to birth. Klaatsch found
a much simpler and more natural explanation. The tribesmen had
tied up the body to prevent its rising later on as a demon from the
grave. This conjecture was supported by the holes found to have
been pierced in the bones of the feet of certain skeletons and also
by the enlightening circumstance that primitive peoples in the South

Seas, New Guinea, and the islands of the Indian Ocean had done exactly the same thing within historical times.

Accordingly, the Ice Age man had neither lived the rude and uncultivated life of a wild beast nor the pious and monogamous one of Adam and Eve in Paradise. Superstition and fear of ghosts, battle and acts of violence, the abduction of women and bloody ceremonials had been as much part of his life as the need for personal adornment, the cult of beauty, and family feeling. In subsequent ages mankind, however unwilling they may be to admit it, have inherited as much of one set of habits as of the other.

Hermann Klaatsch, the first great chronicler and describer of the customs of primitive man, came of a Berlin doctor's family and possessed all the basic traits necessary to enable him to come to grips with Adam's secrets in the cool and sober spirit of an anatomist. He studied medicine under Haeckel's friend Gegenbaur, but soon, as a young professor at the University of Heidelberg, began to oppose the doctrine of the descent of man held by Darwin, Huxley, and Haeckel.

At the 1899 congress of anthropologists he gave a lecture, which attracted much attention, on the relation of man to the anthropoid apes, stating that humanity did not come from this source at all but had developed in a number of mutually independent branches from original primates. The differentiation of various branches of humanity, he said, lay "much farther back than has hitherto been supposed possible. Modern science can give no support to the exaggerated humanitarianism intent on seeing our own brothers and sisters in all the lower races of mankind and conceding rights to them." The anthropoid apes, according to Klaatsch, were "unsuccessful experiments in human evolution, our defeated cousins who have withdrawn of their own accord or been forced to withdraw into the protective darkness of the primeval forest." It is only a slight exaggeration to say that he considered the orangutan an unsuccessful rough sketch for the yellow race, and the gorilla and the chimpanzee failures, respectively, to initiate the black and white varieties. He added: "The complete separation of these types of anthropoid apes from the human types especially closely related to them may have first arisen as soon as all interbreeding ceased. In view of the highly sexed character of all primates this is likely to have taken an extremely long time. Once the anthropoid apes had been repudiated and entered upon hostile relations with mankind, they had no resource but to continue to evolve along uncivilized lines."

The essential contribution of Klaatsch to the science of the growth of mankind was not, however, this much disputed theory, but his thorough stocktaking of the entire body of scientific knowledge of primitive and early man in his day. He examined the bones from Neanderthal and the new finds of Neanderthal remains. He visited the Vézère valley where Lartet had excavated, and Trinil, where Dubois had discovered the *Pithecanthropus*. He explored Australia and Tasmania, finding that the fifth division of the globe was a great museum of natural history and ethnology surviving from primitive times. He brought about final recognition of Neanderthal man, the ape man of Java, and later of Heidelberg man. He checked the pedigree of man back to the fishes and believed he had found, in the primitive Coelacanthidae family of fish the original ancestors of all the higher vertebrates. As early as 1896 he suggested that the first legs, the organs that led to the conquest of land, had evolved from the fins of these fish.

Fifty years later everyone was talking about Klaatsch's coelacanth. Loose sheets illustrating the "fish with legs" passed from hand to hand in South Africa. Every fisherman who caught one of these most interesting and venerable creatures was assured of a substantial reward. For it had been discovered that they had not departed this life sixty million years ago, as had formerly been assumed. Some species survive to this day in the bays of Africa. England's greatest ichthyologist, J. R. Norman, observed at a meeting of the London Linnean Society: "It is as though a living dinosaur had suddenly been discovered. And there is more to it than that even. We men come ultimately, just as herrings do, from the coelacanth."

About Christmastime in the year 1938 a South African named Goosen, captain of a steam trawler, took a fish between four and five feet long out of his dragnet. It had four leglike fins and was a kind he had never seen before. Of course by the time he submitted the creature to the curator of the East London Museum, Miss Courtenay-Latimer, the fish was half rotten, but the South African zoologist J. B. L. Smith recognized it as a representative of the oldest known group of vertebrates. It was a true coelacanth that had survived through the ages. Such creatures had inhabited the globe for 350,000,000 years. Goosen's fish, *Latimeria chalumniae*, had remained practically unchanged throughout this unimaginably long period.

Professor Smith put all the coastal stations on the alert. It was not until Christmas 1952 that the second coelacanth to survive from the misty beginnings of time right into the Atomic Age was captured. A Negro saw a bluish, glittering creature, with its fins situated on what were obviously the stumps of legs, in the fish market of Anjouan, one of the Comoro Islands, in the basket of a trader named Achmed Hussein. It reminded him of Smith's leaflet. He at once hurried to a certain Captain Haunt and suggested that he should rescue the coelacanth. Haunt injected all the preservation substances he could find in Anjouan into the fishy ancestor of all quadrupeds and bipeds and sent a wire to Smith. A government plane brought Smith to the island. He closely inspected the fish, knelt down in front of it, and, according to one of his companions, burst into tears of joy. It was the most important zoological discovery of the last few decades, and was also of special importance in the history of the descent of man.

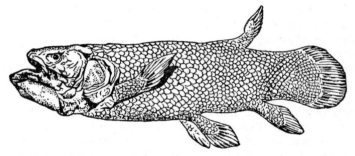

A living fossil that has survived practically unchanged for 350,000,000 years, the coelacanth, or *Malania anjouanae*.

The coelacanth of Anjouan, *Malania anjouanae*, had already changed its air bladder into a lunglike organ. Apparently it produced its young alive, like the higher vertebrates. The muscular system of its fins showed how the leg muscles of land animals had evolved. And that was exactly what its forefathers of the antique world looked like, those who had succeeded in the greatest pioneering act in zoological history, the conquest of dry land. Klaatsch's hypothesis of 1896, which had been so much disputed at the time, was brilliantly confirmed by the unexpected capture of this "living fossil."

It is a far cry from the exploration of "crouching position" graves to the pursuit of prehistoric fish of great importance for the history of evolution. But such leaps back into the twilight of the earliest days of earth are characteristic of the science that deals with the origins of Man. Prehistorians have to have all-round ability. Klaatsch was a prime example. He was an expert on fish and mammals, wrote on the psychology and religious history of primitive peoples, wielded the spade as paleontologist and prehistorian, and, like Virchow, knew his way about human anatomy. Every fossil that fell into his hands was treated as a petrified document and also was given a place in the perpetual tidal movement of growth and decline.

In the course of his investigations Klaatsch also stumbled upon a most interesting field of research, hitherto mainly the preserve of sociologists. He collected data on the erotic ceremonies of primitive man and the origin of marriage. The principle of sexual selection laid down by Darwin was again brought into prominence by Klaatsch. He compared the tattooing recognizable in the cave paintings with the decorative marks borne by Australian aboriginals and the scars of the members of German students' clubs. He maintained that the underlying meaning of such rigorous customs was to be found in the endeavors of males to make an impression on women and in the tendency of the latter to give battle-scarred warriors the preference over smooth-skinned weaklings. All primitive conflicts, according to Klaatsch, were not quarrels over the possession of land, since there was land enough for all, but fights over women. Every man with a good conceit of himself would try to look like an experienced champion in order to appear to the other sex as a hero and conqueror. The custom remained in being even after it had ceased to be necessary to compete for Eve's favors with hand axes.

Mars, therefore, was the ideal of virility in primitive times. The aspect of the Ice Age Venus and the aesthetic opinions that Adam professed in this connection became clear when, in addition to drawings, statues from the Aurignacian, Solutrean, and Magdalenian periods were found.

The prolific Venus of Willendorf

In the valley of the Danube in Lower Austria, opposite the Aggstein ruins, stands the small village of Willendorf. Johann Veran, who turned up the soil with his pickaxe near this village, did not do so for scientific reasons, but because he earned his living that way. Although he was only a roadbuilder's laborer, he had sharp eyes in his head. One day in 1908 he found a small spherical object among the lumps of clay and gravel. It looked to be a very odd sort of stone. He picked it up and showed it in some bewilderment to his mates.

The stone resembled a fat woman, with rounded breasts and broad thighs. To their disappointment Veran quickly thrust the thing into his pocket, saying it might not be a stone at all, but a carved figure, a heathen idol such as was exhibited in museums. He put down his pickaxe on the embankment of the road, slipped on his jacket, and went down into Willendorf to ask Herr Szombathy about his find.

Herr Szombathy was at that time traveling through the loess country of soft porous rock in the Danube region of Lower Austria because he had found traces of antique mammoth-hunters there. He collected hand axes, bone tools, the remains of mammoths, and everything else that still furnished evidence of the activity of primitive man in the district between Krems and Wagram. He saw at the first glance that Johann Veran's find was a female figure from the Aurignacian period, the first representation of a human being that had come down from a very remote era. The men of those days must have had very peculiar ideas of beauty. The Venus of Willendorf had little in common with the Venus of Milo. She bore a striking resemblance to a well-fattened Hottentot female, only attractive to perverse tastes.

In reporting the discovery to prehistorians Szombathy wrote:

It is a small figure about four inches high, made of finely porous limestone, in perfect condition, bearing irregularly distributed traces of red paint. It represents an excessively mature, stout woman, with big breasts, the belly conspicuously prominent, the hips and upper part of the thighs full, but without actual formation of fat on the buttocks. The genitals are powerfully developed, the anatomy of the back correct and furnished with a number of naturalistic details. The hair of the head is rendered by a quantity of rolls wound round the bulkiest part of the head in concentric circles. The face is left quite featureless, without the slightest indication of eyes, nose, mouth, ears or chin. The arms are of reduced proportions, the forearms and hands being only shown in flat strips of relief laid across the chest. The knees are excellently modeled and the lower leg provided with calves, though these are drastically abbreviated. The front parts of the feet are entirely missing. There is no sign of clothing or ornament on the figure except that a roughly serrated wristband is visible on each forearm.

A vigorous dispute soon flared up among scholars over this Venus of Willendorf. The genuine character of the piece could not be doubted. The prehistorians argued all the more over the question whether the woman represented was to be understood as personifying the female sex or as a ritual figure. Breuil's colleague Hugo Obermaier took the former view. He stated his opinion in the following words: "The whole of this little figure shows that its maker had a first-rate comprehension of the build of a human body but was only concerned in this case with bringing out the primary and secondary female sexual characteristics. The rest is ingeniously reduced to the indispensable minimum required for representation." More prudish spirits disagreed and took less notice of the sexual features of the Venus than they did of the others, those that had been reduced. They declared that the bent head, the hands laid across the chest, and the legs closely pressed together showed clearly that the attitude was one of prayer.

The Venus of Willendorf was soon joined by other statues of women collected from the Aurignacian and subsequent cultural stages. In southern France the Venus of Brassempouy came to light. She was also a very corpulent lady, with clearly recognizable decorative scars on the body. A rather slimmer type was discovered near the French village of Sireuil. This was a splendidly modeled female figure, depicted as rising abruptly from a crouching position, the breasts boldly standing out skyward. Female statuettes carved out of jet had probably been worn by Ice Age man as ornaments, strung together to form garlands. Such accessories, representing only the female abdomen, highly stylized, were mainly found in the Petersfels cave near Engen in Baden.

The most prolific source of Ice Age statues proved to be the Moravian loess region. If the yeoman farmer Chrometschek of Predmost had been rather more observant and less acquisitive, the world would have discovered, as early as the seventies of the last century, an extremely ancient cultural area only comparable in its importance with the caves of southern France and northern Spain. Near Predmost, a village lying southwest of the Moravian Gate, while leveling a loess hill Chrometschek came upon a great deposit of the bones of animals and human beings, stone tools, and ornaments. He wondered what use he could make of them and eventually sent for his laborers and ordered them to pulverize the heap of bones and distribute them over his fields as fertilizers. The expedient apparently proved a success. Chrometschek went on fertilizing his land with the skeletons of mammoths and the bone relics of Ice Age culture until some scientists found out what he was doing and with government backing put a stop to it.

In the Predmost region and that of the second center of prehistoric research in Moravia, the Polava Hills near Brünn (now Brno), whole schools of scientists have now been excavating for many generations.

Even today the end of this extensive work cannot yet be forecast. Traces of settlements and permanent residential areas were found, full of ashes and charcoal and surrounded by piles of refuse containing the remains of over two thousand mammoths and innumerable other Ice Age fauna. Wolves, jackals, and cave hyenas had at one time besieged these settlements and rooted about in the refuse. It is

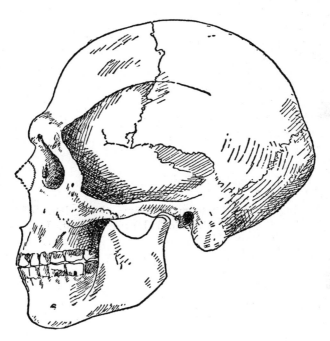

A skull from Predmost.

possible that the whelps of these four-legged thieves were captured by man, reared by him, and domesticated, even at this early period.

The interpreter and recorder of the Moravian cultures, the pre-historian K. Absolon, worked alone for fourteen years in the more remote environs of the village of Unter-Wisternitz, now Dolní Věstonice. Here, too, a Venus was found, not indeed quite as stout as that of Willendorf, but in other respects closely similar. The representations of men dating from that era, however, looked altogether different. In these cases the Moravian artists had not emphasized the physical nearly as strongly. The model in miniature of a man's head, dug up by Absolon, shows delicate, almost intellectual features, and a very long skull, narrowing considerably at the forehead. Eight statuettes of women, some ingeniously carved from mammoth's tusks, and many engravings of women, with the sexual characteristics highly stressed and exaggerated, had hitherto been exhumed from the Predmost and Unter-Wisternitz districts. They all show clearly that their makers possessed very detailed and naturalistic ideas of the female sex and that the Venus of the Ice Age was in fact a symbol of fertility.

Moravia provided prehistoric research with yet a further surprise. The people who had been hunting the mammoth, the woolly rhinoceros, the cave bear, the bison, the musk ox, and similar arctic animals in this region ever since the Aurignacian period and creating attractive works of art on a small scale made quite a different impression from that of the broad-headed, high-browed representatives of the well-known Cro-Magnon race. As early as 1878 that enemy of science Herr Chrometschek had been obliged to yield up certain human skulls and skeletons from his stock of fertilizers. In 1891, during excavations in the town of Brünn, the skeleton of a man, painted red and resplendently adorned, came to light. In 1894, near Predmost a burial ground was revealed which contained the bones of eight adults and twelve children. Further finds were added. Although these early inhabitants of Moravia, as Absolon emphasized, had reached the same cultural level as those of the Cro-Magnon type and buried their dead just as reverently and carefully, they looked far more primitive. Particularly striking in the male skulls were the prominent ridges above the eyes, the long occiput, the low forehead, and the jutting oral formation. One of the Predmost men looked exactly like a Neanderthal half-breed.

It appeared that in the latest glacial period at least two culturally creative races had lived in Europe: in the west the somewhat more progressive, broad-headed people of Cro-Magnon type, and in the east the more primitive, long-headed beings, possibly evolved from Neanderthal man, and belonging to the "Brünn race." Both groups were capable of outstanding performances in art; for in Moravia, too, there were cave paintings — magnificent pictures of bisons were found in the Pekarna cave. Both were addicted to ritual customs recalling those of the Australian aboriginals, and both admired women with well-developed figures.

Certain naïvely naturalistic sketches in obscure recesses of the caves — those, among others, of Les Combarelles, Laussel, and Laugerie-Basse — disclose something of the part played by women in the ceremonial and everyday life of the man of the Ice Age. According to Klaatsch female beauty is "the result of a long breeding process confined to humanity, the consequences of which have led to different ideals, owing to the very different tastes of various races and communities. This process of breeding began among primitive peoples by the males preferring women whose build indicated that they would have plenty of children. And when they set about representing such women they stressed in their representations what they felt to be important, as applied art and fashion have done in various ways at all times."

Fertility was not only a matter of importance to primitive man. As he did not yet recognize the connection between the sexual act and conception, he considered that there was something mysterious and supernatural about fecundity. The special processes in the sexual life of a woman — which always, somehow or other, seem gruesome to the male — inspired primitive man, as Simone de Beauvoir writes in *The Second Sex*, with "a respect mingled with fear, this feeling being reflected in his rituals. All alien Nature was incorporated, for him, in woman. He regarded children as supernatural gifts. He believed that the mysterious emanations of the female body could bring into the world treasures lying at the heart of the hidden sources of life." In this way pictures of women became ritualistic and magical objects in the cave era, representing personified secrets, rather than individuals.

In a cave drawing at Les Combarelles, representing a love scene, the woman is only drawn in the most casual outline, apart from the breasts and abdomen, whereas the man's body is executed in the utmost detail. Strangely enough, even today the separate figure of this man, taken in isolation from the rest of the picture, is for some obscure reason still described as a "sorcerer" in certain scientific works. Pictures that had played some part in a fertility rite depict women shortly before childbirth. In these cases the head and limbs are only lightly suggested, while the body is naturalistically rendered throughout and shown lying close to a bear or under a reindeer, since according to the magical ideas of antiquity the strength of the animal in question could be transferred by certain ceremonies to the child about to be born.

Quite a different ideal of beauty and quite a different cult of women developed after the close of the Ice Age. Female figures as slender as wands, walking with a dancing step that gives an almost athletic impression, suddenly appear in pictures reminiscent, in their bold abstraction, of modern art. Man had now left the caves and started to migrate. Woman had begun to emancipate herself, and had become a traveling companion and comrade. Instead of the mysterious

Cave paintings from eastern Spain dating from after the close of the Ice Age and showing the new ideals of beauty and physique.

ancestral mother, the confident amazon appeared, busy with her weapons, helping in the search for food and playing the man in the conquest of new territory as well as any spear-flourishing warrior. The Venus of Willendorf was succeeded by the Diana of Valltorta.

The expressionist painters of Valltorta

In the mountain gorges of eastern Spain exist many recesses of jutting rocks, which the peasants and shepherds pass with nervous glances. The country people say that they contain the hoarded gold of the Moors and if anyone could succeed in deciphering the red marks on the walls he would find the treasure and become a rich man.

By the year 1903, when Breuil and Cartailhac were starting to investigate the southern French and northern Spanish cave paintings, it had long been known that man had once painted on sunlit rock walls as well as in dark caverns. Throughout northern Europe and at many places in northern Asia, rock engravings could be found, rigid and lifeless, incised on horizontal planes. They seemed to show decidedly less talent than the splendid pictures of Altamira, Font-de-Gaume, and Les Combarelles. The first finds of this description were made in 1848 on the eastern shore of Lake Onega. Similar rock engravings — stylized representations of elks, reindeer, whales, birds, and fish, all kinds of magic symbols, and also a few human figures — were later discovered in Sweden and Norway, in the Urals, on the shore of the White Sea, and along the upper course of the Yenisei River. They were at first wrongly thought to belong to the Bronze Age and it was supposed that at that time human beings simply could not draw any better.

In the same year in which Breuil and Cartailhac rediscovered Altamira, a Spanish photographer named Cabré Aguiló came across quite different and far more artistic rock frescoes near the city of Teruel. Three stags and an auroch were painted in red on a rugged wall of rock under an overhanging ledge, not naturalistically as at Altamira, nor to a formula as in northern Europe, but ingeniously simplified, full of movement, in the expressionist manner. Cabré Aguiló at first did not know what on earth to make of these pictures. But when he heard shortly afterwards about the Ice Age cave paintings found in northern Spain, he became convinced that early man must also have left his traces in the mountain ranges bordering the Iberian tableland. In the mild climate of eastern Spain he had probably not lived in caves but under projecting ledges of rock and evolved quite a different style of art in the open air, characterized by glittering sunlight and clean-cut shadows. In 1907 the art-loving photographer informed the scientists Breuil and Obermaier of his discovery. They immediately set out for the rocky regions of eastern Spain and found an unexpected surprise waiting for them.

Within a period of ten years they discovered, especially in the Valltorta gorge but also at Minateda, Albacete, Cogul, Alpera, and other places, on open walls of rock exposed to sun, wind, and weather the most imposing collection of expressionist pictures imaginable. Moreover, they discerned faded paintings in the naturalistic style which the ancient artists had not hesitated to paint over. They perceived the way in which expressionism gradually passed into abstraction and even cubism. They were able to distinguish thirteen different periods of painting. Men with bows and arrows, brilliantly red on a yellow ground, raced and hunted. Women dressed in bell-shaped skirts danced round a male puppet. Animals pranced, arrows whizzed against them. At the edges of forest paths the hunter, the picture of vigilance, braced himself in ambush, with his new magical weapon, the bow. A honey gatherer climbed a tree and smoked out a hive. A man struck by arrows dropped to the ground, his head ornament falling from his brow. Two groups of warriors

A drawing of fighting archers from the east coast of Spain. All is life and movement and the style of the figures is one of ingenious simplification.

rushed upon each other, bounding along at full speed. Amid a throng of wild horses, stags, aurochs, and ibexes there were the most varied groups of men and women, often only half delineated. The recesses of the rocks were covered with "snapshots" of this kind. Everything was lifelike, in movement, dashing and whirling about inextricably. The pictures gave an impression of being as rapid as thought, as transient as existence, and at the same time as having the authentic invocation and abstraction of a moment that vanished tens of thousands of years ago.

Breuil and Obermaier had already noticed the transitions in many cave paintings to expressionist and abstract styles. They had no doubt that the rock paintings of eastern Spain also belonged to the Ice Age. Obermaier assumed that two peoples with different customs, cultures, and stylistic tendencies had lived in southwestern

Further development in technical and artistic expression. The hunter is using a bow whose enhanced range and accuracy represent a technical advance. The painting is almost impressionistic in style.

Europe during the Ice Age. In France and northern Spain a cave-dwelling folk, hunters of the mammoth, bison, and bear, had developed its arts and cults in the twilight depths of the caverns. In eastern Spain a people living in the open air and hunting the aurochs, stag, and ibex had been influenced in its art and ritual by light, sunshine, and distance.

This view, however, was not confirmed. The expressionist pictures in the Valltorta style did not include typical Ice Age animals.

The clothing, ornaments, and weapons of the persons represented pointed to a later epoch. The individual creature no longer predominated. It was now the turn of the mass in movement. Perspective disappeared. Each scene resembled a silhouette. "Everything is so

Among the famous archers of Cueva del Civil in the Valltorta gorge of eastern Spain artistic expression changed to pure expressionism on the very verge of abstraction.

completely different from the productions of the Ice Age," wrote the prehistorian Herbert Kühn, who had made an intensive study of the rock pictures and compared them with the cave paintings, "the style has changed so much, that it cannot belong to the same period. The Ice Age world is completely real and based entirely on the contemporary. But the other world has been translated into intellectual terms. All the running, hurrying, and racing figures are abbreviated, summarized, altered to suit an idea and this idea is the guiding principle."

Cabré Aguiló and the Spanish scientist Hernandez-Pacheco, after thoroughgoing investigation, came to the same conclusion. Today it is generally assumed that the rock drawings of eastern Spain did not start until after the Ice Age. They began in that restless epoch when man set about conquering the vast spaces of the globe.

Seals were important game for the ancient Scandinavians. Had Man already discovered at this early date their fondness for play? This scene from a Swedish rock drawing gives the impression of a display by trained seals.

In our age we are used to being offered one new style after another by modern artists; each style is the language of a quite distinct spiritual epoch. In the Late Ice Age this was not the case. Some 30,000 years passed before primitive scratchings on walls of rock developed into the naturalistic cave paintings of southern France and northern Spain. Another 20,000 years later the first expressionist pictures appeared. The history of early art confirms the theory of the physical growth of humanity. Every development begins very slowly.

There are long intervals between the separate stages. Then development gradually accelerates like a train that has left the station and can now proceed to full speed. The tempo may be occasionally slowed down by obstacles, but if the way ahead is clear, inventions, discoveries, and intellectual conquests follow in quick succession, like a long-distance runner who strains every nerve to gain ground with spasmodic bursts of speed.

When the frescoes of eastern Spain were discovered, a complete investigation began of the Scandinavian and east European rock pictures, which differ so strikingly in their rigid stylization from the bustling scenes depicted in the Valltorta gorge. The Norwegian Brögger at first considered them to be primitive drawings dating from the Ice Age, but the Swedish prehistorian Hallström, who in a piece of research planned on a grand scale attempted to interpret

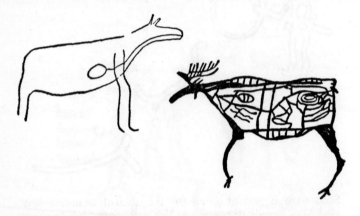

The northern Stone Age man as an anatomist. Norwegian rock drawings showing a female elk with heart line and a male with intestines.

the entire range of early northern art, refuted this opinion. He also referred the northern rock frescoes to the Late Ice Age, declaring correctly that in the case of the fishing and hunting tribes of the north there were natural reasons for stylization necessarily taking a wholly different direction from that of the sunny south. The animal in the north stiffened to a symbol. The artist drew not only its outline but also its heart, bowels, and the lifeline inside the body. In order to obtain luck in the chase and fertility in the animals by means of magic, realistic representations were not required in the strict seclusion of the habitable regions in the Arctic. It was enough to show what was required by using a certain formula. In this way the art of the Ice Age had developed during the subsequent "reindeer period" in two entirely different directions in the south and north of Europe, leading to the expressionism of the art of the Levant and the symbolism of arctic art.

The culture of the north belonged to the tundra. When the ice melted, the hordes of human beings followed their arctic prey. They streamed into the steppes of Scandinavia and eastern Europe, which now became habitable. Some settled on the fiords, living principally on fish, seals, and mollusks. Others made for the forests, occupying the banks of the rivers and living by the slaughter and trapping of game just as some Siberian peoples still do today. Snowstorms and drift-ice, strong contrasts between bright summers and dark winters, and a perpetual struggle for food and existence characterized the

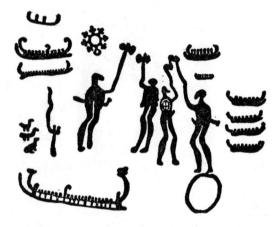

Rock drawings show that Scandinavian man of the Late Ice Age traveled in ships across the sea and conquered new territory in fierce battles. In a land with little sun the latter became the symbol of life. It is to be found in many forms in rock pictures. At this date Man was already accompanied by his dog.

lives of these northern campaigners. Their art grew melancholy and froze into ornament. Then some of the great minds among them invented the ship and freed themselves from imprisonment on the ice and the marshes, in the primeval forests, and among the mountains of the fiords. From the early Bronze Age onward, sunlike wheels, scenes of dancing and festival, and vigorous renderings of everyday life suddenly appear in the Scandinavian rock pictures. A fresco in Sweden even seems to show an elephant and a giraffe. It is possible that some ancient Viking, impelled by longing for the sun, discovered Africa many thousands of years ago.

Those who remained in the south had a far easier time of it. Although the most important animals of the chase disappeared — bison and reindeer — they were replaced by aurochs, fallow deer, wild asses, and other equally useful game that migrated to southern Europe. It became necessary to adopt new hunting methods, in-

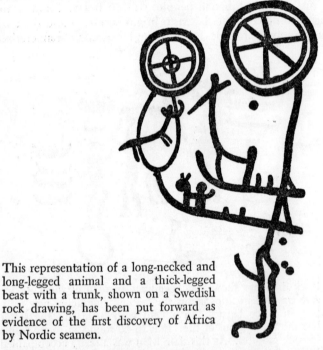

This representation of a long-necked and long-legged animal and a thick-legged beast with a trunk, shown on a Swedish rock drawing, has been put forward as evidence of the first discovery of Africa by Nordic seamen.

vent new weapons, form large mobile groups, and lead the life of a southern people of the plains. Their brothers in the north, fishermen, trappers, eaters of shellfish and builders of boats, traveled great distances. Primeval forests separated them from the Mediterranean paradise, and for this reason Africa suddenly began to interest them. Cro-Magnon men did not confine their settlements to Morocco and the Canary Islands. Rock pictures resembling those of Valltorta have been discovered in the gorges of central Africa. They show how active a cultural connection existed in the postglacial periods between the lands of the Levant and the Black Continent, with links across the Mediterranean Sea.

Herds on African rock faces

The agile little Bushmen of South Africa, considered by those who first discovered and studied them to belong to the lowest stage of human development, were in one respect superior to many other races of mankind. They could draw excellently. At first no one could

The Cro-Magnon men of Spain settled in North Africa. This rock drawing from the Libyan Desert is closely related in its restless style to the Levant art of eastern Spain. It also proves beyond doubt that what is today a wilderness must once have been fertile and stocked with animals.

believe that they possessed this talent, for dwarfs living in the crevices of rocks and hollowed out termite hills and feeding on the eggs of ants, locusts, and wild honey are not usually expected to show artistic impulses.

When the colonists of the Cape district entered the first caves of the Bushmen and discovered extraordinary pictures and engravings on their walls, they shook their heads. For the most part they regarded the uneducated brown Pygmy families with contempt and believed that some other race of mankind must have immortalized itself there. They saw elephants and rhinoceroses, lions, zebras, and giraffes depicted in lifelike attitudes, and small wiry hunters lying in wait for their gigantic prey. They saw herds of animals in flight and game struck down and dying. In short, they saw everything that was later found in the caves of the Ice Age, though drawn in quite a different style. The views of the worthy farmer-trekkers on these strange sights have not been recorded.

But it was not only farmer-trekkers who invaded the land of the Bushmen. Missionaries, government officials, and scientists also

Leo Frobenius discovered at In Habeter, the dried out bed of a river in the middle of the Sahara, an extensive series of rock engravings resembling the rhinoceros hunt shown above.

came. By that time the Bushmen had long ceased to draw. Some of them had been civilized and others exterminated. The uncivilized survivors, leading a terror-stricken and miserable existence in their unproductive wastes, had something else to think about. A man like the Berlin philologist and ethnologist Wilhelm Heinrich Immanuel Bleek felt really sorry for them. About 1870 he started collecting Bushman legends and fables about animals and studying the inarticulate and unique language they employed. He would have been delighted to learn more of their artistic activities. Bleek, the son of a well-known commentator on the Bible, was one of the earliest and most enthusiastic of the supporters of Darwin and Haeckel. He believed that evolutionary and cultural parallels could be drawn between the Bushmen and primitive man. Perhaps the ancient hordes of Ice Age hunters had lived, talked, and decorated the walls of their caves in the same fashion as the strange dwarfish people of the Kalahari gorges. To further his researches, Bleek took a Bushman family to live in his house. He did learn the clucking noises they made and he noted down their myths, but he discovered little or nothing about the history of their art.

After the discovery of Altamira the artistic documents of primitive tribes of natives suddenly became deeply interesting to the scien-

tists. Klaatsch established the fact that even the Australian aboriginals, who stood still lower in the racial scale than the Bushmen,
possessed an extraordinarily highly developed artistic sense. They
used red and white earth-colors to paint animals, scenes of everyday
life and hunting, footprints and symbolical signs on calcareous
rock. They pressed their hands against the rock in the same way
as the people of Altamira. Klaatsch wrote about the Bushman drawings:

> The ancestors of the Bushmen produced rock engravings and

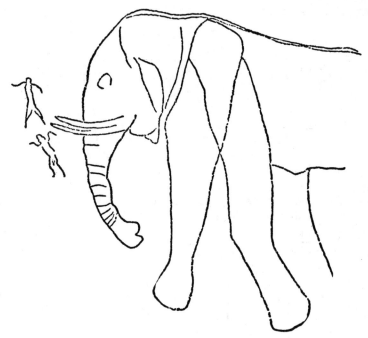

Africans in flight before the monster.

> cave paintings superior in many respects, in their lifelike delinea-
> tion of hunting scenes, to those of the ancient Europeans and
> Australian aboriginals. Moreover, rock paintings have often been
> discovered at places in Africa where the present inhabitants, the
> Negroes, had no idea that they existed. As we know that the
> Bushmen belong to a fairly old substratum of the African popula-
> tion the rock paintings may very well have some connection with
> that layer.

The connection that Klaatsch had in mind had also occurred to other investigators. Magnificent rock frescoes, executed in a boldly abstract manner, were found in the mountain gorges of the Sahara and the Libyan Desert, in Nubia and in Damaraland. They looked quite different from the severely naturalistic drawings of the Bushmen, which often resembled silhouettes, and recalled the

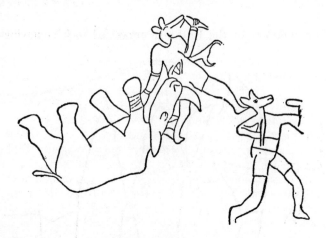

The men with jackal-masks have slaughtered a rhinoceros and are dragging it home.

expressionist pictures of Valltorta and Alpera, the east Spanish art of the postglacial period. They included the "White Woman" of the Tsissab gorge in South-West Africa, which the painter and land surveyor Maack discovered while taking measurements in the district. It represents a running huntress with slender limbs, a bow and arrow in her hand, and a net of pearls in her hair. Other subjects were buffaloes and elephants, standing out in massive relief from the steep mountainsides of North Africa. Gigantic hands containing drawings of human figures and whole scenes were also discovered, and a mythical animal suckling three children and dancing figures of Egyptian type. Could all these drawings still be characterized by the stock phrase "Bushman Art"?

Experienced connoisseurs of Ice Age painting and Levant art like Breuil, Obermaier, and Kühn had already stated, shortly before the First World War, that some connection or other might have existed between ancient European and African expressionism. The archeologist Menghin, best known for his book *World History of the Stone Age,* made a similar conjecture in the opposite direction. In his view the Bushmen, hitherto not considered quite human, had in earlier times occupied the whole of Africa and also Spain, mingling there with the Aurignacian type. The half-breeds, endowed with Bushman talent, had then painted the splendid red-chalk pictures of Valltorta. Menghin went even farther. He mistakenly believed the art of Valltorta to be older than the cave art of France and northern Spain and insisted on referring the paintings of Altamira to the influence of his hypothetical half-breeds. The Bushmen were suddenly elevated to the rank of masters of art and initiators of a substantial part of the ancient culture of southwestern Europe.

It was mainly the work of three men — Leo Frobenius, the African explorer and ethnologist, the Abbé Henri Breuil, and indirectly the anthropologist L. S. B. Leakey, born in Kenya — that put the sequence of events back into their correct order again. Frobenius discovered in his journeys through Africa, especially in the Libyan and Syrtis deserts and in the Sudan, a large number of new rock pictures representing animals, men with bows, masked dancers, and scenes from cultural, hunting, and family life. He described them in collaboration with Hugo Obermaier. They included a drawing of swimmers which permitted the conclusion that at the time of its

Swimmers in the desert.

production there were still rivers or lakes in what is today a waterless waste. Thousands of years ago the Sahara must have been a fertile region with its own culture. And the people who inhabited this ancient land of early civilization did not look like Bushmen but like members of the races of western Europe during the late Ice Age and the postglacial period.

We do not know how far the posterity of the Cro-Magnon and Aurignacian peoples penetrated into Africa. It is possible that the ancient hunter-folk of the Mediterranean reached the south of the continent in the course of milleniums. Their descendants may have settled there and erected in historical times cyclopean strongholds, defensive towers, and gold mines. In 1929–30 Frobenius visited the mysterious ruins of the fortress of Zimbabwe in Southern Rhodesia, the central point of an ancient civilization of advanced type, today half overgrown by the primeval forest. Over a wide area of some ten square miles are scattered the remains of over five hundred buildings. The first explorers of Zimbabwe, Karl Mauch and Karl Peters, had believed it to be Ophir, the legendary land of gold. Why Zimbabwe declined and who destroyed it have remained puzzles down to the

It is difficult to make out the subject of the above drawing. Does it refer to the magical ceremonies of a sorcerer? A love scene? Or a session at the dentist's? It comes from the Libyan Desert and the style clearly proves its connection with the Levant art of eastern Spain.

present day. There is much reason to believe that the small cave dwellers of the Cape region were forced out into the deserts as be-lated stragglers from the main postglacial invasion and that they then degenerated and sank to the level of primitive aboriginals.

By the time Leakey had distinguished the various African Stone Age cultures and found in many parts of the continent graves of the Aurignacian-type ancestors of the Hamitic races, it had once more been confirmed that African expressionism had come from the north. The culture of the postglacial period in eastern Spain and North Africa is today designated "Capsian," from the name of an Algerian town. The Capsian epoch began some 20,000 years ago. It lasted perhaps as much as 15,000 years — in other words three times as long as the entire historical period in the West — to culminate in the advanced civilizations of the Mediterranean area.

Breuil visited Africa on several occasions, even when he was over seventy, and often risked his neck in climbing to study the herds of animals and human figures depicted on the rocky walls of gorges and crags. He recognized three clearly distinct cultural groups. The most ancient was the North African Capsian of the postglacial period, closely related to the art of Valltorta. Then came certain pictures in South-West Africa, including the "White Woman" of Tsissab. These originated some 4000 years ago and recall Egypto-Minoan art. Incidentally, as the result of recent research, Breuil considers the White Woman to represent a man, the king of an unknown light-skinned race of conquerors in South-West Africa. The actual Bushman drawings that led to the discovery of African art are in Breuil's opinion, and that of most other investigators, unlikely to be more than a few centuries old.

All these African cultures have vanished. Where once Aurignacian man swam in sparkling lakes and lay in wait for vast herds of animals, deadly deserts lie today, destitute of humanity. Where Zimbabwe's walls once rose there are now only bare ruins, caught in the stranglehold of the jungle. Where light-skinned conquerors once painted a Diana or a king on alpine heights only the jackal and the lizard now live. And the last of the draftsmen, the little Bushmen, have forgotten the days when their forefathers drew their magic symbols of elephants and rhinoceroses on the walls of caves. They now pin up magazine illustrations in their corrugated-iron huts.

Part Four

ADAM UNMASKED

It would be a good thing if man concerned himself more with the history of his nature than that of his deeds.
FRIEDRICH HEBBEL

XIII

THE DAWN OF HUMANITY

A prehistoric Pompeii

AT A PRIVATE SCHOOL in Zurich about the year 1890, a sickly boy
of sixteen with a lame leg sat listening intently to the words of his
history teacher. He heard about the civilizations of antiquity, about
excavations at Troy and Pompeii, in short, about all those matters
that are taught in history lessons to high school students all over
the world. Once he looked surreptitiously at his watch. Instantly
the schoolmaster snapped, "If this is too boring for you, Hauser,
you'd better clear out!" The boy shook his head. "On the contrary,
sir," he replied with perfect sincerity, "I was only worrying because
we were getting so near the end of the lesson." His eyes were shining.

Otto Hauser subsequently became an archeologist. Unfortunately
the physical affliction that had kept him bedridden until his twelfth
year had made him suspicious and quarrelsome. It aroused an almost
pathological ambition in him to outwit his fellow men and professional colleagues, endowed by fate with a superior physique, and
elbow his way to a place in history. "He was an awful boor, but
devilish honest," so one of his friends described him later. "He was
not even recognized after his death, because he had presumed upon
his success and quarreled with nearly everybody." The "awful boor,"
undoubtedly one of the most colorful and controversial personalities
in prehistoric research, put the quest for primitive man back onto
the right lines again at the turn of the century, thanks to his industry
and honest enthusiasm.

While still a twenty-two-year-old student, he carried out excavations, financed by his wealthy mother, near the village of Windisch
in the Aargau canton, formerly Vindonissa, an ancient Roman en-
campment. He found a large number of weapons, tools, lamps, jars,
rings, and a magnificent silver bowl that Virchow admired. But he
got little thanks for these discoveries. His learned compatriots, to
whom it would never have occurred to dig on that site of the Swiss
headquarters of Roman legions and cohorts without his example,

gave the young dilettante less than his due in their irritation with his excessive zeal. Hauser's only crime had been to anticipate them and this reception of his work had the effect of an ice-cold shower. "Thenceforth," he wrote, "my life was embittered. I saw for the first time that even when one has good intentions the road to achievement can never be absolutely smooth." He suffered the fate of many a tactless outsider, and after this the experts made his life a burden to him.

The Vindonissa case made him take a dislike to the antiquities of his native land. He began to devote himself to a still older civilization and in 1898 took an unauthorized journey at the expense of his willingly self-sacrificing mother into the paradise of primitive man the Vézère valley, explored by Lartet and Christy. There he invested the fortune of his parents in the purchase or renting of extensive strips of territory near Le Moustier, Laugerie-Basse, La Micoque, Combe-Capelle, La Rochette, and other places where prehistoric finds might be expected. He employed gangs of workmen to comb the gorges, grottoes, hills, and clay subsoil of the Dordogne. The French collectors and excavation promoters watched the activities of this unknown foreigner with understandable suspicion. When Hauser actually started to sell abroad the hand axes and bones he found, in order to cover his expenses, they took the offensive, embarking on every conceivable measure to ruin the trade of the "dealer in antiquities," as Hauser's enemies maliciously called him.

In the thirty-odd years that had passed since Lartet's work in this area the valley of the Vézère had turned into a Tom Tiddler's ground for treasure hunters. Everyone with a taste for Stone Age implements burrowed in the ground like a mole. Anything that did not seem worth taking was thrown carelessly away. The documents of remote antiquity were no longer scorned as they had been in the time of Boucher de Perthes; on the contrary, they were worth their weight in gold, and a regular run on relics had set in. All the museums were interested in old skulls, hand axes, and ivory carvings, and many people had the idea of making a living out of this market. Official agents, schoolmasters, priests, and natural scientists strove in vain to dislodge the treasure-hunting moles. In the course of his excavations, Hauser was continually coming across abandoned shafts, rusty pickaxes, candle ends, and breakfast leavings in ransacked Paleolithic layers.

The professionals, who had long been irritated by this brigandage, regarded Hauser simply as a treasure hunter on a grand scale and refused to admit that he was gradually developing into a qualified expert. When he announced that he was now going to put a stop to "the theft of artifacts, the grossest negligence in excavation works and the most reckless demolition," Breuil, Obermaier, Peyrony, and the other connoisseurs and interpreters of the primeval period in France said bitterly, as the result of their experiences, that it was like the fox taking charge of the geese. "Without scientific training and without scruples," as Obermaier put it, "Hauser is merely exploiting the sites of discovery in the interests of trade." The majority of prehistorians, apart from a few like Hermann Klaatsch, shared this opinion. The life and work of Otto Hauser became one long battle. For, obsessed as he was with his researches, confident and not always wholly disinterested, he very often overstepped the mark in his enthusiasm and in the proclamation of his likes and dislikes.

"A Pompeii of the primeval period," was what Hauser called the valley of the Vézère, which he so passionately loved.

This country, which is today buried under rubbish and fallen rock, was once no less great and mighty a landmark of civilization and no less significant than Roman Pompeii in the classical age. No gorgeous marble palaces stood in the valley of the Vézère. Instead, fantastic walls of rock towered up on the riverbank, shielding the simple cave-dwellings of the nomads. The frescoes did not arise upon smoothly coated masonry. They were chiseled by primeval man straight on the rocky wall, deep in the mysterious darkness of antique subterranean passages. Their outlines were colored with yellow ocher and coal. Our spades do not bring golden coins to light or vessels of silver and bronze. We only find stones and bones in the soil. We find the strangest villages and towns in this sunken world, which inform us of the growth of our own race. Hordes of the antique world arise from the twilight of humanity, from their struggle for existence, from their first labors and burdens, to tell us here, in their relics, how they lived. We are confronted by the first stirrings of art and religion.

In this Pompeii of the primeval age, on the hill of La Micoque, Hauser believed he had discovered a whole new civilization, quite different from that of Neanderthal man and the Cro-Magnon race. He called it the Micoquean. He made it the subject of his doctoral thesis, on the grounds that the Micoquean race had contributed substantially to the formation of Western man. He even wrote that he had come across traces of the representatives of the Micoquean culture, meaning the human remains of Neanderthal type found at

Taubach on the Ilm and at Ehringsdorf. These primitive beings are today considered to be pre-Neanderthal, with striking characteristics of *Homo sapiens*. But Hauser insisted on associating them with the implements from the hill at La Micoque, over six hundred miles away, and also with cultural relics from several other sites in western and central Europe. His views, if accepted, would have entailed nothing less than the abandonment of Mortillet's cultural pattern, which had been universally recognized and elaborated by Breuil and Obermaier. As it was, Hauser's opinions only gave rise to fresh irritation, while he himself apostrophized his scientific adversaries in far from flattering terms.

Once more prehistorians were facing each other like gamecocks in a pit. The dispute of scholars over an ancient level of culture turned into a vicious wrestling match, with no holds barred. Hauser, with the morbid conceit that was due ultimately to his disability, had severely criticized the work of the French prehistorians, recognized by the whole world as exemplary. He described them as "dilettanti, sensation-mongers, and picnickers." The great discoverers of the culture and art of the Ice Age read with amazement and vexation, in his essay, that "what no one dared to do in parties of five and ten, I undertook alone. I understand all the difficulties and I never dreamed of cash remuneration. In full recognition of the outstanding magnitude of the task I set out myself, alone, to complete it." This emotional attitude seems to have caused a commotion among the professors. Obermaier confessed that he had received an extraordinarily painful impression. The Munich prehistorian Birkner denied that Hauser had any scientific reliability. The Swiss professor Ackermann observed that the objective truth in Hauser's work "seemed much obscured by the clouds of incense arising from an objectionable egotism." Hauser hit back with a whole arsenal of abuse, verbal missiles, and insinuations — which did nothing to increase his popularity.

Finally the Berlin geologist Emil Werth took a hand. He admitted that Hauser was right in several respects and asserted his belief in the new Micoquean culture. He also revealed a number of mistakes that had escaped the notice of the temperamental "boor" of Zurich. He concluded by advising the embattled prehistorians to take less account of the mote in their brother's eye than of the beam in their own. " 'He that is without sin among you, let him first cast a stone!' " he said to the infuriated scholars, with an emotion that matched Hauser's own.

Today the Micoquean culture has been recognized by science,

though with considerable modifications. Breuil had absorbed it into the current system. But the finds in the German gravel pits, which Hauser fought so fiercely to have associated with it, have been found to bear no relation to it.

Two men sold for 160,000 gold marks

Hauser worked for sixteen years in his prehistoric Pompeii, acquiring in the course of time such a mastery in the technique of excavation and of the interpretation of hand axes, tools, and works of art that the heads of the big museums and scientific institutes eventually paid him the attention he deserved. He had developed in particular the capacity to identify at a glance the forged artifacts that were turning up at that time everywhere in the neighborhood of the sites and were being sold to interested visitors. Meanwhile, however, his mother's fortune had been entirely swallowed up in the purchase and rental of land and the payment of wages, and the cunning farmers immediately put up their prices as soon as the eccentric foreigner showed himself anywhere near their land. Hauser now had to live and finance his further work by selling what he found, and he became, more or less compulsorily, a real "dealer in antiquities."

He was already concentrating on a single purpose at the time he formed the hypothesis of a Micoquean race. He intended to discover the still unknown stages of human development: first, that of pre-Neanderthal man, and second, that of the intermediate step that led from the apparently uncivilized Neanderthal type to the culturally creative cave men. He hoped to find both forms in the Vézère valley.

It was a plan that was bound to be enthusiastically welcomed by anthropologists. Shortly after the turn of the century many investigators had already conjectured that a forerunner of Neanderthal man must have existed in the penultimate period of the Ice Age, about 250,000 years ago, and a forerunner of the Cro-Magnon race in the last glacial period, from 20,000 to 100,000 years ago. They considered this last human or semihuman race to be particularly important. For between the bow-legged, ape-faced Neanderthal type of the Mousterian age, in which neither pictures nor graves had been found, and the intellectually superior types of the Solutrean and Magdalenian cave dwellers, who believed in an immortal soul, far too great a gap extended. It was not filled by the Brünn race, either. The Moravian carvers of Venuses did indeed resemble the Neanderthal type to a certain extent in their physiognomy, but they had already possessed a high culture and it was difficult to derive them straight from primitive barbarians. It was here that the most important link in the chain of proof of the theory of evolution was lacking: that fateful being which represented the transition from the darkness of semibrutish existence to the clear light of civilization, and represented a turning point in the history of the world.

At that time, in opposition to the outsider Klaatsch, consistent Darwinians believed in a direct descent of the human race from the chimpanzee-like *Dryopithecus* through the *Pithecanthropus* and the Neanderthal type down to Cro-Magnon and present-day man. And consistent students of hand axes and stone knives took the view that every early stage of culture was associated with a certain race or type of humanity. This meant that the rise of mankind had been achieved systematically, chronologically, and in accordance with cultural history, without branch lines, parallel growths, and overlapping. Consequently, the pre-Neanderthal period — the Chellean and Acheulean ages — were explored for the transition from the *Pithecanthropus* to the Neanderthal type. Also, the early Aurignacian period — the epoch between Mousterian barbarism and Solutrean culture — was searched for a direct descendant of Neanderthal man, who was bound also to be a direct ancestor of the bison hunters, artists, and sorcerers of Altamira and Les Combarelles.

Hauser's finds between 1908 and 1910, which crowned his much contested life's work so sensationally, seemed to have bridged completely these gaps in the pedigree of man. In 1908 a primitive man was brought to light in the Le Moustier cave. He apparently dated from the Acheulean age and was therefore older than the Neanderthal types hitherto discovered. He was known as Mousterian man. In 1909 a representative of the stage between Neanderthal and Cro-Magnon man turned up in the Combe-Capelle grotto. He was known as Aurignacian man. In 1910, in precise chronological sequence, a much damaged skeleton was found near La Rochette. Hauser called it Aurignacian II, but the French prehistorians very soon classified it with a primitive man dug up thirty-one years before near Chancelade and dating from the Late Ice Age. He was known as Chancelade man.

The scale of human evolution could now be filled in very nicely by those who so desired. *Homo mousteriensis hauseri* had lived, according to this system, a quarter of a million years ago, in the Acheulean age. He was followed 150,000 years ago, in the Mousterian age, by Neanderthal man; who developed 100,000 years ago, in the Aurignacian age, into *Homo aurignacensis hauseri*. The latter's descendants were the races of Chancelade, Brünn, and Cro-

Magnon. Somewhere in the third intermediate Ice Age the Ehringsdorf race — Hauser's alleged Micoquean man — could be fitted in.
It all looked most orderly on paper. The systematizers must have
been delighted.

The discoverer, Hauser, has to be given special credit for not associating himself for long with this "terrible simplification," and
abandoning it soon for the views of the veteran master, Klaatsch.
Klaatsch was convinced that the human family tree had many rami-
fications and had also produced subsidiary branches that were
doomed to die out. He considered all these new types as more or
less variant members of the two long familiar groups of forms, the
Neanderthal and the people of the Late Ice Age. They might well
be races; but they could not be new species, still less bridgers of
gaps. Nevertheless, the Le Moustier and Combe-Capelle skeletons,
particularly because of their good state of preservation, are among
the most important of all the finds of human remains yet recorded.
Their excavation, their interpretation and their later destiny had
wide repercussions throughout France and Germany. Otto Hauser
was now fully assured of renown, ill repute, and immortality.

One evening in March 1908, when Hauser had only just returned
from a tour of inspection of the excavation sites, tired out and wet
through, a workman belonging to the Le Moustier party called on
him in great excitement, reporting that a human bone had been discovered in a wholly untouched cultural layer of great antiquity.
Hauser immediately drove to the site, examined it by lantern light,
and verified the workman's statement. What chiefly agitated and
fascinated him was the fact that the layer in the Le Moustier grotto
must be some 250,000 years old. It was unmistakably Acheulean.
Apart from the *Pithecanthropus,* so early an epoch had not yet
yielded any primitive human remains whatever.

Almost any investigator in Hauser's situation would have instantly
proceeded to further excavations, in a frenzy of eagerness to ascertain what the prehistoric man of Le Moustier must have looked like
and whether any more relics of him were to be found. Hauser was
faced with a difficult decision. Would he not once more be reproached with impropriety, and would not his statements once more
be doubted, if he started digging into the hitherto untouched layer
with no witnesses? He pulled himself together. Then he ordered a
great heap of earth to be piled on the site of the find, sentries to be
posted, and every possible measure to be taken to ensure the security
of the all-important spot. He did not touch the bone.

He spent the following weeks sending out invitations to French and German experts, in whose presence he intended to uncover the site and have every phase of the excavation photographed and recorded in writing. The first to arrive was a delegation from the French government. It verified Hauser's statement that the layer was untouched and established the fact that it contained a skull. Hauser again covered up the site, repressed his curiosity, and went on waiting. The month was now August. Eventually, after Hauser had sent over six hundred invitations to professional people all over the world, a party of nine German scientists arrived to investigate the matter, with more suspicion than real interest. Among them were such great men as Klaatsch, Hans Virchow, the prehistorian Gustav Kossina, and the anthropologist Baelz, private physician to the emperor of Japan.

Klaatsch remained skeptical until Hauser with his own hands had laid bare the vault of the skull. Then he noticed something. He examined the ridges over the eyes as they caught the light and finally exclaimed, "If the region of the jaw shows the same primitive characteristics, we are in the presence of the most important anthropological find that has ever been made!" He took over the work of excavation himself, with Hauser assisting him. Piece after piece of the decayed and brittle skull and bones were exhumed from the soil and every tiny particle recorded. The camera came into action and registered all the stages of the work. The sun beat down on the site and hours passed. At last the skull and skeleton lay exposed to the investigators' gaze. Klaatsch uttered a cry of delight. Shortly before setting out for Le Moustier he had prepared an imaginative reconstruction of Neanderthal man. The bones now before them resembled it in every detail. He embraced Hauser. "We've found it! This is Neanderthal man in the full, the formidable bulk of his primitive frame!" The Mousterian had been a youth of about fifteen, earlier in date and far better preserved than any member of the Neanderthal race hitherto submitted to science.

But the youth from Le Moustier entered history, not as Neanderthal man, but as *Homo mousteriensis hauseri*. The supporters of Klaatsch and Hauser had at that time the confusing habit of giving every newly discovered primitive man of any special importance a scientific name of his own. In the Le Moustier case this procedure was perfectly justified, as Hauser pointed out, for the bones seemed to be about a quarter of a million years old and looked rather different, in a number of details, from those found in the Feldhof grotto which had given rise to the name Neanderthal. Other experts were not of this opinion. They also severely criticized the excavation in other respects. Despite the precautionary measures taken by Hauser, they alleged that the digging had been improperly executed and pointed out that the excavators had not been able to produce any animals' bones at all, though they would have been important for the determination of the age of the find.

The learned world criticized with particular severity Hauser's statement that the "hordes of cave men" had "buried" the lad "reverently, furnished him for his journey with roast joints of bison and finely wrought flint tools and laid his head, as if in preparation for sleep, upon a kind of stone pillow." A tomb at such a remote primeval epoch? Impossible! Serious doubt was expressed about the accuracy of the records kept by the French committee and the German excavation party, in both of which reference was made to deliberate burial. The age of the remains was also considered open to question. Only one thing seemed certain. Hauser had found an absolutely perfect Neanderthal skeleton at Le Moustier.

As luck would have it three French priests had been digging in the little grotto of La Chapelle-aux-Saints shortly before the discovery of the Le Moustier boy. They had come upon remains of a primitive man. They notified the director of the Institute of Human Paleontology in Paris, Pierre Marcellin Boule, one of the most eminent anthropologists of the day. And Boule removed from the site the almost complete skeleton of a fine specimen of an elderly man of Neanderthal type, together with stone tools of especially good workmanship and the bones of a woolly rhinoceros and other animals of the last glacial period. Another perfect Neanderthal man! Investigations were made and the finds of Hauser and Boule compared. The Le Moustier skeleton turned out to belong to the same race and period as the old man of La Chapelle-aux-Saints. The former's deviations from the normal Neanderthal type were merely attributable to its youth.

Today science dates the Le Moustier remains from the same period as all the other Neanderthal specimens. The boy had probably lived in the upper grotto at Le Moustier, his body reaching by chance the ancient Acheulean layer of the lower grotto later on. Hauser's conjecture that it was a case of genuine burial might then afford a genuine explanation of the transfer, but not all prehistorians agree with him. Despite these qualifications, the discovery of the Le Moustier skeleton remained a splendid piece of anthropological documentary evidence until its deplorable end under the hail of bombs dropped during the Second World War.

A year after the removal of the Le Moustier skeleton Hauser

was digging down through four cultural layers in the Combe-Capelle grotto. All sorts of tribes of the Old Stone Age must have lived in that region. They might have included the long sought "intermediate race," the link between Neanderthal and Cro-Magnon man. On August 26, 1909, two of Hauser's workmen came upon a "dark-brown stone" in the deepest layer, the Aurignacian. Suddenly they shouted, "It's a man, it's a man!" Hauser at once jumped to the conclusion that it must be a representative of the intermediate race.

Once more Klaatsch, at Hauser's telegraphed request, dashed from Breslau to the Vézère valley. Once more the pair of them dug up a primitive human being, assisted by the Swiss museum director and cave investigator Baechler. They did not find it very easy work. Water had dripped into the Combe-Capelle soil, forming a kind of putty that had hardened round the bones. The rocky floor showed unmistakable signs of having been artificially hollowed out. There could be no doubt whatever this time that a grave had been constructed. After Klaatsch and Hauser had carefully removed, piece by piece, the cement-like fragments of soil, they saw a skeleton lying in a crouching position, adorned with shells and surrounded with tools of the Aurignacian period. There were clear traces that the body had been tied up. The bones were found soaked in limewater, which had preserved them so marvelously that except for a few tiny pieces the skeleton was complete.

Hauser may be pardoned for having elevated this man to the rank of a particular species, *Homo aurignacensis hauseri*, and having believed him to be a transitional form between Neanderthal and Late Ice Age man. The skull gave the impression, when compared to that of a Cro-Magnon type, of extreme antiquity in many respects: for instance, the low forehead, the powerfully molded jaws, and the thick ridges above the eyes. On the other hand, it was so long that it might have graced an excessively highly bred aristocrat of the present day. The typical, broad Cro-Magnon heads looked almost Mongolian beside it.

The Aurignacian species had a much longer life in science than the Mousterian. A considerable time elapsed before the man of Combe-Capelle was deprived of his specific character and defined as a very ancient specimen of *Homo sapiens diluvialis*. Today he is no longer believed to be a link between Neanderthal and Cro-Magnon, but an extreme western representative of the long-headed race that once accumulated mammoths' bones in Moravia and carved stout female figures from mammoths' tusks.

The subsequent career of both skeletons raised much controversy. Hauser, who wanted to make enough money by their sale to start excavations at last on a grand scale, offered them to the Berlin Ethnological Museum at the exceptionally high figure of 160,000 gold marks the pair. The director of the museum, the eminent archeologist Schuchhardt, eventually agreed to the price after experts had assured him that the teeth alone of the Le Moustier

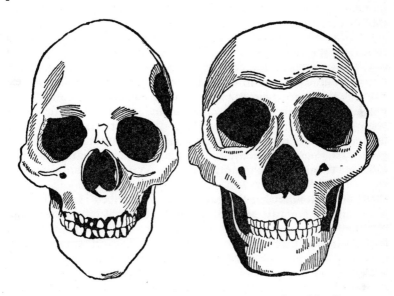

On the left the long skull of Aurignacian man found by Otto Hauser at Combe-Capelle. On the right, for comparison, a Neanderthal skull. The Aurignacian type resembles the Brünn race. Similar long skulls are still found today among the Eskimos. Cannibal fellow tribesmen have tapped the Combe-Capelle skull at the left temple and extracted the brain.

skeleton were worth the money; but the miserly state authorities boggled at the figure. Hauser had by now become quite impossible. In France he was bitterly reproached for sending the precious bones out of the country. In Germany people were furious at having to pay out a fortune for them. And, by a peculiarly unlucky chance, only a fraction of this fortune ever reached Hauser. For the Swiss bank into which Schuchhardt had paid the 160,000 gold marks shortly afterwards failed.

Thereafter misfortune continued to dog the latest explorer and exploiter of the Vézère valley. At the outbreak of war in 1914 Hauser was obliged to leave France. His lands were taken over by the French government. At the latter's request the prehistorian and schoolmaster from Les Eyzies, Peyrony, made a most careful record of the old burial grounds and excavation installations, classifying them in exemplary fashion. Since Hauser's former sphere of work was henceforth closed to him, he now set about the conquest of another one, that of literature. He wrote a series of uncommonly exciting books on the life and activities of primitive man. These works appeared at exactly the right time. The discoveries made in such rapid succession had aroused the curiosity of a wide public. It eagerly devoured Hauser's books in order to learn more about Adam. Even the scientists read them, though with considerably less satisfaction. For, with the exception of Klaatsch and some other friends of Hauser's, many recognized distorted portraits of themselves in these writings. In his coarse, argumentative style Hauser had censured Breuil, Obermaier, Peyrony, the archeologist Schuchhardt, the ethnologist Weule, and the anthropologist Weinert. Hardly anyone escaped.

It was no wonder that the learned world described Hauser's books as unreal and fantastic and no wonder that he fell into even deeper disgrace. This purgatory of criticism did not end with Hauser's life, but extended to his reputation after his death. Nevertheless, ordinary people, who were not interested in these academic quarrels, obtained a glimpse of a new world through Hauser. Many students and amateur scientists turned to prehistory after reading his books. He gave many their very first idea of what Old Stone Age tools looked like. The number of his disciples who are today working in museums and in the field to extend our knowledge of primitive man cannot be estimated.

A true story is told — the prehistorian Karl Brandt took part in it — that shows the remarkable relationship which had existed between Hauser and the primitive beings he resurrected. Periodically he visited Berlin with his wife, bought a large bouquet of flowers in the Potsdamer Platz, and then proceeded to the Ethnological Museum where the glass coffins of the Le Moustier and Combe-Capelle skeletons were on view. To the astonishment of the staff he approached the coffins, laid the bouquet upon them, and stood still for a moment in quiet meditation. The two skeletons were not only scientific objects in his eyes. He saw in them, too, the mortal remains of our ancestors who had once been sentient human beings in the dawn of history.

At the cradle of European man

In the course of the years and decades following Hauser's find at Combe-Capelle several more specimens of Aurignacian type were discovered. They were brought to light not only from the Aurignacian but also from all the Late Ice Age layers and cultural epochs. They could not therefore have been ancestors of the Cro-Magnon race. They were contemporary with it and similarly culturally creative. They were its long-headed cousins and coevals, somewhat resembling Australian aboriginals. Scientists ferreted out cave drawings by them, too. In the autumn of 1953 the Spanish engineer Alfredo García Lorenzo detected on the walls of the hitherto unknown subsidiary cave, the Cave of the Hearth in the El Castillo labyrinth, black, unshaded delineations of wild horses, elk, ibex, and mammoths. They are older than those of Altamira and were attributed to the Aurignac stock.

The types of Aurignacian and Cro-Magnon are basically no more than two extreme types of Late Ice Age man. Their characteristics can be traced down through the ages to the present-day population of Europe, the Near East, and North Africa. Links between the two extremes were formerly composed by many transitional and mixed races, just as is true among European peoples today.

One of these hybrid forms was Hauser's third type, Chancelade man. Opinions about him differed widely. As early as 1879 the French prehistorian Féaux, following in the footsteps of the lawyer Lartet, found an exceptionally long skull near Chancelade in the Dordogne. Nine years later the skeleton belonging to it was discovered. It lay in the familiar crouching position and had apparently been bound with ropes of reindeer sinew. Science began to take notice of the matter when in 1910 Hauser slowly and painfully assembled from the clay at La Rochette in the Vézère valley the remains of another man of Chancelade type, with the bones bitten through by cave hyenas. But the hope that in this case a true forefather of Cro-Magnon man had at last been run to earth proved false, for the capacity of this magnificent Chancelade skull of positively modern aspect was larger by 200 cc. than that of the average European skull of today. A daring theory was advanced to explain this puzzling circumstance: certain racial theorists, delighted with the long skull and its imposing capacity, elevated this problematic type to the status of founder of the Nordic race!

In so doing they were guilty of a colossal oversight, for the body of the Chancelade man made a positively pygmy-like impression.

His clumsy, squat limbs recalled those of Neanderthal man. Beside the model figures of Nordic man which the imaginations of the ancestor-worshipping experts on race created, Chancelade man must have looked like a hydrocephalic idiot. The French scholar Testut at once contradicted his colleagues, the champions of the Nordic race. He turned his attention to a region lying still farther north. Dwarfs with big heads were particularly frequent among the Eskimos. Testut therefore concluded that Chancelade man had been the ancestor of all Eskimos. He circulated a wild story about the descendants of this race having trekked on a large scale to Greenland and North America toward the end of the Ice Age in the tracks of their migrating reindeer.

Meanwhile, many more human remains with diverse characteristics were dug up and classified for the time being as representatives of new races. But most modern anthropologists consider it excessive to give every skull that differs from the rest in certain individual peculiarities a special name immediately. The number of races assigned has now again been considerably cut down. The Chancelade and La Rochette specimens were probably genuine Cro-Magnon types that happened to possess exceptionally large skulls and at the same time rather small bodily frames. Neanderthal man and the present-day races of mankind also include such extreme types.

Generally speaking, the former arrangement of the culturally active races of the Ice Age in accordance with their tribal history has long been given up. Attractive enough as the scale seemed in its time — following the sequence Mousterian, Neanderthal, Aurignacian, Brünn, Chancelade, Cro-Magnon, Modern — it was really no more than an agreeable fancy of the systematizers. Aurignacian and Cro-Magnon man, the Brünn and Chancelade types, and the under-sized human specimen discovered in 1914 at Oberkassel were closely associated contemporaries in the Aurignacian, Solutrean, and Magdalenian ages. Long-headed and broad-headed men, those with high foreheads and those with low, tall and short groups fought one another or intermingled for 50,000 years on end and finally formed the multifarious picture of the tribes and races of today. Now and then, no doubt, they even captured the women of slaughtered Neanderthal males and bred children from them. How great the mixture of races already was by that time in Europe was proved by further finds. Colleagues of that keen investigator Albert I, Prince of Monaco, discovered in the grottoes at Grimaldi certain skeletons which the French anthropologist Verneau described as negroid. Opinions are not yet quite unanimous as to the origin and classification of these Grimaldi specimens.

Did all these races descend from Neanderthal man, as had hitherto been believed? Many scholars began to doubt it, especially as genuine Neanderthal specimens lived far into the age of Aurignacian and Cro-Magnon man. Klaatsch was the first to abandon the idea. After comparing the Le Moustier and Combe-Capelle skeletons he declared: "The differences are so great that there can be no question of the descent of Aurignacian from Neanderthal man. All that can be assumed is a common aboriginal root." A large number of modern anthropologists share this opinion. New finds in Europe, Asia, and Africa, some details of which are given later, appear to suggest that even before the typical Neanderthal man came on the scene people lived in those regions who bore a very close resemblance to the Ice Age races of *Homo sapiens*. Fuhlrott's forest creature from the Feldhof grotto and his numerous counterparts, found in Belgium, France, Italy, Croatia, southern Russia, and central Asia, would therefore probably not be ancestors of our own, but a collateral branch that proved something of a failure.

According to this view there existed in the second intermediate period of the Ice Age, about 300,000 years ago, a highly gifted, intellectually active form of man, occupying what was later to be the cultural area of Europe, the Near East, and East Africa. He was a kind of aboriginal Neanderthal type, developing, in the third intermediate period of the Ice Age, into the evolutionary series comprising genuine Neanderthal man and *Homo sapiens*. The two lines of descent diverged, under the selective influences of environment, to an even greater extent. The more intelligent and adaptable *Homo sapiens* later moved into the regions inhabited by Neanderthal types, as Aurignacian, Cro-Magnon, and Grimaldi man. In the course of the Würm glacial stage he thrust his clumsy and helpless cousin still farther into the background — thanks to his superior weapons and mental capacity — and gradually, under the strain of the competitive struggle induced by the rigors of the severe and to some extent arctic climate, laid the foundations of his culture. Recollection of the encounter with the dwarfish and more primitive Neanderthal race sank into the subconscious mind of the man of the Late Ice Age. Its obscure deposit may perhaps be traced in the folklore and legends that tell of subterranean dwarfs and ogres.

It proved extremely difficult to throw any light on the history of the founders of these two branches of humanity. The men with spades and pickaxes had to grope their way back into the darkness of the Middle Pleistocene and even the First and Intermediate Ice Ages, ending up at the verge of the Tertiary period. In these layers no systematic excavation could be practised, for they offered no clues, no such cultural relics, cave pictures, and burial grounds as were available from the Late Ice Age. The ape man of Eugène Dubois had been an exceptionally lucky find. Investigators could only hope for equally favorable special circumstances and accidents during their future researches. Nor were they disappointed.

In the days of Hauser and Klaatsch theories of the evolutionary career of the human race still relied mainly upon scientific proof by means of circumstantial evidence. The associative links between the Tertiary anthropoid apes and the somewhat isolated phenomenon of the Java *Pithecanthropus* were missing, and above all so were the transitional forms leading from the *Pithecanthropus* to Neanderthal man and the culturally active races of the Late Ice Age. The great finds of the twentieth century provided many a surprise in this connection. They gave rise once more to fierce conflicts of opinion. At times they seemed to be turning the accepted pedigree of the descent of man upside down. In the end they eliminated all doubts of the fundamental accuracy of the doctrine of evolution.

Herr Rösch's sandpit

The romantic city of Heidelberg on the Neckar — where the customs of the students' societies, with their caps of many colors, were considered by their former professor, Klaatsch, to be atavistic and therefore extremely interesting from the point of view of tribal history — had long regarded research on prehistoric man with much favor. Heinrich Bronn, the translator of Darwin, had once taught at Heidelberg, Klaatsch had won his first spurs there, and ever since 1887 the anatomist and paleontologist Otto Schoetensack, a tireless collector and interpreter of fossils who came from the Odenwald, had been following in Bronn's footsteps at the university.

The discoveries in the Neanderthal and in France worried Professor Schoetensack considerably; and he wished he could find a prehistoric man for Heidelberg. He did not cherish the same extravagant hopes as Otto Hauser, nor had he the slightest expectation of a new human species suddenly turning up in the loess of the southern Odenwald. He would have been perfectly satisfied with an unmistakable specimen of Neanderthal man; and if there were anyone who could supply him with antique human bones it would be Herr Rösch.

Herr Rösch owned a number of clay and sand pits near the village of Mauer, just over six miles southeast of Heidelberg. Schoetensack knew the pits well. He often visited them with his students in order to show them what a typical formation belonging to the transitional period between the Tertiary and Diluvial epochs looked like. The clay soil of the pits covered a layer sixty-five feet thick of broken stones, sand, and gravel. This layer interested both Herr Rösch and Herr Schoetensack to an equal extent, although for different reasons. Herr Rösch valued the stones because he carted them away and traded in them, whereas they attracted Herr Schoetensack's attention because he considered that at one time, toward the end of the Tertiary period, the Neckar must have flowed over them. And since a former riverbed is usually an ideal spot to find well-preserved fossils, the two gentlemen discussed the matter together amicably and struck a bargain. The owner of the sandpit agreed to reserve all the fragments of bone discovered on his estate for the University of Heidelberg.

Schoetensack had the good fortune to have picked on an exceptionally intelligent man in Herr Rösch. All workmen employed in the pit received strict instructions to conduct a lynx-eyed search of every truckload of stones carted away, without troubling about the loss of time involved, and to report instantly anything that looked in the least like a bone. For twenty years Herr Rösch performed this service to science and thereby won the right to an honorable place in the record of the achievements of prehistoric research. He delivered to the University of Heidelberg thirty-five species of fossil snails and mollusks and a whole menagerie of prehistoric mammals. Almost every time Schoetensack made the journey to Mauer there was some new triumph to celebrate. The bones of elephants of the forest and the plain were found in the gravel, together with the remains of cave lions, saber-toothed tigers, rhinoceroses, hippopotamuses, and bison, and the skeletons of primeval pigs, panthers, wild cats, lynxes, and cave hyenas. Two species of bears and wild horses, Schoetensack found, had once lived on the banks of the antique Neckar, as well as several kinds of deer, and a large rodent of a peculiar type, the *Trogontherium*, which resembled a beaver. But not until 1907 was the slightest trace of a human being found.

On the evidence of the fauna it was thought possible that man had still not existed at that time. All the species of animals, whose remains Herr Rösch had loyally caused to be fished out of the rubble, belonged to the Late Tertiary or the First Intermediate Ice Age. Not a soul except Schoetensack, and possibly also Klaatsch, considered it feasible for beings of human type to have reached Europe at such an early period. The *Pithecanthropus* had not yet been discovered when Schoetensack began his search. Nor had it been given any recognition at the time his hunt entered upon its decisive phase.

Moreover, Neanderthal man was only known from the Mousterian specimen dating from between 100,000 and 150,000 years ago. The layers near Mauer, however, were at least 500,000 years old.

Nevertheless Schoetensack went stubbornly on with his hunt for a Heidelberg Adam. His methods and final success are described by himself in a few simple and modest sentences that hardly reveal anything about the trouble he had been taking:

For more than two decades I had been watching extractions from the Grafenrain sandpit for traces of human beings. I sought in vain for coal residue or traces of burning on the bones of mammals. The small horn-stone fragments, which came for the most part from the adjacent shell-lime, showed no trace of having been worked on. Tapering bone-splinters, which I carefully separated, at home, from the coating of sand hardened to cement by carbonate of lime, hoping to be able to prove they had been worked on, all turned out to be fragments formed in the natural way. I was accordingly left with the one hope that a human relic might one day be found among the numerous remains of mammals. Herr Rösch, the owner of the sandpits, who was always most interested in and appreciative of scientific effort, very kindly promised, at my request, that he would immediately inform me of any finds made. On October 21, 1907, Herr Rösch found the opportunity to redeem his promise.

Rösch's message, which reached Schoetensack the next day and made him leap to his feet with excitement and dash to the station, ran: "For twenty years you have been making efforts to find traces of primitive men in my sandpit in order to prove that human beings lived in this district at the same time as the mammoth [he meant the antique elephant of early Pleistocene times]. Yesterday we came across this proof. Sixty-five feet below ground level at the bottom of my sandpit the lower jawbone of a prehistoric man was found, in a very good state of preservation."

The finders, two of Rösch's workmen, had an excellent understanding of fossils. They had already been able to supply the university with a number of the teeth of a saber-toothed tiger and several bones of a cave hyena. It was actually at a depth of over seventy-five feet, practically at the bottom of the great layer of rubble, on that historic October day, they came upon a rather large stone. They lifted it up with their shovels and noticed that something else lay below it. As they were freeing with their hands this object, which they immediately recognized as a fossil, it broke in two. "Aha," remarked one of the workmen confidently. "There's the primitive man the professor's been looking for so long." He took up the two halves of the jawbone, turned them this way and that, and observed knowingly to his mate, "See? You can tell that by his tooth. If he was an ape, he'd have a big canine. Tell Herr Rösch what we've found!" This was the sober, unromantic story of the finding of Europe's oldest representative of the human species, Heidelberg man.

Schoetensack continues:

The next train brought me to Mauer, where I found the information given me to be perfectly accurate. The jaw was broken in two, but the halves had still been joined when the workman's shovel came upon the object in the sandpit. They only became separated when it was taken out. The canines and molars were firmly embedded in thick, solidified crusts of rather coarse sand, as in the case of animals' bones taken from the Mauer pits.

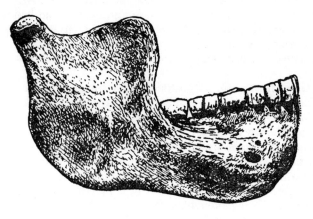

The Heidelberg lower jaw.

The teeth had been broken by the weight of the stone that had been lying on the jaw but were fortunately still in position. They differed hardly at all from true human teeth. All simian characteristics were absent. If they had been found separated from the jaw no one would have hesitated to attribute them to *Homo sapiens*. The underjaw, however, looked altogether different. Massive and coarse in appearance, it lacked the protuberance of the chin and the salient bone of the vocal chords. On the other hand its ends, with the articulation heads, were so heavy and broad that in the absence of the teeth anyone would have taken the jaw for that of an ape, as Schoetensack observed.

Schoetensack now attempted to fit the broken pieces of the jaw together again and reconstruct the creature as it had lived. As his photograph of the jaw had not been properly focused, the anthropologists to whom he sent the print believed as soon as they saw it that the Heidelberg man had been a gigantic gibbon with human teeth.

A gibbon with human teeth would assuredly have had to be accepted as a true "missing link." Certain upholders of the theory of evolution did indeed make use of expressions calculated to suggest that the Heidelberg man might be the oldest of all possible ancestors of the human race. The fauna with which he had been contemporary seemed to bear out this conjecture. Schoetensack considered them Tertiary creatures. Yet he did not believe his find had been an ape man. Humanity was much older, probably, than had hitherto been assumed. He described the Heidelberg man as *Homo,* a true human being, gave him the name of *Homo heidelbergensis,* and regarded him as an extremely primitive type of aboriginal Neanderthal man.

Other scientists, still as hostile as ever to the "monkey theory," felt Schoetensack's view to be altogether too Darwinian. The history of research has been enlivened by the afterthought that at the very time when the jaw of the Heidelberg man was giving an exaggeratedly simian impression in wrongly focused and inaccurate photographs he was being certified by eminent scholars as the aboriginal *Homo sapiens;* whereas after the jaw had been subjected to correct anthropological treatment and so had begun to look more human, Heidelberg man was being brought a few stages nearer to the ape. The anthropologist Johannes Ranke, a stubborn opponent of the theory of evolution in the form given it by Haeckel and Huxley, expressed what many of those who shared his opinions thought and hoped. He put back the earliest beginnings of civilization "at least as far as the oldest Tertiary period" and declared that Tertiary man must have already possessed "the essential features of present-day man in his bodily frame." He pronounced judgment on Schoetensack's discovery as follows: "The Heidelberg find may date the presence of man in central Europe back to the upper limit of the Tertiary period. But it is certain that the Heidelberg underjaw, like all other relics of the Neanderthal race, presents us with a surviving trace of true human beings, representatives of the species *Homo sapiens.* Its characteristic peculiarities do not remove this race from the series of forms already known to us in modern races." Thus, according to Ranke, even Neanderthal man could not yet be regarded as a species apart. On the other hand, the *Pithecanthropus* of Eugène Dubois was considered by Ranke to be a large "anthropoid ape" which had been falsely "proclaimed, even in modern textbooks, to be the long and vainly sought intermediate link between man and monkey."

It so happened that Klaatsch returned from Australia in the very year of the Heidelberg discovery and was thus able to discredit the new myth of a legendary antiquity for civilized man right from the start. He saw that the Mauer fauna did not date from the Tertiary period but from the First Intermediate Ice Age. Hence Heidelberg man had by no means lived as early as the dawn of the world but some time after *Pithecanthropus* and approximately 300,000 years before Neanderthal man. He fitted admirably into Haeckel's pedigree of mankind as a descendant of the ape man and an ancestor of the two branches constituted by Neanderthal man and *Homo sapiens.* This remarkable being, the first of all Europeans, does not seem to have used tools. It is true that a few hollow bones in the Mauer rubble bore a distant resemblance to spear points. But nevertheless, their appearance was highly questionable. "The thoroughly coarse and frankly brutish structure of the Mauer underjaw," said Klaatsch in opposition to the supporters of Ranke, "does not suit the Neanderthal type even on the assumption of a lower grade within this group of forms." And Klaatsch's Italian partisan Bonarelli drew the logical conclusions from this statement when he removed the Heidelberg man from the genus *Homo,* where Schoetensack had placed him, and invented a new genus, that of the *Palaeoanthropus* — "antique man" — to receive him.

The category to which the underjaw found in Herr Rösch's sandpit probably belonged was first recognized by the present professor-in-ordinary of the medical faculty of the University of Kiel, Hans Weinert. He had attracted much attention, shortly after the First World War, by a brilliant flash of intuition. He had found out that the offensive sting of wasps and bees was merely intended as a means of making the hole in which to lay their eggs, as with the more primitive types of hymenopters — ichneumon flies, wood wasps, and ground wasps. Later his taste for research led him to prefer the study of the science of Man to the study of stinging insects, which had first caused his recognition by the learned world. In 1925 he published a striking essay called *Frontal Cavities as an Indication of Racial History*. It set him in the front rank of German evolutionists. He had ascertained that chimpanzees and gorillas were the only apes to possess frontal cavities like those of men, and for this reason necessarily derive from a common stock. Weinert's researches showed that the two African anthropoid apes were not, as Klaatsch had supposed, abortive attempts at human growths but genuine relatives of mankind.

The clash between the theories of Klaatsch and Weinert was the clash of two generations. About 1900, when Klaatsch was active, Haeckel's outspoken view that men were descended from apes was still widely felt to be somewhat disreputable. And though Klaatsch himself had no prejudices in the matter, his formulation of the theory that apes represented failures to evolve as Man unconsciously betrayed the hope of his contemporaries that Adam had perhaps not looked as repulsive as the "monkey professors" made out. Twenty-five years later, however, when Weinert took up his research work, the public was already regarding the question in a much more sober light. People were beginning to study the psychology of anthropoid apes and to realize that descent from such a family was not necessarily dishonorable.

On the practical side of his work Weinert followed Klaatsch. With the same suitable detective sense that his predecessor had shown in the interpretation of skulls, he rapidly grasped the essence of an apparently barely decipherable fragment. He seemed to look at fossils through X-ray apparatus. He instantly spotted details relating to racial history and could reconstruct entire skeletons from bone-splinters. His reconstruction of the skull of the *Pithecanthropus*, made after his visit to Dubois, became especially famous. It was confirmed at all points later on by von Koenigswald's discoveries near Sangiran.

When Weinert examined the Mauer find in 1937 he stuck the broken teeth back in their proper places with plasticine and photographed the entire jaw with accuracy in four positions of anthropological interest. He then perceived that the Heidelberg man bore an astonishing resemblance to a well-known, much disputed, and now honored specimen of prehistoric man, the ape man of Java.

The Mauer find of course represented a somewhat different, more robust type than that of Trinil, but it seemed, nevertheless, to belong to the *Pithecanthropus* group. If *Pithecanthropus erectus*, as

modern investigations revealed, first appeared in the Middle Pleistocene period, the Heidelberg man was actually even older. This would
mean that relatives of the Javanese primitive man had lived some
500,000 years ago, in the Günz-Mindel Intermediate Ice Age, and in
Europe. As we shall see later, they were probably distributed all over
the Old World in at least four forms. A great many anthropologists
assume today that they developed into all the higher types and races
of mankind.

In the sands of Mauer a tireless and most enthusiatic search was
still being kept up, as in Herr Rösch's time, for further traces of the
ancestral Heidelberg being, and a complete skull was actually found.
Tragically, it was not preserved for science. During the Second
World War the bodies of prisoners from a concentration camp were
buried in the neighborhood of Mauer. Workmen who were given
the task of exhuming them after the war suddenly discovered, in the
same geological layer from which Rösch had taken the lower jaw, a
queer-looking skull without a skeleton that belonged to it. They
naturally supposed it to form part of the remains of one of the
prisoners. But as they were afraid of being called to account for careless work they smashed the telltale evidence to pieces. The affair was
not made public until 1953, when a Göttingen scientist ascertained
with the aid of tiny splinters what a unique treasure-trove had here
been lost.

An imitation coconut

Four years after the discovery of the Mauer lower jaw another per-
plexing find in Europe caused a stir, and eclipsed the fame of the
Heidelberg man for decades. The showpiece of Schoetensack's collection was mistakenly denied the right to be regarded as the first
progenitor of European man, while at the same time the find of the
English lawyer Dawson was just as mistakenly claimed as the skull
of the genuine, most ancient Adam of all — Eoanthropus, or "dawn
man."

This affair, in which nearly all the prominent anthropologists and
prehistorians of Europe gradually became involved, began with the
digging for gravel on the outskirts of the village of Piltdown near
Brighton in the southern English county of Sussex. The intention
was to obtain materials for road improvements from the pits. Charles
Dawson, an Uckfield solicitor who took a great interest in matters
of natural science and spent his leisure in collecting fragments of the
bones of extinct reptiles and other fossils, happened to be passing the

pits one day, probably in the year 1908. As far as can be gathered, events were somewhat as follows. He watched the workmen for a time. Then he suddenly noticed, lying in the ditch at the roadside among various types of gravel, the splinters of a brown, spherical object, which had apparently been smashed to atoms by the men with their pickaxes.

"What have you got there?" Dawson asked. He thought it might be something interesting. He knew that natural scientists could always find something or other in gravel pits.

"It's a coconut, sir," answered one of the workmen. "No good to anybody. It's quite empty." He indicated, with a vague gesture, that he had pitched the thing away from the rubble. Then he gave the fragments another blow with his pick, sending them flying in all directions.

In an authoritative tone Dawson ordered the startled workmen not to touch the alleged coconut with either their picks or their fingers. He told them it was a human skull, petrified and turned brown by ferric oxide, and probably of the utmost value. He took it back with him to Uckfield, treated it with potassium dichromate in order to harden it (which he ought not to have done), and then added it to his collection.

During the ensuing months and years he tirelessly searched the neighborhood of Piltdown in order to discover from which geological layer the skull vaulting had originally come and unearth more details of the "Piltdown man." He relates that in 1911 he found some further fragments of the vaulting in the soil heaps of the gravel pit, and eventually in 1915 parts of the brain case of another individual, found in ill-defined circumstances in fields two miles from the original pit.

It was not until 1912 that he visited the Keeper of the Department of Geology at the British Museum, Arthur Smith Woodward, a most distinguished scholar, to whom Dawson had been sending fossils for the last thirty years, and a high authority on primitive fish and reptiles. Dawson submitted his finds to his old friend at the British Museum and anxiously demanded his professional opinion.

He was very excited by what he heard, for it seemed to confirm his own conjectures. Did he get overexcited about it? Did he, while in this state, allow himself to commit a highly unscientific act? Woodward stated that the layer beneath the gravel rubble of Piltdown, from which the workmen had apparently brought the bones to light, was Tertiary. Highly petrified remains of Tertiary animals had been unearthed there, including the bones of the antique elephants

Mastodon and *Stegodon*. Had Dawson really discovered an early type of man who had lived in the epoch of the Tertiary period, the Pliocene? The fragments alone hardly justified that conclusion. They did not give a particularly ancient impression. Nor had their treatment with potassium dichromate, as Woodward observed in a sternly censorious tone, exactly improved their condition.

The real thrill was still to come. Smith Woodward and Dawson undertook further excavations near Piltdown. They were accompanied by the French prehistorian Father Teilhard de Chardin on several occasions. And their discoveries burst upon the scientific world like a thunderbolt. Later in 1912 Smith Woodward brought to light at the original site a fragment of skull that fitted the Piltdown skull number one and was only differently colored because it had not been treated with potassium dichromate. Shortly afterwards, at the same spot, Dawson, in Woodward's presence, unearthed an extremely simian underjaw and a few teeth. The jaw was apparently similar in mineralization to the skull fragments, and it was also discolored with potassium dichromate! Had Dawson been in possession of it before it was dug up? Strangely enough, no one voiced such a suspicion. The Uckfield solicitor was universally regarded as an absolutely honorable, upright, and modest man.

The surprises continued as primitive flints came to light. Then Father Teilhard de Chardin discovered in the pit an apparently semihuman, semisimian canine, which he at first believed to be that of an ancient chimpanzee; but it obviously belonged to the jawbone. Further fragments, apparently from a second skull turned up in 1915. The excavations were crowned by the discovery of a very queer-looking object resembling a large petrified cudgel.

Smith Woodward and other scholars who were asked to give an opinion made desperate attempts to fit the fragments together like a jigsaw puzzle, but in vain. None of the joints fitted properly. Which went with the first and which with the second skull? They first tried to reconstruct skull number one, supplying the missing parts by guesswork — the forehead, the upper jaw, the front teeth, the cheekbones, and a piece of the occiput. At this point they found to their astonishment that the "Piltdown man," to put it crudely, resembled a cross between a chimpanzee and a civilized man. The lower jaw, when they had patched it up as well as they could, looked like that of a large ape. The skull vaulting, on the other hand, had an extremely modern appearance owing to the absence of the ridges above the eyes.

Consequently, despite the abundance of concrete evidence — in comparison with which the Heidelberg underjaw, only available in a single example, paled into insignificance — no one felt quite at ease with the "Tertiary man" of Mr. Dawson. To be sure, Woodward baptized the creature *Eoanthropus dawsoni* — Dawson's dawn man — and promoted it to the rank of the missing link. But his reconstruction made much too odd an impression. If it were correct, Man had possessed at the earliest stages of his development the muzzle of a beast and at the same time a brain capacity as large as that of Neanderthal man, his successor about half a million years later! Neither the Darwinians nor the anti-Darwinians, who were now engaged in a fierce dispute over the monster, could accept such a statement.

The leading English anthropologists, Arthur Smith Woodward, J. H. McGregor, Elliot Smith, Arthur Keith, and others, spent a number of years trying out every possible combination of the cranium of human type and the simian underjaw. Later on German scholars like Hans Weinert, Heinz Freiderichs, and Franz Weidenreich devoted themselves to the same task. Again and again casts of the pieces of Dawson's find were taken apart and put together afresh. But the results were not very successful. The reconstructions remained questionable, and one contradicted the other.

Klaatsch, who had been following the course of the affair intently until shortly before his death, disassociated himself from the *Eoanthropus* with the cautious announcement, "After a thorough examination of the case I consider an absolutely indubitable classification of these interesting skull fragments impossible." Twenty years later Weinert observed in equally cautious terms, "Nothing can be stated, in any case, with certainty. Consequently the *Eoanthropus* ought not to be used to advance new theories of the growth of mankind." Every expert knew what theories he referred to. The capacious prodigy of a skull might lend itself to arguments against the "monkey theory."

Eventually a majority of scientists agreed to regard the Piltdown monstrosity, which had thrown the whole system of classification into confusion, as a unique error of nature. The *Eoanthropus* was dismissed from the human evolutionary series. He was proclaimed to have been a creature "with no past and no future" which had got stuck in a blind alley of evolution and thus died without posterity. Nevertheless, he was still considered to have actually existed; it was still believed that the skull and jawbone went together; and he was still credited with a high antiquity of at least 500,000 years. By 1916 his discoverer, Dawson, was already dead at the age of fifty-two. The scientific world ensured that he would be remembered with honor in the future. His name gleamed in large letters on the glass case in the British Museum which exhibited the unorthodox "human brute" to inquisitive visitors from all over the world.

The violent contrast between the number one cranium and the mysterious underjaw remained. Could there have been some error in reconstruction? Once more Weinert divided the casts into their component parts. Once more he fitted them together again, replacing the underjaw in a different manner. Then he saw that the whole skull, including the large canine which had induced Teilhard de Chardin to make the comparison with the chimpanzee's tooth, now looked decidedly more human.

The results of further investigations undertaken at the site seemed to suit this view. After prolonged study of the Piltdown rubble the French anthropologist Marcellin Boule, discoverer of the Neanderthal specimen of La Chapelle-aux-Saints, affirmed his conviction that the dubious bones did not originate in the Tertiary period but in the Middle Pleistocene epoch, in other words the Middle Intermediate Ice Age. They thus deprived Dawson's find of much of its glory. Later investigations made the skull still more recent, placing it at a time when *Homo sapiens* had already arisen in the shape of the Cro-Magnon and Aurignacian races. As for the antique bones of animals from Piltdown, it was proved they came from far older layers and had probably been washed by mountain streams into the gravel now used for road repairs.

And what did the petrified club, the apparent weapon of Piltdown man, amount to? It was now finally unmasked as simply an ancient elephant's bone. Nearly all the prehistorians had been taken in by its peculiar shape and believed it to be the handiwork of *Eoanthropus*. Breuil thought an Ice Age beaver had made an irritating mistake. The beaver had supposed the enormous bone to have been the trunk of a tree and had nibbled at it for so long that it came to look like something made by man.

The skull of a *Homo sapiens* with an underjaw of primitive type! Such was the way in which the majority of scholars, though somewhat reluctantly, summed up the results of the affair. A favorite of prehistoric research thus was out of the running. Was the action premature? Science felt a little uneasy about it. But scientists shed no tears over the grotesque reconstructions made in Dawson's time, which had a monstrous appearance with their jutting simian jaws and modern thinkers' foreheads and seemed to turn all knowledge hitherto gained upside down. In fact they showed positive relief

that it had proved possible to give the obnoxious jaw, no matter
by what means, a form of *sapiens* type.

In the last weeks of 1953, however, the "Piltdown man" was news
once more.

Comedy of errors

On November 25, 1953 the members of the House of Commons
were called upon to decide a question unique in parliamentary history. Five Conservatives and one Socialist, sinking all party differences, had together presented a bill, praying the House to put it
on the Order of the Day for debate and Division. The bill read:
"The House is requested to pass a vote of no confidence in the Trustees of the British Museum for their delay in ascertaining that the
skull of the Piltdown Man is partly a forgery."

Mr. Dawson's find thus became a matter of national importance.
The fifty-one trustees in question, who controlled on behalf of the
nation the greatest assembly of treasures in the world and who were
now, in the opinion of the six proposers of the bill, to be held
responsible for the Piltdown business, included such men as Prime
Minister Churchill, Foreign Secretary Eden, the Speaker of the
House of Commons, the Lord High Chancellor, the Archbishop of
Canterbury, Lords Derby and Elgin, and a member of the Royal
Household. In what way had these highly placed persons incurred
such guilt as to expose themselves to declared suspicion of this
kind? They had simply not kept a sharp enough eye on science.
The six members considered they were to blame for allowing an old
skull — or rather an old underjaw — to trick humanity for forty
years.

The Speaker, whose name had been deliberately excluded from
the bill, had to decide whether it should be accepted for debate.
Amid the laughter of the House he stated that Parliament, the
statesmen of England, and the trustees of the museum had more important things to do than testing the authenticity of a heap of old
bones. A majority of the members agreed with him. Mr. Morrison,
while the House smiled and applauded, proceeded to shelve the bill,
thus liberating the Archbishop of Canterbury and Messrs. Churchill,
Eden, Derby, and Elgin from the charge of levity and neglect.

The charge still applied to other people, to those who had tried to
interpret the Piltdown monster to the best of their knowledge and
conscience and in so doing had omitted to take fraudulent possibilities into consideration. In their view the Piltdown skull was not

an uninteresting heap of old bones, but the incentive to a most painful hoax and the cause of a huge scandal. A number of different things had been happening during the years between the dismissal of *Eoanthropus* from the pedigree of mankind and the sensational session of the House of Commons; and the prominent personalities of anthropological science had by no means played a brilliant part in them. Yet, as we shall see, Sherlock Holmes himself might have been misled by the evidence that the anthropologists had to face.

The interpreters of the Piltdown fossil, who regarded *Eoanthropus* as either a perverse mistake on nature's part or else an Ice Age man of irregular form, had meanwhile been joined by many skeptics, especially outside England. They shook their heads over the reconstructions and refused to believe that the cranium and the jawbone went together. The degree of fossilization seemed, indeed, to favor the conjunction, and the underjaw and skull also "fitted" when they were brought into contact. But the resultant picture could not be accepted. It did not suit the theory of evolution or current knowledge of the growth of mankind. Nor could the new reconstructions of *sapiens* type be accepted, in which the Procrustean method of forcing the two parts to correspond was being exerted.

For these reasons some scholars had begun to believe that by an uncommon accident the remains of a Late Tertiary anthropoid ape and a *Homo sapiens* of the Late Ice Age had become associated. Well-known American, French, and German scientists were of this opinion, including among others the systematizer Gerrit Miller of Washington, D.C., and the Frankfurt anthropologist Franz Weidenreich, of whom we shall hear much later on in connection with subsequent finds in eastern Asia. A few years after the discovery Miller was already declaring that the jawbone had belonged to a Late Tertiary or Early Diluvial chimpanzee. Weidenreich went farther. He stated categorically, after examining the fifth reconstruction, that the skull vaulting was that of a modern human being, while the underjaw had nothing whatever to do with it, being that of a present-day orangutan. Other specialists, who were not quite so sure, declared that at any rate the two parts belonged to different geological periods.

These skeptics were vigorously opposed by Sir Arthur Keith, the Nestor of the British anthropologists. He continued to support, as before, the views of Smith Woodward, and after the latter's death he presented himself as counsel for the defense of *Eoanthropus*. In 1935, almost at the same time as scientists were proving the Piltdown bones to be of considerably more recent date and Weinert was affirming their *sapiens* character, Keith's theory received a heavy blow, which turned out to be mortal. The dentist and prehistorian Alvan Theophilus Marston, who had known Dawson the solicitor personally, discovered in a gravel pit near Swanscombe, just under twenty miles southwest of London, the remains of the skull of an incontestable British primitive man. It was accompanied by some six hundred wonderfully well wrought stone tools, dating from the Acheulean period. The circumstances of the find were not in doubt. The extremely ancient hand axes dated unquestionably from the same geological period as the fragments of the skull. Accordingly, the "Swanscombe man" must have lived at least 300,000 and possibly even 500,000 years ago. And, unlike the *Eoanthropus*, he fitted perfectly into the system, into the doctrine of evolution, the edifice of current theory.

Marston, highly delighted with his success and now determined to unmask the monster of Piltdown once and for all, joined the ranks of the skeptics. His judgment of the *Eoanthropus* was, intelligibly enough, primarily based on his examination of the Piltdown teeth. The teeth and the jawbone, he stated, summarizing the views of those who declined to accept the conjunction of skull vaulting and jaw, were not only unmistakably simian: they were the remains of a true ape, to wit, a prehistoric chimpanzee of the Tertiary period, whereas the cranium, equally unmistakably, was to be attributed to an Ice Age man of a geologically late period.

Marston's interpretation, despite his triumph at Swanscombe, was not accepted. It sounded too improbable that the underjaw of a prehistoric chimpanzee, which had never been proved to have lived in England, could have been found in the very place where the underjaw of a human skull ought to have been found, quite apart from the similarity of the state of preservation of both specimens. But Marston retained his opinion, fighting a lonely battle for Swanscombe against Piltdown.

The wheel of time continued to turn, and people would probably still be racking their brains today over the "coconut" of the Piltdown roadmenders and still trying somehow to combine cranium and jawbone, still wondering whether the old monster were really an abortion or a *sapiens*-type form, if the English scientists Oakley and Hoskins had not some years ago introduced the fluorine test into prehistoric research, a method by which objects found could be examined microchemically for their fluorine content. This system of ascertaining the age of fossils by chemical means relied upon the fact that the fluorine content of a bone increases in proportion to the length of time a bone has lain buried. It is true that this method is not perfectly reliable in the determination of absolute age, as chemical conditions in the soil vary greatly at different places and times. But the relative age of a number of problematical bones found at the same site can be determined by it with complete certainty. And it was in fact the relative age, the question of the like nature of skull vaulting and jaw, that had to be decided in the Piltdown case.

Kenneth P. Oakley was a member of the research staff at the British Museum. Marston immediately got in touch with him, believing that now at last he would have a chance to prove the truth of his views. In 1949 Oakley subjected certain small bone-splinters from Swanscombe and others from Piltdown to the fluorine test. The result of the test was, as anticipated, a brilliant victory for Swanscombe and a crushing defeat for Piltdown. Marston's Swanscombe man was in fact an early Neanderthal specimen, dating from the Middle Intermediate Ice Age and a true forefather of both the branches of mankind that subsequently culminated in Neanderthal man and *Homo sapiens*. After the somewhat older Heidelberg man he was by far the most important find dating from the earliest history of mankind. But Dawson's Piltdown man was at most 50,000 to 100,000 years old, probably an ordinary Late Ice Age specimen, many of which had been found in England itself.

Marston was not yet satisfied. He insisted on knowing more. Had Oakley also made a thorough test of the jawbone, the dubious lower jaw which he, Marston, was convinced should be attributed to a Tertiary prehistoric ape? Was it not now about time to abandon the senseless conjunction of a *sapiens* type and a simian jaw? Marston was convinced that Dawson had made a mistake in combining under one heading two different things that happened to have been thrown by workmen into the same gravel pit. And this uncertainty ought now to be cleared up irrespective of the state of preservation of the bone.

Was it only a mistake that Dawson had made? Was it only by chance that the jaw had turned up at the site where the skull had been excavated? Did the jaw really come from a genuine prehistoric ape? Oakley gave in to Marston's pressure, although he had his own suspicions about the results.

Meanwhile the fluorine test had been supplemented with tests for nitrogen, radioactive carbon, and iron content, as well as having been substantially improved and elaborated in other respects. Oakley had been testing the jawbone and teeth, like a criminologist, by this latest method. The results of his investigation were no longer a matter for anthropologists but for Scotland Yard. The jaw had not belonged to a Tertiary ape at all; it belonged to a modern one, an orangutan or chimpanzee, as Weidenreich had already suspected. It had been artificially turned into a fossil with extreme skill and professional knowledge, and made to resemble the cranium by having been polished and subjected to treatment with potash and iron. The jaw was the most subtle forgery ever perpetrated in the annals of prehistoric research!

It was out of the question to communicate this statement to the public without being able to prove it up to the hilt. The two leading anthropologists of the University of Oxford, Wilfrid E. Le Gros Clark and J. S. Weiner, made a further study of the case, together with Oakley. Problem after problem called for a solution. One was that of the potassium dichromate, which had been forgotten for forty years. Dawson had used the stuff to color the skull fragments first found; but the jawbone, when it was found, had been colored in the same way. By Dawson? Had he been in possession of the thing before the "excavation" took place? Had he acquired it somewhere, falsified it, given it certain treatment, and then placed it like a legitimate find, so to speak, under the nose of his patron, Smith Woodward? If so, why? Or had he simply been the unwitting victim of some swindler, fanatic or facetious student, like the unlucky Professor Beringer long ago?

Light only gradually penetrated the darkness. The canine found by Teilhard de Chardin was that of a young anthropoid ape. Real precision work had been employed to file it to a replica of a prehistoric human tooth. The ducts of the canine contained tiny grains of fossilized ironstone. It looked as though some masterly technician of a dentist had introduced them from outside. The skull splinters, unquestionably genuine, were impregnated with iron through and through, like the bones of all human fossils. Yet exactly the same treatment with iron had been applied to the falsified jaw, though only in the form of a thin exterior coating. The interior of the jawbone was "modern." What sort of a genius, what exceptionally gifted expert had performed this operation on the bones, the discoloration with iron, the grinding of the teeth?

Where did the jawbone come from? How had the forger been able to procure in a relatively short time the jaw of an anthropoid ape corresponding in its entirety to the old skull? "I know the skulls of apes in most museums," wrote an anthropologist shortly after the revelation of the Piltdown forgery, "but I should not expect to be able to find such a jaw in a few months." Had the business, then, all been arranged long beforehand, had the unknown unearthed the ape's jaw years before the research operations at Piltdown? Had he falsified it, adapted it to fit the cranium of an Ice Age man that happened to be in his possession, and then taken all the other steps so cunningly that the luminaries of science were bound to fall into the trap? Had he been a master paleontologist, a master artist, and a master stage manager rolled into one? And why had he taken all this trouble? For what reason?

On November 21, 1953, Oakley, Le Gros Clark, and Weiner submitted to their contemporaries in the *Bulletin of the British Museum* (Natural History) all the evidence they had of this "perfectly executed and carefully prepared fraud." For the next few days the affair was on everyone's lips. The caricaturists of the daily newspapers, the comedians in the music halls, and the comic papers took up the matter. Debates took place in the British House of Commons on the subject, professors all over the world puzzled over the identity of the forger, his methods, and his motives, and an English wit consoled the disgusted experts with the remark, "At any rate science did manage to discover the first man who had false teeth."

Since a matter of science had now become a matter of law, the most interesting question was the identity of the guilty party. It was the "finder," the solicitor Dawson, who seemed most to blame. Yet everyone who had known him described him as an honorable man. He had made no sort of financial or other profit out of his "dawn man," and although he was a very keen amateur research student, he could not be considered a master paleontologist. He would hardly have been capable of the artificial fossilization of a modern ape's teeth. And yet who could tell what might go on in the mind of a discontented solicitor in a small town? What technical knowledge might not a gifted dilettante, devoted to his hobby, acquire on the sly? What incredible feats may not be performed by some obsessed, eccentric fellow thirsting for world fame?

The view of the English professor Fleure that this was a case of a carefully and learnedly executed students' prank was soon repudiated by the experts, for what student would ever have perpetrated so ingenious a paleontological master forgery and then forever held his peace? The fun to be got out of a hoax could not have been the motive for an act so momentous in its consequences and so difficult to carry out. There could only have been two motives. Either the forger, perhaps seduced by some very far-fetched anthropological theory that had become a fixation with him, had meant to cause a scientific sensation that would make him immortal, or else, being a fanatical opponent of the theory of evolution, he had been concerned to expose prehistoric research to ridicule.

Both explanations were unconvincing. The thing had been done for one or other of those reasons, but it also might have been done for quite a different one. The question caused a serious dispute early in December 1953 during a meeting of the London Geological Society. Alvan Theophilus Marston, the dentist, declared that the whole case had been misunderstood, that Oakley and his colleagues were wrong: the jaw had not been falsified. He continued to believe that the jawbone had belonged to a Tertiary anthropoid ape and had been found in the gravel pit by sheer accident during the road-mending works. "The proof is inside," he exclaimed, "right inside the tooth. The teeth are those of a young prehistoric ape. They contain hollows not yet filled with properly developed nerve ducts. Such teeth regularly become filled with ironstone grains in a perfectly natural way during the process of fossilization."

Oakley quietly retorted that according to the fluorine and nitrogen content of the jaw the anthropoid ape in question had died a bare fifty years ago. Marston said he doubted it. The fossil might have come from a different district, where different chemical conditions had prevailed in the soil. Moreover, he added emphatically, no one in 1912 would have been able to operate upon a tooth-duct in such a manner as to compel the conclusion that the tooth was between 20,000,000 and 35,000,000 years old. Twenty to thirty-five million years? Those attending the session exchanged blank looks. "Yes!" cried Marston. "The jaw is that of a *Proconsul,* a prehistoric chimpanzee dating from the Middle Tertiary period. You professionals have no idea what you are talking about!" The chairman, Professor King, requested him to moderate his language.

The final truth about the "Piltdown man" has yet to be discovered, and we may never learn it. Some things have been established. The Swanscombe man is a genuine early Neanderthal specimen, a human fossil of perfectly ordinary appearance dating from the Middle Pleistocene epoch and possessing features already suggestive of *Homo sapiens.* The Piltdown cranium, on the other hand, belongs to the Late Ice Age, being a direct ancestor or contemporary of the Aurignac and Cro-Magnon peoples. And the Piltdown jawbone is simian. But whether Dawson was guilty of a crime against science or only made a pardonable mistake remains a secret that the Uckfield solicitor who was so enamored of prehistory has carried with him to the grave.

The comedy even had a sequel. The protagonists were no longer anthropologists, but journalists. Skillful writers not overburdened with technical knowledge seized upon this sensational material in all countries and tried to persuade their readers that the theory of evolution, after the revelation of the *Eoanthropus,* had lost one of its most important witnesses, the "final proof of Darwin's doctrine" and the "most eminent of the missing links." Immediate revision of the current textbooks was essential. They were thus encouraging the very action that the forger had intended to bring about — if he really had been, as was still suspected by some people in England, a fanatical opponent of the evolutionary thesis.

The anthropologists smiled indulgently at this eagerness for revision. They were greatly relieved at having at last rid themselves for ever of the disturbing fellow from Piltdown, who had absolutely refused to fit into the theory of evolution. They devoted themselves henceforth, with all the more enthusiasm, to the concrete evidence of prehistory.

Storm over Oldoway

The Berlin paleontologist Hans Reck was anything but impetuous and overzealous: he was distinguished, on the contrary, by a lofty consciousness of scientific responsibility. His excavation work in East Africa — in the course of which he discovered a number of prehistoric elephants, hippopotamuses, and antelopes — was described as exemplary in scientific circles. And yet this most excellent man was destined to administer a severe shock to anthropological and prehistoric research.

In 1913 Reck, with a staff of native assistants, was reconnoitering the Oldoway gorge at the edge of the Masai plain. What he was after in this gorge he described later in a lively and attractive book.

The Oldoway series of strata is divided with great regularity into five main horizontals, which lay open before our eyes like five volumes of enigmatic geological history. Each of them revealed to us documents which it alone possessed. These were never incoherent, but embodied a continuous range of development, leading us like a scarlet thread from the first page to the last. The Oldoway layers were piled neatly one on another, so that, as rarely happens, they were easy to survey, the oldest being at the bottom and the latest at the top. There were no gaps between them, nor had mountain-forming agencies anywhere ruffled or distorted their disposition.

It is necessary to quote Reck in detail because in the bottom layer but one — the age of which was estimated at more than 300,000 years — a strange discovery was made. One evening the explorer's two black assistants, Manjonga and Bakari Omari, turned up, evidently suffering from the effects of some kind of shock.

"Boss, we've found something we've never taken out of the ground yet."

"What was it?" asked Reck, thinking it might be a new sort of fossilized mammal.

"I think it's an Arab, boss," said Manjonga. "He's lying asleep on his side."

Reck looked up in astonishment. Bakari Omari explained.

"I climbed down the cliff and saw a little piece of bone sticking out from under a bush. I scraped with my knife and some more bones showed up. They looked like a head, in the end. The head is certainly that of a man."

"What did you do then?"

"We cleared a bit more of the topsoil away till we could see plainly that there was a man lying there. We didn't touch him after that."

Reck immediately summoned his excavation party and hurried off to the site. It was unmistakably in the last layer from the bottom. And Manjonga's "Arab" really did resemble a modern human being of Semitic or Hamitic origin. It was a skeleton painted red and in a complete state of preservation, lying buried in a crouching position. "It is impossible," Reck wrote, "to describe my feelings at the sight of it. Delight, hope, doubt, caution and eager excitement all surged through my mind at once. For it was immediately clear to me that if this skeleton were contemporary with its layer and the Oldoway fossilized animals the find was of enormous importance for the history of the earliest of mankind. It would have to be dated far back into the Diluvial age and would not only be the oldest specimen found on African soil but one of the oldest human remains ever discovered."

Reck checked the layer and the grave with the meticulous accuracy of a criminologist. He found nothing that could justify skepticism. Accordingly, on his return he announced to the learned world with a clear conscience that he had discovered a *Homo sapiens* dating from the Middle Diluvial age, a human being of the type of a present-day Nubian or Masai native and more than twice as old as the oldest Neanderthal specimen. In two lectures given to Berlin scientists on March 17 and May 15, 1914, he stated the reasons for his opinion and exhibited the skeleton in its bed of soil.

Thirty-six speakers said what they thought about it, in a long debate. Most of the scholars considered it out of the question for Man in his present shape to have lived before the time of prehistoric man. But they had no satisfactory answer to the facts presented by Reck. Before the debate ended reporters from the big local and foreign newspapers were queueing up outside the hall. During the next few days the tidings spread like wildfire from one country to another that the "monkey theory" had been dealt a crushing blow, that Man did not descend from bestial cave dwellers and monsters, but on the contrary had made his appearance in the world much earlier than all the so-called prehistoric forms and missing links. Some contemporaries even drew the bold conclusion from Reck's lecture that Man's earthly paradise had been situated in East Africa.

Reck was much alarmed by all this uproar. He had never intended to stab the theory of evolution in the back. And yet, when one took the circumstances of the find into consideration, one was almost obliged to admit that those who argued against the hitherto accepted pedigree of mankind were, to a certain extent, justified. Reck arranged further expeditions to throw more light on the matter, but not one of them ever reached its goal. The disputes over the Oldoway affair were lost sight of in the chaos of the First World War.

Fifteen years later the Oldoway case was taken up by a man who resided in Africa and is still regarded as the highest authority on East African prehistory, culture, and ethnology. L. S. B. Leakey, the son of an English missionary, was born in Kenya. He had found some skeletons east of Lake Victoria which much resembled that of Oldoway but were at most 20,000 to 30,000 years old. They were probably Aurignacian and may well have been the ancestors of the Hamitic plainsmen of East Africa.

But as the Oldoway man was still being put forward as a witness against the theory of evolution, Leakey visited Berlin, got into touch with Reck, and urged him to undertake a further exploration of the mysterious gorge. Reck at once agreed. As the original discoverer he naturally felt a particular interest in solving the puzzle once for all. In 1931 the second Oldoway expedition started from Nairobi, led by Leakey and Reck. It was accompanied by English geologists, naturalists, prehistorians, and a few enterprising students. They all carried first-rate equipment for the final unmasking of Manjonga's Arab.

This expedition opened a new field of prehistoric investigation. Leakey and his men discovered the African Stone Age cultures, finding that the development of weapons and tools from the simple hand axe to the obsidian knife had proceeded in Africa on the same lines as in Europe. They even discovered still more primitive implements, which indicated a race of human beings far below Neanderthal standard, such as simple spherical pebbles only slightly flaked on one edge. Had the Oldoway man perhaps produced these "spheroids"? All the members of the expedition considered it out of the question. A still less known specimen of early man must have left such traces of his existence, a being who had only just crossed the threshold leading from animals to humanity. Leakey and Reck were unable to ascertain what he had been like, and it was not until a few years ago that such remains were found in South Africa.

The riddle of the man of Oldoway was eventually answered quite simply. It will be recollected that Cuvier and Virchow in their time had described many finds of prehistoric remains as those of later graves that had sunk to lower geological levels. Precise investigations later on proved that they had been wrong. But they would actually have been right in the present case. East Africa was still being subjected to violent earthquakes in the Late Pleistocene epoch. And the geologists proved that an earthquake of this kind had forced the Oldoway grave down to Reck's bottom layer but one. The alleged primitive man was no older than the skeletons discovered by Leakey near Lake Victoria.

Reck himself did not survive to see the matter cleared up. He had returned home some time before and died soon afterwards, without learning that his much discussed primeval ancestor had belonged to an old tribe of Hamitic warriors.

Ironically enough, it was Leakey himself who, after unmasking the man of Oldoway and proceeding to further investigations near the villages of Kanam and Kanjera, not far from Lake Victoria, once more dug up human remains of highly progressive type in an extremely ancient layer. He believed them to have been contemporary with the *Dinotherium* monster whose bones he found in the same deposit. Much doubt was expressed of the accuracy of this conclusion and no exact verification proved possible, since the site, although diligently searched for, could never be found again. Opinions are still divided on the question today. One party assumes that in this locality as almost everywhere in the great East African valley geological upheavals displaced and intermingled the various levels of the soil and that earth tremors brought ancient Hamitic bones into association with those of a *Dinotherium*. The other party keeps to Leakey's view and puts the two fossils into a single group with the Swanscombe man and his Middle Ice Age relatives.

Africa did not only produce fossils which upset the learned world: it also presented science with superb collections of Old Stone Age tools, extremely interesting rock drawings, and finally with the most ancient and therefore the most important finds ever made of prehistoric human remains. We shall have much to say about them later. As early as 1921 anthropologists got a foretaste of what was in store for them in Africa. This happened ten years before the unmasking of the Oldoway man — in other words, at a time when no other prehistoric human being apart from him had come to light in Africa.

Deep in a shaft of the Broken Hill tin mine in Rhodesia, and therefore at a spot that does not permit of precise geological dating, all sorts of remarkable bones were found in the course of removing the metal. It is certain that they included a complete human skeleton and it is even alleged that there were several. However that may have been, the deposit of bones must have been dispersed during work at the mine, so that the experts eventually received only one very large, apparently extremely ancient skull with a low forehead, enormous ridges over the eyes, and what a contemporary describes as a "strikingly brutish facial bone formation." A few long, flattened upper thighbones of clearly modern aspect also arrived.

On November 17, 1921, the first report on this Rhodesian man was published in London. The creature was given the name of *Cyphanthropus rhodesiensis*. For some time it played an even bigger part on the scientific stage than the *Pithecanthropus*, which Dubois was at that time keeping strictly under lock and key. For four years it was officially held to be the oldest find of a prehistoric man ever made. Leading scholars studied it closely. Some of them considered the Rhodesian man to be a direct descendant of the gorilla. Others, like the Parisian anthropologist Marcellin Boule, declared that in all probability it belonged to the Neanderthal group of forms, though the structure of the skull looked far more primitive and that of the limbs far more advanced. Perhaps, then, it was a kind of pre-Neanderthal specimen, already possessing the legs of a *Homo sapiens*?

At a later date certain scientists denied this and said it was a late Neanderthal type that had proceeded still farther on the road of evolution than the Neanderthal men of Europe. They called attention to the fact that the oldest members of the Neanderthal race were the least "brutish" of aspect and suggested that the alleged primitive features of this race were in reality newly inherited characteristics. From this point of view the *Cyphanthropus* was an exceptional case that had died out without posterity, like the venturesome saurians of the Cretaceous period.

The mine-shaft deposit offered no clue to geological classification. The bones themselves had to be more closely examined for this purpose. In this process something really very extraordinary occurred. Marks were found indicating that the Rhodesian man was of far later date than the European Neanderthal specimen and might even have lived in historical times. Certain peculiarities of the facial bones were amazingly reminiscent of *Homo sapiens* and contrasted absurdly with the heavy osseous formations above the eyebrows and the allegedly primitive occiput. The creature from Broken Hill had also unmistakably suffered from dental decay, a disease of civilization that had never been detected in any Ice Age man. Last of all came the biggest surprise. The Berlin professor Mair and other scholars asserted positively that the two queer-looking holes at the sides of the skull represented the entrance and exit of a modern bullet! Had a white or Arab conqueror of modern times shot the *Cyphanthropus* and thus wiped out a "surviving human fossil"? Or had some hunter used the skull for target practice? At any rate it looked as though the fossil could not be referred to the deeper, Middle Pleistocene layers. Hauser called it "a superb example of atavism, resuscitated evidence of ancient conditions." Weinert observed that it was "not impossible for the Rhodesian to have been still alive, as a single individual, by chance retaining features of Neanderthal type, in our own time." Other investigators advanced the hypothesis that it was a primitive Negro that had survived through the ages down to the present day.

This theory gave rise for the first time to the question of whether Negroes are descended directly from Neanderthal man. Almost all scientists today think not, but very little is yet known about the origin of the black race. The suggestion that it evolved during the last glacial period from Aurignacian or Cro-Magnon man is only supported by the existence of a skeleton in an almost complete state of preservation found by the explorers Besnard and Monod in 1927 near Asselar, some three hundred and forty miles north of Timbuctoo, in a layer of sand exposed by rainfall. So far as the structure of the skull is concerned present-day Negro tribes may just as well have descended from Neanderthal or Rhodesian types as from the long-headed peoples of the Late Ice Age. This is new ground for anthropological research. Primitive jungles and savannahs still no doubt hold many secrets that may yet reveal the pedigree of the Negro.

The man of Broken Hill, too, remained a mystery until a short time ago. Was he the last atavistic descendant of an old cross between Neanderthal and Aurignacian man? Was he a halfwit, a monstrosity in whom the long forgotten characteristics of the gray dawn of the world had cropped up again? Did the ancient sagas and those modern reports of encounters with "beast-men" retain, after all, a grain of truth? Technical literature was haunted for a long time by weird hypotheses concerning the Rhodesia man. But eventually a second skull of the same sort was found in South Africa which belonged — unquestionably this time — to the Late Pleistocene epoch. It represented a southern branch of the Neanderthal race, reminiscent in certain respects of the *Pithecanthropus*. The puzzle of the bullet hole was also solved in an extremely unromantic manner. An ancient hyena had dug its teeth into the Broken Hill skull, making the two holes that had puzzled many scientists all over the world for more than thirty years.

Oldoway and Rhodesia attracted the attention of anthropologists and prehistorians to the Black Continent. Its limestone caves and rocky fissures still concealed far more important human fossils, dating from an entirely different and bafflingly distant age, which were to come to light later.

XIV

THE PROTOTYPE

The Dayton Monkey Trial

DARWINISM had taught that mankind, like all creatures, has a long history. Man evolved from forms of life not yet human and in so doing passed through a "critical phase," a "transitional stage from beast to Man." Twentieth-century research took over this cornerstone of the doctrine of evolution, tried to close the gaps in the theoretical edifice and clarify procedure during the "critical phase" of the making of Man. Science succeeded in producing a picture — very full in many particulars — of the development of vegetable and animal life in prehistoric times. One of the fullest of these passages was the scientific account of the history of mankind. At the very beginning of this new development in paleontology certain curious fossils from the days of our forefathers were resuscitated in remote corners of the world innocent of even a tincture of science. Such were the much discussed, much ridiculed, and for that very reason historically significant, "Monkey Trials." The far-famed trial at Dayton obtained the greatest amount of publicity.

By July 21, 1925, the day on which the Dayton Monkey Trial ended, scientists in various parts of the world were on the point of solving some of the remaining puzzles about Adam. Zoologists were comparing the physical features and mental capacities of the chimpanzee with those of man. Anthropologists were beginning large scale excavations in China and Africa in order to discover the true transitional forms between Tertiary anthropoid apes and primitive man. At New Haven Robert Yerkes, director of the Yale Institute of Animal Psychology, was compiling a dictionary of the chimpanzee's language. At Suchum on the Black Sea the Russian Nina Kohts was detecting reason and intuition in the apes she studied. At Jena the Dutch anatomist Ludwig Bolk was investigating simian and human embryos. In Berlin Hans Weinert was discovering similarities between Man and chimpanzee, especially in the structure of the frontal cavities, cardiac arteries, and spermatozoa, and Hans

Friedenthal was providing chemical proof of blood relationship. The French prehistorian Marcellin Boule was busy with the unusually primitive skull found in the Rhodesian tin mine at Broken Hill. The South African anatomist Raymond A. Dart was brooding over the "Taungs child," a fossil that even the greatest luminaries of science could not determine to be human or simian. The Swedish geologist J. G. Andersson was looking in the cave district near Peking for a Chinese Prometheus who had presented mankind with fire. All these men heard of the Dayton affair. They thought of Lamettrie and Wolff, who had been driven from their homes like criminals; of Lamarck, who had been expelled from his professorial chair; of Boucher de Perthes and Don Marcelino de Sautuola, who had been ridiculed. They thought of legions of pioneers who had fallen on the battlefields of science. And they glanced at the calendar. Yes, it really was July 21, 1925.

At Dayton, a small town in Tennessee inhabited by farmers, backwoodsmen, and petty traders, a young elementary schoolteacher named John Scopes stood in court, accused of having taught his pupils something about the theory of evolution and research on primitive man. Apparently the worthy Mr. Scopes had forgotten that there was a law in Tennessee according to which any mention in public educational establishments of Darwin's theory and the fields of learning associated with it could be punished; or perhaps he ignored the law intentionally. He may have thought that since the greatest naturalists in the United States, the paleontologist Henry Fairfield Osborn, the zoologist William Beebe, the geneticists Thomas Hunt Morgan and Joseph Muller taught the same things as he did, why should anything be untrue in Dayton which was accepted as true in New York and Chicago, at Harvard and Yale, and everywhere else on earth? He could not dream that his modest attempts to give American farmers' boys some ideas of the struggle for survival and the ape man of Java would give rise to such tremendous excitement.

A puritanical inspector of schools had called attention to the infringement of the law by Mr. Scopes. A worthy provincial judge, who had probably never even heard of Darwin, meditated over the case for weeks. He searched the statutes of Tennessee, found that Scopes really had defied a prohibition, and eventually resolved to give the lad who told innocent children fairy tales about monkeys the lesson he richly deserved. But meanwhile the public had got wind of the affair. Leading scientists traveled to Dayton and demanded that Scopes be left in peace. Indignant farmers, cattle dealers, and small-town citizens belonging to the most various religious sects also gathered in the little country town, formerly so quiet, and demanded wth equal firmness a severe sentence on the transgressor. Dayton became world-famous overnight. Real estate prices rocketed. Traveling salesmen put up their booths around Scopes's house. Journalists, photographers, movie-camera men, clergymen, and speculators flocked into the town. Soon there were no beds available anywhere. Those who understood how to take advantage of the market made a good thing out of John Scopes's mistake.

The governor of Tennessee intervened. He assured the citizens of Dayton that the theory of evolution was harmless. In vain. The honest puritans were determined to fight the matter out to the end. The opponents of Mr. Scopes were joined by the sternest of America's public prosecutors, the former democratic candidate for President, William Jennings Bryan, who hated scientists, Free Churchmen, Negroes, and monkeys like the plague. The men of science entrusted America's coolest counsel, Clarence Darrow, with the defense of the accused. John Scopes himself had long ceased to count. The main point at issue in Dayton, with its eight thousand white and black inhabitants, its four churches, equal number of schools, twelve drugstores, and two hotels, was the question of all questions, the origin of mankind. Which was right, biology or Genesis? The population of Dayton intended to have this matter settled once and for all by a provincial judge and a jury of a dozen rustics.

Many of those, both learned and unlearned, who followed the course of the Dayton trial were not quite satisfied with the alternatives thus proposed. They maintained that Genesis could perfectly well be reconciled with the data of biological research. And they were ready to prove their words. But Bryan, the prosecutor, and the farmers, citizens, and evangelists of Dayton refused to admit such proofs. So far as they were concerned there could be no compromise between a lump of clay and the ape, Adam and the *Pithecanthropus*.

On July 10, 1925, the trial of John Scopes began. It lasted twelve days. The small courtroom could only accommodate a fraction of the spectators thirsting for sensation. Anyone who had managed to obtain a seat could sell it for good ready cash at any time. The trial of science had turned into a carnival.

The defending counsel, Darrow, tried several times to get certain naturalists who were present to give evidence. It proved impossible. As soon as one of the gentlemen in question began to speak and made any reference to cells, mutations, primitive human beings, and natural selection, he was answered by bellows of laughter from the farmers. The floorboards of the room cracked and split under the overcrowded courtroom. The judge, sweating and utterly helpless, was then forced to continue the hearing out of doors. When the accused attempted to justify his conduct to the jury, canned-food tins, empty bottles, and lumps of filth were hurled at his head. And even the hard-boiled defense counsel, who had so often conducted many a difficult case to a successful outcome, found his carefully prepared speech completely ruined by shouted oaths and personal insults. He sighed, turned his eyes skyward, and gave it up as a bad job.

The court found Scopes guilty of infringing the school regulations of Tennessee and sentenced him to be fined a hundred dollars. Science had lost its case. No sooner had sentence been pronounced than thousands of men and women in Dayton fell to their knees and sang psalms.

Next day an epidemic of typhoid fever broke out among the tightly packed masses of people in Dayton and there were more than a hundred deaths — a horrible epilogue to this exotic carnival.

Although John Scopes was obliged to give up his schoolteaching the step turned out to his advantage. His monkey trial had made him so popular that his future was assured. He became not a biologist, but a car salesman.

The scientific world, also found guilty on this occasion, learned from the lips of the prosecuting counsel, Mr. Bryan, that man differed from the beasts by his logical intelligence and moral sense in behavior. That was exactly what we, too, had hitherto assumed, thought the biologists, anthropologists, and animal psychologists of the year 1925. But when we think of Dayton, we can't be quite so sure.

The affair at Dayton was a last grotesque revolt against the new conception of history which America itself, apart from its remote recesses, had long since generally accepted. The world laughed, and soon forgot the trial. And the natural scientists, profoundly shocked, once more stated emphatically that a picture of humanity which left out of account its historical and biological basis resembled a tree without roots or a house without a substructure.

Do you speak Chimpanzee?

Man, so runs an old objection to the theory of evolution, can laugh, weep, speak, and think. The apes, however much they may resemble

ADAM UNMASKED

man physically, cannot do these things. In the mental and psychological field, therefore, an unbridgeable gulf yawns between humanity and the simian species. This fact makes a common origin at least dubious.

An attempt was made as early as 1877 by the German animal psychologist Johannes von Fischer to weaken the force of this objec- tion. He studied the imitative behavior and the sounds made by the gorilla M'Pungu, which was at that time kept in the Berlin Aquar- ium, and finally announced that he had learned the language of apes. So one day he entered M'Pungu's cage, talked gorilla dialect to him, and waited for an answer. In his own words: "M'Pungu looked at me in astonishment. Finally, he grinned, gave me a box on the ear and immediately afterwards bit my nose." Presumably Johannes von Fischer had made a frightful mistake in what he said!

Greater success attended the efforts of the psychologist Wolfgang Köhler, who was in charge of an establishment for the study of anthro- poid apes which the Prussian Academy of Sciences maintained on the island of Teneriffe between 1912 and 1920. Seven chimpanzees were kept there in relative freedom. Köhler watched their be- havior, subjected them to various tests, and concluded from it all that they had intelligence. He perceived that, without guidance, they piled boxes one on top of another and thrust hollow rods into one another in order to reach bananas suspended from the ceiling or lying outside the cage. One chimpanzee would often even help another, although the first one would derive no advantage from so doing. According to Köhler this was "indubitably sensible behavior of the kind familiar among human beings." The objects of his experi- ments also laughed and wept, communicated intelligibly by tones and gestures, and were quick to understand the sense of human speech.

When Köhler published his observations in 1921, the majority of psychologists at first greeted them with reserve. But intelligence tests of anthropoid apes soon became a widespread fashion. Chimpanzees and orangutans were placed by American, Russian, and German scientists in the most difficult situations, which they could only master by the use of reason and judgment. The chimpanzees made a far better job of it than the orangutans. The former distinguished colors and shapes, used appliances much too complicated for human beings at the ABC stage, and found their way out of mazes in which other animals became hopelessly lost.

Other mammals of the higher orders, too — such as capuchin monkeys and raccoons — proved at the experimental stations that they knew all sorts of tricks. But they "think and act at the same time," while the big anthropoid apes, as the Viennese animal psychologist Konrad Lorenz stated in commenting on an impressive case of this kind, "behave in a way that no one who has seen them will ever forget." An orang was placed in a room from the ceiling of which a banana dangled on a string. In one corner of the room stood a box high enough to serve the ape as a ladder. The orang looked first at the banana, then at the box, scratched its head just like a perplexed human being, finally flew into a rage, fidgeted with its arms and legs, uttered loud cries, and turned its back on the box and the banana, as though offended. In Lorenz's words:

> But the thing still worried him. He tackled the problem again and his previously sulky features suddenly did what I can only describe as "clearing." His eyes now turned from the banana to the empty space below it on the floor, thence to the box and then back to the space again and from it up to the banana. Next moment, with a shriek of delight, he somersaulted over to the box in the highest of spirits and immediately began shoving it under the banana with every sign of confidence . . . no one who has seen such a thing can doubt that a genuine realization of the solution of a problem, equivalent to the mental exclamation "Aha!" occurs in anthropoid apes.

The chimpanzees that Robert Yerkes kept in the laboratory of Yale University even learned to appreciate the value of money, and in this respect showed themselves true cousins of that good businessman, *Homo sapiens*. One of the staff at the Institute of Animal Psychology, John B. Wolfe, trained them to set automatic machines going which contained special tidbits, by putting disks representing coins into the slot. He experimented with three kinds of these disks. A blue token elicited two bunches of grapes from the machine, a white one only obtained a single bunch, and the yellow tokens produced nothing. This difference was particularly well and rapidly grasped by the two young female chimpanzees, Bimba and Bula. They would also work for wages, lifting up weights, for example, in order to receive blue and white disks, and working out accurately what was due them. Yellow disks were immediately thrown in Mr. Wolfe's face. As soon as Bimba and Bula had had enough of the contents of the automatic machines, they stored up their "money" for future use.

The intellectual activity of the chimpanzees tested at Yale,

Suchum, and elsewhere diminished with their age. During the first years of life, human and chimpanzee infants were found to be absolutely equal mentally. In order to ascertain the extent of this resemblance the American scientists Mr. and Mrs. Winthrop Niles Kellogg undertook an uncommonly risky experiment. They brought up their little son Donald, as soon as he was a few weeks old, with a female infant chimpanzee of the same age, Gua. The two got on excellently together. At first Donald learned much more from Gua than she did from him. The chimpanzee retained her lead until both were three years old. The two playmates then entered upon separate courses of development, which differentiated the human child from the little chimpanzee. Some American scientists believe that this experiment may throw light upon racial history.

Among the animal psychologists working in the laboratory of Robert Yerkes and training anthropoid apes by extremely subtle methods to develop special mental capacities was the young Blanche Learned. She was particularly concerned with two extraordinarily intelligent young chimpanzees named Jim and Pansy. With true patience she noted down all the sounds they made, compared one with another, watched to see on what occasions Jim and Pansy uttered readily identifiable noises, and discovered that her nurselings actually conversed together in a kind of primitive language. She could even herself talk to Jim and Pansy without risking, like Johannes von Fischer, a box on the ear or a bite on the nose. In 1925 she published, in collaboration with Yerkes, a dictionary of the chimpanzee language containing seventy-five distinct sounds and detailed explanations of their meanings.

A still more comprehensive phrasebook with the title *Do You Speak Chimpanzee?* was brought out by Georg Schwidetzky, who considered the lemurs called *Indris* to be the ancestors of the higher apes and of mankind. Schwidetzky, a decidedly fanciful person, believed the chimpanzee language to be the mother of all the tongues of Man. But he suspected other apes, too, of having made contributions to the idioms spoken by human beings. "The long-tailed monkeys click their tongues," runs one of his unconsciously humorous statements, "and the tongue-click brings us to the primitive Mongols and bushmen." Schwidetzky's vocabulary was used by many visitors to zoos who desired to converse with their cousins from the primeval jungle. But in practice it did not turn out to be much good. At any rate, chimpanzees of mature age hardly took any notice of it.

The explanation of the mind of the chimpanzee represents an advance into new scientific territory. Its results have often been exaggerated and often deprecated in popular writing. The truth, as usual, lies between the two. The kind of importance the investigations of Yerkes and other scientists have for human racial history is emphatically stated by the Berlin animal psychologist Günter Tembrock.

The chimpanzee, too, plays and discovers tools and their uses, consequently the beginnings of self-conciousness occur in his case also. Though we may still be very far from having achieved a precision in psychology which may permit us to make a comprehensive comparison between man and the chimpanzee, we are nevertheless justified in affirming today that of all the animals which have hitherto been fairly closely studied the chimpanzee is not only physically the nearest to man but also shows evidence of the powers which mental evolution made generally available to mankind.

Thus, in the opinion of the zoologists named, the psychology of anthropoid apes not only bridges the gulf between the psychology of animals and that of mankind but also completes the picture presented by comparative anatomy of the origin of man. But a fundamental intellectual difference between anthropoid ape and primitive man does at the same time appear. Although anthropoid apes are quite capable of using tools, they never make them. After prolonged gnawing, one of Köhler's chimpanzees was able to straighten a broken wall bracket into a kind of fishing rod that could be exactly fitted into a hollow bamboo. Of this feat Lorenz rightly says: "But in order to make a proper tool, a hand axe for instance, an incomparably higher type of differentiation and a treatment continuously regulated by checking the success obtained, is required. And it really seems as though this very close connection between action and recognition is conditioned beforehand by a special central of his brain, possesses." Such centers have not yet been identified in anthropoid apes.

Do animals come from men?

Scientific theories are the product of their epochs, and since man's field of knowledge and his intellectual horizon change from age to age his theories are usually "dated" and seldom contain irrefutable truths. This is just as much the case with theories of the evolutionary process of humanity as it is with any other working hypothesis. Prehistorians in particular have to be especially careful not to become fossils themselves by sticking to old views to which they have grown attached. Paradoxical as it may sound, paleontology is an extremely active science, perpetually moving from one exciting phase to the next.

The "classical monkey theory" of Darwin's period mainly relied on morphological, embryological, and physiological evidence. It had however only relatively few finds of primitive human remains at its disposal. Even the Darwinians of the nineteenth century soon noticed the conspicuous contrast between the anthropoid apes with their special faculties for suspended movement, horizontally or vertically, and man with his upright walk. Yet the lack of other evidence caused them to conclude that man had formerly descended from trees in the primeval jungle and was, as Buffon put it, "an ape come down in the world."

In the twentieth century, however, it was proved that in the Tertiary period, long before the anthropoid apes of the primeval jungle appeared, there existed lightly built, nimble primates of a very low degree of specialization. They had no equipment for suspended movement and inhabited open grassy plains where few trees grew. The primeval jungle was not therefore the earlier epoch. On the contrary, the anthropoid apes had in the course of ages developed special adaptation to life in the jungle, thus separating from the stem type of primitive man far sooner than the Darwinian group of scientists had ever suspected.

Did it follow, then, that human beings did not descend from apelike ancestors but, conversely, that anthropoid apes descended from progenitors of human type? Various opinions were expressed and the primate stem was explored in all directions in the search for a human primary form. A new theory, that of the "exclusive" line of human development, went still farther. Permeated through and through with romantic feeling and emotional reservations, it claimed to detect human traits even in antique mammals and the most archaic forms of life right back to the beginning of things. In 1926 the anatomist and pathologist Max Westenhöfer, a pupil of Rudolf Virchow, published in Austria an essay with the astonishing title, *Man As the Oldest Form of Mammal*. It revived one of old Lorenz Oken's basic ideas. The uniquely special position of Man in nature, distinguishing him from all other living beings, must imply, so Westenhöfer stated, an equally unique and special kind of evolution.

"Although I at first took the conventional view of the descent of man," Westenhöfer writes, "I progressively abandoned it under the pressure of the results of my investigations and for more than ten years now have been of the opinion that Man does not descend from apes or apelike ancestors but is a race apart, going back directly to the mammalian root and only slightly differing from the presumptive primary stem of the mammals, which I consider to be his origin."

According to Westenhöfer the process of growth of every species has been determined and laid down in advance from the earliest beginning by means of the hidden aptitudes it is destined to develop. Breeds of animals have not evolved in the course of geological history one from another, but side by side, coming from an unknown root. The Darwinian family tree must be replaced by a "shrub" of life, the branches of which grow separately from a single point without touching one another. And the situation with regard to mammals is also a special one. They did not arise from the primeval mammals of reptilian type that have been extracted from the Jurassic and Cretaceous deposits of former times. Their root, their primary stock, was nothing less than Man himself.

Similar views, though somewhat more temperately expressed, were advanced by the curator of the Munich public collections, the paleontologist Edgar Dacqué. He considered that animals were unsuccessful attempts to evolve Man. "At the moment in the history of nature," he wrote in his book entitled *The Prototype,* "when the anthropoid apes, as often happened, split off from the primary anthropoid stem still unknown to us and formed their own genera, specialized in various ways, the character of the fully developed human being was revealed. For it was only then that he could be represented in pure form, as a type. In this way that which had previously impeded the rise of the essential and kept it hidden was stripped away from the phenomenon as a whole."

There are still today, especially in theosophical circles, many disciples of Westenhöfer and Dacqué who confidently affirm that the evolution of species has not proceeded in the serial form hitherto assumed but in the opposite direction. There first appeared in the world a prototype, still undifferentiated, which carried within itself the image of future Man. Then, as early geologic times progressed, this undifferentiated type gradually gave birth to all the other creatures still retained in the womb of earth, some surviving and some dying out, till *Homo sapiens* had reached perfection in his present form.

This theory, which was announced in a variety of extreme and less extreme terms, appears fascinating at first sight, like so many philosophical systems. Like them, too, it flatters human pride but is not susceptible of proof. Exact natural scientists, moreover, immediately pointed out that the allegedly "unknown roots" had in fact for the most part long been known, and that primitive unicellular organisms, worms, coelacanths, Ichthyosauria, Insectivora, and monkeys — whether or not they contain the germ of the idea of mankind — must continue to be considered by scientists what they have hitherto been: genuine unicellular organisms, worms, coelacanths, Ichthyosauria, Insectivora, and monkeys.

Other theories of evolution, which rely less upon speculation and sophistical argument than on concrete facts, were much more cordially welcomed by the learned world and led to a thoroughgoing revision of the ideas hitherto accepted of the development of the human race. They did not, as was occasionally asserted in partisan publications, deal Darwin's doctrine its deathblow. The "classical monkey theory" was completely overhauled, extended, corrected, and brought into line with contemporary knowledge. This metamorphosis, scarcely noticed by the public, occurred in the seclusion of libraries, museums, and laboratories, but its stages were just as stormy and full of surprises as those of historical Darwinism.

Was our original ancestor a lemur?

About the year 1918 the Australian scientist Frederic Wood Jones entered the limelight with an astonishing hypothesis. He had for a long time been closely concerned with the Indonesian dwarf lemur, a little prosimian already studied by Alfred Russel Wallace and designated by him as a possible ancestor of the higher apes. This attractive animal was found by Wood Jones to possess certain features distinguishing it from all prosimians and apes, with the exception of the anthropoids, and relating it closely to mankind. There were, moreover, a large number of extinct members of the family which were still more like human beings. The natives of the region called it by the somewhat creepy name of "ghost creature."

The director of the Sarawak Museum in Borneo, Eric Mjöberg, who had been keeping up a lively correspondence with Wood Jones about this curious little creature, suddenly received a flood of inquiries from all parts of the world. Scientific institutes, mammal specialists, anatomists, and anthropologists required at all costs, as soon as possible, skeletons and specimens of the ghost creature preserved in spirits. "If you can let me have three and a half gills of ghost-creature blood," ran the gushing request of one scientist, who wished to establish a blood relationship between the dwarf lemur and man, "I shall be grateful to you for the rest of my life!" Owing to Wood Jones and his book *The Problem of Man's Ancestry*, the ghost creature had become famous overnight.

The fame was due to the highly developed, twofold accommodation center in its brain, this being a group of nerve cells which directed the correct focusing of the eyes upon the object under observation. The animal could stare, and he had plastic vision. These were the very faculties that zoologists believed had given the first impetus to the development of the refinements of the human brain. Apart from this, much in the bodily frame and physical activity of the dwarf lemur seemed very human. For this reason Wood Jones ventured to designate the little prosimian as the direct radical form of mankind.

An era of "lemur theories" then began. The philologist in charge of the German Library at Leipzig, Georg Schwidetzky, preferred another prosimian, one that belonged to the true lemur family — the indri of Madagascar, which had no tail and walked upright. He compared the shape of the nose, ears, and lips of this prosimian, its hands, growth of beard, and voice with those of *Homo sapiens* and maintained that the aboriginal indri could still be discerned in any human being.

Strangely enough, many people found it much more agreeable to be descended from lemurs than from anthropoid apes. Indris and dwarf lemurs were not as a rule familiar to the average citizen and he could not form any very exact idea of what they looked like. Anthropoid apes, on the other hand, were well known and for some reason the notion that we might once have looked something like them offended the pride and self-confidence of mankind. Prosimians grew steadily more and more popular, while the dwarf lemur easily outstripped the indri in the race, and its ancestor does in fact seem to have been a hopeful sprig on the human family tree.

This view was confirmed even by those scientists who remained loyal to the "classical monkey theory." They find room, today, for the dwarf lemur and its fossil brothers as a suborder between the prosimians and the apes. But they consider the little creature a far less important animal than the chimpanzee, which is still at present regarded by a majority of zoologists and anthropologists, despite its peculiar evolution into an acrobat of the primeval forest, as man's nearest blood relation in the literal meaning of the word.

Blood is a very special kind of fluid

All attempts to eliminate anthropoid apes from the ancestry of mankind emphasize the obvious difference between man and the inhabitants of the jungle, just as all opposing attempts emphasize the many features that are common to both. Criticism was leveled at the "lemur" and "separate development" theories very early along these lines. If Man were to be regarded as directly descended from prosimians of the early Tertiary period or even from archaic aboriginal mammals, it was argued, the anthropoid apes must have inherited the features and modes of behavior in question independently of man, although this could not be reconciled with the data of genetics. Comparative anatomy has assembled a great deal of evidence that points to a true blood relationship between man, chimpanzee, and gorilla. Weinert, the most consistent champion of the classical monkey theory in Germany, deduced that these three forms could only have issued from a common root and classified them together under the name of Higher Primates. The circumstantial evidence he adduces is impressive.

Man and chimpanzee are the only primates that share with the gorilla the possession of frontal cavities and a peculiar formation of large cardiac arteries. But they differ from the gorilla in lacking the central wristbone, in having lost the intermaxillary and the palatal folds, and in the form of the ear. The kidneys, the spermatic cords, and blood groups are the same, according to Weinert, in man and chimpanzee. Even the duration of pregnancy is identical. Finally, the most striking proof is provided by the blood itself. The method of diagnosis of blood serum used in criminal cases to assist in the determination whether a suspicious bloodstain is animal or human seems to incriminate the chimpanzee beyond doubt. Its blood darkens the serum of an experimental animal, previously injected with human blood, to such an extent in the test tube that scarcely any difference can be noted between it and the human blood.

Weinert's theory of the higher primates culminates in the following argument: "The chimpanzee is related to no other animal, but is related to man, through the common possession of a number of inherited attributes. It follows that at one time a race of anthropoid apes existed, descendants of which survive today in the forms of chimpanzee and man, all other present-day anthropoid apes having detached themselves before this last separation took place."

What, then, did this genealogical tree of anthropoid apes look like and where did it come from? When did the climbing specialists become detached from it? It appears from a wealth of paleontological evidence that toward the end of the geological Middle Ages primitive Insectivora evolved from aboriginal mammals of marsupial type, which still retained many of the attributes of reptiles. These Insectivora became the ancestors of all the "higher primates" of Linnaeus. Even today animal forms exist such as the tree shrews of southern Asia which could be just as well classified insectivores as prosimians. The prosimians spread over the whole world at the beginning of the Tertiary period. They were the ancestors of the fox-faced lemur in Madagascar and the spider monkeys and capuchin monkeys in America. Only the dwarf lemurs retained their aboriginal characteristics. In compensation, they developed brain and visual capacities. They, or close relatives of them, were the ancestors of a whole host of Old World monkeys, including the Mesopithecus, whose skull King Otto's Bavarian soldier had carried off from Pikermi to Munich. Most of these Old World monkeys became specialized, branched off by themselves, and lost the opportunity of higher evolution. They include the baboons, long-tailed monkeys, black lemurs, and the *Semnopithecus* groups. Later on the gibbon, too, branched off and is still regarded by many zoologists, following Haeckel, as the closest relative of mankind. And finally the "wild man of the woods" of Linnaeus' time, the orangutan, also left the human genealogical tree.

If all these terms of the equation are canceled out mathematically we are left with a relatively unspecialized group of anthropoid apes with many potentialities for living in trees, on grassy plains, or in caves, and also for physical or mental development. In Europe, in addition to many bones of the *Dryopithecus* discovered by Lartet, a fossil ape — at first supposed human — was found as early as the beginning of the nineteenth century. Today it is called the *Paidopithex*. Remains of various types of *Dryopithecus* are also frequent in Tertiary strata in Asia. The members of this group have many of the same attributes as the gorilla, the chimpanzee, and Man but the majority of them make a more human impression than the anthropoid apes and a more apelike one than human beings. Weinert describes them as the point of departure for his Higher Primates.

The gorilla, in Weinert's opinion, occupies a special position. Its ancestors seem to have gone their own way at an early stage before the forefathers of mankind and the chimpanzee had separated. It is considered probable by the adherents of the classical monkey theory that the common progenitor of primitive man and the prim-

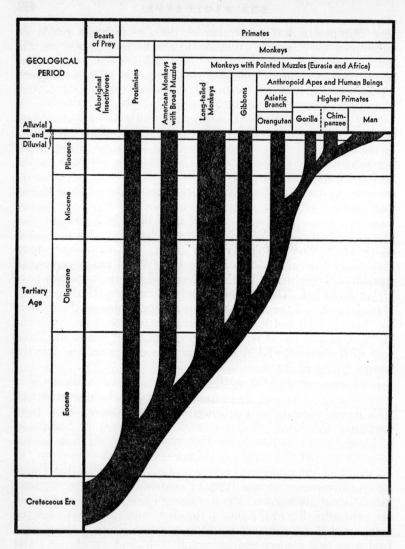

Weinert's genealogical tree of the higher animals.

itive chimpanzee was a member of the *Dryopithecus* group, an anthropoid ape of simple structure but also of lively disposition and great adaptability. Those of his descendants which took to the jungle developed their climbing aptitudes and became chimpanzees. Those which overran the savannahs developed the upright posture and mental powers. They became primitive men.

This theory explained a good deal, and yet it did not seem completely satisfactory. The species of *Dryopithecus* which was known by the middle of the century did indeed include unspecialized forms, but no creature of so simple a structure as to represent the common progenitor convincingly. The one fact remained that Man was in many respects a more original type than any anthropoid ape known and that he had nevertheless, or possibly for that very reason, managed to become cosmopolitan, prudent, and intelligent and actively carve out a career for himself. Only one creature existed which was just as original in type as Man: that was the unborn anthropoid ape while still in the womb. Here anatomy once more stepped in with a hypothesis at the first glance surprising and even alarming. It led up to the statement that Man was physically, at bottom, nothing but an ape that had remained infantile.

The baby ape in Man

Herder, in his rough sketch of a theory of evolution, had once put the question: "What prevented the animal most resembling a human being [the ape] from becoming one?" In the twentieth century this question was inverted. "What prevented Man from remaining an animal?" Science found that there was a good deal to prevent him. To be candid, Man is a defective creature, unable to adapt himself to special purposes and lacking the equipment to do so. He is compelled to make his own tools and clothing, with which animals are endowed forthwith by nature. He is not a "complete" being, set upon a definite course like a mature anthropoid ape. He remains all his life in a process of growth. What could be more typically childish a trait? A young animal *grows*, making eager trial of its environment and perfecting its adaptability thereto. The adult animal, on the other hand, *is*. It has hardly anything else to learn.

Even physically Man has preserved many attributes that in apes only occur as embryonic or infantile characteristics — for example, hairlessness, faint coloration, and the proportion of the head. The Dutch anatomist Ludwig Bolk was referring to these conditions when he wrote a remarkable book in 1926 entitled *The Problem of Human Incarnation*. Bolk asserted in so many words that from the anatomical point of view human incarnation was not an advance but a regression. He alleged there were mutations that initiated repressions and might keep the animate being they affected at a childish stage right into old age. He said that human beings had crystallized from a series of such mutations. Even as an adult, Man still showed signs of the stage of early youth passed through by his animal forebears. Thus, according to Bolk, Man had been arrested at the level of growth of the embryo of an ape, and the embryo of a primitive chimpanzee at that, his development into a specialist had been delayed and it was only for this reason that he had acquired a versatility unrivaled by any other animal.

The animal kingdom contains a number of instances of neoteny — the retention of larval or youthful conditions beyond the period of sexual maturity right up to death — which supported Bolk's theory. The animal hitherto found to exhibit this phenomenon in its clearest form is a Mexican salamander, the axolotl. This strange creature has been known to zoologists ever since the discovery of America. It looks like a large gill-bearing larva of its own species, but propagates itself in this state and invariably, so it was thought until 1865, remains in this condition for the rest of its life. Cuvier, Alexander von Humboldt, and many other investigators had once racked their brains over the mystery of the axolotl. What was really the matter with the creature did not become evident until suddenly, in 1865, in the Jardin des Plantes, certain young axolotls kept in open water lost their gills, dorsal and caudal fringes, and turned into proper land salamanders. Thereupon attempts were made wherever axolotls were kept in aquariums to accelerate this change by cutting away the gills and radically varying living conditions. And soon the French zoologist Dumeril, the German geneticist Weismann, and in particular Fräulein Marie von Chauvin at Freiburg actually succeeded in artificially turning aquatic, larva-shaped and gilled salamanders into the terrestrial and lung-possessing variety.

The axolotl had thus at one time, no doubt under pressure from variation in its living conditions, carried out a retrogressive evolution. It did not in this case, as usually happened with other salamanders, turn into a perfect terrestrial amphibian, but remained arrested at its infantile larva stage. A somewhat similar transformation was observed later in other batrachians and several species of insects. Bolk concluded that it might also have been so with Man. Man resembles the embryo of an ape, with his similarly large head and similar development of the limbs, and he was thus given the great chance of perfecting his brain as a unique organ.

This theory not only took account of the hitherto disconcerting fact that the human anatomy is extremely primitive compared with that of the ape: but it also agreed with the observations of the psychologists. As Konrad Lorenz put it:

> Every study undertaken by mankind is the genuine outcome of curiosity, a kind of game. All the data of natural science, which are responsible for Man's domination of the world, originated in activities which were indulged in exclusively for the sake of amusement. When Benjamin Franklin drew sparks from the tail of his kite he was thinking as little of the lightning conductor as Hertz, when he investigated electrical waves, was thinking of radio transmission. Anyone who has experienced in his own person how easily the inquisitiveness of a child at play can grow into the life work of a naturalist will never doubt the fundamental similarity of games and study. The inquisitive child disappears entirely from the wholly animal nature of the mature chimpanzee. But the child is far from being buried in the man, as Nietzsche thinks. On the contrary, it rules him absolutely.

Ludwig Bolk's "foetal theory" and its psychological complement stormed many scientific strongholds. Jean Rostand, the greatest biologist in France, praised its ingenuity and discernment. The Belgian evolutionist Lucien Cuenot revived it in 1945 in an acute form, maintaining that man was "an example of neoteny in a chimpanzee or gorilla" with the physical characteristics of an infant and retarded growth, while modern chimpanzees and gorillas on the other hand had passed rapidly through this stage and become expert acrobats.

There were, however, skeptics who pointed out that accelerated as well as delayed development characterized human beings and that the apparently repressive limitations should be regarded as signs of domestication, because man had domesticated himself of his own accord and in so doing retained, like many domestic animals, certain childish traits and an unprejudiced childish outlook on phenomena.

Science accepted and made use of Bolk's discoveries up to a point. Nevertheless, the idea that humanity might be derived directly from a sexually mature chimpanzee or gorilla embryo seemed rather perverse to most investigators. The restrictions in development were admitted, at least in part; yet this still meant that the creature affected by them, the very first of all primates, the mysterious earliest progenitor of anthropoid apes as of mankind, had not yet been discovered. Would it be necessary to grope still farther back into the Middle Tertiary period for the crossroads? Had some animate being existed in those days which fulfilled absolutely all the preliminary conditions necessary to traverse the transition stage between beast and Man in times to come?

Going even farther back into the Middle Tertiary meant leaving chimpanzee and gorilla cousins behind, turning one's back on Uncle *Dryopithecus*, and seeking the real source of the higher primates. According to the conclusions reached about the middle of the twentieth century, it was there that fossil evidence might be found for the historic and fateful epoch of transition.

Back to the gibbon

Some of the many African expeditions that Leakey undertook with his wife and his colleagues in the region of Lake Victoria after 1948 brought particularly valuable finds of fossil anthropoid apes to light. But were they actually anthropoid apes? According to their teeth they certainly were, but the skulls recalled the lower primates, and the limbs were proportioned like those of very early specimens of humanity.

One of these unique prehistoric apes, *Limnopithecus*, looked like a highly simplified ancestor of the gibbon. The other, the *Proconsul* discovered by Hopwood and Mrs. Leakey on the East African island of Rusinga (many remains of its bones being afterwards found at other places), was apparently the descendant of a type resembling the *Limnopithecus* and to all appearance might just as well have been the forefather of the chimpanzee as of mankind. The scientists Leakey, Le Gros Clark, and Thomas, who made a thorough examination of the proconsuls, estimated them to be about 20,000,000 years old. They would thus be far older than *Dryopithecus* and the other anthropoid apes that preceded the chimpanzee, and they were decidedly "more human." They did not have eyebrow ridges, acrobats' arms, or climbers' feet. In another respect, too, they bridged the gulf to the pure monkey. There were no compact forests in the Victoria valley region in their day. They had undoubtedly lived on the plains, racing on all fours through the bare landscape from one group of trees to another, and perhaps they could already walk half erect if necessary.

"But the erect gait is the preliminary condition for the characteristic human enlargement of the brain," wrote the Göttingen anthropologist Gerhard Heberer in an account of the proconsuls, "so the acquisition of this posture represents the first decisive stage of the long process of metamorphosis which culminates in the crossing of the Rubicon between beast and Man." The finds at Lake Victoria

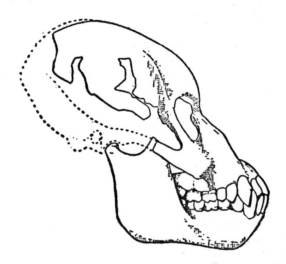

The oldest prehistoric primate known. Skull of the middle Tertiary *Proconsul africanus,* about half lifesize. The *Proconsul* group probably stood at a decisive parting of the ways. At this point the arboreal forest creatures separated from the erect rovers of the plains. This primitive anthropoid ape still retained all the faculties required for both kinds of movement. It was slender and lightly built, could climb well, and also run and leap with agility. The position of the eyes in the skull and the occipital gap placed far back in it indicate that the animal walked on all fours. Its limbs prove that it could not have been so highly specialized a climber and swinger as the present-day anthropoid ape.

are not perhaps in the direct line of our ancestors, but they do represent the start of this transitional stage. They are accurate "ancestral models" for the creature that bore within itself the chance of becoming human. This new paleontological evidence does not transform the picture of humanity twenty or twenty-five years ago into a primitive chimpanzee swinging from a branch, nor into an impish little lemur, but a creature of the *Proconsul* type. The proconsuls were the common historical basis for both anthropoid apes and human beings. The racial line which was to lead eventually to the large primates of the primitive jungle began its isolation from the branch of evolution which produced man in close proximity to the *Proconsul* group.

In an old number of *Chambers's Journal*, dated November 1927 and rescued from oblivion by Willy Ley, a certain Captain W. Hichens relates all sorts of rumors and conjectures dealing with legendary and still undiscovered animals in the heart of Africa. The most interesting of the fabulous beasts mentioned in Hichens' article are the Agogwe, little pygmy-like "furred men" also referred to by other hunters and travelers. The captain writes that he saw them with his own eyes.

> Some years ago [his article states] I was sent on an official lion-hunt in the Ussute and Simbiti forests. As I was waiting for a lion in a clearing I noticed two small brown hairy creatures emerge from the jungle, run across the clearing and disappear again into the thicket on the other side. They resembled small human beings, were about four feet high, ran along upright and were covered with brownish-red hair. My native hunter stared at them in mingled fear and astonishment. He said they were Agogwe, little furred men, who were hardly ever seen alive. I made desperate attempts to find them but failed to do so in the almost impenetrable jungle. They might have been monkeys; but if so they were no common ones, neither baboons nor marmosets nor long-tailed monkeys nor any other species found in Tanganyika. What were they?

What were they, really? All sorts of rumors are current which describe "beast-men" of this kind in the dense rain forests of Africa. They can of course all be dismissed as hunters' gossip. But there are a few people, like the African explorer Attilio Gatti, who are convinced of the existence in Africa of small hairy creatures, for the most part walking erect. Although there may be nothing in those tales, it is nevertheless interesting that the region alleged to be inhabited by the mysterious Agogwe is that in which excavation brought the proconsuls to light.

What did the ancestors and the posterity of the proconsuls look like? A thoroughgoing inventory of all the remains found resembling those of anthropoid apes and dating from the Oligocene and Miocene ages, in other words the Middle Tertiary, upwards of

30,000,000 years ago, leads to an astonishing vindication of the old master, Haeckel. He had at one time wrongly described the gibbon as the first cousin of mankind, but he had also suggested that a prehistoric gibbon might have been the ancestor of the higher primates and thus eventually of man. He now seems to have been proved correct. All the archaic prehistoric anthropoid apes whose remains have been found in central Europe, Egypt, and East Africa — including the *Propliopithecus*, the *Pliopithecus*, and the recently discovered *Limnopithecus* — were prehistoric gibbons, though admittedly without the special equipment peculiar to the modern species of gibbon. The gibbon, which is the most graceful and attractive of primates, is today an accomplished arboreal trapeze artist, a "bird in the form of a monkey," and yet not a genuine anthropoid ape. But at one time it lived in unspecialized form, full of promise for the future, on wooded plains; and from this agreeable, affectionate, and ingenuous creature, which lacks entirely all the familiar vices of the monkey, it seems that the proconsuls and thus the anthropoid apes and also the human race directly or indirectly proceed. If Bolk's foetal theory could be accepted Man might be a sexually mature prehistoric gibbon or *Proconsul* foetus, but certainly not a chimpanzee or gorilla arrested at the embryonic stage. For prehistoric chimpanzees and gorillas appeared on the scene long after the transition stage of the forefathers of mankind.

It may reconcile many people to the theory of evolution to learn that our first parents of the Middle Tertiary were not fierce and brutish but childish and amiable. However, as the naturalist Fritz Kahn said, "We have to face a second fact which cannot unfortunately be disregarded. Between our gibbon-like forefathers and the human beings of today comes the procession of those ancestors which developed not only good but also bad qualities. Man acquired not only reason and morality but also immorality as his brain evolved."

The gap between the forms represented by the prehistoric gibbon and *Proconsul* and the first human beings was not filled, as all the subsequent finds of semihuman and early human types prove, by such arboreal creatures as the "classical monkey theory" postulated, but by denizens of open country running on two legs. It is assumed today that this mode of progress was begun by the "human animal," between approximately 12,000,000 and 15,000,000 years ago. It is not so very difficult to deduce from the fossil remains of bones the kind of gait employed by the creature in question. The shape of the bones of the pelvis and limbs discloses the attitude of the body as a whole. The position of the occipital gap indicates whether the skull was balanced by gravity and, finally, the inclination of the eye cavities gives the angle at which vision was directed to the earth's surface. All the finds hitherto collated show clearly that the upright posture had evolved some millions of years before the enlargement of the brain. The phase of transition to humanity began in the Miocene period with the development of the two-legged creature and ended at the threshold of the Pleistocene with the "Prometheus" who knew fire, after between four and six hundred thousand generations.

The present phase of the investigation of the descent of man, the most active since the days of Darwin and Haeckel, has accordingly led to a rearrangement of its conceptions. However, it has not called into question the principle of the derivation of the human race from the primate stem. To ignore this fact would be, in Heberer's words, to put oneself "on practically the same level as a man who declared there was no sense in the Atomic Theory." The wide difference between present-day anthropoid apes and *Homo sapiens*, which some decades ago afforded pretexts for the theories of "exclusive development" and "lemur origin," becomes perfectly intelligible in the light of the long autonomous history of humanity dating from the Middle Tertiary. Our new knowledge has been acquired at the very time when we are making strenuous efforts to explain the position and significance of mankind in the global scheme. The knowledge is opportune. For our conception of man would be suspended in a void, unrelated to anything, were it not firmly anchored in that understanding of human origins which biologists, anthropologists, and prehistorians, by their gropings, conjectures, research, and calculation, have gained in two hundred years of painful investigation among details.

By what process of crystallization, then, did the primates give rise to humanity as we know it? Was it a gradual and smooth succession of mutations and metamorphoses? Many students of heredity assume that it was, but others are skeptical. They have introduced two new ideas into genetics: that of "gross mutation," an abrupt variation bringing about a particularly important change, and "key mutation," involving fresh creation. They believe that only such variations, or "creative acts," which may not be accessible to our understanding, can break new ground in racial history. After the pattern of future development has once been drawn, the normal "petty mutations" set about further evolution of the new type and its perfect adaptation to the environment.

The zoologist Wilhelm Ludwig, a leading German exponent of

the theory of natural selection, made an interesting comparison to explain the process by which the "beast-man" was humanized. He compared the production of the human figure with the construction of an automobile. A key mutation, in the shape of the gasoline engine that replaced the horse, was first necessary to enable the motor vehicle to arise at all from the horse-drawn cart. This key mutation was only realized in a few factories and drafting rooms. Further gross mutations followed in quick succession, which produced serviceable types suited to conditions and demand. It was only then that development, properly so called, began. The vehicle proved a success, a steep increase in the number of cars ensued, the original type produced many subsidiary forms, large and small, open and closed, cheap and expensive, racing cars, and transport trucks. Those that proved capable of surviving and found buyers eliminated their less valuable competitors. Environment, fashion, and requirements effected further subdivision and selection of the subsidiary types until at last the modern makes of car could make their appearance in the market.

It is only very seldom that paleontological research discovers the bearer of a key mutation, in other words a true connective link between two groups of forms. Ludwig's illustration of the automobile explains this too. If ashes, dust, mud, or lava were now to cover the earth, excavators a thousand years hence might well find complete motor vehicles of innumerable subsidiary types all over the place. But their links with the horse-drawn cart would only be discovered if an archeologist especially favored by fortune were to stumble by chance upon a fossilized factory-museum.

The island of Rusinga, where the bones of the proconsuls were found, was a "fossilized factory-museum" of this kind, in which the very first preliminary sketch for the figure of a higher primate able to walk upright had been preserved. However, still more elaborate and enlightening "workshops for construction of the human figure" have been discovered in the last few decades, some of them long before the proconsuls were unearthed, in the Far East and South Africa. They indicate the course of later events, the traversal of the transitional stage between beast and man, the development of the use of tools and implements, the recognition of the purposes for which fire could be employed, the eating of the fruit of the tree of knowledge and the crime of Cain. Finally the soil of Europe disclosed how from a profusion of prehuman and early human types and subsidiary forms the strongest and most active scion of all, *Homo sapiens*, evolved.

XV

PROMETHEUS AND THE GIANTS

Racial politics and the Steinheim skull

BERCKHEMER, Chief Curator of the Natural History Museum of Württemberg and a modest and most discerning scholar, maintained relations with the owner of a gravel pit, just as Otto Schoetensack had once done. Herr Sigrist of Steinheim on the Mur occasionally supplied him with interesting fossils of the Middle Pleistocene age. On July 24, 1933, Herr Sigrist called on Berckhemer in considerable excitement and reported that he had found a highly petrified primitive human skull in his pit. The rubble had hardened round the skull to such an extent that it could not be extracted.

Berckhemer at once left for Steinheim. He expected to find a more recent specimen of Heidelberg man. He was led to this conclusion both by the layer in which the skull had been found and by the animal remains hitherto obtained from the pit. When Böck, his mounting assistant, had extracted the skull in masterly fashion from the rock, all sorts of surprising facts emerged. At first glance the Steinheim man looked surprisingly like a female chimpanzee. He had massive eyebrow ridges like an "ape man." His skull capacity was practically equal to that of the *Pithecanthropus*. The smoothly rounded shape of his occiput and certain other features were nevertheless very reminiscent of those of modern man. Was he a primitive Neanderthal specimen, as Weinert considered? Or a primitive *sapiens?* Or might he actually be the common ancestor of both these human types? At any rate his features were a queer mixture of chimpanzee, ape man, Neanderthal type, and modern human being.

The discovery of the Steinheim man had certain political consequences, since it occurred at the time when the doctrine of race, up to that time a most respected scientific preoccupation, was being used as a political weapon in Germany. The powers of the Third Reich turned their attention to those who knew most about the faces of humanity — anthropologists.

They found that even in Germany the anthropologists believed all the races of mankind formed a sort of hereditary community and no doubt went back to a common stem. According to the doctrine, therefore, the Nordic man belonged to the same hereditary community as those fellow citizens of other races whom, precisely on account of their difference of race, it was intended to eradicate. He was the same as they were and had the same original ancestor. This was an exceptionally painful discovery for the German race-politicians, for it was absolutely opposed to the National Socialist ideology and its practices of extermination.

How could this dilemma be solved? Should Darwin's theory be scrapped? Some people were actually heard to damn Darwinism as a "theory of racelessness." Others literally turned their eyes to the moon in the hope of detecting the cradle of Nordic man there. A book was circulated called *Lost Civilization*. It had been written by a man called Eugen George and asserted nothing less than that the Nordic race had reached the earth the last time the moon hit it. Other hypotheses, rather less fantastic, denied the unity of the human race or attempted to relegate the origin of the modern races of mankind to the remotest mists of antiquity.

All such endeavors to rehabilitate the officially recognized flower of races were received by anthropologists with extreme distaste, to their great credit. They adhered unswervingly to the theory of evolution in its contemporary form and frankly described their views, even to the authorities, although it was not easy for them to do so. The political authorities repeatedly requested them to provide serviceable scientific foundations for the National Socialist view of life. Since they could not find any such foundations, German anthropologists worked on, as any scientist does under any dictatorship, in an extremely sultry intellectual climate. Meanwhile, every ancient skull, every crumbling hand axe they disinterred suddenly acquired a political significance.

In these explosive circumstances scientists had to take notice of the Steinheim man, the puzzling fossil, part *Pithecanthropus*, part Neanderthal type, and part *Homo sapiens*, discovered by the modest and thoroughly unpolitical Professor Berckhemer: for the skull from Herr Sigrist's gravel pit had suddenly become quite especially popular with German race-politicians. He must surely be the long sought ancestor of the Nordic race! The Nordic race would then be some 200,000 or 300,000 years old, which would be reason enough for distinguishing it from the other races.

A flat-nosed primitive man with massive eyebrows, thus spotlighted by the highest authorities in the state, naturally attracted a good deal of attention. Soon the troubled waters subsided and the pipedream of the Nordic Adam faded like all illusions conceived under similar circumstances. The same sort of human remains were found in England, France, Italy, and East Africa. Even hybrid forms of these and primitive Neanderthal types were discovered in Asia Minor. And all these finds appeared to belong to an extremely interesting group, that from which *Homo sapiens* directly evolved.

The Steinheim man and his relatives probably represent the ancestral group of all the modern races of mankind, including of course the forefathers of the Nordic race, though they cannot be given any special position in it. The unmasking of the much discussed man of Steinheim began a new chapter in prehistoric research.

Homo sapiens *rises from the mist*

When the English dentist Alvan Theophilus Marston discovered his Swanscombe man two years after the find of Steinheim, together with some six hundred stone tools from the Acheulean period, the two primitive types were at once compared. "To all appearances, the skulls of Swanscombe and Steinheim resemble each other very closely," wrote the anthropologist Morant, who examined the Swanscombe fragments. "It is not improbable that they belong to the same Acheulean group. It may be conjectured that this group either included the direct ancestors of *Homo sapiens* or was at least more nearly related to the latter than Neanderthal man."

This undeniably important statement did not agree with the current views of a direct line of human development. For the *sapiens*-like Swanscombe and Steinheim men were some 200,000 or 300,000 years old and consequently twice the age of the much more primitive-looking Neanderthal men. They did resemble early types but had already clearly undergone further evolution in the direction of modern man. They had first appeared, as was proved by further finds and research, in the warm climate of the Second Intermediate Ice Age and had then vanished during the ensuing glacial period. Did they really vanish? Or were the Aurignacian and Cro-Magnon men their grandchildren and great-grandchildren? Was there, as the French anthropologist H. V. Vallois said, a "second line" of the evolution of humanity? Or were there, as his German colleague Heberer assumed, actually three such lines, one that had led to *Pithecanthropus*, a second from which the Neanderthal type had arisen, and a third that culminated in *Homo sapiens*? One thing at any rate was certain: the finds at Swanscombe and Steinheim could only be fitted with difficulty into the graduated system hitherto accepted.

The same objection applied to other primitive human remains brought to light in very recent times. In the cave of Fontéchevade

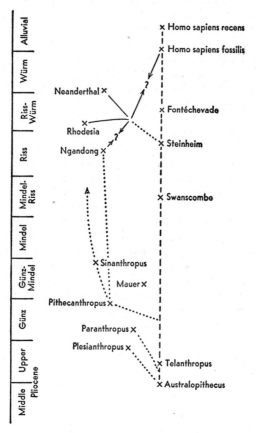

Probable evolution of the *sapiens* type according to Falkenburger. The time scale bears no relation to the various durations of the epochs.

the Frenchwoman explorer Germaine Henri-Martin discovered beneath a solid stalactite deposit a skull and some remains of a frontal bone which had an extremely modern aspect. Here too some flint implements were also unearthed which Henri Breuil considered dated from the oldest Stone Age, prior to the advent of Neanderthal man. The Fontéchevade man must have come on the scene shortly after the men of Steinheim and Swanscombe, but a good 50,000 years before the Neanderthal type. He would certainly have fascinated the race-politicians still more than the Württemberg showpiece, for he even lacked the apelike ridges above the eyes. By 1947, when he appeared, history had long since made a clean sweep of exaggerated racial theories.

Heberer gave the name of "Pre-sapiens Group" to all these specimens. They were a very mixed lot, including Leakey's strange finds at Kanam and Kanjera, as well as an occipital bone discovered by the Italian Battaglia near Quinzano, not far from Verona. Heberer declared that the (genuine) Piltdown skull ought also to be added to the series of *sapiens*-like types. They included specimens of a thoroughly modern aspect, though undoubtedly dating from the Middle Pleistocene period, such as those of Fontéchevade and Kanjera, the Frenchman Vallois being convinced of the former's identity with the culturally creative Late Ice Age Man. But specimens of Neanderthal type like those of Swanscombe and Steinheim were also included. To all appearance a new "workshop for the production of mankind" had been set up in the Middle Pleistocene epoch and developed the "early man" model into that of *Homo sapiens*.

It seemed as though there had been very strange happenings in the general evolution of humanity before the rise, some 150,000 years ago, of the two clearly distinguishable forms of the typical Neanderthal specimen and the *Homo sapiens* of the Ice Age. In Palestine, on Mount Carmel, on the shores of Lake Tiberias and near Nazareth, an Anglo-American expedition in charge of the explorers Theodore McCown and Dorothy Garrod unearthed eighteen primitive human beings between the years 1925 and 1935. They resembled Neanderthal man, but on the one hand their skulls were much more primitive and on the other their limbs were far more modern. These "Sukhul men" varied to an extraordinary extent. A female skeleton found at Tabun was only four feet nine inches long, while a male one discovered near Carmel was a foot taller. In addition to skulls of Neanderthal type others were found with high foreheads, well rounded occiputs, and pronounced chins. In addition to *sapiens*-like thighbones others were collected which recalled those of the *Pithecanthropus*. And all these Sukhul men were older than the Neanderthal specimens of Europe. They are believed today, no doubt correctly, to have been half-breeds deriving from pre-Neanderthal and pre-*sapiens* types. The Near East region, the great land bridge between Europe, Asia, and Africa, was a likely place for such hybrids to have arisen during the climatically occasioned migrations of the Last Intermediate Ice Age.

The unique finds, half approximating to Neanderthal type and half resembling the *sapiens* group, and very ancient into the bargain, which were made at Taubach in the valley of the Ilm, have already been mentioned. With these were associated in 1914 the remains of the skeleton of a child that had probably been drowned, firmly embedded in the limestone of the riverbank in the neighboring village of Ehringsdorf, and in 1925 the shattered skull of a young woman. In the opinion of the anthropologist Weidenreich these fragments, showing a mixture of extremely ancient signs and others indicative of progress, were also pre-Neanderthal. The people of Taubach and Ehringsdorf may have been the descendants of Steinheim man, in which case the lateral branch of true Neanderthal man might have been derived from them at a later stage.

Science has not yet delivered its final verdict on pre-*sapiens* man and his relation to other semihuman and early human types. All that is certain is that he stood quite near to our genetic line of evolution, that his geological age lies relatively far back but at most no farther than the Middle Ice Age, and that interbreeding occurred between him and the pre-Neanderthal types and possibly also descendants of *Pithecanthropus*. The few traces of him available for study are not enough to justify the statement recently made that all other early specimens of humanity were abortive nephews and grandnephews of *Homo sapiens*, recessive to animality; or the statement made in an article of 1952 on the racial history of mankind to the effect that these other early specimens were "extinct at an incomplete stage at the beginning of the Quaternary period" (the Ice Age). Such traces are still insufficient to support wild conjectures of a legendary age of *Homo sapiens* reaching right back to the Early Pleistocene or Tertiary period and to promote present-day man to the rank of "firstborn," ancestor of all semihuman types or even of the whole stem of Primates.

In reality the discovery of Steinheim, Swanscombe, and Fontéchevade man made no essential difference. The evidence for the theory of evolution was only enriched by a few new transitional forms, filling yet another gap in the human family tree. The recognition that certain races of mankind already possessed features indicative of progress 200,000 or 300,000 years ago does not disprove our ancestral kinship with an early type of man twice as old, with a semihuman being ten times as old, and with the proconsuls, seventy times as old. At most it dethrones Neanderthal man, already in any case long suspected of having traveled — in his pronounced late form — a separate road. It also may remove to some extent the *Pithecanthropus*, which had developed a few special peculiarities on its island, from the direct genetic series of the ancestors of present-day humanity. But all that does not amount to very much. It is indeed assumed today that certain apparently primitive characteristics of the *Pithecanthropus* and Neanderthal man which were formerly described as "apelike," such as the heavy eyebrow ridges, were really acquired at a late stage by "parallel evolution," complicated processes affecting inherited structure; and that consequently, in this case, something of the ape had come out at a higher evolutionary level. Nevertheless, in the principles governing their structure the remote Early Pleistocene progenitors of pre-*sapiens* man could not have been very different from the ape man of Eugène Dubois, as indeed some splendid recent discoveries have confirmed. And the ape man's ancestors of the Tertiary period, as has also been indicated during the last few years, must anatomically have formed a connecting link between the small denizens of wooded plains — belonging to the *Proconsul* group — and the long-limbed, erect, semihuman types dating from the first glacial period.

All discoveries of *sapiens*-like bones of unspecified antiquity soon turned out to have been misinterpreted. The latest find of this description, which also promptly gave rise to all sorts of speculations, occurred in northern Persia. In 1952 the American prehistorians Carleton Coon and Louis Dupree were exploring, in dramatic circumstances, the cave of Hotu near the Caspian Sea. Just as they came upon the first traces of human activity in the cave, the Persian oil dispute broke out. Hatred of foreigners blazed up among the natives, and the explorers were in peril of their lives. They continued their excavations with feverish haste in hourly expectation of being attacked by a fanatical horde of the adherents of Mossadegh and thrown into the nearest jail. Dupree described their predicament as a race against time.

They won the race. At a depth of about twelve yards they came upon the skulls of three human beings. Each had been killed by blows from a stone. Coon is said to have fainted with excitement at the sight of them — not, as might be supposed, because the Hotu men were of such antique and singular aspect, but because they looked so modern. The two Americans would not have been surprised if they had stumbled upon primitive Neanderthal specimens or even more primitive ancestors of man at that level, which they considered to be very ancient. But the Hotu skulls appeared almost contemporary. When Coon came to himself again he could not help exclaiming: "I believe I've discovered Adam!" And he rather unwisely added, "If that's not so, I'll eat the things!"

The press reported the discovery of this new remote ancestor in banner headlines. Only a few weeks later H. L. Movius, one of the highest authorities on early Asiatic cultures, perceived that the tools found with the Hotu men dated from the Middle Stone Age. In other respects, too, the alleged Adam proved to be a very late sprig of the human genealogical tree. Whether Coon thereupon in fact ate up the bones he had found is not known.

The secret of the Chinese chemists' shops

"It is a medical work dating from the time of the Emperor Ch'ien-lung," said Herr Wilzer, a German customs inspector at Tientsin, to his globe-trotting compatriot Dr. Haberer. "It was probably written about the middle of the eighteenth century." He swallowed a mouthful of green tea and sighed. "Difficult to translate. But I'll try. Do you want to take the manuscript back to Germany with you, doctor?"

Haberer nodded, examining the wavy symbols. "We doctors would certainly be interested in it. The Chinese have been good physicians ever since very early times. Science may be able to make something of the secrets of their prescriptions." He spelled out with an effort, "*Fung-lung-tschih*. What does that mean exactly, Herr Wilzer?"

"Big, white dragons' teeth," explained Herr Wilzer. "Small, black dragons' teeth are called *tsing-lung-tschih*, dragons' bones *lung-ku*, and subterranean dragons themselves *tin-schu*. They're very important in medicine."

"Dragons?" repeated Dr. Haberer in surprise. "How on earth do the Chinese suppose they can make drugs out of dragons' teeth? There are no such things as dragons anyway."

The customs inspector smiled. "By dragons' remains our yellow medicine men of course mean fossils. The *tin-schu* is really the mammoth. This animal is still the subject of the most extraordinary conceptions among the masses of the people here. In the *Pen-ts'ao Kang-mu*, the great Chinese natural history book composed in the sixteenth century in which the village quacks still believe as implicitly as ever, we are told: 'The *tin-schu* only lives in dark, lonely places. It dies the moment the rays of the sun or moon fall on it. Its feet are short in relation to the size of its body, so that it can only walk with difficulty. Its tail is a Chinese ell long. Its eyes are small and its neck curved. It is extraordinarily dull-witted and sluggish. During a flood in the Tan-schuan-tuy district these animals appeared in great numbers on the plains and fed on the roots of the Fu-kia plant.' The teeth and bones of the mammoth and other prehistoric creatures," Wilzer went on, proud of his knowledge of Chinese customs, "are boiled in rice wine, fried in fat, or eaten in powdered form. I am informed that they have a sourish but rather faint flavor."

"Then these subjects of the Son of Heaven annually devour an enormous quantity of valuable fossils!" Haberer cried indignantly. He was immediately reminded of his former schoolfellow in Munich, Max Schlosser, with whom in the days of his youth long ago he had often teased salamanders and who had now taken up the study of prehistoric animals. "Do you know what I think, Herr Wilzer? The shops of all Chinese chemists ought to be thoroughly searched and everything bought up that has a smack of the prehistoric about it. There might be some highly sensational results for science."

"The stuff's devilish expensive," Herr Wilzer warned him. "A hundredweight of *tsing-lung-tschih* costs approximately two hundred gold marks of our money. And most of the material would probably be worthless. You might have to buy dragons' bones by the ton, doctor, before you could get hold of an interesting tooth."

"By the ton?" exclaimed Haberer in amazement. "Are there really as many fossils in the Middle Kingdom as all that?"

"Every year," replied the inspector, "traders set out for the caves and gorges of the mountains inland and come back with treasures of immense value. The last annual report of the Imperial Customs authorities shows that in twelve months over twenty tons of dragons' remains were loaded at Chinese ports."

Haberer shook his head. "What valuable scientific material must have been lost in that way for millenniums!" he exclaimed. "You see the damage superstition can do, Herr Wilzer!"

Herr Wilzer poured out some fresh tea. "I have heard," he remarked, "that until a short time ago we did much the same sort of things in Europe. We have no business to laugh at the Chinese charlatans. Their written accounts of the uses to which fossils can be put are surprisingly reminiscent of the pronouncements of our own old authorities."

He read out a translation he had made of an order given to chemists in the time of the Emperor Ch'ien-lung.

Dragons' bones are effective in the diseases of the heart, kidneys, intestines, and liver. They improve vitality and have an astringent effect. Their influence on the kidneys is especially beneficent. In cases of nervous affections this medicine is particularly recommended to persons suffering from timidity and shyness. Dragons' bones have also been found to be good remedies for constipation, nightmares, epileptic fits, fever, diarrhoea, consumption, and haemorrhoids. Bladder trouble, respiratory disturbances, and boils are also cured by partaking of this medicine. Dragons' bones are equally effective as astringents or as laxatives. The best quality of this drug can be identified if, when wrapped in thin silk, it sticks to the tongue.

"Enough!" cried Haberer. "You get that translation done, Herr Wilzer! That book will delight medical men everywhere, as well as historians of civilization! Meanwhile I'll scrape together my last few coppers and buy myself astringent and laxative *lung-ku, fung-lung-tschih,* and *tsing-lung-tschih* in the chemists' shops of Tientsin. My friend Schlosser will be amazed — "

Between 1899 and 1902 Haberer not only ransacked the Tientsin chemists' shops and wholesale druggists' establishments but also visited Peking and Shanghai, in his enthusiasm over the great quantities of valuable remains of ancient mammals supplied to him by the yellow Sons of Heaven. He invested all his money in fossils and returned to Munich in 1903 with empty pockets but many chests full of dragons' bones. His friend Schlosser then labored for years sorting out and identifying the sour-tasting miraculous drugs. Wilzer's translation of the medical work published in the reign of the Emperor Ch'ien-lung proved very useful to Schlosser. It not only described the effects but also the composition of the Chinese patent medicines.

The outcome exceeded all expectations. A new view of prehistory was obtained. As soon as Schlosser published his reports on Haberer's sample collection the Far East became an important meeting place for investigators of all nations. America's leading paleontologist, Huxley's pupil Henry Fairfield Osborn, initiated expeditions on a large scale to the Chinese loess districts and Mongolia. He discovered, in addition to many hitherto unknown mammals of the Tertiary period, Sauropoda and other dinosaurs dating from the geologic Middle Ages, and even saurians' eggs containing embryos. He found that certain species of saurians inhabiting the Jurassic and Cretaceous plains of the East had positively specialized in egg stealing. Other expeditions, led by Americans, Englishmen, and Frenchmen, penetrated to the caves of the mountain ranges — to the annoyance of the industrious traders who supplied the Chinese druggists — and snapped up the coveted articles of commerce under the very noses of the native merchants. Search was also begun for the fossilized remains of human beings, the reason being a very precise one.

Schlosser had found a certain molar in Dr. Haberer's chests. It might have been that of an extinct anthropoid ape or even that of a prehistoric man. Its age could not be exactly determined by the means then available. Schlosser considered it must date from the Pliocene, the last epoch of the Tertiary period. It therefore attracted a great deal of attention. People scented, so to speak, a new missing link in China. Paleontologists followed up like detectives the slightest clue that might indicate prehistoric activity. The Swedish geologist J. G. Andersson was the first to collect, near the village of Chou-kou-tien, thirty miles southwest of Peking, certain evidence implying that the tooth acquired by Haberer probably came from that neighborhood.

Since 1918 Andersson had been collecting the fossils of mammals in the crevices and caverns of the chalky hills near Chou-kou-tien. The fossils occasionally made a peculiar impression. It was as though they had been smashed by tools used by man. In 1921 this suspicion became greatly reinforced. On the floor of a cave that had been filled with rubble from a landslide there were found, in addition to fragments of the bones of animals dating from the Early Diluvial age, splinters of quartz, that had apparently been worked upon and shaped. And two years later two teeth came to light which exactly resembled the tooth in Schlosser's collection from the chemists' shops.

The story of this find sounds quite a simple one. But before the discovery was made, Andersson and his Austrian collaborator, Otto Zdansky, the man who actually found the teeth, had to contend with the greatest difficulties imaginable. Although both men worked in close association with the official Chinese geological survey service, the local Chinese population showed no sympathy whatever with the explorers' interest in "dragons' bones." The inhabitants of Chou-kou-tien squatted impassively everywhere on the excavation sites, went in for passive resistance, and could only at most be persuaded to retire for a time when Andersson flourished a camera and threatened to take their photographs. Their fear of the camera did not last long, and Andersson often literally had to pull out his finds from beneath them.

On October 22, 1926, the Crown Prince Gustaf Adolf, now king of Sweden, visited Peking. In the course of a reception he heard about the secrets of the Chou-kou-tien hills. Andersson's report to the Crown Prince aroused an immense amount of interest both in scientific and lay circles. Newspaper articles were written and a scribe with a vivid imagination, Maurus Horst, at once embarked upon fictitious narratives of a "Half-man of Shansi," a weird sort of missing link in the loess and chalk soil of China.

Most interest was shown by a man who had been on the track of the remains of primitive man in the Far East for years. The Canadian Davidson Black, professor of anatomy at Union Medical College in Peking, was one of the scientists who had been concerned with the strange affair of the Piltdown skull, about the year 1914. A burning enthusiasm for the prehistory of mankind had been kindled in him as a result. He had accepted the academic appointment in Peking solely because he believed that the human race must have originated in Asia.

He got in touch with Andersson and suggested an examination on a grand scale of the neighborhood of Chou-kou-tien. The official Chinese authorities gave the project their support. It was stipulated that any finds made were to remain in Chinese possession. Thus, in 1927, an operation began which was to prove a model instance of international collaboration. Black superintended the undertaking from Peking. The actual excavation works were supervised by the Swedish geologist Birger Bohlin. The scientific institutes of China, Sweden, and the United States put large funds at the disposal of the expedition and sent competent paleontologists, anatomists, prehistorians, and anthropologists to Chou-kou-tien in order to join in the hunt for the creature that had manufactured weapons from quartz rubble and broken up animals' bones.

While civil war raged through China, with robbery and murder in its wake, the representatives of six nations stood shoulder to shoulder and dug deep holes in the rubble and clay, hardened by chalk deposits, of the "Deep Crevasse," the cave of Ko-tse-tang and other localities in the Wu-tai-schan Mountains. Marauders took refuge in the neighborhood. Unsympathetic military commanders made all sorts of difficulties, and bullets often whistled over the roofs of Chou-kou-tien, but the explorers took hardly any notice of them.

Andersson's view had been correct. The spot had at one time been used as a camping ground by primitive men of extremely early date. In a layer over fifty yards deep were found all the remains of meals, sweepings, and refuse which a primitive horde of human beings is wont to leave behind. There were traces of charcoal, very ancient stone implements, and the calcined bones of animals. Each of the American, Canadian, English, Chinese, Swedish, and French participants in the expedition was firmly convinced that one day their spades and pickaxes would lay bare an unmistakable human fossil.

On October 16, 1927, they were able to record their first success. Birger Bohlin, discovered a tooth resembling those found by Haberer and Andersson, in the same cave. In shape it looked as though it might be that of a man, but the deeply wrinkled enamel of the tooth suggested a chimpanzee's. Without further delay Black thereupon gave this enigmatic being the name of *Sinanthropus pekinensis* — Chinese man of Peking. It was a risky thing to do. In Virchow's time anyone who announced a scientific genus on the strength of a few teeth would have been considered both rash and eccentric. Black had already seen so much in Chou-kou-tien that he knew what he was doing.

The broken and occasionally calcined fragments of animals' bones in the chalk caves belonged to much the same species as the fossils in the Mauer sandpit. They included antique elephants, primitive rhinoceroses, saber-toothed tigers, and the large rodent *Trogontherium*. Geological conditions were identical with those of the Early Pleistocene period, the first glacial period. The Peking man was therefore apparently a contemporary of the *Pithecanthropus* of Java and the Heidelberg specimen. The peculiar hybrid formation of the teeth suited this view. Black deduced that early human types like those of Trinil and Mauer had at one time settled in North China. They had probably dragged slaughtered game into their cave dwellings and roasted it over a fire. If so, Chou-kou-tien might come to be of far greater importance for science than Trinil or Mauer, for it would then be there that the very first beginnings of human civilization had been revealed, those fateful hours in which the beast governed by instinct and impulse became the thinking, self-conscious lord of his environment.

Davidson Black's bold hypothesis was confirmed two years later. Meanwhile the Rockefeller Foundation had intervened and assumed financial responsibility for continuation of the undertaking. The entire world waited excitedly for the Chinese Prometheus who had discovered fire 500,000 or 600,000 years ago and thus initiated the history of humanity.

The Dragons' Mountain

Black's collaborators included an able young Chinese called Weng Chung Pei. He was a professional paleontologist, and had been trained for years as an excavator. Weng Chung Pei had as little in common with those Chinese of Dr. Haberer's time who had tried to relieve their stomach troubles with mixtures of fossils and rice wine as his white-skinned colleagues had with those honest villagers who had appreciated powdered "unicorn" as late as the eighteenth century. Even in China knowledge of natural science had long ceased to be drawn from the dusty *Pen-ts'ao Kang-mu*. Chinese professors had learned in a few decades all the practical remedies and skills of Europe and America without forgetting in the process the true wisdom of their poets and philosophers. They were rapidly catching up with the advanced guard of Western scholars. Weng Chung Pei was a typical representative of the new China, open to all foreign influences, intelligent, unprejudiced, and endowed with an instinctive and subtle talent for research into the bargain, such as only a very ancient tradition of culture can develop.

When Birger Bohlin left on an expedition to Sinkiang in 1929, Weng Chung Pei took over the leadership of the excavation party. Meanwhile, in addition to innumerable fossils of mammals, some twenty teeth, two fragments of lower jaws, and a few splinters of skulls and temporal bones of the Peking man had been found. They were not enough to give a clear picture of the Chinese Prometheus. Famous scholars had arrived in Peking, including the American Roy Chapman Andrews and the French paleontologist Father Teilhard de Chardin. The study of the strange teeth was also now being taken up by Germans and Russians, so that eight nations were participating in the hunt. Nevertheless, during the bitterly cold winter of 1929, after two and a half years of not very profitable work, the research party had at last grown very disheartened. They were already wondering whether it would not be better to drop the whole project. Only Weng Chung Pei remained optimistic.

As if guided by a sixth sense, he concentrated his investigations upon a cave in the Dragons' Mountain which had already been reported to be without relics. The roof had fallen in. He blasted away one after another the hard strata of sand, rock, and red clay, which had become rigidly cemented together. He analyzed them, tested every scrap of material for residues of bone. In Peking on December 6, 1929, with a proud smile he handed to his chief, Davidson Black, the well-preserved, highly petrified skull of a young "Peking man." Although the expedition had been counting on such a find for two and a half years, an indescribable scene of rejoicing took place. Weng Chung Pei was congratulated, embraced, and given the reception of a hero. Davidson Black was more pleased than anybody. For his diagnosis had been confirmed in every detail. The skull was so like that of Trinil that the Java and Peking types really seemed to belong to the same species.

The bones were massive and thick, utterly different from those of Late Diluvial and modern human beings. Black was above all struck by the heavy eyebrow ridges, standing out prominently from the forehead, by the slightness of the convexity of the parietal bones, and by the steep slope of the occiput. The head tapered upward, in contrast to that of a *Homo sapiens*, from a point directly above the ears, thus forming a true boat-shaped skull. In all these features the Peking man bore an astonishing resemblance to a chimpanzee. But the curves of the skull were less pronounced, more rounded, and the brain capacity seemed to be twice as big. The heavy underjaw, as chinless as that of Mauer, was provided with the familiar semi-human, semi-chimpanzee-type teeth, which had the peculiarity, however, of growing larger as they retreated from front to back. Considered as a whole, the creature still remained physically at the intermediate stage between chimpanzee and man; but mentally it had already crossed the threshold of humanity. It represented the most interesting and significant find of prehistoric human beings yet made.

When Black published his illustration of the first Chou-kou-tien skull it was immediately obvious that this time he had proved his point. Not a single word of criticism was heard. The scientific world, the press, the churches, and the public unanimously accepted *Sinanthropus*, exactly as they had acknowledged the truth of the theory of evolution. Simultaneously the last traces of opposition to the genuineness of the Javanese counterpart of the skull, Dubois's ape man, were also silenced. Boule and Weinert consequently at once inquired of Black why he had not named this skull *Pithecanthropus pekinensis* — since it was of precisely the same type as that of Trinil — so as to confirm once more and this time for good the status of the find of Eugène Dubois. Black, like a sensible man, did not insist on retaining the name he had given and agreed to the correction. A little later Weng Chung Pei made some new finds that considerably diverged in many of their characteristics from the Javanese *Pithecanthropus*, and for this reason the designation *Sinanthropus* was eventually retained.

In 1930 the Chinese paleontologist excavated a second skull out of the solid chalk block in which the first skull had been embedded. This had a more highly convex forehead and a larger brain capacity. There could be no doubt whatever that both finds belonged to the same geological era and also to the same kith and kin. The second skull, however — the discovery of which had by this time attracted

swarms of interested persons from all quarters of the globe to Peking
— already showed clearly a further step in development to a higher
type of humanity. In Chou-kou-tien, it was obvious that a "workshop for evolutionary models of mankind" had been uncovered.

The energetic and indefatigable Davidson Black did not live to
see any later progress. He suffered from heart trouble and had completely exhausted himself in Peking as planner and organizer of the
undertaking, while at the same time describing and reconstructing
the finds. In 1934 he succumbed to a heart attack in the midst of
his activities. At the request of the Rockefeller Foundation he was
replaced by a rising anthropologist of great sagacity, the German emi-
grant Franz Weidenreich, who exchanged the University of Chicago
for the Peking institute.

Discoveries now came thick and fast. Up to the year 1939 Weidenreich, Pei, and their collaborators extracted from the Dragons' Mountain the remains of at least forty-five (some scientists actually mention eighty) "Peking men" of all ages. They found skulls, lower jaws,
the bones of limbs, and some one hundred and fifty separate teeth.
The people of Chou-kou-tien seem to have been extraordinarily diverse in type. Brain capacity varied between 900 cc. and 1200 cc.
Some lower jaws were much more primitive than that of the Heidelberg man. Others showed features that can still be observed today
among the Mongol races. Apparently prehistoric man had entered
at that time upon a period of mutations when all kinds of progressive characteristics were formed in certain individuals, only coming
to be the common property of humanity at a later epoch.

Even mentally everything must have been in a state of flux and
commotion in that Promethean age. The Peking man walked upright. Consequently his brain was better supplied with blood than
that of the anthropoid ape and the results of this newly aroused
cerebral activity appeared in every cave and crevice of the Dragons'
Mountain. Not only pieces of quartz but also fragments of the skulls
of game were found which had been knocked into shape as tools and
weapons. Unmistakable hearths, too, were discovered, in which the
Chinese Adam had burned brushwood and roasted meat. Finally,
even suspicious signs of cannibalism were noted, for as with the
people of the Late Ice Age, all the Chou-kou-tien skulls had an artificially opened occipital gap into which the hand could be inserted
to extract the brain. Most of the cylindrical bones looked as though
they had been split to enable the marrow to be sucked out.

Franz Weidenreich, the new chief of the excavation staff, studied
these bloodthirsty but interesting antique head-hunters of the

Dragons' Mountain very thoroughly. A lively and restless spirit, he
was one of the most striking personalities of the modern researchers
into prehistory. He gained his first laurels at Strasbourg and Heidelberg as an anatomist and adherent of the theory of evolution. His
reconstructions of the skulls of early man were famous throughout the
world, and he was also one of the very first to give an approximately
correct explanation of the Piltdown mystery. In 1935, at the age of
sixty-two, he was obliged to resign, on racial and political grounds,
his post at the University of Frankfurt. He emigrated to the United
States and soon began to play a leading part among anthropologists
here, but in the same year he went to Peking to continue Black's
work. Later on, during the Second World War, he made von Koenigswald's Javanese finds known and published some strange data
relating to a prehistoric race of giants, culminating in the startling
hypothesis that they were the ancestors of mankind. He died in 1949
in New York, after sharing to a great extent in the discovery of the
Peking man, the delight it aroused, and its eventual triumph, and
also watching helplessly from a distance the bitter end of the finds
he had made.

As soon as Weidenreich had made a thorough examination of the
bones of Chou-kou-tien he declared that these Peking men had
been slaughtered in a body, dragged into the caves of the Dragons'
Mountain, and there roasted and devoured. Exhaustive investigations seemed to prove him right. But what sort of beings had overcome the *Sinanthropus?* Would they have been more highly organized human types? In that case perhaps the cooking hearths
and the quartz and bone implements were not made by early man,
but by genuine human beings? The question gave rise to vigorous
discussion. And when the prehistorian Movius, after a fresh examination of the soil deposits of the Dragons' Mountain and
their fauna, made the date of the Peking men 100,000 years later,
placing them in the Middle Intermediate Ice Age, Weng Chung
Pei's finds were for the first time subjected to serious analysis.

Meanwhile extremely interesting human and cultural relics, resembling those of the European Ice Age, had been found in other
caves near Chou-kou-tien. Skulls of Cro-Magnon type were discovered, together with animals' bones, kitchen waste, and stone
tools. Here, too, cannibalism had evidently been practised. Could
these Chinese Stone Age men have been the evildoers who had
exterminated *Sinanthropus?* Surely not — for between their time
and that of the Peking men lay at least 250,000 years. Their implements were altogether different, and the animal fossils in their

caves were dissimilar in many respects to those of the *Sinanthropus* period.

Apparently the Dragons' Mountain, like certain European and Javanese sites, had been from very ancient times a dwelling place of early man. The *Sinanthropus* had constructed cooking hearths there, worked stone implements, disembowelled animals, and ventured out to collect hackberry fruits and wage war against his fellows. His successors of the Late Ice Age had done the same sort of thing by improved methods and a more refined technique.

In 1939 the great Chou-kou-tien operation came to an abrupt end. The Japanese occupied the village and made further scientific work difficult, and two years later, when Weidenreich was in New York, one of the most tragic events in the history of paleontology occurred. Wong Wen Hao, the head of the Chinese institute where the bones of the Peking men were kept, felt uneasy at the attitude of the Japanese and requested the American embassy to have these valuable objects removed from the country without delay. The Americans agreed, and on December 5, 1941, a train left Chou-kou-tien with the boxes of fossils, took American consignments aboard at Peking, and proceeded toward the harbor of Ching-wang-tao. There the boxes were to be transferred to a steamer for shipment to the United States.

They never reached their destination. On December 7, Japanese bombers raided Pearl Harbor. The war in the Far East broke out. The last positions on Chou-kou-tien were evacuated, nor could the excavation works in other parts of China be continued. It was only in Yunnan that a few Chinese paleontologists remained until 1942, menaced by military attack, hunger, epidemics, and catastrophic floods. They eventually managed to escape with their precious animal fossils to Chungking.

Meanwhile, what had happened to the American train and the boxes from the Peking institute? After the war, Americans, Chinese, and Japanese combined in a strenuous effort of detection to discover the fate of the Peking men. It turned out that the Japanese had confiscated the train at Ching-wang-tao and taken the American transport personnel prisoners. A lighter that had been loaded up with part of the booty sank shortly afterwards in the straits of Chile. Were the boxes containing the *Sinanthropus* bones also aboard that vessel? Or had they already been thrown away by the Japanese troops, who could make nothing of their contents?

No trace of the *Sinanthropus* could be discovered in the Japanese collections, and nothing had been left behind in Peking. Today the scientific world possesses no relics of the Peking man apart from a few teeth found in Chinese chemists' shops. Weng Chung Pei, at present China's leading paleontologist, can only count on the one slender chance that enterprising inhabitants of Ching-wang-tao may have found the boxes and sold the bones in a hurry to the nearest chemist. It is possible, though not very probable, that the remains of the Far East ancestors of the human race, to which Andersson, Black, Pei, and Weidenreich had dedicated a great part of their life work, may now be gathering dust, as "dragons' bones," in some Chinese shopping quarter.

Such was the end, aeons after his own physical death, of the most famous witness to the dawn of our culture, the Peking man.

A race of giants

Weidenreich was still at work on the site where the Peking man had been found when he heard of a discovery that promised to be one of the greatest paleontological sensations of the century. The expert on Java man, von Koenigswald, had identified in his extensive collection of Chinese fossils the teeth of a huge and lordly animal, either a super-gorilla or perhaps even a primeval giant in human form.

Von Koenigswald had been impelled by the same interest as had formerly guided Haberer to visit the big Chinese chemists' shops in Indonesia and China itself. They still contained, among all sorts of other drugs, dried lizards and tattered rhinoceros hides, and the "dragons' teeth" that had meanwhile become famous. "These drugs," von Koenigswald complacently reported later, "only look strange to us. They are probably cheaper than many European specifics and just about as ineffective." His acquisitions had grown far more plentiful than those of Dr. Haberer, which he had known and studied in Munich. The fossil relics from a Hong Kong chemist's shop were particularly interesting. He had come across them in 1935, some time before the discovery of the *Pithecanthropus* of Sangiran.

They included bones of the prehistoric elephant *Stegodon*, jaw and skull fragments of ancestors of the tapir and orangutan, the teeth of a rhinoceros and a bamboo bear, and all kinds of other treasures. The places of origin and the ages of these "dragons' bones" could be approximately guessed. They might be referred to the "yellow earth" of Kwangsi or Kwangtung, cave deposits and the contents of crevices dating from the Late Tertiary period or the first glacial periods in China. And the peculiar tooth which the Chinese chemist had also ferreted out from among his treasures probably belonged to the same layer.

At the first glance this molar resembled the masticator of a very large anthropoid ape, though the embossed crown and the rest of

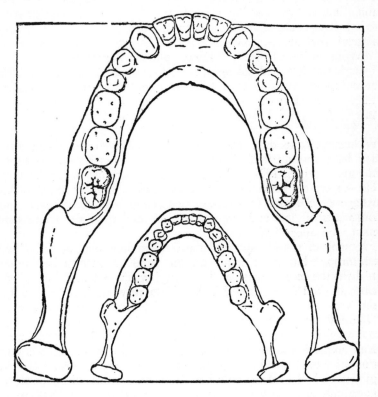

Weinert's reconstruction of the jaw of the Kwangsi giant as compared with the underjaw of a man of today.

its shape in many respects recalled typical features in human teeth. It was three times the size of any of the latter and must, if its bulk is any indication of that of the rest of the creature, have been set in an underjaw seven inches long and two and a half high. It followed — von Koenigswald almost took fright as he made the calculation — that the entire monster had been nearly twice as big as a gorilla. Could it have been a man? Impossible! Men of so gigantic a size could never have existed. Accordingly, in his first publication von Koenigswald cautiously described the giant of Kwangsi as a large ape and gave it the name *Gigantopithecus blacki* — Black's giant ape — in honor of the deceased explorer of Chou-kou-tien, Davidson Black. Some years later he found two more molars, gnawed by porcupines, of the *Gigantopithecus* in Hong Kong. He showed them to Weidenreich on a visit to the latter in Peking.

Weidenreich at first refrained from giving expression to the hypothesis that had immediately and forcibly occurred to him: could there really once have been giants? Soon more reports of huge jaws and teeth began to come in, and the temperamental interpreter of the Peking man became a student of giants.

Once more an amazing stroke of good fortune came to the aid of science. The three teeth from the shelves of the Hong Kong apothecary would never have been sufficient foundation for a new theory. Between 1937 and 1941, while von Koenigswald was searching for further remains of the *Pithecanthropus* near the Javanese village of Sangiran, he came upon some very remarkable large fragments of skull and jaw which did throw quite a different light upon the alleged giant ape of Kwangsi. He first discovered the fragment of a primitive underjaw, resembling that of the *Pithecanthropus*, but larger than the Mauer underjaw, which had hitherto held the record for size. The new jaw did not fit the *Pithecanthropus* skull found in 1937. Was it a new species? Or had the skulls of Trinil and Sangiran belonged to females of the Javanese type and the jaw fragment to a male?

Two years later one of von Koenigswald's collectors dug up a large upper jaw containing indubitably human teeth. But between the incisors and canines there was a gap, the famous "monkey gap" that had hitherto only been found in anthropoid apes, never in primitive man. Von Koenigswald was at the time about to go to Peking in order to compare the original *Pithecanthropus* material with the Chou-kou-tien finds in that city. For the stubborn Dubois, on hearing the news, had doubted the relationship between the two forms and described the *Pithecanthropus* of Sangiran as a fraud. Consequently von Koenigswald took both of the imposing jaws with him to Peking to show Weidenreich. He instructed his collaborators in Java to send on any further finds to him forthwith.

After a few weeks, while von Koenigswald and Weidenreich were still studying the jaw with the monkey gap, the two investigators actually did receive another badly shattered but again very large skull. Weidenreich reconstructed it later in New York and added the jaw fragments to it. They fitted! It really looked like a male *Pithecanthropus*. If so the other, apparently female finds — that discovered at Trinil in 1891 and that at Sangiran in 1937 — must at least belong to the same type. Yet the discrepancies were far too great to be accounted for on the grounds of sex alone.

Von Koenigswald continued his explorations with his collaborators at Sangiran. Up to 1941 he had found two more fragments of a quite notably gigantic lower jaw. One of them contained teeth almost as large as those from the Hong Kong chemist's shop. Both fossil relics belonged quite unmistakably to primitive men. This could not be said of the Kwangsi giant. And their size far exceeded that of the jaw that was to have been attributed to a male *Pithecanthropus*.

The question again arose which was male and which female. Was the gigantic jaw a male counterpart to the big 1939 skull, which would then have to be defined as female? Should a distinction therefore be drawn between a smaller *Pithecanthropus erectus* and a larger *Pithecanthropus robustus*? Or had there actually been three forms of early primitive man in Java, one of normal size, one above the average, and one of gigantic type? Von Koenigswald reflected on these problems for weeks, studying the finds. He grew more and more inclined to think that giants must at one time have existed on our planet. He gave the two jaw fragments the name *Meganthropus palaeojavanicus* — the big man of ancient Java.

As in China, so also in Java Pearl Harbor Day had a formidable effect upon research into the origins of mankind. At the last possible moment von Koenigswald, who feared the worst, sent casts of his finds to New York. Thereupon the curtain of silence descended upon him and his field of operations for four long years. No one could imagine what was happening to him. A rumor went round that he had been dead a long time. Accordingly, Weidenreich, who was now working at the American Museum of Natural History in New York, felt it his duty to inform the scientific world — with the aid of the casts of the finds of giants — what he thought.

He studied the casts, comparing them with the teeth of the *Gigantopithecus*, the Kwangsi giant. He found there were a few hard nuts to crack. First of all, it was clear that unmistakably human giants had also lived in Java. Next, it was evident that these Javanese giants resembled the *Pithecanthropus erectus* of Eugène Dubois. And finally, the size of the skulls, jaw fragments and teeth proceeded as though in accordance with a graduated scale, beginning with the Trinil man, going on to the big skull of Sangiran and the two even larger lower jaws of the *Meganthropus* until it reached the Kwangsi giant. The Sangiran skull seemed to represent a stage of transition from giant to early man. Weidenreich gave it the name of *Pithecanthropus robustus*. With regard to the probable size of the *Meganthropus* he stated: "We shall not be far wrong if we assume that this gigantic human being resembled a large gorilla in height, weight, and muscular strength." As for the *Gigantopithecus* — which had perhaps been twice as big — the ridges and grooves in his teeth, their shape and relative proportions did not apparently indicate a gorilla type of ape at all but probably a being of human characteristics. Weinert accordingly baptized him *Giganthropus* at a later date. What, then, was the course of evolution? From the Trinil man to the *Meganthropus*, as von Koenigswald believed, or conversely from the giants to the men of Trinil and Peking and from the latter in their turn to the present races of mankind? This second astonishing theory was now presented to American scholars by Weidenreich.

On May 9, 1944, he submitted in a striking report to the American Ethnological Society in New York, brilliantly phrased and boldly conceived, his belief in the descent of man from giants. He cited in this connection the well-known passage in the Bible referring to "giants in those days." Willy Ley wrote that his lecture was "received by the meeting with exclamations of incredulity which politeness could hardly disguise." But it was precisely the sort of thing newspaper readers of our century enjoy, and the daily and illustrated magazines immediately took up the matter. They described the ancestor or early contemporary of man as a monster that might have given rise to the legends of titans and cyclops, a Polyphemus fifteen feet high and weighing half a ton, able to tear up trees by the roots and play ball with great pieces of rock. The public shuddered at this disclosure.

Weidenreich's theory of giants was, in fact, more plausible than it sounded in the newspapers. He stated in his book *Apes, Giants, and Man* that in the course of evolutionary history, many kinds of animals diminish in size, such as the dwarf elephant of Malta, numerous domesticated animals like the dwarf Indian bull, dwarf donkey, Shetland pony, bantam and small breeds of dogs, and finally the Pygmies and Bushmen of Africa. Domestication has a specially favorable effect on the production of dwarf species. And as the development of humanity is nothing more, in principle, than a long process of domestication, the primitive, so to speak untamed, forefathers of *Homo sapiens* have to be imagined as gigantic monsters. Moreover, Weidenreich continued, most dwarf forms have abbreviated jaws, a higher forehead, and a larger brain capacity — in other words, exactly the same characteristics as humanity.

This was the situation when the world once again heard of von Koenigswald. The Japanese occupying forces in Java, it was learned, had interned him as a member of the Dutch army. His wife and daughter had been obliged to take refuge with Indonesian friends. His collection, including the valuable giant finds, had been cleverly hidden by himself and his collaborators, part of it actually in milk bottles. Only one of the skulls from the Solo River had found its way to Tokyo, as a birthday present to the Emperor Hirohito, who was very interested in biological, anthropological, and prehistoric matters. The emperor examined the skull, made private notes about it, and returned it to its owner after the war.

In 1946 American scholars were able to welcome in New York von Koenigswald and his pupils, so long thought to be lost. They were able to study the finds made and take up the problem of the giants afresh. Until the spring of 1948 von Koenigswald stayed in the United States working on his collection. It was so extensive that part of it, even today, still remains to be described. He then accepted a teaching appointment in Utrecht. Scientists all over the world now began to concern themselves with the genealogy of the giants. They examined the embossed teeth, endeavored to reconstruct the appropriate skulls from precise measurements and proportional figures, and estimated their age at about 500,000 years. The large forms had therefore probably been contemporary with the early human type of Trinil. It remained an open question which form had descended from the other.

Gradually Weidenreich's sensational hypothesis yielded to a somewhat soberer theory, propounded by Weinert in the words: "Such extreme forms as those of giants do not initiate any kind of evolution. They are much more likely to be the final terms of a genealogical series." A comparison between Javanese and Indian fossilized mammals showed that Java must first have been settled from India. Early man, too, probably reached eastern and southeastern Asia by way of India, though it was not yet clear whence he came or by what route. Some groups migrated to China and others to

Indonesia across a land bridge that then still existed. And these migrations took place at the very time when climatic conditions of a quite special character prevailed — at the beginning of the Pleistocene epoch.

Did early humanity, under the influence of the weather of this fateful epoch, divide into two groups of forms, giants and men of brain? It might have been so. The onset of low temperatures in the Early Ice Age could have been better withstood by large bodies, more capable of resistance than small bodies. It was for this reason that many gigantic animals then arose, such as the mammoth, the giant elk, and the cave bear. All these animate beings of excessive dimensions soon grew overspecialized, lost their evolutionary chances, and perished; the forms of normal build found other means of protecting themselves against the cold and survived. This fact had long been known. It could be applied without difficulty to the prehistory of mankind. And if this view were correct there might well have been battles of the titans in the Early Pleistocene epoch, as described by the legends of the gods of antiquity.

The interpretation of the giant fossils has not yet been concluded. Scholars still continue to differ on many points. Was the giant of Kwangsi fifteen feet high or only eight? Ought he to be described as an anthropoid ape or as a primitive man? The most recent investigations of further dental material in von Koenigswald's collection have convinced him that the giant was human. Does a child's skull of peculiar form and great antiquity — found in 1936 near the Javanese village of Mojokerto — belong to the *Pithecanthropus* or to the primitive giant group? There are more than enough theories in this connection. On the other hand, factual material is still in very short supply. We do not know how long the giants lived on this earth or in what epoch they died out. We cannot imagine what their physique and limbs were like.

Only one thing is certain. Beings resembling man inhabited the earth in many different forms as the Tertiary period gave place to the First Ice Age. A definite trend to human evolution must at that time have prevailed among erect semihuman primates. Competition suppressed the extreme forms, leaving the healthy average to survive — types such as those of Trinil, Chou-kou-tien, Mauer, Swanscombe, and Steinheim. Thence the line descended to the Cro-Magnon race and modern man. Some recent surprising discoveries have helped the interpretation of the giant fossils. The trail led to an entirely different part of the globe, Africa. In that quarter, too, a gigantic form came to light, actually in the same year in which von Koenigswald discovered the first Javanese giant, a remarkable coincidence such as often occurs in prehistoric investigation. The monster from the Black Continent, named *Meganthropus africanus* by Weinert, did not appear before the footlights for another ten years, however.

The German doctor and ethnologist Kohl-Larsen had undertaken at the request of the *Berliner Zeitung* in 1935 a journey to East Africa. He had collected there, on the shores of Lake Eyasi, a great quantity of blackish-green, metallically hard bone-splinters. Weinert declared them to be the remains of an *Africanthropus*, an African counterpart to the Peking man. In search of further relics of the kind Kohl-Larsen started four years later on a second expedition to the same neighborhood, but the war and the restless postwar years in Germany delayed the scientific examination and identification of his new acquisitions for a long time. At last, in 1949, the finds reached Weinert. They included a large fragment of an upper jaw containing several teeth. Weinert, after investigating it, realized that the Asiatic giants had possessed a cousin on the shores of Lake Eyasi.

The African *Meganthropus* turned out to be a particularly important and enlightening giant fossil. The nostril bone and part of the palate had been preserved. Consequently oral formation and that of the lower half of the face could be reconstructed with some degree of certainty. The giant of Lake Eyasi had probably possessed a gorilla-like muzzle and nose, but with the teeth of a primitive man.

Where could such beings be found? Similar "semihuman" types had long constituted a puzzle. And these ape-headed creatures with human teeth had lived in the same continent in which the new giant had been found! The most exciting, interesting, and significant finds of the last few decades, the true missing links, as they had long been called in the literature of popular science, seemed to be very closely related to the giants, even actually in part to be identical with them.

This realization caused some investigators to draw the conclusion that the giants had not been anything like so big as had hitherto been assumed. If they were identical with the polymorphous, semihuman, semisimian stock with which they were now being compared they may have only had the mouths and not the stature of giants. Their skulls, moreover, were adorned by a bony ridge that had supported appended layers of powerful chewing muscles. And that meant, as Heberer explained, that despite the massive jaw and teeth their bodies had not been to any notable extent larger than that of a normal human being.

The trail the eccentrically stubborn Dubois had picked up in Java and which von Koenigswald had followed up on the banks of the Solo River and in Chinese chemists' shops now led to Africa, to chalk caves and rock crevices of great antiquity, and the same shrubgrown plains where the proconsuls too, the presumed ancestors of the higher primates, had once been at home. It was there that the world began to have an inkling of the earliest steps in human evolution. The discovery of this African Garden of Eden, the story of which is told in the following pages, ends for the time being the two-hundred-year-old search for Adam. It was the work of three investigators, the South African professor of anatomy Raymond A. Dart, the Scottish doctor and paleontologist Robert Broom, and the South African anthropologist John Talbot Robinson.

Dynamite in Sterkfontein

A Bechuanaland Negro was busy at the priming cable. The foreman of blasting operations, de Bruyn, sounded his horn. The workmen took cover. Then came the roar of an explosion. Chalk dust whirled up and the precipices of Taungs * gave back the echo of the detonation. R. B. Young, the geologist in attendance on the quarrying operations, sprang quickly to one side. A small fragment of rock had been hurled right at his feet. Something induced him to pick it up. He looked at it and found himself staring at the toothy grin of a child's skull.

A few weeks later, at the end of 1924, fourteen scholars from all quarters of the globe had begun to study the "Taungs child" that the geologist Young had accidentally discovered. The explosion had to some extent shattered the bones of the skull but it could still be clearly discerned that this enigmatic creature must have borne some resemblance to a chimpanzee or gorilla cub, though it must also have had a far greater brain capacity. Young considered that the layer from which the dynamite had flung it was to be ascribed to the Middle Tertiary period. It followed that the Taungs child was much older, much more prehistoric, and — if the exact truth must be told — much more simian than any semihuman type yet discovered. Did it then deserve the designation "human" at all? Or had it really only been an erect anthropoid ape? The skull had no eyebrow ridges, and that made it look very human. This impression was contradicted

---

* Until recently this name has been spelled (somewhat confusingly) with the final *s*. It now appears, however, that "Taung," in addition to being more pleasing to the ear, may be the correct spelling.

by its lower part, the nostrils and the size of the teeth. The faint suspicion dawned on one of the scholars that the Taungs child might come to have a greater importance for mankind than all the diamonds extracted from the mines of Kimberley, an hour's run south of Taungs.

Raymond A. Dart was the name of this scholar. He was the Johannesburg anatomist to whom Mr. de Bruyn had brought the skull. He made a close examination of the Taungs child. It possessed, with the exception of a single permanent molar, an absolutely human set of milk teeth. It could not be a prehistoric chimpanzee or gorilla, as the majority of experts believed. Dart did in the end give this find the name of *Australopithecus africanus* — southern ape of Africa —

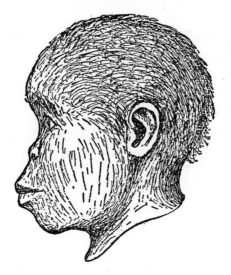

"Dart's Baby" was the facetious name given by scholars to the Taungs skull described by Raymond A. Dart as the missing link. But Dart was right: this enigmatic creature was no ape. It was semihuman, as this reconstruction shows.

but in so doing he stated that it was probably a connecting link between anthropoid ape and Man.

The other gentlemen greatly enjoyed themselves at his expense and that of his "Baby." Their jokes went on so long that at last Dart gave up his investigations in disgust. Thereupon, however, another scientist took a hand, the Scot-born doctor, Robert Broom, who practised in the little village of Maquassi at the edge of the Karoo desert and collected fossils as a hobby. He was the right man for the job. He had not only discovered in the Karoo the transitional forms leading from reptiles to mammals but was also an intimate friend of the Prime Minister, Smuts. By 1929 Broom was already calling attention to the astonishing similarity of the Taungs teeth to those of a human being. He determined to do his utmost to find mature specimens of the *Australopithecus* in order to prove its evolutionary position beyond doubt.

Twelve years passed. A Taungs official, Mr. Barlow, who had been present at the discovery of the child's skull, was meanwhile transferred to Sterkfontein. At the latter place and the neighboring villages of Swartkrans and Krugersdorp, some thirty miles from Johannesburg, certain caves that tourists were fond of visiting existed near the quarries. These caves ran deep into the hard limestone cliffs of the valley. Neither spade nor pickaxe can be used in them, the rock being as solid as concrete. For this reason paleontologists and prehistorians, until 1936, took little interest in the Sterkfontein valley. They had no idea that Barlow, the foreman of the blasting works, had been doing a lucrative business with fossils there for some considerable time.

One day Broom, who had since been appointed curator of the natural history museum at Pretoria, discovered in a roundabout way that Barlow was actually selling the old bones he had blasted out of the limestone pits to rich tourists as souvenirs. It was rumored that fossilized human teeth had also been found and sold in this way at Sterkfontein. A guide to the city of Johannesburg even contained at that time the attractive invitation, "Come to Sterkfontein and find the missing link!"

Broom at once scented a unique opportunity. He jumped into his car, drove off, and called on the blasting works foreman. Barlow admitted that now and again during blasting operations the remains of mammals had come to light. They consisted of fragments, smashed to pieces, and so firmly embedded in the limestone that in his view they could be of little use to anybody. He agreed that, unless his memory were at fault, a human tooth had also turned up among them.

"Now listen to me, Barlow," said Broom urgently. "You know about the Taungs skull, don't you? If you find anything of that sort I most earnestly beg of you to keep it for me. It might be of incomparable importance. Perhaps this Sterkfontein limestone conceals" — his voice shook with excitement — "the first member of all mankind — "

"I'll see what I can do for you, sir," replied Barlow calmly. "How long will you be staying in Sterkfontein?"

"About a week," said Broom. "I shall really have to make a closer examination of this district. Can you show me over the caves and quarries?"

Barlow nodded. Then he smiled, with some embarrassment. "Did you say the first of all mankind, sir? It certainly would be a pity if he were now lying at the bottom of some globe-trotter's trunk. Excuse me, sir, but I didn't know."

"It might be the most manlike of all apes," said Broom, "which comes to practically the same thing."

Broom examined the cliffs of the Sterkfontein valley. He realized that if fossilized human beings or anthropoid apes lay buried in the limestone they could only be extracted with a great deal of trouble. The crevices in the rock were full of broken stones and rubble. Probably heavy rains ever since primeval times had been carrying away at intervals all the loose objects lying about in the open and depositing them in the clefts of the rock. There would be all sorts of rubbish, stones, and the remains of meals made by beasts of prey, and the bones of various types of animals that had succumbed in the struggle for existence. Later on the water had bolted the gates leading to that remote world by dissolving the minerals in the crevices and enveloping the rubbish and bones in a pulp like that of plaster of Paris, which had eventually hardened to a slag of the consistency of glass. The Sterkfontein clefts had accordingly been well and truly cemented up. Their contents could only be reached with the aid of dynamite, which would destroy a great part of them. It would also be extremely difficult to decide to which era fossils thus blasted out should be ascribed.

While Broom was still wondering whether it might not be possible to clear the clefts inch by inch by precision work with the chisel, Barlow appeared with an object under his arm which he had wrapped in a cloth. He winked.

"I guess I've found what you're looking for, sir," he said with a grin. "Unfortunately that first man of yours is a bit smashed. Couldn't be helped. He looks rather an ugly devil in any case."

He undid the knots of the cloth. It contained five skull fragments firmly stuck together with crystalline rock precipitate. They consisted of the vaulting of the skull and facial bones, remains of the upper and lower jaws, and in particular a wonderfully well preserved brain cast. It was August 17, 1936, the third day after Broom's arrival in Sterkfontein and a notable date in prehistoric research. For apart from the Taungs child — as to which opinions still varied —

the bones in Barlow's cloth had belonged to the first of all human beings hitherto known to have lived on this earth.

At first the scholars, with the exception of that tireless investigator Broom, considered the Sterkfontein fossil to belong to another anthropoid ape, though of a different species than the Taungs child. When blasting operations extracted further parts of the alleged ape from the cliffs, including the remains of a thighbone and a pelvic bone, they had to revise their opinion. The creature must have walked upright. It also lacked the long canines and other dental features characteristic of modern anthropoid apes. The capacity of the skull, however, barely exceeded that of a chimpanzee's. In fact, the creature had been of pygmy size, had walked on two legs, and possessed a thoroughly simian head containing human teeth and a brain already almost human. It was a "half-man." Broom christened it *Plesianthropus transvaalensis*, indicating by this description "a being from the Transvaal closely allied to man" — the unique intermediate position occupied by the Sterkfontein man.

Two years after the discovery of the *Plesianthropus*, while Barlow was making a fresh investigation of the caves and quarries of the Krugersdorp valley, a fifteen-year-old boy named Gert Terblanche appeared on the site, shyly approached the foreman, took a bone out of his trouser pocket, and handed it to Barlow. Then he vanished. A little while later Broom examined the bone. It was a fragment from a human palate, including a first grinder. Barlow looked on with interest.

"Another First Man, sir?" he inquired dryly. "Bit bigger than the one I found, eh?"

"Yes, it is bigger and if I'm not mistaken even more unusual," exclaimed Broom excitedly. He made Barlow tell him the story of the find. Then he hurried off at once to Kromdraai Farm, where the boy lived, only to find that he was at school.

It thus happened that a famous museum curator suddenly burst into a Boer village school and announced that he must speak to one of the pupils at once. The teacher, tremendously impressed and yet clever enough to take advantage of the occasion, said he would gladly release the boy if South Africa's great fossil hunter would be good enough first to say a few words about his researches on prehistoric man.

When Broom at last had Gert of Kromdraai Farm to himself, he shook the bone under the lad's nose and demanded excitedly: "Where did you get this from? Come on, tell me! Take me immediately to the place where you found it!"

Gert Terblanche rummaged in his pockets and pulled out something else. It was a handful of teeth. They were fossilized human teeth.

"Didn't lose any of them, boy, did you? Who told you, anyway, that you had to bring us bones like this?"

"The whole district," retorted the boy with a laugh, "talks of nothing but that primitive man of yours. There's lots more of the stuff lying about at our farm, Kromdraai."

Half an hour later they were at Kromdraai. The schoolboy showed Broom a precipitous wall of rock, corresponding to that at Sterkfontein in every detail. Here, too, there were many crevices filled with rubbish and sealed off by hard precipitate. An upper-arm bone of human type was sticking out of one of them. "That's the place," Gert explained eagerly. "The best thing to do," he said innocently, "would be to pour gunpowder into the hole and blow the whole show up. We always do that when we need stones for building." He was already beaming with enjoyment at the prospect of the big bang.

"For heaven's sake!" cried Broom. "You'd better help me, instead, to chisel the bones out. Sure you haven't got anything more in your pockets?"

"Yes, I've got one more tooth," the boy confessed. "Can't I keep just that one?"

"Well, of course, it would be a premolar!" groaned Broom. "Look here, I'll give you five slabs of chocolate for it!" And the youthful discoverer agreed to the bargain.

They extracted the larger part of the skull, nearly all the teeth, substantial portions of the arm and an anklebone. This Kromdraai man had been an extraordinary fellow. He had possessed massive nutcracker jaws, a foot (with a turned-out big toe) shaped for leaping, human though very large teeth, and also clearly human arms without the least simian characteristic. Unfortunately he did not seem to belong to the ancestral stock of mankind. The crevice also contained remains of the saber-toothed tiger, only known to paleontologists to have existed during the Ice Age in Europe. If the Kromdraai man had been contemporary with the saber-toothed tiger he would have to be ascribed to a far later epoch than the early human types of Java and Peking. Broom considered him to be a backward side-branch of the human stem, a *Paranthropus robustus*, or robust collateral line that had died out some time in the Pleistocene epoch. It was not discovered until later that saber-toothed felines had already existed in the African Tertiary period.

The South African finds, interesting as they were, remained overshadowed by other discoveries for ten years. In the interval von Koenigswald had excavated his Java men and giants near Sangiran. Weidenreich had come before the public with his theory of giants. All conjectures about the birthplace of mankind centered as before on southeastern Asia. Though anthropologists in the course of time

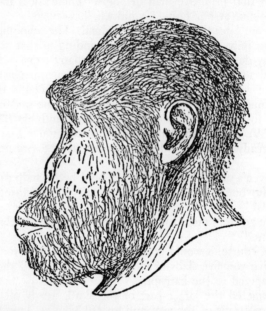

A strange ape-headed type belonging to the semihuman group, *Paranthropus robustus*.

came to incline more and more to see a semihuman type even in the Taungs child, they remained cautious. They assumed that the entire group of South Africans had evolved independently of the main human stream. No agreement could be reached as to the time in which they had lived. The dates given varied between 5,000,000 and 500,000 years ago. It was no use working on such variable data. In order to illuminate the darkness of the caves of the Transvaal it would have been necessary to make a close examination of the contents of the rock crevices, attract chemists and prehistorians to the work, and apply laboratory tests to the geological layers and mammal fossils. However, during the Second World War hardly any dynamite was available to prehistoric explorers. Blasting operations in the caves had accordingly to be postponed and the explanation of the mystery delayed.

Not until after the war were operations resumed, when the trail of the enigmatic South African creatures was taken up strenuously on a grand scale. It was the Transvaal blasting operations that were to disclose at last the misty era, millions of years ago, in which mankind escaped the charmed circle of the animals.

The Transvaal Garden of Eden

Ever since the days of Scheuchzer the investigators of prehistory have been groping their way backward along the path trodden by early man. In 1868 they came upon the first traces of civilization dating from the Ice Age and upon its creators themselves, the Cro-Magnon men. About the year 1880 recognition was accorded to a still older human race of remote antiquity which had already begun to produce highly effective tools. These were the Neanderthal men. (The original discovery of the bones of a manlike being with features we now list as typical of Neanderthal man was made at Neanderthal in Rhenish Prussia in 1856.) Around 1890 an ape man was discovered in Java and considered to be the true transitional form between beast and Man. About 1930 it was proved in Chou-kou-tien that even the alleged ape men might well have possessed a certain culture and could not therefore be described as the very first men. So the chief aim of the science of primitive man had still not been achieved by 1945. Evidence from the earliest stages of human history was lacking, as were also proofs of the existence of an animate being that still remained an animal and yet had already become Man. A true semihuman type had not yet been found.

It was now being sought not only by Broom but also by the South African paleontologist John Talbot Robinson, who succeeded Broom on his death in 1951. Robinson shared Broom's views and had suspected from the beginning that there was something altogether wrong about the three "collateral branches" of Taungs, Sterkfontein, and Kromdraai. There were many indications that these relics were older than those of Asiatic early man. The Taungs child, considered to be in part the most manlike of apes and in part the most apelike of men, appeared to have already existed in the Tertiary period. Perhaps the *Plesianthropus* of Sterkfontein had been a direct descendant of the Taungs creature. If so, the South African group would have to be looked at in quite a new light. They were not backward side-branches, but the most important of all semihuman types yet found. It is possible, thought Robinson, as he studied over and over again the mysterious skulls from the limestone caves, that the cradle of mankind existed in South Africa.

There was one scholar in the world who could determine the age of the South African specimens with precision, the father of cave research, the Abbé Henri Breuil. Broom, Robinson, and their supporter Dart corresponded with Breuil, gave him an exhaustive description of their finds, and urged him to come to South Africa at the earliest opportunity. They cherished the secret hope that the great expert might even succeed in discovering traces of civilization dating from the epoch of the alleged semihuman types. Should the Sterkfontein culture prove much more primitive than that of Chou-kou-tien the creatures themselves must also have existed at a much earlier date. The attitudes of scholars were still evenly divided between curiosity and skepticism, noncommittal expectation

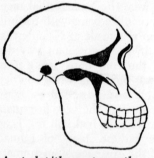

Australopithecus prometheus
(Makapansgat)

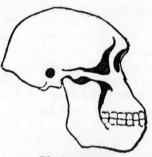

Plesianthropus
(Sterkfontein)

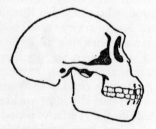

Pithecanthropus erectus
(Trinil)

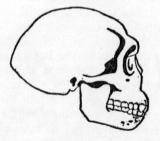

Sinanthropus
(Peking)

and anxious conjecture. Broom, Dart, and Robinson, however, remained firmly convinced that their hypothesis was correct.

Immediately after the war Breuil arrived in Pretoria. He had followed the trails of primitive man for half a century and spent a great part of his life in subterranean caverns, but except for his white hair he showed no traces of his age. He climbed the cliffs of the Sterkfontein valley and scrambled about in the narrow caves and crevasses shown him by Broom, Dart, and Robinson as nimbly as when in his youth he had explored with Cartailhac the wonders of Les Combarelles and Font-de-Gaume.

He did not find any Old Stone Age implements or hand axes such as occur in every Pleistocene deposit in South Africa. Consequently the Sterkfontein and Kromdraai beings had not lived in the Pleistocene epoch and had to be ascribed to earlier layers. In these older layers — of the Late Tertiary period — Dart had found a great many bones of antelopes and shattered baboons' skulls. Without exception they had all been violently cracked and split.

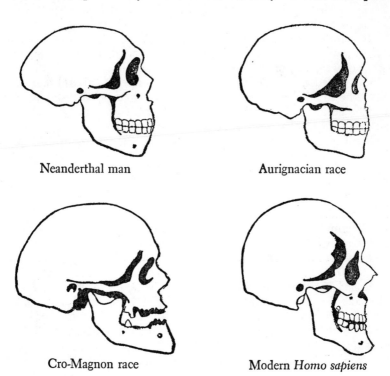

Neanderthal man   Aurignacian race

Cro-Magnon race   Modern *Homo sapiens*

Dart picked up a big antelope's thighbone and brought it down hard on the skull of a baboon. Right enough! The two protuberances at the leg joint fitted exactly into the holes made by the blow in the skull vaulting.

The explorers gazed with profound emotion at the first implements of humanity thus brought to light in the South African chalk rubble. They were weapons automatically available to a semihuman creature still ignorant of what a stone could do, and they did not need treatment of any kind. Had the first glimmerings of humanity started when an animal that walked upright, exasperated by its longing for fresh meat and blood, ceased to rely on its bare hands and seized a bone in order to slaughter a stubborn prey? Weapons of bone — clubs made of the legs and jawbones of animals — had also been used in hunting by the Peking man. He knew how to adapt this raw material for certain purposes and had gone farther, using flaked stone implements. These South African creatures, however, had taken up whatever came to hand without concerning themselves any further with it. Their culture was improvised. It only surpassed in a single decisive respect the skill shown in handicraft by chimpanzees at the anthropoid-ape establishments. The Sterkfontein men had begun pursuing and overcoming the animal kingdom by the employment of weapons, mastering the beasts by intelligence.

The question of date still remained to be solved, but Breuil believed he could clear up the matter. Of the fifteen species of animals which had left traces in the rock crevices of Sterkfontein, his investigations showed that by far the greater number belonged exclusively to the Tertiary period. The others, including the saber-toothed tiger, had appeared on earth toward the end of the Tertiary period and had lived far into the Pleistocene epoch. All the game hunted by Sterkfontein man originated in the Late Tertiary period. Some had probably died out while he still existed. Other newly immigrant species had then replaced them. It was a purely arithmetical problem to determine the length of time during which all the animals associated with the *Plesianthropus* had been contemporary with him. The result of one calculation gave Mr. Barlow's find an age of at least 1,000,000 years.

As had happened previously in Chou-kou-tien, a staff of scientists checked the layers, deposits, and fossils and subjected the South African finds to the most modern methods of chemical analysis. There is still no absolute certainty about their geologic age. But it is assumed that the oldest skull, that of Taungs, had lain in the soil for some 2,000,000 years. The semihuman types of Sterkfontein seem to be about 100,000 years younger, and the Kromdraai "nut-crackers" over 1,000,000. On this view the South African specimens are four times as old as the ape man of Java, fourteen times as old as Neanderthal man, thirty times as old as Cro-Magnon man, and a hundred times as old as the enlightened Late Ice Age type.

Africa had now suddenly come to be a primary focus of research on prehistoric man. Oakley, Le Gros Clark, Teilhard de Chardin, and many other prominent scholars declared themselves to be of Broom's opinion. New and surprising discoveries were reported from the most diverse districts of East and South Africa. On the African island of Rusinga the wife of the anthropologist Leakey had found the *Proconsul* and the *Limnopithecus*, the primitive anthropoid apes already mentioned, which lived 20,000,000 years ago. They already resembled in some of their characteristics the South African semihuman types that walked upright and carried weapons. In the Transvaal many counterparts to the Taungs, Sterkfontein, and Kromdraai skulls were dug up. In Germany Hans Weinert published reports on Kohl-Larsen's baggage from Lake Eyasi, the *Africanthropus njarasensis* and the *Meganthropus africanus*. Africa showed the scientists the entire evolution of mankind from the simian *Proconsul* through the baboon-hunting semihuman type, the promising stock of early man, and the giants that died out without posterity down to the Neanderthal-like Rhodesian man and the cliff-painting progressive races.

The most important of all these finds were the semihuman types of the Transvaal. They proved to have been closely associated with the diversion process that separated human beings from the anthropoid apes, so according to the anthropologists they represent the transition stage from beast to Man. Those most resembling human beings — the prehominids, as the South African specimens were called — probably already occupied a position well this side of the field of transition. The Taungs child was considered by certain investigators to stand rather farther over toward the simian side.

Among the caves and crevasses of rock along the Witwatersrand and between the rivers Vaal and Limpopo blasting has been going on since 1945. New skulls and bones have been coming to light everywhere. Up to 1947 Broom and Robinson had collected the remains of twelve Sterkfontein men, including one almost complete skull. In the same year Dart, who first described the child of Taungs, opened up a new site just under a hundred and ninety miles north of Johannesburg, the district of Makapansgat. He extracted a whole series of bones from the rocks in that neighborhood. They resembled in every respect those of the Taungs creature. Among them he discovered something extremely astonishing. Hidden in heaps of ashes were the bones of animals that showed traces of what looked like burning. So the primeval being that Dart believed to be the true missing link might already have been acquainted with fire. His discoverer confidently gave him the name of *Australopithecus prometheus.*

A year later Broom and Robinson came across "nutcrackers" near Swartkrans, a place not far from Sterkfontein. They resembled the

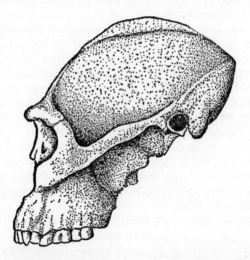

Cranium of "nutcracker" *Paranthropus crassidens.* This constituted the hinge on which the muscular apparatus of the chewing mechanism was hung. Similar formations are still to be seen in the orangutan and chimpanzee species. Presumably the "giants" of eastern Asia belong to a related type.

Kromdraai type but came from an older geologic level and had even more massive jaws and larger teeth. They bore a small ridge on the skull that served to suspend the powerful chewing muscles. And on April 29, 1949, Robinson obtained from the same lime-cemented crevasse the most interesting of all South African human fossils. It was a lower jaw which resembled that of the Heidelberg man, except that it had a stronger set of teeth.

Thus the most diverse forms had become available in positively embarrassing abundance. There were ape-headed creatures, somewhat more human Pygmies bringing down baboons with clubs, uncouth beings of colossal size with little ridges on their skulls, and African "Heidelbergers." For 1,500,000 years the prehominids were the only creatures on earth that resembled human beings. This enormous period is three times as long as that allowed before their discovery by science for the entire evolution of mankind. "It stands to reason," Weinert stated emphatically, "that during such lapses of time, which are utterly inconceivable to us, variations must also have occurred." Some of these variations — giants and dwarfs, nutcrackers and beings of the Heidelberg type — seem to have lived at the same time and in the same places. Which of them was the real Adam?

The question cannot be answered with any certainty. There is much reason to suppose that the *Telanthropus capensis* of Swartkrans, with an underjaw amazingly reminiscent of that of the Heidelberg man, played a very special part in the process of human evolution. At first Robinson could make little or nothing of his find. He estimated that the *Telanthropus* had lived between 250,000 and 500,000 years before the early human types of Trinil, Peking, and Heidelberg — at an epoch and in a district in which, according to all the data hitherto accepted, only the far more ancient prehominids belonging to the Sterkfontein and Kromdraai groups of forms might have been expected. In addition, he had been a contemporary of the biggest and most extraordinary of the "nutcrackers," the *Paranthropus crassidens*. Were there already at that time in the Tertiary period cousins of the *Pithecanthropus*? And where did they come from?

The puzzle was solved in 1952. Robinson discovered near the first site another typically human palate fragment of the *Telanthropus*, and a year later another extremely human-looking bone. On the basis of the jaw, the palate, and the five teeth that were now available, a very good idea of the aspect of this new Swartkrans man could be obtained. He combined the characteristics of the semihuman type of Sterkfontein with those of Asiatic early man and the Heidelberg specimen to such a convincing extent that there can hardly be any doubt of his true classification. Although he obviously still belongs to the prehominid group and shares many of their primitive features, he had been evolving for a long time in quite a different direction from that taken by the big-mouthed, ridge-headed *Paranthropus* man alongside whom he had lived. There is every indication that with his appearance toward the close of the Tertiary period a great stretch of the road leading to true humanity had been left behind. In this case, therefore, one of the many related forms in the limestone caves of the Transvaal has at last been identified which, as Heberer writes, "can serve as a model for the stage we must assume the direct forerunners of mankind to have reached."

The genealogy of semihuman types and thus the history of the growth of man now seem to be somewhat as follows, according to the current data available. Somewhere in the tropics of the ancient world, perhaps on the plains of Africa, perhaps also in the area that subsequently became the seat of oriental civilization, the first man-shaped creatures appeared in the form of diminutive rovers of the savannahs. They resembled the Taungs and Makapansgat types. It is impossible to be sure whether they still were monkeys or already men. They probably lived in hordes on open ground, digging up rodents from holes in the earth, also collecting lizards and crayfish, and gradually learning the use of fire. Whether they were already able to kindle it themselves or whether on each occasion they had to wait for a grass fire, we do not know. They developed in the course of some hundreds of thousands of years into the semihuman types of Sterkfontein and Kromdraai — and probably into other hitherto undiscovered species also — which obtained a living in similar fashion but by that time employed superior weapons. They instituted mass hunting expeditions after monkeys and small antelopes, evolved into confident masters of their environment, and probably survived far into the Pleistocene epoch in their paradisal South African game reserve, which produced all they needed to live. One of these species is the forefather of the *Telanthropus* and may thus well have been the presumptive ancestor of the human race. Although the rovers of the savannahs and the "nutcrackers" gradually died out, their posterity became the conquerors of the world.

THE EARLY CULTURES

Brain, club, and stone

SOME ELEMENTS of the technical accomplishments that have made Man so powerful have long been practised by animals. Termites and ants erect ingenious buildings, cultivate plants, and breed domestic animals. Birds and beavers are gifted architects. Insects possess eyes that can be compared with our telescopes and microscopes. Bats developed the first supersonic equipment, cuttlefish the first rocket propulsion mechanism. No submarine can compete with a shark, no jet aircraft with a swift.

In one respect the technical dexterity of animals differs fundamentally from that of mankind. The apparatus used by an animal is its own body. Each technician of the animal world became a specialist in its own field, a living rocket or reverberating or flying device. It is chained like a galley slave to a contrivance applicable to a definite purpose. Other worlds are closed to it. Even the crustaceans, insects, fish, and birds that use foreign bodies as instruments do not overstep the bounds set to their own physical capacities. They cannot do so because they are irrevocably committed to their individual spheres of action. The most wonderful equipment in the animal kingdom, the fully developed upper portion of the brain, was the first to enable a relatively unspecialized group of animate beings to break the chains, construct complicated instruments from the raw material provided by nature, and thus occupy the most extensive areas of living space.

Man, in a phrase of Freud's, is a "god of prothesis." He is the only creature who has forced the phenomena of his environment into his service. He no longer represents technical devices in his own person but replaces them by appliances that relieve his body of strain. He himself grows less efficient. But his instruments improve. Without them he would today be as naked and helpless as a mussel with its shell broken open.

The gray mass of cells composing the modern brain, that arbitrator and creator of worlds, exists in all mammals. But in the human case it became a directing headquarters, controlling its own organs and the data of its environment and making independent decisions. Man thinks and judges. He has left the warm security of animal life for the ice-cold realm of personal responsibility. But his body and the antique part of his brain are retained on the animal level. The animal in us refuses to yield and this disunion renders man a split personality with two souls within the same breast, as the psycho-analysts say.

All primates — the prosimians, the vast army of genuine monkeys, and the anthropoid apes — already exhibit such split traits of character. They want, so to speak, to stop being animals; and they have in fact, if we consider their psychological and mental endowment, ceased to be animals in the true sense that applies to other mammals.

> If a barrel-organ man's monkey collects money for his master [writes Fritz Kahn in his *Book of Nature*], it does so with human gestures and a look in its eyes which will not be forgotten even if fifty years pass and meanwhile one looks into the eyes of twenty thousand people, some honest but most of them deceitful. In that deeply melancholy gaze of the monkey, more eloquent than a dozen sentences which any beggar-boy can learn by heart, can be read four momentous words: "Primates are not animals!" It is a gaze more significant than that of the most faithful dog. We are looking into the soul of a being arrested upon the way to becoming human, like the water-sprite Gottfried Keller imagined he could see in the ice of the frozen lake beneath his feet. "She groped this way and that, choking and desperate, at the rigid layer above her."

This urgent and groping intellectual unrest drove certain primates — which had not evolved into peaceful, vegetarian specialists in climbing — into the wide open spaces. They were obliged to adapt themselves and walk on two legs. Their hands were left free for other purposes. The growing brain began to make all sorts of experiments. Sticks and bones were lying about on the plain. They could be picked up and used to knock fruit off the trees. Some of the sticks were not good for much and were thrown away. Others proved serviceable, were retained, and gave pleasure. Thus the history of civilization began, perhaps as long as 20,000,000 years ago, in the time of the *proconsul*, perhaps not until shortly before the appearance of the Taungs and Makapansgat creatures.

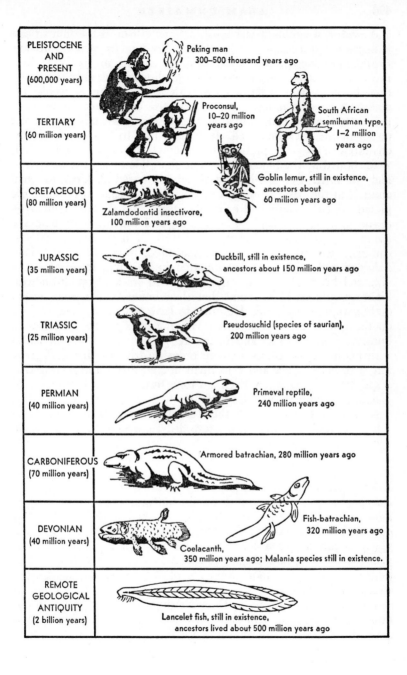

PLEISTOCENE AND PRESENT (600,000 years)	Peking man 300–500 thousand years ago
TERTIARY (60 million years)	Proconsul, 10–20 million years ago — South African semihuman type, 1–2 million years ago
CRETACEOUS (80 million years)	Goblin lemur, still in existence, ancestors about 60 million years ago — Zalamdodontid insectivore, 100 million years ago
JURASSIC (35 million years)	Duckbill, still in existence, ancestors about 150 million years ago
TRIASSIC (25 million years)	Pseudosuchid (species of saurian), 200 million years ago
PERMIAN (40 million years)	Primeval reptile, 240 million years ago
CARBONIFEROUS (70 million years)	Armored batrachian, 280 million years ago
DEVONIAN (40 million years)	Fish-batrachian, 320 million years ago — Coelacanth, 350 million years ago; Malania species still in existence.
REMOTE GEOLOGICAL ANTIQUITY (2 billion years)	Lancelet fish, still in existence, ancestors lived about 500 million years ago

A stick is a splendid instrument. It lengthens the owner's reach and gives him a feeling of proud superiority. The primate became a lord and master. If another animal crossed his path, perhaps intending to seize a fruit he wanted for himself, he only needed to raise his stick and strike a blow with it. The animal would immediately cease to move. It was obliterated, dead, gone forever from the battlefield of competitive struggle. The self-confidence of the owner of the stick increased. It amused him to frighten his fellow creatures. He grew presumptuous, cruel, tyrannical. His hands were stained by the blood of those he slew. He licked the blood and liked its taste. Perhaps he had already devoured all kinds of small animals in the past, as many apes do. He now learned to enjoy the pleasures of the chase and of eating meat. And the first animals — apart from insects, land crabs, lizards, and rodents — that he systematically pursued and slaughtered were of necessity his helpless cousins, the lower primates. He was in daily contact with them. Baboons and other monkeys squatted in the trees from which he obtained his food. It was easy for him to strike them down with his stick, and he soon found that their brains in particular tasted quite exceptionally good. He came to have an entirely new outlook on the world. He experimented with the most various methods of hunting, hurling sticks and stones at his quarry, joining in bands with his ingenious companions in order to drive the herds of game into a confined space and hem them in, and finally discovering that a splinter of bone when given a strong thrust would be capable of piercing an animal right through.

A creature capable of all these accomplishments no longer considered himself an animal. He regarded the fruit-eating anthropoid apes with contempt, as only able to kill, at best, a bird on its nest or a little tree frog. And he took every opportunity of exhibiting his strength to the pacific primitive chimpanzee. However much the latter might resemble him physically it feared the stick as much as the timid natives of newly discovered countries were millions of years later to fear the firearms of the white conquerors. A deep gulf had opened between the rovers of the plains, who could employ their newly acquired reason for both good and evil purposes, and the primates of the primeval jungle, which had preserved their mental innocence. And the more Man ate of the tree of knowledge the wider the gulf grew.

The old idea of history in Darwin's time, according to which our beastlike forefathers had been barbarous and immoral and only gradually worked themselves up to a high ethical level, is a charming illusion, a fairy tale. Today we think quite differently on the subject. "I do not see how nowadays any man can look a monkey in the face and claim any sort of relationship to it on the ground of his behavior," wrote the anthropologist Earnest Hooton some years ago with remarkable candor. "Any decent monkey would repudiate the suggestion of a common ancestral kinship with mankind." This is the bitter truth. As the gray cells of the upper portions of the brains of the erect primates multiplied and their clever hands began to wield the stick, humanity entered upon a dangerous road. It was bordered not only by intellectual feats, discoveries, inventions, and services to civilization but also by intellectual misdeeds and violent and criminal acts. The split mentality of the master animal made it a creature that bore both heaven and hell within its breast.

As the anthropologists had not yet quite made up their minds whether the South African specimens were to be classified with the apes or with mankind Weinert wrote down the following much quoted sentence: "To slaughter, roast, and devour members of one's own species is a thing no ape ever does. It is the action of a human being." And he added: "It would be pleasant if we could regard the act of Prometheus as the first proceeding in the growth of humanity. But we cannot help recognizing that the act of Cain preceded it." This sounds severe, but it is true in principle. The old legends say exactly the same in their narratives of the origin of the human race.

In the course of time, when *Telanthropus* came on the scene, the weight of the brain increased, exceeding that of the ape. Attainments and abilities improved. The semihuman types came to inhabit larger and larger areas. At the beginning of the Pleistocene epoch they were already occupying all the warmer zones of the Old World. And there, in a new environment, they were faced by problems which they could only solve by further strains on their intelligence and the invention of superior weapons and tools. They found the shaped stone the best of all killing devices. "A brain weight of nine hundred grams [just under two pounds]," remarks that pessimistic critic of civilization, Hooton, "is adequate as an optimum for human behavior. Anything more is employed in the commission of misdeeds." The large-brained predecessors of mankind had not yet come anywhere near this optimum. But with the aid of that new and miraculous weapon the stone, they doubtless perpetrated all sorts of bloody massacres at this period. They were the first foreign conquerors to set foot on alien soil and establish a stern dominion over it.

The stone which enabled them to conquer the world was not

yet a hand axe, but a large pebble that had been given a cutting edge by a few blows. It was the size of a cricket ball and fitted into a robust masculine hand. Such "spheroids" were found in southern and eastern Asia and especially, in improbably large quantities, in the desert sands of North Africa. In 1952 and 1953 the French prehistorian Camille Arambourg alone dug up near the Algerian village of Aïn-Hanech more than three hundred, together with bones of mammals dating from the transition period between the Tertiary and Pleistocene ages. At two congresses of natural scientists in Algiers it was proved beyond doubt that the stones had been shaped by men. Their age was estimated at 600,000 years.

Similar stones, worked into the shape of chopping knives, were still being used by the Peking man 100,000 years later. One is emboldened to ask whether the descendants of the semihuman types settled on the Mediterranean coast and thence, over a period ten times as long as that of the whole epoch of our own civilization, penetrated the Old World in all directions. The Mediterranean occupies a central position, is easy to cross, and has remained down to our own day the artery of culture. The great decisions could have been taken there which led to the inventions of the hand axe and the stone knife, to great achievements in arts and crafts, to the creating of values, and to abstract thought.

This hypothesis was brilliantly confirmed in 1954. Camille Arambourg of the prehistoric museum in the Jardin des Plantes, the discoverer of the Algerian spheroids, turned up the evidence near Palikao in Algeria. He struck a sandhill permeated with horizontal stone beds. Underneath there was a stratum that to all appearances was the ancient sea floor. Arambourg expected surprises. In the big digging net brought up full of animal bones there were primeval Atlantic elephants and camels and the forerunners of swine that must be 500,000 years old. Finally, in the middle of this Early Pleistocene menagerie he found two human jawbones.

One jawbone, which lay under the skull of an Atlantic elephant, is very big and powerful. It appears to have belonged to a male and shows a disconcerting similarity to the lower jaw of Heidelberg man. The other, smaller and presumably that of a female, reminds one strongly of Peking man. This primitive human, therefore, who fills the gaps between *Telanthropus*, Heidelberg man, and Peking man is at least 100,000 years older than Asiatic early man. It was named *Atlanthropus mauretanicus*. Almost more important, however, than the excavation of these two jawbones was the discovery of the sandstone artifacts that *Atlanthropus* had once made.

Another Algerian site in the neighborhood of Mascara yielded new fragments of *Atlanthropus* and in addition a stock of sandstone implements. There were no more spheroids, no simple killing devices, but there were tools of the next stage of development, the Abbevillian and Early Clactonian. Man had learned to use a big boulder as an anvil, on which he had laid his raw material of stone and shaped it with the aid of a cuttingstone. Implements for the most varied uses could be produced, far superior to the old killing devices. Such primitive wedges and blades had been recognized by science since Lartet's time but nothing had been known of their manufacture until now. They are found throughout North and central Africa, in southern Europe, and the Near East, the classic lands where higher types of civilization subsequently arose. At the time of their production about 500,000 years ago, neither Neanderthal man nor any other human creatures possessing technical skill existed on earth. Only the most primitive early man existed, recognized in fragments like the lower jaw of Mauer and the somewhat misleadingly delicate fragments of *Pithecanthropus robustus*.

It had been suspected for a long time that such creatures must have been the bearers of the Early Clactonian and Abbevillian cultures. Now finally we know how they looked, and we know that they as the first men laid aside club and pebble and struck instead with quartzite, sandstone, and flint.

As not only skull fragments but also the successive steps of stone culture show, there is a direct line from *Atlanthropus* to European pre-Neanderthals with their heavy Acheulean axes. However, there appears to be still another line leading to Asia — where the ancient hand axe and blade cultures intersect the chipping-knife cultures of Peking man and his relatives — as far as India and Malaya. With stone in hand primitive man conquered the world.

As early as the First Intermediate Ice Age pioneering groups of these people, far ahead of the main body, were occupying positions at the edge of the world, on the coasts of the Pacific Ocean.

If we try to grasp the idea of the time taken for this greatest, most wonderful, and most momentous of events in the history of the earth to develop, our powers of imagination go on strike. We have to call comparisons to our aid. If we calculate, as paleontologists are fond of doing, the period that elapsed between the first appearance of Tertiary anthropoid apes and the present era as a twenty-four-hour day, we get the following figures: the phase of human growth lasting from the adoption of the erect posture to the use of fire extended over from 400,000 to 600,000 generations, in other words 12,000,000

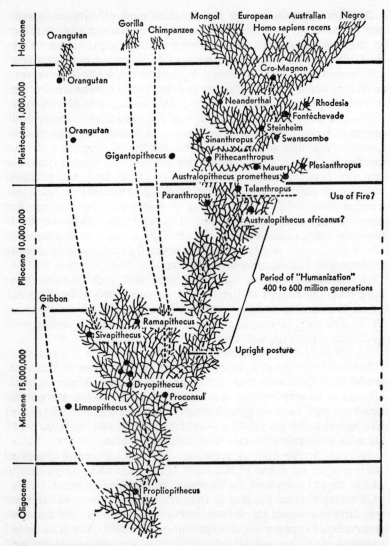

The descent of Man from the *Proconsul* to *Homo sapiens*, according to Heberer. The time scale bears no relation to the various durations of the epochs.

to 20,000,000 years — or, on the basis of convertibility indicated, from twelve to twenty hours. Thus at five o'clock in the morning the half-erect proconsuls arrive. Seventeen hours pass before they evolve into the armed semihuman types of Taungs and Swartkrans. Half an hour later, at half-past ten in the evening, Robinson's Adam, the *Telanthropus*, appears, followed after another half-hour by the Prometheus ape man acquainted with fire. At half-past eleven early man — the Trinil, Peking, and Heidelberg specimens — enter; at a quarter of twelve those of Steinheim and Swanscombe; at ten to twelve Neanderthal man; at five to twelve the Cro-Magnon and Aurignacian races; and at one minute to twelve present-day European man. Our own cultural epoch, accordingly, bears the same relation to the whole duration of the growth of humanity as one minute does to twenty-four hours.

All the ideas, productions, and achievements of this one final minute of human history, from the pyramids to Homer, Beethoven, and atomic physics, are based on the previous twenty-three hours and fifty-nine minutes, during which manlike beings gradually — at first with infinite slowness and later faster and faster — learned to employ their hands and walk upright, to use fire, develop their minds, and manufacture tools from bone and stone.

The conquest of the fifth continent

A decisive turning point in the history of the early cultures of mankind was that at which the first primitive human beings brought animals beneath their sway. Thenceforth man began to exercise his dominion over nature by subtle intellectual means as well as by clubs and stone weapons. He chose certain creatures to be his servants and slaves, thereby relieving himself of many problems connected with the struggle for existence. The nomadic hunter became a settler, breeding cattle.

Most kinds of domesticated animals were not in existence before the postglacial epochs. One animal however, had become familiar with primitive man long before that time. It was not forced into his service but came of its own accord, in the expectation of deriving advantage from the association. This animal was man's most faithful friend, the protector of his home and the companion of his hunting expeditions, the dog.

Packs of wild dogs at one time swarmed round the settlements of primitive man, rummaged among his heaps of refuse, announced the approach of game and beasts of prey, and gave valuable practical aid in repelling hostile attacks. Thus arose in the course of infinitely prolonged periods a true symbiosis — a living together — which benefited both partners. Primitive man took pleasure in his four-legged followers, fed and tamed them. He suddenly discovered that the elusive animal world, if it were properly treated, could be induced to obey him. It was a revelation of tremendous importance. For the first time nature, in the shape of an agile carrion-eating creature, became truly subject to the rule of man.

This friendly relation between man and dog seems to have evolved

For tens of thousands of years, the dog has accompanied the hunting expeditions of Man.

in Europe during the last glacial period, about the time of the Solutrean or Magdalenian epochs. But in another quarter of the globe, in southeast Asia, there existed to all appearance during the Riss Glacial Age some 200,000 years ago a breed of half-tamed dogs that followed the migrations of humanity and even took part in the conquest of a new continent. The boldest, most imposing, and most adventurous warrior expedition primitive man ever undertook was the crossing from Asia to Australia. It was accompanied by packs of red-haired dogs the size of wolves. They are today well known for their attacks on sheep and are called dingoes, and they have already caused the zoologists a great deal of trouble.

The story begins on the island of Java, where Eugène Dubois once dug up his ape man. Java proves what happened during the Pleistocene epoch, just as South Africa provides evidence of the earliest stages of human history. In the Günz Ice Age, the first glacial period, the water level of the Sunda Sea dropped. Anthropoid apes, wild dogs, saber-toothed tigers and bears, and also early specimens of Man and "giants," migrated from the mainland of Asia to the islands. The giants died out, but early man found the living conditions favorable and evolved there, as he did in Africa, China, and Europe, into long-headed, tall, primitive Neanderthal types, clever with their hands. In the neighborhood of Trinil, near the village of Ngandong, since 1931 Dutch geologists under the engineer Oppenoorth have dug up eleven skulls belonging to this race of ancient Javanese of Neanderthal type. Von Koenigswald investigated these "Ngandong men" and came to the conclusion that the almost pentagonal heads, tapering toward the top, with saddle-type vaulting, were clear evidence of their descent from *Pithecanthropus*. A little later the "Wadjak men" discovered by Dubois made their appearance. It was at this time that humanity must have succeeded in crossing the six-hundred-odd miles of the Timor straits and settling the continent of Australia, which had been lying in a charmed sleep since the beginning of the Tertiary period.

Australia became separated from the mainland of Asia 75,000,000 years ago. It drifted away, carrying its primeval fauna with it. Only marsupials and duckbills occupied the grassy plains, the eucalyptus groves, and the lakes. Higher mammals did not exist. There were no wild dogs or predecessors of Man. But suddenly, probably as early as the Riss Glacial Age, brown and agile primitive men penetrated the fifth continent. They resembled the Javanese men of Ngandong and Wadjak. Red-haired dogs chased the startled kangaroos. They looked like the wild dogs of Java, those of the Tengger district. Human and canine fossils have been found in Victoria and New South Wales, together with the bones of long extinct giant marsupials. This might be taken as a sign that the invasion of Australia could have taken place as early as the Middle Pleistocene epoch.

Geologists have calculated that sea level between Java and Australia dropped over three hundred feet during the Riss Glacial Age; but in places depths in the straits of Timor amount to over three thousand feet. Neither man nor dog can cross such places by swimming. Even drifting logs could not transport whole families of people and packs of dingoes. If a temporary land bridge between Indonesia and Australia had existed at that time, other higher mammals would also have been able to migrate to the new country. Yet only human beings and dogs succeeded in doing so. We must therefore assume, astonishing as it may sound, that the primitive man of Java had already, at the very same time that the first Neanderthal men were roaming the forests of Europe, built rafts or dugout canoes, tamed the wild dogs of Tengger, and started large-scale voyages of discovery.

Such an achievement presupposes high technical skill and genuine civilization. The modern inhabitants of the Australian bush show little trace of either. The nautical knowledge of their ancestors was lost and the dingo ran wild, reverting to a ravening beast of prey. The people themselves sank, among the primeval animals of the fifth continent, to a cultural level their adventurous forefathers had far surpassed. Only their boomerangs, skill in drawing, and magical practices still convey some idea of that mysterious epoch of humanity when direct descendants of Javanese early man for the first time dared to advance across the seas into the unknown.

Comrade cave bear

After the First World War the Austrian farmers' fields yielded little produce because of the absence of artificial manure. Some intelligent farmers then had the idea of using the guano of the Alpine caves for agricultural purposes. The caves began to be cleared and their contents sold in the markets. The expedient proved successful. Layers of nitrogenous bats' dung three feet thick were to be found in many of the rock grottoes. And beneath these layers the Austrian collectors of guano came upon even better fertilizers. The carcasses and bones of large animals came to light there in great numbers. They were cave bears that had never awakened from their winter sleep.

The scientists heard about these finds and began to take an interest in the fossilized fertilizers of the Alpine caves. Zoologists, paleontologists, and prehistorians traveled to Styria, climbed up through narrow openings into the interior of the mountains, started excavation, and discovered the second form of community living with an animal which primitive man had practised. The cave-bear cult of Neanderthal man stood revealed.

As late as the time of Klaatsch research workers and all scientific circles interested in their investigations had regarded the cave bear as a terrible beast of prey, the fiercest adversary of the weak, inadequately armed man of the Neanderthal age. Observations taken and examinations carried out in the Austrian grottoes, especially in the Dragon's Cave near Mixnitz, present quite a different picture. As the hunter flourished his hand axe he had no need to be particularly frightened of his huge shaggy next-door neighbor. He could even let the animal share his cave without risk. For the cave bear fed peacefully on grass and other plants, as was proved by the way in which its teeth were worn smooth, by the contents of the stomachs of the carcasses which had been preserved, and above all by veterinary medicine. Many cave bears had suffered from severe diseases of the jaw. The remarkable deformation of their heads indicated that the disease was the same as that known today by the name of actinomycosis, which only affects grass-eating animals such as sheep, cattle, and goats. Not a single cave bear's den contained any animal bones showing traces of biting by this primeval giant. The fine old dramatic pictures of the Ice Ages, in which cave bears were represented as attacking the settlements of early man, are therefore just as inaccurate as the drawings of dragons and unicorns dating from the centuries of fantasy.

A ponderous, relatively harmless grass-eating animal, and one that spent a third of its life in a winter sleep, must have been the ideal prey, a kind of living larder, for Neanderthal man. Bears' meat and fat tasted delicious, bearskins were a protection against rain and cold, bears' bones could be made into weapons and tools. If one felt hungry, one explored the underground maze till one found a recess with a cave bear sleeping in it, hit him on the head with a club, disembowelled him, and dragged the carcass away. Primitive man behaved like a modern pig-breeder when he goes into the sty and slaughters an animal.

> Two animate beings have to some extent "domesticated" themselves [writes the animal psychologist Konrad Lorenz]. They are the cave bear and Man. The cave bear seems, at the period of its widest distribution, to have become, like Man, a lord of the earth. This species in particular exhibited the typical signs of "domestication" during the years when it was most prevalent, which immediately preceded its disappearance. In the Dragon's Cave near Mixnitz a number of bears' skeletons were found lying together. They showed pretty nearly all the changes which the house-dog has undergone in the process of "domestication." Some were enormous, some quite small. There were long-legged specimens with heads shaped in much the same way as those of greyhounds and others with abbreviated skulls unmistakably reminiscent of bulldogs and pugs. They were bow-legged like dachshunds. One does not have to be very imaginative to suppose that the cave bears with such skulls were lop-eared and spotted when they were alive.

The Göttingen paleontologist Othenio Abel, one of the highest authorities on prehistoric animals, has collected abundant factual evidence of the great importance of the cave bear in the life of Neanderthal man. Primitive Europeans did not indeed keep this shaggy monster in their dwellings as the primitive Javanese did the dog of the Tengger district. But their whole culture was based on exploitation of the bear. It was to slaughter bears, perhaps, that Mousterian man invented the stone axe. Possibly it was to cut up their carcasses and prepare their skins that he evolved some of the new techniques in the shaping of flint and quartzite, setting up regular workshops for the production of knives and scrapers. He made wooden shafts, fastened rough-hewn sharp fragments of stone to their ends, and thus manufactured the first spears, which enabled him to slaughter his comrade the cave bear even when the beast was otherwise inaccessible.

The historic moment at which Man succeeded in getting into his power an animal that was ten times as strong and heavy as himself needed not only a technical but also an intellectual revolution of decisive significance. It was in the time of cave bears that the first cultural and religious ideas arose, that the first magicians appeared, that Man achieved dominion over nature and began to believe in the support of supernatural powers. Very puzzling deposits of bears' bones have been discovered in certain caves. At first no one could think of a satisfactory explanation. In the Dragon's Hole overlooking the village of Vättis in the Engadine stood rectangular stone chests, carefully covered with flat slabs. Each chest contained a number of cave bears' skulls. Large bones of the limbs had been thrust through the openings of the eyes and mouth. There was clear evidence that the Neanderthal men had effectively beheaded the animals and treated the heads in a special manner. In Peter's Cave, in central Franconia, the lateral recesses were filled with neatly arranged cave bears' skulls and bones. In other caves primitive man appeared to have set up the heads of slaughtered bears on poles and danced round them.

There are still some tribes today that practise a similar ritual concerned with bears — for example, the Ainu of northern Japan, the Gilyaks at the mouth of the Amur River, and the primitive Siberians inhabiting the banks of the Yenisei River and the Asiatic shores of the Arctic Ocean. Their peculiar ceremonies are considered by most ethnologists to represent a last reflection from Neanderthal times. Among these peoples the bear is regarded as a being of a higher order and as sacred. Though its meat is eaten and its hide is worn it is at the same time revered as a divinity. The skulls of slaughtered bears are hung on the topmost branches of high trees to enable the bear-god to turn them into living animals again. Captured bears are adored, invoked in terms of magic, and finally sacrificed with much solemnity at the great popular festivals.

Bear sacrifice was probably the first cultural ceremony of mankind. Neanderthal man regarded the bear as more important than any human being. For 100,000 years ago, when it had long been the custom ceremoniously to behead slaughtered cave bears and put the carcasses in coffins, the mortal remains of members of the tribe itself were far from being treated with any particular respect by their own kindred. The corpses were thrown out of the cave or dragged into remote corners of it, where they gradually acquired a covering of clay. It is true that Neanderthal man — as the reports of discoveries by Hauser and other explorers reveal — was also in the habit of making graves for human beings; but it is not known whether a regular cult of the dead was already being practised, as in the cases of the highly developed races of Aurignac and Cro-Magnon. It might have been so. A surprising find in Italy suggests as much.

In 1929 the skull of a Neanderthal female was discovered in a gravel pit near Saccopastore, a suburb of Rome. Six years later Breuil visited the site, accompanied by the prehistorian Baron Blanc. By an extraordinary coincidence at that very moment the wall of the pit collapsed, disclosing a second skull. Large-scale excavations were immediately undertaken in Italy and in the course of them Baron Blanc opened up a five-chambered grotto at Guattari near San Felice on Cape Circeo. In the last chamber lay the skeleton of a Neanderthal man buried some 60,000 years ago. It had been treated in exactly the same way as a sacrificed cave bear. It was surrounded by a circle of stones. Near it stood stone receptacles full of the bones of animals. The primitive occupants of Cape Circeo had beheaded the dead man and bored a hole in the skull in order to remove the brain. Bear sacrifice had developed into human sacrifice.

The culturally advanced races of the Late Ice Age took over the bear ritual of Neanderthal man, although they really had no further need of it, since they mainly hunted other animals such as bison, mammoths, wild horses, and deer. The close domestic association that had lasted 100,000 years between primitive man and the cave bear had made so deep an impression on the human spirit that bear festivals, bear ceremonies, and hunting and fertility magic involving the drawing and sculpture of bears remained important activities in the lives of the tribesmen right down to the end of the Ice Age and left traces — in the shape of their art — in all directions. When the cave bear grew rarer it was replaced by the smaller but much more dangerous brown bear. The custom survived among the last representatives of the Stone Age culture of Europe and northern Asia, the peoples of Siberia.

The cave bear only outlived Neanderthal man by some 10,000 years. It could no longer resist the improved weapons and hunting methods of the Aurignacian and Cro-Magnon races. It also happened that the steadily increasing severity of the climate of the Würm Ice Age unnaturally prolonged the animal's winter sleep. The grass and herbs it needed for food were only available for a few months in the year. For the rest of the time it remained shut up in its dark cave as in a prison. Its teeth were too little used; they grew to such a size in many young cave bears that they literally locked the jaws. Most skulls of cave bears of the last period of their existence show signs of serious inflammation of the jaws, and most of the bones found indicate that the animals suffered, in their oppressive isolation, from rank growths and deformities, rickets and arthritis. It was easy for the expert hunters of Altamira, Les Combarelles, and Brünn to deal with such miserable wrecks. They routed out the bear from his last refuge, drove the limping colossus with great clamor into recesses and narrow passages, and there pitilessly exterminated him.

Such is the tale of the extinction of the first totem animal of mankind, the deified giant of the primeval world, on whom the early cultures of Europe were founded.

The battle of Krapina

When the first Europeans set foot on the American continent the natives stared with mixed feelings upon the "white gods." They trembled with awe, fear, and hate. A whole world had collapsed about them. They dimly apprehended that a superior civilization acts like a ravening Moloch and that all resistance would be vain to the white men's claim to rule them. Mighty empires capitulated almost without striking a blow.

More highly developed races have never had difficulty in conquering and partly annihilating their less advanced cousins. The Tasmanians died out. The Australian aboriginals, the Veddas, Melanesians, Negritos, aborigines of the Philippine Islands, Pygmies, ancient Siberians, and many American Indian tribes have diminished to a few insignificant survivors. The victors deprived them of their own culture and fathered mixed races that were usually able to adapt themselves better to the new conditions than the original inhabitants of the country. Darwin's opinion that the struggle for existence is the stimulus to evolution is painfully underlined by the history of the human race, its peoples, and tribes.

There is no ground for the assumption that the men of the Ice Age behaved any better than the men of the present day. When, 75,000 years ago, progressive and well-armed races of the type of the Javanese explorers descended upon the lands occupied by Neanderthal man in Europe and central Asia, their intentions can hardly have been particularly peaceful. They probably behaved no differently from the Boers at the Cape of Good Hope, the roughriders of the American Indian frontiers, or the colonists of the Tasmanian bush. The Neanderthal men were helpless against their spears and boomerangs. All our knowledge of the evolution of the human race proves with shocking clarity that Man has always concentrated his inventive spirit above all on the construction of weapons of greater and greater range. He has now at last carried this process to such dazzling perfection that his latest weapons threaten the entire earth.

Extremely significant events had occurred during the Last Intermediate Ice Age in the ancient areas of civilization in the East. Hordes of primitive men had advanced into the north and west as well as into Australia. The most various races came into existence, including the Kiik-Koba type, found on the Crimean peninsula, possessing uncommonly mobile hands with fingers of almost equal length. Swift-footed, climate-resisting peoples of the steppes invented the first throwing devices and began setting traps for big game such as bison, deer, and wild horses. They continuously diverged in their physique and ways of life from true Neanderthal man. Some races — for instance, the Kiik-Koba type with its skilled fingers — disappeared for unknown reasons, while others survived when the first waves of cold in the Würm Ice Age put them to the test. Their hunting trails led them to new districts. There they encountered queer, awkward creatures who had taken refuge from the cold in bears' caves and begun to live in close association with their shaggy fellow tenants. The Aurignacian and Cro-Magnon men observed their Neanderthal cousins with appraising, somewhat scornful looks, as Captain Cook's sailors 75,000 years later were to observe the people of the Australian bush. But it is certain that their leaders were not in the least like the humane Captain Cook. They unslung their spears and boomerangs and dashed to attack the terrified cave men.

In the valley of a small river near the Croatian village of Krapina the professor of paleontology at Zagreb, by name Gorjanovic-Kramberger, found over five hundred remains of Neanderthal skeletons between 1899 and 1905. Their condition indicated that a cruel cannibalistic orgy had at one time taken place at the spot. The skulls

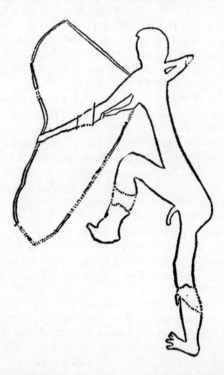

Against the intellectually far superior and culturally advanced *Homo sapiens diluvialis* and his long-range weapons Neanderthal man with his hand axes was helpless and doomed to destruction, just as tens of thousands of years later primitive colored people were helpless against the white Europeans.

and bones, some of them even more massive than those of Neanderthal and Spy, had been smashed to pieces. They bore traces of fire and some bones seemed to show the imprint of human teeth. Most of the stone weapons found amid the debris of the cannibal feast did not belong to the Mousterian age — the cultural epoch of Neanderthal man — but to the Aurignacian, the oldest of the cultural levels of *Homo sapiens*.

Klaatsch examined the Croatian finds and subsequently published a report, which has since been much criticized, maintaining that a battle had taken place at Krapina between Neanderthal and Aurignacian man. According to Klaatsch a highly organized tribe of hunters had attacked a settlement of Neanderthal men in the Krapina valley and massacred the unfortunate cave men. The conquerors had assaulted the natives with spears, stone axes, clubs, and missiles, brained them and afterwards roasted and devoured all who had fallen in battle, whether friend or foe, man, woman, or child, at a banquet in celebration of the victory.

It later transpired that Klaatsch had mistaken certain Neanderthal children's bones for those of Aurignacian adults, and this shook the theory of the battle of Krapina considerably. Many investigators today consider the alleged battlefield to have been an ancient site of ritual proceedings where Neanderthal men had sacrificed and devoured their own fellow tribesmen. Perhaps they are right. But the idea of such battles is not invalidated. Conflict between Neanderthal man and members of the civilized Ice Age races would have occurred — unless the Aurignacian and Cro-Magnon men were perfect patterns of meekness — throughout Europe and the Near East during the Last Ice Age. In such conflicts the weaker side was gradually exterminated, as has always been the case in human history.

When he died out, however, the typical late Neanderthal man left more traces behind than his brother the bear. Near the Moravian village of Ochos, on the Hollow Rock near Happurg in Franconia, in the neighborhood of the north Caucasian city of Pyatigorsk, and at several other places human remains have been discovered which look like crosses between Neanderthal and Aurignacian man. Some date from the postglacial age and some even from the early period of the age of metals. There can be no question, therefore, of transitional forms. Their ancestors were probably enterprising youths of the victorious race who had fraternized with the women and girls of the defeated natives. The half-breeds assumed, much as they do today, the progressive traits of the more advanced stock, became absorbed into it, and preserved certain features of Neanderthal man in their descendants.

My house is my castle

Near the village of Le Moustier in the Vézère valley four projecting cliffs are piled almost vertically upon one another, occupying a rocky ledge of the hills. Each of these projecting slabs forms the entrance to a grotto. In front of the one at the bottom there stood until 1907 a small house. Otto Hauser had it demolished in order to clear the way to the underground dwellings of primitive man. While Hermann Klaatsch and Hans Virchow, son of the famous doctor and expert on cells, were assisting in the excavation of the youthful Le Moustier skeleton from the depths, they had a good look around. They found to their astonishment that for the last 100,000 years the most various human groups had regularly lived and made their homes on this tiny spot of earth.

At first Neanderthal man lived in the bottom grotto. Later on Cro-Magnon men took possession of the upper floors. Postglacial hordes used the caverns as larders and built rough huts of wattle and clay before their entrances. Celtic settlers followed. At last a French farmer came along who knew nothing of his predecessors of the Ice Age. He closed the entry to the place where the Mousterian youth was lying by putting up a stone building.

The development of architecture followed the same lines as that of graphic art. For several hundred thousand years mankind was quite content to dwell in caves and ravines. Toward the end of the Ice Age the first attempts were made to enlarge the grottoes by means of stone buildings or erect artificial dwellings in some other way. Thus the spell was broken. No more than 15,000 years later huge edifices arose in the valleys of the Nile and Euphrates which are today a source of wonder and admiration to the whole world.

The way in which the cave became the house has been painstakingly explained by two eminent French investigators, the prehistorian Henri Martin and the schoolmaster Peyrony. These two Frenchmen belonged to the great host of disinterested idealists who explore crevices in the rocks and layers in the soil with antlike industry all over the world, obsessed with the desire to become acquainted with the beginnings of human civilization. Innumerable workers of this type prepare the way for the study of prehistory and their achievements and careers would fill many volumes.

Peyrony and Henri Martin concerned themselves, beginning in the year 1900, with burial places in the south of France, the former concentrating on the Vézère valley and the latter on the department of Charente. They found a number of remains of Neanderthal skeletons, including the famous skulls of La Ferrassie and La Quina. Above the Mousterian layers they discovered traces of the cultures of later times. It was the same picture as that of Le Moustier. Cro-Magnon men had taken possession of the dwelling places of the defeated natives, adorned the caves, and provided them with the appurtenances of their own civilization. The caves were not always adequate for their purpose. The new tenants experienced the need to enlarge them. They built on annexes, just as a modern householder does when his premises grow too small for him.

The first signs of an architecture of the Ice Age were claimed by Henri Martin while he was examining two small cave dwellings. Between them stood a kind of platform, seven and a half yards across. A double layer of large stone slabs was built out in front of the mountainside, composing a regular terrace, roofed over half its extent by a projecting ledge of rock. The bottom layer of stone, forming the base of the terrace, was unhewn. Henri Martin discerned on the top slabs a series of sculptures of animals, including a mare being covered by a stallion. The place may accordingly have been used for fertility rites. Perhaps the small caves had not been roomy enough for the celebration of festivals and ceremonies.

In the district of La Madeleine Cro-Magnon men had taken an even longer stride forward into modern times. Toward the end of the Ice Age caves suitable for habitation in that area seem to have grown rarer. For this reason many groups of hunters, it was ascertained by Peyrony, established their dwellings under the shelter of big projecting ledges of rock. An improvised refuge of this kind was of course not so easy to defend as a grotto, as the old settlers soon discovered. They carried rubble and fragments of rock to the place, erected walls, and even covered them with engravings. After having thoroughly examined the dwellings of early man in La Madeleine, Peyrony stated, "it is probable that this withdrawn and dark retreat was also shut in by hides and branches arranged in front of it." Such was the beginning of genuine domestic building.

Later, in the time of the great migrations, there was not much point in having permanent houses if the tribes were always on the move. They were content with mere roof shelters to keep off the rain and windbreaks made of plaited boughs to protect the fireplaces. Primitive nomads in Africa and Australia continue to employ these methods to this day. Men did not become sedentary until they no longer needed to go in search of their food. The course of events is disclosed by the "Shell-mound Cultures" found in northern Europe, so called because the camping grounds of families can be identified by great refuse heaps of the shells of mollusks. The descendants of the bold bison hunters lived modestly in these places on all sorts of seafood. It might seem a step backward, but really it was a great stride forward — for the Nordic mollusk collectors founded the first village. They replaced the nomadic mode of life by that of the stationary citizen.

The break with nomadic life brought about in the New Stone Age (Neolithic) by the occupants of the fen and lake districts of Switzerland was even more complete. They drove their four piles into the water a fair distance from the bank. In these dwellings the family could enjoy relative security from roving bands and wild animals. The first lake dwellings were discovered as early as 1854 by the Swiss

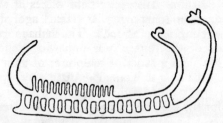

Scandinavians living between the Stone and Bronze Ages used a kind of horned sledge with broad runners in their snowy regions and made the discovery that the vehicle could float. Such was, perhaps, the origin of the open boat with runners, which then developed into one with a hull.

Aeppli. For a long time they excited more interest than any other prehistoric finds. Renowned investigators, including Virchow, made a close study of these structures, then believed to be the oldest ever created by mankind. They were large dwellings, ingeniously built of uncut tree trunks, with room for a few domestic animals as well as the human inmates. Narrow footbridges, which could easily be demolished, connected them with the bank and its jungle of reeds, beyond which lay the lake dwellers' fields.

Villages and lake dwellings are the work of a new type of human economy, the Neolithic. Farmers and cattle breeders replaced hunters and food-gatherers. Nature, hitherto so moody and rebellious, and often actually dangerous, was at last partly subjugated by humanity. Wild forms of oxen and sheep were domesticated. The farmers of the New Stone Age developed their various cereals from wild grasses and manufactured clothing from the fibers of plants by means of the distaff and loom worked by hand. Suddenly, even before the Bronze Age had started, highly bred domestic animals and cultivated plants appeared all over Europe. Where did they come from? Many were strangers from a warmer climate. All the evidence goes to show that the agricultural peoples from southern and southeastern Europe had made a peaceful penetration of the forests and tundras of the north, having come by very ancient routes.

In the Mediterranean lands and in the Near East agriculture was being generally practised, at a time when north of the Alps mankind was still living on game, seals, fish, and mollusks and gathering acorns, beechnuts, and roots. Large settlements were founded in what are today Egypt, Mesopotamia, and India especially. The remains of clay walls, cooking-hearths, and pits full of fragments of pottery, bones, and stone tools indicate the places at which the peoples of the East, some 10,000 to 12,000 years ago, were gradually coming to adopt the social habits of today. Perhaps the first farmer

One of the most interesting rock drawings of the north from the point of view of the history of civilization. Ships, fat oxen, reindeer, and a plow drawn by dogs are represented. Man had gained control over the soil, water, and animals. A snake is also depicted.

was a man who had formed a large collection of the seeds of wild grasses in his dwelling. Part of his store was lost, carried off by animals or children and dropped on the ground near the hut, where it began to send up shoots. The man realized that the seeds could be sown. He started to grow grasses systematically. Since he was successful, other members of the tribe hastened to follow his example.

The great rivers of the Orient — the Nile, the Euphrates, and the Indus — periodically overflowed and deposited fertile mud. When Neolithic man threw a handful of seeds onto this mud he soon noticed that one such sowing resulted in the growth of particularly sturdy and productive plants. Accordingly, he made his way to the riverbank, built himself a substantial house there, and profited by the rich yield of the mud. Such was the origin of the great river-civilizations. At the beginning of the Neolithic period, when central

Europe was only populated by scattered bands of nomads, settlement after settlement of farmers could be found ranged along the Nile Valley, from the delta to the first cataract. The population grew rapidly. Land-hungry colonists migrated, taking agriculture to Syria and Persia, Spain and the Danube region. Egyptian emmer and the spelt of Asia Minor and of Persia were finally acclimatized in Europe, becoming the forerunners of wheat. The wild mountain grasses of the East and of North Africa developed into barley. Many other field plants were tried out near the great rivers and added to the rest. Animals from foreign lands, moving lazily and reluctantly, were driven north, to the astonishment of the hunters, who had hitherto only known game that was shy and elusive.

According to one ingenious theory the evolution of domestic animals is to be referred to the postglacial change of climate in the Near East and North Africa. The melting of the great ice fields in the north altered the geographical incidence of rain. Meadowland

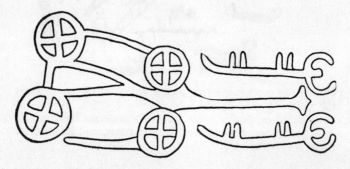

The greatest, most important and far-reaching technical invention ever produced was the wheel. This result of human ingenuity exercised more influence than any previous or subsequent discovery upon the inventor's own evolution. It initiated the conquering career of *Homo sapiens*.

turned to steppe and steppe to desert. Men and animals had to retreat to the neighborhood of oases. The hunters, unwilling to allow their sources of food to dry up, soon began to slaughter in the oases only enough animals to meet their immediate needs for meat and to preserve the rest. Later on they proceeded to drive the herds into large enclosures to prevent their running away and falling into the hands of neighboring tribes. In the Neolithic period attempts were made to domesticate nearly all the species of animals that lived

33. Le Moustier in the Vézère valley. The boy's skeleton was found by Hauser in the lower grotto, today masked by a house (behind the trees). *Below*: Otto Hauser setting out from Laugerie-Basse to excavate the skeleton.

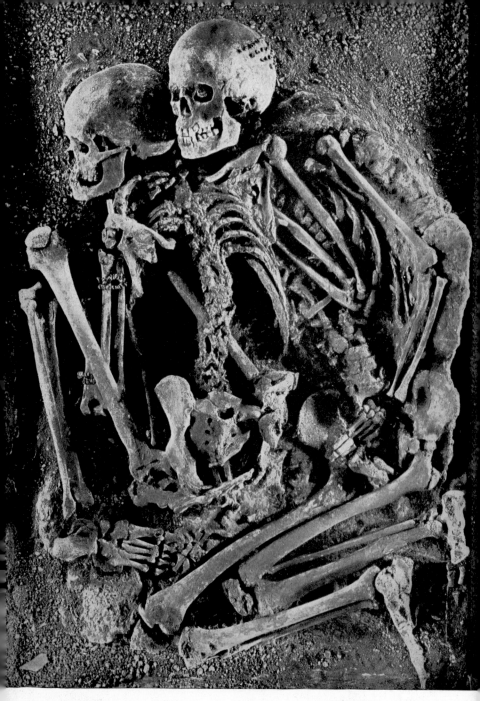

34. Double grave in the Grimaldi Grotto near Monte Carlo. *Left:* an old woman; *right:* a young man. The ingenious methods of burial and the double graves themselves prove that the men of the Ice Age possessed notions of ritual and theories of a life after death.

35. An orangutan, a pair of pincers, and an apple under the grating.

36. *Right:* a goblin lemur of the homunculus among the lower primates. Its brain already shows a number of features otherwise peculiar to the higher primates and to mankind.

Below: the archaic anthropoid ape *Proconsul.* Such was approximately the appearance of the common ancestor of the anthropoid apes and mankind. A modern reconstructive drawing from the Museum of Natural History, London.

37. It was Professor Weng Chung Pei (*above*) who extracted the Peking man from the Dragons' Mountains at Chou-kou-tien.

Right: Weidenreich's reconstruction of the *Sinanthropus* skull.

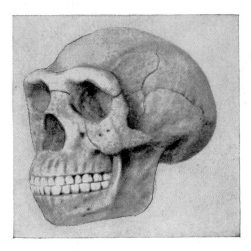

38. The landscape of Sangiran (central Java) exhibits, as in a diagram, the hard sandstone of the Middle Pleistocene epoch above the soft clay of the Old Pleistocene. It was in this district that von Koenigswald and his assistants (*below*) found the Javanese early specimens of man and the giants.

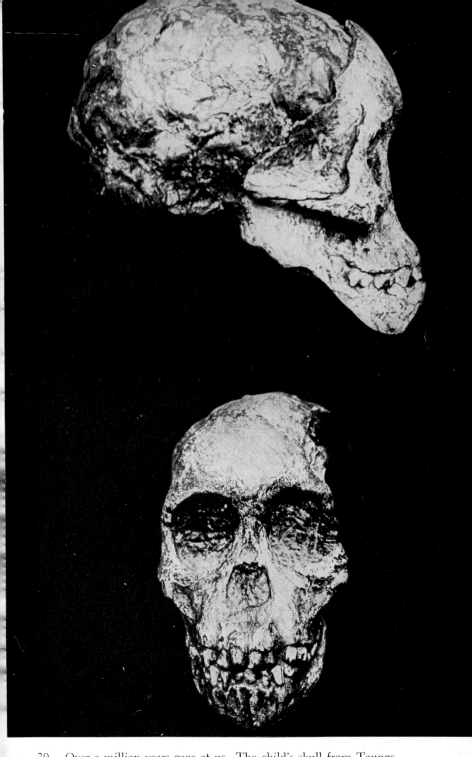

39.　Over a million years gaze at us.　The child's skull from Taungs.

40. Half man, half ape: *Plesianthropus*. Such drawings are no longer fanciful today. Science has identified the most important components of the skeleton of the half-man and discovered many traces of this creature's mode of life. Scientists are thus able to compose serviceable and relatively accurate reconstructions.

41. The skeleton found by Hans Reck in the Oldoway Gorge (*above*) attracted the attention of investigators to Africa. A quarter of a century later Professor John Talbot Robinson (*below*) discovered in South Africa the connecting links between anthropoid apes and man.

42. The steppes of the Tertiary bush resembled the African savannahs of today. The half-men of the Tertiary epoch lived in such places among antelopes, antique horses, and baboons.

43. The first domestic utensils: millstones and primitive bone needles.

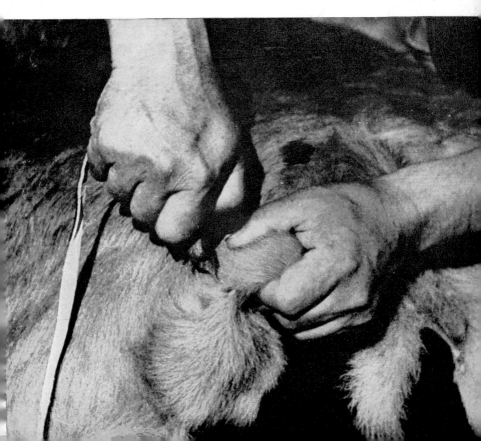

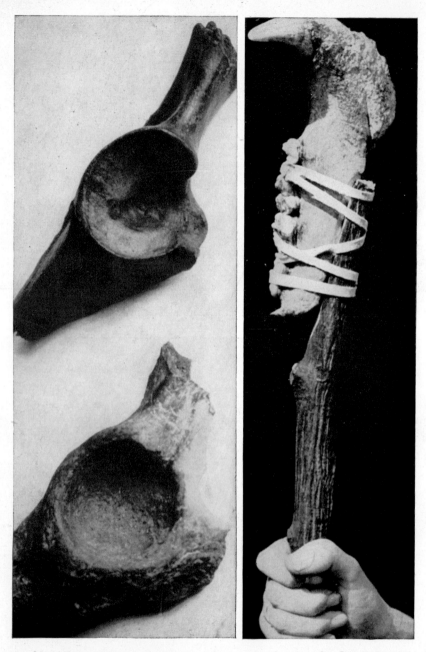

44. The sockets of the joints of large animals were the first dishes of primitive man. The underjaw of the cave bear made a massive striking weapon.

45. *Above*: the dingo, the oldest domesticated animal of humanity, has today reverted to the wild state. Early Javanese man once took the animal to Australia on his great voyage of discovery. *Below*: these mysterious pictures of the mouthless divinity Vondina were found by Leo Frobenius in the Central Kimberley Division of Australia.

46. The bear's figure above never had a head. The cave bear played an important part in the ritual practice of Ice Age man. The head and hide of the slaughtered animal were placed on its plastic representation, and the participants then danced round it. Footprints made in such dances can still be seen in the clay of the cave. *Below:* the Ainu of eastern Asia still perform ritual ceremonies with slaughtered bears.

47. It was in La Mouthe (Dordogne) that the Early Stone Age drawing of a building of hut type was found. At the beginning of the age of metal, architecture had already progressed to such an extent that stable structures like the lake dwellings of Unteruhldingen on the shores of Lake Constance, shown here in a modern reconstruction, could be erected.

48. Out of the dim prehistoric ages Adam and Eve come forth to the light: a painting from the Hoggar Mountains of the Sahara.

in the oases. Five thousand years ago the Egyptians were still keeping large herds of antelopes and gazelles. The Sumerians yoked to their war chariots a yellow Asiatic species of wild ass, which bears no relation to the modern donkey. The Indians succeeded in taming the elephant, the water buffalo, and the gayal and banting species of ox. There were plenty of animals to choose from, and those that proved unsatisfactory were eliminated. By the year 5000 B.C. the civilized peoples of the East already possessed cattle which supplied them with milk and drew their carts, sheep and goats whose hides they utilized for making fine fabrics, pigs that provided them with pork, and donkeys and camels which carried their goods.

The revolutionary changes of the Neolithic period represent a climax of human cultural evolution. Humanity had needed 2,000.000

Two-wheeled cart drawn by reindeer.

years to progress from the use of the club to the invention of the first machines, the bow, and the catapult. Yet within 5000 years men had learned how to use the power of the wind and that of domesticated animals. They constructed the plow, the wheeled cart, and the potter's wheel. They built stone houses, manufactured new kinds of weapons and tools from copper, and began to write, calculate, and measure. Rivers were embanked, mines established, fruit trees grafted, and seals cut from precious stones. Between 8000 B.C and 3000 B.C. the foundations of cities and states were laid and the two new forces of science and politics grew more and more conspicuous.

During this epoch of invention and discovery bridging the gap between prehistoric and historical times, it also occurred to mankind to domesticate his own species. Capital in the form of herds, victuals, tools, and ornaments accumulated among the groups that were exceptionally fortunate. In order to protect this wealth its owners had to erect fortifications, and in order to increase it they had to engage in trade or military expeditions. The result was a series of conflicts on a hitherto unprecedented scale. An age of wars and raids began that produced the first social orders and privileges. The prosperous became aristocrats, the military leaders kings, and they consolidated their power by inducing others to work for them.

In early times slaves were members of defeated tribes who built fortifications for the conquerors, attended to their fields, and looked after their cattle, from which the dominant races gradually bred a new and uncommonly useful body of domestic animals. Their condition consequently improved very much. They no longer needed to suffer under the manifold burden of the tasks necessary to gain a livelihood. They began to feel a longing for luxury, and they had the time and leisure to satisfy it.

The domestication of Man was one of the most important proceedings in the history of civilization. It created the preliminary conditions for the foundation of mighty empires. It initiated a refined cult of luxury. It decided the course that led the peaceable primate to become the tyrannical master of the earth. It was the beginning of modern times.

The Flood once more

The small Austrian market town of Hallstatt is situated on the western shore of a large lake in the Salzkammergut district, amid melancholy and wildly romantic scenery. It is famous not only for its natural beauty but also for its production of salt. This fame has already been enjoyed by the environs of Hallstatt for nearly 4500 years. Salt was just as important for man in early times as flint, obsidian and quartzite, ivory and amber, hides and the first metal. Wherever salt was obtained trade routes converged and merchants of all races and languages met.

"In studying prehistoric commercial and cultural societies," wrote the Swedish prehistorian Montelius, "one must always remember that the influence of any trade is always more conspicuous at commercial centers than in the intervening regions. This is the case today. And it was obviously also the case in very ancient times. Such is the explanation of the fact that during the Bronze Age southern Europeans [and also Eastern] influences were far stronger in the salt-producing districts of the Alps and the Saale River and in Jutland, with its rich supplies of amber, than in many countries lying between the north and the Mediterranean." In the Stone Age commercial and cultural exchanges were concentrated at the places where prehistoric miners had come across copious flint deposits. In the age of metal copper and tin mines formed the centers of business activity. We may add, too, the trade in fur, amber, and other simple commodities. Finally, salt assumed a dominant position in these early trading ventures.

The environs of Hallstatt have brought to light a number of graves of inhabitants who had grown rich through the salt trade. The graves were full of valuable objects and finely wrought ornaments but also some obvious trash. The term "Hallstatt civilization" is actually used today to designate a culture prevalent at the beginning of the Iron Age and characterized by various objects which are evidence of trade and contacts with other regions. This Hallstatt civilization is estimated to be about 2500 or 3000 years old. More than 1000 years before that date trade routes were converging upon the Salzkammergut. There Etruscans bargained with Scandinavians, Cretans with Celts, and Illyrians with the brown-skinned peoples of the East. The newly rich swaggered and filled their houses with bronze trinkets.

Cowries from the Orient, ornaments from Egypt, furs from the north, Cretan alabaster, and the latest fashion in currency standards — Baltic amber — found their way into the coffers of the Hallstatt traders. Their wives hung corals from the Red Sea round their necks. The men put away the long swords that had hitherto been customary in central Europe, and followed the southern example by sticking elegant short daggers in their belts. Treasures were hoarded, foreign countries and districts came to be esteemed in accordance with the value of their products and all the attributes conspicuous ever since among international businessmen developed.

Hallstatt is only one example among many. Centers of trade and civilization arose, after the Neolithic revolution, wherever copper or salt mines, river valleys, seaports, and traffic junctions offered favorable preliminary conditions. The great cities of ancient Egypt, the Sumerian royal capital of Ur of the Chaldees, Mohenjo-Daro in the valley of the Indus, whose technicians discovered bronze — all these early settlements, and many others which became world-famous through archeological research, were not only centers of political and religious life but also, to varying degrees, had merchant classes.

This period of human evolution is no longer a part of primeval or prehistoric times. It belongs to history. One event that occurred at the inception of the early metal age nevertheless bears a unique and significant relation to the science of the beginnings of the human race. Described in the sixth to the ninth chapters of Genesis, the First Book of Moses, and responsible for the start of the search for Adam two hundred years ago, this was the Flood.

The legend of the Flood, as we know today, is based upon an actual occurrence. The great deluge did not indeed burst upon the world in the dawn of humanity, as all the Diluvians from Scheuchzer to Buckland maintained; nor did it lay waste whole continents, or by any means exterminate all life on earth, except that of the animal and human passengers aboard Noah's Ark. However, it did represent an extremely important intervention in the history of early cultures. For it affected a race of people, whose name it must be confessed we do not know, although results of excavations in Mesopotamia give us extensive proof of their existence. All the evidence shows that they were the real founders of Western civilization.

A local catastrophe in the delta of the Euphrates and Tigris, but nevertheless one of formidable dimensions doubtlessly unique even for that frequently flooded district, made so deep an impression on the civilized minds of that era that the traditions relating to it have remained living to this day. The raging of unchecked waters has always meant a frightful and deadly peril for mankind, bringing terror and alarm with it. Legends of floods have therefore always been current among peoples living near seas or rivers. But one flood in particular, the Biblical one — of which, incidentally, there is an even more detailed description in the great Gilgamesh epic of Babylonia and Assyria than is given in the First Book of Moses — occupies a very special position. It destroyed the first and historically the most important of all the Near Eastern cultures known up to that time. The destruction was indeed not complete, for Noah's contemporaries were already acquainted with ships. They and their civilization were thus enabled to escape utter annihilation and thereafter to lay the foundations of a new cultural development, traces of which can still be discerned today.

Is all this merely a hypothesis? No. We now have just as much documentary evidence of the Flood as we have of the series of ancestors of Man. Archeologists have given the working designation of "Sumerians," derived from the ancient rule of Akkad and Sumer in Mesopotamia, to the people who experienced the catastrophe. Proofs of a high level of Sumerian civilization between 5000 and 6000 years ago, in the shape of finely wrought gold ornaments and jewelry, chariots, and other magnificent works of craftsmanship, have been brought to light since 1927 in the so-called "Graves of the Kings" at Ur, especially by the English archeologist Sir Leonard Woolley. It was established that the Sumerians had already possessed eminent doctors, lawyers, astronomers, and mathematicians, while the rest of the world "was still sunk in the depths of barbarism," as Woolley puts it. He considers the Sumerians to have been the predecessors of all civilized peoples. "The importance of their culture lies in its having been one of the first forces making for progress in the world."

In the deep layer of cultural relics below the soil of Ur, Woolley suddenly came upon a deposit of clay some seven feet thick which made an abrupt break in the ascending scale of cultures. It was an unmistakable inundation-layer, undoubtedly caused by a great flood. The clay contained no ashes, ornaments, or tile fragments. Historians and archeologists are convinced that it constitutes a clear trace of the cataclysms of which the Bible states: "And all flesh died that moved upon the earth, both of fowl, and of cattle, and of beast, and of every creeping thing that creepeth upon the earth, and every man." After the waters had subsided cultural evolution was at once resumed, as is also disclosed by the soil of Ur. The man Ut-napishti (corresponding with Noah in the Bible), who steered his vessel to the mountains that had escaped the flood, symbolizes Sumerian energy and genius. The primitive Bedouins beyond the boundaries of the Sumerian settlement were probably for the most part drowned.

It is stated that the Flood was a Divine judgment. This opinion becomes intelligible on a close study of the finds at Ur. We are confronted in the graves by an advanced civilization of a gruesome kind, terrible in its dimensions, shocking in its perversity. War chariots rumble over human bodies, hecatombs of men and women are sacrificed to their deified masters. Each king's grave not only contains the body of the monarch but also the remains of brutally massacred warriors, attendants, musicians, slaves, and girls. "There were tyrants upon the earth in those days," states the Bible, "and the earth was corrupt before God's eyes and full of wickedness."

From where, then, did the Sumerians come? They were called "black-headed foreigners" by the Semites who inhabited the Euphrates Valley and afterwards took over their civilization. Noah's people, according to their own traditions, had reached Mesopotamia by ship long before the Flood. Archeology shows distinct evidence of trade connections between Sumeria and the Indus Valley, though we cannot say more as yet.

The Sumerians have bequeathed to us one document that completes the circle of our observations and also illuminates the record of generations in the Bible. It is the chronology of the human race enshrined in the "lists of kings." Unfortunately this chronology has only come down to us at second hand, fancifully metamorphosed and embellished by a Babylonian. It states that the epochs from the creation of mankind until the Flood make up a period of 465,000 years — an amazing assertion, which, curiously enough, has a rough agreement in the findings of modern research. For anthropologists and prehistorians also assume a period of about 500,000 years to have elapsed between the first appearance of early man in Europe and the Near East and the inception of the age of metal. According to the Babylonian version of the Sumerian lists of kings, only ten rulers reigned during the whole of this long epoch, a number that corresponds with the ten patriarchs of the Bible from Adam to Noah. Consequently each of these rulers apparently attained an average age of forty-five thousand years.

We may assume that the "rulers" were intended to refer to some dim notions of earlier epochs. Ideas regarding the growth of humanity which had once been grasped and raked together in meditation, by conjecture, and by early science were later given permanent form in the shape of legendary kings and reconstituted as a saga. And at a still later time, when the Mosaic story of creation originated, the text of the "chronology" underwent a further revision, in which each of the ten patriarchs since Adam was given a slightly less fantastic age of nine hundred years. In the eyes of those who stuck to the letter of the tradition, the age of the human race must have shrunk to a mere fraction of that formerly assumed by the Sumerians.

When we look up the references to the antediluvian patriarchs, the descendants of Cain and Seth, the separate stages of human evolution revealed by prehistoric research impose themselves of necessity upon our attention. We find Lamech, through whom the crime of Cain is passed on; we find Jabal, whose tribe built the first huts and bred the first cattle; Tubal-cain, the "artificer in brass and iron"; and Jubal, the first artist, from whom the "harp and organ" come. The later patriarchs, too, are distinguished by similar features. Does not every word that relates to Nimrod, the "mighty hunter before the Lord," inevitably recall the great slaughterers of game who lived in the Late Ice Age and postglacial period? Does not the figure of Enoch symbolize the first beginnings of ritual and religion? And does not the story of the hairy Esau, who sold his birthright for a "mess of pottage," suggest once more the earliest of mankind? The mythology of the Mesopotamian cultures has left us yet another piece of poetic evidence. In the greatest of the Babylonian epics the "god-man" Gilgamesh kneads the furry human being Wabani from an animal that has eaten forest plants and drunk with wild beasts and then he sets out with Wabani on his expedition to conquer the world.

It would be an exaggeration to affirm that the Sumerians already knew in broad outline the essential features of what modern Western science has ascertained of the origin and growth of mankind. At any rate, the epics, legends, and chronologies prove that the dwellers in Mesopotamia had some inkling of it. A people who determined the motions of the moon and the planets to within a few fractions of a second of the results calculated by our modern astronomers, and whose mathematics operated with figures higher than those used in the West until the seventeenth century, must be confidently allowed that much proficiency.

The excavations that provided our evidence for the Biblical Flood took place at the same time as the discovery of the Peking man and the investigation of the Taungs skull. A gulf was thus bridged which had separated the opinions of the learned for centuries. The statements of Genesis were substantiated by the findings of scientific research. The shell of legend revealed a kernel of truth. That Western humanity has looked to the highly significant events which took place in the early part of the age of metal between the Euphrates and the Tigris as the true start of its history is no more surprising than the fact that the enormous periods preceding that epoch almost wholly disappeared from the memory of man. We know today that the Flood was not a world-wide catastrophe, as Cuvier maintained, and is not, as Buckland had believed, to be identified with the Diluvial age. It did not take place in the dim days of early antiquity when Man first began to evolve, but at the opening of the Bronze Age, when civilization flourished between the Euphrates and the Tigris — almost at the same time as may be calculated with the aid of Biblical and Sumerian sequences of generations.

History before that date has been bequeathed to us in the form of myths and symbols. It lasted during those 465,000 years of the Sumerian chronology which the hairy beast-man Eabani took to become the builder of the ark, Ut-napishti.

The Maya and the mastodon

One of the great fossil hunters of America, Chester Stock, was told in 1882, to his utmost astonishment, that a large sandstone slab that bore the recognizable footprints of prehistoric human beings had been found during the building of the State Prison of Nevada near Carson City. How was it possible? The higher apes did not exist in America, so no special forms of mankind could have evolved there either. Science taught that Man had only taken possession of the New World in historical times, coming from northern Asia. But in addition to the alleged traces of human beings the sandstone slab of Carson City clearly depicted the tracks of Tertiary and Early Diluvial animals.

Stock racked his brains for a long time over those strange footprints. Rumors became current that Man, contrary to all evolutionist doctrine, might after all have arisen on American soil. Geologists and anthropologists dug out old half-forgotten finds from their collections and conducted heated debates on their antiquity. A human pelvis had been discovered as early as 1846, consequently ten years before Fuhlrott's Neanderthal man, in a clay layer of the tablelands of the Mississippi, among the bones of mastodons and giant sloths. Twenty-six years later the American archeologist Charles Abbott had extracted from the bed of the Delaware River fragments of the bones of human beings and mastodons, as well as a number of very ancient hand axes. These fossils suddenly became extremely interesting. Things almost seemed to show that American primitive men had been contemporary with the Tertiary and Early Diluvial monsters, the mastodon and the *Megatherium*. Stock, who had at first considered the Carson City footprints to be the tracks of bears, began to waver. For the time being he leaned toward the rebellious view that the sandstone slab was the petrified relic of a riparian oasis formerly frequented by primeval animals and early man. He began, though with reservations, to believe that *Pleistocene* types of mankind had lived in America.

For some years the Carson City man made periodical appearances in the newspapers, much as the mysterious snowman of the Himalayas did about 1950. The "Abominable Snowman" is explained by some investigators as a large *Semnopithecus* ("sacred monkey," or hanuman) and by others as a "frilled" bear. The same thing happened in the case of the Nevada puzzle. It finally occurred to Chester Stock himself that the manlike footprints on the stone slab might have been made by the giant sloth called *Mylodon*, a creature that walked upright. Further study proved him right. The resemblance between human feet and those of a mylodon was amazing. Nevertheless, this ancient monster had nothing to do with the evolution of an American Adam.

Yet the theory of a remote antiquity of the American races persisted in many quarters. About the turn of the century the Argentinian paleontologist Fiorino Ameghino discovered in the pampas of Patagonia the bones of small apelike creatures of such weirdly human aspect that he gave them the name "homunculus." The Patagonian homunculi had lived during the first third of the Tertiary period, some 40,000,000 years ago. Ameghino considered that they might very well have evolved into genuine human beings. He continued his investigations assiduously, and shortly afterwards published the news of a discovery that caused a sensation throughout the world. He declared that he had identified, in the loess of the pampas, unmistakable traces of primitive human beings dating from the Tertiary period.

Ameghino's "Tertiary men" ultimately turned out to be figments of his imagination. The homunculi proved to be ancestors of the South American capuchin monkeys, closely related to the archaic group of the lemurs. Further remains on the American continent of what seemed to be primitive human beings and anthropoid apes were also soon revealed as masqueraders. But the suggestion that America had made at least a contribution to the prehistory of mankind still cropped up. It was given fresh support when in the thirties of the present century the petroleum geologist de Lois shot and killed a large ape in the forests of Venezuela. De Lois was sure he had bagged an American anthropoid ape and supplied the press with a photograph of the enigmatic beast. He had lost the actual carcass. All the big illustrated papers published the picture and built up a series of rash conjectures in connection with it. The "anthropoid ape of Venezuela" became nearly as popular as the Loch Ness monster. The zoologists, however, remained skeptical. They examined the photograph, and perceived that it was that of a dead ape of slender physique, seated on a chest and propped up by a stick. They concluded that the creature did not look very different from an ordinary sapajou (small prehensile-tailed South American money), and that de Lois might have in fact discovered a new species of sapajou, a particularly large representative of the South American "three-quarter monkey" which had diverted at an early date from the other primates and gone its own way. In any case the depressing body on the chest was not in the slightest degree related to the anthropoid apes. Willy-nilly the newspapers were obliged to banish the topic from their columns.

During the seventy years following Chester Stock's meditations on the Carson City footprints many human skeletons and relics of civilization were discovered all over the American continent, from Minnesota to the Strait of Magellan. Every one of these primitive Americans belonged to the *Homo sapiens* species. They combined the characteristics of Cro-Magnon man with Mongolian and Indian features. Their age could be fairly accurately established by the aid of radioactive-carbon and fluorine tests. None of the skeletons had lain in American soil for longer than 12,000 years. The stone tools often made a very primitive impression. Obermaier actually classified some of them as being Acheulean. But they lay at such recent levels that prehistorians considered they had probably been made at earliest during the last glacial age, but in all likelihood not until the postglacial period. It is perfectly possible that the first conquerors of America encountered conditions that obliged them to make an entirely fresh start, culturally and technically, with simple hand axes.

During the Würm Ice Age and the intervals of rising temperature, toward the end of the great glaciations, the level of the Arctic Ocean several times dropped well over a hundred and fifty feet. Broad tracts of the Bering Strait between northeastern Asia and Alaska became dry land. It was not difficult for ancient tribes of hunters to cross the shallows and descend from the northwest into the wide spaces of the New World. The various races and cultures of ancient America reveal the fact that Stone Age men advanced into Alaska. across the Bering Strait in several waves, the last probably taking place actually in historical times. It is difficult to estimate how long they took to reach the most southerly point of the continent. A human skeleton found in the cave of Palli Aike on the shores of the Strait of Magellan seems to be about 9000 years old. If this calculation of age is correct, the whole of the Americas had been occupied by descendants of northern Asiatic hunters of big game 3000 years before the founding of the civilized Egyptian, Assyrian, and Babylonian empires.

American primitive men, therefore, never existed. The first man to set foot in the New World was an explorer, a Stone Age pioneer. How could this fact be reconciled with the circumstances that human remains were continually discovered in America in association with the bones of prehistoric animals? At almost all the places where human bones were found — on the banks of the Mississippi and the Delaware, in Brazilian caves and Argentinian clay deposits — paleontologists and prehistorians also came upon large elephants of *Mastodon* type (such as had lived in Europe during the Tertiary period), and mylodons, Grypotheria, and other relatives of the giant sloth famed in song — the *Megatherium* — as well as primitive cattle

and horses. Human beings had hunted and killed them, living on
their meat. These species of animals could not have died out in the
Tertiary or Pleistocene ages. They must still have existed a few millenniums ago. Had the two-legged immigrants finished them off for
good with hand axe and spear? It looks like it. But it is one of the
great curiosities of early American history that that was not the
only way in which they treated them.

Alfred Wegener's theory of alterations in the position of continents has contributed to the solution of many zoological problems
and other problems concerned with the geographical distribution of
animals. According to this theory it was the land of marsupials, Australia, that first broke off from the floating continents; it was followed
by the land of lemurs, Madagascar; and finally, in the first half of
the Tertiary period, South America too came away from the large
continental block and drifted slowly to the west, like an immense
clod of earth. An archaic fauna, elsewhere long since extinct, maintained itself on this Noah's Ark. It comprised mastodons, giant
sloths and giant armadillos, tapirs, predatory marsupials, and primitive primates. They developed into forms so one-sidedly specialized
that they were thus deprived of all chance of further evolution. Such
were giant Megatheria, tortoise-like glyptodons and acrobatic sapajous and capuchin monkeys. When several million years later North
America made contact with the South American ark and formed
a land connection with it, a wave of more highly organized animals
overran this primeval world, which time had forgotten. Horses, stags,
bison, bears, wild dogs, and saber-toothed felines established themselves, after a struggle, among the "living fossils" of the land that
had floated away. American fauna thus became a unique mixture of
primeval and progressive forms of life.

A sinister and appalling picture of the world of Tertiary animals
is provided by the bituminous lake of La Brea, today situated within the municipal area of Los Angeles. Several million animals were
there submerged, during many millenniums, within the narrow limits
of a region of absorbent, treacly, and pulpy tar. Their remains have
been preserved in the pitch. They include tiny primitive horses the
size of a fox, hunchbacked forerunners of the llama, knife-toothed
predatory felines, mighty elephants of the mastodon type and man-
footed sloths of the *Mylodon* genus. Such were the animals, for the
most part of extremely strange and unexpected aspect, encountered
by Man during his great migrations in the postglacial age across Alaska
and Canada as he moved steadily south into the mysterious unknown. These beasts were quite different from the game he had

hunted in his old home and also quite different from the creatures from which the civilized peoples of the East had bred their domestic animals. They could of course be slaughtered and utilized for domestic purposes. But could they be domesticated? At some time or other the American tribes, like all the other races of mankind, began to see the advantage of overcoming the animals that shared their occupation of the country, taming them and utilizing their strength. The giant sloth and the mastodon were of course, as one may well imagine, utterly unsuitable objects for the experiments of budding breeders. Nevertheless, the Americans tried them out.

In 1890 a cave was discovered in the department of Ultima Esperanza in Patagonia. A party of scholars, including the Swedish brothers Otto and Erland Nordenskjöld, Arthur Smith Woodward, who was subsequently to be connected with the Piltdown man, and the Argentinian Ameghino, were kept busy for some years examining the contents. The clay deposits covered bones of the giant sloth *Grypotherium*. They had been split open by human agency. Pieces of the hide of the same animal were also found. They were scorched and heavily charred at the edges. A wall had been built across the cave as though to separate part of it as a stable. Bales of hay and thick layers of *Grypotherium* dung were found in this enclosure. The animal must have been kept shut up and fed by the aboriginals of Patagonia for a long period as a domesticated creature.

The mastodon, the antique elephant of America, was even more useful. The ancient Americans were not yet acquainted with the wheel at the time of their immigration. They first came to know it in the time of Columbus. Although primitive species of the horse did exist in America and remained long enough to be encountered by Man, as certain finds prove, they soon died out. It does not appear that the peoples of the early civilizations of America ever made any attempt to tame them. All the horses that roam the pampas and prairies of the New World today came originally from Europe. Powerful draft animals were therefore more needed in America than anywhere else for the conveyance of loads. On the high tablelands of Peru, where the Inca civilization originated, llamas existed, suitable for this purpose. In Central America, where the Mayan culture developed, there was only one creature that could be employed to carry riders and heavy baggage. This was the shaggy, mammoth-like mastodon.

When the archeologists laid bare the temples, palaces, fortresses, and terraced cities of the Mayan people in Guatemala and Yucatán, they were astonished by the magnificent sculptures and reliefs representing elephants with their riders and drivers. They believed for a long time that the Maya were immigrants from Asia or that at any rate there had been an ancient cultural connection between India and Central America. Many extremely interesting theories were published of the origin of the Mayan civilization. It is also perfectly possible that the imposing builders of the cities and inventors of the calendars of Central America — who far exceeded their Western conquerors from an intellectual, cultural, artistic, or moral point of view — formed a foreign community on the soil of America. But it is quite certain that their elephants did not come from India. The animals were mastodons.

There is plenty of documentary evidence to support the theory. The skeletons of mastodons were found at many sites among fragments of Mayan pottery. The prehistorian Franz Spillmann excavated in 1928 an entire workshop of Mayan ware dating from the second to the fourth centuries of our era. Its owner must have kept a mastodon, for among the smashed bowls and jars lay the bones of the mighty beast. It looked as though a primeval elephant had broken into a shop that dealt in pottery. Traces of a mastodon cult have also come to light in North America, especially in the Missouri district, where layers filled with charcoal, interspersed with domestic utensils, tools, and elephants' bones were found. In Jacob's Cave near Pineville the paleontologist Jay L. B. Taylor actually discovered the bone of the forequarter of a stag, bearing the engraved picture of a mastodon.

If the English adventurer David Ingram is to be believed, the mastodon was still roaming the North American prairies in the sixteenth century, though no longer as a domestic animal. It probably went out of fashion, owing to the drastic cultural revolutions of the pre-Columbian period. Ingram was one of the hundred and fourteen seamen put ashore by Sir John Hawkins in 1568 somewhere between Mexico and Florida. Soon afterwards they had to retreat northward under hostile pressure from the Spaniards. In the course of wanderings that lasted for years in utterly unknown regions, these men attempted to cross the continent of North America. Most of them disappeared as time went on, either starving to death, being killed by the natives or joining Indian tribes. Only Ingram and two of his companions at last reached the coast. A French ship brought them home. And in 1582, after his two comrades had at length succumbed to their sufferings, Ingram, the last survivor, appeared before Sir Francis Walsingham, state secretary to Queen Elizabeth, and told him what he had seen in the forests and prairies.

Ingram's report has never been taken particularly seriously by historians. It is made up mostly of typical seaman's yarns. What the blunt sailor had to say to Sir Francis about the animal world of America, however, sounds perfectly credible. He described precisely and drew accurate pictures of bison, wapiti, and grizzly bears native to the country of the Indians. His account of the great grassy prairies and rivers is quite unexceptionable; and there is really no reason to suppose that the brown, long-haired elephants that he said he had observed near the herds of bison only existed in his imagination. Ingram in fact encountered so many strange beasts that he had not the slightest need to add any fabulous creature to their number. Moreover, he could probably scarcely have known what real elephants looked like and what countries they came from. Sir Francis himself was no better informed. He was not surprised to hear about the hairy elephants. He simply made a note of them without wasting any words on the subject.

Two hundred years later further evidence supported Ingram's narrative. According to this second testimony the huge beasts that had once been driven through the streets of Mayapán, Uxmal, and Chichén Itzá had survived to the time of the founding of the United States. The third President of the United States, Thomas Jefferson, received in 1800 a number of Indian chiefs from regions in the interior of the country, then very little known. They gave him information as to the game that could be hunted where they came from. And these red warriors, who lacked even a veneer of civilization, described to their "White Father," who listened to them with amazement, animals, among others, which resembled elephants. Since they had never heard of the elephants of India and Africa it would have been difficult for them to have invented such creatures.

America, the great double continent with two faces, inhabited until a short time ago by monsters of immense size side by side with primitive hunting tribes and peoples of advanced civilization, was the last section of the globe to be subjected to the rule of the restless, brain-bearing primate, Man. This virgin soil remained a land of contrasts. At the time the Mayas were evolving their 40,000-year calendar and covering whole aeons as no people ever did before or since, the majority of the American immigrants continued to represent the Cro-Magnon level. And today, in the epoch of gigantic cities and atomic physics, television transmitters, radar apparatus, and space rockets, there are still empty tracts on the map of America where tribal peoples practise rituals not unlike those that were in vogue among the Old Stone Age peoples of Europe.

A visit to Adam

Rubbish lay half a yard thick in the cellars. Among twisted iron girders and collapsed walls I could see broken urns, calcined flints, and charred fragments of bone. An old man was crouching over one of the piles of rubbish, picking piece after piece out of the debris, turning the pages of a book, and trying to fit the pieces together.

It was May 1953. Many European museums and collections that had held the bones and artifacts of our ancestors had been reduced to blackened ruin by the war. I visited one of these rubble heaps, the Ethnological Museum of Berlin. I wanted to find out what had become of the primitive men and the great collection of prehistoric tools and ornaments assembled by Otto Hauser. The curator, Gertrud Dorka, was so unnerved that she could hardly utter a word. A short time before children had scrambled through window openings and over heaps of rubble into the catacombs. They had carried off the last of the bronze swords that had been preserved. The weapons of the ancient German warriors might now be adorning the leaders of a band of youngsters who had no idea of their value. Or perhaps the swords had long since fallen into the hands of a junk dealer.

"Things that generations of scientists of every nationality have collected have vanished irretrievably," Frau Dorka told me at last. "We have lost evidences of the culture of the Ice Age, tools from ancient barrows, Trojan domestic utensils, vessels and works of art from the most various countries and eras. And innumerable articles of value that escaped destruction in the war disappeared later in the chaos of the postwar years. We only recovered a very few of them. Urns two thousand years old were being used by ignorant people as flower vases. Flint knives were serving as paperweights. Boys were decorating the lapels of their jackets with engravings on mammoth-tusk. There were yawning gaps all over the ruins of the museum. Metal thieves, the modern grave robbers, keep breaking in. We shall have to make a completely fresh start."

We walked through the cellars. Twilight reigned, as in those caverns in which the men of the Ice Age had once painted, danced, and practised magic. The old man brought a tiny piece of pottery close to his eyes, studying it attentively in order to discover if possible to which cultural epoch and type of vessel it had belonged. Tens of thousands of such fragments lay scattered in a single room, producing an effect of bewildering confusion among the stones, chalk, and ashes that surrounded them. Suddenly the old man smiled. Referring to an illustration in one of his many books he gave the potsherd a number and with quiet pride laid it carefully on a rack.

I was reminded of the many investigators who had opened up the earth all over the world with their spades and pickaxes in order to penetrate to the secrets of prehistory. Their careers passed before me like a film, from the first hesitant advances, through the conflicts and disputes they had to engage in to get their discoveries recognized, down to the final submission to the public of their work. And here in Berlin the film suddenly broke and the work of the men who had labored for the Ethnological Museum started all over again. Suddenly it seemed to me as if these ruins, just as examples among so many, had a symbolic significance for the rise and fall of human cultures. In a weirdly shadowy cave produced by the twentieth century an old man sat collecting potsherds found and classified long ago.

The outlines of hand axes showed in the ashes. Heat had distorted them. "We had better not touch them," said Frau Dorka. "They crumble at the slightest contact." Primitive man had slaughtered mammoths and cave bears with them, used them in his battles and in his pertinacious struggle to survive. Now these weapons and tools that had lasted 100,000 years were no more than fragile shapes in the dust of ashes. A child's finger could have broken them.

A black thighbone, which looked like a piece of charcoal, lay in the rubble. It was the Le Moustier boy, sold with another skeleton by Otto Hauser to Berlin forty-five years ago for 160,000 gold marks. Near it reposed another primitive man discovered by Hauser. It had been burned to a cinder.

Frau Dorka shrugged her shoulders in reply to my question. "The skulls," she said in a low tone, "were taken away by the Russians. We don't know what happened to the skeletons. We shall have to draw up a report on their condition."

Particles of dust from the ashes filled the air. The old man was bending over another potsherd. There is a grim irony in fate, I thought. When Otto Hauser discovered the Le Moustier boy he got the French authorities to certify in writing that the skeleton had remained undisturbed in an ancient Acheulean layer ever since primeval times. Forty-five years later the charred relic of the same skeleton is again made the subject of an official report and duly recorded.

"For the time being," said Frau Dorka, her eyes on the slender rays of light from outside that fell delicately upon the boy's thighbone, "that is all we can do. The prehistoric men must lie where they are for the present. We shall have to wait for the professionals to dig them out."

Index

AND PHOTOGRAPHIC CREDITS

PHOTOGRAPHIC CREDITS

INDEX

Abel, Othenio, 501–2
Abominable Snowman, 520
About, Edmond, 303
Absolon, K., 361–62
Acheulean age, 229–31, 388, 389, 450, 522
Agassiz, Alexander, 268
Agassiz, Louis, 83, 116, 195–96, 209, 270–71
Agogwe tribe, 444
Agriculture, prehistoric, 510–14
Aguiló, Cabré, 365, 369
Aldrovandi, Ulisse, 24
Alexander, Grand Duke of Weimar, 283, 287
Altamira caves, 327–33, 335, 377, 504
Ameghino, Fiorino, 521, 524
Andersson, J. G., 458–60
Anthropoid apes, 75–76, 169–70, 260–61, 273, 291–92, 295, 355, 403–4, 414–17, 427–31, 435–47, 485, 492–93, 521
Apes, Giants and Man (Franz Weidenreich), 470–71
Aristotle, 6, 7, 25, 26, 29–30, 34, 41–2, 57, 75, 132, 133–34, 305
Arrhenius, Svante, 304–5
Artedi, Peter, 43–44, 48–51
Aurignacian man, 230, 354, 377–79, 388, 392, 395, 396–97, 483, 497, 507
Australopithecus prometheus. See Makapansgat man

Averroës (Mohammed ibn-Rushd), 7
Avicenna, 6, 7, 8, 13

Baer, Karl Ernst von, 95
Bajer, Johann Jakob, 12, 13
Banks, Sir Joseph, 100–102, 112 113
Bathybius Haeckeli, 303
Battel, Andreas, 76
Bebel, August, 278, 279
Bégouen, Count, 340–43
Benoît de Maillet, 27, 28
Berckhemer, 448–49
Beringer, Johannes Bartolomäus, 17, 18
Bexon, Gabriel-Leopold, 106
Bible, 3, 5, and *passim*
Black, Davidson, 459–63, 468
Blumenbach, Johann Friedrich, 39, 83, 105, 129, 153, 156, 173–75, 176–77, 192
Boccaccio, Giovanni, 8
Boerhaave, Hermann, 44–47, 53, 60, 74
Bolk, Ludwig, 439–41
Boltunov, 38
Bonnet, Jacques de, 88, 91, 124
Boucher de Perthes, Jacques, 201, 202–7
Bougainville, Louis Antoine de, 101–2
Boule, Pierre Marcellin, 391, 409, 462

Bourgeois, Abbé, 344–45
Breton, André, 351–52
Breuil, Henri, 228, 229, 332–37, 343–44, 352, 364–65, 367, 376–79, 386–87, 409, 482–84, 503
Brisson, 106, 109, 111
Brongniart, Alexandre, 169, 170, 302
Bronn, Heinrich Georg, 280, 398
Bronze Age, 208, 514
Broom, Robert, 474–86
Brünn race, 360–62, 388, 396, 504
Bruno, Giordano, 130, 133, 136, 284
Büchner, Ludwig, 189
Buckland, William, 193–96, 209
Buffon, Georges Louis Leclerc, Comte de, 63–67, 70, 72, 76, 78–84 *passim*, 104, 105, 139, 146, 432
Buffon, Leclerc de, 108–11
Buildings, prehistoric, 507–14
Burial grounds, prehistoric, 352–54, 362, 502–3
Bushman drawings, 373–79

Camper, Peter, 73–74, 77, 84, 123, 127–29, 150, 156
Cannibalism, prehistoric, 353–54, 463, 503
Capsian Age, 379
Cartailhac, Emile, 330, 331–35, 364–65
Casteret, Norbert, 346–49
Catastrophes, theory of, 83–4, 147–49, 154, 155, 164, 192, 248
Cave bear, 97, 500–504
Celsius, Olaf, 32–33
Cesalpino, Andrea, 41
Chancelade man, 388, 395–96
Charles XII, King of Sweden, 35, 40
Chellean age, 229–31
Chou-kou-tien, 458–66, 472

Christy, Henry, 209–11
Claudius, Roman Emperor, 23
Clifford, George, collection of, 49, 51
Coelacanth, 356–57
Combarelles, cave of Les, 332, 337, 343, 363, 504
Commerson, Philibert, 101–3
Condorcet, Marquis de, 107, 110
Conyers' discovery, 21–24, 40, 99
Cook, Captain James, 101–3, 113
Cope, Edward Drinker, 267–68
Correlation, Cuvier's law of, 145, 147, 149
Correns, Karl, 313
Cro-Magnon man, 171, 196, 212–14, 215, 352, 362, 372, 373, 377, 395, 396–97, 422, 464, 472, 483, 485, 497, 508–9
Cross breeding, 68–70
Cuvier, Georges, 39, 83, 116, 144–71 *passim*, 195–96, 200, 201, 236, 269, 301, 519
Cyphanthropus rhodesiensis. See Rhodesian man

Dacqué, Edgar, 433
Dames, William, 297
Dart, Raymond A., 425, 474–75, 482–86
Darwin, Charles, 116, 118–19, 196, 235–74 *passim*, 274–77, 280, 284–86
Darwin, Charles Galton, 277
Darwin, Emma (*née* Wedgewood), 239, 250, 253, 254
Darwin, Erasmus, 112, 114–19, 235–36, 239, 274
Darwin, Robert Waring, 119, 235–38, 250–51
Daubenton, Edmée-Louis, 106
Daubenton, Jean-Marie, 106, 110
Dawson, Charles, 405–17
Dayton Monkey Trial, 424–27
d'Azyr, Félix Vicq, 77
d'Epinay, Madame, 79–80, 84

Descartes, René, 31, 57–58, 86, 134–35
Diderot, Denis, 78–9, 107
Diluvial age, 5, 10–11, 15–17, 28, 83, 96–7, 98, 156, 192–97, 202, 206, 230, 299
Dinosaurs, 267
d'Orbigny, Alcide, 169–71 passim, 196, 202
Dryopithecus, 202, 388, 437–39
Dubois, Eugène, 292–301, 462
Du Bois-Reymond, Emil, 188–90, 286, 290
Duckbill, 101, 499

Eckart, Johann Georg von, 24, 207
Empedocles, 8, 83
Encyclopedists, 78–80, 82, 107, 129
Engis skeletons, 171
Environment, Theory of, 138–39, 160–66, 307–8, 320, 322–25
Eoanthropus dawsoni. See Piltdown man
Esper, J. F., 97–99, 156, 200
Exhibition, Paris International of 1867, 210–11; of 1878, 327
Expressionism in prehistoric art, 365–70, 378–79
Eyasi giant (Meganthropus africanus), 473

Falconer, Hugh, 206, 208
Fertility rites, prehistoric, 334, 363
Feuerbach, Ludwig, 189
Fitzroy, Captain Robert, 239–47 passim, 249, 262, 266
Flood, The, theories concerning, 5, 15–18, 192–96, 516–19. See also Diluvial Age
Fluorine test, 412–16
Foetal theory, 439–41
Font-de-Gaume cave, 332, 336, 343
Fontéchevade man, 451–52
Fossil ivory (ebur fossile), 96–97

Frederick the Great, of Prussia, 60, 62, 93
Freicine, 151
French Revolution, 108, 160
Frere, John, 99, 156, 193, 208
Frobenius, Leo, 374, 377
Fuhlrott, Johann Karl, 215, 217–23, 291, 296

Gassendi, Pierre, 56, 57–9
Gay-Lussac, Joseph Louis, 162, 318
Gegenbaur, Karl, 285–86
General Morphology (Ernst Haeckel), 284–85
Gesner, Konrad von, 7
Gibbon. See Anthropoid apes
Gigantopithecus blacki. See Kwangsi giant
Godin, Henri, 150–51, 347
Goethe, Johann Wolfgang von, 71, 78, 116, 123–29 passim, 137–40, 173, 179, 181, 192, 272, 280, 284
Göttingen University, 172–73
Greek theories of evolution, 130–34
Grimaldi man, 396, 397
Guericke, Otto von, 8–9, 28, 53
Guettard, Jean Etienne, 20–21, 53, 83

Haberer, Dr., 455–58, 461
Haeckel, Ernst, 93, 127, 183, 186, 236, 278–90, 292, 298, 303, 305, 404, 437, 445, 446
Haggquist, 319
Hale, Matthew, 27
Haller, Albrecht von, 45, 87, 90–91, 93–95, 104, 124
Hallstatt civilization, 514–15
Hallström, 370
Hanno, the Carthaginian, 75–76
Hauser, Otto, 383–94, 395
Heidelberg man, 398–405, 487, 497

Helmholtz, Hermann Ludwig von, 186, 304
Henri-Martin, Germaine, 451–52
Henslow, J. S., 237–39, 242
Herder, Johann Gottfried von, 116, 124, 125, 127, 137, 138
Heredity, laws of, 308–14
Herodotus, 8
Het Loo Zoo, 72–73
Hoff, Karl Ernst von, 192
Hoffman, Friedrich, 150, 152
Holbach, Baron von, 107–8
Hollman, Samuel Christian, 83
Homer, 3
Hooker, Joseph Dalton, 254, 257, 264
Hoskins, C. R., 412
Hotu skulls, 454–55
Hoxne man (John Frere's discovery), 99, 156, 193, 208
Hrdlička, Aleš, 299
Humboldt, Alexander von, 172, 237, 280
Hume, David, 63, 115–16
Hutton, James, 191–92, 194
Huxley, Julian, 277, 326
Huxley, Thomas Henry, 257–58, 260–64, 272–74, 275, 276

Ice Age, 167, 193, 202, 209–11, 228, 397–98, 453
Ichthyosaurus, 13, 153
Ingram, David, 525–26
Intermaxillary bone, 77, 123–29, 173
Iron Age, 208
Isis case, 183–84

Jardin des Plantes (formerly Jardin du Roi), 53, 76, 107, 110, 118, 144–47, 150, 151
Java, the ape-man of (Meganthropus paleojavanicus), 404, 460, 462, 468–71, 485, 497, 499
Jemmy Button, 241–47
Julia Pastrana, 272–74
Jussieu, Bernard de, 53, 63, 109

Kagg, Baron, 35, 37, 83
Kahn, Fritz, 445, 490
Kammerer, Paul, 321–25 passim
Kant, Immanuel, 116, 137, 140–43, 259
Keith, Sir Arthur, 408, 411–12
Kingsley, Charles, 262–63
Kircher, Athanasius, 8
Klaatsch, Hermann, 297–98, 353–58, 375–76, 385, 389, 390, 392, 397, 398, 403, 408, 500, 507
Klagenfurt, dragon of, 9
Klopstock, 90
Knorr, Georg Wolfgang, 19
Koenigswald, G. H. R. von, 299–301, 404, 464, 466–71, 499
Köhler, Wolfgang, 428
Krapina, battle of, 505–7
Kühn, Herbert, 368
Kwangsi giant (Gigantopithecus blacki), 467–74

La Brea, lake of, 523
Labastide grotto, 346–48, 350
Lakhovsky, Georges, 305
Lamarck, Jean Baptiste de, 109, 111, 117, 145–46, 149, 159–66, 258, 259, 307, 315
Lambert family, 307
Lamettrie, Julian Offray de, 45, 47, 59–63, 90, 94, 107, 129, 141
Langius, 12
Laplace, 157, 162
Lartet, Edouard, 200–202, 209–15, 225, 229, 344
Lascaux, cave of, 342
Lavaillant, François, 103–4
Le Gros Clark, Wilfred E., 414–15, 442, 485
Le Moustier skeleton, 389–94, 397, 400, 508, 528
Leakey, L. S. B., 377–78, 419–21, 442, 452
Leeuwenhoeck, Anton van, 87
Leibniz, Baron Gottfried Wilhelm von, 9, 28, 85–86, 89, 124, 136

Leiden University, 44, 296–97
Leidy, Joseph, 267
Lemur, dwarf, 435, 437
Leonardo da Vinci. *See* Vinci, Leonardo da
Lever, Ashton, 103
Leverian Museum, 113
Levi, Robert, 347
Lichtenberg, Georg Christoph, 172–73, 192, 307
Linnaeus, Carolus, 25–53 *passim*, 54, 56, 60–61, 65, 68–72, 86–87, 94, 99–100, 104, 139, 146
Linnean Society, 254, 255, 256, 356
Lorenz, Konrad, 429, 431, 441, 501
Loubens, Marcel, 347
Lubbock, John, 276, 292, 330
Ludwig, Wilhelm, 446–47
Lyell, Charles, 190, 191–97, 200, 203, 208, 223, 239, 245, 248, 251, 255, 256, 264, 275, 276, 283
Lysenko, Trofim Denisovich, 277, 325–26

McEnery's discovery, 169, 193, 208
Magdalenian age, 230, 329, 337, 340, 354, 396, 498
Mairey, André, 347
Makapansgat man (*Australopithecus prometheus*), 482, 485
Malthus, Thomas Robert, 235, 251, 255–56
Mammoth, 34–40, 53, 83, 105, 167, 360, 456, 472; of Cahors, 351–52
Manoncourt, Sonnini de, 106
Marsh, Othniel Charles, 267–68, 297
Marston, Alvan Theophilus, 412–16 *passim*, 450
Martin, Henri, 508–9

Martinus, Friedrich Heinrich Wilhelm, 76
Mastodon, 524–26
Materialism, doctrine of, 89, 107, 189, 278, 286–87
Mazurier (French surgeon), 8
Meganthropus africanus. *See* Eyasi giant
Meganthropus paleojavanicus. *See* Java, the ape-man of
Megatherium, 152–53, 248
Meier, G. F., 90, 92
Melbourne, William Lamb, Viscount, 238, 240–42
Mendel, Johann Gregor, 309–14
Menghin, Oswald, 377
Merck, Johann Heinrich, 124–25
Mesopithecus pentelicus. *See* Pikermi, monkey of
Messerschmidt, 37
Michurin, Vladimirovich, 321–25 *passim*
Micoquean man, 385–87, 389
Mill, John Stuart, 264–65
Miocene age, 446
Monaco, Albert I, Prince of, 343, 396
Monboddo, Lord, 118, 119
Montaigne, Michael Eyquem de, 56, 59
Montbeillard, Philibert Gueneau de, 106
Montespan cave, 347
Moraeus, Sara Lisa, 43
Morgan, Thomas Hunt, 317–20, 425
Mortillet, Gabriel de, 210, 212–14, 225–30, 345
Mousterian man, 230, 387–94, 396, 502
Muller, Joseph, 319, 425
Müller, Johannes, 185–88, 218, 280
Mutability of species, 26, 49, 68–70, 86, 146, 157, 164–65, 266, 302

Mutation Theory, The (Hugo de Vries), 316
Mutations, 141–42, 316–19, 439–47

Napoleon Bonaparte, 112, 157–58
Napp, Abbot Cyrillus, 309–14 *passim*
National Socialism (Nazis), influence on anthropology, 449–50
Natural History of Creation (Ernst Haeckel), 285, 288
Natural selection, theory of, 126–27, 252, 256, 260, 265, 271, 305–306, 308, 447
Neanderthal man, 196, 216–24, 230–31, 276, 288, 291, 292, 301, 337, 388, 391, 396, 413, 421–23, 453, 481, 483, 485, 497, 501–3, 504–7
Neolithic age, 510–13
Noble, 324–25

Oakley, Kenneth P., 412–16, 485
Obermaier, Hugo, 229, 343, 359–60, 365, 367, 376, 377, 385, 386, 522
Oenothera Lamarckiana, 314–15
Oken (Okenfuss), Lorenz, 93, 175–85, 258, 259, 280, 289, 432
Oldoway skeleton, 417–23
Orangutan. *See* Anthropoid apes
Origin of Species, The (Charles Darwin), 258–59, 265, 280
Owen, Richard, 196, 260

Palissy, 8 3
Pallas, Peter Simon, 101–3, 104
Pantheism, 278, 283–85
Pascal, Blaise, 134
Pasteur, Louis, 302–3
Paul et Virginie (Bernardin de Saint-Pierre), 109
Pausanias, 8
Paviland, Red Lady of, 169, 171, 193

Peking man (*Sinanthropus Pekinensis*), 460–66, 473, 482, 494, 497
Peloria, 69–70
Peter the Great, of Russia, 35, 37
Peyrony, 508–9
Pikermi, monkey of (*Mesopithecus pentelicus*), 197–200, 437
Piltdown man (*Eoanthropus dawsoni*), 405–17, 464
Pithecanthropus, 292–301, 356, 388, 398, 403, 404, 421, 453, 468–70, 482
Pleistocene age, 299, 397, 409, 446, 453, 472, 483, 498. *See also* Diluvial age
Plesianthropus transvaalensis. See Sterkfontein man
Pliocene age, 458
Polyp, fresh-water, 87–88
Pouchet, 302–3
Preformation, theory of, 87–92
Prehominids, 487
Pre-Socratic philosophers, 130–32
Preyer, Wilhelm, 304
Principles of Geology, The (Charles Lyell), 194, 239, 245, 251
Proconsul, 442–47, 474, 485, 490, 497
Pterodactyl, 154

Racial characteristics, 174–75
Radiolaria, 280
Raleigh, Sir Walter, 26–7
Rank, Johannes, 402–3
Ray, John, 41–42, 85
Réaumur, René-Antoine Ferchault de, 66, 67, 70–72, 88
Reck, Hans, 417–20
Reding, David, 15
Rhodesian man (*Cyphanthropus rhodesiensis*), 421–23
Riddles of the Universe, The (Ernst Haeckel), 285–86

Rituals, prehistoric, 338, 340, 341, 363

Robinson, John Talbot, 474, 481–87

Rösch, Herr, 398–401

Rostand, Jean, 441

Rousseau, Jean Jacques, 20, 64, 102, 108

Rudbeck, Olof the Older, 32–33

Rudbeck, Olaf the Younger, 32–33

Rydelius, Anders, 31–32

Saint-Hilaire, Geoffroy, 111–12, 147–48, 152, 158–59, 162, 168, 170–71, 236, 259

Saint-Pierre, Bernardin de. *See Paul et Virginie*

Saurians, 150–52

Sautuola, Don Marcelino de, 327–33

Scandinavian rock drawings, 370–72

Schaafhausen, Hermann, 218–24

Schelling, Friedrich Wilhelm Joseph von, 180–82, 185

Scheuchzer, Johann Jakob, 3–6, 10–19 *passim*, 29, 52, 55, 74, 96, 98, 150, 156, 200

Schiller, Johann Christopher von, 138–40, 143

Schipka cave, 224

Schleiden, Jakob, 186–87

Schlosser, Max, 456–58

Schlotheim, Baron Ernst Friedrich von, 166–69

Schmerling, 171, 214

Schoetensack, Otto, 398–403

Schopenhauer, Arthur, 142, 259

Schultze, Max, 187

Schumachov, Ossip, 38–9, 83

Schwalbe, Gustav, 224, 297

Schwann, Theodor, 186–87

Seba, Albertus, collection of, 45, 48

Sexual selection, 117, 274–77, 358

Sinanthropus pekinensis. See Peking man

Six, Dr., 314–17

Slavery, abolition of, 240

Smith, Adam, 115, 129, 235

Smith, William, 147–48, 155

Solander, Daniel, 101, 112

Solutrean age, 230, 337, 354, 396, 498

Sonnerat, Pierre, 103

Sorbonne, School of Theology, 21

Spallanzani, Lazzaro, 87–89

Spencer, Herbert, 257, 263–65

Spinoza, Benedict, 44, 129, 134–37, 139, 284

Spontaneous generation, 53, 85, 95, 301–6

Spy d'Orneau cave, 224, 292

Stein, Frau —— von, 125, 129, 137, 138

Steinheim man, 448–50, 472, 497

Sterkfontein man (*Plesianthropus transvaalensis*), 478–80, 482, 484–85, 488

Stobaeus, Kilian, 32

Stock, Chester, 519–20, 521

Stone Age, 208

Strahlenberg, Philipp Johann Tabbert von, 35–36, 37, 83

Sukhul man, 452

Sumerian civilization, 516–19

Swammerdam, 87

Swanscombe man, 412–17, 421, 450–52, 453, 472, 497

Swartkrans man (*Telanthropus capensis*), 486–87, 497

Sylvius, Jacobus, 77

Systema naturae (Carolus Linnaeus), 42–44, 45–48, 49, 52–53, 68–70, 72

Szombathy, 359

Taungs child, 425, 474–78, 485, 488, 497, 519

Teilhard de Chardin, Father, 407, 414, 461, 485

Telanthropus capensis. See Swartkrans man

Teutobochus, 8–9
Thomsen, Christian Jürgensen, 207–8
Thompson, William, 304
Tools, prehistoric, 169, 204, 206, 225–31, 344, 384, 387, 403, 420, 431, 489–97
Trembley, Abraham, 87–88
Trinil man. *See* Java, the ape man of
Trois Frères cave, Les, 338, 340–42, 343
Tschermak-Seysenegg, Erich von, 313
Tuc d'Audoubert cave, 340–41, 343

Unicorn, 36
Ur of the Chaldees, 515, 517

Valltorta caves, 364–70, 376, 377
Venus of Willendorf, 358–60
Vertebral theory of the skull, 178–82
Vézère valley, 210–11, 214–15, 229–30, 328, 332, 384–94, 507–8
Vinci, Leonardo da, 10, 12, 83
Virchow, Rudolf, 127, 186, 188–90, 218–24, 290, 288–91 *passim*, 292, 296–97, 330, 331, 420, 432, 510
Vis plastica theory, 6, 7, 11, 18
Vivisection, protests against, 105
Vogt, Karl, 189–90, 195, 219, 282
Voltaire, 19–21, 60, 64, 82

Vries, Hugo de, 313–17

Wagner, Rudolf, 219
Walch, Johann Ernst Immanuel, 19
Wallace, Alfred Russel, 254–57, 273–74, 275, 434
Wegener, Alfred, 523
Weidenreich, Franz, 411, 463–71
Weiner, J. S., 414–15
Weinert, Hans, 299, 403–4, 408–9, 412, 422, 436–39, 471, 487
Weismann, August, 308–9, 440
Wells, Dr., theory of, 253
Weng Chung Pei, 460–66
Werner, Abraham Gottlob, 191–92, 194
Werth, Emil, 386
Westenhöfer, Max, 432–33
Wilberforce, Samuel, Bishop of Oxford, 261–63
Wolff, Kaspar Friedrich, 91–96, *passim*, 139
Wood Jones, Frederic, 434–35
Woodward, Arthur Smith, 406–8, 524
Woodward, John, 11, 12
Woolley, Sir Leonard, 517

Xenophanes, 8

Yeflichev, Adrian ("Little Father"), 271–74

Zioberg (Sjöberg), 68–69, 70